D1237545

THE
BOLSHEVIKS
IN POWER

THE
BOLSHEVIKS
IN POWER

THE FIRST YEAR OF
SOVIET RULE IN PETROGRAD

ALEXANDER RABINOWITCH

INDIANA UNIVERSITY PRESS

Bloomington and Indianapolis

This book is a publication of

Indiana University Press
601 North Morton Street
Bloomington, IN 47404-3797 USA

http://iupress.indiana.edu

Telephone orders   800-842-6796
Fax orders   812-855-7931
Orders by e-mail   iuporder@indiana.edu

The paper used in this publication meets the minimum requirements of American National
Standard for Information Sciences—Permanence of Paper for Printed Library Materials, ANSI
Z39.48-1984.

Manufactured in the United States of America

Library of Congress Cataloging-in-Publication Data

Rabinowitch, Alexander.
The Bolsheviks in power : the first year of Soviet rule in Petrograd / Alexander Rabinowitch.
p.   cm.
Includes bibliographical references and index.
ISBN 978-0-253-34943-9 (cloth : alk. paper) 1. Rossiiskaia sotsial-demokraticheskaia
rabochaia partiia (bol'shevikov)—History—Sources. 2. Saint Petersburg (Russia)—History—
Revolution, 1917–1921—Sources. 3. Soviet Union—History—Revolution, 1917–1921.
4. Kommunisticheskaia partiia Sovetskogo Soiuza—History—Sources.
5. Lenin, Vladimir Il'ich, 1870–1924. I. Title.
JN6598.S6R33 2007
947'.210841—dc22

2007007276

1 2 3 4 5 12 11 10 09 08 07

For Victor
Twin brother, best friend, global humanitarian

CONTENTS

PREFACE AND ACKNOWLEDGMENTS

THE BOLSHEVIKS came to power in Russia in October 1917. The regime they established, which was dedicated to the universal triumph of communism, controlled Russian politics and society for more than seventy-five years. It can reasonably be argued that this outcome, more than any other single event, shaped world history for much of the twentieth century.

Most of my professional research and writing has been devoted to studying the October 1917 revolution and its immediate outcome in Petrograd, now St. Petersburg, the capital of Imperial and revolutionary Russia. In my first book, *Prelude to Revolution: The Petrograd Bolsheviks and the July Uprising* (Indiana University Press, 1968), I explored the causes, development, and results of the abortive July 1917 insurrection in Petrograd as a means of clarifying the sources of popular dissatisfaction with the liberal/moderate-socialist Provisional Government, and the program, structure, method of operation, and strengths and weaknesses of the Bolshevik party (in comparison with other contemporary political parties). In my next book, *The Bolsheviks Come to Power* (1976), I utilized the insights provided by *Prelude to Revolution* to better understand the nature of the October 1917 Russian revolution, the reasons for the failure of Western-style democracy, and the triumph of Lenin and the Bolsheviks. Most fundamental, my goal in both books was to study events in Petrograd as a means of addressing basic, then inadequately studied, questions relating to the Bolsheviks and the course of the October revolution.

The Bolsheviks Come to Power, together with *Prelude to Revolution,* challenged prevailing Western notions of the October revolution as no more than a military coup by a small, united band of revolutionary fanatics brilliantly led by Lenin. I found that, in 1917, the Bolshevik party in Petrograd transformed itself into a mass political party and that, rather than being a monolithic movement marching in lock step behind Lenin, its leadership was divided into left, centrist, and moderate right wings, each of which helped shape revolutionary strategy and tactics. I also found that the party's success in the struggle for power after the overthrow of the tsar in February 1917 was due, in critically important ways, to its organizational flexibility,

openness, and responsiveness to popular aspirations, as well as to its extensive, carefully nurtured connections to factory workers, soldiers of the Petrograd garrison, and Baltic Fleet sailors. The October revolution in Petrograd,
I concluded, was less a military operation than a gradual process rooted in
popular political culture, widespread disenchantment with the results of the
February revolution, and, in that context, the magnetic attraction of the
Bolsheviks' promises of immediate peace, bread, land for the peasantry, and
grass-roots democracy exercised through multiparty soviets.

This interpretation, however, raised as many questions as it answered.
For if the success of the Bolshevik party in 1917 was at least partly attribut-
able to its open, relatively democratic, and decentralized character and operational style, as seemed clear, how was one to explain the fact that it was so
quickly transformed into one of the most highly centralized, authoritarian,
political organizations in modern history? Further, if soviets, in 1917, were
genuinely democratic, embryonic organizations of popular self-rule, as my
studies also suggested, how was it that the independence of soviets and other
mass organizations was destroyed so quickly? Most fundamental, perhaps,
if the goal of many of the dissatisfied lower-class citizens of Petrograd who
spearheaded the subversion of the Provisional Government and facilitated
the Bolshevik seizure of power was the creation of an egalitarian society
and a democratic-socialist, multiparty political system, and if this goal was
shared by many prominent Bolsheviks, as my research also showed, how was
one to explain the extraordinary rapidity with which these ideals were sub-
verted and Bolshevik authoritarianism became firmly entrenched?

These are the key questions posed in this book. My efforts to complete
it have taken an inordinately long time, ironically partly because of the cultural liberalization begun by Mikhail Gorbachev. I had completed pertinent
research during trips to Leningrad and Moscow libraries by the early 1980s.
Well before Gorbachev and the collapse of the Soviet Union in 1991, I had
begun drafting the main chapters. I was dissatisfied with the results, however, especially for the period after much of the non-Bolshevik press was
shut down during the first half of 1918, which eliminated one of my main
sources. Even the limited kinds of published documents on events, institutions, social groups, and political figures and parties, especially the Bolshevik party organization in Petrograd, that were crucial for my work on 1917
were unavailable for 1918. Thus, to complete this book, I needed access to
Soviet government and Communist party archives, which were then still
tightly sealed.

The first strong hint of the immense change that liberalization under
Gorbachev would have on my situation as a Western historian of the Rus-

sian revolution and earliest Soviet period came in 1989, when *The Bolsheviks Come to Power* became the first Western study of the revolution published in the Soviet Union. I remember the presentation of the book in an auditorium at the Progress Publishing House in Moscow as one of the most satisfying in my life. All the same, even after the book's publication in the Soviet Union, the possibility that a "bourgeois falsifier" like me might soon have the opportunity to work in Soviet historical archives still seemed farfetched.

This changed abruptly in June 1991, when I went to Russia to do some supplementary research in Moscow and Leningrad libraries. With the support of Soviet colleagues, I requested, and to my great surprise received, permission to work in government and Communist party archives in Moscow and, a bit later, in Leningrad. Although it was immediately clear that some materials of greatest interest to me remained classified, my potential source base was now expanded immeasurably. Moreover, it grew even larger in 1993, when I was first allowed to work in the former KGB archives, and also during the remainder of the 1990s, as an increasing number of documents was gradually declassified. That was the positive side. The negative side was that, for practical purposes, I had to begin my research over again.

A bibliography of the sources upon which this work is based can be found at the end of the book. Important unpublished sources relating to the first year of Soviet power in Petrograd that were available to me include minutes of meetings of the Bolshevik Petersburg Committee for 1918, as well as of other citywide party forums; minutes of meetings of Bolshevik district party committees; protocols of meetings of the Council of People's Commissars (Sovnarkom); stenographic records of key sessions of the Petrograd Soviet and its leadership bodies; minutes of meetings of Petrograd district soviets; internal memoranda; correspondence; unpublished memoirs; extensive records for other parties and government, administrative, and civic bodies; and the personal files of key Bolshevik leaders for this period. In addition, I have been able to examine some, though by no means all, pertinent case files of the All-Russian Extraordinary Commission for Combating Counterrevolution, Speculation, and Sabotage (VCheka), as well as those of local investigative agencies, for this period. Of similarly great value to me have been meticulously annotated, comprehensive collections of previously classified records pertaining to the history of political organizations other than the Bolshevik party during the revolutionary and immediate postrevolutionary eras published in Russia in the last decade and a half.

Taken together, these newly available sources have made it possible to examine, for the first time, Bolshevik internal debates and decision making in Petrograd from top to bottom, the development of party and government institutions and their relationship at all levels, and the evolution of popular political opinion during the first year of Soviet power. Based on this analysis, I have tried to reconstruct the dynamics of the earliest development of the repressive, ultra-authoritarian Soviet political system against the backdrop of Petrograd's profound post-October political, economic, social, and military crises. My hope is that this reconstruction, however imperfect, will shed useful new light on one of the central historiographical issues in early Soviet history, namely, the relative importance of developing circumstances and responses to them as opposed to a preconceived Bolshevik revolutionary ideology or a firmly established pattern of dictatorial behavior, in shaping Soviet Russia's highly centralized, authoritarian political system.

The Bolsheviks in Power is organized into four parts. Part 1 covers the period from the October revolution to the dissolution of the Constituent Assembly in January 1918. During this time the Petrograd Bolsheviks consolidated power in Petrograd, and Lenin successfully stifled Bolshevik moderates who were dubious about prospects for early socialist revolutions abroad and looked to a socialist friendly Constituent Assembly to further the revolution in Russia. The central focus of part 2 is the course and impact of the fierce controversy over the Treaty of Brest-Litovsk, a separate peace with Germany, that began in January 1918 between a majority of leading Petrograd Bolsheviks and Lenin, and ended the following March with the advance of German forces to the very gates of Petrograd, the Soviet government's frenzied flight to Moscow, and the treaty's ratification. Part 3 explores Petrograd's catastrophic domestic and military crises during the spring and early summer of 1918, responses to them by workers, and the ways in which these crises shaped the Bolsheviks' approach to government in what was now Russia's "second city." This part concludes with an examination of the disintegration of the Bolshevik-Left SR alliance in the Northwest and the turn to one-party rule in early July. In part 4 primary attention is devoted to the Petrograd Bolsheviks and political developments in July–August 1918, leading to the proclamation of mass "Red Terror" in the fall, as well as on the dynamics and impact of the Terror in Petrograd. The final chapter of part 4 focuses on the organization and staging of the grand celebration marking the first anniversary of the October revolution in Petrograd. The festivities are used as a vehicle for evaluating the condition, revolutionary hopes, and self-identity of the Petrograd Bolsheviks, as well as the changed structure of Petrograd government, after twelve months of desperate struggle to retain power until the eruption of expected, decisive socialist revolutions in the West. Throughout the book, I focus on certain events and moments that provide particularly illuminating insights into the answers to central, still puzzling questions about the changed nature of the Bolshevik party and the soviets following the October revolution, as well as the disparity between the revolution's initial goals and its early results.

*   *   *

The system of transliteration employed in this work is the one used by the Library of Congress, with some simplifications, such as in the case of well-known proper names (e.g., Trotsky, not Trotskii).

On 1 February 1918, Russia switched from the Julian calendar to the Gregorian calendar of the West, which was then thirteen days ahead of the former. Unless otherwise indicated, all dates in the text accord with the calendar in use in Russia at the time.

Over the many years I have worked on this book, so many people and institutions have aided me in my work that it is impossible to express my appreciation to them all. My work on it could not have been completed without generous support from the John Simon Guggenheim Memorial Foundation; the John D. and Catherine T. MacArthur Foundation; the International Research and Exchanges Board; the National Council for Eurasian and East European Research; the American Council of Learned Societies; the Harriman Institute, Columbia University; the Hoover Institution, Stanford University; and the Office of International Programs, the Russian and East European Institute, and the Office of the Vice President for Research, Indiana University.

I am deeply grateful, as well, to the staffs of the Hoover Institution; the New York Public Library; the Library of Congress; the Indiana University Library; the National Library, London; the International Contemporary Documentation Library, Nanterre; the Russian National Libraries, Moscow and St. Petersburg; the State Public Historical Library of Russia, Moscow; the Institute of Scientific Information on the Social Sciences of the Russian Academy of Sciences, Moscow; the Russian Academy of Sciences Library, St. Petersburg; the State Museum of the Political History of Russia, St. Petersburg; the National Archives of the United Kingdom (TNA), Public Records Office (PRO); the State Archive of the Russian Federation (GARF); the Russian State Archive of Social and Political History (RGASPI); the Central State Archive of St. Petersburg (TsGA SPb); the Central State Archive of Historical-Political Documents, St. Petersburg (TsGAIPD); the Leningrad Oblast Archive in Vyborg (LOGAV); the Central State Archive of the Military Naval Fleet, St. Petersburg (TsGA VMF); the Archival Administration of the Federal Security Service, the Russian Federation, Moscow (AU FSB RF); and the Archival Administration of the Federal Security Service for St. Petersburg and the Leningrad Oblast (AU FSB SPb i LO).

Beginning in the 1980s, my research and writing profited greatly from interaction with historians in Moscow and St. Petersburg, especially Genrikh Ioffe, Mikhail Iroshnikov, Viktor Miller, Albert Nenanorkov, Genadii Sobolev, Vitalii Startsev, Pavel Volobuev, and Oleg Znamenskii. Since the collapse of the Soviet Union, contacts between Western and Russian scholars have been normalized; as much as anyone, I have benefited from this welcome development. Beginning with my first days of work in the Leningrad [Communist] Party Archive (now TsGAIPD), Irina Il'marovna Sazonova, Senior Researcher and Archivist, and Taissa Pavlovna Bondarevskaia, Senior Researcher and Chief Archival Specialist, took me under their wing, shared their vast knowledge with me, and aided my research in countless other ways. Taissa Pavlovna, whose primary scholarly interests coincide with mine, remains as generous to me today as at the start. The Petersburg Branch of the Institute of History, Russian Academy of Sciences, is blessed with a group of distinguished historians whose interests also overlap with mine. At the Institute, I am particularly grateful to Boris Ananich, Tamara Abrosimova, Vladimir Cherniaev, Raphael Ganelin, Boris Kolonitskii, Sergei Potolov, and Nikolai Smirnov for their encouragement, scholarly insights, and friendship. Special thanks, as well, for their advice and assistance, to Barbara Allen, Stanislav Bernev, Richard Bidlack, Nadezhda Cherepinina, Sergei Chernov, Barbara Evans Clements, Pete Glatter, Leopold Haimson, Vladlen Izmozik, Aleksandr Kalmykov, Svetlana Koreneva, Anatolii Kraushkin, Carol Leadenham, Sergei Leonov, Iaroslav Leontiev, Moshe Lewin, Aleksei Litvin, Nikita Lomagin, Vladlen Loginov, Andrea Lynn, Michael Melancon, Larissa Malashenko, Vladimir Naumov, Oleg Naumov, Michaela Pohl, Toivo Raun, Anatolii Razgon, Larissa Rogovaia, Jonathan Sanders, Richard Spence, Mikhail Shklarovskii, Stanislav Tiutiukin, Phil Tomaseli and Rex Wade. Over the years, my students in the Department of History at Indiana University have been a never-ending source of inspiration. I am also deeply in their debt. Let me add that Mary McAuley's pioneering study, *Bread and Justice: State and Society in Petrograd, 1917–1922,* has helped me to better understand the broader context of which my work is a part. The same is true of Donald J. Raleigh's *Experiencing Russia's Civil War: Politics, Society, and Revolutionary Culture in Saratov, 1917–1922;* Peter Holquist's *Making War, Forging Revolution: Russia's Continuum of Crisis, 1914–1921;* and Richard Sakwa's *Soviet Communists in Power: A Study of Moscow during the Civil War, 1918–1921.* A rich post-Soviet collection of essays edited by V. A. Shishkin,

Petrograd na perelome epokh: Gorod i ego zhiteli v gody revoliutsii i grazhdan-skoi voiny, provided me with the stimulating insights of contemporary Petersburg historians of especially great interest to me.

Thanks are due to the staff of Indiana University Press for their thoughtfulness and efficiency in editing and producing my book. Last but by no means least, it would not have been finished without the constant support, encouragement, and invariably sound advice of my wife, Janet. She has read and made suggestions for improvement of successive drafts of each chapter, and they have been invaluable in revising them. I alone, of course, bear responsibility for shortcomings which remain.

ABBREVIATIONS

ACS	All-Russian Committee for Salvation of the Homeland and Revolution
CEC	Central Executive Committee
GPU	State Political Administration
EAD	Extraordinary Assembly of Delegates from Petrograd Factories and Plants
FSB	Federal Security Service
Kadet	Constitutional Democrat
kombedy	Committees of the Village Poor
KGB	Committee for State Security
Komuch	Committee of Members of the Constituent Assembly
Left SR	Left Socialist Revolutionary
MRC	Military Revolutionary Committee
PCheka	Petrograd Extraordinary Commission for Combating Counter-revolution, Speculation, and Sabotage
PTK	Petrograd Labor Commune
SIS	[British] Secret Intelligence Service
SK PTK	Council of Commissars of the Petrograd Labor Commune
SK SO	Council of Commissars of the Northern Oblast (Region)
SNKhSR	Supreme Council of the National Economy for the Northern Region
SOK	Northern Oblast [Bolshevik] Committee
Sovnarkom	Council of People's Commissars
SR	Socialist Revolutionary
UDCA	All-Russian Union for Defense of the Constituent Assembly
VCheka	All-Russian Extraordinary Commission for Combating Counter-revolution, Speculation, and Sabotage
VSNKh	Supreme Council of the National Economy
Vikzhel	All-Russian Executive Committee of the Union of Railway Workers

THE
BOLSHEVIKS
IN POWER

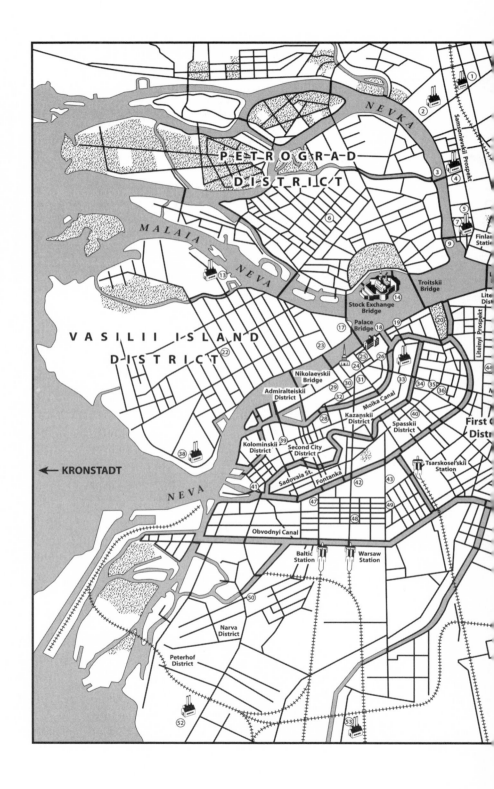

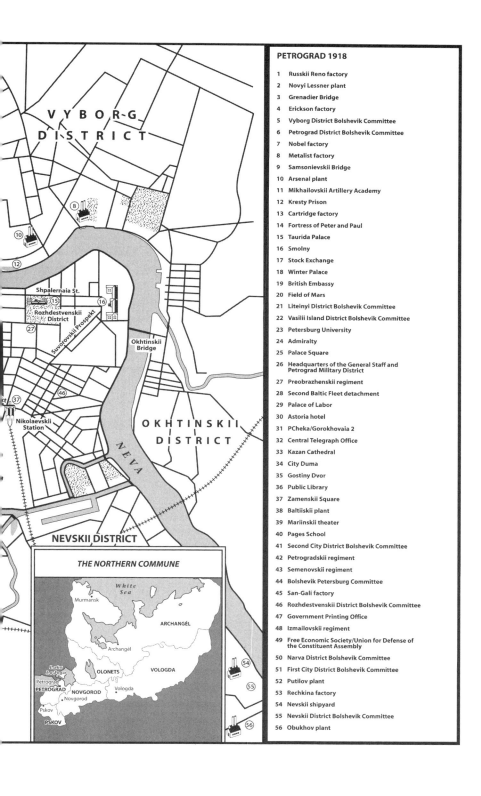

PETROGRAD 1918

1 Russkii Reno factory
2 Novyi Lessner plant
3 Grenadier Bridge
4 Erickson factory
5 Vyborg District Bolshevik Committee
6 Petrograd District Bolshevik Committee
7 Nobel factory
8 Metalist factory
9 Samsonievskii Bridge
10 Arsenal plant
11 Mikhailovskii Artillery Academy
12 Kresty Prison
13 Cartridge factory
14 Fortress of Peter and Paul
15 Taurida Palace
16 Smolny
17 Stock Exchange
18 Winter Palace
19 British Embassy
20 Field of Mars
21 Liteinyi District Bolshevik Committee
22 Vasilii Island District Bolshevik Committee
23 Petersburg University
24 Admiralty
25 Palace Square
26 Headquarters of the General Staff and Petrograd Military District
27 Preobrazhenskii regiment
28 Second Baltic Fleet detachment
29 Palace of Labor
30 Astoria hotel
31 PCheka/Gorokhovaia 2
32 Central Telegraph Office
33 Kazan Cathedral
34 City Duma
35 Gostiny Dvor
36 Public Library
37 Zamenskii Square
38 Baltiiskii plant
39 Mariinskii theater
40 Pages School
41 Second City District Bolshevik Committee
42 Petrogradskii regiment
43 Semenovskii regiment
44 Bolshevik Petersburg Committee
45 San-Gali factory
46 Rozhdestvenskii District Bolshevik Committee
47 Government Printing Office
48 Izmailovskii regiment
49 Free Economic Society/Union for Defense of the Constituent Assembly
50 Narva District Bolshevik Committee
51 First City District Bolshevik Committee
52 Putilov plant
53 Rechkina factory
54 Nevskii shipyard
55 Nevskii District Bolshevik Committee
56 Obukhov plant

Prologue: The Bolsheviks and the October Revolution in Petrograd

To MAKE SENSE of the evolution of the Bolshevik party in Petrograd during the first year of Soviet rule, and the factors shaping the authoritarian, one-party political system which emerged then, it is necessary to take account of the results of the February revolution that overthrew Tsar Nicholas II and, even more, the character and makeup of the Bolshevik party in 1917 and the dynamics of the October revolution which brought it to power.

The February 1917 revolution, which grew out of prewar political and economic instabilities, technological backwardness, and fundamental social divisions, coupled with gross mismanagement of the war effort, continuing military defeats, domestic economic dislocation, and outrageous scandals surrounding the monarchy, resulted in the creation of two potential national governments. One was the officially recognized Provisional Government, initially dominated by prominent liberals and, after April, by an uneasy coalition of liberals (primarily Constitutional Democrats or Kadets) and moderate socialists (most importantly, representatives of the moderate social democratic or Menshevik party and of the agrarian Socialist Revolutionary or SR party). The second was the Soviet—initially the Petrograd Soviet, created during the February revolution and, by mid-summer, national Soviet executive committees: the All-Russian Central Executive Committee of Soviets of Workers' and Soldiers' Deputies (CEC) and the All-Russian Executive Committee of Soviets of Peasants' Deputies. Formed by national congresses representing a countrywide network of urban and rural soviets, these national soviet bodies were politically stronger than the Provisional Government by virtue of their vastly greater and constantly growing support among workers, peasants, soldiers, and sailors.

Under the control of the moderate socialists, the national soviet executive organs recognized the legitimacy of the Provisional Government and, with some qualifications, supported its policies of delaying fundamental political, economic, and social reform, as well as convocation of a Constituent Assembly, in the interests of continued partnership with the liberals. Participation of the liberals in government, they believed, was essential for Russia's military security and national revival. However, beginning in the spring and summer of 1917, as popular frustration with the results of the February revolution deepened, pressure from Petrograd's rebellious masses on the moderate socialist–controlled national soviet bodies to take power into their own hands grew apace. Events would show that the elemental social forces that erupted during the February revolution could not be reversed or stopped in midstream and that, at a popular level, soviets were viewed as the harbinger and engine of social progress.

Virtually alone among Russia's top political leaders Vladimir Il'ich Lenin, the founder and chief leader of the Bolshevik Party, instinctively sensed this. From its outbreak, he believed that the world war would inevitably lead to socialist revolutions in all the warring countries. At the time of the old regime's overthrow, Lenin was in Switzerland. Returning to Petrograd in early April 1917, he called for an immediate second, "socialist" revolution in Russia. Although he backed off this goal as an immediate objective after acquainting himself with the prevailing situation (including little support for precipitous, radical revolutionary action even among many of his closest colleagues), his historically momentous achievement at this time was to orient the Bolshevik Party toward preparation for the replacement of the Provisional Government by a leftist "soviet" government as soon as the moment for such a step ripened.

Nonetheless, in assessing Lenin's role in the October revolution, it is critically important to keep in mind that he was either away from the country or in hiding and out of regular touch with his colleagues in Russia for much of the time between February and October 1917. In any case, top Bolshevik leaders were divided into three groups. On the left were Lenin and Leon Trotsky, among others, for whom the establishment of revolutionary soviet power in Russia was less an end in itself than the trigger for immediate worldwide socialist revolution. In the center was a group of often quite independent-thinking leaders whose views on the development of the Russian Revolution tended to fluctuate in response to their reading of existing conditions. And on the right was a highly influential group of significantly more moderate national party leaders led by Lev Kamenev and including Grigorii Zinoviev, Vladimir Miliutin, Aleksei Rykov, and Viktor Nogin (all members of the Bolshevik Central Committee), and Anatolii Lunacharskii. Its numbers and influence increased significantly after the Sixth All-Russian

Bolshevik Party Congress in late July, when such influential left Mensheviks as Iurii Larin, Solomon Lozovskii, and the independent-minded trade union leader, Marxist scholar, and humanist David Riazanov joined the party. This group was skeptical about the likelihood of early, decisive socialist revolutions in the West. During the second half of 1917 it viewed transfer of power to the soviets as a vehicle for building a strong alliance of left socialist parties and factions which would form a caretaker, exclusively socialist coalition government to begin peace negotiations and prepare for fundamental social reform by a Constituent Assembly. In Lenin's absence, this group's outlook, *more than any other,* shaped the Bolsheviks' public political platform.

Then too, events often moved so rapidly that the Bolshevik Central Committee had to develop policies without consulting Lenin. Beyond this, circumstances were frequently such that structurally subordinate party bodies were forced to develop responses to evolving realities without guidance or contrary to directives from above. Also, in 1917 the doors to membership were opened wide and the Bolshevik organization became a mass party. More than this, Bolshevik programs and policies in 1917 tended to be developed with strong, timely inputs from rank-and-file members and therefore reflected popular aspirations.

Meanwhile, the revolution among factory workers, soldiers, sailors, and peasants had a dynamic of its own, so much so that at times the Bolsheviks followed its constituency rather than the other way around. For example, on 1 July the Bolshevik Central Committee, influenced by party moderates, directed regional committees to begin the most energetic preparations possible for an early left socialist congress aimed at unifying all elements of the Democracy, including trade union leaders and representatives of internationalist wings of organizations that had not yet broken with the defensists (such as the Left Socialist Revolutionaries [Left SRs] and Menshevik-Internationalists).[1] At the same time, regional committees were instructed to prepare for elections to the Constituent Assembly.[2] Yet, only two days later, radical elements of the Bolshevik Petersburg Committee and Military Organization, responsive to their ultra-militant constituencies, played key roles in organizing the abortive July uprising against the wishes of the moderates as well as Lenin and those closest to him.

*   *   *

The July uprising ended in an apparent crushing defeat for the Bolsheviks. Even most moderate socialists turned against them. Lenin was forced into hiding, many Bolshevik leaders were jailed, the growth of the party temporarily stalled, and preparations for a left socialist congress were shelved. On the other hand, fierce attacks on the Bolsheviks had the un-intended effect of further radicalizing and strengthening such left groups within the moderate socialist camp as the Menshevik-Internationalists and the Left SRs. This, in turn, reawakened the appetite of a majority of the Bol-shevik Central Committee (though not of Lenin) for the formation of a left socialist bloc and, in mid-July, led it to invite "internationalists" from other parties to the coming Bolshevik national party congress with a consultative vote. Actually, at the local level, Bolsheviks, Mensheviks-Internationalists, and Left SRs were already working together productively in such grass-roots institutions as district soviets. However, in light of the successful tactics pur-sued by the Bolsheviks in the October revolution, perhaps the most telling aspect of the July uprising was the great popular attraction for the Bolshevik revolutionary program that it reflected.

What was the Bolsheviks' public program? Contrary to conventional wisdom, in 1917 the Bolsheviks did not stand for a one-party dictatorship. Rather, at a popular level they stood for democratic "people's power," exer-cised through an exclusively socialist, soviet, multiparty government, pend-ing timely convocation of the Constituent Assembly. They also stood for more land to individual peasants, stronger worker influence in factory man-agement ("workers' control"), prompt improvement of the food supply, and, most important, an early end to the war. All these goals were neatly pack-aged in the slogans "Peace, Land, and Bread!"; "All Power to the Soviets!"; and "Immediate Convocation of the Constituent Assembly!"

The interplay and political value of these two key factors—the attrac-tiveness of the Bolshevik political platform and the party's carefully nurtured links to revolutionary workers, soldiers, and sailors—were evident in the fall of 1917, after the Left's quick defeat of an unsuccessful rightist putsch led by the commander-in-chief of the Russian army, General Lavr Kornilov. The march of Kornilov's forces on Petrograd was halted by the action of all so-cialist groups working together under the aegis of the soviets. However, the role of the Bolsheviks was especially critical because of the party's ability to quickly mobilize factory workers, garrison soldiers, and Baltic fleet sailors in defense of the revolution. Thus the swift defeat of Kornilov had the dual ef-fect of enhancing the Bolsheviks' stature at a popular level and providing a powerful stimulus to the moderate Bolshevik position of all socialist groups banding together for the fulfillment of the revolutionary goals embodied in the party's platform.

On 1 September, the Petrograd Soviet adopted a resolution proposed by Kamenev calling for exclusion of the bourgeoisie from state power and the creation of a new, exclusively socialist government. Although Kamenev's resolution was widely interpreted as a call for transfer of political power to the soviets, he did not insist on this. In the short run, Bolshevik moderates sharing his views would have been satisfied with a socialist coalition government which would include representatives of all socialist parties, and of such "democratic" institutions in addition to soviets as trade unions, zemstvos, municipal dumas, and cooperatives.

Passage of Kamenev's resolution enabled the Bolsheviks to gain effective control of the Petrograd Soviet, a development that would greatly facilitate their assumption to power in October. Of more immediate consequence, however, the national soviet executive committees rejected it. Moreover, the Democratic State Conference, a national conference of "democratic" organizations which met in Petrograd from 14 to 22 September to reconsider the government question, rejected the creation of an exclusively socialist, soviet-based government. Still, the Democratic State Conference reflected the striking growth within the moderate socialist camp of left Menshevik and left SR groups who supported much of the Bolshevik program embodied in the resolution adopted by the Petrograd Soviet on 1 September. Consequently, the failure of the conference to respond to popular demands for an immediate change of governments refocused attention on the soviets as the arbiter of Russian national politics.

Later in September, this swing was reflected in the overwhelming majority that the Left SRs, whose immediate political program now dovetailed with that of the Bolsheviks, won at the Seventh City Conference of Petrograd Left SRs. On 21 September, the Bolsheviks and Left SRs joined forces in calling for early convocation of a second national congress of soviets of workers' and soldiers' deputies which, at the insistence of delegates from soviets at the Democratic State Conference, was scheduled for 20 October (later postponed until 25 October). The basic orientation toward the creation of a homogeneous socialist government by the Second All-Russian Congress of Soviets that this decision reflected defined the political activity of the Bolsheviks, as well as of the Left SRs and Menshevik-Internationalists, during the latter part of September and the first week and a half of October.

* * *

In August and September, Lenin tried his best to influence Bolshevik policy from a hideout in Finland. After the fiasco of the July uprising, and the criticism heaped on the Bolsheviks by the moderate socialist soviet leadership for its role in it, he had campaigned with only very mixed success to persuade his party colleagues to abandon the goal of transferring power to the soviets and to prepare for an independently organized armed uprising. Subsequently, even he was so impressed by the ease with which the Bolsheviks, Mensheviks, and SRs, working together, defeated Kornilov that in an essay of early September, "On Compromises," he allowed for the possibility that the revolution might yet develop peacefully if the national soviet leadership took power into its own hands without further delay.

Lenin's mood of moderation was short-lived. In mid-September, he renewed his emphasis on the absolute need for an armed uprising to further the revolution. Such factors as the strong position of the extreme Left in Finland, the winning of majorities in the Petrograd and Moscow soviets, the massive social upheaval among land-hungry peasants in the countryside, the continuing disintegration of the army at the front and the soldiers' increasingly insistent demands for immediate peace, and signs of revolutionary unrest in the German fleet encouraged Lenin to hope that the seizure of power by the Bolsheviks would have strong support in the cities, that it would no longer be opposed by the provinces and the front, and, most important of all, that a violent popular explosion in Russia and the creation of a genuinely revolutionary government there would serve as the catalyst for immediate, decisive mass rebellions in other European countries. Primarily for these reasons as well as others, on 12 and 14 September, just as the Democratic State Conference was getting under way, Lenin wrote two blistering letters to the Central Committee demanding that the party walk out of the conference and begin organizing an armed uprising "without losing an instant."[3]

To party leaders in Petrograd, these letters came as a bolt out of the blue. The Bolshevik Central Committee met in emergency session on the evening of 15 September, within hours of receiving Lenin's letters. Participants in this meeting included not only members of the party's top leadership customarily in Petrograd but also several Central Committee members temporarily in the capital for the Democratic State Conference. All were cool to Lenin's entreaties. Indeed, what appears to have concerned the committee members most of all was to ensure that the substance of Lenin's messages be kept secret. Moreover, undeterred by these messages, the Bolshevik leadership, in concert with the Left SRs and other left groups, maintained a steady course aimed at the creation of a homogeneous socialist government at the coming nationwide Congress of Soviets. At the same time, with the approval of a majority of Bolshevik delegates to the Democratic State Conference, the party leadership decided to convene an emergency party congress on 17 October, on the eve of the Congress of Soviets.[4] This was to be the forum in which the party's tactics in connection with the soviet congress, and the closely related question of the nature and makeup of a future government, were to be decided.

Lenin reacted to this rebuff with fury. First from Finland, and beginning at the end of September from a hideout on the northern outskirts of Petrograd, he delivered a series of stinging rebukes to his party colleagues, accompanied by ever more strident demands that the Provisional Government be overthrown at once. Lenin argued his case in person at a historic meeting of the Central Committee on 10 October. At issue was the reversal of the strategy aimed at peaceful transfer of power to multiparty soviets that had been the key to the party's extraordinary rise in influence and authority among the revolutionary masses since April. Beyond this, the party leadership had to somehow be persuaded that the existing situation was so critical that a decision on this question could not be delayed until the party congress, then only a week away, which, judging by closely related intraparty debates during the Democratic State Conference, would have strongly resisted the seizure of power before the Second All-Russian Congress of Soviets. Only twelve of its twenty-one members attended the meeting of the Bolshevik Central Committee, which skewed the discussion in favor of the Leninists. Ultimately, ten of twelve participants (all but Kamenev and Zinoviev) yielded to Lenin and agreed to make the seizure of power "the order of the day," effectively preempting the scheduled party congress—which was never held.

*   *   *

Despite this green light for the organization of an armed uprising, little was done to accomplish this goal for roughly three weeks. For one thing, moderate party leaders led by the indefatigable Kamenev continued to vigorously oppose Lenin's course. In part because of the correspondence of their views with the views of other left socialist groups (with whom they were in continuing contact), as well as with the aspirations of the lower classes, these moderate Bolshevik leaders (Kamenev, Zinoviev, Rykov, Nogin, Riazanov, and the like) were among the party's most authoritative spokesmen in 1917.

Another factor that worked against the organization of an independently organized immediate armed uprising was the opposition of Central Committee members such as Trotsky and radically inclined Petrograd party leaders who were attracted to the idea of an early socialist revolution in Russia but skeptical about whether workers and soldiers could be mobilized behind the kind of "immediate bayonet charge" demanded by Lenin. Nonetheless, despite these concerns, in response to the Central Committee's decision of 10 October, local-level Petrograd Bolsheviks earnestly explored possibilities for starting an armed uprising at once. After several days, however, many

were forced to conclude that the party was technically unprepared to ini-
tiate an immediate uprising and, in any case, that most workers, soldiers,
and sailors would probably not be responsive to an uprising before the Congress of Soviets. Moreover, they were forced to recognize that by usurping
the prerogatives of the national Congress of Soviets, they would jeopardize
possibilities for collaboration with such important allies as the Left SRs and
the Menshevik-Internationalists. Further, they risked loss of support in such
mass organizations as trade unions, factory committees, and the Petrograd
Soviet. Most ominous of all, they would increase the danger of opposition
by troops from the nearby northern front.

Consequently, with considerable wavering caused largely by pressure
from Lenin for bolder direct action, the Bolshevik leadership in Petrograd,
both Lenin's partisans and those of Kamenev, pursued a strategy based on
the following principles—that the soviets (because of their stature in the eyes
of the masses), and not party bodies, should be employed for the overthrow
of the Provisional Government; that for the broadest possible support, any
attack on the government should be limited to actions that could be justified in terms of defending the soviets; that action should therefore be delayed
until a suitable excuse for giving battle presented itself; that to undercut potential resistance and maximize the possibility of success, every opportunity
should be utilized to subvert the authority of the Provisional Government
peacefully; and that the formal removal of the existing government should
be linked with and legitimized by the decisions of the Second All-Russian
Congress of Soviets. At the time, Lenin considered it "sheer idiocy" to wait
for the congress.[5] However, considering the development of the revolution
to that point, as well as the views of a majority of leading Bolsheviks around
the country, it appears to have been a natural, realistic response to the prevailing correlation of forces and the popular mood.

Between 21 and 24 October, Bolshevik leaders staunchly resisted immediate, open offensive revolutionary action, as demanded by Lenin, in favor of preparing for a decisive struggle against the Provisional Government
at the approaching national congress of soviets. In the party's press and at
huge public rallies, they attacked the policies of the Provisional Government
and reinforced popular support for the removal of the Provisional Government by the soviet congress. Simultaneously, using the Provisional Government's announced intention of transferring the bulk of the Petrograd garrison to the front as justification, and grounding its actions as defensive
measures against the counterrevolution, the Bolshevik leadership utilized
the Bolshevik-dominated Military Revolutionary Committee of the Petrograd Soviet (MRC), established on 9 October to monitor the government's

troop dispositions, to take control of most Petrograd-based military units. Weapons and ammunition from the city's main arsenals were distributed to supporters. Although the MRC did not cross the boundary between defensive moves and steps that would appear to infringe on the prerogatives of the congress, for practical purposes the Provisional Government was disarmed without a shot being fired.

In response, early on the morning of 24 October, a day before the scheduled opening of the Second All-Russian Congress of Soviets, a majority of which was poised to vote in favor of forming an exclusively socialist, soviet government, Kerensky attempted to curb the Left. Orders were issued for the re-arrest of leading Bolsheviks who had been detained after the July uprising and released at the time of the Kornilov Affair; loyalist military school cadets and shock battalions from the suburbs were called to the Winter Palace, seat of the government; and the main Bolshevik newspaper, *Rabochii put'*, was shut down. Soon after, however, revolutionary troops liberated the paper's press. Similarly, revolutionary forces countered efforts by loyalist cadets to control movement over the strategically critical Neva bridges. They also took over key communication and rail facilities. All this was done in the name of defense. Not until Lenin's direct, personal intervention at the party's headquarters in Smolny did the unilateral effort to overthrow the Provisional Government, which he had been demanding for a month, begin. This occurred before dawn on 25 October. At that time, all pretense that the MRC was simply defending the revolution and attempting most of all to maintain the status quo pending expression of the congress's will was abruptly dropped. Rather, an open, all-out effort was launched to confront congress delegates with the overthrow of the Provisional Government *prior* to the start of their deliberations.

During the morning of 25 October, military detachments directed by the MRC seized strategically important bridges, key government buildings, rail and power stations, and communications facilities not yet in their hands. They also laid siege to the Winter Palace, defended by only meager, demoralized, and constantly dwindling forces. Kerensky managed to flee to the front in search of troops before the ring was closed. The "storming of the Winter Palace," dramatically depicted in Eisenstein's classic film *October,* was a Soviet myth. After nightfall, the historic building was briefly bombarded by cannon from the Fortress of Peter and Paul and occupied with little difficulty, after which remaining members of the government were arrested. Hours earlier, a proclamation drafted by Lenin announcing the Provisional Government's overthrow was telegraphed around the country.

In retrospect, it is apparent that Lenin's basic purpose in insisting on the violent overthrow of the Provisional Government before the opening of the Congress of Soviets was to eliminate any possibility that the congress would form a socialist coalition in which the moderate socialists might have had a significant voice. This strategy was successful. On the eve of the opening of the congress, prior to the initiation of open military operations that culminated in the occupation of the Winter Palace, the political affiliations of arriving delegates and their positions on the government question made it all but certain that efforts to establish a multiparty democratic socialist government pledged to a program of peace and fundamental reform at the congress would bear fruit.[6]

It is important to keep this in mind in order to grasp the full import of the Bolsheviks' overthrow of the Provisional Government before the opening of the Congress of Soviets. The immense political impact of this act became apparent the moment the Second All-Russian Congress of Soviets began. As a sign of protest, the Mensheviks and SRs refused to participate in the Presidium of the congress. No sooner had a Bolshevik-dominated Presidium headed by Kamenev taken its place in seats vacated by the "old" moderate socialist soviet leadership and announced that the question of state power would be first on the congress's agenda than the leader of the Menshevik-Internationalists, Iulii Martov, a fervent supporter of a change in governments, rushed to the speaker's platform for an emergency announcement. Amid the ominous sounds of nearby cannon fire, his voice cracking with emotion and raspy from the tuberculosis that was to take his life a few years later, Martov implored delegates to stop the warfare that had broken out in the streets and to superintend immediate negotiations among all socialist parties aimed at the formation of a "democratic" government acceptable to all sides.[7]

Given the strong desire of a majority of congress delegates, Menshevik-Internationalists, Left SRs, most Bolsheviks, and, however hesitant, even many centrist Mensheviks and SRs, for intra-socialist collaboration, it is not surprising that Martov's plea was greeted by waves of applause. Representatives of the United Social-Democratic Internationalists[8] and of the Left SRs immediately rose to express solidarity with him. So did Lunacharskii for the Bolsheviks. Accounts of the congress indicate that Martov's proposal was quickly passed by a unanimous vote. For a fleeting moment it appeared that the congress might yet be put back on a track leading to the creation of an all-socialist coalition government.[9]

But this was not to be. Before any steps could be taken along the lines proposed by Martov and approved by the congress, a succession of Mensheviks and SRs rose to denounce the Bolsheviks as usurpers and to declare their intention of walking out of the congress in order to fight them. The collaborative spirit that had blossomed among a broad spectrum of socialists on the eve of the congress evaporated and the opening session quickly degenerated into a verbal free for all, during which most of the Mensheviks and SRs in the hall went off to help coordinate resistance to Bolshevik-led military operations.[10]

Not long after, Martov made a last futile attempt to persuade remaining delegates to proceed along the lines he had proposed. By this time, however, the atmosphere at the congress was so inflamed that his remarks were lost in the din. If earlier the prevailing atmosphere favored Bolshevik moderates seeking accommodation with all socialist groups, the reverse was now the case. Trotsky took advantage of this shift to further widen the breech with the moderate socialists. The left Menshevik and unsurpassed chronicler of the revolution Nicholas Sukhanov recalls Trotsky declaiming: "A rising of the masses needs no justification . . . Go where you belong—into the dustbin of history," to which Sukhanov quotes Martov as retorting, "then we will leave!"[11]

Waving Martov away, Trotsky introduced a resolution endorsing the insurrection in the streets and condemning the Mensheviks and SRs as servants of the bourgeoisie.[12] Many years later the distinguished historian Boris Nicolaevsky, then a Menshevik who left the hall with Martov, recalled that Martov walked out silently, not looking back. A young worker-Bolshevik dressed in a black shirt belted at the waist turned to him and, with undisguised sadness, exclaimed: "You know, among ourselves, we thought that some might leave us but not Martov." These words gave Martov pause. He stopped for a moment, tossed his head in a characteristic manner, and seemed on the verge of a retort. Then he thought better of it and, walking out the door, quietly murmured: "Someday you will understand the crime in which you are participating."[13]

Meanwhile, the opening session of the congress, continually interrupted by exultant reports of revolutionary triumphs, dragged on. Speaking for the Left SRs, Boris Kamkov implored the delegates not to adopt a sharply worded resolution such as Trotsky's. In his view, the support of moderate elements of the democracy and especially of the peasantry, among whom the Bolsheviks had little support, was vital for success in the struggle against the counterrevolution. "In the interests of creating a united revolutionary front, organization of the broadest possible democratic state power is an absolute necessity," Kamkov declared.[14]

Around 3:00 AM, it was announced that the forces under the control of the MRC had captured the Winter Palace and arrested the Provisional Government ministers meeting there. At this point, the Menshevik-Internationalist Naum Kapelinskii returned to the hall and made a last unsuccessful attempt to persuade delegates to explore peaceful ways of resolving the crisis. The best Kamenev could do was to quietly table Trotsky's inflammatory resolution condemning the Mensheviks and SRs, thereby leaving the door ajar for future collaboration. A short while later, the congress turned its attention to a manifesto written by Lenin, "To All Workers, Soldiers, and Peasants," endorsing the uprising in Petrograd; decreeing the transfer of supreme political authority into the hands of the congress and local soviets everywhere in Russia; and pledging that Soviet power would propose immediate peace, facilitate transfer of land to the peasantry, stand up for soldiers' rights, implement a program of complete democratization of the army, establish workers' control over industry, arrange for the timely convocation of the Constituent Assembly, supply grain to cities and manufactured goods to the countryside, and grant the right of self-determination to all nationalities. The historic first session of the Second All-Russian Congress of Soviets ended at 5:00 AM, 26 October, with the approval of this manifesto. The Soviet era in Russia's history had begun.

*   *   *

The October revolution in Petrograd has often been viewed as a brilliantly orchestrated military coup d'état without popular support, carried out by a tightly knit band of professional revolutionaries brilliantly led by the fanatical Lenin and lavishly financed by the Germans. This interpretation, which was undermined by Western "revisionist" social history in the 1970s and 1980s, was rejuvenated after the dissolution of the Soviet Union at the end of the Gorbachev era, in spite of the fact that data from newly declassified Soviet archives reinforced the findings of the revisionists. At the other end of the political spectrum, for nearly eighty years Soviet historians, bound by strict historical canons designed to legitimate the Soviet state and its leadership, depicted the October revolution as a broadly popular uprising of the revolutionary Russian masses. According to them, this upheaval was rooted in Imperial Russia's historical development and shaped by universal laws of history as originally formulated by Karl Marx and adapted by Lenin.

In truth, the October revolution in Petrograd cannot be adequately characterized as either a military coup or a popular uprising although, as we have seen, it contained elements of both. Its roots are to be found in the peculiarities of prerevolutionary Russia's political, social, and economic development, as well as in Russia's wartime crises. At one level, it was the culminating event in a drawn-out political struggle between an expanding spectrum of left socialist groups supported by the vast majority of Petrograd workers, soldiers, and sailors dissatisfied by the results of the February revolution, on the one hand, and the increasingly isolated liberal-moderate socialist alliance that had controlled the Provisional Government, together with the national Soviet leadership bodies between February and October 1917, on the other. By the time the Second All-Russian Congress of Soviets convened on 25 October, the relatively peaceful victory of the former was all but assured. At another level, the October revolution was a struggle, at first primarily within the Bolshevik leadership, between proponents of a multiparty, exclusively socialist government that would lead Russia to a Constituent Assembly in which socialists would have a dominating voice, and Leninists, who ultimately favored violent revolutionary action as the best means of striking out on an ultra-radical, independent revolutionary course in Russia, which would trigger decisive socialist revolutions abroad.

Muted on and off during much of 1917, this conflict erupted with particularly great force during the run-up to the October revolution and just after it. Such developments as the Bolsheviks' overthrow of the Provisional Government before the Second All-Russian Congress of Soviets, the walk-out of Mensheviks and SRs, and, as we shall see, their intransigence during negotiations over the formation of a broad socialist coalition government after the congress, coupled with the Bolsheviks' first military victories over loyalist forces, decisively undermined the efforts of Bolshevik moderates to share state power and ultimately facilitated the ascendancy of Soviet-style authoritarianism. Lenin's wager on international revolution took center stage. However, these outcomes should not obscure the fact that the October revolution in Petrograd was in large measure a valid expression of widespread disenchantment with the results of the February revolution and of popular aspirations for a brighter, more just future.

PART ONE

THE DEFEAT OF THE MODERATES

1

Forming a Government

THE SEVERE SETBACK that Bolshevik moderates suffered at the opening session of the Second All-Russian Congress of Soviets did not end their efforts, or those of other left socialist groups, to form a multiparty, homogeneous socialist government at the Soviet Congress and in its immediate aftermath. During these days, they sought to restore the movement toward creation of a broad socialist coalition that had been destroyed by the violent overthrow of the Provisional Government engineered by Lenin just before the opening of the Congress of Soviets. When that failed, they strived mightily to ensure that the exclusively Bolshevik cabinet ultimately approved by the congress, the Council of People's Commissars (Sovnarkom), would be strictly accountable to the multiparty Central Executive Committee (CEC).

* * *

The chaotic opening session of the congress during the night and early morning of 25/26 October had adjourned after endorsing transfer of power to the soviets but before defining a new government. In effect, Russia was temporarily without a functioning national government. On 24 October, at the last meeting of the Bolshevik Central Committee before the overthrow of the Provisional Government, Kamenev and Ian Berzin had been appointed to conduct negotiations with the Left SRs on their entry into a Soviet government,[1] and the next day, leading Left SRs were sounded out about forming a coalition with the Bolsheviks.[2] The issues of staying or withdrawing from the congress and of whether to join the new government were the main topics of discussion at Left SR fraction caucuses on 26 October. Although sympathetic to the Bolsheviks with whom they had been collaborating closely for weeks, Left SR fraction, or caucus, members remained true to the principle that the survival of the revolution dictated the formation of a broad coalition government which included all Soviet parties proportionate to their representation at the Congress of Soviets. To facilitate this outcome, they insisted on the importance of maintaining links to the Bolsheviks and the revolutionary masses but rejected the idea of joining with the Bolsheviks in the government.[3] At a gathering of members of the Bolshevik Central Committee and leading Left SRs in the early evening of the twenty-sixth, the Left SRs declined cabinet posts pending construction of a broadly inclusive socialist coalition.[4]

Finally, at 9:00 PM on 26 October, efforts to form a government with Left SRs having failed, Kamenev opened the second session of the Soviet Congress. To shouts of approval, he announced that the Presidium, expressing the decisions of the congress, had issued orders for the elimination of the death penalty at the front and the release of soldiers jailed for political crimes; the liberation of members of land and peasant committees jailed by the previous government; and Kerensky's arrest. Perfunctory decrees authorizing these steps were approved by acclamation.[5]

The first main agenda item of the evening was to be the government question, but resistance from the Left SRs to forming a coalition with the Bolsheviks alone complicated its resolution. Evidently, in order to establish the program of a Soviet government before considering its composition, the agenda was rearranged, and Lenin took the podium to present a peace declaration to the "Peoples and Governments of All the Warring Powers." It was Lenin's first appearance at the Congress, and all sources agree that he received a thunderous ovation. His declaration, interrupted by explosions of applause, pledged an end to secret diplomacy and proposed that all warring peoples and their governments immediately arrange a truce and begin negotiations for a just and democratic peace, without annexations or indemnities. The declaration also provided for the right of self-determination to subject nationalities everywhere in the world, regardless of when their forced incorporation into larger states occurred.[6] In a later speech, Trotsky made it plain that the declaration was primarily directed to the revolutionary masses around the world. "It is understood that we do not expect to influence imperialist governments with our proclamations but as long as they exist, we cannot ignore them," he said. "We are placing all our hopes on our revolution unleashing the European revolution. If uprisings by the peoples of Europe do not crush imperialism, we will be crushed."[7]

In the peace declaration and the ensuing discussion, Lenin took pains to emphasize the "October 24–25 revolution," rather than the Congress of Soviets, as the source of the Soviet government's legitimacy. Subsequently, this would be one of his major themes. Moreover, association with the mythical October armed uprising became central to Bolshevik identity. As was the case with all the decrees of the Soviet Congress, Lenin also stressed that the peace declaration was "provisional," pending confirmation by the Constituent Assembly. Nonetheless, following the Congress, support for its program became the standard by which the acceptability of all political groups and institutions, including the Constituent Assembly, would be judged. Everything in the peace declaration had been a staple of the extreme left for years. It is not surprising, therefore, that it was adopted without a dissenting vote. The assembled delegates gave Lenin another resounding ovation and sang the *Internationale,* the worldwide socialist anthem, before proceeding to the next item of business.[8]

Lenin next presented a decree on land reform that would abolish private ownership of land and would transfer all private and church lands to land committees and to soviets of peasant deputies for distribution to individual peasants according to need. Contradicting fundamental tenets of the communal land program long championed by the Bolsheviks, this decree was, in fact, modeled after the popular SR land program. After several delegates pointed this out, Lenin retorted, "So be it. . . . As a democratic government we cannot ignore the feelings of the masses even if we don't agree with them." After a break, during which the Left SRs reviewed the decree, it was adopted by an overwhelming vote without discussion.[9]

Not until close to 2:30 AM, 27 October, did the Congress finally begin to consider the structure and composition of a new national government. The task of presenting Lenin's position fell to Kamenev, who had led opposition to a unilateral Bolshevik seizure of power and who remained firmly committed to the creation of a broad socialist coalition on both theoretical and practical grounds.[10] That position was contained in a brief decree to which the makeup of a new "temporary," exclusively Bolshevik government was appended. According to this decree, the Sovnarkom, the worker and peasant government to be established by the Congress, was to function only until the convocation of the Constituent Assembly. Each major department or "people's commissariat" in this government was to be headed by a governing board. The chairs of each of these boards, along with the head of the government, were to make up the Sovnarkom. In close collaboration with mass organizations, it was pledged to implement the program of the Soviet Congress. Control of the Sovnarkom and the right to remove individual commissars was to rest with the new CEC to be elected by the Congress. Kamenev ended by presenting the proposed, exclusively Bolshevik slate of people's commissars, headed by Lenin, as chair of the Sovnarkom, and Trotsky, as people's commissar for foreign affairs. Conspicuously missing from the slate was Zinoviev, one of Lenin's closest comrades-in-arms in earlier times.[11]

Following Kamenev's presentation, Boris Avilov, representing the United

Social-Democratic Internationalists and a cluster of Menshevik-Internationalists who had not yet withdrawn from the Congress, articulated a remarkably prophetic argument against the immediate formation of an exclusively Bolshevik government, a view shared by a significant number of Bolshevik delegates, including roughly half the proposed cabinet. Avilov expressed grave doubts about the ability of an exclusively Bolshevik government to alleviate food supply shortages. Nor could such a government bring peace, as the allied governments would not recognize it, and European workers and peasants were still a long way from decisive rebellion. Therefore either a peace would be arranged between the Central Powers and the Entente at Russia's expense, or Russia would be forced to accept a separate onerous peace with Germany. Avilov offered a resolution calling for a delay in confirmation of a Bolshevik government and for the creation instead of a Provisional Executive Committee to form a government in agreement with all groups from the revolutionary democracy participating in the Soviet Congress, including those who had walked out of it.[12] However, the resolution was defeated.

Avilov's emphasis on the creation of a government representing the entire revolutionary democracy was similar to the position of Left SRs as well as of moderate Bolsheviks. Vladimir Karelin, a leading Left SR, rose next to declare that "circumstances demand the creation of a homogeneous democratic government" and that "without the support of the parties that have left the congress, a homogenous [socialist] government will find it impossible to implement its policies." At the same time he absolved the Bolsheviks of blame for the previous day's Menshevik-SR walkout and declared that "the fate of the entire revolution is [now] inextricably linked to their [the Bolsheviks'] fate and that their destruction will mean the destruction of the revolution." Still, he criticized the Bolsheviks for forming a "ready-made government" rather than temporary committees that would try to resolve critical issues that brooked no delay; for their hostile actions toward other revolutionary-democratic parties, including the Left SRs; and for their violations of freedom of speech. Moreover, he articulated the enduring Left SR principle that any new national executive body should be subordinate and strictly accountable to the multiparty CEC.[13]

Since Kamenev, who was still in the chair, sympathized with the views of Avilov and Karelin, Trotsky was called on to defend the immediate appointment of an exclusively Bolshevik government. Now that the latter was a practical possibility, Trotsky, no less than Lenin, was disinclined to let the opportunity slip. Trotsky dismissed Avilov's insistence on the need for a broadly based coalition to overcome Russia's deepening crises. Far from strengthening the revolution, he declared, coalition with the likes of Fedor Dan and Mikhail Lieber, both prominent Mensheviks, would lead to its inevitable downfall. Trotsky was similarly dismissive of Karelin. He warned that the Left SRs would lose their support among the masses and isolate themselves from the poorer peasantry if they attempted to contest the Bolsheviks with whom the poorer peasantry had united. Moreover, he claimed that the Bolsheviks had openly "raised the banner of an uprising," and he brushed aside accusations that the Bolsheviks had preempted the Soviet Congress by blaming Kerensky for the military action undertaken on 24–25 October. Branding Mensheviks and SRs who had left the Congress as "traitors to the revolution with whom we will never unite," he professed to welcome any group willing to help implement the Congress's program and to stand on the Bolsheviks' side of the barricades to the end.[14]

Following Trotsky's statement, a representative of the Executive Committee of the All-Russian Union of Railway Workers (Vikzhel) pushed forward to read a telegram expressing firm opposition to the "seizure of power by any one party" and strong support for the establishment of a "revolutionary socialist" government responsible to the "entire revolutionary democracy." The telegram made it clear that until such a government was created, Vikzhel intended to take control of the entire Russian railway network. Even more menacing for the Bolsheviks, the Vikzhel representative made it quite clear that in the struggle between the old Soviet leadership and the new, Vikzhel's loyalties rested with the former.[15] After he yielded the floor, two rank-and-file railway workers challenged Vikzhel's right to intervene in national politics, one of them declaring unequivocally that Vikzhel was a "political corpse that no longer represented the sentiments of its constituents."[16] Lenin's decree appointing an exclusively Bolshevik government passed without difficulty, with only about 150 of roughly 600 votes cast for Avilov's motion.[17] Nonetheless, the threat of a potentially disastrous railway stoppage if the government was not broadened cast an ominous cloud over the closing moments of the Second All-Russian Congress of Soviets.

After electing a new CEC consisting of sixty-two Bolsheviks, twenty-nine Left SRs, six United Social-Democratic Internationalists, three Ukrainian Socialists, and one SR Maksimalist, the congress agreed that this body, to be chaired by Kamenev, could be expanded with representatives of peasant soviets, army organizations, and the groups that had walked out the day before.[18] The potential entry into the CEC of representatives of peasant soviets was especially significant in terms of broadening the government, because most soviets in the countryside were still dominated by SRs. With this, the historic Second All-Russian Congress of Soviets came to an end.

＊　＊　＊

As the Second All-Russian Congress of Soviets closed on the morning of 27 October and delegates from around the country departed from Smolny, most of them, including Bolshevik moderates, expected that once tempers cooled the Sovnarkom would be restructured according to the model reflected in the party's pre-October political program, that is, as a multiparty, exclusively socialist coalition government reflecting the relative strength of the various parties and groups in the Congress of Soviets at its start. Only such a broadly based central power under the aegis of the soviets, they believed, would be capable of avoiding economic disaster, fending off counterrevolution, and averting full-scale civil war. Lenin and Trotsky, however, did not share this view. They were now concerned most of all with retaining freedom of action for themselves, so as to maximize the galvanizing effect of violent social upheaval in Russia on revolutionary workers abroad.

Most of the departing delegates also left Smolny with the impression, embodied in the Congress's decree on the structure of the new, temporary government, that it would be responsible to the CEC in which Left SRs, United Social-Democratic Internationalists, Ukrainian Socialists, and SR Maksimalists, a smaller, radical SR splinter group, were already represented, and in which all other Soviet groups, including those that had either left the Congress or were inadequately represented there, would participate. In any case, the decree establishing the Sovnarkom seemed to leave no doubt that it would soon yield its authority to the Constituent Assembly which, with the bourgeoisie swept aside, would confirm and build upon the first steps toward a bright future which the delegates felt they had taken. We have Trotsky's testimony that, in the first hours after the Congress of Soviets, Lenin leaned toward postponing elections to the Constituent Assembly and to structuring them to favor the extreme left.[19] Most party leaders insisted, however, on making good on their commitments with respect to the Constituent Assembly either because, like Kamenev, they rejected Lenin's theoretical views and strategy, or because, like Iakov Sverdlov, they feared the popular outcry that reneging on pre-October pledges and disrupting the elections would provoke. Consequently, a decree issued by Lenin on 27 October confirmed that the elections would be held as scheduled on 12–14 November, and that the Constituent Assembly would convene on 28 November.[20]

Efforts to undo the exclusively Bolshevik Sovnarkom were most intense in the first days after Kerensky's overthrow. At that time, both in Petrograd and Moscow, supporters of the deposed Provisional Government and proponents of Soviet power clashed in fierce armed combat. To most internationalists, regardless of party, it seemed that the revolution was on the verge of disintegrating into a bloodbath unless a truce was arranged and some kind of comprehensive socialist "united front" government was established immediately. On the one hand, the Kadets and right and centrist Mensheviks and SRs considered the Bolsheviks unscrupulous usurpers. For them, the Bolshevik government and the very idea of a dictatorship of the proletariat and poorer peasantry were an abomination. At the height of the October days, these opposition groups, supported by officers, military school cadets, and Cossack forces, coalesced around the Petrograd City Duma, which viewed itself and a national, broader, moderate socialist–dominated body which it created, the All-Russian Committee for Salvation of the Homeland and the Revolution (ACS), as Russia's preeminent functioning national political authority.[21] On the other hand, from the moment it was confirmed by the Second Congress, Lenin and also Trotsky (now second only to Lenin in the Bolshevik hierarchy) presented their government as revolutionary Russia's sole legitimate political authority. All individuals and institutions that opposed it were counterrevolutionary by definition and fair game for attack by the Petrograd Soviet's MRC, which was supported by armed factory militias (the Red Guards), Baltic Fleet sailors, and, less dependably, by elements of the Petrograd garrison.

Most newspapers in the capital sided with the ACS against the Bolshevik government and could fairly be charged with incitement to overthrow it. The MRC wasted no time in dealing with this problem. On the evening of 26 October, while the Second Congress of Soviets was still in session, it raided and shutdown several opposition papers.[22] In the days that followed, other newspapers especially hostile to the Bolsheviks were shut down. On 27 October, in the name of the Sovnarkom,[23] Lenin issued a decree endorsing all the press closures, explaining that temporary infringements on freedom of the press were justified because, at such a critical moment, opposition papers were "no less dangerous than bombs and machine guns."[24]

By 28 October, government in Petrograd was at a standstill as a large part of the national and municipal bureaucracy, with encouragement from the ACS and the central city and most district dumas, refused to recognize the authority of the Sovnarkom and municipal and district revolutionary institutions, and either staged sitdown strikes or walked off the job. General Petr Krasnov, with Kerensky in tow, stood at the head of a reportedly disciplined, anti-leftist force of seven hundred or so Cossacks who had brushed away disorganized groups of Petrograd soldiers, sailors, and Red Guards on the way from Gachina to Tsarskoe Selo, less than twenty miles from Petrograd. At this point, units of the Petrograd garrison, which had been unreliable and unstable throughout 1917, ignored the MRC's mobilization appeals. Moreover, many Red Guard units were disorganized and lacked leadership. Lenin and Trotsky had to intervene personally to bring some semblance of order to the existing chaos among revolutionary forces and, most important, to get some of them to move into a defensive line hurriedly established along the Pulkovo heights overlooking the southern edge of Petrograd.[25] Concurrently, efforts were initiated to deploy female factory workers to shore up support for the Soviet government among peasants in rural areas of the Petrograd region.[26]

On the twenty-ninth, Krasnov and Kerensky waited for reinforcements in Tsarskoe Selo, and announced their intention of mounting an all-out assault on the capital the next day. To aid them, the ACS, in collaboration with the SR Military Commission, laid plans for an insurrection inside Petrograd timed to coincide with Krasnov's assault. Primary participants in this insurrection were to be cadet officer-trainees from several Petrograd military academies. Taking advantage of the MRC's preoccupation with Krasnov, they were to take control of key military installations and communications facilities. However, the MRC found out about these plans late on the twenty-eighth, when, quite by accident, one of its leaders was detained with a copy of the plans. Consequently, it was decided to start the rebellion a day early, without Krasnov's diversion. Even so, the several hundred cadets and officers involved had some initial success. However, regular troops of the Petrograd garrison and Petrograd-based Cossack units ignored appeals for support from representatives of the ACS. In these circumstances, the ACS forces were doomed. Their rebellion was brutally suppressed by nightfall on the twenty-ninth. All told, an estimated two hundred combatants were killed or wounded during the street fighting in Petrograd on 29 October.[27] These casualties were much higher than those suffered in the capital during the February and October revolutions.

At this time, the armed force at the disposal of Bolshevik authorities in Petrograd was spread too thin to compel compliance with orders. Many of the opposition papers which had been shut down in the immediate post-October days quickly resumed publication under slightly revised titles. Their pages were filled with lurid accounts of Bolshevik excesses, indiscriminate searches and arrests, widespread looting and street violence, and shooting that lasted long into the night. It was widely reported that many of the women soldiers arrested during the occupation of the Winter Palace had been raped, that MRC prisoners were being executed in the street, and that the situation of all detainees defied description. Similarly frightening reports circulated at round-the-clock sessions of the City Duma.[28] Even today, separating fact from fiction with respect to early Bolshevik "terror" is difficult. Petrograd was a battle zone, gripped by anxiety, fear, and fierce antagonism. Although the new authorities were too weak and disorganized to control Cossack patrols who still routinely abused workers and Red Guards in privileged central districts of the capital, "people's power" had been officially proclaimed. Better-off citizens, the "exploiters" from whom power had been seized, watched from their balconies as columns of soldiers, sailors, and Red Guards armed with rifles and shovels streamed southward. Warships of the Baltic Fleet dropped anchor on the Neva and pointed their guns toward targets in the southern suburbs occupied by Krasnov's modest Cossack forces. Barricades were hastily erected, barbed wire strung, and trenches dug in the city itself. In such an environment, often irrational rumors acquired instant credibility.

Some of the most sensational charges against the Bolsheviks at this time were investigated and proven false. Nonetheless, a portion of what the opposition press reported about Bolshevik excesses is supported by reliable evidence. Following suppression of the cadet insurrection, with most of its hastily organized forces at "the Krasnov front," the MRC, to maintain order in Petrograd itself, had to rely largely on such institutions as district soviets, which themselves depended for order on radicalized and frequently unruly and vengeful worker Red Guards.

The MRC placed Petrograd under martial law on the morning of 29 October, at the start of the planned insurrection by the ACS. Later that same day it appointed a Left SR, Lieutenant Colonel Mikhail Muraviev, to direct Petrograd's defenses. Muraviev, a talented but fanatic military leader who nine months later was shot for betraying the Bolsheviks, appears to have been the highest-ranking officer willing to assume this responsibility. An "Order No. 1" which he issued upon assuming his post gave workers free reign to lynch suspected counterrevolutionaries.[29]

The situation was chaotic enough in Petrograd, but late reports from Moscow suggested that the situation there was far worse. In Moscow, the outcome of an all-out struggle for power between a loyalist Committee of Public Safety and a Bolshevik-dominated Military Revolutionary Committee was in doubt for more than a week. Savage street fighting and heavy artillery bombardment that had begun on 28 October badly damaged buildings, several of them in and around the Kremlin, and casualties numbered in the hundreds. In response to news of this warfare in Moscow, major labor organizations and left socialist political groups in Petrograd not yet firmly allied with either of the two major warring sides issued ever more urgent pleas for a cease fire and the immediate start of negotiations aimed at forming a mutually acceptable, inclusive homogeneous socialist coalition government. Among the most important of these were the Menshevik-Internationalists and especially the Left SRs. In the 31 October issue of *Znamia truda,* the voice of Petrograd Left SRs, Boris Kamkov lamented, not without foundation, that "the old coalition government has fallen but we don't have a new government. You can call the Sovnarkom what you will—a general staff to combat Kerensky, the Bolshevik Central Committee—but a viable government it is not." A front-page appeal alongside Kamkov's editorial called on "everybody" to end the civil war and, "all as one, to demand the immediate establishment of a homogeneous revolutionary government composed of representatives of all socialist parties."

*   *   *

In addition to the Left SRs, Vikzhel was another key organization that sought to reconcile the warring sides at this time. As foreshadowed by its telegram to the Second All-Russian Congress of Soviets, on 29 October it invited representatives of all major "democratic" groups to participate in political negotiations under its auspices beginning that very day, aimed at creating an all-inclusive, homogeneous socialist government from the Bolsheviks on the extreme left to the Popular Socialists on the right. Moreover, Vikzhel declared its intention of calling a nationwide railway strike starting at midnight that very day unless a military truce was proclaimed in Petrograd and Moscow, and serious talks on reconstruction of the government were begun before then.[30] Vikzhel's demand for an immediate halt to armed civil conflict and reconstruction of the government on a broad, exclusively socialist basis was echoed by the Petrograd Soviet of Peasants' Deputies, by individual trade unions, as well as by the Petrograd Trade Union Council and the Central Soviet of Factory-Shop Committees, in which Bolsheviks had majorities.[31]

At this point, Lenin and Trotsky were preoccupied with stamping out the revolt by the ACS and mounting a defense against Krasnov's Cossacks. In their absence, soon after the announcement of Vikzhel's ultimatum, the Bolshevik Central Committee hastened to endorse the party's participation in the proposed negotiations and to define its position in them. Most important, the Central Committee, at its meeting on 29 October, unanimously agreed that the government should be broadened and that the participation in it of all Soviet parties was acceptable. In the spirit of the Soviet Congress's mandate, it was agreed that any new government should be formed by the CEC and be responsible to it, and that it should be bound by the decrees of the Second All-Russian Congress of Soviets. With regard to the inclusion of specific individuals in the new government, inevitably an especially sensitive issue because of demands by the moderate socialists and the City Duma that Lenin and Trotsky be disqualified from holding top government posts, by a vote of 5 to 3 with 1 abstention, the Central Committee reached the ambiguous conclusion that "some reciprocal give and take on party nominations was permissible."[32] At a plenary session of the CEC a few hours later, Kamenev was more explicit on this point, declaring that "with respect to the creation of a homogeneous socialist government," the brunt of the problem did not lie in its composition or personal groupings but in "recognition of the Second [Soviet] Congress's basic propositions."[33] In the prevailing circumstances this statement, which was consistent with Kamenev's position before the overthrow of the Provisional Government, was a signal that Lenin and Trotsky were not untouchable and that even a Bolshevik majority in a government which included all socialist parties might not be an absolute requirement. Lenin subsequently claimed that Bolshevik interest in a negotiated settlement of the government question during these days was a "diplomatic smokescreen for military operations."[34] No doubt this was the way he and Trotsky saw it. In their absence, however, this was clearly not the view of a majority of the Central Committee. The position on the Sovnarkom adopted by the Central Committee on 29 October was immediately circulated to major party organizations around the country as official party policy.[35]

Although support for significantly broadening the Sovnarkom was at its peak in the Bolshevik Central Committee during the first chaotic days following the Soviet Congress, the same cannot be said of the socialist groups, primarily centrist and right Mensheviks and SRs, who had supported the Provisional Government throughout 1917 and who had walked out of the Second Congress of Soviets to protest its overthrow by the Bolsheviks. Indeed, the main factors that pushed "swing" members of the Bolshevik Central Committee toward compromise—the threat from Vikzhel, the party's isolation from all other political groups, and its seeming incapacity either to govern or to successfully defend the revolution by itself—encouraged moderate socialists to believe that the Bolsheviks were on the brink of defeat and that therefore it made more sense to resist them rather than meet their terms.

A hard-line resolution adopted by the Menshevik Central Committee on 28 October reflected this view. The resolution prohibited negotiations of any kind with the Bolsheviks until their "adventure" had been completely liquidated. Moreover, it called on the ACS to enter into discussions with the Provisional Government, the Preparliament, and worker organizations on construction of a new government. So confident were centrist and right Mensheviks that things were going their way that in this resolution they called on the ACS to propose to the MRC that it surrender at once—in exchange for which its leaders would receive guarantees of personal safety until the Constituent Assembly had an opportunity to decide whether they should be tried.[36]

This staunchly anti-Bolshevik stance was reflected in the behavior of representatives of moderate socialist groups and of the ACS at the first three sessions of the Vikzhel talks on 29–30 October, and in the work of a "Special Commission" delegated by participants in the talks to formulate a draft agreement on the makeup and program of a new government on the morning of the thirtieth.[37] In these forums, Menshevik and SR leaders demanded the immediate removal of Lenin's government and its replacement by an exclusively socialist coalition cabinet from which both the Bolsheviks and representatives of privileged society would be excluded; the disarming of workers; the dissolution of the MRC; and acceptance of the principle that everything done by the Second Congress of Soviets, including its very existence, should be declared null and void. In return, efforts would be made to insure that, upon entering the capital, Krasnov's forces would refrain from reprisals.[38]

To the contrary, Bolsheviks at the Vikzhel talks argued forcefully for the creation of a new, broadly representative Soviet government. Responding to the Mensheviks and SRs the night of 29/30 October, Kamenev insisted that workers would not support a government from which Bolsheviks were excluded.[39] Later, when it appeared that the moderate socialists were extinguishing any possibility of agreement, Grigorii Sokolnikov, representing the Bolshevik Central Committee, declared that the party was not "seeking power" and "accepted the proposal of the railroaders" on condition that the new government would be responsible to the CEC and [committed] to the program of the Second Congress of Soviets. "We do not intend to delay the Constituent Assembly," he insisted. "Soviet power will be conveyed to it."[40] The Bolshevik moderate David Riazanov, who participated in these talks as a representative of the trade union leadership, was ready to forego retention of a Soviet-based government in the interest of socialist unity.[41] He feared, however, that disarming workers, as Dan was then demanding, would lead to their slaughter. Consequently, his remarks at this session of the Vikzhel negotiations focused on this danger.[42]

Negotiations over the formation of a new government at this juncture were constantly interrupted by reports of savage battles in the streets of Petrograd and Moscow, and in the Pulkovo region south of Petrograd. The cadet insurrection and its brutal suppression during the first day of the talks (29 October) also undermined them. From the start, consideration of the structure and composition of the government became intertwined with mutual recriminations and a desperate search for acceptable terms for an immediate military truce.[43] Appealing to supporters of the ACS for reason were A. A. Blum, speaking for the United Social Democratic-Internationalists, Martov on behalf of the Menshevik-Internationalists, and Boris Malkin for the Left SRs. "Have you given any thought to what the defeat of the Bolsheviks would mean?" asked Blum. "The action of the Bolsheviks is the action of workers and soldiers. Workers and soldiers will be crushed along with the party of the proletariat. . . . The creation of a united revolutionary front is essential."[44] "A peaceful liquidation of the crisis through a negotiated settlement between the two sides is absolutely necessary," echoed Martov. In his view, only the formation of a government uniting the entire democracy, not just the soviets, but excluding representatives of privileged society, offered the hope of heading off a terrible civil war, the destruction of the democracy, and the imposition of a rightist dictatorship.[45]

Malkin also made a passionate plea for support of the Vikzhel initiative. Although seconding the insistence of the Bolsheviks that any new government should be controlled by the CEC and should endorse the decrees of the Second Congress of Soviets, he tried to make this stipulation a bit more palatable to the moderate socialists by proposing that the CEC as well as the government be reformed so as to equalize the representation of Bolsheviks and "defensists" and give significant power to the middle (specifically, that 40 percent of the membership be allotted to Bolsheviks, 40 percent to "defensists" [i.e., largely Mensheviks and SRs], and 20 percent to "internationalists" [i.e., primarily Left SRs and Menshevik-Internationalists]).[46] Bearing in mind that at the start of the Second Congress of Soviets the Bolsheviks did not have a majority without help from other "internationalists," this proposal was not as farfetched as it may appear. More important, however, is that at the first two Vikzhel plenary meetings and in the meeting of the "Special Commission" on 30 October, the Mensheviks and SRs stymied all efforts at compromise by insisting that Bolsheviks be eliminated from the government altogether.

After the suppression of the uprising organized by the ACS (the evening of 29 October), the unexpectedly quick elimination of the threat of forces supposedly loyal to Kerensky near Pulkovo and, of no less consequence, insistent demands for a compromise agreement by a broad cross-section of representatives of rank-and-file workers,[47] at a CEC meeting the night of 30/31 October, the Menshevik position on absolute exclusion of the Bolsheviks from the government softened.[48] On 31 October, by a one-vote margin, the Menshevik Central Committee endorsed participation in efforts to form a socialist coalition government that included Bolsheviks (although both the Mensheviks and SRs remained adamantly opposed to the inclusion of either Lenin or Trotsky in a new government).[49] For their part, with agreement in sight, Bolshevik moderates went a step further in the direction of compromise. Menshevik and SR representatives in the Vikzhel talks the night of 30/31 October proposed the creation of a wholly new representative body, to be called the Provisional People's Council, to which the new all-socialist cabinet would be responsible. Designed to eliminate the possibility of a Bolshevik majority, it was to include representatives from, among others, the first CEC, the Petrograd and Moscow city dumas, the All-Russian Executive Committee of Soviets of Peasants' Deputies, the Central Trade Union Council, and Vikzhel. Kamenev and his colleagues responded by insisting that the new CEC should be the core of this new entity. They were subsequently accused by Lenin of backing off this principle. Although the evidence in this regard is contradictory, there is no doubt that a general plan for the Provisional People's Council to which a government including representatives of all socialist parties would be responsible was accepted by a majority of participants at this meeting.[50]

The next night (31 October/1 November) Kamenev, Sokolnikov, and Riazanov participated in the deliberations of yet another commission formed to prepare recommendations for the makeup of the new government to be responsible to the Provisional People's Council. These deliberations were abruptly interrupted by thirty angry representatives of Obukhov plant workers who demanded an end to procrastination and immediate agreement on a socialist coalition government responsible to the CEC and committed to implementing the program of the Second All-Russian Congress of Soviets.[51] One of the Obukhov delegates banged his fist on a table and shouted: "Finish up, do you hear, finish . . . People are already going at each other with bayonets . . . To hell with leaders and parties . . . String up all the Lenins, Kerenskys, and Trotskys . . . We need an agreement and we won't leave without it!"[52]

After several more hours of fierce arguments, this commission's deliberations culminated with a decision, by majority vote, to eliminate Lenin and Trotsky as candidates for ministerial posts, and to limit Bolshevik representation in the proposed new cabinet to the Ministry of Education (Lunacharskii), Commerce and Industry (Leonid Krasin), and possibly also Labor, and Foreign and Internal Affairs (where Bolsheviks were listed among alternative candidates—respectively, Aleksandr Shliapnikov, Mikhail Pokrovskii, and Rykov). According to the preliminary ministerial slate drafted at this meeting, Viktor Chernov was the leading candidate for prime minister and his SR colleague, Nikolai Avksentiev, a leader of the ACS who had been publicly implicated in its insurrection, was the primary nominee to head the foreign ministry.[53] Many years later Raphael Abramovich, a prominent Menshevik commission member, recalled that Bolsheviks on the commission consented to dropping Lenin and Trotsky as ministerial candidates.[54]

Vikzhel officials, with Kamenev's encouragement, now announced their acceptance of the basis for a final agreement on the form and construction of a new government. Vikzhel also announced that all participants had acknowledged the necessity of establishing an immediate military truce.[55] At this point, in messages to their counterparts in Moscow, Vikzhel officials in Petrograd expressed confidence that a mutually satisfactory settlement was all but certain.[56] Even the Soviet press in Petrograd seemed confident that an agreement was close at hand. Thus, on 1 November, the lead editorial in the Petrograd Soviet's *Rabochii i soldat,* which was controlled by the Bolsheviks, informed its readers that "agreement among all fractions [at the Vikzhel talks] has been reached based on the principle that the government should be composed of all socialist parties in the Soviets." "In promoting the idea that power should belong to the revolutionary democracy," the editorial continued, "the Bolsheviks always understood this to mean a coalition of all socialist parties . . . not the domination of a single party."

* * *

Lenin apparently first became fully alert to the extent of efforts by his Central Committee colleagues to reach a compromise agreement on construction of the government the night of 29/30 October, following the suppression of the insurgent cadets. Supremely confident that social revolution and civil war in Russia were on the verge of igniting decisive socialist revolutions in Europe, he had spent the previous month and a half frantically pushing his party to a unilateral seizure of power and, with Kerensky's help, succeeded at the eleventh hour. Subsequently, he had outmaneuvered Bolshevik moderates and Left SRs at the Congress of Soviets, in this case thanks partly to the withdrawal of the Mensheviks and SRs. Moreover, with the support of workers, soldiers, and sailors excited by the bright perspectives in the Soviet Congress's program, he and Trotsky had superintended the suppression of the ACS insurrection and were poised to stop Krasnov's attack.

A flood of resolutions from factories, labor organizations, and garrison military units indicated that, in the wake of these initial successes, popular support for homogeneous socialist Soviet power, and aversion to anything that smacked of collaboration with the bourgeoisie, was stronger than ever. The Bolshevik Petersburg Committee, for one, had first considered the party's position toward the Vikzhel negotiations on 29 October.[57] Prior to meeting that day, it had solicited and received brief reports from party district committees on prevailing political sentiment in their neighborhoods. A minority of these reports strengthened the argument for retreat. In the centrally located, upper-class Liteini district, for example, even rank-and-file Bolsheviks strongly favored significant concessions to the moderate socialists in the interest of reaching agreement on broadening the government. But significantly more typical was a message from the Narva district, an area dotted with factories, where it was reported that "the masses view a settlement from the point of view of keeping and implementing the victories of the October revolution . . . [F]eelings toward the SRs and Mensheviks are hostile."[58]

The Petersburg Committee meeting of 29 October itself began with additional local reports. This was at precisely the time when the ACS insurgency was most threatening and when a clash with Krasnov's forces near Pulkovo appeared imminent. Consequently these reports focused on such questions as control of strategically important railways, available weapons and vehicles, and the strength and fighting spirit of Red Guards and workers generally, as well as on conditions in district soviets germane to military operations and neighborhood security. Nonetheless, taken together, the reports suggested that, in the wake of their gains at the Second Soviet Congress, the workers' fighting spirit was high. Partly influenced by these reports, members of the Petersburg Committee, although hopeful of broadening the government to include other internationalist groups such as the Left SRs and Menshevik-Internationalists, expressed little support for the principle adopted by party moderates at the Vikzhel talks of obtaining an agreement at almost any cost. Rather, most members were adamant that the party had to continue to champion Soviet power and the program of the Soviet Congress. They ended their discussion by adopting a resolution affirming that the primary task of the moment was to realize the slogan "All Power to the Soviets" both at the center and locally, and that the goal of Soviet power was to implement the program adopted by the Second All-Russian Congress of Soviets. Any compromise from that goal was unacceptable.[59]

Without question, as in the pre-October period, the prevailing popular mood was not specifically pro-Bolshevik in the sense of advocating or even favoring Bolshevik one-party rule. However, judging from these reports and the vehement protests of worker delegations at sessions of the Vikzhel talks, Lenin was on safe ground in arguing, as he now did, that the revolutionary masses would view compromises undermining Soviet power and the gains of

October as a betrayal of Bolshevik promises. Yet here party colleagues who had rejected his basic theoretical tenets and had opposed many of his most fervently argued strategic directives from the time of the February revolution were steering the party toward a political settlement which, as Lenin viewed it, would restore the moderate socialists' strong influence in government and thereby destroy his wager on Russia setting off decisive revolutionary outbreaks internationally.

On 1 November, Lenin vented his rage at this state of affairs at meetings of the Petersburg Committee (in which several members of the Central Committee participated) and the Central Committee (in which representatives of the Petersburg Committee, the Bolshevik Military Organization, and Bolshevik trade union leaders participated).[60] At the Petersburg Committee meeting, evidently struggling to maintain his composure with only mixed success, Lenin charged that the behavior of the Central Committee's representatives in the Vikzhel meetings was treasonous. The only Bolshevik leader he singled out for praise was Trotsky. "Trotsky recognized long ago that unification is impossible and from that time on there has been no better Bolshevik. . . . If there must be a split [in the party], so be it," Lenin fumed. "If you get a majority [in the full Central Committee] take power in the CEC and carry on. But we will go to the sailors."[61]

Members of the Petersburg Committee sat transfixed as the bitter struggle within the national party leadership over the future government unfolded before their eyes. It was rare enough for Lenin to attend one of their meetings; in fact, he had done so only three times in the preceding seven months. Now, however, the committee heard, firsthand, Lenin's views on government, on the future of the revolution, and on the crisis within the upper echelon of the party. Lunacharskii then rose to defend the views of the moderates. Trotsky continued the ferocious, unrelenting attack on Kamenev, Zinoviev, and their supporters launched by Lenin, and Nogin followed Trotsky with a final impassioned plea for compromise.

Lunacharskii insisted that a homogeneous socialist government rather than an exclusively Bolshevik or even Soviet government was a necessity. In response to Lenin's categorical rejection of compromise, he argued that if the Bolsheviks did not obtain the cooperation of the existing state apparatus they "would not be able to manage anything." He acknowledged that the party had the option of "resorting to terror." "But why?" he queried. To him arrests would solve nothing—the state bureaucracy was just too big and complex to harness by means of terror. The only viable course, he insisted, was to "take the path of least resistance," rather than "taking each station with a bayonet charge."[62]

Bolshevik moderates Lev Kamenev, Viktor Nogin, and Anatolii Lunacharskii. Drawings by Iu. K. Artybushev, in *"Diktatura proletariata" v Rossii: Nabroski s natury Iu. K. Artsybusheva* (Moscow, 1922).

To Trotsky, Lunacharskii's preference for negotiation rather than armed violence and terror, as well as his emphasis on gradualism rather than on immediate decisive action, was a legacy of "petty bourgeois psychology." The "middle-class lice" who were then refusing to take sides, including Vikzhel, would swing to the Bolsheviks as soon as they saw the strength of their government. "The bureaucracy has its own interests and habits," he said. "It must be smashed and rejuvenated. Only then will we be able to work." Compromising with moderate socialists in government would just bring continued vacillation and the evaporation of Bolshevik authority among the masses.[63]

Nogin was a key leader of the party's Moscow city organization and, since 2 October, had been chairman of the Moscow Soviet. During the run-up to the Congress of Soviets, he had been an especially ardent supporter of linking the creation of a homogeneous Soviet government to its deliberations. He had left for Petrograd at the very moment when the Bolsheviks' situation in Moscow was at its grimmest to report on this state of affairs, to weigh in on the side of compromise, and to assume his post as people's commissar for trade and industry. The record of a speech he made at the first Sovnarkom meeting on 3 November reveals that the savage brutality of class warfare in Moscow and the anarchy reigning there had convinced him that unless the Bolsheviks split the opposition by coming to terms with Vikzhel, they were "doomed to destruction, after wasting all their forces in a prolonged civil war."[64] At the Petersburg Committee meeting of 1 November, he appealed for an immediate end to bloodletting. Moreover, he wondered aloud about why the word "conciliation" grated so on the ears of Lenin and

Trotsky. In his mind, the party simply could not survive alone, and the attempt to do so by what he referred to as "the minority in the Central Committee" would inevitably result in a long civil war, hunger, the breakup of the Soviets, the destruction of the party, and the triumph of the counterrevolution.[65]

The debate at this meeting between opposing members of the Central Committee was so long and heated that the consistently radical journalist and member of the Executive Commission Anton Slutskii was one of only a few Petersburg Committee members able to get in a word. Siding with Lenin and Trotsky, Slutskii attacked compromise as a "camouflaged retreat from power," and loudly reaffirmed the cardinal importance of continuing to champion exclusive Soviet power. The revolutionary masses, he suggested, would be unresponsive to anything else.[66] After his speech, it was agreed to convene a broader gathering of the Petersburg Committee with additional representatives of district committees to explain the city party leadership's position the next day (this meeting was not held until 4 November), and, a short while later, the meeting broke up so that several of its participants could attend the expanded meeting of the Central Committee which was about to begin.

As was the case in the Petersburg Committee, at the 1 November Central Committee meeting Lenin, again arm in arm with Trotsky, led the attack on the proposed Vikzhel compromise. Arguing that parties which had not even participated in the insurrection were taking advantage of the negotiations to seize power from those who now had the upper hand, Trotsky insisted that Bolsheviks should predominate in any new government and that Lenin should stand at its head.[67] Trotsky, as much as Lenin if not more, was then obsessed with instigating immediate decisive socialist revolutions in the more advanced countries of Europe by means of a big revolutionary bang in Russia. Judging by his statements, it is no exaggeration to suggest that most of his thinking about Russian politics was shaped by this overarching concern.[68] Lenin, for his part, again made it quite clear that he was unalterably opposed to *any* further negotiations with the Mensheviks and SRs.[69]

Under the weight of this onslaught, moderate Bolshevik leaders, including Kamenev, Rykov, Lunacharskii, and Riazanov, distanced themselves from some aspects of the pending Vikzhel agreement. However, in arguing for the necessity of significant compromise with other socialist groups along the lines agreed upon by the Central Committee on 29 October, they were as fervent as Lenin and Trotsky. Take Riazanov, for example. Like Kamenev, Rykov, and Lunacharskii, Riazanov had been a leader in the fierce, often successful struggle to curb the influence of Lenin's radicalism in the late summer and early fall of 1917. Based on this experience and discussions with party colleagues during the Second All-Russian Congress of Soviets, he was confident that a majority of Bolshevik leaders in Moscow and the provinces shared his views. In making the case for a broadly representative government Riazanov, as chairman of the Petrograd Trade Union Council, could justly purport to represent Petrograd's 450,000 unionized workers. He would emphasize this point during a bitter confrontation with Lenin at a meeting of the Petrograd Trade Union Council on 6 November.[70] On 1 November, before the Central Committee, he made a particularly forceful plea for compromise: "If we abandon an agreement," he declared at one point, "we will be utterly and hopelessly alone . . . without the Left SRs, without anything . . . we will be faced with the fact that we tricked the masses, having promised them a Soviet government. . . . [Some] agreement is a necessity."[71]

The categorically negative views of Trotsky and Lenin on negotiations with the opposition were also rejected by centrist Central Committee members, including Ian Berzin, Moisei Uritskii, Andrei Bubnov, and Iakov Sverdlov, all of whom had voted in favor of participating in the Vikzhel discussions on 29 October. Nonetheless, emboldened by the sudden improvement in the party's situation locally, and by prodding from Lenin and probably also from mid-level party leaders from the Petersburg Committee, even they felt that Kamenev and other Bolsheviks who had participated in the Vikzhel talks had exceeded the Central Committee's mandate of 29 October and that several provisions of the preliminary agreement were unacceptable. Uritskii, for one, declared: "We must not yield on either Lenin or Trotsky for that would constitute renunciation of our program."[72]

At the expanded Central Committee meeting of 1 November, Slutskii was the designated spokesman for the Petersburg Committee. Again allying himself with Lenin and Trotsky, he insisted that the party's negotiators were acting "in opposition to all workers." The question [i.e., of Soviet power] is settled as far as the masses are concerned, he added, "and it behooves us not to talk of broadened Soviets of any kind."[73]

Toward the close of this meeting, by a vote of 10 to 4, the Central Committee rejected Lenin's demand that the Vikzhel talks be aborted at once. It was decided, instead, that the party should participate in the talks one last time, couching its minimum demands in the form of an ultimatum, if only to demonstrate the unfeasibility of an agreement to the Left SRs. This ultimatum asserted that, among other things, a new government would recognize the inviolability of the decrees of the Second Congress, and would also acknowledge the Second Congress and the CEC as the sole government authority. It also reiterated the principle that only groups previously in the Soviet could be represented in a broadened CEC. Thus, representation from municipal dumas and the creation of some hybrid organ like the People's Council was not allowed.[74] Significantly, V. Volodarskii (Moisei Gol'shtein) rather than Kamenev was designated to announce the party's rejection of the Vikzhel commission's proposal and its new ultimatum to a meeting of the CEC that night (1/2 November).

Although Volodarskii was only twenty-six years old, he was a veteran revolutionary renowned for his polemical skills, energy, and ability to stir large crowds. After his return to Russia from the emigration in May 1917, he became an influential member of the Bolshevik Petersburg Committee. A Leninist at heart, Volodarskii, in the immediate pre-October period, had been among tactically pragmatic Petrograd Bolsheviks urging caution and careful preparation before any attempt to overthrow the Provisional Government. This position was conditioned by his unease about the possibility of providing bread to the Russian population and either ending the "imperialist" war or mobilizing support for a revolutionary war. He was also skeptical about the likelihood of early socialist revolutions in Europe. "We must understand that having taken power we will be forced to lower wages, to increase unemployment, to institute terror," he had warned. "We do not have the right to reject these methods, but there is no need to rush into them."[75] In the CEC meeting of 1 November, which began soon after the Central Committee adjourned, he declared, disingenuously, that among us [Bolsheviks] "there is scarcely anyone who does not want an agreement." "However, we cannot conclude an agreement at any price." "We must not yield positions which have been fought for by hundreds of thousands of workers, peasants, and soldiers." Volodarskii then put before the CEC, still chaired by Kamenev, a resolution which adhered closely to the terms of the Central Committee ultimatum just described.[76]

Clearly taken aback by this abrupt retreat from the significantly more conciliatory Bolshevik stance in the Vikzhel talks the day before, Vladimir Bazarov, for the United Social-Democratic Internationalists, introduced a sharply worded resolution condemning the Bolsheviks for reneging on earlier commitments and announcing his group's intention of withdrawing from the CEC until Bolshevik intransigence ceased. No less dismayed by the abrupt collapse of previously bright prospects for a peaceful political settlement than Bazarov, Karelin struggled to find a new basis for agreement. He proposed that representation in the revolutionary parliament to which a reconstructed government would report be weighted much more heavily in favor of soviets than had been tentatively agreed on the previous night, and also that any new government be pledged to the principles embodied in the Second Congress decrees. In an initial vote, Volodarskii's resolution received thirty-eight votes against twenty-nine for Karelin's. However, after the adoption of a few minor amendments, the Left SRs, still concerned most of all with creating a broad socialist coalition which included the Bolsheviks, voted for Volodarskii's proposal.[77]

Meanwhile, the struggle for leadership of the Bolshevik party raged on. Reconstruction of this phase of the conflict over the government issue and its reverberations within the Central Committee is complicated by the fact that no protocols are available for meetings of the Central Committee that are known to have taken place on 2, 4, and either 5 or 6 November.[78] Undoubtedly the Vikzhel negotiations were the subject of long and fierce debate at the meeting of the Central Committee on 2 November. This debate culminated in the adoption, by a one-vote margin, of a resolution proposed by Lenin that berated the moderates for bowing to pressure for reconstruction of the government by a minority in the Soviets, thereby frustrating the will of the Second All-Russian Congress of Soviets, and endorsed the policies of the existing government as the only ones consistent with the triumph of socialism in Russia and Europe.[79]

Lenin's method in achieving even this close victory, however, is dubious. Two earlier votes on the acceptability of significant concessions to the moderate socialists ended in ties, after which Lenin turned to the Petersburg Committee for aid.[80] A cryptic entry in the minutes of a meeting of the Petersburg Committee on 2 November indicates that early on it was abruptly interrupted by the reading of an urgent note from Lenin indicating that a resolution against compromise should be adopted immediately and brought to a meeting of the Central Committee then in progress. Iakov Fenikshtein, who delivered Lenin's appeal, explained that "the Muscovites," obviously Nogin and Rykov, were demanding agreement with the Mensheviks and SRs, and that the Petersburg Committee's help was needed to rebuff them.[81]

Viacheslav Molotov, Stalin's future foreign minister, was in the middle of a report on the "current moment" when Lenin's note arrived. The Petersburg Committee responded by sending Gleb Bokii, one of its leaders throughout 1917, to inform the Central Committee of the former's strong opposition to concessions which would dilute Soviet power or stray from the reform program adopted by the Second Soviet Congress. Following Bokii's departure, a parade of militantly inclined local-level leaders took the floor to oppose inclusion of moderate socialists in the government. No one supported continuation of the Vikzhel talks. In the end, the ultimatum which the Central Committee and CEC had passed the day before was endorsed. A bit later,

Bokii returned from the Central Committee meeting with the news that he had been unable to get the floor to express the Petersburg Committee's solidarity with Lenin. Consequently, Molotov and Slutskii were hurriedly dispatched to inform the Central Committee of its most recent action.[82]

Did the Petersburg Committee's intervention help swing the Central Committee Lenin's way? We do not know. What is known is that Lenin's attacks on the behavior of the moderates did not deter them from trying to keep alive the negotiations over reconstruction of the government. This became apparent at a late-night meeting of the CEC on 2 November.[83] When the meeting turned to the Vikzhel negotiations, Malkin, who appears to have been aware that Lenin was getting the upper hand over the moderates, rose to read a Left SR declaration attacking the Bolsheviks for their lack of flexibility in government negotiations and for "plunging the country into the abyss of civil war." The declaration ended with an ultimatum to the Bolsheviks: either you adopt more acceptable negotiating terms or you are on your own.[84] It is conceivable, indeed probable, that Bolshevik moderates encouraged the Left SRs to issue this ultimatum in order to strengthen their position. At the First Left SR Congress a few weeks later, Kamkov recalled that at precisely this time "responsible representatives" of the [Bolshevik] party came to them and said: "Comrade Left SRs, pursue your cause with energy—we support you and hope that we can reach agreement."[85]

At the 2 November CEC meeting, responding to Malkin, Zinoviev dutifully presented Lenin's position rejecting agreement with the moderate socialists adopted by the Central Committee earlier in the evening. However, he immediately made it clear that this was not the Bolsheviks' final word, explaining that the position had yet to be considered by the party's CEC fraction and requesting an hour's recess so this could be done. No account is available of the meeting of the Bolshevik fraction which took place during this recess. But a proposal on construction of a new government cobbled together there and immediately presented to the CEC by Kamenev leaves no room for doubt that, through what he and Zinoviev later referred to as "extraordinary effort," they succeeded in persuading a majority of the fraction to soften the Central Committee's new, harder negotiating position. Although still including many of the minimum demands in the Central Committee's 1 November ultimatum (those relating to the primacy of the CEC, recognition of the decrees of the Congress of Soviets, and rejection of the creation of any wholly new parliamentary body), it was made more palatable to the Left SRs by a provision allowing for the inclusion in the CEC of representatives of socialist fractions in the Petrograd City Duma (thereby opening the door to broadening the CEC to include non-Soviet groups), and by the stipulation that "no less than half" of government portfolios would go to Bolsheviks (rather than a preponderance, as the 1 November Bolshevik ultimatum implied). The proposal insisted on the inclusion of Lenin and Trotsky in a new government. The positions they would hold, however, were not specified.[86]

Most significant of all, the Central Committee's ultimatum of 1 November, as well as Lenin's unequivocal attack on the moderates, was aimed at bringing negotiations over reconstruction of the government to an immediate halt. The primary purpose of the proposal Kamenev presented was to continue the negotiations. For the Left SRs, these were forward steps. They withdrew their own ultimatum and, in principle, committed themselves to support of the new Bolshevik proposal.[87] Kamenev, Riazanov, and Zinoviev for the Bolsheviks and Karelin and Prosh Proshian for the Left SRs were to represent the CEC in further negotiations over the makeup of a new government.[88]

Riazanov presented the proposal to participants at the next session of the Vikzhel talks on 3 November. The meeting had begun inauspiciously for the moderate socialists. They had assumed that the preliminary agreement reached by the Vikzhel commission the night of 31 October/1 November would be the basis for construction of a new government, and consequently that it would be controlled by the People's Council in which Bolshevik influence would be minimized. However, the chair, A. Malitskii, read a resolution just presented to him by a delegation representing thousands of Putilov factory workers. Like the demands of the Obukhov workers a few days earlier, the resolution affirmed that the creation of a homogeneous socialist government was essential but that it had to accept the program of the Soviet government as reflected in decrees on land, peace, workers' control, and immediate convocation of the Constituent Assembly; recognize the necessity of merciless struggle against the counterrevolution; acknowledge the Second Congress with participation by the peasantry as the sole legitimate source of political power; accept that the government was responsible to the CEC; and reject participation in the CEC of organizations that were not part of the Soviet. In short, as was the case with the CEC's proposal subsequently presented by Riazanov, the resolution of the Putilov workers was a rejection of many of the more important concessions tentatively agreed upon at the Vikzhel negotiations the night of 31 October/1 November. Abramovich, representing the United Social-Democratic Internationalists, probably also spoke for the Menshevik-Internationalists, not to mention mainstream Mensheviks and SRs, when he declared that the proposal presented by Riazanov precluded an agreement and that the responsibility for the consequences of this outcome fell on the CEC. The remainder of this meeting was devoted to attacks by the moderate socialists on Bolshevik "terror" and the passage of a resolution demanding the formation of a comprehensively representative socialist government, responsible to a body representing the entire "democracy" (i.e., the Provisional People's Council).[89]

* * *

The apparent collapse of the Vikzhel talks notwithstanding, one can well imagine Lenin's fury upon learning that the party's fraction in the CEC led by Kamenev and Zinoviev was continuing political negotiations aimed at forming a new government. For Lenin, this public act of disobedience was the last straw. The preceding days of bitter intraparty debate testified to the great attraction that a compromise agreement still had for some of his most authoritative colleagues. Therefore, he now asked each individual member of the Central Committee not openly allied with Kamenev to sign a formal statement pledging to bring the dispute with the moderates before top party committees regionally and nationally, including, if necessary, before an emergency party congress if the "Central Committee minority" did not agree categorically in writing to adhere to the letter and spirit of his resolution of 2 November endorsing the structure and policies of his government.[90] Trotsky, Sverdlov, Stalin, Uritskii, Dzerzhinskii, Sokolnikov, Bubnov, Adolf Ioffe, and Matvei Muranov, in addition to Lenin, signed the statement.[91] Analysis of available evidence suggests that although some of the latter remained sympathetic to compromise (and, obviously, had voted for significant compromise on 29 October), few were prepared to challenge Lenin on the impermissibility of gross violations of party discipline in time of incipient civil war.

On the other hand, feeling deeply about the absolute importance of their cause, the leading moderates—Kamenev, Rykov, Zinoviev, Nogin, and Vladimir Miliutin—promptly resigned from the Central Committee so that, as they wrote in a response to Lenin's statement, "we will be free to lay out our views before the masses . . . and to appeal to them to support our call for immediate agreement on a government representing [all] Soviet parties."[92]

Kamenev and his colleagues obviously hoped that their resignations would rally support for them within the party. According to Sverdlov, their step touched off some shock waves.[93] In retrospect, however, they would probably have been better served by remaining in the Central Committee, where there were still critically important battles to be waged and possibly won (for example, over policies toward the Constituent Assembly), and by taking Lenin up on his offer of a party congress or conference to adjudicate the split in the party leadership. For it is by no means certain that a national party gathering would have sided with Lenin. By leaving the Central Committee and not responding positively to the idea of convening an emergency national party meeting, moderate Bolsheviks left one of the revolution's most important arenas of battle and helped "ensure the victory of Lenin's whole line," no less than did the Mensheviks and SRs in quitting the Second Congress of Soviets.

As it was, continuing excesses by the MRC at this time again hardened moderate socialist attitudes toward collaboration with the Bolsheviks. Also, the Mensheviks and SRs interpreted resignations from the Bolshevik Central Committee as a sign that the expected disintegration of the Bolsheviks had begun.[94] Naturally, such thinking undermined whatever residual interest still existed among them for compromise with the Bolsheviks. They showed up for a previously scheduled Vikzhel meeting the night of 5/6 November from which the Bolsheviks and Left SRs were absent, but not with any inclination to negotiate. On this note, the Vikzhel talks were postponed indefinitely.[95]

Unfortunately for the Mensheviks and SRs, the Bolsheviks' initial revolutionary decrees, and their apparent toughness in dealing with the internal and external counterrevolution, had rejuvenated the revolutionary spirit of Petrograd's lower classes, a fact reflected in the expansion of support for Lenin's position at the local level. The Petersburg Committee's conference with delegates from district party organizations on 4 November provided a graphic example of this. At this meeting, some 112 party activists from all districts of the capital listened to a rousing account by Trotsky of the greatness of the Bolshevik party and of the struggle within it over compromise on the government question. Only the Bolsheviks, he declared, had the boldness to lead a popular armed uprising—over the objections of a minority of party moderates who had opposed an armed uprising during the October days and had even rejected the slogan "All Power to the Soviets." Only under the leadership of the [Leninist wing of the] Bolshevik party could workers achieve the goals for which they had long strived. "Taking place now," he went on, "is a socialist revolution, a revolution of the working class, when realization of our maximum program is just days away."[96] It was all very heady. A resolution adopted at this meeting affirmed that, "to realize its program the Bolsheviks, standard bearers of Soviet power, needed the wholehearted support of the laboring and downtrodden masses rather than collaboration with petty bourgeois groups" and that circumstances necessitated a "steady revolutionary course, a maximum degree of discipline . . . and no desertions from responsible positions."[97]

A similar swing toward support of Lenin's position took place at the opening session of a Bolshevik-sponsored conference of factory women on 5 November (dubbed the First Conference of Female Workers in Petrograd). Organization of the conference by several leading Bolshevik women grouped around the journal *Rabotnitsa* had begun before October,[98] primarily to mobilize female workers in support of Bolshevik candidates in elections to the Constituent Assembly. The roughly five hundred women at the first session leaned strongly toward supporting the position of Bolshevik moderates on the construction of the government until Liudmilla Stal', a fiery orator, one of the editors of *Rabnotnitsa,* and a staunch Leninist, persuaded them of the crucial importance of retaining the existing, exclusively Bolshevik government and of putting an end to intraparty bickering.[99] That night, a delegation of women chosen at the session went to Smolny to convey these sentiments to Bolshevik leaders.[100]

Nowhere was the swing from support of the position of Bolshevik moderates to that of Lenin demonstrated more clearly than in the proceedings of the Petrograd Trade Union Council. On 31 October the Council, led by the Bolshevik moderates Riazanov and Lozovskii, had adopted a firmly worded resolution calling for the immediate creation of a homogeneous socialist government representing all parties in the Soviet and responsible to the CEC.[101] Analogous resolutions had been adopted by most of the individual unions represented in the Council. On 6 November, that is, after Lenin's crackdown on the moderates and the breakdown of the Vikzhel talks, the position of the Trade Union Council's leadership on the critical importance of a quick agreement between warring socialist camps remained unchanged.[102] However, this view no longer represented that of rank-and-file unionists. This became apparent on 9 November, when the Council convened a meeting of the representatives from all its member unions. Close to two hundred Petrograd trade unionists participated. Lenin gave the main address, "On the Current Moment," after which members of the Council jumped on him for focusing the brunt of his attack on Mensheviks and SRs rather than on the Kadets. An unidentified Menshevik-Internationalist insisted that the repressive policies of Lenin and Trotsky were signs of weakness rather than strength, and of obsequiousness toward the masses, and that "a party which placed impossible challenges before the proletariat was not its friend." Judging by the protocol of this meeting, nobody spoke out in Lenin's defense. Yet, at its close, a Leninist resolution endorsing the existing government as "a true reflection of the interests of the vast majority of the population" was adopted by a vote of 112 to 33.[103] Clearly, for the time being at least, in the eyes of union locals and rank-and-file workers, Bolshevik firmness in dealing with class enemies was attractive.

This was the last time the issue of intraparty negotiations aimed at creating a broad, exclusively socialist government was discussed by the Petrograd Trade Union Council. The question had been considered by the CEC for the last time on 6 November, a couple of days after the Vikzhel talks broke down, without any progress being made.[104] Thus, the net result of week-long, often round-the-clock negotiations on the government question, and a fierce Bolshevik intraparty struggle over them, was nil. For now, all members of the Sovnarkom were Bolsheviks.

* * *

Despite the lack of progress in reconstructing the Sovnarkom through Vikzhel negotiations during the first weeks of Soviet power in Petrograd, proponents of the multiparty socialist government, moderate Bolsheviks included, drew solace from the fact that, according to the decree establishing the Sovnarkom, it was responsible to the CEC in which all Soviet parties, groups, and institutions, including those that had withdrawn from the Second Congress of Soviets, or were unrepresented in it, were entitled to participate. In Bolshevik Central Committee resolutions on the government question during this period, regardless of whether they were proposed by the moderates or Leninists, the CEC's primacy *over* the Sovnarkom was consistently reaffirmed. Further, Bolshevik moderates and Left SRs alike interpreted this to mean that the CEC would be the primary legislative body and the Sovnarkom would be an executive organ, primarily implementing its policies.[105] Taken for granted, at the very least, was that no policy would become law until confirmed by the CEC.

Even Lenin acknowledged, in principle, that the Sovnarkom was accountable to the CEC. In practice, limitations on the independent power of the Sovnarkom, and the prerogatives and sensibilities of the CEC, were ignored by the Sovnarkom from the start. Before mid-November, when the Sovnarkom first began to meet regularly, Lenin and other peoples' commissars issued decrees on their own, without reference to the CEC. Indeed, during these first weeks, a steady stream of decrees, primarily hastily drafted statements of revolutionary principle, were issued. Their main purpose was to solidify support for Soviet power in Petrograd and the rest of Russia, and to help trigger decisive revolutionary uprisings abroad.

Similar arbitrariness characterized the behavior of the MRC. In the first weeks after Kerensky's overthrow, the MRC became the main command post for security in Petrograd and for expansion of Soviet rule nationally. Beyond this, in Petrograd, for reasons examined in the next chapter, the MRC became responsible for many civil services, and quickly evolved into a government within a government.[106] The independent role of the MRC in national and local political life following the overthrow of the Provisional Government has yet to receive the scholarly attention it deserves. But without question, in response to the unwillingness of government ministries, financial institutions, and municipal agencies to recognize the legitimacy of Soviet power, the MRC issued decrees and orders, often implemented by force, that were not and, in some instances, would not have been approved by the Sovnarkom, let alone the CEC.

In declaring that Russia was without a functioning national government on 29 October, Kamkov was close to the mark. Where Kamkov erred was in implying that the Bolshevik Central Committee might be integrally involved in the government.[107] By and large, neither the Central Committee nor local-level party organs began to play significant, policy-making roles in government for some time. The relationship of party to government institutions in this earliest stage of Soviet rule was implicitly acknowledged at the time by Sverdlov, director of the Central Committee secretariat. In a letter of 28 October to local party organizations he advised that "if you need to know the Central Committee's line, we commend the decrees of the Sovnarkom."[108]

In the first few days after October, amid internal and external counterrevolutionary threats, the ad hoc nature of Bolshevik government could perhaps be justified. Much of the CEC, including most Bolsheviks and all Left SRs, viewed the first repressive decrees issued in the Sovnarkom's name, as well as those of the MRC, as extraordinary measures to deal with temporary emergencies. They continued to consider the CEC as revolutionary Russia's main legislative body and source of political authority, and also expected that once the political situation in Petrograd stabilized, the Sovnarkom would function as the CEC's executive arm.

By the beginning of November immediate threats to the survival of the revolution in Petrograd appeared to have been overcome. Nonetheless, rule by arbitrary decree imposed by force showed no signs of abating. Within the CEC, among the first to formally object to this situation was the moderate Bolshevik Iurii Larin. He did so at the start of the CEC meeting of 2 November. Larin was one of the influential left Mensheviks who had shifted allegiance to the Bolsheviks soon after the Sixth All-Russian Bolshevik Party Congress. Already at that time he had expressed implicit support for the Kamenev wing of the party as well as opposition to "rash methods" and Bolsheviks who favored them.[109] In the CEC, on 2 November, Larin focused his attention on Muraviev's infamous "Order No. 1," which had been published in bold type on the front page of *Izvestiia* that morning without clearance from either the CEC or the Sovnarkom.[110] To him and like-minded party colleagues, not to speak of most Left SRs, Muraviev's endorsement of lynch justice was utterly repugnant. Mindful of the CEC's prerogatives as stipulated by the Second Congress's decree on government, Larin, seconded by Riazanov, urged the CEC simply to revoke it. Such action was seriously considered. However, at this delicate stage in intraparty and intragovernmental relations, a majority of the CEC backed away from an immediate, head-on collision with Lenin and the Sovnarkom. The CEC requested rather than ordered Rykov, people's commissar for internal affairs, to rescind Muraviev's decree, which was done a few days later.[111]

The issue of the relationship between the Sovnarkom and CEC arose again at the very next CEC meeting on 4 November, this time in conjunction with Lenin's decree endorsing press curbs.[112] Again, Larin initiated the discussion. Acknowledging that tight controls over the press might have been justified during the unstable, immediate post-October days, he insisted that this was no longer the case and that the news media should remain free of restrictions as long as it did not directly incite subversion or insurrection. He introduced a resolution revoking Lenin's press decree and prohibiting repressive acts of any kind not sanctioned by a special representative tribunal to be created by the CEC expressly for this purpose.[113] Notably Left SRs at this meeting were prepared to go further than that. They urged that the press decree be dealt with as an aspect of a broader consideration of the Sovnarkom's usurpation of the CEC's legislative powers and demanded that all repressive measures decreed by Lenin and other people's commissars since the October days be rescinded.[114]

In response, the Bolshevik secretary of the CEC, Varlaam Avanesov, a Leninist, contended that the Sovnarkom still needed unlimited powers, as the struggle to defend the revolution was by no means over. He introduced a resolution prohibiting restoration of press freedoms and endorsing all measures of the Sovnarkom to date.[115] Subsequently first Trotsky, and then Lenin, both of whom rushed to the CEC meeting upon hearing of the conflict brewing there, rose to defend the press decree as an absolute necessity in time of extreme emergency. Thus, very quickly, Larin's initiative evolved into a second bitter structural clash between the CEC and the Sovnarkom, as well as a direct confrontation between Bolshevik moderates and Left SRs on the one hand, and Leninist Bolsheviks on the other, over fundamental governmental powers.

When the issue was voted on, Avanesov's resolution won out over Larin's, but the matter did not stop there. Frustrated in their hope of broadening the Sovnarkom, or of moderating its behavior through the CEC, the Left SRs announced their withdrawal from the MRC and from all other government institutions except the CEC.[116] The sensation this caused paled by the reaction to what came next. Nogin made an emotional plea for a compromise on the government issue, following it up with an announcement that was as prophetic as it was startling. As he put it, the only alternative was "a purely Bolshevik government maintained by political terror . . . this will lead to the estrangement of proletarian mass organizations from those who direct our political affairs, to the establishment of an unaccountable regime, and to the destruction of the revolution and the country." Declaring that Bolshevik moderates could not accept responsibility for such a course, he disclosed the resignations from the Sovnarkom of four people's commissars—Rykov, Miliutin, Ivan Teodorovich, and Nogin himself—as well as the association of seven additional prominent Bolshevik officials with their protest.[117]

To be sure, three of the officials who resigned (Nogin, Rykov, and Miliutin) were members of the Bolshevik Central Committee who stood close to Kamenev on theoretical and tactical questions. Their departures from the government followed logically from their withdrawals from the Central Committee. Moreover, most of those who formally endorsed the statement but did not resign also belonged to the moderate wing of the party. However, this was not true in all cases. For example, Aleksandr Shliapnikov, people's commissar for labor, had, until then, usually allied himself with the Leninists.

One of the most eloquent moderate Bolshevik indictments of the hardline toward political compromise that Lenin and Trotsky were pushing for at this time was delivered by Lozovskii at a Bolshevik caucus preceding the 4 November CEC meeting. Prefacing each indictment with the refrain "in the name of party discipline, I cannot remain silent," Lozovskii attacked the Leninists for supporting the extremism of the MRC reflected in Muraviev's incitement of mob violence; for the suppression of the opposition press, harassment, persecutions, searches, and arrests; for curbs on the right of association; for the MRC's usurpation of civil government; for cheating the toiling masses who had fought for [multiparty] Soviet government only to discover that for reasons unclear to them this government turned out to be purely Bolshevik; and for making agreement on reconstruction of the government conditional on inclusion of specific individuals [i.e., Lenin and Trotsky] when every moment of delay in reaching agreement brought further bloodshed.[118]

Lozovskii's indictment of the Leninists in the Bolshevik caucus was stirring and captured the tense, emotional atmosphere which obviously prevailed there. Larin's move against curbs on the press, and the impending resignations from the Sovnarkom, were undoubtedly discussed by the fraction at the caucus. For non-Bolsheviks at the subsequent CEC meeting, however, Nogin's announcement of resignations from the government had the effect of an exploding bomb. Suddenly, it was apparent that both the Bolshevik Central Committee and the Sovnarkom were in shambles. The Left SRs sought to exploit this circumstance in order to try once again to assert the authority of the CEC over the Sovnarkom. In a formal written interpellation to Lenin, an unidentified Left SR pointedly noted that the Congress of Soviets had designated the CEC as the supreme authority to which the Sovnarkom was wholly responsible. He asked for an immediate explanation of the grounds upon which the Sovnarkom had issued decrees neither authorized nor discussed by the CEC and whether the Sovnarkom intended to desist, in the future, from the impermissible practice of ruling by decree.[119] Lenin responded with the claim that the prerogative of removing ministers was quite sufficient to enable the CEC to maintain control over the Sovnarkom's policies and that all the decrees in question were essential for dealing with emergencies. Should this not be enough, he said, the CEC had the option of calling another national Congress of Soviets whenever it wished.[120]

The Left SRs immediately moved to declare this response unsatisfactory. A resolution to this effect failed by a vote of 25 to 20, with 6 Left SRs and 6 Bolsheviks abstaining.[121] The climax of this clash came on a subsequent confidence vote on Lenin's government introduced by Uritskii for the Bolshevik Central Committee. With historical perspective, one can see that this was a critical moment in the earliest evolution of the Soviet system. The primary source of the Bolsheviks' popular authority lay in the identification of the party with the Soviets and defense of the Soviets as the embodiment of the revolution. An open break between the Sovnarkom and the CEC at this point, even if only temporary, might have significantly undermined the authority of the former and enhanced the possibilities for resumption of the Vikzhel talks.

So close was the relative strength at this meeting of Bolshevik moderates, Menshevik-Internationalists, United Social-Democratic Internationalists, and Left SRs, on the one hand, and Bolsheviks upon whom Lenin could rely, on the other, that in order to assure a plurality Lenin was driven to insist that Bolshevik people's commissars in attendance be permitted to participate in the balloting—in effect, allowing members of the government to participate in a vote of confidence in themselves.[122] A roll-call vote ended up 29 to 23, with 3 abstentions. Riazanov and other leading moderate Bolsheviks at this meeting—Larin, Nogin, and Kamenev, among them—do not appear to have voted. This circumstance, coupled with the "yes" votes of four people's commissars—Lenin, Trotsky, Stalin, and Nikolai Krylenko—was decisive.[123]

* * *

After weathering the CEC meeting of 4 November, Lenin personally sent an ultimatum to Kamenev, Zinoviev, Riazanov, and Larin threatening to expel them from the Bolshevik party unless they either immediately agreed in writing to support the policies of the Central Committee unswervingly and promote its policy in all their speeches or withdrew from all public activity pending the decisions of a party congress.[124] Kamenev, Riazanov, and Larin, though not Zinoviev, immediately replied with a defiant joint response challenging Lenin's right to insist that they promote Central Committee policies with which they radically disagreed as an unprecedented demand to speak against their own consciences.[125]

At the same time, it is important to note that when several of his most prominent allies resigned from government posts, Kamenev had remained in his still potentially very powerful position as chairman of the CEC and even refrained from formally expressing solidarity with the defectors as had several other Bolshevik officials sympathetic to them. However, this caution was insufficient to save him from Lenin's wrath. Once Lenin decided to break with party moderates irrespective of cost, it was inevitable that he would seek to remove Kamenev from leadership of the CEC and of the Bolshevik CEC fraction, and to substitute a more pliant, dependable party comrade in his place. Primarily by virtue of his unswerving loyalty and subservience to Lenin as director of the Central Committee secretariat, the obvious individual for the job was Sverdlov.

At Lenin's instigation, participants in a morning meeting of the Bolshevik Central Committee on 8 November agreed to remove Kamenev from leadership of the CEC.[126] No record is available of the fraction meeting which dealt with the issue later that day. Did Kamenev go down without a struggle? In view of his decision to remain at his post a few days earlier, that seems unlikely. Judging by a report in *Novaia zhizn'* on 9 November, Kamenev, in announcing his resignation as chair of the CEC, left no doubt that he was stepping down under pressure. That said, in picking Sverdlov as Kamenev's replacement Lenin got what he wanted. Under pressure from the Left SRs, the struggle for the prerogatives of the CEC vis-à-vis the Sovnarkom briefly reemerged and the Left SRs appeared to make some headway in it.[127] Over the longer term, however, under Sverdlov's tight rein, the CEC was reduced to a "fig leaf."[128]

* * *

The endorsement of the program of the Second All-Russian Congress of Workers' and Soldiers' Deputies by the Emergency Second All-Russian Congress of Soviets of Peasants' Deputies and the subsequent merger of the All-Russian Executive Committee of Peasants' Soviets with the All-Russian Central Executive Committee of Workers' and Soldiers' Soviets also strengthened the strategic position of Lenin's government in mid November. The history of the Emergency Second All-Russian Congress of Soviets of Peasants' Deputies, which was convened in Petrograd on 11 November, is complex. Here it will suffice simply to note that the Congress was convened largely at the initiative of the Bolsheviks and Left SRs, expressly for the purpose of further legitimating Soviet power, in part by facilitating the merger of the All-Russian CEC of Soviets of Workers' and Soldiers' Deputies with the All-Russian Executive Committee of Soviets of Peasants' Deputies. It also bears recording that, in contrast to the First All-Russian Congress of Peasants' Soviets in May 1917, which was dominated by centrist and right SRs, this second national gathering of peasant representatives had a solid Left SR majority.[129]

The question of forming a combined CEC was discussed at a joint gathering of the Bolshevik Central Committee and the Bureau of the Left SR CEC fraction the night of 14/15 November and, a bit later, at an assembly of the CEC and the emergency peasant congress. The terms of the merger were agreed upon at a joint meeting of the Presidiums of the Congress and the CEC the same night and confirmed by the full congress the next day, thereby making Soviet power symbolically representative of the bulk of the Russian people. According to these terms, 108 members of the existing CEC would be joined by an equal number of representatives from the peasant congress, 100 representatives of soldier and sailor committees, and 50 trade union representatives. The 108 representatives from the peasant congress formally joined the CEC amid great pomp and ceremony on 15 November.[130]

A preponderance of the new CEC members from the peasant congress was Left SRs. Consequently, for nearly two weeks, they had numerical superiority over the Bolsheviks in that body. The Left SRs had agreed not to exercise their majority to reorganize the government pending the arrival of other new members.[131] The Bolsheviks predominated, as it turned out, among incoming delegates to the CEC from trade unions and from soldier and sailor committees. Thus, by the end of November, the Bolsheviks had a majority in the combined CEC. In view of the traditional SR authority among peasant-soldiers, it is natural to ask whether the restoration of a Bolshevik majority in the new CEC as finally constituted was a legitimate expression of popular sentiment or the result of some sleight of hand by the Bolsheviks, especially with respect to new members from the armed forces. And regardless of the answer to this question, one must still ponder why the Left SRs, having acquired a temporary majority in the CEC, chose not to exercise it, and, in particular, why they made no attempt to form a cabinet with a Left SR majority.

Regarding the legitimacy of new representatives from the armed forces, a massive shift of troop support from moderate socialists to Bolsheviks commensurate with the latter's preponderance among incoming soldier delegates to the CEC had taken place at the end of the summer and fall of 1917.[132] As for the second question, the apparent willingness of the Left SRs to forego exercising their majority in the merged CEC, it appears that at this time the Left SR leadership simply lacked the confidence and will to challenge the Bolsheviks for leadership of the government. In this connection, it is important to note that this was precisely the time when the Left SRs held their founding congress (19–28 November). Referring to this period at the Left SR Fourth All-Russian Congress in October 1918, Karelin attributed what he termed the Left SRs fear of power (*vlasteboiazn'*) at the end of 1917 to the fact that, despite their growing influence, they were just beginning their existence as a separate entity and lacked a developed party organization. "This fear of power and the asceticism and monasticism which it produced," he recalled, "were characteristic of us [Left SRs] for a long time."[133]

The impact of this self-perceived weakness, coupled with a desire to maintain involvement in the revolution, was so strong that, in spite of repeated signs that a Soviet government led by Lenin would behave as it pleased, the Left SRs now entered into negotiations over participation in a coalition with the Bolsheviks. The question of joining the government was apparently first raised at the joint meeting of the Bolshevik Central Committee and the Bureau of the Left SR CEC fraction the night of 14/15 November, where the formation of a combined CEC was considered.[134] This discussion resumed two days later, when Sverdlov participated in a meeting of the Left SR fraction in the merged CEC.[135] At a session of the First Left SR Congress at precisely that time, in a comment that typified Left SR sentiment, Maria Spiridonova justified close collaboration with the Bolsheviks. A legend among Russian peasants since 1906, when, at the age of twenty-two, she had assassinated a high police official in Tambov Province and suffered greatly for it,[136] Spiridonova, in 1917, was one of the Left SR's most prominent figures. At the Left SR Congress, she asserted that "we are on the threshold of a tremendous social upheaval. We will experience much that cannot be foreseen. This is the point of view from which we must approach the Bolsheviks. However alien their crude behavior is to us, we are maintaining close contact with them because the masses . . . follow them."[137] "We entered into a bloc with the Bolsheviks to moderate them," recalled another leading Left SR nearly a year later, after this approach had failed.[138] For these reasons, by mid November 1917, orientation toward partnership with the Bolsheviks was so strong among Left SR leaders that revulsion toward this or that repressive measure by Bolshevik authorities only reinforced it. Thus, at a CEC meeting on 17 November, Spiridonova publicly signaled the desire of Left SRs to enter the Sovnarkom in a speech in which she lambasted the Bolsheviks for having dissolved the Petrograd City Duma without the CEC's prior approval.[139]

Sverdlov followed Spiridonova's attack by introducing a draft constitution regulating the future relationship between the CEC and the Sovnarkom drawn up at the insistence of the Left SRs as a precondition for further negotiations over the makeup of a coalition cabinet. According to this constitution, which was adopted with minimal discussion, the Sovnarkom was to be wholly responsible to the CEC. Prior to enactment, "all legislative acts, as well as ordinances of a major political character, were to be submitted [by the Sovnarkom] to the CEC for review and confirmation." An exception could be made for measures connected with combating counterrevolution, on condition that the Sovnarkom be accountable for them to the CEC. Each people's commissar was obligated to make weekly reports to the CEC, and interpellations by the latter had to be responded to immediately.[140]

On 22 November, several days before the reestablishment of a Bolshevik majority in the CEC, Kamkov triumphantly reported to his colleagues at the First Left SR Congress that henceforth "not a single decree can be published unless it has been passed in advance by the CEC. Thus, the CEC is the legislative authority, and the Sovnarkom the executive power. This is a tremendous victory for the position of the Left SRs."[141] It was not quite that. As time would show, the understanding depended on good faith on the part of the Bolsheviks and left extensive discretionary power in the hands of the Sovnarkom. Nonetheless, for some time, people's commissars dutifully made reports on their work to the CEC.[142] Also, many major decrees, though by no means all, were transmitted to the CEC for confirmation after adoption by the Sovnarkom.

* * *

The period between 25 October and 4 November 1917 marked a major turning point in the development of the Russian revolution. During this time, the movement toward the creation of a multiparty, exclusively social-ist government by the Second All-Russian Congress of Soviets of Work-ers' and Soldiers' Deputies was stopped, and an all-Bolshevik government was established. Popular support for the Bolsheviks in Petrograd was solidi-fied by the Soviet Congress's adoption of much of the party's revolutionary program, as well as by the Soviet government's first military victories over the counterrevolution. Attempts by Bolshevik moderates to curtail the Sov-narkom's arbitrary power, which was supported by Left SRs, Menshevik-Internationalists, and other left socialist groups in the CEC, were rebuffed. Moderate Bolsheviks were pressured out of the party Central Committee and withdrew from the Sovnarkom. Moreover, the legitimacy of the So-viet government was enhanced by the endorsement of the program of the Second All-Russian Congress of Peasants' Deputies and by the merger of their executive committees.

Certainly such factors as Kerensky's belated attack on the Left, the with-drawal of the moderate socialists from the Second All-Russian Congress of Soviets, and their unrealistic positions at the Vikzhel talks paved the way for these developments. Clearly, however, the most important factor shap-ing them was Lenin (supported by Trotsky)—his supreme confidence in his ability to gauge the revolutionary situation in Russia and internationally, his iron will and dogged determination to achieve his goals irrespective of the strength of the opposition, his consummate political skill, and his lack of scruples. The popular impulse behind the October revolution in Petro-grad notwithstanding, political developments in Petrograd between 25 Oc-tober and 4 November 1917 illustrate the sometimes decisive role of the in-dividual in history.

2

Rebels into Rulers

THE COLLAPSE OF efforts to broaden the Sovnarkom or even make it account-able to the multiparty CEC, coupled with the unwillingness of all Russian political groups, except for the Bolsheviks and Left SRs, to recognize the le-gitimacy of Soviet power, meant that in the wake of the October revolution the Bolsheviks bore exclusive responsibility for maintaining order and pro-viding municipal services, and food and fuel, to Petrograd and the surround-ing region. In proclaiming the transfer of all government power in Russia to the soviets and rejecting broad political alliances, Lenin and Trotsky were not particularly concerned with the practical implications of their acts. They were absorbed, instead, with defending and consolidating Soviet power, and with stimulating the decisive worldwide socialist revolutions that they be-lieved were necessary for the survival of the Russian revolution, by the most dramatic measures possible. The consequence of their stance, however, was that Bolsheviks in the city party organization, the Petrograd Soviet, and Petrograd district soviets were forced to transform themselves from rebels into rulers and to reshape or construct new local government and adminis-trative bodies. Moreover, they had to do so without having given any con-crete thought to how they would govern, at the same time that they were obliged to furnish personnel for service in new institutions of national gov-ernment and to spread and defend the revolution around the country. These burdens led inexorably to the fundamental transformation of the Petrograd Bolshevik party organization's composition, structure, method of operation, and relationship to its constituencies.

* * *

Considering that, during the October days, government power every-where in Russia was, in principle, transferred to soviets, from top to bottom, it might have been expected that, in Petrograd, city soviets and district sovi-ets would promptly begin taking over the responsibilities of the institutions of local government created in the late tsarist era, such as the City Duma and district dumas, and their panoply of administrative boards (*upravy*). Yet, for several reasons that are important for understanding the evolution of Soviet government in Petrograd, and the relationship between it and the role of Bolshevik party committees in government, this did not occur. Take the leadership bodies of the Petrograd Soviet, for instance. Beginning as early as September 1917, the Executive Committee of the Petrograd Soviet and its Presidium, in which the Mensheviks and SRs still had considerable strength, was largely paralyzed by political infighting and, in October, by the transfer of authoritative Bolsheviks such as Trotsky to the MRC and national commissariats. This dysfunction persisted until late November, when a new Executive Committee and Presidium were elected, both chaired by Zinoviev and dominated by Bolsheviks and Left SRs. Only then, more than a month after the Bolsheviks assumed formal power, did the executive organs of the Petrograd Soviet begin to play a meaningful role in governing revolutionary Russia's capital city.[1] By virtue of being chair of the newly elected Executive Committee and Presidium, Zinoviev, who had restored himself to Lenin's good graces by abandoning the moderates, became head of the Petrograd Soviet. He was to hold that post until the end of 1925.[2]

In the opening stage of Soviet power the Petrograd Soviet itself met regularly. However, composed of more than a thousand elected representatives of factories and military units, several hundred of whom showed up for most meetings, it was simply too big to serve as an agency for meaningful discussion and decision making. With few exceptions, its plenary sessions were mobilization rallies aimed at disseminating information and building popular support for Bolshevik positions on national and international issues rather than serious business meetings to resolve important issues.[3]

The MRC took the initiative in preparing for the dissolution of the Petrograd City Duma on 9 November because of its active opposition to Soviet power.[4] It was officially dissolved by order of the Sovnarkom on 16 November.[5] The next day, the Petrograd Soviet adopted a resolution proposed by Trotsky calling on members of the Petrograd Soviet and district soviets to break with "the rotten bourgeois prejudice that only bourgeois civil servants could run a state," and providing for the immediate creation of separate departments attached to the Petrograd Soviet, as well as to district soviets, "for this or that branch of [local] civil administration."[6]

Nonetheless, rather than implementing this directive, elections for a new City Duma calculated to retain the bourgeois civil servants who staffed duma administrative boards were scheduled for 26 November; this was specified in the Sovnarkom's decree dissolving the existing duma. Trotsky's predilections notwithstanding, as a practical matter neither the Petrograd Soviet nor district soviets had the expertise, stable composition, or infrastructure necessary for municipal government and administration. When the existing City Duma was dissolved because it became apparent that effective collaboration with it would be impossible, there was no thought of not electing a new one. The Sovnarkom's primary concern was to hold elections for a new City Duma as quickly as possible so as to keep intact duma boards and their specialized departments and commissions at all levels. These elections were held on 27–28 November. Boycotted by the Kadets and moderate socialists, they resulted in the creation of a Petrograd City Duma dominated by Bolsheviks.

Also figuring prominently in efforts to preserve old institutions of city government after October was the fact that Bolshevik Soviet leaders had precious little taste for day-to-day municipal administration. Having devoted their lives to fomenting revolution, at the outset they perceived soviets less as organs of popular self-government than as political institutions whose task of consolidating the revolution was by no means over and which would at most define public policy, not implement it. Privately, this was candidly acknowledged by local Bolsheviks. Typical was the response of a member of the Bolshevik Committee in the Okhtinskii district to a colleague who asked why district soviets did not simply take on the work of district dumas. "Institutions of local self-government are purely organizations for economic management, whereas district soviets are political institutions," he said firmly. "Soviets should not take on managerial functions, as this will only complicate their political work which is difficult enough."[7]

To be sure, district-level Bolshevik activists worried about the possibility that local dumas and their administrative boards were so intrinsically hostile to radical revolutionary change that soviets would have no choice but to assume direct responsibility for municipal government. But for most of them, this was a thoroughly distasteful last resort. Some local party activists favored gerrymandering and decreasing the number of districts in Petrograd as a means of circumventing especially intransigent local dumas and boards.[8] Although this idea was not pursued, it illustrates the depth of their desire to keep the functions of district soviets and dumas discrete, and to retain professional duma boards for daily municipal administration.

In the aftermath of the October days, except for the duma in the Vyborg district, all district dumas, as well as the central City Duma, were controlled by Kadets and moderate socialists who actively resisted Soviet power. All the same, initially district soviets limited themselves to maintaining close watch over district dumas and boards, and attempting to influence them through

Bolsheviks in their ranks. Not until late November and December (by which time virtually all Petrograd district soviets were headed by Bolsheviks), in the face of strikes by civil servants partly directed by district dumas, did district soviets begin dissolving them.

The process of dissolving district dumas was often begun by the local Bolshevik party committee which, in response to complaints about sabotage by civil servants, adopted a resolution calling for dissolution of the local duma and election of a new one, and providing for a vote on it by a broader meeting of party members, or an assembly of Bolshevik representatives from district factories and military units, and implementation by the local district soviet.[9] At this early stage in the organization of Soviet power in Petrograd, party decision making at city and district levels was decentralized. The structure of district party organizations and even the locus of power in them varied greatly. Also, their operation was still relatively democratic and fluid. Decisions of Bolshevik committees in at least some districts were not binding on general meetings of local party members, which were the highest party authority locally.[10]

District party committee and district soviet resolutions dissolving district dumas provided for their reelection. Preparations for these elections were often initiated, but none were actually held. The predilections of their leaders notwithstanding, circumstances forced Petrograd district soviets, gradually and unevenly, to assert control over duma boards as best they could, and to transform themselves into institutions of local self-government. Meanwhile, work stoppages by veteran civil servants petered out in early January, not because they were smashed or replaced by freshly trained representatives of the revolutionary masses, as Trotsky advocated, but because ultimately most of them were dependent on wages for survival. When the city employees' resources were used up, they returned to work.[11] District soviets throughout Petrograd drew on these employees, beginning in December 1917 through the first half of 1918, to form separate sections for key municipal services.

Upon the advent of Soviet power in Petrograd, it might also have been expected that the Bolshevik Petersburg Committee would become centrally involved in defining broad public policy, and that it and party district committees would superintend city and district level government, respectively. However, the process leading to this outcome did not begin for some time, and it was drawn out, difficult, and divisive. Meetings of the Petersburg Committee following the October days were primarily devoted to such national issues as the Vikzhel talks, elections to the Constituent Assembly and its fate, assessments of the current moment, and narrow organizational matters. More often than not, agenda items that might have triggered general discussion of the committee's role in local government were tabled for lack of time.

During this initial period of Soviet rule, Bolshevik district party organizations, irrespective of their structure, also devoted much of their time to assessing national issues.[12] They played direct roles in mobilizing forces to combat Krasnov's expected march on Petrograd and in implementing the party's electoral campaigns for the Constituent Assembly and City Duma, and, without benefit of direction from above, they began developing ad hoc relationships with factory collectives, district soviets, and district dumas. These links varied by district and were unsystematic. As reflected in their periodic reports to the Petersburg Committee, district committees strove to keep higher party authorities informed of popular political opinion at the grass-roots level. Their most important function was to serve as labor pools and personnel agencies for positions in national and local government, revolutionary courts, the Red Guards, workers' militias, and Red forces helping to spread the revolution across Russia and defending it from forces hostile to Soviet rule organized on the periphery of Central Russia.

The first major hostile force of this kind emerged in the Don Territory even before the collapse of the Vikzhel talks over the creation of a socialist coalition government. General Mikhail Alekseev, commander-in-chief of the Russian army during the first several weeks after the February revolution and Kerensky's chief-of-staff following General Lavr Kornilov's attempted coup at the end of August, had rushed to Novocherkassk, capital of the Don Territory, at the beginning of November. In an uneasy alliance with General Aleksei Kaledin, ataman of the Don Cossacks, he immediately began organizing the nucleus of an anti-Bolshevik, pro-Allied army, soon to become known as the Volunteer Army. In succeeding weeks, Alekseev was joined in Novocherkassk by General Anton Denikin and, of more immediate importance, by General Kornilov who, having fled from the monastery in which he had been held since his failed coup, agreed to share leadership of this first major White movement with Alekseev and Kaledin.

Lenin exaggerated the seriousness of the Volunteer Army's threat to the survival of the revolution, perhaps because he underestimated the desire of younger Cossacks for an end to the war and their coolness toward Kaledin, as well as the latent support for Soviet power among local factory workers concentrated in the industrial town of Rostov, Donbas coal miners, and non-Cossack peasants, a high proportion of whom were of Russian origin. Also probably contributing to Lenin's anxiety about the Volunteer Army was the swelling number of officers, cadets, university students, and top conservative and liberal political leaders who became associated with it. Beginning in late November, in response to Lenin's urgent appeals to suppress the bourgeois counterrevolution on the Don, thousands of Petrograd Bolsheviks, Red Guards, Baltic Fleet sailors, and ordinary workers, many of them mobilized by district party committees, joined the growing rag-tag Soviet forces bound for the south. As January turned to February 1918, these forces, commanded by Vladimir Antonov-Ovseenko, who had directed seizure of the Winter Palace during the October days and, subsequently, had served as co-people's commissar for army and naval affairs, overwhelmed the still relatively meager Volunteer Army and pushed it out of the Don Territory deep into the frozen Kuban steppe.

This first episode in the Russian civil war was typical of the post-October period with respect to the drain of Bolshevik personnel from Petrograd. At this early stage of Soviet power, in response to endless civil and military emergencies, many party district committee meetings and other local-level Bolshevik assemblies already devoted significant attention to appointments and transfers. Any thought of systematic control of Bolshevik duma and soviet fractions went by the boards. Even political agitation among the great mass of Petrograd workers and soldiers was curtailed. This potentially disastrous situation for party control of governing bodies developed with stunning speed.

As early as 29 October, reports to the Petersburg Committee from representatives of district party committees documented the decline of party strength, as did records of grass-roots party meetings throughout Petrograd. From the Okhtinskii district word came that "[political] life is centered in the soviet, where a struggle is taking place . . . the party organization is playing no role at all." "Party work is declining," reported a representative of the Narva district. "[Party] workers have been drawn to duty in the Red Guard or someplace else." A representative from the Nevskii district echoed that "party work has ground to a halt."[13]

When the Bolshevik committee in the Kolpinskii district selected twelve candidates for the Petrograd Soviet on 11 November, the appointment list included several of its most experienced leaders, headed by its chairman and secretary. Many of those selected were members of the local district soviet or district duma. Yet, at this same meeting, twenty-five additional candidates were selected for the district soviet.[14] At a party committee meeting in this same district on 22 November, four additional members were picked for the executive committee of the local district soviet, three for the local food supply board, and one to become head of the district duma and duma board.[15]

The record shows that during the first year of Soviet power in Petro-

grad massive outflows of the most effective party workers, leading to organizational dysfunction, were the rule in all districts. No doubt, it was often
initially assumed that many assignments were temporary or part-time, and
a small percentage was. However, because those assigned often held several
positions outside the party, and also because the responsibilities of Bolsheviks in government agencies such as district soviets, revolutionary tribunals,
and the like, tended to expand exponentially, in practice most assignments
resulted in the complete withdrawal of the individual party member from
active party agitational and organizational work. At a Petersburg Committee meeting on 16 November Slutskii worried aloud about this problem.
In a report on the current moment, he referred to the way the SR party had
been swallowed up by power during the previous summer and warned that
the same thing was happening to Bolsheviks. "What do we see happening
in the districts?" he asked. "Everyone is being dispersed and everybody is
being devoured by power," he said, warning that "we need to take steps to
avoid being overwhelmed by 'October Bolsheviks' [i.e., by inexperienced
post-October recruits]."[16] Lower-level party veterans everywhere shared this
anxiety but were helpless to do anything about it.[17]

In December, if not before, the Petersburg Committee, working through
district party committees, began enrolling new recruits into crash party
training programs, which were held off and on throughout 1918.[18] However, even before completing these programs, especially bright and competent new Bolsheviks received assignments unrelated to party work. In addition to sending new members to party schools, district committees tried to
compensate for the loss of veteran cadres by hiring full-time, paid responsible organizers to rebuild factory collectives and to coordinate membership
recruitment and agitation among workers. Thus, it was not coincidental that
on 11 November, after assigning many of its most competent members to
government agencies, the Kolpinskii district committee selected a full-time
organizer to rebuild shop collectives crippled by losses. But even such steps
did not really help. Very quickly, district party committees and their carefully nurtured networks were in disarray, and the close interactive ties that
had been a key to the Bolsheviks' popular support in the summer of 1917, as
well as their development of successful strategies and tactics before and during the October revolution, were broken.

As for the Sovnarkom, even before it began to meet regularly, that is, before 15 November, Lenin and other people's commissars had begun to issue decrees in its name pertaining to Petrograd, for example, the decree on
press restrictions. After mid November, beginning with the dissolution of
the Petrograd City Duma, the Sovnarkom did not hesitate to issue decrees

dealing with local government in the capital without consulting local authorities. Nonetheless, the burden of existing evidence shows that from the October days until its dissolution on 5 December 1917, the MRC was the primary governing authority in Petrograd. Originally created by the Petrograd Soviet to monitor the Provisional Government's disposition of troops of the Petrograd garrison, it had been deftly utilized by the Bolsheviks for Kerensky's overthrow.[19] To be sure, it was technically still an arm of the Petrograd Soviet. In reality, following the seizure of power it became a national institution, largely independent of outside controls. Willy-nilly, in the course of combating anti-Bolshevik forces and attempting to maintain security and order, in the vacuum created by work stoppages on the part of experienced civil servants that staffed duma boards and never ending crises caused by disorder at all levels of government, the MRC expanded its activity from directing military operations and policing into such areas as the procurement, delivery, and distribution of food, fuel, and other basic necessities; transport and travel; labor relations and wages; public health; prison administration; and the allocation of housing.[20]

The MRC was headed by a bureau intended to coordinate a plethora of constantly changing sections with overlapping responsibilities. Its commissars, mostly Bolsheviks and Left SRs drawn from party committees and directly from factories and military units, were dispatched by the dozens with unlimited powers over government agencies, enterprises of every kind, and military and police forces. It is clear that the MRC's operations were haphazard and primitive despite continuing efforts to streamline them. Around 22 November Sergei Gusev, secretary of the MRC and head of its secretariat, quit his posts because of the organization's enduring "chaos." In a bitter resignation letter, he explained his action. "The question of organizing the MRC's work has been discussed incessantly, resolutions have been adopted providing for sections and commissions and the appointment of MRC members to each of them. . . . All these resolutions have remained unfulfilled and the work of the MRC has been carried out in its previous disordered, chaotic way." Declaring that he no longer had any hope of reforming the MRC, he asked to be relieved of his responsibilities within twenty-four hours.[21]

Gusev was persuaded to stay on, partly, perhaps, because the Sovnarkom scaled down the MRC's responsibilities.[22] In any event, the MRC's organizational problems ought not to obscure the enormous independent power and reach it had acquired during the first several weeks after October. At a popular level, the suppression of the cadet uprising on 28 October and the defeat of Krasnov's forces at Pulkovo a few days later enhanced its stature as the local command post for Soviet power. Starting then, district soviets controlled by Bolsheviks looked to the MRC for support and direction. In as much as it had at its disposal worker Red Guards, soldiers of the Petrograd garrison, Baltic Fleet sailors, and large stores of arms and munitions, it was the only agency in Petrograd with the military strength to enforce orders. Moreover, organizational shortcomings aside, the cream of the Bolshevik leadership was active in the MRC at one time or another. The critical role of the MRC in governing Petrograd, to the extent it was governed at all, is clear. In this sense, it is impossible to argue with the conclusion of the contemporary Petersburg historian A. N. Chistikov regarding the government of Petrograd in the aftermath of the October revolution, namely, that "the MRC embodied Soviet power . . . taking the place of the Petrograd Soviet and, to a large degree, also the central City Duma."[23]

* * *

Arbitrary, disorganized Bolshevik policies and actions during the first weeks of Soviet power, many of them carried out by the MRC, antagonized all major opposition political groups. Moreover, their result, at least in the short term, was to speed up and deepen Petrograd's political, social, and economic disintegration. The Bolsheviks blamed the expanding chaos on their predecessors and insisted that the decisive steps Bolsheviks were taking were the quickest and surest way to make things better. But would impatient workers, peasant-soldiers, and sailors whom these policies were partly meant to attract accept this contention? Or was their loyalty to the Bolsheviks and to Soviet power unstable and wavering, as Mensheviks and SRs insisted?

A comprehensive expression of political opinion in Petrograd and among troops on the nearby Northern front was provided by the results of the 12–14 November elections to the Constituent Assembly.[24] In this connection, it is important to note that despite widespread civil turmoil following the Bolshevik seizure of power, by and large the overall fairness of these elections is not in dispute.[25] Restrictions on the press and on circulation of leaflets and posters were loose enough to allow all the contending parties and groups an opportunity to present their programs and visions of the future, although much of the campaigning was negative. As already noted, the Bolsheviks had the supposed advantage of being able to issue revolutionary decrees which would, so they hoped, bind the revolutionary masses more closely to them. Beginning with the seemingly epoch-making resolutions of the Second All-Russian Congress of Soviets, the Bolsheviks tried to utilize this advantage to the fullest. However, communication problems limited its value. Indeed, for many weeks after October large parts of Russia had only a murky sense of events in Petrograd. At a meeting of the Sovnarkom on 25 November Viacheslav Menzhinskii, acting people's commissar for finance, worried aloud that "the decrees of the government are not being telegraphed around the country, they only appear in the Petrograd press."[26] The Sovnarkom agreed on steps to combat the problem, but whatever their eventual result, they obviously came too late to influence the elections nationally.

On the eve of the overthrow of the Provisional Government, the Bolshevik Petersburg Committee had formed an election campaign committee for the Constituent Assembly.[27] Its work, however, was naturally interrupted by the October days and was not resumed until a few days before the elections. The Bolshevik Petersburg Committee considered the party's approach to the campaign only once—at an emergency meeting with active party workers on 8 November. In an opening report on behalf of the committee's leadership, Volodarskii conveyed its concerns about the campaign. Evidently bothered by the possibility that consolidation of Soviet power in the capital might diminish the importance of the election in the eyes of potential Bolshevik voters, Volodarskii emphasized the importance of transmitting the message that realization by the Constituent Assembly of the Soviet program was wholly dependent on the party's success in the electoral campaign.

What would happen if the Bolsheviks were defeated? Early on in his report, Volodarskii declared that elections to the Constituent Assembly were inevitably an aspect of the struggle for power among classes and that therefore the revolutionary masses should be oriented to the fact that a third revolution would be necessary if the Bolsheviks did not win a majority of delegates. This comment by Volodarskii caused a public furor after it was leaked to the press.[28] However, at the Petersburg Committee meeting of 8 November, fundamental questions relating to the appropriate course in the event opponents of Soviet power gained the upper hand in the Constituent Assembly were put aside. A majority agreed with the leadership that mounting the strongest possible campaign and holding the elections as scheduled were essential and deserved highest priority. Therefore, attention turned to maximizing the Bolshevik vote so that it would, in Volodarskii's words, "reflect the will of workers, soldiers, and peasants."[29]

In nonstop rallies and factory meetings, in punchy leaflets with which they inundated factory districts, and especially in the party press, the Bolsheviks presented themselves as the party of immediate peace, fundamental social revolution, and firm decisive action—the party of the revolutionary proletariat, single-handedly leading the fight against the Kadets, the party of bourgeois counterrevolution.[30] The main parties in the middle, the SRs and Mensheviks, did not matter. On 10 November Trotsky began to fulfill the Bolsheviks' pre-October pledge to expose the imperialist character of the war by publishing secret correspondence relating to war aims between Russia and her allies. Moreover, it was just at this time that the Soviet government's campaign for immediate peace appeared to be working; the Germans seemed to be open to an armistice. A major Bolshevik campaign theme, captured in a front-page *Pravda* headline and editorial on 13 November, was that a vote for the Bolshevik list was an endorsement of these efforts and the best way to ensure an early end to the war. According to the editorial, a vote for list 4, the Bolshevik list, was most of all an expression of solidarity with the October revolution and with Soviet power.[31]

The Petrograd Bolsheviks made a special effort to retain the support of factory women. This effort was well reflected in the proceedings of the 12 November session of the Bolshevik-sponsored First Conference of Female Workers in Petrograd. A primary purpose of this conference, as noted in the previous chapter,[32] was to mobilize factory women in support of the party's electoral list. During an impassioned speech laying out the reasons why female laborers should vote only for Bolsheviks, Klavdiia Nikolaeva, a printer by trade, the conference chair, and another of *Rabotnitsa*'s editors despite only four years of formal schooling, explained that of the nineteen electoral lists, only one list, that of the Bolsheviks, was committed to representing workers and would strive to consolidate their hard-won revolutionary gains. She specifically warned her listeners not to be fooled into voting for list no. 7, the list of the primarily Kadet League for Women's Equal Rights. Campaigning in factories, the League's spokeswomen pledged to defend the interests of working women, she explained. In reality, if elected to the Constituent Assembly, the League's delegates would represent privileged women. "We [class] conscious women know that we do not have any unique women's interests, that there should not be separate women's organizations," Nikolaeva declared. "We are really strong only when we are united in one brotherly proletarian family with all workers fighting for socialism."[33]

Before this conference session ended, one citizen Doroshevskaia, of the League for Women's Equal Rights, asked for the floor. At Aleksandra Kollontai's insistence, she was given a chance to speak. Her message was that women from all over the world had visited the League to praise its efforts; that the League was, in fact, *leading* the successful struggle for women's rights in revolutionary Russia; and that it was impossible for men to defend women's interests as they had no understanding of them. "I am a laboring woman myself, a physician, my husband ran out on me, [and] so I must feed my children through my own labor," she ended.[34]

None of the assembled factory women appeared to have any sympathy for Doroshevskaia. Rather, they were clearly in agreement with a delegate who scoffed at the idea that all women had common interests, suggesting that "comrade-maids" who worked for people like Doroshevskaia be asked if this was true. The factory women were obviously also in agreement with a second delegate, who wondered aloud about where the League for Women's Equal Rights was when the working day for factory women was as long as fourteen hours and when pregnant women lost their babies at their work benches. They responded positively to another delegate, who insisted that it was unfair to fight men just because they were men, that "there was not and could not be conflict with male workers with whom we work at one bench, and with whom we are fighting for a free life and an honest democratic peace, in the ranks of one class." Judging by Kollontai's combative response to Doroshevskaia, the latter's plea for support of the League for Women's Equal Rights momentarily obscured fundamental distinctions that emerged during the conference between Kollontai, who believed that women workers did indeed have unique interests and therefore favored separate party entities to advance them, and most Petrograd Bolshevik women leaders like Nikolaeva and Konkordia Samoilova, who excluded the very idea of gender-based issues, who concentrated most of their time on general party work, and for whom special publications for women or party women's sections were no more than a practical means of attracting female workers to participation in a common socialist cause.[35]

The Bolshevik campaign message to women was also reflected in leaflets and newspaper appeals, among them a *Rabotnitsa* editorial, "The Constituent Assembly and Women Workers" by Samoilova. As a consequence of the February revolution, revolutionary female workers, in tandem with male workers and soldiers, had won such rights as freedom of speech, the press, and assembly, as well as the right to vote regardless of gender, Samoilova wrote. Since the Constituent Assembly would define a wholly new state order, and pass a host of new laws, it was critical for women workers that these laws protect their rights along with those of workers generally. Only genuine defenders of the interests of male *and* female workers, the Bolsheviks, could ensure that women's labor would be protected through the passage of laws regarding maternity, health, and old-age insurance, and the establishment of an elected women's factory inspectorate to keep close watch over working conditions for women.[36]

In their campaign, the main enemy, the Kadets, like the Bolsheviks, portrayed the elections as primarily a choice between diametrically opposed visions. As a Kadet editorial of the time put it, "Two paths lie before the country—the path of profound class struggle and destruction of the state, on the one hand, or the gathering together of Russia and the establishment in it of strong state order, on the other. The first path is most clearly represented by the Bolsheviks, the second by the Party of People's Freedom [the Kadets]. It is only necessary that the choice be made firmly and definitely."[37] A Kadet campaign leaflet entitled "Lists" made it quite clear that a vote for its list, list no. 2, headed by Paul Miliukov, was a vote for the transfer of full governing authority to the Constituent Assembly and a vote against the Bolsheviks and Soviet power: "Elections to the Constituent Assembly are approaching. This body is the only true Lord of Russia. . . . Citizens, you must make it clear that it is not for them [the Bolsheviks], whose hands are soiled with the blood of their brothers, to build a new Russia, but for those who are endowed with true statesmanship, who genuinely love their country, who are ready to free her from the [foreign] foe, and who respect the people's freedom. . . . Cast Your Ballot for the Party of People's Freedom, the only truly national, non-class, and democratic party."[38]

The Mensheviks also championed the Constituent Assembly; they lambasted both the Bolsheviks and the Kadets. "Today is Election Day—Vote for List No. 16—Not One Vote for the Bolsheviks!" trumpeted *Rabochaia gazeta*'s banner front-page headline on 12 November. That newspaper's lead editorial on that day explained that the elections were revolutionary Russia's last hope for survival. Only a Constituent Assembly in which parties representing the true democracy, in other words, all socialist parties, labor organizations, zemstvos, municipal dumas, and the like, would be able to put an end to the Bolshevik seizure of power and establish an authoritative, legitimate government, equally respected in Russia and abroad. Only a Constituent Assembly led by genuine social democrats would bring real peace, a democratic republic, and land for the peasantry. The Kadets were not opposed to the restoration of the monarchy; they continued to resist land expropriations without compensation and were ready to sacrifice Russia in the interests of allied imperialism. The Bolsheviks promoted anarchy and civil strife, and were prepared to accept shameful peace terms that would bring about Russia's total disintegration and collapse as a nation.[39]

Like the Mensheviks, the SRs focused much of their campaign fire on the Bolsheviks and Kadets, in equal measure. It was as if the previous months of close collaboration with Russia's chief liberal party never happened. This venom against both the Bolsheviks and Kadets was captured in editorials titled "Don't Vote Bolshevik" and "Not One Vote for the Kadets," published side by side in the SR daily *Delo naroda* on 12 November. Nobody should vote for the Bolsheviks as they had seized power by means of an armed conspiracy and had been, or were currently, in the process of reneging on all

Petrograders examine campaign posters for elections to the Constituent Assembly.
Jonathan Sanders Collection.

their promises. Moreover, they threatened to disperse the Constituent Assembly if it differed from what they wanted.[40] Nobody should vote for the Kadets because they had shown that they were not revolutionaries, genuine democrats, or even reliable republicans. Instead of an early democratic peace without victors or vanquished, the Kadet ideal was still a victorious end to the war. For them, any system in which things went well for the classes that were privileged and dominant before the revolution was good.[41]

Despite negativity about Kadet reformism, by contemporary standards there was very little in the SR campaign platform that was radical. Indeed, apart from a revolutionary agrarian program which provided for socialization of land (i.e., the permanent expropriation of all farmland for utilization by rural "toilers" without compensation to owners), there was little in what the SRs offered that was incompatible with the modern welfare state. Key planks in the SR platform included transfer of all state authority to the Constituent Assembly; arrangement of a quick and mutually just peace (although exactly how such a peace was to be arranged was unclear); confirmation of a democratic republic; passage of laws to guarantee basic civil rights and equality before the law; equal rights for women (like the Bolsheviks, the SRs targeted the women's vote);[42] and enactment of such liberal economic and social legislation as an eight-hour day, a minimum wage, and state subsidized unemployment and accident insurance.

By contrast, the electoral platform of the Left SRs really did call for revolutionary political and social change. Certainly, for now, the Left SRs continued to uphold the sanctity of the Constituent Assembly as revolutionary Russia's supreme political authority. But to them, as for the Bolsheviks, both elections to the Constituent Assembly and the proceedings of the Assembly itself were natural arenas for waging class struggle. Moreover, at bottom, the Left SRs did not feel any more constrained by parliamentary forms of struggle for the realization of revolutionary goals than the Bolsheviks did. Their campaign promises included an immediate end to government by Lenin and Trotsky; creation, finally, of a homogeneous, broad, united socialist coalition government, responsible to the soviets; arrangement of an immediate peace without victors or vanquished (if necessary, through direct appeals to the peoples of warring states); struggle for the triumph of socialism internationally; and workers' control of factories. In short, the Left SRs stood for undoing political damage caused by the Bolsheviks' "premature" seizure of power and the realization, through the Constituent Assembly, of the principal decrees of the Second All-Russian Congress of Soviets.

Unfortunately for the Left SRs, in elections to the Constituent Assembly they were saddled with a major structural handicap. At the First Left SR [National] Congress, convened exactly a week after the elections, the Left SRs organized themselves into a separate party. But as things stood, their candidates to the Constituent Assembly were sandwiched in among centrist and Right SRs on list 9. This list, rank-ordered, had been composed in September before differences among SRs became unbridgeable. There was no way for voters to indicate preferences among candidates (assuming they understood their differences), and by virtue of their control over the composition and rank ordering of most SR lists around the country, centrist and right SRs were able to insure that election of their candidates was maximized.

How, then, did the elections turn out? With preponderant strength among peasants in the countryside, nationally the SRs received the largest number of votes. In combination with other moderate socialist and liberal groups (altogether 62 percent of the total), they were well positioned to control the Constituent Assembly. But in Petrograd and its environs, electoral results, indicative of political attitudes locally, turned out differently.

Voter participation in the capital was very high; some 942,333 citizens, or nearly 80 percent of eligible voters, turned out. Attracting strong support in the central bourgeois districts of the capital, the Kadets finished second, garnering some 246,506 votes, or 26.3 percent of the total.[43] The League for Women's Equal Rights received 5,231 votes, constituting 0.5 percent of the overall vote.[44] In comparison with earlier citywide elections, the moderate socialists lost considerable ground to the Kadets on the right and the Bolsheviks on the left (the SRs received 152,230 votes, or 16.2 percent of the total vote, and the Mensheviks 29,167, or 5 percent). The Bolsheviks, with 424,027, or 45.2 percent of the total vote, were the clear winners.[45] Winning twelve of the city's eighteen electoral districts overall, they completely dominated Petrograd's working-class areas. Moreover, they did similarly well among soldiers of the Petrograd garrison, previously the preserve of the SRs, receiving 75 percent of the soldier vote. It is also noteworthy that the party demonstrated impressive strength among Baltic Fleet sailors and soldiers on the strategically critical Northern front. In the remaining six electoral districts, the Kadets led.[46]

In sum, the results of elections to the Constituent Assembly were a strong endorsement of revolutionary Bolshevik policies and Soviet power by lower classes in the Petrograd region. Significantly, in the wake of the elections, Vikzhel finally admitted defeat. It formally acknowledged the governmental authority of the CEC, and turned its attention to gaining control over the People's Commissariat for Transportation.[47] A disappointed *Novaia zhizn'* correspondent was not far off the mark when, commenting on the election results in Petrograd, he wrote that, "however we may feel about it, we cannot but admit one thing: even with respect to the Constituent Assembly, the workers of Petrograd recognize the Bolsheviks as their leaders and spokesmen for their class interests."[48] Lenin could now be hopeful that Petrograd workers, soldiers, and sailors, as well as troops on the Northern front, would support the Bolsheviks in the event of a confrontation with the Constituent Assembly over the future of Soviet rule.

*   *   *

After the results of the elections to the Constituent Assembly became known, the Leninist Bolshevik Central Committee leadership gradually developed a two-pronged policy toward it. First, it encouraged the recall of elected Constituent Assembly delegates opposed to Soviet power. A decree providing for recall elections drafted by Lenin was adopted by the CEC shortly after the election results became known. It placed the right of recall and reelection of delegates to the Constituent Assembly in the hands of local soviets.[49] Although recently published data suggest that the recall movement had promise,[50] the time was so short before the scheduled opening of the Constituent Assembly, and, in any event, its life was so fleeting, that it had little practical impact. Second, the central Bolshevik leadership sought to undermine efforts by the SRs, Kadets, Mensheviks, and other groups and institutions hostile to Soviet power to direct preparations for the Constituent Assembly and to mobilize popular support and protection for it. In pursuit of this objective, the Bolsheviks sought to control all matters relating to the opening and operation of the Constituent Assembly, to brand and incarcerate prominent opponents of Soviet power as enemies of the people, and to prepare party organizations and Petrograd's lower classes for the Constituent Assembly's possible dissolution.

The Petrograd City Duma, a national center for resistance to Soviet power and for support of the Constituent Assembly,[51] was shut down by Sovnarkom decree on 16 November. Its dissolution triggered a fresh explosion of protest by liberal and moderate socialist groups and even by the Left SRs. The City Duma responded by passing a joint SR-Kadet resolution rejecting the authority of the Soviet government, and continued its activity as if nothing had happened. Matters came to a head on 20 November. Deputies arriving at the City Duma for an evening meeting were greeted by armed sailors and Red Guards who tried to prevent them from entering. The deputies pushed their way in and proceeded with their scheduled business but were quickly and forcibly dispersed.[52] Resuming their deliberations at another location, they ended their session by declaring 28 November, the opening day of the Constituent Assembly, a national holiday. Later that night, the MRC searched the apartments of opposition duma leaders, several of whom were arrested. Except for the mayor, Grigorii Shreider, and a close associate of his, all those detained were quickly deposed and released.[53] Stenographic records indicate that the old City Duma continued to meet occasionally in various underground locations at least until mid January.[54]

On 22–23 November, prominent opposition leaders from the old City Duma and the ACS, primarily SRs and also Kadets, Popular Socialists, and Menshevik Defensists, collaborated in the formation of an organization called the Union for Defense of the Constituent Assembly (UDCA). Headquartered in the building of the venerable Free Economic Society, it formed branches in several districts of Petrograd and also established itself in other major Russian cities. Its declared purpose was to be a national center for strengthening and expanding popular support for the Constituent Assembly as Russia's legitimate supreme political authority and for organizing security for it. This was also the goal of the semi-autonomous SR Military Commission, which had helped organize the insurrection against Soviet power on 29 October. As 28 November drew near, the UDCA took the lead in planning mass demonstrations around the country on the day of the public holiday scheduled by the old City Duma to celebrate the Constituent Assembly's opening. Roughly simultaneously, SR delegates, most of them housed in an overcrowded, makeshift dormitory on Bolotnoi Street, began preparations for the Constituent Assembly's work.[55]

* * *

During these days, the Leninist Bolshevik leadership pursued the general directions developed when the outcome of the elections to the Constituent Assembly became known, namely, organizing recall elections, doing everything possible to undermine the Constituent Assembly at a popular level, and asserting control over arrangements for the assembly. In connection with the latter, a key problem was what to do about a national commission which the Provisional Government had established in August to coordinate Constituent Assembly elections and preparations. This commission, the All-Russian Commission on Elections to the Constituent Assembly, was controlled by groups opposed to Soviet power, primarily Kadets and SRs. As a sign of opposition to the Bolsheviks, it had suspended activity during the October days. On 6 November, after it became clear that elections to the Constituent Assembly would probably be held on schedule, the commission resumed operations. However, it steadfastly refused to recognize Soviet power and resisted the Sovnarkom's attempted intrusions into its work. On 23 November, in response to the commission's continued stonewalling, Soviet authorities arrested several commission members, all told some twelve to fifteen Kadets and SRs, and detained them for four days.[56] At the same time, Moisei Uritskii, a member of the Bolshevik Central Committee then serving in the Commissariat for Internal Affairs, was appointed special commissar responsible for strict control of the Commission on Elections.[57] However, this arrangement lasted only a couple of days, after which the commission was dissolved, ostensibly because of its unwillingness to work with Uritskii.[58] In truth, a new office for arrangements connected with the Constituent Assembly, headed by Uritskii, had been formed a day or two earlier.

It had become apparent even to Kadets and SRs in the now disbanded Commission on Elections that voting and tabulation of election results around the country were running far behind schedule and consequently only a small fraction of certified delegates would arrive in Petrograd by 28 November. Lenin saw the absence of anything approaching a quorum as a convenient excuse for delaying the Constituent Assembly. On 26 November he issued a decree stipulating that it would be convened when four hundred delegates—roughly half the elected delegates—arrived in Petrograd. This decree also stipulated that the first session of the assembly would be opened by an individual designated by the Sovnarkom.[59]

Meanwhile, without consulting the Sovnarkom or the leadership of the Petrograd Soviet, the MRC organized a march of its own to counter the demonstration planned for 28 November by the old City Duma. However, the Sovnarkom forced the MRC to abort the march.[60] Unfortunately for the MRC, the cancellation was missed by *Rabochii i soldat*. On a day when *Pravda*'s front page contained a huge blank space where the MRC's appeal for support of its countermarch had been, the front page of *Rabochii i soldat* featured such provocative, unauthorized parade slogans as "Down with the Kadets, Kornilovites, Kaledinites–Enemies of the People!" "Down with the Compromising SRs and Mensheviks–Servants of the Bourgeoisie!" "Down with Kadets in the Constituent Assembly!" and "Down with the Bourgeoisie! Long Live the People!"[61]

The scheduling and cancellation of this march, and Bolshevik approaches to the Constituent Assembly in general, provide insights into decision making on important policy issues at this juncture, generally confirming the picture that emerged in the first weeks after the Bolsheviks came to power. The policies of the Leninist leadership toward the Constituent Assembly were defined by the Sovnarkom and Bolsheviks in the MRC, both of which met daily. Essentially, the party Central Committee, meeting irregularly, limited itself to consideration of issues connected with the stance of Bolshevik delegates. Indeed, the Central Committee does not seem to have considered *any* matters relating to the Constituent Assembly until 29 November, that is, a day *after* its scheduled opening. At that meeting, Uritskii appealed to his colleagues for guidance on how the Constituent Assembly should be handled. Nikolai Bukharin responded with the rhetorical question, should the Assembly even be convened? His answer was yes, as "constitutional illusions were still very much alive among the masses." He proposed convening the assembly, driving out the Kadets, and organizing left deputies into a "revolutionary convention." Although Trotsky echoed the idea of a revolutionary convention, it was not voted on. Out of concern about drawing effective regional leaders away from outlying areas prematurely, and perhaps also not wanting to contribute to the total of four hundred delegates required for opening the Constituent Assembly, a proposal to call the entire party delegation to Petrograd at once was also rejected. For the most part, however, the Central Committee, which was responsible for defining the party's policy on such fundamental political issues, was content either to postpone decisions on the Constituent Assembly until the domestic and international revolutionary situation was clearer, or to leave it to the discretion of the Sovnarkom and, in the meantime, to harass the opposition and let it make the first move.

This wait-and-see approach was reflected in a report on the party's policy toward the Constituent Assembly that Uritskii delivered to the Bolshevik Petersburg Committee on 12 December. "We are now entering the moment of greatest tension relative to the Constituent Assembly. . . . It will be impossible to define our tactics even an hour beforehand," he declared. "How we act, what we do, everything will depend on how and what they [the opposition] do. . . . Will we convene the Constituent Assembly? Yes. . . . Will we disperse it? Perhaps. Everything depends on how the situation develops."[62]

It is essential to note that within the Bolshevik Petersburg Committee and district party committees, as in the Central Committee minus the moderates, temporizing pertained to tactics, not to the fundamental principle that the Constituent Assembly should not be allowed to supersede Soviet power. Minutes of the meetings of the Central Committee on 29 November and the Petersburg Committee on 12 December leave no doubt on that score.[63]

This position was fully shared by the Left SRs. Their strong stance against the Constituent Assembly emerged at sessions of the first national Left SR congress in the second half of November. During discussion of the "current moment" on 23 November, Ekaterina Kats, a member of the key Petrograd Left SR committee, spoke for a majority of delegates when she declared that "the Constituent Assembly must take account of the will and tactics of the soviets. In so far as the Constituent Assembly opposes their will, we will not support it and no fetishes will change us." Even more menacing was Prosh Proshian's declaration that, "if we believe and see that the socialist revolution has begun, then state power must belong to the soviets of workers', soldiers', and peasants' deputies. . . . [O]bviously we cannot and should not lay down our arms and give state power back to the Constituent Assembly . . . if the Constituent Assembly starts off by attempting to organize state authority . . . we won't allow it."[64]

Although there were different opinions about the Constituent Assembly among Left SRs at their first national congress, these pertained less to whether its prerogative to create a permanent new political system for Russia should be respected even if it meant the end of Soviet power than to the mechanics and timing of the Constituent Assembly's dissolution in the event a majority of deputies could not be persuaded to endorse the supremacy of Soviet power. Most leading Left SRs felt that the Constituent Assembly should be allowed to convene as elected, with the exception of substitutions by recall. Many agreed with Evdokim Murav'ev, a delegate from Voronezh, that if a clear stand against the Constituent Assembly was not adopted at the outset, "the masses will distance themselves from us just as they had left the Right SRs and Mensheviks earlier . . . and then we will [also] be without an army." However, tactically more cautious leaders such as Shteinberg, Karelin, and Kamkov felt that popular support for the Constituent Assembly was still so great that any thought of direct action against it had to be delayed until the assembly had had ample time in which to bankrupt itself in the eyes of the masses. At a congress session on 27 November, the day before the Constituent Assembly was originally due to open, Kamkov speculated that this might happen in as little as a week. The congress's resolution stipulated that immediate implementation of worker and peasant power was essential and that, to the extent that the Constituent Assembly constituted such a power and pursued the fundamental positions of the Second All-Russian Congress of Soviets of Workers' and Soldiers' Deputies and of the Emergency Congress of Soviets of Peasants' Deputies, it should be fully supported. However, any attempt by the Constituent Assembly to transform itself into an organization for struggle against soviets of workers', soldiers', and peasants' deputies as organs of state power would be considered an attack on the achievements of the revolution and would need to be decisively rebuffed.[65]

* * *

Fully aware of the hostility toward the Constituent Assembly among Bolsheviks and Left SRs, opponents of Soviet power in the UDCA concluded that Lenin's announcement of a postponement, on 26 November, was part of a Bolshevik conspiracy to abort the assembly altogether. Thus, despite anxiety about their own weakness and poor organization, they went forward with arrangements for popular demonstrations on behalf of the Constituent Assembly and for its ceremonial opening on 28 November.[66] At a meeting of the Kadet Central Committee on the evening of November 27 it was agreed to proceed roughly as planned, with one difference: inasmuch as so few elected Constituent Assembly delegates had actually arrived in Petrograd, daily preparatory conferences of delegates should be arranged until a sufficient number of delegates had arrived to justify convening the assembly proper.[67]

The pro–Constituent Assembly march on 28 November revealed the immense rift that divided the population of Petrograd after six weeks of Soviet power. Around midday, a procession of mostly well-dressed citizens, variously estimated at from ten thousand to one hundred thousand,[68] many

Postcard depicting heroes of the October revolution in Petrograd. Top row: L. D. Trotsky, V. I. Lenin, A. V. Lunacharskii, M. A. Spiridonova; bottom row: A. M. Kollontai, F. F. Raskolnikov, L. B. Kamenev, and G. I. Zinoviev. Lockhart Collection, Lilly Library, Indiana University.

having just come from special thanksgiving religious services, marched from the City Duma building southeastward along Nevskii Prospekt to the sound of pealing church bells. Petrograd's "Fifth Avenue" was decorated with brightly colored flags and banners bearing inscriptions hailing the Constituent Assembly. The procession was led by the head of the old City Duma, Grigorii Shreider, just released from jail, and pro–Constituent Assembly colleagues from the city and district dumas, the entire SR party congress (including more than three hundred delegates from fifty-one provinces); moderate socialist members of the old All-Russian Central Executive Committee of Peasants' Soviets and the All-Russian Executive Committee of Workers' and Soldiers' Soviets, who had continued to meet in secret; prominent Menshevik-Defensists; and members of the Popular Socialist and Kadet central committees still at liberty. Eyewitness accounts agree that the appearance of workers, soldiers, and sailors was rare.[69]

As the marchers turned north on Liteinyi Prospekt, they were greeted by a huge banner displayed above the street: "Make Way for the Electors Chosen by the People!" Arriving at the Taurida Palace and finding the gates in the wrought iron fence surrounding it locked and heavily guarded, they clambered over it and stormed into the palace gardens. There they listened to fiery speeches calling for an immediate end to Soviet rule by the SRs Chernov and Pitirim Sorokin (the future founder of the sociology department at Harvard) and by the leading Kadet Fedor Rodichev. Pushing past Uritskii, the crowd forged into the palace. There, at 4:00 PM, a meeting was convened of some 60 of the estimated 127 Constituent Assembly delegates then in Petrograd (4 of them Kadets and the rest SRs). After electing Chernov their chairman, the delegates listened to more oratory and ended their meeting, dubbed the First Unofficial Conference of Constituent Assembly Delegates, with a pledge that they would reassemble in the Taurida Palace daily until a sufficient number of delegates was seated, at which time they would set a date for the Constituent Assembly's opening.[70] On 29 November, they managed to reassemble in the Taurida Palace. However, their meeting was forcibly dispersed, and, from then on, they were barred from reentering the palace.

The events of 28 November and their implication were discussed at a Sovnarkom meeting later that evening. Trotsky took center stage, portraying the day's events as nothing less than an armed uprising against Soviet rule by the Kadet Central Committee, the coordinating center for counterrevolution and rebellion against Soviet power nationally.[71] Intelligence reaching Bolshevik leaders may have led them to exaggerate the Kadets' influence on opposition to Soviet rule in Petrograd and on the organization of resistance movements around the country.[72] Kadet leaders, Paul Miliukov among them, were just then prominently involved in the counterrevolution on the Don led by Generals Kornilov, Alekseev, and Kaledin. However, that the Sovnarkom regarded the Kadets' actions at the Taurida Palace as merely a pretext to repress them is indicated by the fact that soldiers and Red Guards armed with MRC arrest warrants began a roundup of their top leaders on the morning of 28 November, several hours before the demonstrations occurred.[73]

Be that as it may, upon the conclusion of Trotsky's report, participants in the Sovnarkom meeting the night of 28/29 November—all Bolsheviks, as the Left SR people's commissar for agriculture Andrei Kolegaev was absent—approved the text of a government proclamation branding the Kadets as "enemies of the people" for "organizing a counterrevolutionary insurgency."[74] They also adopted a decree proposed by Lenin authorizing the immediate arrest of Kadet leaders and their trial before revolutionary tribunals. The decree made local soviets around the country responsible for "keeping the Kadet party under close surveillance because of its close links to the Kornilov-Kaledin civil war against the revolution."[75]

Both the proclamation branding Kadets "enemies of the people" and Lenin's decree authorizing their immediate arrest were published in *Izvestiia* the following morning. Most Petrograd workers and soldiers appear to have taken the Bolsheviks' attack on the Kadets at face value. However, to moderate socialists, not to speak of Kadets, it reinforced the belief that the Bolsheviks were intent on either aborting the Constituent Assembly or destroying its integrity. Thus, in Gorky's *Novaia zhizn',* Vladimir Bazarov speculated about the possibility that rather than calling off the Constituent Assembly altogether, the Bolsheviks and their "Left SR henchmen" had in mind reshaping it into a docile instrument of their will.[76]

Although Bazarov relegated the Left SRs to Bolshevik "henchmen," in reality they were as disturbed as the moderate socialists, if for different reasons, by the outlawing of the Kadets and its political implications for the Constituent Assembly. They felt the act was ill advised, as it lent credence to the widely held assumption that Soviet power was intent on suppressing the Constituent Assembly before it had had an opportunity to reveal its true face. By reinforcing this belief, the Bolsheviks had hurt the soviets much more than they had the Constituent Assembly.[77] The Left SR CEC fraction immediately filed an urgent interpellation to the Sovnarkom regarding the violation of the Kadet delegates' immunity from arrest.[78] At the next CEC meeting, on 1 December, Isaac Shteinberg initiated the Left SR attack on the decree outlawing the Kadets, arguing that such arbitrary repressive measures as outlawing and arresting Kadets were unacceptable methods of waging class warfare. A European-educated, longtime revolutionary activist, jurist, and publicist, Shteinberg, along with Karelin and Spiridonova, was the Left SRs' most outspoken public critic of arbitrary Bolshevik repressions. Now, on their behalf, he demanded that the revolutionary struggle be waged openly and honestly, insinuated that the Sovnarkom's decree outlawing the Kadets reflected a willingness to disrupt convocation of the Constituent Assembly, and voiced categorical opposition to such action.[79]

Lenin himself rose to answer the interpellation and to respond to Shteinberg. Repeating and embellishing the now familiar charge that the Kadet Central Committee had become the general staff for the counterrevolution, he declared that all political and social elements formerly to the right of the Kadets had now joined them in one grand anti-Soviet conspiracy. Using support for the Constituent Assembly as a cover, the Kadets were openly fomenting civil war. "To this there can be but one reply," Lenin declared. "Prison! That is how [the Jacobins] acted in the great French revolution; they declared the bourgeois parties outside the law."[80]

Lenin's response to Shteinburg was tame in contrast to Trotsky's brief but bombastic remarks. Moments earlier, Trotsky had interrupted the meeting to announce, with obvious exhilaration, that the German government had just accepted the Bolshevik armistice terms.[81] Perhaps this apparent concession by German imperialism stirred Trotsky's revolutionary ardor and flair for the dramatic. If Lenin's speech was largely directed toward the immediate task at hand—justifying the Sovnarkom's actions in response to a formal interpellation and criticism by Shteinberg—this was not the case with Trotsky's speech. For him, repression of the Kadets was a harbinger of terror on a significantly grander scale. Pounding the podium for emphasis, he thundered: "There is nothing immoral in the proletariat finishing off a class that is collapsing . . . You [the Left SRs] wax indignant at the naked terror which we are applying against our class enemies. But let me assure you that in one month's time at the most, it will assume more frightful forms, modeled after the terror of the great French revolutionaries. Not the fortress [of Peter and Paul] but the guillotine awaits our enemies."[82]

The Left SR Sergei Mstislavskii responded to Lenin's and Trotsky's references to the French revolution with the rejoinder that, for all their talk about a socialist revolution, the Bolsheviks were in fact "entrapped in purely bourgeois forms of political revolution." At the same time, he was critical of the moderate socialists for separating themselves from the movement of the masses, which the Left SRs felt duty-bound not to do. In the face of Lenin's and Trotsky's powerfully articulated disdain, Mstislavskii signaled the intent of the Left SRs to push ahead with negotiations over their entry into the government. "Confronted by Bolshevism, which is not of our creation," he declared, "we will do everything possible to minimize the harm it is doing to the revolutionary cause."[83]

Mstislavskii introduced a resolution prohibiting the Sovnarkom from interfering in the convocation of the Constituent Assembly as elected. The resolution provided for repeal of the decree outlawing the Kadets and reaffirmed the principle of the Sovnarkom's accountability to the CEC embodied in Sverdlov's Constitution of 17 November.[84] In pressing for the adoption of this resolution, Shteinberg literally begged the Bolsheviks to "free themselves of their [senseless] nightmares about the Kadets." However, without further discussion, by a vote of 150 to 98, with 3 abstentions (apparently strictly divided on party lines), the CEC adopted a Bolshevik resolution endorsing convocation of the Constituent Assembly upon the registration of four hundred delegates, and not only sanctioning blanket repression of the Kadets but also authorizing whatever other measures the Sovnarkom deemed necessary to combat the counterrevolution in the future.[85]

Ongoing negotiations over the entry of Left SRs into the Sovnarkom not-withstanding, the resolution did not concede anything to their sensibilities.

* * *

In the immediate aftermath of the October days, as a result of policies successfully pressed by Lenin and Trotsky, the Petrograd Bolsheviks bore ex-clusive responsibility for all aspects of government in Petrograd. However, they lacked the training, experience, or taste for this task. In these circum-stances, they tried to rule through existing political institutions—primarily the Petrograd city duma and district dumas and their networks of admin-istrative boards and agencies. Only after it became clear that this approach would not work were government and administrative functions gradually transferred to soviets. In the interim, the MRC, more than any other body, filled the existing vacuum in local government. Willy-nilly, it became the primary governing agency for the city of Petrograd.

Simultaneously, growing numbers of the Petrograd Bolshevik party or-ganization's most effective personnel were appointed to full-time positions in soviets or the military, or transferred out of Petrograd to consolidate the revolution around the country. Consequently, party activity among Petro-grad factory workers and lower-ranking military personnel came to a vir-tual standstill. To be sure, continued popular support for the Bolshevik pro-gram, coupled with a last-minute propaganda blitz, enabled the Bolsheviks to do quite well in elections to the Constituent Assembly in Petrograd and surrounding regions. Moreover, this strength was to be of inestimable value in enabling the Bolsheviks, allied with the Left SRs, to control the convoca-tion of the Constituent Assembly. But over the longer term, the Bolshevik organization's increasing isolation from its social base was to have most un-fortunate consequences.

3

Gathering Forces

In December 1917, in spite of tension between hard-line Bolshevik policies and Left SR ideals reflected in conflict over repression of the Kadets and the structural relationship between the Sovnarkom and the CEC, the Left SRs agreed to accept posts in the Sovnarkom. Contrary to accepted wisdom, directly connected to this development was the founding of one of the pillars of early Soviet repression, the All-Russian Extraordinary Commission for Combating Counterrevolution, Speculation, and Sabotage (VCheka).

According to traditional interpretations of the creation of the VCheka, by the first week of December 1917 the MRC, recognizing that its mission of seizing and consolidating Soviet power in Petrograd had been fulfilled, voluntarily liquidated itself. This step was implemented at a meeting of the Sovnarkom on 5 December which established a group to coordinate dissolution of the MRC within seven days. The next day, so these interpretations go, a nationwide civil servants strike prompted Lenin to propose to the Sovnarkom that Felix Dzerzhinskii form a special commission to explore means for fighting such political sabotage by forceful revolutionary measures. The great urgency attached to this task was reflected in the fact that at the Sovnarkom's meeting on 7 December, when it became known that Dzerzhinskii's commission was still in session, the Sovnarkom agreed not to disperse until it had finished its work. That evening, Dzerzhinskii called for the creation of a powerful temporary agency attached to the Sovnarkom to combat counterrevolution and sabotage. His idea was accepted on the spot and the VCheka was born.[1]

Documents from Soviet archives that shed light on the development of the MRC during the last weeks of its existence, and on its relationship to the Sovnarkom during this time, prompted me to question this interpretation. In the aftermath of the October days, the MRC had filled the void created by work stoppages in government agencies and assumed responsibility for providing basic municipal services and coordinating the security and defense of the revolution in Petrograd. Especially between 4 and 17 November, when, following Rykov's resignation, the position of people's commissar for internal affairs was vacant, the MRC accumulated vast powers to fight counterrevolution, sabotage, and speculation.

In mid November, as well, the merger of the All-Russian Executive Committee of Peasants' Soviets with the All-Russian Executive Committee of Workers' and Soldiers' Soviets was successfully completed, and negotiations over a Bolshevik–Left SR coalition in the Sovnarkom began.[2] It remained uncertain for the next two weeks which of the left socialist parties, the Bolsheviks or Left SRs, would end up in control of the combined CEC. During that interval the Left SRs had particularly great leverage vis-à-vis the Bolsheviks. Among other things, the Bolsheviks now accepted a Left SR demand for parity in the MRC, an unappealing concession for Bolshevik leaders.[3] The Left SRs, immediately after the October days, had fiercely attacked the MRC's violence against political opponents and the curtailment of civil rights. Now, Left SR equality in the MRC threatened to obstruct the Bolsheviks' freedom of action in repressing political enemies. At a meeting of the Sovnarkom, on 15 November, sentiment for abolishing the MRC was voiced. Sverdlov, chair of the CEC, vigorously opposed such a step. Instead, he proposed that the MRC's responsibilities be narrowed significantly and that funds for combating counterrevolution and other funds not subject to accounting should be transferred to the MRC from the Commissariat for Internal Affairs. To preclude Left SR equality in the MRC from interfering with repression of political enemies, he also urged that the MRC's Military Commission, which the Bolsheviks would try to retain under their control, have the right to make independent arrests without interference from the full MRC.[4]

The record of the 15 November Sovnarkom meeting does not indicate any action on these recommendations. However, at a meeting of the MRC on 21 November, the Bolshevik leadership in the MRC initiated steps to form a wholly new agency to fight counterrevolution from which Left SRs would be excluded. This step was negated the next day, when the Left SRs forced the Bolsheviks to include them.[5] Recognizing that the MRC had become a pawn in negotiations over the formation of a Bolshevik–Left SR coalition government, the Bolshevik MRC leadership postponed reorganizing it.[6]

Although intense Left SR criticism of Bolshevik "terror" continued unabated throughout these weeks, and although it was now clear that the Left SRs would be strongly represented in both the MRC and its special agency to combat counterrevolution, at a Sovnarkom meeting on 25 November

Lenin still looked to the MRC as the fledgling Soviet government's primary organ for domestic security. Three proposals regarding the future disposition of the MRC were presented at this meeting. Lenin, echoing Sverdlov's proposal of the 15th, urged that all of the MRC's responsibilities not directly concerned with combating counterrevolution and sabotage be immediately transferred to appropriate government commissariats. Martin Latsis suggested that the MRC be incorporated into the CEC's section for combating counterrevolution, and Uritskii recommended that the MRC be liquidated. In the inflamed political atmosphere surrounding the scheduled opening of the Constituent Assembly and intensified work stoppages by civil servants, Uritskii's recommendation was probably deemed premature. Very likely, Latsis's motion was undermined by lingering uncertainty about which party would control the CEC after it was reconfigured. Lenin's proposal to narrow the MRC's tasks was adopted.[7]

Nonetheless, little more than two weeks later, the MRC was liquidated and the embryonic VCheka took its place. How did this come about? Some of the top MRC leaders were independent-minded Bolshevik zealots who quickly came to resent curbs on their freedom of action imposed by Lenin and the Sovnarkom. They were profoundly disturbed by the Sovnarkom's catering to the Left SRs at the expense of the MRC's capacity to combat counterrevolution. Tension between the more radical MRC and the more tactically cautious Sovnarkom was reflected in the armed demonstration organized by the MRC without authorization from the Sovnarkom to counter the demonstration on behalf of the Constituent Assembly scheduled for 28 November.[8] The Sovnarkom, unprepared for this frontal attack and probably fearful that a physical, possibly bloody confrontation between opposing demonstrations might boomerang, aborted the counterdemonstration. No doubt, many Bolsheviks in the MRC were enraged by this public humiliation, exacerbated by the publication in *Rabochii i soldat* of their appeal to workers and soldiers to participate in the countermarch, and by a formal rebuke by Vladimir Bonch-Bruevich, acting on instructions from the Sovnarkom.[9] Judging by an announcement by Viacheslav Molotov at a meeting of the Executive Committee of the Petrograd Soviet on 29 November, the MRC resolved to liquidate itself either on that day or the previous night.[10]

What does the question of Bolshevik–Left SR relations have to do with the MRC's dissolution and the VCheka's formation? It now appears likely that the MRC decided to disband not because it considered its role finished but because its radical Bolshevik leadership was frustrated with the Sovnarkom. It is also clear that the decisive factor dictating the Sovnarkom's approval of the MRC's self-liquidation and the creation of the VCheka was its perceived need for a temporary agency, free from meddling by the Left SRs, to deal decisively with the threatened nationwide strike of civil servants and, even more fundamental, to contend with the danger posed by supporters of the Constituent Assembly to the survival of Soviet power. In a long-suppressed report on organizational issues relating to the VCheka prepared for internal use in 1922, Latsis, one of the VCheka's top leaders, acknowledged the significance of the "Left SR problem" in the decision to form the VCheka. As he put it, the Left SRs "greatly impeded the struggle against counterrevolution by pressing their 'universal' morality, humanism, and resistance to placing limitations on the right of counterrevolutionaries to enjoy free speech and freedom of the press. For Soviet leaders, it became clear that the presence of Left SRs made combating counterrevolution impossible. This gave rise to the idea of creating a new agency for fighting counterrevolution that would be separate from the MRC and would exclude Left SRs."[11]

To assess the significance of the Left SR factor in the dissolution of the MRC and the creation of the Cheka, it is necessary to reconstruct the course of negotiations between Bolsheviks and Left SRs over the formation of a coalition government. At a meeting of the Sovnarkom on 16 November, Sverdlov presented an encouraging report on discussions he had that day with the Left SR fraction in the newly merged CEC regarding formation of a Bolshevik–Left SR coalition. Attracted by the prospect of broadening the government as the day of reckoning with the Constituent Assembly neared, and heartened by collaboration with Left SRs in the CEC, the Sovnarkom responded by appointing a delegation to build on Sverdlov's deliberations.[12]

The discussions of this delegation began the next day. By then, the Left SRs had become infuriated by the Bolsheviks' dissolution of the Petrograd City Duma the day before. They were confident that they would still have a majority in the new, combined CEC when it was fully reconstituted. Moreover, they were hopeful of winning more than enough nominally SR peasant delegates to the Constituent Assembly to acquire decisive influence in the assembly. Thus, they made it clear that the price of their entry into the Sovnarkom would be high. At the outset, they insisted on the appointment of Left SRs to head the commissariats for internal affairs, military affairs, railways, and justice (in addition to agriculture, which was already directed by a Left SR, Kolegaev). Along with issues relating to the peasantry and land reform, the Left SRs' overriding concern with the buildup of military forces to defend the revolution at home and to support socialist uprisings abroad impelled them to press especially hard for control of the people's commissariat for military affairs. They gave similar high priority to establishing a just system of revolutionary law, which explains the importance they attached to the appointment of Shteinberg as people's commissar for justice.

Yielding all these key posts was obviously unacceptable to the Bolshevik negotiating team. At the same time, several additional provocative acts by the Bolsheviks during the second half of November further roiled the Left SRs, frequently bringing government talks to a standstill and, on occasion, threatening to scuttle them entirely. These acts, all vehemently protested by the Left SRs, included the detention of members of the All-Russian Commission on Elections to the Constituent Assembly, the branding of all Kadets as "enemies of the people," the arrest of leading Kadets, and the dispersal by armed force of the Unofficial Conference of Constituent Assembly Delegates. Consequently, the talks dragged on for nearly three weeks. Finally, as its first order of business on 7 December, the Sovnarkom concluded that the latest Left SR conditions for entry into the government were acceptable with some changes. The Russian émigré historian Anatolii Razgon, who has reconstructed these negotiations in greater detail than anyone else, argues that still in dispute was a Left SR demand for *equality* with the Bolsheviks in the allocation of key commissariats.[13] Although that may be, by then it was apparent that the Bolshevik majority in the CEC would be restored. Left SR leaders operated on the assumption that participation in Lenin's cabinet afforded them the possibility, perhaps their only one, of moderating Bolshevik behavior and playing a prominent role in advancing the revolution domestically and internationally. Petrograd workers, soldiers, and sailors sympathetic to the Left SRs were pressuring them to enter the Sovnarkom.[14] Moreover, one of their main conditions, support for their land reform program, was accepted by the Bolsheviks.[15] For these reasons, on 9 December, they accepted Bolshevik terms for entry into the Sovnarkom that amounted to considerably less than equality. Soon afterward, Shteinberg (people's commissar for justice) joined Kolegaev (people's commissar for agriculture) and six other Left SRs as people's commissars.[16] Left SRs were also named to the collegiums of all other people's commissariats and other central government institutions. As a result, on the eve of the Constituent Assembly, the Left SRs held roughly a quarter of the posts in the Sovnarkom and about a third of the seats in the CEC, and had a significant presence in all other key Soviet bodies.

Framed against this background, the primary reason becomes clear for jettisoning the MRC and creating the VCheka, as well as for the Sovnarkom's haste in forming the new agency on 7 December—the day that Left SR conditions for reconstructing the government were accepted "with some changes." Shortly, Shteinberg would head the potentially troublesome Commissariat for Justice. To Lenin it was essential that the VCheka, composed exclusively of reliable Bolsheviks and responsible directly to the Bolshevik-dominated Sovnarkom, be up and running before that happened. An official announcement about the creation of the VCheka appeared in *Izvestiia* on 10 December.[17] It informed readers that the headquarters of the new body was Gorokhovaia 2. In tsarist times, Gorokhovaia 2 had housed offices of the governor of Petersburg, the municipal police, and the notorious tsarist security service, the Okhrana.

It is worth noting that Lenin's concern about Shteinberg was fully justified. On 15 December, less than a week after taking office, without consulting the Sovnarkom, Shteinberg published a decree stipulating that all prisoners held in Smolny or in the premises of the revolutionary tribunal be immediately transferred to one of five main Petrograd prisons. There, temporary commissions specifically constituted in agreement with the Petrograd Soviet and district soviets were to review the justification for the arrest of these prisoners and either remand them for trial or free them within twenty-four hours. These commissions were also to conduct, immediately, a similar review of all prisoners in other Petrograd jails.[18] This decree, if allowed to stand, would have aborted the practice already begun by the VCheka of rounding up and isolating political opponents to *prevent* them from causing trouble rather than for specific counterrevolutionary acts. Consequently, for Lenin, Dzerzhinskii, and like-minded Bolsheviks, the publication of Shteinberg's decree amounted to a declaration of war. Moreover, in a press interview the same day, Shteinberg announced his intention of visiting Smolny and the Revolutionary Tribunal for the stated purpose of releasing prisoners not guilty of specific crimes.[19]

The next day, Shteinberg issued another decree which listed the agencies that were allowed to permit and carry out searches and arrests, and ordered that improper actions by any of these investigating bodies be reported both to him and to the institution to which they were attached.[20] The VCheka was on the list. However, the provision that complaints be reported to him clearly staked out Shteinberg's intention of overseeing the VCheka according to criteria set by the People's Commissariat for Justice. A short time later, this aim was made even more explicit when Shteinberg ordered that all materials in the VCheka's possession be sent to him for review.[21] After this request was denied, Shteinberg formally petitioned the Sovnarkom for permission to conduct an inspection of the VCheka. This petition was also rejected.[22] Next Shteinberg, again in the spirit of eliminating arbitrariness in the exercise of revolutionary justice, assigned Aleksandr Shreider, his deputy and a fellow Left SR, to supervise preparation of a compendium of Russian revolutionary laws and guidelines for revolutionary tribunals aimed at systematizing their structure and procedures.

Meanwhile, amid escalating tension caused by the delay in convening the Constituent Assembly and by the start of separate peace talks with Germany, the VCheka had, if anything, intensified harassment of political opponents. Thus, on 16 December, fifteen moderate socialists were arrested at the headquarters of the Union for the Defense of the Constituent Assembly.[23] Little more than twenty-four hours later, the VCheka superintended the arrest and incarceration of Nikolai Avksentiev.[24] The next day, Dzerzhinskii issued an order for the immediate arrest and trial by the revolutionary tribunal of eleven other opposition leaders and delegates to the Constituent Assembly, including Iraklii Tsereteli, Viktor Chernov, Fedor Dan, L. M. Bramson, Matvei Skobelev, Abram Gotz, and Vladimir Rozanov.[25] That evening (18 December) an armed detachment headed by a Chekist raided a workers' conference of some 135 representatives of opposition parties and moderate socialist delegates from factories, trade unions, military units, district dumas, and the Petrograd Soviet at the headquarters of the UDCA, evidently in the hope of catching some of the leading opposition figures named in Dzerzhinskii's order. Organizers of this conference had agreed in advance that they would not identify themselves and that they would try to proceed with their deliberations in the event of another raid. Therefore, they refused an order to register their names and addresses in writing and proceeded with their business unfazed. The Chekist then proclaimed that all the conferees were under arrest and stationed guards at the doors to prevent anyone from leaving.

Word of the arrests at the UDCA's headquarters was announced by Lenin at an early evening session of the Sovnarkom.[26] Although not recorded in the minutes of this meeting, it is apparent that the Sovnarkom resolved that after the detainees had identified themselves, all those not specifically named in Dzerzhinskii's arrest order would be released.[27] Armed with this mandate, Shteinberg and Karelin hurried to the scene to try to resolve what was fast becoming a highly explosive situation. Ignoring the Chekist and his detachment, they explained that their group also opposed "terror" but was obliged to enforce orders of the legitimate government and appealed to the conferees to identify themselves so that what was obviously a misunderstanding could be settled peacefully. Their pleas were also rejected, and the assembled representatives defiantly insisted on being taken to jail. Next, Shteinberg turned to the conference chair and asked him to certify, if only orally, that none of the individuals specified in Dzerzhinskii's arrest order was present. After he was refused, Shteinberg and Karelin ended the standoff by taking personal responsibility for attesting that this was the case and freeing everyone.

An early showdown over the prerogatives of the VCheka between Shteinberg and his Left SR colleagues in the government, on the one hand, and Dzerzhinskii and Bolshevik people's commissars led by Lenin, on the other, was now inevitable. It came at a Sovnarkom meeting on 19 December, after Lenin belatedly added to an already crowded agenda the issue of "the release on 18 December of members of the Union for Defense of the Constituent Assembly arrested on Dzerzhinskii's order by people's commissar Shteinberg."[28] Six of seven Left SRs in the government attended this meeting— an unusually good turnout. They were outnumbered, however, more than two to one by Bolsheviks, Lenin and Trotsky among them. Dzerzhinskii led off the discussion with the claim that Shteinberg's action the previous evening had humiliated and demoralized his agency.[29] The terse protocol of this meeting masks the furious debate that took place there. Predictably, it ended with the passage of a resolution affirming that the directives of Dzerzhinskii's commission could only be revised by appeal to the Sovnarkom. The resolution also reprimanded Shteinberg and Karelin.[30]

The Left SR people's commissars fought back. At one point in the meeting, Shteinberg threatened to resign.[31] Still, the best the Left SRs could achieve was an agreement to table implementation of the motion, Shteinberg's reprimand included.[32] Shteinberg was undeterred by this defeat. Subsequently, for example, he telegraphed soviets around the country directing them to bring systematic repression to a halt on the grounds that Soviet power had been stabilized and, consequently, it was time to integrate control of counterrevolution into a new, revolutionary legal system.[33] However, the Sovnarkom continued its efforts to fetter him. In December and January alone, issues relating to the behavior of the VCheka raised by Shteinberg were discussed at eleven meetings of the Sovnarkom—without any positive result.[34]

In the end, however, Bolshevik hopes of maintaining the VCheka as a kind of party praetorian guard were short-lived. In early January 1918 Shteinberg, having tried without success to make the VCheka accountable to him, attempted to moderate Cheka behavior from within by forcing the Bolsheviks to admit Left SRs into the VCheka leadership. On 4 January, after individual Left SRs who tried to join the VCheka were brushed off with the claim that membership was by election only, Shteinberg, in a letter to Dzerzhinskii, courteously but firmly insisted on the right of Left SRs from the Petrograd Soviet and the CEC to occupy places in the VCheka

leadership without delay or elections.[35] The Sovnarkom considered Shteinberg's demand on 7 January. At that point, the Third All-Russian Congress
of Soviets, in which Left SR support for Bolshevik policies was critical, was
about to convene. This consideration, as well as gratitude for Left SR collaboration in the dissolution of the Constituent Assembly (5/6 January), probably explain the Bolsheviks' concession to Shteinberg despite Dzerzhinskii's
objections.[36] Indeed, four Left SRs were confirmed the next day as members
of the VCheka collegium. Viacheslav Aleksandrovich, a nationally prominent member of the party, became Dzerzhinskii's deputy.[37]

* * *

During the first week and a half of December 1917, at the time Bolsheviks and the Left SRs cobbled together a coalition and the VCheka was
founded, the Bolshevik Central Committee took steps to impose control
over its own sizable Constituent Assembly delegation. At first blush, this may
appear to have been the least of its problems. However, to anyone familiar
with the heated debates among Bolshevik leaders throughout 1917 over fundamental issues relating to the development of the revolution, as well as the
relative independence of major, nominally subordinate party bodies at that
time, profound intraparty conflict over the role of the Constituent Assembly
is not at all surprising. Again, at issue in this case were drastically differing
theoretical and strategic views between Lenin and his comrades in the Central Committee, on the one hand, and, on the other, Bolshevik moderates
still led by Kamenev.

As we have seen, at the end of October and the beginning of November,
the moderates had been frustrated in their efforts to facilitate construction
of a broad, democratic socialist, unity cabinet and even to make the Sovnarkom effectively accountable to the CEC. Following the failure of these
efforts, they had either withdrawn from or been forced out of high positions
in the party and national government. Nonetheless, they had not lost faith
in the critical importance of their cause, or their resolve to do whatever was
necessary to put the party back on a less extreme and violent tack. If anything, deepening political conflict and chaos in the economy during the balance of November strengthened their conviction that Lenin and Trotsky
were leading the revolution and the country to inevitable ruin. Their last
hope lay with the Constituent Assembly, which they had consistently viewed
as the only institution in which revolutionary Russia's future political and
social order could legitimately be defined.

Toward the end of November, as the question of the Constituent Assembly's fate began to take center stage, Kamenev, Rykov, Miliutin, and Nogin

sent a statement to the Central Committee requesting reinstatement. Neither the Letter of the Four, as the statement of the moderates was referred to, nor a written reply by Lenin has been published or declassified. There is little doubt, however, that the moderates sought reinstatement in order to fight for their views on the Constituent Assembly within the party's top leadership. The record of the Central Committee's meeting on 29 November, at which the moderates' request was discussed, indicates that their appeal was denied because their stance had clearly not changed and, as Uritskii put it, "we have no guarantee that if left in the minority, they will not behave in the same way [as they had before the October revolution and at the Vikzhel talks]."[38]

Nonetheless, the four still had cards to play. Virtually all the leading moderates were elected delegates to the Constituent Assembly, the Bolshevik delegation having been formed according to electoral lists compiled in late September when their influence was at its peak. How the delegation as a whole would view the Constituent Assembly in the prevailing circumstances was impossible to predict. However, the moderates drew encouragement from the fact that during the Democratic State Conference in late September 1917 a sizable majority of what had been the last formal assembly of party leaders from around the country (the numerical equivalent of a party congress) had sided with them against Trotsky and the Leninists on the party's participation in the Preparliament.[39]

Much about the campaign of Bolshevik moderates to uphold the sanctity of the Constituent Assembly within the party at this time remains unclear. What is apparent is that at an initial organizational meeting of the party's Constituent Assembly delegates in the Taurida Palace in early December, following remarks by Lenin on the attitude of the Central Committee and the Sovnarkom toward the Constituent Assembly, the moderates won a majority in the fraction's elected Provisional Bureau. Among its members were Kamenev, Nogin, Rykov, Miliutin, Riazanov, and Larin—in sum, a high percentage of the key party moderates who had left high party and government posts in early November.[40]

Under the direction of this moderate-dominated bureau, the fraction set out on an independent course based on the principle that the Constituent Assembly should be the ultimate arbiter of Russia's political destiny. Ignoring the decision of the Central Committee at its 29 November meeting, surely conveyed by Lenin, that for the time being the main body of Bolshevik Constituent Assembly delegates should not be called to Petrograd, the fraction authorized the bureau to send for absent delegates at once. In the meantime, it authorized the bureau to begin preparing legislation for the Constituent Assembly's consideration. The fraction also voted to call for the immediate convocation of a national party congress or conference to define the party's approach to the Constituent Assembly. Pending the decisions of this gathering, the delegation opposed efforts by the Sovnarkom to assert control over the Constituent Assembly's convocation and structure.[41]

The divergence between the policies of the Bolshevik Central Committee and the party's Constituent Assembly fraction, as reflected in these actions by party moderates, was the main topic of discussion at a meeting of the Bolshevik Central Committee on 11 December.[42] There it was decided to call the party's Constituent Assembly delegates to Petrograd at once. It was also agreed that the party's policy toward the Constituent Assembly as embodied in a set of Theses on the Constituent Assembly drafted by Lenin would be presented to the fraction for adoption the next day (12 December). According to these theses, the existing republic of soviets was a significantly higher form of democracy than a bourgeois republic and a Constituent Assembly. The only possibility for resolving the crisis caused by contradictions between the overall results of Constituent Assembly elections and the aspirations of the people lay in the broadest possible use of recall elections and the unequivocal recognition of Soviet power by the Constituent Assembly.[43] In short, these theses constituted a firm prohibition against treating the Constituent Assembly as a legitimate expression of the popular will, as moderate Bolsheviks were doing. The Constituent Assembly was to be marginalized but not eliminated. Nikolai Bukharin and Grigorii Sokolnikov were appointed to ensure that henceforth the work of the Bolshevik Constituent Assembly fraction was conducted in this spirit. Before adjournment on 11 December, the Central Committee also adopted a resolution drafted by Lenin calling for election of a new Provisional Bureau. The old Provisional Bureau's demand for a party congress or conference was not even discussed.[44] Surely it is no coincidence that on this same day (11 December) Kamenev, Riazanov, Rykov, Larin, and Miliutin were purged from the bureau of the Bolshevik fraction in the CEC.[45]

Information on the 12 December meeting of the Bolshevik delegation to the Constituent Assembly is thin. According to an announcement that Sverdlov sent to the Provisional Bureau, the meeting was to be held in Smolny rather than the Taurida Palace so that members of the Central Committee could participate.[46] This circumstance, coupled with the fact that delegates not already in Petrograd would not have enough time to get to the meeting, gave the Leninists an immense advantage. An agenda for the meeting approved by the Central Committee on 11 December specified that the delegation would hear a report from that committee (undoubtedly a dressing down), consider Lenin's theses, and elect a new bureau, in that order.[47] Lenin personally presented his theses, and they were adopted.[48] All that is known about the results of elections to a new bureau is that Alexander Shliapnikov was chosen as the new chair in place of Kamenev.[49] Party moderates had suffered another devastating blow.

*   *   *

The main point of Lenin's Theses on the Constituent Assembly, that any form of government the Constituent Assembly might create would be an intolerable step backward from the republic of soviets formed by the people in the course of the October revolution, was the central motif of a vigorous propaganda campaign conducted by the Bolsheviks as well as the Left SRs among Petrograd factory workers and garrison troops during the second half of December 1917 and the first days of the new year. Early in this campaign, on 20 December, under pressure from the Left SRs, the Sovnarkom resolved to convene the Constituent Assembly on 5 January, provided the required four hundred delegates were in place on that date.[50] Two days later the CEC confirmed this resolution. At the same time, obviously as a counterweight to the Constituent Assembly, should one be needed, the CEC scheduled a national congress of soviets of workers' and soldiers' deputies, and a national congress of soviets of peasants' deputies for 8 and 12 January, respectively.[51]

A discussion of questions relating to the opening and operation of the Constituent Assembly was on the Sovnarkom's agenda on 2 January. However, this discussion was deferred until an emergency joint meeting of the Bolshevik and Left SR Central Committees scheduled for later that evening.[52] Little information is available about its proceedings, although Lenin's Declaration of the Rights of Toiling and Exploited People and an accompanying ordinance were surely discussed there. Both were endorsed by the CEC on 3 January without dissent and published in *Pravda* on the 4th. Prepared for adoption by the Constituent Assembly as its first order of business, the declaration was aimed at setting up an immediate, decisive confrontation between the soviets and the Constituent Assembly, and eliminating any possibility that the latter would be able to consolidate its power. Thus, the declaration stated categorically that Russia was and would remain a republic of soviets and that governing authority throughout the land belonged exclusively to soviets. It endorsed without qualification all the major decrees and steps of the Soviet government in both domestic and foreign policy and, in case anything had been left out, it included a repudiation of any claim to governing authority on the part of the Constituent Assembly. The accompanying ordinance specified that attempts by any individual or institution, including the Constituent Assembly, to appropriate any function of state government would be regarded as a counterrevolutionary act and suppressed by all possible means, including the use of armed force.[53] All in all, the message was unambiguous—the Constituent Assembly would either yield its prerogatives and leave the scene at once or it would be forced to do so. This was a significant tactical difference between the declaration and Lenin's earlier theses on the Constituent Assembly, which had envisioned the possibility of an extended supportive role for that body.

*   *   *

While the Bolsheviks and Left SRs were setting the stage for the quick demise of the Constituent Assembly, their opponents—most important the SRs, since only a tiny number of elected delegates were Mensheviks—continued preparations for its work. To be sure, after the events of 28 November the SR Central Committee had doubts about whether the Assembly would actually be permitted to convene.[54] Nonetheless, during the first half of December, SR delegates from the provinces who had arrived in Petrograd still met regularly, often in their makeshift dormitory on Bolotnoi Street.[55] By mid month, at which time roughly 150 SR delegates were on hand, the fraction gathered daily to review, debate, and revise draft legislation, pick and instruct floor leaders, and even rehearse main speakers. Several commissions concentrated on such specific tasks as coordinating agitation and propaganda in Petrograd; establishing and maintaining communications with soviets and party organizations in the provinces; coordinating activity with other fractions in the Constituent Assembly including the Left SRs (this was to be the task of an interfractional commission); preparing and publishing daily bulletins, brochures, and leaflets; and formulating drafts of fundamental laws on such questions as the political form and structure of the new Russia, as well as basic economic and social reform. The critical importance of revealing the true face of the majority in the Constituent Assembly as quickly as possible was first acknowledged in a resolution adopted by the Fourth SR Congress in early December.[56]

Thus, together with the Commission on Fundamental Laws, the most important special commission was the Committee for the First Day, whose sole purpose was to develop plans for opening the first session of the assembly and coordinate strategy and tactics for it.[57] The SR fraction, as early as 18 December, approved a draft declaration proposed by the Committee for the First Day which formally endorsed the overthrow of the tsarist political and legal system; disavowed the monarchist system forever; proclaimed Russia a democratic, federal republic; and specified that, pending adoption of fundamental laws, all state power belonged to the Constituent Assembly.[58]

At the end of the month, the bulk of the reform legislation drafted by the Commission on Fundamental Laws was reviewed and approved by the centrist-dominated leadership bureau of the fraction, and the gist of it was incorporated into a succinct programmatic manifesto that was widely circulated.[59] This manifesto highlighted the measures prepared or being prepared by the fraction for immediate implementation by the Constituent Assembly. A peace plank provided for the appointment of a high-level delegation to conduct negotiations with all the warring powers. The aim of these negotiations was to arrange a universal peace without victors or vanquished as quickly as possible. Even before these negotiations were completed, all military personnel who wished to do so were to be released from duty and service in the Russian armed forces was made voluntary. A plank on nationalities provided for self-determination of minority peoples within a federative Russian democratic republic. Regarding agricultural reform, which was of central importance to the SRs, the manifesto specified that prior to the fall harvest all private lands would be redistributed by land reform agencies based on the principle of equality of land use by the working peasantry without compensation to owners. In the industrial sector, provision was made for state regulation and control of industry with the broadest possible participation by worker organizations. In time, the toiling people themselves were to direct industrial production. Also provided in the manifesto was legislation aimed at shifting the burden of paying off war debts from toilers to the propertied classes; establishing an eight-hour day, a minimum wage, and all forms of social insurance; conducting a vigorous fight to combat unemployment; and supplying the masses with basic necessities. The manifesto revealed how far left the majority of the fraction and bureau was prepared to go to capture the popular attraction of Soviet power. Comparing the provisions of the manifesto with the program of moderate Bolsheviks before and immediately after the overthrow of the Provisional Government, about the only thing missing was the explicit exclusion of non-socialist parties from the government.[60] Small wonder that the agrarian specialist Nikolai Oganovskii, a staunch Right SR, scorned the bureau's efforts as "Vikzhelish" [*vikzhelistoi*].[61]

Around 20 December, when the opening date of the Constituent Assembly was announced, emissaries from the SR Interfractional Commission met with Shteinberg, Karelin, and Kolegaev to sound them out about possible collaboration. Nikolai Sviatitskii, one of the emissaries, later recalled that after a long, tense argument the Left SRs responded with a clear signal that they would be "on the other [the Bolshevik] side of the barricades."[62] No doubt! At the same time, it should be noted that many Left SRs hoped to attract the support of enough nominally SR peasant delegates to play a decisive *independent* role in the Constituent Assembly. Before and after this setback, the leadership of the SRs endorsed civil servants' strikes in support of the immediate convocation of the Constituent Assembly and sought to expand agitation on its behalf among Petrograd workers, soldiers, and sailors, in part through the Union for Defense of the Constituent Assembly.[63] Also, it sought to bring pressure to bear on the Bolsheviks by peasants who supported the Constituent Assembly. This effort was reflected in a telegram from the old SR-dominated CEC of Soviets of Peasants' Deputies circulated to rural areas under Chernov's name toward the end of December. In the telegram, Chernov contended that the scheduling by Soviet authorities of the Third All-Russian Congress of Soviets of Peasants' Deputies for 15 January, well after both the Constituent Assembly (5 January) and the Third All-Russian Congress of Soviets of Workers' and Soldiers' Deputies (8 January), was intended to marginalize peasants and facilitate suppression of the Constituent Assembly. Ignoring the new combined CEC, the old peasant CEC rescheduled the Third All-Russian Congress of Soviets of Peasants' Deputies for 8 January, so as to coincide with the Third All-Russian Congress of Soviets of Workers' and Soldiers' Deputies. Further, it appealed to peasant soviets loyal to the Constituent Assembly to have their representatives in Petrograd, by 5 January, armed with political instructions providing for upholding its sanctity, obviously to counter any attack on the Assembly by supporters of Soviet power.[64]

That was all, however. Efforts by the UDCA and the SR Military Commission to provide for the security of the Constituent Assembly notwithstanding, the SR leadership was obsessively fearful of preparations for defense that might possibly provoke government retaliation. When pressed by its Military Commission to turn from listening to reports and preparing resolutions to security matters, its response was that, since the Constituent Assembly was popularly elected to build a new political system and life for Russia, its defense was the people's responsibility.[65]

Then, too, many SR leaders considered the Constituent Assembly so sacred that they simply could not envision an attack on it.[66] Boris Sokolov, a member of the Military Commission, later acknowledged that individuals like him who favored pro-active, even preemptive measures for defense of the Constituent Assembly constituted a small minority in the SR Constituent Assembly fraction and were viewed with unease by the majority. So it was that after the Military Commission signed off on a plan by Fedot Onipko, another member of the Military Commission, to kidnap or assassinate top Bolsheviks, the idea was immediately vetoed by the SR Central Committee on the grounds that "insane, terrorist acts" would "trigger such fury among workers and soldiers that they might well end in a general pogrom against the intelligentsia."[67] As early as 12 December, the SR Central Committee became so concerned about the possibility that aggressive moves of people like Sokolov might give the Sovnarkom an excuse to abort the Constituent Assembly that it specifically banned terrorist acts and formed a special commission "to investigate the activities of comrades engaged in arranging for the defense of the Constituent Assembly [the Military Commission]."[68]

Still, on the same day (12 December) the Military Commission probably drew some encouragement from a resolution, adopted by the Semenovskii regiment, registering support for the Constituent Assembly as "all-powerful master of the Russian land,"[69] Around this same time, the UDCA managed to organize publication of a daily newspaper (*Biulleten' vserossiiskogo soiuza zashchity uchreditel'nogo sobraniia*). Moreover, toward the end of the month, the Military Commission managed to publish a few issues of its own rabidly anti-Bolshevik newspaper for soldiers, *Seraia shinel'.*[70] Representatives of numerous Petrograd factories regularly participated in a workers' conference, as well as lectures and workshops, organized by the UDCA. Although the significance of these measures is impossible to quantify or evaluate in terms of readiness for political action, clearly the SRs had considerable influence in several key factories, among them the Government Printing Office and the Obukhov steel and armaments plant. On 28 December, Obukhov workers rejected a resolution pledging unconditional support for Soviet power, after which they adopted a statement that condemned the Sovnarkom's foreign and domestic policies for leading the country and the revolution to unavoidable ruin. Declaring that the Constituent Assembly constituted the revolution's last hope, the statement demanded that it be convened at once.[71]

The Military Commission aspired to form a kind of Red Guard of its own, but as Sokolov ruefully acknowledged: "We may have recruited up to two thousand guardsmen, but this figure existed only on paper."[72] The SR Military Commission managed to get several hundred armed officers and soldiers transferred from the front to Petrograd, intending to use some of them to strengthen support for the Constituent Assembly in the Semenovskii and Preobrazhenskii regiments, and to officially attach the rest to a fictional soldiers university where they would form into roving combat squads for use on 5 January. These steps were also aborted by the SR Central Committee as too dangerous.[73]

Simultaneously, the leadership of the UDCA began laying plans for a peaceful mass military and civilian demonstration of support for the Constituent Assembly timed to coincide with its opening on 5 January. These plans were approved at the fourth session of the UDCA-sponsored workers' conference on 29 December. Their implementation began at this session and was continued at another on 3 January.[74] Apparently, at least some of the instigators of this march hoped it might develop into an armed insurrection on behalf of the slogan "All Power to the Constituent Assembly." Describing plans for the march in considerable detail, Boris Sokolov claimed that, as the time for the opening of the Constituent Assembly neared, prospects were encouraging for substantial worker and soldier participation. The latter was centered on the Semenovskii and Preobrazhenskii regiments and also the Fifth Armored Car Division. Yet even he acknowledges that nothing was certain.[75] In any case, when these plans were brought to the SR Central Committee for endorsement, the latter, completely unpersuaded by arguments regarding their potential, issued an absolute ban on an armed march, insisting that even soldiers should leave their weapons behind so as to avoid any possibility of bloodshed.[76]

* * *

At the same time, Soviet authorities appealed to workers and soldiers to refrain from participating in any demonstrations on the Constituent Assembly's behalf. Leading Bolshevik party bodies were not involved in decision making on security issues. Like the Central Committee, the Petersburg Committee was already preoccupied by the implications of a possible separate peace being considered by Soviet and German negotiators on prospects for socialist revolutions abroad.[77] In general, security agencies and forces at the government's disposal were disorganized. The MRC had been dissolved, and the formation of the VCheka was rudimentary. Despite its designation as a national agency, its reach did not extend beyond the capital, and, even there, its impact was limited for several reasons. In Petrograd, there existed several permanent agencies whose functions and powers overlapped with those of the VCheka. Among these were the Investigating Commission of the Petrograd Soviet's Revolutionary Tribunal (previously, the Military-Investigating Commission of the MRC),[78] the Emergency Commission for the Security of Petrograd under Georgii Blagonravov, Bonch-Bruevich's Committee to Combat Pogroms—all of which had only recently been formed[79]—and district-level investigating commissions of one kind or another, some still on the drawing board. These security agencies and others operated independently and were in varying states of disarray.

At this time, as well, the VCheka had virtually no military forces at its direct disposal. Even for modest operations, it had to rely primarily on undisciplined, largely untrained, and loosely controlled Red Guard detachments, many of them attached to district soviets. Also, in the beginning VCheka leaders, including Dzerzhinskii, eschewed "Okhrana methods"—the use of secret agents, agent provocateurs, and the like—on principle. Their hope was that vigilant workers would suffice as the VCheka's eyes and ears.[80] Hence, the value of the VCheka was limited even for intelligence. This initial aversion to anything that smacked of the hated Okhrana also helps account for the great difficulty the VCheka encountered at this early stage, and indeed for much of 1918, in recruiting loyal and qualified staff. Of course, an acute shortage of reliable cadres was common to all Soviet institutions. Still, Iakov Peters, a member of the VCheka's Presidium in 1918, later recalled a unique feature of the VCheka's recruitment problem. He remembered that, for veteran Bolsheviks, recollections of special security agents who fought the proletariat, conducted searches, sent victims to Siberia, drove them into prisons, and dispatched them by hanging, were still very fresh. And here a new power was organized, and once again a fresh cycle of searches, arrests, and violence was beginning. Many simply did not differentiate between repressions in the past and those in the present, and were reluctant to serve in organs of the VCheka.[81] Difficulties connected with the recruitment of Bolshevik party members and even unaffiliated factory workers into the VCheka help explain why so many former Okhrana agents and blatant criminals successfully wormed their way into the VCheka, as well as its initial limitations as a security agency from the point of view of the Soviet government. In an official report several months later a high VCheka official, Ivan Polukarov, recalled that in this period "we did not have strength, ability, or knowledge, and the commission's size was insignificant."[82]

In view of this, a prominent role in providing for the protection of Soviet power in Petrograd during the Constituent Assembly fell to the Presidium of the Petrograd Soviet, which in turn looked to district soviets, Red Guards, Latvian Rifle Regiments, elements of the Petrograd garrison, and Baltic Fleet sailors for military support. Protocols of Presidium meetings at the end of December 1917 and the beginning of January 1918 reflect this situation.[83] On 31 December, less than a week before the scheduled convocation of the Constituent Assembly, the Presidium met to discuss security arrangements. In response to the blunt conclusion of the main speaker on this subject that existing military forces could not be relied on, it resolved to ignore the holidays and begin emergency recruitment of five hundred of the most dependable, steadfast, and experienced comrades available for service in the so-called Colt Battalion no later than 2 January. The sense of this meeting was that, if supplemented in this way, the battalion could be relied on to carry out particularly critical missions. The Bolshevik Petr Zalutskii, a member of the Presidium, was appointed to alert district soviets to the security crisis without delay.[84]

Late on the night of New Year's Day 1918, an event occurred that stirred the anxieties of Soviet authorities in Petrograd even more, and further inflamed the already highly explosive political situation. A car in which Lenin was riding, returning from delivering a speech to Red Guards about to depart for the Don to combat the forces of Generals Kornilov, Alekseev, and Kaledin, was fired upon. Neither Lenin nor his passengers, his sister Maria and the Swiss social democratic leader Fritz Platten, was seriously injured, and the perpetrator escaped. However, Soviet authorities immediately concluded that the Right SRs were responsible for the attempted assassination. The next day the offices of *Volia naroda,* the main Right SR newspaper, were raided, and Pitirim Sorokin and Andrei Argunov, both members of the paper's editorial board and of the bureau of the SR fraction in the Constituent Assembly, were arrested and imprisoned.[85]

At Lenin's request, investigation of the incident was assigned to Vladimir Bonch-Bruevich's Committee to Combat Pogroms rather than to the VCheka or to the Emergency Commission for the Security of Petrograd.[86] Information on the results of its investigation in the original case file is incomplete. In response to a request for a clarification from the NKVD in 1935 regarding one of the alleged participants in the conspiracy against Lenin who was then under arrest, Bonch-Bruevich, in a secret written memorandum, replied that the attempted assassination had been organized and carried out by a small idealistic group of young army officers from the front who had come to Petrograd to help protect the Constituent Assembly.[87] They had been successfully rounded up on 22 January. Those directly involved had confessed, and the others, among them several active members of the Union of Cavaliers of St. George, were soon released. The Investigating Committee of the Revolutionary Tribunal was to investigate the cases of those who confessed, but, during the German advance on Petrograd toward the end of February 1918, the prisoners formally requested an opportunity to redeem themselves by going to the front to fight. With Lenin's approval, they were amnestied and allowed to do so.[88]

During the first days of January 1918, significant numbers of Petrograd workers and lower-ranking military personnel interpreted the attempted assassination of Lenin as an aspect of the struggle between the Constituent Assembly and Soviet power. Nonetheless, even now some major garrison units reconfirmed their support for the Constituent Assembly. Because of the closeness of its barracks to the Taurida Palace, probably most troubling for the Bolsheviks was a pledge of support for the Constituent Assembly proclaimed by the Preobrazhenskii Regiment.[89] Although its support was conditional on the Constituent Assembly adopting decrees providing for an immediate democratic peace, equal redistribution of land without compensation, and popular control over industrial production and distribution, guarantees for promulgation of these measures by the majority SR fraction in the Constituent Assembly had already been widely publicized.

The Bolshevik and Left SR Central Committees held an emergency joint meeting the night of 2/3 January that centered on the Constituent Assembly.[90] A subsequent joint discussion of the same question by the Left SR Central Committee, the party's fraction in the CEC, and Left SR delegates to the Constituent Assembly affirmed, "almost unanimously," that an attack on Soviet power by Right SR Assembly delegates would need to be met with a decisive, organized rebuff on the part of the "revolutionary democracy," and that "in so far as the Constituent Assembly was subordinate to the revolution, implementing its triumphs, it would not break with the soviets." If this were not the case, "a conflict with the Constituent Assembly, or more accurately with the Right SR fraction, was inevitable."[91] Clearly, the focus of the Left SR leadership was on politics aimed at establishing the supremacy of Soviet power.

This was also the Bolsheviks' approach. On 3 January, after listening to an intelligence report by Zinoviev on the demonstration being planned by the UDCA for 5 January, which Zinoviev described as part of a conspiracy to overthrow Soviet power, the Presidium of the Petrograd Soviet agreed that it would not try to ban the march. At the same time, it issued a public appeal to workers and soldiers not to participate, along with a warning to citizens generally to expect the most extreme measures if the demonstration were not peaceful.[92]

At the outset of a major address to the Petrograd Soviet later on 3 January, Zinoviev declared that the Bolsheviks were not blaming an entire party for trying to kill Lenin. Yet in his lengthy speech he did precisely that, attributing responsibility directly to the Right SRs. According to Zinoviev, individual terrorist acts and shooting behind the back were their trademarks. The Right SR press had explicitly sanctioned all forms of combat in the life and death struggle against the Bolsheviks. This was understandable, he explained, as the Right SRs had so bankrupted themselves before the revolutionary masses that the only tactic left to them was to take up arms against the leaders of the working class. Bonch-Bruevich followed Zinoviev to the podium, ostensibly to clarify facts about the attempt on Lenin's life. However, perhaps because he had been in Finland on 1 January and his investigation of the case had not even begun, he largely ignored the shooting, enumerating instead a litany of threatening moves by the Right SRs. "Everything will be done to avoid bloodshed [on 5 January]," he declared, "but be assured that we are prepared to combat every blow against us without the slightest mercy," adding that each worker and soldier should be ready to defend the revolution by his own hands if that became necessary.[93]

A resolution adopted by acclamation following Bonch-Bruevich's tirade condemned the Right SR press for instigating acts of terror against representatives of Soviet power. The resolution implicitly put "the bourgeoisie and its servants, the Right SRs," on notice that further violence by them would be answered with mass terror.[94] A second resolution adopted at this session called on workers and soldiers to remain on the job and soldiers to stay in their barracks on 5 January. Toward the close of this meeting, representatives of several military units came forward to deny reports that garrison troops were wavering in their support of Soviet power and swinging toward supporting the Constituent Assembly. By unanimous vote, the deputies gave Blagonravov carte blanche to take whatever measures he deemed necessary to maintain order on 5 January.[95] A resolution passed by the CEC with virtually no debate was similarly unequivocal. "All power in the Russian Republic belongs to the Soviets and Soviet institutions," the CEC resolution read. "Attempts by anyone or any institution to usurp this or that function of state government will be considered a counterrevolutionary act . . . and will be crushed with all of the means at the disposal of the Soviet government."[96]

That evening (3/4 January), Blagonravov placed Petrograd under martial law, justifying the step as a safeguard against the attack on Soviet power *planned* for January 5. Blagonravov's proclamation warned citizens that all attempted pogroms would be suppressed by armed force; that failure to obey government directives would be severely punished; and that beginning on 5 January all efforts by counterrevolutionary groups to enter the area of the Taurida Palace and Smolny would be stopped by armed force.[97] Clearly, then, Soviet authorities were firmly bent on avoiding pressure, at any cost, from a large hostile crowd such as that manifested on 28 November. Instructions to participants in the demonstration organized by the UDCA specified that they were to march past the Taurida Palace, without stopping.[98] However, the prohibition on even entering the neighborhood of the palace made a bloody confrontation between pro-Assembly and pro-Soviet forces inevitable.

According to an *Izvestiia* report on 5 January, mass meetings in all units of the Petrograd garrison during the previous days ended with pledges of support to the Soviet government in any conflict with the Constituent Assembly. The reality was not as conclusive. Soldiers of the Semenovskii and Preobrazhenskii regiments were still a potential source of trouble for Soviet power. The Preobrazhenskii Regiment, for one, was on record as having decided not to participate in the march on behalf of the Constituent Assembly; at the same time, it had vowed to come out if needed to combat any attempt to disrupt it.[99]

In view of such continuing threats, the Presidium of the Petrograd Soviet organized an emergency conference with representatives of district soviets and factory committees on the afternoon of the 4th.[100] The Bolshevik military commissar Mikhail Lashevich, who worked closely with Blagonravov, opened the meeting: "No attempt has been made to ban demonstrations," he said, "because they will take place in any case." "Our overall strategy," he explained, "is to have a strong concentration of force at every [strategically important] location so that, should they [supporters of the Constituent Assembly] try to seize installations, we will be able to [repel them]." "Special measures have been taken to protect Smolny and the Taurida Palace," he continued. "Beginning in the morning, we will have reconnaissance planes in the air, and they will be in communication with the naval staff." To avoid panic, Lashevich urged that the districts be alerted to the reconnaissance flights. "We may be confronted with an offensive tomorrow," he warned. "We need to be ready for trouble at any moment."[101]

As Lashevich finished, Zinoviev, whose usual treble was pitched higher by panic, cried out: "We are experiencing a third revolution," adding that, to restrain workers from participating in the demonstration, agitators would need to be shuttled from factory to factory. By contrast, district soviet representatives who participated in this meeting were generally calm. To be sure, a few of them conveyed unsettling news. The representative of the outlying Kolpinskii district warned that "we don't have anybody to defend us because the best of our Red Guards have been sent to the front." "There will be participation in the demonstration but whether with arms or peacefully is unknown." In a similarly disturbing vein, the representative of the Nevskii district characterized his area as a "defensist nest" and warned that some workers would participate in the pro-Assembly demonstration. According to him, the local Red Guard was under anarchist influence and consequently would neither attack nor defend the Petrograd Soviet.[102]

To the relief of the conference participants, this exhausted the list of apparent problem spots. The Petersburg district representative informed the gathering that, although street rallies and student demonstrations on behalf of the Constituent Assembly were even then in progress, worker participation in the protests was not a worry. In the central First City District, it was reported that, although ample local security forces were available, the close proximity of the district to the Taurida Palace made it prudent to send an armored car and machine gun there. The representative of the Second City District Soviet was also reassuring, as he believed that, for now, the situation in that heavily bourgeois quarter was good. The local police had been disarmed, the Red Guard was on alert, and factory workers would not demonstrate.

Most reassuring of all, the representative of the critical Vyborg workers' district confidently declared that everything was quiet and that "a coming out" was not anticipated. Similarly encouraging were the words of the representative of the Novoderevenskii district: "There would be no demonstrations [in his area]," he asserted firmly, "[even] the police is with us." The representative from the Vasilii Island district, home to several major factories, reported that a day earlier petitions calling for support of the convocation of the Constituent Assembly had been circulated in neighborhood churches, but they had been stopped. Announcements of pro-Soviet meetings on the 5th had been posted in local plants. Workers would go to them, he implied, and not to the pro-Assembly demonstration. According to the spokesman from the Okhtinskii district, the situation there was similarly calming. With obvious pride, the representative from the suburban Sestroretskii district noted that, at a general meeting of factory workers there, "defensists" were not even allowed to speak. "The militia is ours," he continued, adding that "there won't be any demonstrations, there is too much snow."[103]

Even this generally encouraging picture apparently did little to calm Zinoviev. As soon as the Sestroretskii district representative finished, Zinoviev urged that street meetings be banned. Moreover, he took great pains to persuade the representatives of the importance of maintaining the closest possible communications the next day. "Our plans could change," he said. "We might decide to organize our own demonstration." This comment by Zinoviev came as a shot out of the blue. In view of his anxiety, it was agreed that the district representatives would return to Smolny at 1:00 PM the next day for the latest information.[104]

A few hours later, the people's commissar for military affairs Nikolai Podvoiskii, and his deputy, Konstantin Mekhanoshin, formed an Emergency Military Headquarters to direct defense of the Soviet government during the Constituent Assembly.[105] It immediately issued an Order No. 1, which prohibited obeying any military directives by security agencies other than the Emergency Military Headquarters. Exceptions were made for orders signed by Bonch-Bruevich in the Smolny neighborhood and for Blagonravov's orders around the Taurida Palace and at the Fortress of Peter and Paul.[106] However, this eleventh-hour attempt to impose control over the disparate bodies and forces already set in motion to fend off attacks on Soviet power in the city of Petrograd during the Constituent Assembly came too late.

*   *   *

On the eve of the Left SRs' entry into the Sovnarkom, the Bolsheviks, led by Lenin, dissolved the MRC and created the VCheka to serve as a reliable security force free of interference by the Left SRs. During the second half of December, at the time of the VCheka's harassment of prominent Kadet and moderate socialist delegates to the Constituent Assembly, Isaac Shteinberg's determined but ultimately unsuccessful efforts to curb the VCheka's arbitrary power demonstrated the validity of Lenin's concern. Then, in early January, Shteinberg decided to try to reign in the VCheka by pressing the Bolsheviks to allow Left SRs into its leadership. Although the Bolsheviks' concern for retaining Left SR support on the eve of the Constituent Assembly forced them to accede to Shteinberg's request, the relatively modest numbers of Left SRs involved were insufficient to significantly influence the VCheka's policies. The same situation obtained in respect to the Left SR leadership's hope that, by entering the Sovnarkom, its representatives, even if a minority, would be able to moderate government policies. In the Sovnarkom, as in the leadership bodies of the VCheka, majority ruled. Consequently, in questions such as repression of opponents in the Constituent Assembly, on which Bolsheviks and Left SRs differed, the Left SRs were bound to lose.

Meanwhile, during the period when negotiations over the entry of Left SRs into the Sovnarkom were finalized, the Bolshevik moderates resurfaced as a potentially significant political force by virtue of their dominant influence in the leadership Provisional Bureau of the Bolshevik Constituent Assembly delegation. Contrary to the position of the Bolshevik Central Committee, as well as of the Left SRs, that the Constituent Assembly should not be allowed to supersede Soviet power, they initiated steps to restore the legitimacy of the Constituent Assembly within the Bolshevik delegation as a whole. However, the Central Committee nipped their effort in the bud. Moreover, the Central Committee's stance on the primacy of Soviet power over the Constituent Assembly, coupled with the reluctance of the SRs even to try to provide for the Constituent Assembly's security, along with the indifference of the bulk of Russian population to its fate, all but assured its quick demise.

4

The Fate of the Constituent Assembly

THE DAY HAD arrived, 5 January 1918, that was to mark the end of efforts to establish a Western-style, multiparty democratic system in Russia for most of the twentieth century. The Constituent Assembly was scheduled to convene at 1:00 PM. According to plans developed and widely circulated by the UDCA, participants in its mass demonstration were to gather at nine assembly points during the morning. From there, they were to march to the communal grave on to the Field of Mars, merge into one grand procession, proceed to the Taurida Palace, march by its vast, snow-covered gardens without stopping, and continue on to Nevskii Prospekt and through the heart of the capital before returning to their starting points.

Late the previous night, Soviet authorities had heard disquieting rumors of last-minute swings in sentiment toward support of the Constituent Assembly in some units of the garrison.[1] This apparent confirmation of instabilities among Petrograd-based soldiers prompted a frenetic search for additional loyalist forces from outside the capital. With the disorders at the Taurida Palace on 28 November fresh in mind, and believing that the UDCA's planned march was part of a conspiracy to overthrow Soviet power, the primary aim of Soviet authorities in Petrograd was to maintain control of key government buildings, the state bank, and communications facilities. They also were determined to prevent demonstrators from congregating close to the Taurida Palace so that they could manage events there. Log barricades were erected at the intersections of Liteinyi Prospekt and the main east-west approaches to the palace (at the corners of Shpalernaia, Zakhar'evskaia, Sergeevskaia, Furshtatskaia, and Kirochnaia streets), and also at strategically located points on the small square in front of the palace. In the early morning government forces—mostly worker Red Guards, Baltic Fleet sailors, and modest numbers of soldiers from the Petrograd garrison—dug in behind these fortifications; smaller armed detachments began patrolling adjoining side streets and alleys; and machine-gun firing points were set up on

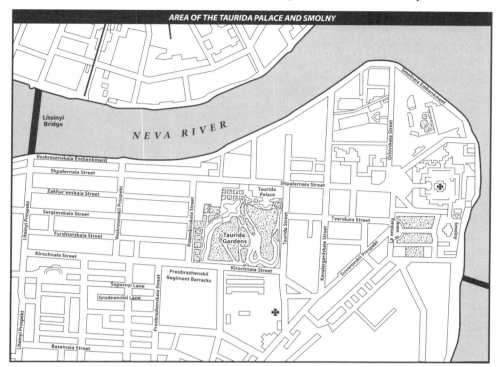

the roofs of nearby buildings. Later in the day, as additional sailors arrived from Helsingfors and Kronstadt, they were rushed to perceived weak spots.

Most of these security forces had been hastily recruited and assembled, because significant numbers of the most competent and reliable military detachments had already been shipped out of the capital to help consolidate the revolution in the provinces or to join Antonov-Ovseenko's forces combating counterrevolution in the south. With no experience or training in controlling crowds or dealing with civil disobedience, they were simply sent off with weapons and ample supplies of ammunition, imbued with the idea that they were responsible for defending Soviet power from enemies grouped around the Constituent Assembly bent on restoring the injustices of the past. Their commanders, also technically unprepared, received the same orientation and were provided with only flimsy instructions, if that. They were to organize perimeters and patrols in specified zones, be prepared to rush reinforcements to trouble spots, and not allow anyone without authorization access to the Taurida Palace and Smolny neighborhoods. The unpublished memoir of a sailor from the battleship *Zaria svobody* testifies to these realities. Before dawn on 5 January, he was appointed commander of a composite detachment of several hundred men and, periodically, was given brief orders more appropriate for troops under hostile fire at the front than for those maintaining domestic order. Demonstrators who refused to stop were to be disarmed and arrested (it was assumed that marchers would have weapons). If shooting broke out, fire was to be returned "without mercy." An exception was to be made for workers, for whom every possible means of persuasion was to be used before resorting to violence.[2] These instructions did not specify appropriate action in the event large *unarmed* crowds attempted to breech or circumvent barriers, and, as nearly as one can tell, there was no established system of communication between security forces, or between those forces and the belatedly constituted Emergency Military Headquarters.

Beginning in the early morning, supporters of the Constituent Assembly, singing revolutionary songs and carrying aloft banners inscribed with slogans such as "All Power to the Constituent Assembly!" "Away with Political Terror!" and "Long Live the Brotherhood of Peoples!" had begun to funnel to nine assembly points designated by the UDCA. Most of the demonstrators were university students, civil servants, office workers (many of them women), shopkeepers, and professionals. All accounts agree that with scattered exceptions (for example, workers from the Government Printing Office, the Obukhov plant, and other industrial enterprises in the Nevskii district), factory workers and soldiers obeyed the appeals of the Petrograd Soviet and remained in their factories and barracks. Demonstrators also observed the ban on carrying weapons that organizers of the march had insisted upon. Even armored cars that were to provide an escort for the demonstrators were successfully commandeered by Bolshevik workers, leaving them completely defenseless.[3]

Initial confrontations with government patrols occurred when marchers from the suburbs were interdicted en route to the city.[4] The biggest and bloodiest confrontations, however, erupted at the log barricades blocking the main arteries leading from the Field of Mars to the Taurida Palace and on side streets in the neighborhood of the palace and surrounding park. These appear to have begun at around 10:00 AM, when an estimated one thousand demonstrators who had crossed the Neva from the Petrograd side were stopped on Sergeevskaia Street by a detachment of Red Guards. Ordered to halt and turn back, the marchers, singing the *Marseillaise* and carrying red banners, continued moving forward. The Red Guards fired a few warning shots into the air and, when that did not stop the procession, they fired wildly at the marchers.[5] An hour later, Red Guards and soldiers sprang from

Demonstrators supporting the Constituent Assembly on Palace Square, 5 January 1918. State Museum of the Political History of Russia, St. Petersburg.

behind a barricade at the corner of Liteinyi and Shpalernaia, cocked their rifles, and ordered some two hundred demonstrators from the Vyborg district who had just crossed the Neva to turn back. Yet, with scarcely a pause, they fired shots into the air scattering them. Seizing the demonstrators' banners, they ripped them from their sticks and tossed them on bonfires or off the Liteinyi bridge.[6] Count Louis de Robien, the French military attaché, watched as the banners fluttered "on to the glittering, frozen surface of the Neva, like great scarlet butterflies."[7] The leading Futurist writer Victor Shklovskii later saw yardmen (*dvorniki*) using the sticks as broom handles.[8] The demonstrators' conscious retention of such revolutionary symbols as red banners, on the one hand, and the spontaneous, triumphant appropriation of these banners by guardians of Soviet power, on the other, figured prominently in the major clashes in Petrograd on 5 January 1918.

Incidents such as these in which nobody was killed were the prelude to several bloodier assaults on peaceful demonstrators in roughly the same area. Indeed, between midday and sunset the northern end of Liteinyi Prospekt, especially at the corners of the main east-west streets leading to the vicinity of the Taurida Palace, was a battle zone where the glistening knee-high snow was soon reddened by the blood of fallen marchers. Halted by a barricade at Kirochnaia Street, an estimated ten thousand demonstrators, holding banners aloft and singing revolutionary songs, tried to break through to the Taurida Palace via Furshtatskaia Street but were stopped by Red Guards and soldiers in full battle gear. Virtually without warning, they were scattered by rifle and machine-gun fire. Intense shooting lasted a good fifteen minutes, during which several demonstrators were hit.[9]

Among the first known dead was G. L. Logvinov, who had come to Petrograd from Tambov to participate in the All-Russian Congress of Soviets of Peasants' Deputies supporting the Constituent Assembly.[10] Carrying a large red banner, he marched at the head of one of many processions that left the Field of Mars soon after 1:00 PM. Upon reaching the barricade on the corner of Liteinyi and Kirochnaia, he and his comrades were ordered to turn back. Then, almost instantly, they came under rifle fire from behind the barricade and from machine-gun fire from the roof of a nearby building. Five demonstrators were reported to have been killed in this event (Logvinov, two students, and two Red Cross aid workers). Eight were injured.[11] At roughly this same time, demonstrators walking to the Field of Mars from assembly points at the Tsarskosel'skii railway station and at the Aleksandrinskii Theater in the south central Moscow district were fired on by snipers in the vicinity of the duma building as they passed the corner of Sadovaia and Nevskii Prospekt. A bit later, an estimated fifteen thousand demonstrators from the southeastern Nevskii district, including sizable numbers of workers from the Obukhov plant, Pal', and other Nevskii district industrial enterprises, paused and held an impromptu rally on Znamenskii Square before continuing on to the Field of Mars. Whereas demonstrators in outlying districts of the city were frequently greeted by pro-Soviet soldiers and workers (some with their families) who harassed and hooted at them, in this more prosperous commercial district they were cheered. This procession, led by the Obukhov plant brass band, came under fire twice. The first attack ended harmlessly, a government patrol only firing into the air. In the second, near the northern end of Liteinyi Prospekt where most of the day's bloodiest incidents occurred, nine of these demonstrators were hit, seven of them seriously.[12]

Marchers who attempted to bypass this area by circuitous side streets fared little better. For example, several thousand demonstrators who tried to reach the Taurida Palace from the south, along Preobrazhenskaia Street, were blocked by soldiers at Sapernyi Lane. When they refused demands to turn away, the soldiers opened fire, killing two and injuring eleven.[13] Around the same time, one of the day's largest processions also attempted to skirt the barricades at the northern end of Liteinyi Prospekt and to reach the Taurida Palace from the south, in this case via Baseinaia Street. Initial warning shots failed to stop the marchers. But at the intersection of Preobrazhenskaia Street and Grodnenskaia Lane, almost within sight of the Taurida Palace grounds, they were fired upon and dispersed by the rifle fire of Red Guards dug into the snow. Several demonstrators were killed or seriously wounded in this incident; others were roughed up.[14]

By evening, signed written complaints describing some of these confrontations had been filed with the SR and Menshevik Constituent Assembly fractions in the Taurida Place. The text of one of them was read into the record by the prominent Menshevik Matvei Skobelev. "At 4:00 PM, while driving along Liteinyi Prospekt, at the corner of Panteleimonovskaia, I personally saw how some groups of Red Guards shot into a crowd of defenseless people, among whom were soldiers, women, and children . . . marching peacefully to the Taurida Palace to express their needs," this complaint read. "Those doing the firing acted without warning, aiming directly into the crowd. I saw those injured—one soldier, two workers, and some women—being taken away by stretchers and horse-drawn cabs."[15]

Although available descriptions of shootings on 5 January 1918 are imprecise, overlapping, incomplete, and impossible to verify, there are enough of them to conclude that, together, they capture many of the chief characteristics of the attacks on demonstrations in support of the Constituent Assembly. First, the number of marchers appears to have been a good deal higher than the ten thousand estimated by Soviet authorities but significantly lower than the one hundred thousand subsequently claimed by the UDCA. Second, although the implication of Soviet authorities that factory workers and soldiers boycotted the demonstration altogether was misleading, it is also clear that they constituted a relatively small minority of marchers. Third, although the leaders of the march and its participants were obviously unwilling to obey the Soviet government ban on demonstrations in the vicinity of the Taurida Palace, there is no evidence that any of them had weapons or behaved in a threatening manner. Even after being fired upon, they made no effort to resist their attackers beyond trying to circumvent them. Finally, the Red Guards, sailors, and soldiers behaved with striking brutality. They shot at demonstrators from behind barricades and fired machine guns from windows and rooftops; they beat them as well and made a triumphant ritual out of seizing and destroying their banners. It is also apparent that once Soviet authorities became aware of the bloodshed, they neither rescinded their ban on demonstrations in the vicinity of the Taurida Palace nor ordered a halt to the shooting; instead, they did nothing. According to a report by Sverdlov at a session of the Third All-Russian Congress of Soviets on 11 January, twenty-one demonstrators were killed. Since this figure is higher than the fifteen estimated to have been killed by Gorky's pro—

Constituent Assembly *Novaia zhizn'* based on a survey of Petrograd hospitals after the clashes had ended, it would appear that Sverdlov's count was closer to the mark.[16]

* * *

As the time for the opening of the Constituent Assembly neared, a second military perimeter was established in the area immediately adjacent to the Taurida Palace. Here the crowd was thin and the space in front of the low, elongated, pale-yellow palace was filled by armed Red Guards and soldiers, field guns, machine-gun emplacements, and belts and crates of ammunition. All the gates in the wrought-iron fence surrounding the palace were locked.[17] Machine guns protruded from ground-floor palace windows facing avenues of approach.

Around 1:00 PM, a single side gate was opened for arriving delegates, and each was carefully screened by sailors dressed in pea jackets, machine-gun belts slung across their chests. Also allowed in were large numbers of guests—mostly selected workers, soldiers, and sailors, many of them carrying rifles with bayonets and grenades and also draped with ammunition. Among the first delegates to arrive was the entire SR fraction fresh from a morning caucus. Marching six abreast, the delegates sported distinctive rosettes and carried candles and sandwiches. Approximately half were attired in business suits and were protected from the biting cold by heavy overcoats and galoshes. The rest were peasants wearing rough sheepskin jackets and felt boots. Nikolaii Sviatitskii subsequently noted that his colleagues appeared lifeless, "like condemned prisoners."[18] Vladimir Zenzinov was later to recall: "We entered the building certain that the Bolsheviks would use force against the Assembly . . . [and] that we would not return home alive."[19]

For some time yet, entry into the ornate White Hall of the palace, a spacious glass-domed amphitheater surrounded by a gallery, was barred by still another phalanx of Red Guards. The meeting place of the Imperial State Duma in the late tsarist years, after the February revolution it had been the scene of the first national conferences and congresses of soviets. For the Constituent Assembly it had been redecorated and adorned with black banners "as if for a funeral" (Zenzinov's words). The color for the banners was probably consciously chosen by Soviet authorities to further the image of the Constituent Assembly as reactionary. The SR delegates, their majority status notwithstanding, were shunted off to a back room. The previous night and that morning, they had fine-tuned their program for the first day. Ballast had been eliminated from the party's platform, and legislation on peace and agrarian reform had been abstracted for rapid-fire presentation and passage.[20] There was nothing left to do. So the SR delegates bustled about, nervously bemoaning their helplessness and listening to periodic, at times hysterical, accounts of massacres in the streets. The much smaller Bolshevik delegation arrived after the SRs and caucused in a spacious sitting room brightened by the shimmering snow visible through the windows.[21]

No records have been published or are available in Russian archives of the caucuses of the Bolshevik Constituent Assembly fraction, including a joint meeting with Left SRs[22] and a long separate meeting preceding the formal opening of the Constituent Assembly. Memoir accounts indicate that, although Lenin participated in the Bolshevik gathering, it was chaired by Sverdlov. Bolshevik moderates were impeded by the absence of Kamenev, who was part of the Russian peace delegation at Brest-Litovsk. Soviet accounts claiming that the caucus proceeded quickly and smoothly are belied by the fact that it lasted much longer than expected and caused a long delay in the opening of the Assembly. The fraction meeting began with a discussion of the agenda and operation of the Constituent Assembly. Several factors make it likely that fundamental questions relating to the role of the Constituent Assembly and the relationship between it and Soviet power were also discussed. Communication difficulties and, even more, Lenin's success in blocking efforts of party moderates to arrange for national party congresses in November and December had prevented earlier consideration of approaches to the Constituent Assembly among Bolshevik leaders nationally. Many Bolshevik delegates from the provinces went straight to the fraction meeting upon arriving in Petrograd, and, in any case, there had not been any systematic effort to bring them up to date on recent policy changes relating to the Constituent Assembly, let alone to debate them.[23] Then, too, the presence at the fraction meeting of such independent-minded Bolsheviks as Riazanov and Lozovskii insured that Lenin's position would be challenged. Raskolnikov's recollections of this meeting suggest that at least some of the party's delegates envisioned a protracted existence for it. He notes that Bukharin, who had by then given up the idea of forming a breakaway Revolutionary Convention, scoffed at this idea. He spoke in terms of a possible three-day life span for the Constituent Assembly.[24]

At some point the Left SRs, who were holding a separate caucus, requested changes in the Declaration of the Rights of Toiling and Exploited People. Although the specifics of these requests are unknown, it seems reasonable to speculate that they were aimed at the primary concerns of the Left SRs at this time, namely, making the declaration more palatable to SR peasant delegates still open to supporting it and letting the Constituent Assembly run long enough to discredit itself. Whatever the case, the changes were rejected. After Sverdlov read the declaration, which had been designed expressly to preclude compromise and to provoke a decisive break with the Constituent Assembly at the outset, the idea of letting the Constituent Assembly run at least until the start of the Third All-Russian Congress of Soviets of Workers' and Soldiers' Deputies was scrapped.[25] Instead, it was agreed that Sverdlov, acting on behalf of the CEC, would integrate presentation of the declaration for immediate implementation into his statement formally opening the Constituent Assembly. After the declaration was ignored, as was certain, the Bolsheviks (and, they hoped, the Left SRs) would make a quick exit to prevent any possibility that the SRs, armed with their new "Vikzhelish" program, would be able to make inroads into support for Soviet power.[26]

*　*　*

At around 3:30 PM, the doors of the White Hall were opened, and half an hour later close to four hundred delegates were seated in the sections assigned them, Bolsheviks on the extreme left, Right SRs and Mensheviks on the extreme right, Left SRs in the middle, divided by the center isle, and the Kadets excluded altogether. On the one hand, with Bolshevik moderates under a tight reign, the party's fraction was set to stay with its prepared script and the Left SRs remained committed to the primacy of soviets over the Constituent Assembly. On the other hand, the SR majority was primed to begin constructing a new democratic order and, that very day, to pass legislation on peace, land, and the future Russian political system as if the Soviet government did not exist.

This drastic polarization of views toward the Constituent Assembly, and the basic weakness of the Constituent Assembly's SR majority in the prevailing situation, was revealed at the very start in a clash over who would formally open the Assembly. The SRs were naturally intent on controlling proceedings from the opening bell. Viewing themselves as representatives of Russia's only legitimate revolutionary authority and the Constituent Assembly in its existing form as an anachronism, the Bolsheviks and Left SRs were equally fixed on exerting control over it from the outset. So it was that promptly at 4:00 PM the oldest delegate in attendance, the Right SR and former *narodnik* and *zemstvo* worker from the Don, Sergei Shvetsov, following instructions from SR floor leaders and taking advantage of Sverdlov's absence, mounted the tribune to call the delegates to order. As the right benches applauded, Bolshevik and Left SR delegates exploded in protest, swarmed to the tribune, and engulfed the unfortunate Shvetsov. At precisely this moment, Sverdlov appeared, elbowed Shvetsov aside, and briskly

Left SR delegates to the Constituent Assembly in the White Hall of the Taurida Palace, 5 January 1918. Maria Spiridonova is at bottom, center. Prosh Proshian is on her right. State Museum of the Political History of Russia, St. Petersburg.

swung the bright nickel-plated chairman's bell. Then fighting broke out among delegates on opposite sides of the aisle. Bonch-Bruevich, who managed Lenin's office, recalled that during this chaotic interval when the Constituent Assembly appeared on the verge of dissolving into a free-for-all, Lenin suddenly became more worried and paler than he had ever seen him.[27] Somehow, however, amid deafening hoots and jeers from the right, a thunderous ovation from the left, and roars of approval from rifle-waving soldiers, sailors, and workers in the galleries, Sverdlov, standing at the tribune "like a marble monument," managed to achieve enough quiet to open the Assembly.[28] Not having any physical force at its disposal, the SR majority had no alternative but to accept this unpropitious start.

With these first unseemly images in mind, it is not surprising that the life of Russia's first Constituent Assembly was stormy and brief. Taking immediate advantage of his position as temporary chair, Sverdlov read out the Declaration of the Rights of Toiling and Exploited People and, in the name of the CEC, proposed that consideration of the declaration be the first item of business.[29] Reportedly at Lenin's instigation, when Sverdlov finished, the Left burst into a lusty rendition of the *Internationale*. Even the Right SRs evidently felt obliged to make a pretense of singing.[30]

Following this musical interlude, the SRs, determined to avoid unneces-

Iakov Sverdlov, left, and Sergei Shvetsov at the opening of the Constituent Assembly.
Drawings by Iu. K. Artsybushev.

sary provocation until their program had been laid out, made no comment
on the declaration. They garnered a pyrrhic victory when Victor Chernov
defeated Maria Spiridonova for the Assembly chairmanship. Spiridonova's
nomination by the Bolsheviks may have been a concession to Left SR hopes
that enough nominal SR peasant delegates might vote for her to offset the
SR majority. Whatever the case, the results of the balloting—244 votes for
Chernov, 153 for Spiridonova[31]—were an accurate measure of the relative
strength of the contending sides.

By the time Chernov began his keynote address, it was nightfall and
the lights were switched on (the SRs, it turned out, had brought candles for
nothing). He sketched in broadest outline an ambitious program of reform
that sounded very much like the pre-October Bolshevik platform—down to
an insistent plea for "immediate deeds, not just words."[32] ("An acrobatic act
on Bolshevik slogans," Oganovskii called it.)[33] Carefully skirting direct criticism of the Bolsheviks or of the soviets, which upset some of those who had
just voted for him as much as anything he said, Chernov pointed to revolutionary Russia's socialist-controlled Constituent Assembly as the one body
in the world with the prestige and authority to superintend an international
peace conference leading to an early universal, democratic, and just peace.

For the benefit of war-weary Russian troops, he called for the organization of a wholly new revolutionary volunteer army which would replace front-line soldiers and protect the nation as it went about the task of transforming outmoded institutions and ways of life. In connection with chaos in industry and expanding unemployment, now further complicated by demobilization, Chernov proposed a grand program of public works and temporary state control of industrial production, pending the time when workers would be qualified to take control of industry into their own hands. In the area of nationality policy, after dutifully paying homage to the aspirations of each minority delegation individually, Chernov drew a picture of a free association of equal, semi-independent peoples and territories within a Federative Russian Republic, in which a network of territorial Constituent Assemblies and local self-governing institutions would work in concert with the All-Russian Constituent Assembly to design a new political system protective of minority rights and consistent with popular aspirations.

On the all-important land issue, Chernov endorsed the immediate systematic redistribution of all land to the "working peasantry" without compensation. Moreover, cleverly countering the Soviet government's charge that the Constituent Assembly was unrepresentative, and even Lenin's earlier emphasis on recall elections to update the vote, Chernov proposed liberal reliance on national plebiscites to assure that actions of the Constituent Assembly harmonized with the people's will. Indeed, he challenged the Bolsheviks to request an immediate nationwide plebiscite on attitudes toward the Constituent Assembly if they had doubts about its right to express the will of the people.[34]

Although Chernov's speech constituted a plea for unity of democratic forces, compromise, and an end to civil war, he made no mention of alliances with the Kadets or other liberal groups. Implicit in what he said was the assumption that although socialism would continue to be the dominant force in revolutionary Russia, the era of Soviet rule was over and that of new institutions to be created by the Constituent Assembly was about to begin.

To the Left SR Sergei Mstislavskii, Chernov's address was "a dead collage of bookish quotes, verse, and pedantically turned phrases."[35] Right SRs were furious at Chernov for having blurred the lines between them and the Bolsheviks. Analyzing the speech, Oliver Radkey, the Western historian of the SRs, came to a far different conclusion. To him, Chernov performed a great service to his party by helping to get legislative proposals on the record that should have been there long before.[36] Perhaps. The essential point is that now, with the eclipse of Bolshevik moderates and with Leninists in control of the party, it was too late. Even before Chernov finished, Bolshevik members of the Sovnarkom drifted out of the White Hall, gathered in an anteroom, and reconfirmed that the Constituent Assembly should be cut off that day.[37]

With Trotsky en route to Petrograd from Brest and Lenin preferring to remain in the background, orchestrating rather than participating in the official proceedings, it fell to the thirty-year-old Bukharin to respond to Chernov.[38] In an impassioned speech that ran almost as long as Chernov's, he appealed for immediate adoption of the Declaration of the Rights of Toiling and Exploited People, arguing that, although it was difficult to quarrel with the lofty goals Chernov had sketched out, the crux of the matter was which classes would hold power while these aims were pursued. The Provisional Government experience had clearly demonstrated that the grande bourgeoisie would have decisive influence in any government controlled by the centrist socialist parties and, consequently, that in each of the key areas touched on by Chernov, rule by the Constituent Assembly would only lead to the reenslavement of workers and peasants in no way different from their servitude under the tsars. What revolutionary Russia required, Bukharin insisted, was not civil peace under a government of national unity sponsored by the Constituent Assembly but rather an exclusively soviet workers' and peasants' dictatorship, as provided for in the declaration Sverdlov presented.[39]

Next, Nikolai Pumpianskii outlined the agenda developed by the Committee for the First Day.[40] So that its views would be public without any delay, the first session of the Constituent Assembly, prior to adjournment, was to take preliminary action on the central issues of the revolution, starting with the questions of peace, land, and the structure of the national government. The Left SR commissar for justice Shteinberg answered Pumpianskii with a demand that the Constituent Assembly stop beating around the bush and consider and endorse Sverdlov's declaration. "All the questions facing the revolution have been identified and are being dealt with hourly by the existing Soviet power," he said. "A Constituent Assembly that wishes to harmonize its will with the aspirations of soviets of the laboring masses cannot avoid the primary obligation of immediately discussing and affirming the declaration of the CEC."[41]

Shteinberg was followed to the tribune by the Georgian Menshevik Iraklii Tsereteli. An urbane, articulate veteran of the Russian social democratic movement from its earliest days, Tsereteli was a revered martyr of Stolypin's infamous assault on the Second Duma in June 1907. Freed from Siberian exile by the February revolution, he was arguably the most authoritative figure in the moderate socialist Soviet leadership in 1917, and its most influential advocate of collaboration with the liberals and staunch opposition to Bolshevism. "One of the few members of the enemy camp who was always honest," was how Mstislavskii remembered him.[42] Largely because of his reputation for candor and hostility to Bolshevism, and perhaps also because, apart from Chernov, other prominent "defensists" were either in jail or in hiding, Tsereteli symbolized the main enemy of Soviet power. His appearance drove the Left benches and the galleries into a frenzy.[43]

Tsereteli was not in the least bit intimidated by the uproar. If anything, he appeared to be energized by it. Previous moderate socialist speakers, following Chernov's tack, consciously shied away from confronting the Bolsheviks directly. Explaining this strategy, Oganovskii wrote that we felt "we first had to entrench ourselves in the Taurida Palace and only after that should we attack."[44] With his customary straightforward manner, Tsereteli would have none of that. Deriding the very suggestion that the Constituent Assembly should blindly endorse Soviet rule, he insisted that the delegates had yet to hear a single argument indicating that any Soviet program was yielding positive results. After more than two months in power, the Bolsheviks were still trying to blame all problems on sabotage by the bourgeoisie and were doing everything possible to stifle legitimate criticism.

Responding to shouts from the Left that "you reinstated capital punishment," Tsereteli acknowledged that "perhaps we made mistakes or even worse, but while we were in power at least we knew how to answer every question and justify our actions without fear."[45] For the most part, however, he ignored ear-splitting heckling and insulting allusions to this or that policy of the Provisional Government and boldly attacked, one by one, what he perceived as major failures of Soviet policy. "You promised bread for all the people but can you now say hand on heart that Petrograd is guaranteed against starvation even for the next few weeks?" he asked. "You gave the people land," he observed, "but are you sure that the poorer peasantry has received the land acquired by the revolution?" "And in the area of foreign policy, are you satisfied with the developing situation?" he inquired. "If the outside force you are counting on to come to the aid of the Russian Revolution doesn't materialize, isn't your position such that the cause of socialism in Russia, and of strengthening and confirming the elemental basis of Russian democratization, will be defeated for years to come?" "Do you really believe the Germans will take account of you in the way they would inevitably have to respect a universally representative and recognized supreme authority, not dependent on an extended civil war for its survival?"[46]

Each time hecklers sought to stifle Tsereteli, he had a ready rejoinder and refocused attention on the business at hand. Thus, after a particularly raucous delegate reacted to his emphasis on inherent Soviet weakness in peace negotiations, with the cry, "I suppose you want us to call on Kerensky for help?" Tsereteli shot back, "Let's suppose Kerensky was worse than you, but that doesn't prove you are better than the Constituent Assembly. At the present time you are fighting neither Kerensky nor Tsereteli but the expressed will of the entire population."[47]

Toward the close of his speech Tsereteli, like Chernov, rejected future collaboration outside the ranks of the democracy (for both Tsereteli and Chernov, this represented a major break with their positions in 1917). Still, to Tsereteli the bourgeoisie was too weak to mount a threat to the revolution. The real danger to the revolution came from divisions in the ranks of the democracy caused by the Bolsheviks. The one hope for ending chaos and assuring the fulfillment of the revolution lay in the unity of "all responsible elements of the democracy" in the Constituent Assembly.

The Menshevik view of the seminal role of the Constituent Assembly in the creation of a democratic republic was fully elaborated in a formal party declaration, "On the Tasks of the Constituent Assembly," with which Tsereteli ended his speech. In some respects, the reforms advocated in this declaration paralleled those articulated earlier by the SRs. However, these reforms challenged Soviet power head-on. Explicitly rejecting the assumptions and policies embodied in the Declaration of the Rights of Toiling and Exploited People, they appealed directly to Russian workers to reject the Soviet dictatorship and, instead, to defend to the death the unrestricted power and authority of the Constituent Assembly. Rather than the Constituent Assembly being a support for Soviet power, as Lenin had demanded in early December and which most top Left SRs still favored, they called for transformation of soviets and other working class institutions into strong bastions of assistance for the Constituent Assembly.[48]

Tsereteli's powerful speech was widely praised, even by his adversaries. Mstislavskii later recalled that, "of all the speeches made in the Taurida Palace that day, Tsereteli's was clearly the best in terms of both its content and the strength of its convictions." "The true tribune of the people showed himself in all his majesty" was Oganovskii's evaluation. The American journalist and socialist Albert Rhys Williams remembered that, at Tsereteli's first words, Louise Bryant, also a U.S. correspondent, whispered to her husband, John Reed (the three were seated in a gallery), "he has that majestic air."[49] Following his speech it appears that even Lenin accorded Tsereteli grudging respect. Indeed, several days later, after a group of drunken sailors and Red Guards killed two leading Kadets (Fedor Kokoshkin and Aleksandr Shingarev), Lenin recommended to Tsereteli, through intermediaries, that he return to the safety of Georgia, this according to a Menshevik colleague of Tsereteli's, Iurii Denike.[50]

As Tsereteli finished and stepped away from the podium, the center and right benches exploded in cheers—this was their moment. A bit later, Zenzinov requested a decision on the agenda proposed by Pumpianskii and attempted to justify acting on the questions of peace and land before deciding on the structure of the government. Clearly his purpose was to assure the adoption of the SR position on peace and agrarian reform before a decisive confrontation with the Bolsheviks and Left SRs over Soviet power. The Moscow Bolshevik Ivan Skvortsov-Stepanov, former editor of *Sotsial Demokrat,* announced that his party would not present a declaration separate from that of the CEC's Declaration of the Rights of Toiling and Exploited People. But to the surprise of most delegates, this was not the stance adopted by the Left SRs. Rather, an elderly peasant named Fedor Sorokin,[51] from the Far Eastern Amur Region, who hobbled to the podium on crutches, presented a separate Left SR declaration despite the fact that the Left SRs, like the Bolsheviks, were pledged to support the CEC declaration read out by Sverdlov.[52] The declaration Sorokin presented dovetailed with the CEC's Declaration of the Rights of Toiling and Exploited People in several key respects. It explicitly recognized the legitimacy of the October revolution and the Soviet political system, and rejected the validity of all claims to independent political authority on the part of the Constituent Assembly. But, instead of requiring the Constituent Assembly to vote itself out of existence at once, it envisioned that it would have a protracted role as a facilitator of revolutionary reconstruction directed by soviets.

This difference between the two declarations may simply have reflected lingering objections of tactically moderate Left SRs to the immediate, forced dissolution of the Constituent Assembly because of their conviction that, if given the opportunity, the Constituent Assembly would quickly discredit itself; their preference for such a natural, peaceful process over the course advocated by more radical Left SRs such as Proshian; and their desire, which they may have persuaded a majority of the Left SR fraction to accept, to distinguish themselves from what they viewed as the overly rigid, dictatorial tendencies of the Bolsheviks. A wish to assert a separate identity may also have prompted the emphasis in the declaration presented by Sorokin on individual human rights, namely, on the firmest possible support for the liberation of individuals who devoted themselves to worthwhile labor, on the right of such individuals to the realization of their full potential, as well as on their right to adequate living conditions and to social welfare in time of need.[53] Missing from the elaboration of rights delivered by Sorokin was the rigid categorization of all people, irrespective of their behavior, as unalterably good or bad, that was implicit in the CEC's declaration and in Leninist thought.

Yet, perhaps the most interesting aspect of Sorokin's presentation was his personal remarks after he finished reading the Left SR declaration. To thunderous cheers from the Right and an explosion of protest from the Left, he purposefully blurred distinctions between the two sides, declaring unequivocally that all peasant delegates to the Constituent Assembly, *irrespective of party*, had been dispatched to Petrograd with instructions to obtain land and freedom. Only after that had been accomplished could they return to their villages with honor. In this respect, he said, that "among us peasants, there are no differences. We of the Right and Left are all alike." "My hope, comrade peasants," he added, "is that we will fulfill our mission to the end." This was interpreted by the majority as indicating a determination to settle the land question within the Constituent Assembly, and, by most of his fellow Left SRs, not to speak of the Bolsheviks, as "sabotage!"[54] Be that as it may, Sorokin's declaration and remarks suddenly triggered intense discussion between peasant delegates on the SR and Left SR sides of the aisle, and renewed hope for the possibility of compromise.[55]

Available sources do not provide evidence of discussion of Sorokin's presentation in the Constituent Assembly or in party caucuses that began soon after he finished. That Sorokin's personal remarks were an embarrassment to Left SR leaders is suggested by the fact that they were not even mentioned in a detailed account of the proceedings of the Constituent Assembly published in *Znamia truda*.[56] Were his remarks about commonalities among peasant delegates, regardless of political affiliation, no more than a spontaneous outburst reflecting the weariness of fractional strife among millions of peasants and their thirst for immediate peace and land? Or did his speech represent more than that? There is no way to tell. Only two agenda proposals were actually brought to a floor vote, the Declaration of the Rights of Toiling and Exploited People endorsing Soviet power and policies without qualification, and the proposal for the first day's agenda introduced by Pumpianskii, ignoring soviets altogether, implicitly recognizing the Constituent Assembly as the supreme political authority in Russia, and calling for immediate consideration of SR legislation on peace, land, and state power based on this assumption. Tsereteli's stirring speech and Sorokin's remarks notwithstanding, the breakdown in relative voting strength between the chief contending sides remained unchanged. Without discussion, by a vote of 237 to 146, Pumpianskii's proposal was adopted.[57]

Immediately following this vote, first the Left SRs and then the Bolsheviks demanded a recess; in Mstislavskii's words, this was not so much to decide "what to do but rather to agree on how and in what order to withdraw [from the Assembly]."[58] Information on the subsequent deliberations at Left SR and Bolshevik caucuses is scanty. According to a report in *Novaia zhizn'*, at the former a proposal from the Bolsheviks that the Left SR fraction withdraw immediately was firmly opposed by peasant representatives who argued that their constituencies would not understand why it was necessary to break up the Constituent Assembly simply because it would not give priority to discussing the CEC's declaration. Debate over this issue was sharp. Some of these peasant delegates threatened to remain in their seats if the Bolshevik proposal to withdraw at once was accepted. Ultimately a compromise was reached whereby Shteinberg would present only the peace plank of the declaration as an ultimatum. Either it was accepted or the entire Left SR fraction would also walk out.[59]

The deliberations of the Bolshevik fraction were apparently dominated by Lenin, who had spent most of the previous eight hours observing the proceedings on the floor of the Assembly from a curtained gallery, hidden from public view, and huddling, alternately, with the Sovnarkom and the Bolshevik Central Committee.[60] Did the reformist track outlined by Chernov and Pumpianskii or the commonalities among peasant deputies emphasized by Sorokin intensify his impatience to be done with the Constituent Assembly? Again, we simply do not know. The party leadership went to extraordinary lengths to keep this fraction caucus private and closed. Before it began, the Bolsheviks' meeting room was cleared and only fraction members were allowed back in, after careful screening of their credentials.[61] All that can be gleaned from available sources is that Lenin arrived armed for bear and, in the name of the Central Committee, demanded an immediate Bolshevik walkout and dissolution of the Constituent Assembly after the first session.

It is highly unlikely that everybody agreed with this strategy. Again, Riazanov and Lozovskii, both fraction members, most certainly argued against it. In the end, however, Lenin's proposals were accepted. Raskolnikov and Lomov, from Kronstadt and Moscow, respectively, were delegated to go back to the hall to present a withdrawal statement drafted by Lenin and given to the fraction already typed.[62] The fraction as a whole was not to return, reportedly to avoid a possible melee. According to Raskolnikov, after the caucus ended he and members of the government present were called to the ministerial wing of the palace for a hurried gathering of the Sovnarkom. He recalls that at this meeting Lenin proposed, and everyone agreed, that under no circumstances should the remaining delegates be forcibly dispersed;

rather, they should be permitted to talk as long as they liked, and then, in Lenin's words, "Let them just go home," after which they would not be allowed back.[63]

Meanwhile, at around 1:00 AM, the Assembly had finally reconvened. With the Bolsheviks and Left SRs still absent from the hall, the delegates began a discussion of the peace issue, the first item on Pumpianskii's agenda. Discussion of this question was constantly interrupted by extraordinary declarations of one kind or another—by the Ukrainian SR Afanasii Severov-Odoevskii relating to conflict between Ukrainian nationalist and Soviet authorities over the future of Ukraine; by a peasant SR from Voronezh on the impatience of peasants for immediate settlement of the peace and land questions; and, finally, by Raskolnikov on the Bolshevik walkout.[64]

During the previous declarations there was continued talking and movement in the hall, as delegates and observers reacted to the proceedings, idly chatted with one another, or wandered off to a nearby buffet for tea and snacks. However, upon Raskolnikov's appearance at the podium, the hall suddenly became hushed, with the empty Bolshevik benches providing unmistakable evidence of his purpose. As a few curious Bolsheviks clustered at the doorways straining to hear, Raskolnikov delivered Lenin's withdrawal statement:

> The vast majority of laboring Russia—workers, peasants, soldiers—presented the Constituent Assembly with the demand that it recognize the triumphs of the great October revolution . . . and, most important of all, the authority of Soviets of Workers', Soldiers', and Peasants' Deputies. . . . However, a majority of the Constituent Assembly, in agreement with the pretensions of the bourgeoisie, rejected this proposal, thereby defying all Russian toilers. . . . Not for a minute wishing to hide the crimes of enemies of the people, we [Bolsheviks] hereby announce our withdrawal from this Constituent Assembly in order to let Soviet power decide on a policy toward the counterrevolutionary part of the Constituent Assembly once and for all.[65]

Raskolnikov's final words were drowned out by furious roars from the SRs. "Nonsense!" "Lies, all lies!" "Blockhead" "Pogromists," they screamed, as the Left SRs and the gallery exploded with cheers and applause.[66] In the ensuing chaos, a sailor on guard raised his rifle and took aim at a stout SR delegate from Moscow, Osip Minor, only to be stopped from squeezing the trigger at the last second by a more sober comrade.[67] Moments later Left SR delegates pounced on an impulsive young Ukrainian colleague, Vasilii Feofilaktov, who, Browning at the ready, was about to dispose of a heckler in the adjoining Right benches.[68] After a semblance of order was restored, another peasant delegate and former deputy in the State Duma, Lavr Efremov, pleaded with the Bolsheviks and Left SRs not to abandon the Constituent Assembly until people's aspirations had been realized. Who other than the Constituent Assembly can fulfill all our dreams, who other than the Constituent Assembly can bring an end to the civil war? he cried out in despair.[69]

Next Shteinberg, fulfilling the instructions of his fraction, demanded that the delegates immediately express themselves on the Declaration of the Rights of Toiling and Exploited People. He argued that, by refusing even to discuss the declaration in favor of adopting Pumpianskii's agenda, the majority of the Constituent Assembly seemed to be indicating that it was against soviets and intended to create some other state authority of their own directed against the triumphs of the revolution. Nonetheless, so Shteinberg said, the position of the majority had not been made sufficiently explicit to lay the matter to rest. Hence he now issued his fraction's ultimatum: either the Constituent Assembly put aside the agenda of the SRs and indicate its solidarity with Soviet power and the achievements of October by immediately discussing and voting on that section of the Declaration of the Rights of Toiling and Exploited People dealing with the peace issue (the question then under discussion), or the Assembly majority's counterrevolutionary character and intent, as well as the need to disassociate from it, would be decisively confirmed to the Left SRs and the Russian people.[70]

Although the SR Constituent Assembly leadership now accepted the critical need for immediate peace, it was understandably unwilling to yield to Shteinberg's "ultimatum," which, as Shteinberg himself acknowledged, would have constituted de facto recognition of Soviet authority. Not long after this became apparent, at around 4:00 AM, 6 January, the Left SRs followed the Bolsheviks out of the hall. As was the case with the Bolsheviks, the Left SRs justified their withdrawal on the skewed composition of the Constituent Assembly and its unwillingness to endorse Soviet power. As the Left SRs filed out, Karelin declared: "We go so that at this critical moment in the great Russian Revolution we may devote all our energies to work in Soviet institutions . . . in the cause of the laboring classes . . . to assure their triumph."[71]

After the last Left SRs departed, noise from the balconies became deafening. Spectators filled the now empty Left benches and shouts of "Enough—away with all of you!" merged with the clang of bayonets being fixed and rifle bolts clanking open and shut. Struggling mightily to be heard above the din, Chernov began frantically reading a draft resolution on the land question—the product of weeks of careful study and debate by the SR fraction land commission made up of many of the country's leading agrono-mists. Midway in his presentation, Chernov was tapped on the shoulder by the captain of the guard, later identified as the notorious Kronstadt Anarchist-Communist Anatoli Zhelezniakov. "The guard is tired," Zhelez-niakov declared. "We have been ordered to clear the hall!"[72] Amid roars of approval from the galleries, Chernov responded that "all the members of the Constituent Assembly are tired, but no degree of fatigue can interrupt the reading of the land law for which all Russia is waiting." "The Constituent Assembly," he added, "will only disperse by force of arms!"[73]

Understandably, the two hundred or so remaining delegates proceeded with their business with greater urgency. A representative of the Ukrainian SRs, offended by Zhelezniakov's brazenness, announced that, because of what had just transpired, his fraction, which numbered eighty, was switch-ing from advocating the planks on peace and land in the Declaration of the Rights of Toiling and Exploited People to supporting the corresponding SR resolutions. Chernov then brought all the preliminary legislation pre-pared for the first day to hurried votes. Included were preliminary state-ments pertaining to the SR peace platform and land program, and Russia's reorganization into a "federal republic."[74] All these measures were adopted unanimously, without discussion, the harried deputies desperately attempt-ing to register their intentions and, in a sense, achieve in minutes what they had been unable to accomplish during seven months of governing with the Kadets. "We simply had to end the session so that something tangible would remain after it was over," Mark Vishniak, a Right SR and lawyer, later ob-served.[75]

Finally, at close to 5:00 AM on 6 January, the Constituent Assembly ad-journed and the delegates were allowed to leave, to the obvious surprise of many of them. As they hurried home in the bitter cold, with only the ca-cophony of church bells interrupting the early morning still, Sviatitskii and an SR companion pondered the day's events. "We will see—perhaps this is not the end," the two concluded glumly. Recalling this moment a decade later, Sviatitskii observed that the Constituent Assembly had died that night, not because of a lack of courage on the part of its supporters to die with it, or because of the sailors' demands, but "as a consequence of the indifference with which the people responded to our dissolution, which permitted Lenin to dismiss us with a wave of his hand: 'Let them just go home!' "[76]

* * *

The formal dissolution of the Constituent Assembly was accepted by the Sovnarkom and confirmed by the CEC later that same day (6 January).

Approved at the meeting of the Sovnarkom was yet another set of theses on the Constituent Assembly drafted by Lenin. Prepared as a decree for presentation to the CEC, these theses endorsed the dissolution on the grounds that after the withdrawal of the Bolsheviks and Left SRs the Constituent Assembly was nothing more than a smokescreen for attempts by the counterrevolution to overthrow Soviet power. An amendment proposed by the Left SRs called for the Third All-Russian Congress of Soviets of Workers' and Soldiers' Deputies to consider establishing a wholly new permanent legislature, the Federal Convention. Intended finally to transform the Sovnarkom into an executive body, to broaden the Soviet government's base and thereby increase the power of the Left SRs vis-à-vis the Bolsheviks, and also to soften popular perceptions of the Constituent Assembly's dissolution, the amendment was defeated by the Bolshevik majority.[77] In his capacity as people's commissar for justice, Shteinberg also urged that a commission be appointed to investigate the previous day's shootings.

The dissolution of the Constituent Assembly by the CEC, which was the first item on the agenda of its meeting on 6 January, was delayed by an emergency statement from Riazanov. He took the floor to protest in the strongest terms possible the shootings of the previous day and to demand that the CEC suspend its deliberations until the coming Soviet Congress had an opportunity to decide whether the Sovnarkom had acted properly in permitting such excesses. As Shteinberg had done earlier, Riazanov also urged that, in the interim, a committee be appointed to investigate the shootings. This step was approved without discussion. However, Riazanov's demand that the CEC suspend its work was ignored—perhaps partly because even Shteinberg felt that the shootings were being blown out of proportion.[78]

Following Riazanov's intervention, Lenin took the floor to justify the dissolution of the Constituent Assembly. "The conflict between Soviet power and the Constituent Assembly was foreshadowed by the entire history of the Russian Revolution," he declared at the outset. Assertions that the deepening of the revolution was the work of a single party or individual were "ridiculous." "The revolutionary conflagration had come about exclusively as a consequence of the terrible sufferings to which Russia had been subjected by the war." Acknowledging that "all kinds of blunders and mistakes would be made in the course of deepening the revolution," he insisted that "every revolutionary movement was invariably accompanied by chaos, destruction, and disorder." "Socialist revolution could not be served up to the people in a neat, smooth package," he continued. "It was bound to be accompanied by civil war, sabotage, and resistance . . . The people had wanted the Constituent Assembly to be convened. But they had quickly realized what it amounted to . . . The Constituent Assembly had shown that it would postpone decisions on all of the urgent questions which the soviets had presented to it." Therefore, delaying its dissolution was intolerable.[79]

According to *Pravda,* Lenin's speech received "stormy applause, which turned into a prolonged ovation."[80] By contrast, Vasilii Stroev, for the United Social-Democratic Internationalists, was jeered when he accused Lenin of countermanding the will of the Second Congress of Soviets which had committed itself to uphold the prerogatives of the Constituent Assembly. While fending off deputies who were physically manhandling him, Stroev managed to blurt out a resolution calling on the CEC to insist that the Constituent Assembly be allowed to proceed without interference. The resolution was not voted on. No less courageously, Riazanov declared that he had never made a fetish of the Constituent Assembly, but that since it had been convened, it should have been given time to show its true face. Sukhanov made the technically valid point that it was inaccurate to suggest that the Constituent Assembly had refused to acknowledge the achievements of the October revolution and urged that the dissolution of the assembly not be confirmed. Lozovskii did the same, insisting that endorsement of the dissolution "would be a mistake, indeed a crime"—to no avail. The Left SR Karelin was given the dubious honor of introducing Lenin's decree dissolving the Constituent Assembly, and, on the early morning of 7 January, it was passed by an overwhelming vote.[81] Riazanov and Lozovskii were among those voting no.[82]

This historic step, along with all other measures of the Sovnarkom and the CEC, was retroactively endorsed by the Third All-Russian Congress of Soviets of Workers' and Soldiers' Deputies[83] which met in Petrograd from 10 to 18 January 1918. The congress merged with the Third All-Russian Congress of Soviets of Peasants' Deputies on 13 January 1918. The joint congresses' decree on the structure of the government reconfirmed the combined CEC as the supreme national governmental organ between national congresses of soviets. However, the systemic relationship between the Sovnarkom and the CEC was again blurred. The decree specified only that the CEC had the right to appoint or remove the latter (either wholly or in part).[84] At the insistence of the Left SRs, a semi-autonomous Peasant Section attached to the combined CEC was established as a substitute for the Executive Committee of the All-Russian Congress of Soviets of Peasants' Deputies.[85] The Peasant Section was to refine the Left SR land reform project ("socialization of the land") for confirmation by the CEC, to oversee its implementation, and, more broadly, to coordinate peasant-related programs generally.[86] Led by Spiridonova and destined to be the citadel of the Left

SRs, it was not even mentioned in the decree on the structure of the government. In the decree, the task of defining a more precise constitutional structure was left to the new CEC, in which the Bolsheviks retained an absolute majority, and to the next national Congress of Soviets.[87] Perhaps because of its preoccupation with more pressing issues connected with fighting a revolutionary war or accepting an "obscene" peace, the CEC that was elected by the Third All-Russian Congress of Soviets never got around to considering revision of the Soviet government's structure.

* * *

In mid December 1917, Lenin thwarted the efforts of Bolshevik moderates to respect the prerogatives of the Constituent Assembly, thus marking the end of their existence as an influential, cohesive, intraparty force. His dissolution of the Constituent Assembly less than a month later ended the hopes of Russian liberals and moderate socialists that the 1917 revolutions might yet culminate with the establishment in Russia of a democratic political system on the Western model. Certainly, contributing to this result was the Bolsheviks' strong popular support in the Petrograd region, as reflected in the mid-November elections to the Constituent Assembly, and the SR leadership's rejection of efforts to provide military security for the Constituent Assembly coupled with the Bolsheviks' and Left SRs' readiness to resort to force of arms to defend Soviet power. Most important, however, Sviatitskii was probably on target when he pointed to the Russian people's fundamental indifference to the fate of the Constituent Assembly, allowing Lenin to command that they all simply go home.

PART TWO

WAR OR PEACE?

5

Fighting Lenin

To WAR-WEARY Russian peasants, workers, and soldiers, the promise of immediate peace without annexations or indemnities had been one of the most engaging aspects of the broadly popular Bolshevik program in 1917. After the collapse of efforts by the moderate socialists to arrange a peace conference in Stockholm during the summer of 1917, the Bolsheviks, alone among major Russian political parties, stood for immediate peace. An abiding concern with arranging the quickest possible end to the nightmare of world war helps explain why such left Mensheviks as David Riazanov, Solomon Lozovskii, and Iurii Larin joined the Bolshevik party in the late summer of 1917, and why they and leading Bolshevik moderates like Kamenev did not withdraw from the party in early November, despite their fundamental differences with the Leninist majority in the Central Committee over the makeup of the government.

Lenin's peace declaration, one of the very first decrees adopted by the Second All-Russian Congress of Soviets on 26 October, called on all warring states to begin peace negotiations at once. When the Entente failed to respond positively to the first peace initiatives of the Soviet government, the Sovnarkom entered separate armistice and peace talks with the Central Powers. These negotiations began on 20 November 1917 in the city of Brest-Litovsk, the site of German headquarters in occupied Poland, and two days later (22 November) the two sides agreed on a ten-day armistice, subsequently extended for twenty-eight days with the proviso that it would automatically be continued until one side rejected it seven days in advance. During the truce, a permanent peace was to be negotiated.

The approach of separate peace negotiations between the Soviet government and the Central Powers stirred great anxiety among Russia's former allies, domestic critics of Soviet power, and important segments of the Bolshevik party. Leaders of the radical Bolshevik Moscow Oblast Bureau are usually credited with having been the first to voice concern on this score.[1]

However, similar unease emerged simultaneously in Petrograd. At the Petersburg Committee session on 16 November, which initially focused on issues related to dissolution and reelection of the City Duma, individual committee members voiced concern about the imminent negotiations with the Central Powers. After Slutskii, in an update on the current moment, suggested that Lenin and Krylenko were intent on concluding a separate peace treaty with Hindenburg, Viktor Narchuk, a representative of the Bolshevik committee in the Vyborg workers' district, warned that if the party did not make good on its commitments regarding pursuit of universal peace, it would lose its popular following. To most participants in this meeting, however, the idea that Lenin and Trotsky might behave treacherously in negotiations with the Germans seemed preposterous. Still, they registered their strong views on peacemaking by electing a new Executive Commission, their main leadership body, which was dominated by ardent opponents of a separate peace— the future "Left Communists."[2]

Anxieties among Petrograd Bolsheviks over the possibility that the goal of a "universal proletarian peace" might be perverted in the course of peace talks with the Central Powers intensified as they proceeded without any sign that Britain and France would join in the talks or that workers abroad were responding in significant ways to Soviet appeals that they take peacemaking into their own hands. This heightened concern was reflected at a meeting of the Petersburg Committee with district agitators on 23 November to which Karl Radek had been invited to present his views on foreign affairs. A prominent party leader well known for his internationalism, Radek was convinced by his own wartime experiences in Central Europe that workers and soldiers in the German and Austro-Hungarian empires were ripe to follow revolutionary Russia's lead and, indeed, that all Europe was on the verge of decisive revolutionary convulsions. His message to the Petersburg Committee on 23 November constituted a passionate call for the rejection of any "deals with capitalists." Russia was now pointing the way for the masses throughout the world, he declared, emphasizing that the fate of the Russian and world revolutions was inseparable. The government was right to enter into separate talks with the Germans as long as this step was coupled with an intensified campaign to revolutionize workers abroad and insofar as a relentless struggle was waged against compromisers in the party.[3]

Most local-level leaders participating in this meeting were in full agreement with Radek's conclusion that deals with capitalists were unacceptable. In his remarks, however, Radek took it for granted that there were still significant numbers of Russian soldiers at the front capable of fighting a revolutionary holy war. During the discussion that followed, this assumption was challenged by Dmitrii Manuilskii (Bezrabotnyi), who declared unequivocally that "for Russia further fighting is impossible." However, he did not find this worrisome, because international revolution would quickly liquidate the consequences of an unfavorable peace. Among others, Grigorii Evdokimov, another representative of the Vyborg district, and Pavel Pakhomov, from the Second City district, took issue with Manuilskii's pessimism regarding the possibility of mobilizing Russian soldiers and workers to wage revolutionary war. Evdokimov felt that demobilizing unreliable elements and better supplying remaining troops would raise morale in the army in case the resumption of military operations became necessary. He emphasized the importance of speaking out candidly about the possibility of a revolutionary war so that workers, soldiers, and sailors would be prepared for such an eventuality. Pakhomov echoed these sentiments, insisting that "if revolutionary war becomes unavoidable, the masses will understand." On the other hand, Moisei Kharitonov, Pakhomov's Second City district colleague, implicitly dismissed the very idea that revolutionary war might become a requirement, remarking that he could not imagine the Germans insisting on unfavorable peace terms. While no formal resolution on the peace issue was adopted at this meeting, the discussion laid bare the strong opposition to a separate peace by a majority of the Petersburg Committee, as well as by district-level activists.[4]

*   *   *

Formal peace negotiations at Brest-Litovsk began on 9 December.[5] On that day Adolph Ioffe, head of the Russian delegation, reiterated the Soviet government's firm commitment to peace without annexations or indemnities. He then presented the main principles on which, according to the Soviet government, the negotiations should be based. These included the speedy withdrawal of foreign troops from all occupied territories; the restoration of independence to all nations who had lost it since 1914; and completely free referendums on the political future of all subject nationalities desiring independence from existing states of which they formed a part. They also provided for the protection of the rights of national minorities everywhere, and excluded annexations and indemnities in any form.

On behalf of the Central Powers, Count Czernin, the Austro-Hungarian foreign minister, responded to these principles at a negotiating session on 12 December. At the outset, his remarks encouraged the Soviet side. He declared that the Central Powers wanted to conclude a just and general peace as soon as possible and that the principles articulated by Ioffe, including prohibition of annexations and indemnities, provided a basis for discussing such a peace. Czernin, however, had two critical reservations, although their practical significance appears to have been lost on Ioffe: first, that acceptance of the Soviet side's principles was conditioned on all belligerents accepting them without undue delay; and, second, that the Central Powers could not accept the principle of self-determination for all subject nationalities without qualification. The future of such peoples had to be solved by each state in accordance with its own constitution.

Although disappointed about these reservations, Ioffe and his colleagues were delighted with what they interpreted as the forthcoming tone of Czernin's response. Not only did it seem to provide ammunition for intensifying popular pressure on the Entente to join in the negotiations, but they also took it to mean that the Central Powers were prepared to withdraw their forces from occupied territories of the former Russian Empire despite what the Entente did. To disabuse the Soviet side of this interpretation, in a statement clarifying the status of occupied territories two days later (14 December), the Central Powers reiterated that their obligation to evacuate Russian territories hinged on complete reciprocity by the Entente. Moreover, they added the bombshell that, based on the principle of self-determination, the peoples of occupied Poland, Lithuania, and most of Latvia had already expressed a desire to separate themselves from Russia (thereby all but announcing their intention to turn these countries into protectorates).

Word of the ostensibly positive response to the revolutionary peace principles enunciated by Ioffe had been telegraphed to Smolny on 12 December and was accepted at face value as a sensational victory. A front-page *Pravda* headline on 14 December, announcing that the Germans had accepted Russia's principles as the basis for peace negotiations and had agreed to conclude a general peace without annexations and indemnities, demanded that soldiers of France, Italy, and England respond to these concessions by rising against their governments.

Soviet leaders were still euphoric at a meeting of the CEC late that night (14 December). When Trotsky rose to report on the progress of the negotiations, he received a long standing ovation and did not try to dampen the excitement. Rather, he, too, viewed developments at Brest as a spectacular vindication of revolutionary diplomacy. "Germany has accepted the peace conditions set by the [Second] Congress of Soviets in full," he exalted. "Even our enemies . . . who so recently prophesied that the German diplomats would not so much as talk to us but would make war on us instead now see that the German proposal is a tremendous success for our policy." Isaac Shteinberg, who usually took the floor to scold the Bolsheviks, also heaped praise on their revolutionary peacemaking. "This is the first big triumph for our diplomacy," he exclaimed. "Unarmed, we entered the enemy camp and spoke not as equals but as superiors. A mortal blow has been inflicted upon imperialism." He introduced a resolution, adopted without dissent, enthusiastically endorsing the Sovnarkom's peace efforts. Not to be outdone, Zinoviev proposed that "grandiose peace demonstrations" be held throughout the country on Sunday, 17 December, to mark the great victory at Brest. His resolution also passed unanimously.[6]

First word of the clarifications issued by Czernin on 14 December, essentially negating the Soviet delegation's initially positive interpretation of the Central Power's negotiating stance, was probably received in Smolny on the evening of the 16th. By that time, the talks at Brest-Litovsk had adjourned, and the Soviet delegation was en route back to Petrograd. Arriving in the capital the next morning (17 December), it headed straight for Smolny to report to a morning meeting of the Sovnarkom. Most of the leading members of the government were present.[7] The delegation's presentation as recorded in the relevant Sovnarkom protocol is obscure. However, a lengthy presentation which Kamenev made at an expanded meeting of the CEC on 19 December leaves little doubt about what the delegation had to say in its meeting with the Sovnarkom two days earlier.[8] It remained of the opinion that the initial willingness expressed by the Central Powers to base negotiations on the principles presented by Ioffe was a singular triumph despite the hypocrisy with which they were apparently to be applied. With regard to future economic relations, the delegation probably conveyed its impression that the Germans understood that they would not receive any special advantages or privileges as a result of a separate treaty. However, there was nothing the delegation could do to soften the implications of the German stance on the all-important question of occupied Russian territories—specifically, the clear intention of the Germans to manipulate the principle of self-determination in order to retain control of Poland, Lithuania, and most of Latvia. As Kamenev explained in his report to the CEC, "the Germans have transformed the principle of self-determination from a formula for national liberation into a disguise for annexation."[9]

After receiving the delegation's report, the Sovnarkom requested that the exact text of Germany's terms be delivered as quickly as possible and, in the meantime, proceeded to discuss their implications.[10] It seems fair to speculate, based on indirect evidence, that Kamenev and Trotsky expressed doubts about the Germans' ability to successfully back up their annexationist aims with force (both believed that any attempt to do so would result in the Kaiser's overthrow). The two probably expressed optimism, moreover, about the prospects for an early change in attitudes toward a compromise peace among the Western allies, as well as about the prospects of launching a successful revolutionary war in the event all else failed.

One is left wondering if Lenin entertained such hopes at this point in the peace process. However, surely any hopes he may have harbored for the efficacy of revolutionary war were dashed by a long meeting he had later that same day (17 December) with representatives from Russia's military fronts, major urban garrisons, and naval forces then in Petrograd for a conference on demobilization. This was precisely the moment when the apparent emergence of a major counterrevolutionary threat on the Don prompted mobilization of trainloads of Petrograd Red Guards to fight together with Antonov-Ovseenko's forces on the Don.[11] Organization of a socialist army had not yet begun. Hence, to Lenin, the fighting capacity of the "old army" at the front was the critical issue. He peppered the military representatives with oral queries and had them fill out a questionnaire about the feasibility and likely outcome of a renewed German offensive and advance on Petrograd, and also on the fighting capacity of Russian forces at the front in the event Russia broke off the peace talks.[12]

According to all available sources, the results of Lenin's survey were devastating. Most of the delegates responded that in the event of renewed hostilities, the best they could hope for was that the army would retreat in good order. Even in the best of circumstances, however, its artillery would be lost and spontaneous demobilization would escalate. The bulk of the representatives apparently also felt that if there were a renewed German offensive, Russian troops would be unable to marshal serious resistance and prevent the quick occupation of Petrograd. Thus, an overwhelming majority of them urged that the negotiations at Brest be dragged out as long as possible and, if necessary, that peace be secured at any price.[13]

The results of this survey did not become generally known at the time. However, the deflation of hopes for an early peace on Russia's terms left organizers of the peace demonstration scheduled by the CEC in a quandary. They had begun energetic preparations for the march on 15 December, and these had been intensified the next day. Simply canceling it would have been politically awkward. Therefore, since a high-level German delegation was then in Petrograd, it was decided to impress the Germans by shifting the parade's emphasis from a celebration of peace to a show of military might, popular support for Soviet policies, and broad hostility toward domestic enemies of the revolution. So it was that while the Sovnarkom listened to the Brest delegation's ominous account of Germany's territorial ambitions, some sixty thousand armed soldiers of the Petrograd garrison, hundreds of factory representatives, and several marching bands trooped through the center of

Petrograd before filing by a reviewing stand filled with Soviet dignitaries on the Field of Mars. Banners inscribed with peace slogans were lost among a sea of red flags and placards lauding the Soviet government and condemning the Constituent Assembly, "enemies of the people" of all stripes, "saboteurs," the "Avksentievs and Chernovs," and the "Kornilovite Kadets."[14]

Bearing in mind the implications of Lenin's survey, it is not surprising that the state of the army as it related to the implications of German demands was a major subject of discussion at the next meeting of the Sovnarkom late the night of 18/19 December.[15] At the meeting, Lenin probed Krylenko, then commander-in-chief of the army, for his views and those of representatives of soldier committees regarding whether Russian soldiers would fight if the Germans launched an offensive. Like the military representatives queried by Lenin the previous day, Krylenko responded bluntly that the army had lost its fighting capacity and would not tolerate delays in ending the war—in short, that, militarily, there was no alternative but to accept whatever peace terms the Germans proposed.[16]

Prior to the meeting, Lenin had reviewed the military representatives' written responses to his questionnaire the previous day. For him, personally, they were extremely distressing. He shared the replies with participants in the meeting,[17] including officials of the People's Commissariat for War such as Podvoiskii and Pavel Dybenko. The Sovnarkom's protocol of the 18/19 December meeting contains no clues about the nature of the ensuing discussion, but the presence of several Left SRs, among them Kolegaev, Karelin, Shteinberg, and Trutovskii, and such future Left Communists as Kollontai, Lunacharskii, Valerii Osinskii (V. V. Obolenskii), and Uritskii, suggests that it was lively. Ultimately, the decision was made to consider the results of Lenin's questionnaire "definitive" with respect to the state of the existing army. Also agreed upon, however, was a resolution proposed by Lenin calling for more agitation against German expansionism, allocation of supplementary funds for this purpose, transfer of the peace negotiations to Stockholm, prolongation of the talks and countering of German efforts to bring them to a conclusion, intensification of measures to enhance the army's fighting capacity, adoption of measures to prevent a German breakthrough to Petrograd, and initiation of a domestic propaganda campaign to demonstrate the necessity of revolutionary war.[18]

*   *   *

For the time being, then, despite a consensus about the utter demoralization of the old army, the Sovnarkom attempted to provide for the eventuality of renewed fighting. In this connection, Krylenko issued an order to his commanders alerting them to prepare for a possible resumption of the war. Simultaneously, he appealed for volunteers to join a new socialist army.[19] However, this was definitely not how the Bolshevik Petersburg Committee perceived the Sovnarkom's military policies. The Petersburg Committee remained profoundly wary of the government's defeatism. Significant in this connection is that the primary agenda items for meetings of the committee on 19 and 21 December were reports by Radek on "Western Europe and the Peace Talks" and the "International Situation."[20] Based on Radek's report to the Petersburg Committee of 23 November, and his speeches and writings in the intervening period, there is little doubt that in these reports he would have made fervent pleas for toughness in the negotiations at Brest and, if necessary, for resistance to any German military threats. Radek's obsession at this time was to dissuade the Soviet government from taking any action that might undercut revolutionary movements in Central and Western Europe. It is also clear that the Executive Commission of the Petersburg Committee and a majority of the committee as a whole shared Radek's staunch opposition to making any deals with imperialists.

Following the 21 December meeting, the Executive Commission drafted a set of theses on the peace talks for approval at the next regularly scheduled Petersburg Committee meeting on 28 December. Although the text of these theses has not been found, their intent and thrust are apparent from a speech delivered at that meeting on behalf of the Executive Commission by Iakov Fenigshtein, when he introduced them, and from the subsequent discussion. Fenigshtein began by explaining that the Executive Commission had decided to put the question of Russia's peace strategy to a vote, as it was convinced that such a vital issue ought not to be left to the discretion of the government alone, that control by the broad masses through their revolutionary leadership would provide the necessary direction.

The remainder of Fenigshtein's remarks embodied a sustained assault on the way the peace talks were developing and a passionate plea for the pursuit of revolutionary goals. German soldiers, he said, had no desire to fight. On the other hand, the Russian armed forces were solidly for defense of the revolution. In such circumstances, what should the Soviet government do? To Fenigshtein and, by extension, to his colleagues on the Executive Commission, the answer was obvious. Regardless of the circumstances, absolutely nothing could justify compromising revolutionary principles. "Every concession from our formula [universal peace without annexations or indemnities] will be damaging to workers and peasants," he insisted. "There simply is no alternative to fighting for the kind of peace we have in mind."

"What should we do if we cannot achieve [our] goals at the peace talks?" he asked rhetorically. "We should break them off." In this way, the annexationist aims of German imperialists would be exposed before all the peoples of the world. "The war triggered by such a policy will be different from all previous wars," Fenigshtein went on. "Politically conscious worker, peasant, and soldier masses will understand that there is no other choice." "We made a big mistake when we infused the masses with the hope that the beginning of peace talks insured peace," he added. "Now we have to mount a broad campaign to convince them of the unacceptability of agreeing to Germany's peace terms and to demonstrate the possibility of [waging] revolutionary war against her."[21]

Next, Fenigshtein presented the Executive Commission's theses which, it is obvious from the ensuing lively discussion, were intended to alert the Central Committee to the Petersburg Committee's unequivocal opposition to any form of capitulation. Perhaps most striking about this discussion is that all the participants shared the Executive Commission's anxiety about dealing with representatives of the Kaiser. A few speakers from the districts were considerably less sanguine than Fenigshtein about the willingness of Russian soldiers and workers to fight a revolutionary war. However, most were inclined to place their trust in timely aid from the European proletariat (as was the case with Sarra Ravich and Fedor Dingel'shtedt) or, at any rate, were optimistic that the negotiations at Brest could be dragged out long enough to create more promising conditions for revolutionary war (as was the case with Semon Semkov and Moisei Gorelik).

In fact, with virtually no exceptions, everyone, either explicitly or implicitly, rejected compromise with the Central Powers. The Vyborg district's Ivan Naumov was concerned most of all with the danger that Russia's former allies might try to associate themselves with a revolutionary war against German imperialism. The propriety of accepting aid from capitalist powers in a war against imperialism was already of concern to some, and Naumov felt that this issue should have been addressed by Fenigshtein. Everyone also seemed to agree that the Petersburg Committee's immediate intervention was necessary to stiffen the backbone of the government and the top party leadership. As Stanislav Kossior, from the Narva district, remarked, "We have ample reason to believe that wavering is taking place at upper levels of the party." The situation called for boldness: "We should be attacking, not bargaining with imperialists." "Some comrades [e.g., Lenin], say it is better to hold on to something than to be defeated," Kossior added. "I believe it is better to be defeated than to compromise."[22]

Perhaps the most passionate plea for the traditionally radical Petersburg Committee's staunch commitment to revolutionary principles, irrespective of cost, was made by Volodarskii, arguably the Petersburg Committee's most authoritative and popular figure among the party's rank and file. To him, as to Fenigshtein and Kossior, it seemed clear that with another round of peace talks on the horizon, something was happening at the top that was being kept from the Petersburg Committee, that there was an extremely dangerous tendency within the government to accept an obscene peace that would scandalize Bolsheviks before the entire world peace movement, and that the Petersburg Committee would need to intervene to save the day, as it had at key moments earlier in 1917.

On this occasion Volodarskii was surprisingly optimistic about prospects for resisting the Germans and stimulating decisive revolutions abroad. At the same time, he was fatalistic, observing that people were pointing to economic chaos and the impossibility of feeding an eleven-million-man army as justification for accepting peace at any price. His response was that feeding two or three million soldiers was not the same as eleven million. The Bolsheviks had destroyed the existing economic apparatus and, if they could not find a way to reestablish one, they were done for anyway, war or no war. "Certainly it would be much easier to compromise and to look ahead to signing a peace in two weeks," he concluded, but "where would that lead us?"[23]

Ravich took the floor after Volodarskii to dispute the idea, which she read into his comments, that fighting a revolutionary war would be easy. But she immediately added, "This should not give us pause." To her, revolutionary Russia's hopes for survival lay less with its own forces than with the world's proletariat. The main task was to do everything possible to stir international revolution. The Executive Commission's theses, in her view, could be very helpful to the peace delegation in its negotiations at Brest. At the close of the 28 December meeting, the Petersburg Committee adopted the theses. With minor editing, they were to be transmitted to the Central Committee. Simultaneously, the Petersburg Committee considered the question of calling for a national party conference "to straighten out the policy line of the party." However, after Volodarskii intimated that a national party congress to consider disputed issues was already in the works, the decision to call for a national conference was postponed.[24]

* * *

Between 24 and 27 December, as one of the most momentous years in Russian history drew to a close, Lenin rested in Finland.[25] He returned to Petrograd on 28 December, a week before the opening of the Constituent

Assembly, convinced that revolutionary war meant suicide and that it was absolutely essential to accept an annexationist peace on Germany's terms, the sooner the better. Historians have disputed the evolution of Lenin's thoughts on the peace issue. Some have suggested not only that Lenin was in the pay of the Germans in the spring and summer of 1917 but that October and perhaps even the sell-out at Brest were phases of a joint Bolshevik-German undertaking to destabilize Russia and end hostilities on the Eastern front.[26] Putting aside the question of German subsidies to the Bolsheviks before the October revolution, my reading of the available evidence leads me to conclude that Lenin came to power convinced of the need for immediate peace if revolutionary Russia was to survive but that this concern did not trouble him much because of his absolute confidence in the immediacy of decisive socialist revolutions abroad. However, he began to have doubts about banking on them, and therefore also about the short-run possibilities for an early universal democratic peace in December. Following his sojourn in Finland, he made one of his characteristic 180-degree turns, concluding that there was no alternative to accepting whatever peace terms the Germans offered. The stage was set for the most profound intraparty crisis of Lenin's years as Soviet head of state.

At this point, the Central Powers had already formally announced at Brest-Litovsk that their earlier understandings regarding peace principles were null and void because of the Entente's failure to respond to them. Further, they had presented Trotsky with the text of a treaty for signature. Indeed, they had even provided him with a map upon which formerly Russian areas that were to remain under German occupation were clearly marked. In addition, the Central Powers had begun private, separate peace negotiations with the Ukrainian Rada. After several days of trying without success to persuade his adversaries to budge from their positions, Trotsky wired Lenin informing him that it was impossible to sign the peace that had been presented to him and requesting authorization to announce the termination of the war and to demobilize the Russian army without signing a treaty. In the telegram, Trotsky expressed confidence that the Germans would be unable to resume military operations in the east because of their difficult domestic situation and appealed to Lenin for a decision by return wire.[27] In Lenin's view, however, Trotsky's assumptions were faulty. Having decided that an immediate formal peace treaty acceptable to Germany provided the only means of forestalling a renewed German offensive and the inevitable destruction of the Bolshevik project in Russia, on 3 January he responded to Trotsky with a request that he arrange a recess in the negotiations and return to Petrograd for consultations.[28]

As soon as the immediate crisis over the Constituent Assembly ended, Lenin summarized his views on the absolute need for immediate peace in "Theses on the Question of the Signing of an Immediate Separate and Annexationist Peace" and scheduled an unofficial conference for 8 January of some sixty-three prominent party leaders from around the country gathered in Petrograd for the Third All-Russian Congress of Workers' and Soldiers' Soviets. In these theses, Lenin contended that to defeat the Soviet government's internal enemies and organize the country on a socialist basis would take some time, and that socialist revolutions would inevitably engulf Europe but it was impossible to predict when this would occur. This was a significant retreat from his position during and immediately after October. Consequently, he argued that Russia had two choices—either she could embark on a revolutionary war at once or sign a separate peace involving huge territorial losses and a sizable monetary indemnity.

The reasoning of proponents of immediate revolutionary war was flawed from start to finish, Lenin went on. Contrary to their contentions, by signing a separate peace, the Soviet government would neither betray the cause of international socialism nor renege on pre-October pledges so long as it used the time afforded by peace to prepare for revolutionary war. Most important, so Lenin argued in these theses, proponents of revolutionary war neglected to consider that the peasant army at the front was utterly incapable of fighting and, in any case, would not support a revolutionary war. At the same time, the creation of a socialist army made up of workers and poorer peasantry had barely begun. Without socialist revolutions in Europe, Russia would be overwhelmed and the Soviet government toppled in a matter of weeks, after which Russia would be forced to accept an even more humiliating peace than it was then being offered. Revolutionary war was not an option; painful though it was, global revolutionary interests dictated making peace on German terms at once.[29]

After presenting his theses, Lenin was bombarded by criticism from supporters of revolutionary war who were already being referred to as Left Communists. Notes that he scribbled suggest that Lomov and Valerii Osinskii from the Moscow Oblast Bureau adopted positions analogous to those embodied in the Petersburg Committee's theses of 28 December.[30] In making the case for breaking off the talks and initiating revolutionary war, Osinskii insisted that German soldiers would refuse to participate in an offensive against revolutionary Russia and that, in Germany, an uprising against imperialism was close. Varvara Iakovleva, from Saratov, remarked that everything possible had to be done to start the revolutionary conflagration in Europe, and, to that end, she expressed her own readiness to die with revolutionary banners held high. Evidently referring to Lenin's concern about Russia's military weakness, Evgenii Preobrazhenskii, based in the Urals, declared that any revolution that was unable to defend itself at the front was already dead, contending as well that the French revolution had shown that faith in victory was essential in such situations and, in any case, that the Germans would be unable to attack, because Russia's winter roads were impassable.[31]

At this conference, Trotsky took the middle position reflected in his letter to Lenin from Brest. He agreed with Lenin that Russia was incapable of mounting a revolutionary war. However, in common with Left Communists, he remained skeptical of the Germans' capacity to resume an offensive. He proposed, therefore, simply to declare that the war was over, that the [Russian] army was being demobilized, and that it was going home to build a socialist Russia. In memoirs, Trotsky explains that he was not certain the Germans would be unable to attack but that it was critical to find out before signing an annexationist peace; if necessary, there would be time to capitulate after that.[32] One conference participant recalled that Lenin became so frustrated by the unrelenting attack on his views that he stormed out.[33] At the end of the conference a vote was taken, and the Left Communists won a solid victory over both Lenin and Trotsky (thirty-two participants voted for revolutionary war, sixteen supported Trotsky, and only fifteen voted with Lenin).[34]

Members of the Petersburg Committee (not to speak of the Moscow Oblast Bureau) were doubtless heartened by this vote. Nonetheless, it was not binding. According to party rules, in the absence of an official national party congress, ultimate authority for deciding major national policy issues rested with the Central Committee. Consequently, at a Central Committee meeting on 11 January, Lenin made another stab at winning the party leadership to his side. Prior to this meeting, according to Trotsky, he and Lenin reached an understanding that, if the "no war, no peace" strategy was tested and failed, Trotsky would support "immediate peace."[35] Most of the participants in the 11 January Central Committee meeting had taken part in the 8 January unofficial conference. Thus, Lenin was able to pick up where he had left off. At the start of the discussion, he reiterated the main arguments of his theses regarding the hopelessness of revolutionary war and Trotsky's proposal, concluding that the latter was international political posturing which would do nothing to deter German expansionism. If the Soviet republic did not agree to immediate peace on Germany's present terms, he added, it ran the risk that Germany would launch an offensive, and, in that event, Russia would have to accept significantly more onerous terms for peace.[36]

To Lenin's dismay, the responses to his arguments in the Central Committee were at least as cool as they had been in the broader forum of party representatives from around the country three days earlier. Of the sixteen Central Committee members present at this meeting, only three—Artem (Fedor Sergeev), Sokolnikov, and Stalin—sided with Lenin. Moreover, their comments seem perfunctory when compared to the passion of the Left Communists. Still, this does not mean that sentiment among Lenin's adversaries had not shifted between 8 and 11 January. On 8 January, an absolute majority had voted for an immediate end to peace negotiations with Germany, coupled with the proclamation of a universal revolutionary war against capitalism. At the Central Committee meeting three days later, even the most ardent Left Communists appeared to see merits in Trotsky's idea of walking out of the negotiations following a declaration of "no war, no peace," with the proviso that negotiations would be dragged out as long as possible and that efforts to strengthen revolutionary movements abroad and military forces at home would be intensified.

In the course of the discussion on 11 January Bukharin, the acknowledged leader of the Left Communists, declared flatly that "Trotsky's position is the most correct," adding, "So what if the Germans beat us, so what if they advance another hundred versts—our concern is the effect this will have on the international [workers'] movement." A general strike linked to the Brest negotiations was developing in Vienna; if a peace was signed, it would be wrecked. It was essential to seize every opportunity to drag out the negotiations and not sign an obscene peace. In that way, the West European masses would be energized.[37] Although acknowledging that revolutionary Russia was not in a position to wage an immediate revolutionary war, Uritskii, also an ardent Left Communist, added that acceptance of an annexationist peace would alienate the Petrograd proletariat. "By refusing to sign the peace [and] demobilizing the army . . . we will, of course, be opening the way for the Germans," he observed. "But then, the instinct of self-preservation will undoubtedly be triggered in the people, and revolutionary war will begin."[38]

Lomov rejected Lenin's argument that a breathing space would permit putting social reforms into practice, insisting that German opposition would preclude that. Declaring that, by concluding peace, revolutionary Russia would be surrendering to German imperialism, he contended that "we have to adopt Trotsky's position but with maximum effort to prepare for revolutionary war." Dzerzhinskii interjected emphatically that signing the peace would mean giving up on the entire Bolshevik program and accused Lenin of doing "in disguised form what Zinoviev and Kamenev had done in October," that is, thinking only of Russia and ignoring the great international impact of events in Russia. Only Kossior, who participated in this meeting as the representative of the Petersburg Committee, appeared wedded to the original Left Communist demand for immediate revolutionary war. Using the 28 December Petersburg Committee theses as his guide, he declared that "the Petersburg organization is protesting and will protest Lenin's point of view as long as it can and considers that the position of revolutionary war is the only possible one."[39] Kossior may not have been aware of it, but this was not entirely true. Sentiment in some district party committees in Petrograd was already closer to Trotsky's view than to the Petersburg Committee's.[40]

By the end of the Central Committee's discussion on 11 January, the weak support for Lenin's position was so apparent that it was not even voted on. Launching an immediate revolutionary war was voted down 11 to 2, with 1 abstention. Instead, by a vote of 9 to 7, the top party leadership adopted Trotsky's "no war, no peace" formula, coupled with demobilization of the [old] army. At the same time, by a vote of 12 to 1, it adopted a resolution proposed by Lenin specifying that every effort would be made to drag out negotiations as long as possible.[41] According to newspaper reports, that evening the Bureau of the Left SR fraction in the Third All-Russian Congress of Soviets of Workers' and Soldiers' Deputies and the Left SR Central Committee voted to continue the war by all means possible if a satisfactory peace was not concluded.[42] This position was quickly changed, however. On the night of 12 or 13 January, a majority of participants in a joint meeting of the Bolshevik and Left SR Central Committees ignored the acceptance of an immediate peace on Germany's terms, rejected the proclamation of a revolutionary war, and voted in favor of implementing Trotsky's strategy. For now this resolution appeased all sides. Lenin saw it as meaning that when further delay at Brest became impossible, peace would be signed; Left Communists and Left SRs believed they had been given a green light to prepare for revolutionary war; and Trotsky concluded that he was now authorized to proclaim "no war, no peace." He also assumed that, in the unlikely event Germany renewed hostilities, signing a peace on German terms would be delayed until Germany's ability to launch a successful offensive and the response of European workers were clear.

*　　*　　*

In his report to the Third All-Russian Congress of Soviets on the evening of 11 January on the goals and achievements of his government, Lenin skirted issues relating to the peace negotiations, leaving that topic to Trotsky.[43] In turn Trotsky, who spoke on the 13th, focused on a recapitulation of the negotiations at Brest. According to him, by clearly exposing Germany's imperialist designs, they were raising revolutionary crises in Austria and Germany to new heights.[44] Kamenev echoed this theme in a supplementary address on developments at Brest and their international impact.[45] Judging by the published record, neither Trotsky's nor Kamenev's speech, nor the congress's resolution on peace, even hinted at the "no war, no peace" strategy or the possible need to mount a revolutionary war. The joint Bolshevik–Left SR resolution on the peace policy, which the congress passed on 14 January, endorsed and praised all the pronouncements and steps already made by Soviet power in the interest of achieving a universal and democratic peace; expressed certainty that the revolutionary workers movement in Central Europe was the best possible guarantee against an imperialist peace; and directed the Russian peace delegation to hold fast to the peace principles embodied in the program of the Russian revolution.[46] One is tempted to conclude that the failure to endorse Trotsky's "no war, no peace" formula, as recommended by the Bolshevik and Left SR Central Committees, reflected the belated recognition that disclosing Russia's negotiating position at Brest in advance would have undermined the strategy. However, the reason for this silence may have been more complex. Some Left Communists at the time, including the leadership of the Petersburg Committee,[47] believed that the resolution the congress passed had been intentionally left vague by the Bolshevik fraction in the congress, where Leninists were in a majority, so that the ultimate decision on whether to sign an annexationist peace would fall to the discretion of Lenin and the Sovnarkom. As we shall see, this was precisely the way Lenin and Sverdlov subsequently interpreted the resolution.[48]

At one point in his speech, perhaps in deference to Lenin, Trotsky implied that while worker representatives at Brest would continue to expose German hypocrisy, the possibility could not be excluded that the Russian delegation would be forced to sign a peace with capitalist representatives that clearly contradicted workers' interests.[49] In a later speech to the congress, Zinoviev also raised the possibility that Russia might be forced to sign an annexationist peace, but he immediately added that this peace, in reality, would only be a truce.[50] Although these veiled references to Russia's possible acceptance of an annexationist peace no doubt heightened the apprehensions of Left Communists and Left SRs, they were lost on outsiders. Thus, despite his aversion to Bolshevism (this was, after all, little more than a week after the dissolution of the Constituent Assembly), even Martov, after listening to Trotsky, praised the "amazing steps" toward a universal peace taken by "the cultivators of the worldwide international revolution."[51]

Martov's comment may have reflected the momentary intensification of revolutionary unrest in Europe, which appeared to be linked to Russia's peace policies. While Soviet congress delegates in Petrograd sought to define a revolutionary peace policy, for a fleeting moment the latest news from Vienna, Budapest, Warsaw, Helsingfors, Berlin, and other major European cities appeared to signal the possibility that the impatiently awaited decisive socialist revolutions in the West were at hand. And each snippet of news about this or that sign of revolutionary unrest abroad was enthusiastically highlighted by the Bolshevik press in Petrograd and announced to jubilant congress delegates.

Petrograders reading the Bolsheviks' *Krasnaia gazeta* on 13 January were greeted by the following huge, bold-face headline:

> IN AUSTRIA, HUNGARY, AND WARSAW REVOLUTIONARY WORKERS ARE FORM-
> ING THEIR OWN SOVIETS OF WORKERS DEPUTIES. . . . A GREAT FIRE IS ENGULF-
> ING THE ENTIRE WORLD![52]

And on 17 January:

> WHEN, IN OCTOBER, WORKERS, SOLDIERS, AND PEASANTS OVERTHREW
> THE LANDLORDS AND INDUSTRIALISTS, THEY KNEW ONLY ONE THING: WITH-
> OUT REVOLUTION IN OTHER COUNTRIES OUR REVOLUTIONS COULD NOT BE
> VICTORIOUS. . . . BUT THE INTERNATIONAL REVOLUTION IS CONTINUING TO
> SPREAD. . . . ONLY A FEW DAYS AGO THE EYES OF THE WORLD TURNED TO
> AUSTRIA, HUNGARY, AND POLAND, WHERE POPULAR UPRISINGS SHOOK THE
> THRONES OF TSARS THERE.

Now we have more wonderful news:

> IN VYBORG, HELSINGFORS, TAMMERFORS, AND SEVERAL OTHER CITIES IN FIN-
> LAND, FINNISH RED GUARDS ARE STRIKING BLOW AFTER BLOW AT FINNISH
> CAPITALISTS. . . . THE SAME THING IS HAPPENING IN SOUTHERN FRANCE . . .
> [AND] HUGE STRIKES HAVE ERUPTED IN ENGLAND . . . THE WORLD REVOLU-
> TION IS NEAR.[53]

And the most hoped for news of all came on 19 January:

> THE TELEGRAPH HAS BROUGHT NEWS THAT THE REVOLUTIONARY MOVEMENT
> IN GERMANY HAS BEGUN AND IS DEVELOPING WITH LIGHTNING SPEED. . . . THE
> WORLD REVOLUTION IS MARCHING TRIUMPHANTLY FORWARD, AND NOW THERE
> IS NO DOUBT THAT FINAL VICTORY IS NEAR.[54]

This wave of welcome tidings peaked on 21 January, when *Krasnaia gazeta*'s front-page headline read:

THE UPRISING OF THE PEOPLES OF ALL COUNTRIES AND NATIONALITIES
CONTINUES TO EXPAND. . . .
ONLY A FEW DAYS AGO THE RUSSIAN REVOLUTION SEEMED TERRIBLY ISO-
LATED. . . .
AND NOW?
NOW NEWLY EMERGING FORCES ARE STRIKING AT THE REAR OF OUR COM-
MON ENEMIES. . . . SWING THE BATTERING RAM OF WORLD REVOLUTION EVER
HARDER.[55]

Left Communists were thrilled by signs of expanding revolutionary unrest in Europe, which seemed to vindicate their position on peace. They may
also have been heartened by the decision of the Sovnarkom, on 15 January,
to begin forming a "Worker-Peasant Red Army," and by the creation of a
collegium in the People's Commissariat for Military Affairs to coordinate
the implementation of this decision.[56] At the same time, the treatment of the
peace issue at the Congress of Soviets made them wary of the possibility that
Lenin would yet somehow realize his aim of concluding a separate peace
with imperialist Germany, despite the views of a majority of party members
and the seemingly decisive events abroad. Conclusion of such a peace, in
their view, could not be allowed. On 15 January, a dozen of the most influential Left Communists signed a statement demanding that a national party
conference be called within a week to make a definitive decision on the peace
issue. If a treaty was signed before such a conference was convened, they announced their determination to resign from their high posts in the party and
government.[57]

On the same day (15 January), the Executive Commission of the Petersburg Committee issued a similarly strong declaration. Signed by Kossior,
Gleb Bokii, Fenigshtein, Ravich, and Afanasii Pluzhnikov (all Left Communists), it reflected the Petrograd organization's profound distrust of the
Central Committee:

TO THE CENTRAL COMMITTEE OF THE RSDRP:
The political line [on peace] now being pursued by the Central Committee,
which, judging by the resolution of the Bolshevik fraction in the [Third] Congress, is directed toward conclusion of a so-called "obscene" peace would result in the abdication of our principles . . . and the certain death of our party as
revolutionary vanguard. . . . On behalf of the Petersburg organization, the Executive Commission strongly protests the basic direction [of our peace nego-
tiations] and the practice of secrecy even from responsible bodies of our largest party organizations.
    We have ample grounds for asserting that signing an "obscene" peace
would run counter to the opinion of the majority in the party. . . . If our present peace policy continues . . . a split threatens our party. With this in mind,

the Executive Commission demands that a special party conference be convened immediately. [I]n the present situation, only it can define our stance on peace.[58]

The full Petersburg Committee held a long discussion of the peace issue at a meeting with "active party workers" around 18 January. Successive meetings of the Petersburg Committee to discuss "war or peace" were convened during the second half of January. At the first meeting Bukharin presented the main report on the issue. From his other statements and writings during this period, it is clear that in this report he would have fiercely opposed signing an annexationist peace and may have supported a "no war, no peace" strategy, while appealing for intensified efforts to prepare for early revolutionary war. He may also have encouraged pressuring the Central Committee for an early party conference. However, a statement Bukharin made to the Central Committee indicates he was not sympathetic to the implicit threat of a party split embodied in the Executive Commission's declaration of 15 January.[59]

The Petersburg Committee's consideration of the peace question at its meeting around 18 January concluded with the passage, by a unanimous vote with one abstention, of another set of theses on the matter. These theses, drafted by Bukharin, did not directly address the issue of Trotsky's "no war, no peace" formula or the question of immediate revolutionary war. Nor did they call for a national party conference on peace policy. Rather, they focused on refuting, from an internationalist perspective and in light of the latest news from abroad, Lenin's arguments for concluding an immediate separate peace. Negotiations were in progress at Brest-Litovsk and so this was Bukharin's primary concern.

These theses specified that the only valid criteria for accepting or rejecting an unfavorable, annexationist peace was to follow a course that was best for the development of the proletarian revolution; that the international proletarian movement was at that moment experiencing a decisive breakthrough that had been furthered by the peace negotiations, and this would be destroyed were an "obscene peace" to be accepted; that even revolutionary Russia's defeat at the front would benefit the world revolution by further revolutionizing the forces of her adversaries; and that the idea that peace would provide a breathing space that would insure the survival of Soviet power in Russia was an illusion and that international imperialism would attack revolutionary Russia as soon as it could.[60]

How to respond to the demands for a party conference was at the top of the agenda at a meeting of the Bolshevik Central Committee on 19 January

(1 February).[61] All the participants at this meeting acknowledged the gravity of the intraparty crisis over the question of war or peace and seemed determined not to allow it to develop into a formal split. Beyond this, there was little unanimity over how best to proceed. Early on, Lenin suggested that ultimately his government would probably sign a peace treaty on German terms and that as far as he was concerned he had a mandate to do so from the Third All-Russian Congress of Soviets.[62] Lenin's strategy for dealing with demands to convene an official party conference immediately, as it evolved during this session, was to call for another meeting of the Central Committee with party leaders from major provincial organizations still in Petrograd for the Soviet Congress as soon as possible and to hold out the prospect of an eventual national party congress. Although the decision of a party congress would be authoritative and binding on the new Central Committee elected there, preparing a congress required at least a month's lead time. Consequently, even a congress convened at the earliest possible date would probably be too late to tie Lenin's hands in negotiations with the Germans.

In one way or another Stalin, Sverdlov, Stasova, Artem, and Sokolnikov registered their support for Lenin's point of view. Trotsky was back at Brest by this time. Left Communists participating in this meeting rejected Lenin's premises regarding his government's mandate in peace negotiations. Even before Lenin spoke, Lomov justified convening a conference on the grounds that speeches by Trotsky and especially Zinoviev at the Soviet Congress had led many party members to suspect that a separate peace with Germany had already been decided. Therefore, Lomov said, it was "necessary to hear the voice of the [entire] party, which had been silent for so long."[63] Moreover, as soon as Lenin yielded the floor, Uritskii insisted that "Trotsky's point of view prevailed at the Congress of Soviets" and was "the same one adopted by the Central Committee." The Left Communists unanimously agreed that the Bolshevik peace policy was in chaos and that only an official party conference could straighten it out. At the 19 January Central Committee meeting, Bukharin and Lomov made these points most forcefully. Ultimately the Central Committee scheduled an emergency party congress for 20 February (5 March) and another unofficial conference for 21 January, where all the major differences on the peace issue would again be aired.

The fourteen participants at the Central Committee's conference of 21 January voted on ten questions. Only five participants—Lenin, Stalin, Muranov, Artem, and Sokolnikov—approved signing an immediate, annexationist peace. A large majority, including Lenin, perhaps influenced momentarily by revolutionary events abroad,[64] were in favor of dragging out the negotiations. Only Innokentii Stukov wanted to break off the negotiations at once. A majority felt it would be permissible to sign an annexationist peace if it were presented in the form of an ultimatum. Only the Left Communists Osinskii and Stukov voted no on this question. Bukharin and Uritskii appear to have left the meeting before the voting, but the result on this question would have been the same even had they voted against it. Based on the questions posed, one surmises that the "no war, no peace" strategy guiding Trotsky's actions at Brest was no longer in dispute. Beyond that, the voting pattern accurately reflected the sharp differences over the peace issue then dividing the party.[65]

Everything now appeared to hinge on revolutionary developments in Europe and, of course, the negotiations at Brest-Litovsk. Trotsky had returned to Brest on 17 (30) January. The resumption of negotiations coincided with Bolshevik military successes in Finland and Ukraine. It also coincided with the eruption of revolutionary unrest in Europe—all of which appeared to bode well for the Russians. But this momentarily promising situation did not last long. Most significant, the all-important labor strikes and revolutionary protest movements in Germany were quickly and severely suppressed. This development restored Lenin's conviction of the need to accept Germany's peace terms as quickly as possible. Another written update on the state of Russian troops at the front and in rear garrisons, which Krylenko submitted to the Sovnarkom at this time, reinforced this conviction. Meanwhile, at Brest, Trotsky and his colleagues sparred with their opposite numbers. Concomitantly, the German General Staff was becoming increasingly impatient. During an adjournment on 23–24 January (4–5 February), discussions between the German and Austro-Hungarian governments, on the one hand, and the German high command, on the other, concluded with the former agreeing to expedite the signing of a separate treaty with the delegation from Ukraine and to present Trotsky with an ultimatum as soon as that was done—in short, to wrap up the peace conference at Brest-Litovsk within a week. Trotsky either had to accept the terms he was offered or hostilities would be resumed—such was the ultimatum that German Foreign Minister Richard von Kühlmann would present to Trotsky.

Despite some last-minute wrangling by moderates on the Austro-Hungarian and German side aimed at providing some measure of legitimacy to the annexationist policies of their governments, the increased influence in the negotiations of the German General Staff represented by General Max Hoffman, and therefore the impossibility of dragging out the negotiations much longer, became apparent to Russian negotiators. On 27 January (9 February), the Central Powers signed a separate pact with Ukraine. The moment Trotsky had been anticipating with great relish followed the next

The Soviet delegation arrives at Brest-Litovsk. Lev Trotsky is in the center surrounded by German officers. David King Collection.

day, 28 January (10 February). With representatives of the Central Powers seemingly lulled into believing that Russia was about to capitulate, Trotsky dropped his "bombshell." He announced that, although Russia declined to sign a formal peace treaty, it considered its state of war with Germany, Austria-Hungary, Bulgaria, and Turkey at an end and was demobilizing its forces.[66]

Later the same day, the chief delegates of the Central Powers gathered for a final meeting. With the exception of General Hoffman, all were strongly disposed toward letting well enough alone. Kühlmann and Czernin took the position that since the Russians, by their declaration, had tacitly agreed that the occupied territories would remain in German hands, there was nothing left to fight for. General Hoffman, however, at the instructions of his military superiors, insisted that since the purpose of the armistice with Russia was to arrange a peace, inasmuch as this had not been accomplished, the truce was over and hostilities needed to be resumed in the seven days that were provided for in the truce agreement.[67]

The Germans argued into the night while the Russian delegates went to the railway station for the return trip to Petrograd, confident, if not entirely certain, that for Russia the long, awful nightmare of the Great War was over. Just before leaving Brest, Trotsky dashed off a telegram to Krylenko at Russian staff headquarters in Mogilev informing him of what had transpired and instructing him to issue demobilization orders, which Krylenko promptly did. At Lenin's insistence, the orders were rescinded the next day, but their psychological impact in further undermining the already hopelessly demoralized state of the army could not be undone. Moments before departing, the Russian delegates' hopes for peace were reinforced by word that moderation was being pressed on the military by German and Austro-Hungarian diplomats. And so they chuckled with pleasure as they settled into their railway carriage, congratulated one another on the marvelous trick they had played on German imperialism, and relaxed. "On the return trip to Petrograd we were all under the impression that the Germans would not start an offensive," recalled Trotsky many years later.[68]

*   *   *

At the end of September and the first weeks of October 1917, one of Lenin's main arguments for the immediate seizure of power was that every European country was on the threshold of a proletarian revolution and that the Bolsheviks in Russia, by virtue of their advantageous situation, had an opportunity and obligation to trigger that revolution. The Bolsheviks, he insisted, by waiting for the Congress of Soviets to remove the Provisional Government, were betraying the international revolutionary cause.

In early December 1917, when separate peace negotiations between Germany and the Soviet government began at Brest-Litovsk, Lenin still believed in the immediacy of decisive socialist revolutions in Europe. By the end of the month, however, the answering revolutions he had confidently expected had not materialized, the utter demoralization of the Russian army at the front had been confirmed, and the expansion of counterrevolutionary forces on the Don had begun. In view of all this, Lenin concluded that immediate peace on Germany's terms was essential for revolutionary Russia's survival. Unfortunately for him, however, many of his closest comrades in the party's leadership bodies—in Petrograd, Moscow, and around the country—remained wedded to his earlier fervent internationalism (this was most definitely the case with leaders of the Bolshevik Petersburg Committee). Convinced that a separate peace with the Kaiser's government would undermine the revolution in Germany for years to come, that fighting a revolutionary war, however painful, was feasible, and that the socialist revolution in Russia could not survive on its own, the Left Communists firmly rejected Lenin's insistence on peace at any price.

In these circumstances, Trotsky's "no war, no peace" stratagem—the premise that if revolutionary Russia simply declared that the war had ended and demobilized unilaterally, the Kaiser's government would be unable to get its troops to fight and the war would be over for Russia—won broad acceptance among Bolsheviks and Left SRs. In mid January, majorities in the leadership of both parties (though not Lenin) accepted Trotsky's approach. After the suppression of an initially promising wave of labor unrest in Europe, on 28 January (9 February) Trotsky sprung his declaration on astonished German negotiators at Brest and returned to Petrograd optimistic that his adversaries had been outwitted. But, of course, everything hinged on the German response.

6

"The Socialist Fatherland Is in Danger"

FIRST WORD OF Trotsky's sensational declaration of an end to the war and its apparent acceptance by the Central Powers reached Smolny by direct wire around midnight, 28/29 January. At once, Zinoviev issued an exultant statement to the press that must have been as puzzling to reporters as Trotsky's statement had been to representatives of the Central Powers in Brest. Asked by a mystified correspondent what the phrase "no war, no peace" meant in practice, he confidently explained that it amounted to an extension of the armistice. "In our view the Central Powers will be unable to launch an offensive because their laboring masses will not support such a step," he said, quickly adding that "continually annexing foreign territory is not in Germany and Austria's interests."[1] As Shteinberg recalled, "a proud calm, compounded by anxiety, descended on Petrograd."[2]

The next morning, all Petrograd buzzed with news of the unprecedented developments at Brest. Emergency meetings of the Bolshevik and Left SR Central Committees endorsed Trotsky's move.[3] At a meeting of the Petrograd Soviet, Mikhail Lashevich, a former member of the Bolshevik Military Organization who was then a military commissar, declared flatly, "German troops will not attack those who have proclaimed to the whole world that they are unwilling to shed the blood of their brothers."[4] A resolution "On the Ending of the War," introduced by Zinoviev and adopted at this meeting, endorsed Russia's position at Brest-Litovsk; appealed to workers in Germany, Austria, Bulgaria, and Turkey to prevent the imperialist powers from doing violence to the peoples of Poland, Lithuania, and Kurland; and proclaimed the formation of a new Red Socialist Army as the main task of the day. Nonetheless, the immediate concern of the resolution seemed to be less with the recruitment for a new army than with bringing some semblance of order to the demobilized rabble from the old army now streaming home from the front by the hundreds of thousands.[5]

Predictably, assessments of the implications of Trotsky's act at Brest varied in the Petrograd press. Liberal and moderate socialist dailies, which, from the start, had been wary of separate peace talks with the enemy, condemned Trotsky's move as a disaster, fated to bring new trials, torment, and degradation to an already devastated, defenseless Russia. "The beginning of the end of the revolution," the Mensheviks' *Novyi luch* called it. On the other hand, the Bolshevik press greeted the news from Brest with unrestrained glee. According to a *Krasnaia gazeta* headline, the war was over:

ON THE DAY AFTER THE END OF THE WAR

We are experiencing the day after the end of the war . . . The Russian ploughman can now return to the land for which he has been thirsting. The Russian worker can return to the city he left long ago. All the people of Russia can now occupy themselves with building their new free life.[6]

The Left SR press, like the Bolshevik dailies, tended to dismiss the possibility that the German government would be able to resume offensive operations on the Eastern front, however much it might wish to. "After such a declaration [as Trotsky's] it will be difficult for the German general staff to get its troops to attack Russia, because there is no way to justify an invasion and the German soldier will know that he is only fighting for annexationist spoils benefiting the bourgeoisie," wrote a *Znamia truda* editor on 30 January. "Now that peace negotiations have broken down exclusively because of the Central Powers, revolutionary movements will naturally erupt more powerfully than ever."[7]

Of course, for the Western allies, who were preparing a decisive spring and summer offensive on the Western front, a halt to hostilities in the East was an altogether unhappy prospect. A couple of weeks earlier the British Foreign Office, for one, had dispatched an experienced young Russian hand, Robert Bruce Lockhart, as its special envoy to Petrograd. Lockhart's primary mission was to persuade the Soviet government to maintain the common allied war effort. At the same time, British naval authorities charged their new naval attaché in Petrograd, Captain Francis Cromie, with directing the evacuation of allied war materiel from the Baltic region. Cromie was fresh from illustrious duty as commander of a British submarine flotilla that had operated in collaboration with Russian naval forces in the Baltic.[8] As naval attaché, he reported to Admiral Reginald "Blinker" Hall, the head of Naval Intelligence. Yet, Cromie had no previous experience in espionage, subversion, or even diplomacy. In August, Latvian officers turned Cheka informants would betray his confidence and compromise his efforts to overthrow Soviet power in the Northwest. Cromie was probably also double-crossed

Captain Francis Cromie, British naval attaché in Petrograd, on a sleigh ride during the winter of 1917–18. Moura Benckendorff, alleged Cheka informer, is at left. Courtesy of the RN Submarine Museum, Gosport.

by Maria (Moura) Benckendorff, a seductive Russian national employed as a clerk and translator by the British Embassy. Circumstantial evidence strongly suggests that Moura, who became Lockhart's lover, was a Cheka informer.[9] "A kind of gramophone for all the infernal gossip in the embassy" was how she described Cromie in a letter to Lockhart.[10]

Trotsky, Radek, and Karelin returned to Petrograd from Brest at 5:00 AM on 31 January. Trotsky went at once to Smolny, where he briefed Lenin on the final stages of the negotiations. Trotsky and Karelin also reported on the negotiations to the combined Bolshevik and Left SR CEC fractions and to the Sovnarkom later in the day, and to a special session of the full CEC the next night,[11] 1/14 February, the first day on the new calendar.[12]

Trotsky presented a detailed account of his tactics at Brest to the CEC. The wave of strikes that hit Germany and Austria-Hungary in January had momentarily enhanced Russia's negotiating position and weakened Germany's. However, after the suppression of this unrest, the German delegation had renewed its expansionist demands as forcefully as ever. In the final stages of the negotiations, the position of the Russian delegation had been further undermined by the independence of the Ukrainian delegation and by candid Russian press reports on the continuing disintegration of the Russian army. After consummation of the agreement between the Central Powers and the Ukrainian delegation on 27 January/9 February, it was obvious that the Germans would not budge from their demands and therefore an end to the negotiations could no longer be delayed. This being the case, Trotsky made his withdrawal statement.

With undisguised glee Trotsky described the shocked reactions of his adversaries, as well as the sentiments of hand-picked German soldiers stationed in Brest who, he said, had taken pains to assure him that revolutionary Russia need not fear a German attack. Even their officers declared that it would be impossible to get them to advance against Russia. Although Trotsky warned against wholly excluding the possibility of renewed German military operations, he made it clear that this did not seem likely. He had personally toured the Russian lines and was appalled by the chaos and anarchy he observed among the troops. As a result, he did not share the illusion common to Left Communists that, if attacked, Russian soldiers would defend the revolution. For him, the aim of immediate, open, and comprehensive demobilization was to demonstrate to the entire world Soviet Russia's unequivocal determination to end its participation in the war and to put the burden of protecting the Russian revolution, if that became necessary, squarely on Europe's revolutionary masses.[13]

Karelin emphasized to the CEC that the fundamental problem facing the Russian delegation at Brest was not to expose the rapacious terms offered by the Central Powers, which was easy, but to demand more than simply a return to the prewar territorial status quo. Essentially, the latter did not correspond to socialist principles that called for peace without annexations and indemnities, and the right of self-determination for all peoples, regardless of when they lost their independence, as stipulated in the Decree on Peace of the Second All-Russian Congress of Soviets and subsequently reaffirmed.[14] Trotsky's final statement at Brest had flowed naturally from this conundrum. As a result of Russia's stance at Brest, the Russian revolution had become a beacon for enslaved peoples everywhere, Karelin continued. To illustrate this point, he described the friendly welcome he and Trotsky had received in Warsaw when they visited there during a break in the deliberations at Brest. At a popular level, previous hostility to Russia had been replaced by reverence for the Russian revolution. Acknowledging that the gamble implicit in simply declaring that the war was over and refusing to sign a peace treaty risked provoking a renewed offensive, Karelin, like Trotsky, was dubious about the possibility that German soldiers on the Eastern front could be used in an attack.[15]

Responding to Trotsky and Karelin, Pumpianskii, on behalf of the SRs, praised the Brest delegation for not signing a separate peace; yet he still considered the results of the negotiations unsatisfactory, since they had left the front wide open to German invasion. Just as he had done in the Constituent Assembly, amid derisive shouts he called for the organization of an international socialist peace conference in Stockholm and the formation of a united popular front government through the Constituent Assembly.

Speaking for the Left SRs, Shteinberg gave Soviet diplomacy higher marks, arguing that the toilers of Europe and America were revolutionary Russia's natural allies and that, as a result of Brest, bonds with them would be stronger than ever. Rejecting Pumpianskii's plea for the re-convocation of the Constituent Assembly, Shteinberg nonetheless echoed his call for an immediate, broadly based socialist peace conference in Stockholm, as well as for an end to unnecessary domestic strife in preparation for the possible renewal of hostilities by the Central Powers. Russia must be ready to mount an adequate defense, he warned. "For this to occur, it is necessary, first of all, to end the civil war within the democracy which is now tearing our country apart."

Martov took issue with Trotsky's implication that the Austro-Germans were weaker after the Brest negotiations than they had been at the start. To him, all signs pointed to the contrary. Although implicitly approving of the "no war, no peace" formula, he insisted on the necessity of taking account of the strengthened confidence of the Central Powers vis-à-vis revolutionary Russia and, above all, on the need to create conditions that would make it possible for all Russian citizens to participate in defending the country from a German invasion.

In his concluding remarks Trotsky, responding to Martov, insisted that primary responsibility for preventing Russia's destruction at the hands of the Germans rested with the German people. Nonetheless, he conceded that, "if necessary, we will have to defend ourselves." A Bolshevik resolution adopted at this meeting endorsed the position taken by the Russian delegation at Brest, and expressed confidence that socialist workers in all countries would approve and that Austro-German workers and soldiers would pursue to a triumphant conclusion the struggle against imperialists and usurpers that had begun in Vienna and Berlin. Warning that the Russian revolution was surrounded by enemies, the resolution pointed to the organization of a free Red Socialist army as one of the critical tasks of the moment.[16] To help explain

Russia's peace policy and build support for it among West European social-ists, Kamenev was now dispatched to Great Britain and France.[17]

The next day (15 February), Trotsky seemed more confident than ever that the Germans would not attack. At an evening plenary session of the Petrograd Soviet, he put the odds on the possibility of the Germans attack-ing at 10 percent as against 90 percent that they would not.[18] The wide-spread assumption among Petrograd Bolsheviks that for Russia the war was over and it was time to give top priority to dealing with domestic crises was reflected in the fact that, on this day, Trotsky assumed responsibility for di-recting food procurement and distribution, revolutionary Russia's thorniest and most threatening domestic problem at the time.[19]

Little did Trotsky know how soon his prediction would be put to a test. The decisive moments in the struggle between German civil and military au-thorities over how to respond to Trotsky's declaration of "no war, no peace" had, in fact, come two days earlier (13 February) at a Crown Council meet-ing, where a debate over policy toward revolutionary Russia culminated in a decision to launch a limited offensive in the east. The aim of this offensive was to advance German lines to Narva and Pskov and, more fundamental, to put "the Bolsheviks in their place." The attack was set for 18 February.[20]

Initial word that Germany's armistice with Russia would expire and that a state of war would be reestablished at noon on the 18th reached Smolny the night of 16 February.[21] Trotsky was in Lenin's office, in conference with Lenin, Karelin, and an unidentified party colleague of Karelin's, when a telegram with the news was received. Lenin, obviously deeply disturbed, si-lently passed the telegram to Trotsky. Recalling this episode in his memoirs, Trotsky wrote that Lenin quickly wound up the meeting, rushed the Left SRs out of his office, and blurted: "They have deceived us after all . . . This wild beast will let nothing escape it."[22]

After Lenin reminded Trotsky that, under the terms of their agree-ment, he was obliged to support immediate consummation of a peace treaty, Trotsky answered that the ability of the Germans to actually launch an at-tack on Russia remained to be tested. Perhaps because of this, for the time being the news was not made public.[23] It was not even brought to the atten-tion of senior military officials responsible for Russia's defense nor was the Sovnarkom informed.[24] Not until the evening of the eighteenth, after Rus-sian intelligence intercepted a telegram to German commanders announc-ing that, as Trotsky had broken the truce, they were to resume offensive op-erations, was the Russian military informed of the developing emergency.[25]

* * *

News of the resumption of the German offensive immediately reopened the enormously divisive question of whether to conclude a separate peace with the Central Powers that had been sidestepped by Trotsky's "no war, no peace" strategy. The renewed debate over this issue, which was constantly reshaped by developments at the front and uncertainty about Germany's ultimate intentions, raged virtually nonstop from 17 to 24 February. It was waged in the press, and in the Bolshevik and Left SR Central committees, the Sovnarkom, the Bolshevik and Left SR CEC fractions, plenary sessions of the CEC, the Petrograd Soviet, the Bolshevik Petersburg Committee, the Fourth City Conference of Petrograd Bolsheviks, Petrograd district soviets and Bolshevik district committees, and among ordinary workers in factories, soldiers in barracks, and sailors at installations and aboard ships of the Baltic Fleet.

The debate began the night of 17/18 February, at a meeting of the Bolshevik Central Committee. Published Central Committee documents for these days include a table indicating how the eleven members who participated voted on a series of questions relating to war and peace. From Lenin's point of view, the most important of these questions was the first—whether the government should offer to reopen peace negotiations, which he understood to mean suing for immediate peace on Germany's terms. Lenin lost on this issue by a 6 to 5 vote.[26] Equally important was the last question—if a German offensive became a reality and if no revolutionary uprisings occurred in Germany and Austria, should peace be concluded? Lenin won this vote; Trotsky made good on his commitment by voting with him.

The Central Committee reevaluated the developing situation at a meeting the next morning (18 February), shortly before German military operations were due to resume. By then, numerous signs of intense German military activity in the vicinity of the front had been reported. Enemy planes had been spotted over Dvinsk, just across the German line, and it appeared that a strike on the major Baltic port of Revel was imminent. German radio had begun to focus on the necessity of protection from the threat of "infection" from the east. Worst of all, from the Central Committee's point of view, nowhere was there any sign of protest, either among German front line forces or in the German rear. Still, the attack had not yet begun. Consequently, because so much time had been spent on contingency issues the previous evening, Sverdlov recommended that the meeting be adjourned until the situation on the ground became clearer. Lenin would have none of that, and, in deference to him, it was agreed to continue the meeting and focus solely on the advisability of straight away sending the Germans a telegram proposing immediate peace. At the end of the debate on this issue, Lenin's demand that

Germany's peace terms be accepted without delay was again defeated by a one-vote margin.[27]

This helps explain the behavior of Bolshevik people's commissars at a Sovnarkom meeting that began early that evening (18/19 February), primarily to deal with the exploding military crisis.[28] In addition to Bolshevik and Left SR cabinet members, among individuals participating in this meeting at one time or another were representatives of the CEC Presidium, the Brest peace delegation, and the general staffs of the "old" army and embryonic Red Army and Navy. With interruptions to allow many of the participants to attend meetings of their central committees, this session of the Sovnarkom lasted through the night and early morning. Much of the discussion appears to have centered on ways to overcome the virtual absence of regular armed forces and defend the revolution from the Germans until help arrived from abroad. Among issues considered were the immediate proclamation of universal mobilization (considered premature because "the intervention" of the German proletariat or of the Reichstag still seemed promising); conclusion of an agreement on defense with the moderate socialist parties (proposed by the Left SRs, rejected by the Bolsheviks); the viability of partisan warfare (deemed unusually strong because "practically everybody had weapons"); and the start of an evacuation of Petrograd (not recommended because it would detract from the defense effort).

As time passed, reports about the unfolding German offensive became increasingly alarming. Within hours, the enemy had captured Dvinsk and Minsk and was advancing on a broad front toward Petrograd. Although the attack forces consisted of small, hastily assembled, irregular detachments, panicked Russian soldiers were offering no resistance and, without stopping to destroy railway lines and bridges, were fleeing pell-mell at the first sign of the German approach. Fewer than a hundred German soldiers were all it took to capture Dvinsk.

The Sovnarkom recessed around midnight. A late night meeting of the Bolshevik Central Committee that began soon after was arranged at the last minute, probably in part because of Lenin's impatience to telegraph acceptance of Germany's peace terms to stave off a German march on Petrograd. At this third Central Committee meeting in twenty-four hours, Lenin launched an unrelenting plea for immediate capitulation.[29] "We cannot wait any longer because the situation has become obvious," he insisted. "Things have reached such a state that the revolution will definitely be crushed if we continue to sit on the fence. . . . If the Germans were to require the overthrow of Bolshevik power, then naturally we would have to fight. [But] further delay is out of the question now."

A meeting of the Sovnarkom, January 1918. Left to right: I. Z. Shteinberg, I. I. Skvortsov-Stepanov, G. F. Fedorov, V. D. Bonch-Bruevich, V. E. Trutovskii, A. G. Shliapnikov, P. P. Proshian, V. I. Lenin, I. V. Stalin (standing), A. M. Kollontai, P. E. Dybenko (standing), E. K. Koksharova, N. I. Podvoiskii, N. P. Gorbunov, V. I. Nevskii, V. I. Shotman, and G. B. Chicherin. Jonathan Sanders Collection.

Lenin's main adversary at this meeting, as it was to be throughout the Brest crisis, was Bukharin who, despite his youth, was not in the least intimidated. Taking the floor, Bukharin suggested that Lenin and those who favored peace at virtually any price were succumbing to panic, when, in reality, nothing unexpected was happening. The forces of imperialism were bent on suppressing the revolution before it spread further. Now, it was critical to rise to the inevitable fight. As Bukharin put it, "events are developing exactly as they were bound to. . . . We foresaw everything. We said that either the Russian revolution would spread, or it would die under the pressure of imperialism."

Lenin deemed Bukharin's arguments hopelessly utopian. "If we are not ready [for a revolutionary war], we must agree to peace," he fumed. "Even if the Germans were to tack on such new demands as noninterference in the affairs of Ukraine, Finland, Livonia, and Estonia," he concluded, "it would be absolutely essential to unconditionally accept even that." For Lenin, that was the price of survival! Saving the revolution in Russia as a beachhead for the international revolution was all that mattered.

While agreeing with Lenin that combating the Germans with the rag-tag forces at the Soviet government's disposal was impossible, Trotsky still held out hope that European workers would come to the rescue. At the Central Committee the night of 18/19 February, evidently to buy time, he urged that, instead of Russia capitulating at once, notes should be sent to Berlin and Vienna inquiring into the nature of their demands. Trotsky appears to have believed that articulation of these demands would have propaganda value. However, after it became clear that this idea was unacceptable to either of the contending sides, he again fulfilled his part of the bargain with Lenin. By a vote of 7 to 5, with 1 abstention, Trotsky provided the swing vote and the Bolshevik Central Committee reversed itself, now recommending that the German government be informed immediately of Russia's readiness to sign a peace. Lenin and Trotsky were delegated to draft a message to this effect. A short time later, the Left SR Central Committee, with only six of its fifteen members present, voted for peace and approved dispatch of the surrender message already drafted by Lenin and Trotsky.[30]

Despite these decisions, by all accounts, the strength of opposition to Lenin in the Sovnarkom, after it reconvened, does not appear to have changed appreciably. In the face of deepening gloom over reports of the speed of the German advance, the emphasis remained on resistance.[31] Toward morning, when the possibility of suing for peace was apparently first put forward for immediate action, the idea triggered a fresh round of bitter debate. Lenin, now joined by Trotsky, led the fight for immediate surrender. Shteinberg and Pavel Dybenko emerged as the main proponents of revolutionary war. At times, the atmosphere became so contentious, and the chasm over fundamental principles between the two sides so wide, that it seemed to one observer that some of the people's commissars would have to resign. At the end of the meeting, by which time the number of people's commissars present had dwindled to nine, "immediate peace" was agreed upon by a one-vote margin.[32] Without consulting the CEC, Lenin and Trotsky immediately radioed a message to Berlin conveying the Sovnarkom's readiness to sign a peace treaty according to the terms proposed at Brest-Litovsk.[33]

How did political groups other than the Bolsheviks and Left SRs react? Virtually all of them had responded to news of the German offensive by declaring their readiness to ignore past conflicts and band together to defend the country against the foreign foe. It is not surprising, then, that their response to news of Russia's capitulation little more than twenty-four hours later produced a tidal wave of outrage. In the harshest terms, the Kadet, SR, and Menshevik press condemned the government's acceptance of German peace terms and demanded that the Constituent Assembly be reconvened immediately.

To Lenin, fierce antagonism toward his policies on the part of liberal and moderate socialist groups was to be expected. More troubling and potentially disastrous was the depth of the fury expressed by large and critically important segments of his own party and by the Left SRs, triggered by the decision to give in to the Germans without a fight. The continued explosiveness of the issue was instantly apparent at caucuses of the Bolshevik and Left SR CEC fractions on the afternoon of 19 February, convened to define positions on the government's peace policy which would be considered at a plenary meeting of the CEC that evening. In addition to the already familiar differences over the issue of an immediate annexationist peace versus revolutionary war between the Leninists and Left Communists, and between similar Left SR groupings, bitter complaints emerged at these fraction meetings over procedural matters connected with the dispatch of the already infamous Lenin-Trotsky radio message. Both Bolshevik and Left SR critics of capitulation objected that the Sovnarkom had decided a fundamental, critical policy issue without a quorum, by a one-vote margin, and without the involvement of the CEC. Even Sverdlov, normally Lenin's most trusted and pliant lieutenant, protested the dispatch of the Lenin-Trotsky telegram without the CEC's endorsement.[34] The large Left SR fraction was so incensed that it immediately renewed its efforts to fundamentally strengthen the CEC's powers to control the actions of the Sovnarkom and individual commissariats. Also, although there was no denying that the Left SR Central Committee had agreed to the dispatch of the Lenin-Trotsky message, many Left SR deputies were roiled that their own leadership's action was decided by a tiny fraction of its members.[35]

Thus, the pivotal question at issue in Bolshevik and Left SR caucuses the afternoon of 19 February was whether the Lenin-Trotsky message accepting German peace terms should be rescinded and the entire issue reconsidered. This question was thoroughly divisive in both the Bolshevik and Left SR camps. At the start, advocates of revolutionary war (or, as the Left SRs preferred to call it, an "uprising against imperialism") were stronger among Left SRs than within the Bolshevik fraction. Still, on the night of 19 February, as a result of continuing bitter debate in both fractions, the possibility of getting the full CEC to go along with immediate peace on German terms was so problematic, and the potential so great for a bloody battle with disastrous consequences for the Bolshevik–Left SR governing coalition and even for the existing structure of government, that at the eleventh hour the Bolshevik

CEC leadership canceled the evening plenum. It was replaced by a highly unusual closed joint meeting of the Bolshevik and Left SR CEC fractions.[36]

Lenin delivered a two-hour address at the meeting, marshaling every conceivable argument on behalf of immediate peace. However, his opponents, led by Sergei Mstislavskii for the Left SRs and Radek for the Bolsheviks, remained unconvinced by his reasoning, and reportedly, at around midnight, the two fractions went their separate ways, with the anti-Leninists ascendant. The fractions met intermittently, both separately and jointly, throughout the night and the following day. Both received closed-door briefings by Krylenko, who was adamant on the need for immediate surrender. His presentations appear to have had little appreciable impact. For the time being, neither fraction was able to muster a consensus.[37]

If continuing debate and indecision remained the watchword among Bolshevik and Left SR CEC fractions in the Taurida Palace, the same was not the case elsewhere in Petrograd. Very soon after the resumption of the German offensive, the Bolshevik Petersburg Committee canvased all its district committees. With the exception of the party committee in the Vyborg district, where views were divided, large majorities in all the other party committees opposed surrender.[38] By coincidence, the start of this new military crisis coincided with the deliberations of the Fourth City Conference of Petrograd Bolsheviks. This gathering, in which the Petersburg Committee and elected representatives of district party committees participated, had opened on 17 February. At that time, party membership was estimated to be thirty-six thousand, a drop of around twelve thousand since the beginning of the year.[39] However, this was an approximation, as no effort had been made to track membership—most important, to monitor the continuing outflow from Petrograd of party veterans that had begun with the seizure of power. Then, too, a high percentage of longtime Bolsheviks still in the city was engaged in full-time government or military service; for practical purposes, their ties to the party organization had been severed.

To compensate for these losses, participants in the city conference adopted new party regulations.[40] The Petersburg Committee's size was reduced from forty or more members elected by district committees on the basis of proportional representation to nine members elected at large at quarterly city conferences. Thus, not all of the sixteen district party committees were now represented in the Petersburg Committee. The new statutes provided for the creation of a wholly new representative Delegates Soviet, composed largely of elected delegates from district committees, one per five hundred members, to offset this change. It was to replace the Petersburg Committee as the most authoritative local party body between quarterly city conferences. At about the same time, an advisory body was created that had not even been mentioned in the new regulations, the Assembly of [Party] Organizers. It was to be convened at the discretion of the Petersburg Committee and was composed of paid responsible organizers from each district. Perhaps partly because some of these responsible organizers doubled as district party committee secretaries, a disproportionate number of them were dedicated young women.[41]

Although the Assembly of Organizers endured,[42] the elective Delegates Soviet never functioned as envisioned.[43] As a result, the reduction and reshaping of the Petrograd party organization at the Fourth City Conference of Petrograd Bolsheviks appears in retrospect to have been a major step in the destruction of the relative internal democracy which was a major source of the Bolsheviks' strength in 1917. Still, in the context of the raging controversy over the acceptance of Germany's peace terms, the most germane point is that, like the Petersburg Committee, the city party conference was dominated by Left Communists. It is not surprising, therefore, that on 20 February it turned to the government's controversial decision to sue for peace.[44] After Lenin and Radek presented the contending views on peace or war, the conferees did not even debate them. Discarding as irrelevant Lenin's warning that "the cream of the Petrograd proletariat would be sacrificed in a struggle against the Germans," the conference adopted a sharply worded resolution censuring the Central Committee and demanding that the Sovnarkom's decision to accept Germany's peace terms be revoked.[45]

In many ways, the most ominous protest against the Sovnarkom's peace policy at this time was contained in a statement, in effect a declaration of war on the Bolshevik Central Committee majority, signed by four minority Central Committee members (Bukharin, Uritskii, Lomov, and Bubnov) and seven other prominent party leaders (Iakovleva, Pokrovskii, Smirnov, Piatakov, Mecheslav Bronskii, and Andrei Spunde). Their statement condemned the willingness of the Central Committee majority to conclude peace on German terms as a "particularly vicious blow to the cause of the international proletariat" that would inevitably result "in the destruction of all the work the [Russian] proletariat had accomplished in building socialism since the October revolution." From Lenin's point of view, perhaps most alarming of all was that the signatories declared their determination to agitate within the party against the peace policy pursued by the majority with the avowed aim of reversing it at an early party congress.[46]

Similarly defiant, anti-peace/pro-war resolutions were also adopted at this time by Left SR national and local-level party committees. Most important, on 20 February, a solid majority of the Left SR Central Committee expressed opposition to a separate peace, thereby reversing the position it adopted the night of 18/19 February. The usually reliable *Novaia zhizn'* reported that feelings against acceptance of a separate peace at this meeting ran so high that a majority was ready to immediately distance itself from the Bolsheviks unless Lenin and Trotsky annulled the acceptance of Germany's terms.[47]

Soon after the Left SR Central Committee reversal, a consensus favoring revolutionary war crystallized in the Left SR CEC fraction.[48] Moreover, at roughly the same time, the balance of power in the Bolshevik CEC fraction, allegedly influenced by developments at the Petrograd City party conference, shifted even more strongly toward the Left Communists.[49]

*　*　*

Contributing to the increasing militancy in both the Bolshevik and Left SR camps in the first days after the dispatch of the Lenin-Trotsky surrender telegram was that the German government was clearly in no hurry to respond to it. Its forces were continuing to advance along a broad front, seizing town after town along the major railway lines to Riga, Revel, and Pskov. Very quickly, Petrograd itself appeared in imminent danger of an attack for which it was psychologically and militarily unprepared.

Word of the German offensive caught the Soviet government and authorities at the People's Commissariat for Military Affairs by surprise. More sensitive than anyone else except perhaps Lenin to Russia's vulnerability, military officials appear to have spent the days immediately following Trotsky's proclamation of "no war, no peace" hoping against hope that the Germans would let well enough alone. Efforts to bring some semblance of order to demobilization of the old army and to begin building a new, socialist Red army had gone badly. In memoirs written many years later Il'in-Zhenevskii recalled his feelings during those days of anxious waiting: "Each day that went by peacefully instilled fresh hope and then, as though out of a clear sky, came the thunderclap. The Germans started to advance, and pressed with incredible speed toward Petrograd." "I shall never forget the heavy, oppressed mood that came over our people in the party and soviets," he continued. "It seemed to many that all was now lost, that we were going to be crushed by the armed might of German imperialism, and that the Soviet Republic was doomed to become a German colony." One of the first people to succumb to the prevailing despair was Il'in-Zhenevskii's wife. On 20 February, she shot herself.[50]

Late the night of 19/20 February, the Sovnarkom had discussed possibilities of organizing a defense and waging a revolutionary war in the event this became necessary.[51] Reportedly, this discussion focused less on the feasibility of mounting defensive operations in the traditional sense than on the prospects for surviving until the German proletariat was able to "strike German imperialism from the rear." Moreover, in view of the ongoing debacle in clashes between German forces, on the one hand, and elements of the old army, the Red Guard, and hastily assembled Red Army units, on the other, partisan warfare was again raised as a promising strategy.[52] The successful advance of Antonov-Ovseenko's irregular forces on the Don no doubt strengthened such thinking.

On 20 February, the Sovnarkom listened to reports from Krylenko and Vasilii Altfater, deputy naval chief-of-staff, on the expanding chaos at the front and adopted contingency measures aimed at mobilizing the population of Petrograd for the defense of the capital, building a war chest, and evacuating citizens unsuited for military service. Also, at the initiative of the Left SRs, the Sovnarkom formed a Provisional Executive Committee composed of Lenin, Trotsky, and Stalin for the Bolsheviks, and Karelin and Prosh Proshian for the Left SRs, to act in the Sovnarkom's name between its meetings during the emergency.[53]

A three-hour emergency plenary session of the Petrograd Soviet in Smolny the night of 21/22 February reflected the dilemma then facing Bolsheviks who favored immediate peace, namely, they needed to allow for the seemingly dwindling possibility that the Germans might yet agree to acceptable surrender terms, while at the same time mobilizing workers, soldiers, and peasants for what looked increasingly like a life-and-death struggle for the survival of the revolution.[54] Zinoviev's primary purpose in convening this session was to obtain its backing for acceptance of Germany's terms. The Bolshevik fraction in the Petrograd Soviet hammered out its position on this issue at a bitterly contentious caucus which ran so much longer than planned that it delayed the plenary session for more than two hours. Still essentially free of external party control, the fraction was not constrained by the Central Committee's narrow vote for peace the night of 18/19 February or by the city party conference's resounding commitment to revolutionary war on the twentieth. Zinoviev, aided by Lashevich, pushed hard to swing the group to Lenin's point of view. Radek and Riazanov led the fight for the Left Communists, appealing to the fraction to withhold approval of the Lenin-Trotsky radio message and insist that the Sovnarkom and the CEC cease dealing with the Germans and concentrate on military defense. Judging by the applause, the group's sympathy was with Radek and Riazanov.

However, it voted with Zinoviev and Lashevich. This decision was binding on the entire fraction; as the caucus dispersed, Zinoviev was unyielding on this point.[55]

Zinoviev opened the plenary session with a long and spirited defense of the government's action.[56] "To our great shame," he said candidly, "we must acknowledge that our soldiers are putting up virtually no resistance whatsoever. . . . [W]e have had cases where groups of *unarmed* German soldiers have dispersed hundreds of our troops" (emphasis in original). At the same time, he insisted that if the Germans did not allow Russia a breathing space, there would be no choice but to defend the revolution "to the last man and the last bullet." Throughout his speech Zinoviev shifted back and forth between these two tactically incompatible positions: on the one hand, the absolute necessity of immediate surrender; on the other, the critical importance of putting all other concerns aside in the interests of revolutionary defense. Zinoviev placed particular emphasis on the latter, declaiming "The Socialist Fatherland Is in Danger," a resounding appeal for the defense of the revolution published in the Soviet press earlier that day.

Krylenko further documented the expanding disaster at the front and its economic implications. He described the utter chaos prevailing on Russia's railway network, as millions of Russian soldiers fled the battlefield. If this tidal wave of humanity was not somehow brought to a halt, he maintained, famine in Petrograd would become inevitable and any possibility of building socialism would be lost, regardless of how efforts to bring an immediate end to the war developed. Krylenko called for the immediate recruitment and dispatch to the front of large numbers of agitators from among Petrograd's most experienced and effective workers and soldiers. If these agitators were successful in restoring some order among front troops, he intimated, this would ease the deepening food supply crisis and facilitate the defense of Petrograd, if that became necessary.[57]

Following these speeches by Zinoviev and Krylenko, representatives of all fractions in the Petrograd Soviet were given time to present their positions, and Mikhail Levinson for the Left SRs, and Efrem Berg for the SRs and Mensheviks, introduced resolutions reflecting them. Levinson's resolution demanded annulment of the Lenin-Trotsky message and mobilization of all the country's forces to fight the Germans, prompting Zinoviev to rebuke the Left SRs for breaking ranks with the revolution "at one of its most critical moments." Berg's joint SR-Menshevik resolution called for the immediate appointment of a new, broadly representative government, a "second sitting" of the Constituent Assembly, and the convocation of an international socialist peace conference.

For the Bolsheviks, Anton Slutskii introduced a resolution that mirrored the party's tactical dilemma. After endorsing the dispatch of the Lenin-Trotsky telegram, it expressed certainty that the Germans intended to try to crush the revolution. Consequently, the resolution appealed to Petrograd workers and soldiers to "immediately rise to the defense of socialist Russia and her revolutionary capital." The resolution provided for the formation of a Committee for the Revolutionary Defense of Petrograd to direct and coordinate defense preparations.[58] And, finally, it called on district soviets to form groups of agitators for dispatch to the front, to try to bring some order into the demobilization. Those at the meeting voted on the three resolutions, and the Bolshevik resolution passed. The composition of the Committee for the Revolutionary Defense of Petrograd was also agreed on, and it assumed most functions connected with the direction of defense preparations.[59]

* * *

At 10:00 PM the night of 21/22 February, at precisely the time when the Petrograd Soviet began its consideration of the Sovnarkom's peace policy, Sverdlov convened the long-delayed meeting of the CEC, ostensibly to debate the same question.[60] It is imperative not to lose sight of differences in the political significance and complexion of the two meetings. Most important, conflict between the Left SRs and the Bolsheviks in the Petrograd Soviet over the issue of war and peace was undoubtedly awkward; however, Bolsheviks supporting Lenin had a majority. Such divisions in the CEC would probably have resulted in the breakup of the Bolshevik–Left SR coalition, and, indeed, the possibility cannot be excluded that they might have brought down Lenin's government. For at this CEC meeting, owing in part to the absence of many Left Communists, the Left SRs had a clear majority.[61] The individual most responsible for dodging this potentially lethal bullet was the CEC chair, the tactically astute Sverdlov. More sensitive than any of his party colleagues to the volatility of the peace issue, as well as to the CEC's escalating resentment toward the Sovnarkom for its failure to consult it before dispatching the Lenin-Trotsky surrender message, Sverdlov had postponed a CEC meeting until passions had cooled. He seems also to have played a significant role in persuading Lenin of the possible implications of this resentment, and exacted a commitment from Lenin that the Sovnarkom would take the peace negotiations no further without consulting with the CEC in advance, irrespective of the German response.[62]

That even Lenin was becoming resigned to the necessity for defense at the time the CEC Presidium met to plan that evening's plenary session worked to Sverdlov's advantage. On the understanding that the CEC's prerogatives would be observed in any future decisions relating to peace, members of the Presidium leadership, all Bolsheviks and Left SRs, developed an agenda and procedural steps that all but assured that the plenum would be free of significant rancor. It was agreed, in particular, that Sverdlov would begin the meeting with an introductory report on the peace process to date. The CEC would then be asked to put policy differences aside and to adopt a Presidium resolution containing a pro forma endorsement of the government's peace efforts and also expressing confidence that workers, soldiers, and peasants would unite in the defense of "socialist Soviet power, against any and all attacks."[63] Saving the socialist revolution from foreign and domestic foes was to be the motif of the meeting.

This appears to have been the plan, and it went pretty much like clockwork. Although Sverdlov, in his opening report, did not totally exclude the possibility that the Germans might respond to the Lenin-Trotsky telegram with acceptable peace terms, it was clear that he shared the prevailing assumption that this was unlikely. In this spirit, he read aloud a spate of rousing calls to arms already issued by the Sovnarkom (among them, "The Socialist Fatherland Is in Danger"). The recitation of these appeals was intended to illustrate the government's commitment to defend the revolution despite its striving for immediate peace, and to convey an air of imminent military emergency. Sverdlov then announced that, in agreement with the Presidium, he would not open the floor for discussion "since every member of the CEC had already thought and discussed the existing situation quite enough," at which point he also proposed that a resolution endorsing the government's peace efforts and providing for defense of the revolution be adopted without debate. In vain, the Menshevik-Internationalist Raphael Abramovich protested that the resolution proposed by the Presidium failed to address any of the questions relating to peace and war requiring immediate clarification, and asked why the country's highest government institution was not allowed to speak out for two days—indeed, why "the opposition" was still shushed into silence.[64] Only 6 of the 150 members of the CEC at this meeting voted against the Presidium's resolution; all but 1 of the no votes were cast by moderate socialists.[65] With this, the long-awaited CEC plenum ended. It had lasted less than an hour.

* * *

During the night of 22/23 February, the radio station at Tsarskoe Selo, used by Soviet officials for sensitive transmissions because it was the most secure long-distance communication facility in the Petrograd region, received two messages from Georgii Chicherin, head of the Russian delegation at

Brest. The first informed the Sovnarkom that the German response to Russia's peace offer had been passed on to a Soviet courier who was bringing it to Petrograd. The second notified Trotsky that Austria-Hungary, together with her allies, was prepared to bring peace negotiations to a conclusion.[66] The terms arrived at 10:30 AM and, their harshness notwithstanding, it is doubtful that they surprised Lenin. In addition to the conditions previously insisted upon at Brest, the Germans now demanded that Russia turn over control of Livonia and Estonia; evacuate and recognize the independence of Finland, Ukraine, and Georgia; immediately demobilize the old Russian army, the newly forming Red Army, and the Red Guards; intern or disarm the Russian navy, restore the trade treaty of 1904, and, in effect, pay a sizable indemnity; and refrain from spreading revolutionary propaganda in territory belonging to the Central Powers. The Soviet government was given forty-eight hours to accept. To complicate matters further, by the time the new terms arrived, more than half this time had elapsed.[67]

One wonders at the thoughts that ran through Lenin's mind as he pondered the new German conditions. Could he have been relieved that they were not harsher? After all, they were similar to the terms he had suggested, at the late-night Central Committee meeting of 18/19 February, that Russia might have to accept. On the other hand, the intervening days had revealed the depth and scope of aversion to bowing before German imperialism on the part of many if not most of Lenin's closest comrades-in-arms. Surely there are few better examples of Lenin's legendary tenacity and strength of will than his fierce determination to overcome his opponents at this critical juncture in the history of Bolshevism and of the Russian revolution.

The stakes involved could not have been lost on the members of the Bolshevik Central Committee on the afternoon of 23 February, when they met to consider the new German terms. At issue were two radically different views about how to insure survival of the revolution. Moreover, each side in the intraparty battle about to unfold felt certain that the policies advocated by the other were suicidal.

The brief, mechanical secretarial notes on this meeting seem particularly incongruent.[68] "Comrade Sverdlov reads out the German terms," they begin. Almost at once, Lenin lays all his cards on the table. The notes read: "Comrade Lenin considers that the policy of revolutionary phrase-making has ended. If this policy continues now, he will resign from the government and the Central Committee. An army is needed for revolutionary war, [and] there isn't one. That means the terms must be accepted." Straight off, the Left Communists knew that Lenin's threat to resign was neither a casual remark nor a bluff, and that if they did not endorse acceptance of the German terms, they would have to accept responsibility for governing Soviet Russia and for leading a fight against German imperialism, the Russian bourgeoisie, and that portion of the proletariat responsive to Lenin. Lenin went to great pains to erase any doubts on that score.

One by one, most members of the Central Committee expressed their attitudes about accepting the peace terms. "Lenin's arguments are not all convincing," declared Trotsky. Zinoviev countered with the claim that, "from the experience of the previous few days, it is clear that there is no enthusiasm [for fighting on the part of the proletariat]. . . . [W]e are now at the point where we must accept the [German] proposal." Bukharin blasted the German conditions, adding that they "do not support Lenin's prognosis [about the possibility of utilizing a 'breathing space' in order to prepare for revolutionary war within a short time]." Stalin sided with Lenin. "Either we get a breathing space or the revolution dies—there's no other viable option," he interjected. Sverdlov and Sokolnikov made plain that they would vote with Lenin, Zinoviev, and Stalin. Uritskii and Lomov made it equally clear that they were firmly opposed to signing the peace and would vote that way. Uritskii insisted that "signing the peace will not save Soviet power." Lomov took issue with Zinoviev's assessment of the mood of the masses. "The panic described here doesn't exist," he said. "We can accomplish a lot [by way of mounting a defense]."

Lomov, the only Left Communist openly to accept the possibility of going forward without Lenin, contended that "there is no reason to be frightened by Lenin's threat to resign. We [Left Communists] must take power without V. I. [Lenin]." But clearly, many Left Communists were uneasy about that prospect. This was true of Dzerzhinskii, Krestinskii, Ioffe, and Trotsky. Trotsky did not agree with Lenin that the revolution was doomed if the German terms were rejected. To the contrary, he expressed confidence that the task of organizing for defense against the Germans would have been manageable and fruitful internationally if the party was united. Since it was not, leading a revolutionary war was impossible.

Just before the question of accepting the German terms was put to a vote, Bukharin attacked Lenin and his contingent again, but the battle was lost. The vote was 7 in favor of accepting the German terms (Lenin, Stasova, Zinoviev, Sverdlov, Stalin, Sokolnikov, and Smilga), 4 against (Bubnov, Uritskii, Bukharin, and Lomov), and 4 abstentions (Trotsky, Krestinskii, Dzerzhinskii, and Ioffe). In a written statement read out by Krestinskii immediately following this vote, Krestinskii, Ioffe, and Dzerzhinskii justified their abstentions on the grounds that, although they were opposed to signing the peace, a party split along the lines Lenin threatened was potentially even more catastrophic.[69] Uritskii read a declaration for those who, like him, had voted no. In the declaration Uritskii, Bukharin, Lomov, and Bubnov, along with Iakovleva, Piatakov, and Smirnov, took note of the fact that, instead of yielding to the Germans, a majority of the Central Committee had tendered their resignations from their high party and government posts so they would be free to campaign against the treaty both inside and outside the party.[70] Clearly the immediate concern of the Left Communists was to block approval of the treaty in the party's CEC fraction and in the CEC itself. For Lenin, the issue remained fraught with danger for two reasons: first, there was the added risk that Left Communists might carry the day in the Bolshevik CEC fraction and, together with the Left SRs, Mensheviks, and right SRs, also in the CEC; second, the resignations of the Left Communists in the prevailing circumstances would likely lead to a decisive split in the party and almost certainly would precipitate the breakup of the Bolshevik–Left SR coalition.

In view of this, Lenin was prepared to go the limit to keep the Left Communists in the fold. Early in this part of the meeting, when Lomov asked Lenin whether he would allow the Left to agitate against the peace, Lenin quickly answered yes. Moreover, Lenin did not object when Sverdlov, near the end of this discussion, tacitly accepted Uritskii's offer to delay the resignations if he and his colleagues were given full freedom to lobby and even vote no to the treaty in the CEC. Subsequently, Lenin encouraged the Left Communists to leave the hall during the voting, but he did not insist. As a result, with the implicit understanding that the resignations would be put on hold for greater consideration the next day, the committee members discussed plans for joint sessions of the Bolshevik and Left SR Central Committees and of the Bolshevik and Left SR fractions in the CEC, as well as a joint plenary meeting of the CEC and the Petrograd Soviet, all projected to be held consecutively in the Taurida Palace beginning at once. Toward the end of the Bolshevik Central Committee meeting, Lenin scribbled a note to the radio station at Tsarskoe Selo directing it to be prepared to transmit a radio-telegram to the German government before 7:00 AM, when the German ultimatum was set to expire.[71]

* * *

The joint meeting of the Bolshevik–Left SR CEC fractions began at 11:00 PM, 23 February, with another frightful report on the situation of Russian soldiers fleeing the front and a desperate plea from Krylenko for immediate surrender. Krylenko's remarks were interrupted by shouts of protest from Left SRs, who felt his comments were one-sided. Somebody in the audience shouted "and what about the fleet?"—to which Raskolnikov responded, waving his hand in a gesture of despair: "There is no fleet. . . . The sailors are running home, leaving their ships for the enemy."[72]

Each fraction was allowed only two speeches, one in favor of peace, the other against, and no discussion was permitted. For the Bolsheviks, Lenin spoke in favor of accepting the German ultimatum, and Radek spoke against it.[73] The Left SRs refused to nominate a speaker favoring peace, Kamkov stubbornly insisting that in his fraction there was unanimity against accepting Germany's peace terms. As a result, the only Left SR to speak was Shteinberg, a vehement proponent of revolutionary war. No vote was taken at the end of this joint meeting, since the Left SR fraction had already decided against accepting the new terms and the Bolshevik fraction had not yet discussed them.

With time so short, Sverdlov began a subsequent caucus of the Bolshevik CEC fraction alone by proposing that the assembled Bolsheviks should dispense with further discussion of whether to accept the German peace terms and immediately vote on the issue. "But can't we at least ask questions?" one fraction member cautiously inquired. "By all means," replied Sverdlov. According to L. Stupochenko, a participant in the caucus, "One of the most interesting discussions I have ever heard now took place." Opponents of peace peppered Lenin with questions, "each more venomous than the last."[74] Iurii Steklov led the attack. When a vote was finally taken, Lenin's position reportedly received seventy-two votes against twenty-five for the Left Communists.[75] The latter suffered yet another blow when Steklov's proposal that fraction members not be bound by this decision so they could vote their consciences in the CEC meeting, as tacitly accepted in the Central Committee, was defeated.[76]

In view of all these preliminaries, Sverdlov was unable to convene the CEC plenum until 3:00 AM.[77] By then, only four hours remained before the German ultimatum would expire. Using this as justification Sverdlov, on behalf of the Presidium, proposed that, after hearing the German peace terms and listening to a fifteen-minute report from a Sovnarkom representative, one speaker from each party fraction have the opportunity to express that fraction's view on whether to accept or reject the German peace terms. A vote on the issue would then be taken. This proposal was accepted, effectively eliminating the possibility that the Left Communist view would even be articulated.

After Sverdlov read out the German conditions, Lenin took the floor as head of the Sovnarkom. Perhaps most notable about this procedure is that the new terms had neither been reviewed nor voted on by the cabinet. Technically, Lenin's speech represented his views on signing the peace, and his alone. As it was, three positions on the peace issue emerged at the meeting: (1) the Bolshevik majority's, expressed by Lenin and Zinoviev; (2) the Left SRs', voiced by Kamkov; and (3) the views of the Menshevik-Internationalists, the SRs, and the United Social-Democratic Internationalists, represented, respectively, by Martov, Mikhail Likhach, and Gavriil Lindov.

Lenin's and Zinoviev's presentations require no elaboration, as they added nothing new to points they made earlier.[78] Kamkov's speech for the Left SRs exposed the depth of the chasm in the Bolshevik–Left SR partnership wrought by differences over the peace issue. He clearly and forcefully laid out the case for fighting on and scoffed at Lenin's accusation that opponents of peace were refusing to face unpleasant facts and were behaving irresponsibly. To the contrary, in response to Lenin's claim that there was no alternative to signing the peace, Kamkov insisted that any hope of saving the Russian revolution as a socialist revolution lay in categorically rejecting Germany's new terms and proclaiming a universal "uprising" against the world bourgeoisie, even if that meant that Petrograd and vast parts of the country would need to be surrendered before Russia would be rescued by revolutions in Central Europe.[79]

To Martov, the peace terms themselves proved that acceptance of them would doom the Russian revolution to an early extinction. He termed the idea of a "breathing space," which was the cornerstone of Lenin's hopes for an early renewal of the revolution in Russia, mere "self-deception." As he put it, Germany's conditions practically insure "that Soviet power will be a prisoner of the Germans on the day after signing this peace." And he added, "You must understand this and ask yourselves if it is permissible to pay such a price for the existence of Soviet power." In Martov's view, there were only two acceptable courses of action: to fight, inspired by hope, or, if a victory was not possible, to fight and die with honor as the Paris Communards had done. However, he made it clear that, to his thinking, the situation was not hopeless, that a viable strategy would be to retreat deep into Russia and, from there, organize a defense based on the unity of all the vital, revolutionary forces. On the other hand, the extreme solution Lenin demanded, namely, capitulating immediately, was not a solution but a recipe for disaster.[80] Martov's emphasis on the unacceptability of agreeing to Germany's peace terms and on the necessity of trying to combat the Germans regardless of the difficulties involved was echoed in the speeches of Likhach and Lindov.[81]

During these oppositional speeches, Lenin stood beside the chairman's tribunal waiting nervously for the balloting to begin. All signs pointed to an extremely close vote. Once again, because of the absence of an extraordinarily large number of members, many of them Left Communists, the Bolsheviks did not have a majority among the close to 230 participants at this meeting.[82] Even if all the Left Communists present maintained party discipline as imposed by a majority of the Bolshevik fraction and voted to accept Germany's peace terms, Lenin would still need help from another quarter to assure their acceptance. Meanwhile, behind the scenes, Left SR opponents of the Brest peace were hard at work trying to attract Left Communists to their side.[83] By agreement, a preliminary vote was to be registered by show of cards, followed immediately by a roll-call. First, Sverdlov called for the yes votes—112. The outcome was too close to call. Then the no votes and abstentions were counted—86 and 22, respectively. At the sight of some soldier-Bolsheviks applauding this outcome, Shteinberg screamed in rage and pounded his fists on the railing of the government box where he sat.[84]

At 4:30 AM, two-and-a-half hours before the German ultimatum was due to expire, Lenin had his mandate. As he hurried off to obtain approval of the text of an acceptance message to the German government from the Sovnarkom, roll-call balloting began. One by one, members of the CEC climbed to the podium and announced their votes. The moderate socialists and Left SRs applauded early in this process when Bukharin voted against accepting the peace terms.[85] Lunacharskii is said to have broken into tears, as he rose to cast a yes vote. The results of the roll-call were only slightly different from those of the preliminary vote: 116 in favor, 85 opposed, and 26 abstentions. "You can't sell Russia out by a mere five votes," someone shouted from the back of the hall. Twenty-two Left SR proponents of peace abstained. Clearly, Lenin owed them a lot. Observing party discipline and also voting for acceptance of German peace terms were several of the most fervent Left Communists in the Petersburg Committee, among them Bokii, Volodarskii, Kossior, and Ravich. Riazanov and Piatnitskii joined Bukharin in breaking ranks and voting against accepting the treaty. Kollontai, Dzerzhinskii, Krestinskii, Ioffe, Bubnov, and Uritskii were among prominent Left Communist "no shows."[86]

Just before 7:00 AM, 24 February, the radio station at Tsarskoe Selo dispatched a message to Berlin announcing that, "in accordance with the decision of the CEC . . . the Sovnarkom has agreed to accept the peace terms proposed by the German government and will dispatch a delegation to Brest-Litovsk."[87]

* * *

In the immediate aftermath of Trotsky's "no war, no peace" declaration at Brest-Litovsk, much of revolutionary Petrograd, though by no means all, had celebrated "the end of the war." Even Trotsky had been confident that his gambit had been successful. However, on 18 February, the Germans responded by launching an offensive aimed at advancing their lines significantly closer to Petrograd.

This attack triggered fresh debate over a separate peace in the Bolshevik leadership. Initially, a majority in the party Central Committee, as well as in the Sovnarkom, staunchly opposed suing for immediate peace, as Lenin proposed, in favor of waiting to see how Europe's proletariat would respond to Germany's action. However, the debacle of the Russian army at the front unfolded so quickly that, late on the night of 18/19 February, Trotsky provided Lenin with the vote necessary to push acceptance of Germany's terms through the Bolshevik Central Committee. The same night, by a similarly tight margin, immediate peace prevailed in rump meetings of the Left SR Central Committee and the Sovnarkom, and Lenin and Trotsky dispatched their infamous "acceptance" message to Berlin

Afterward, conflict over a separate peace in both the Bolshevik and Left SR camps raged more fiercely than ever. The Bolshevik Petersburg Committee, for one, remained bitterly critical of the party's and the government's peacemaking. In this spirit, the Fourth City Conference of Petrograd Bolsheviks, which had been devoted to organizational reforms aimed at somehow compensating for precipitous personnel losses while preserving a measure of democracy in decision making, censured the Central Committee and demanded that the Sovnarkom's decision to accept Germany's terms be rescinded.

Meanwhile, the rapid German advance continued. Very quickly, Petrograd seemed in imminent danger of enemy occupation. This harsh reality placed the Leninist majority in the party and government leadership into the contradictory position of simultaneously trying to maintain support for a separate peace and organizing Petrograd's defenses. Ironically, on the night of 21/22 February, in the CEC, this conundrum enabled Sverdlov to divert attention from decisions on peace to defense, thereby smoothing the way for passage of a resolution which, after perfunctorily endorsing the Sovnarkom's conciliatory policy, called on the Russian masses to defend the revolution to the last.

Yet, no sooner was this accomplished than the receipt of Germany's harsher peace terms again ignited fierce debate over the question of war or peace. At this juncture, Lenin's threat to resign from the government and the party leadership appears to have been decisive in persuading a majority of the Bolshevik Central Committee to endorse acceptance of Germany's new terms. Nonetheless, the Left Communists, led by Bukharin, and the Left

SRs remained bitterly opposed. These profound rifts emerged most starkly at the historic meeting of the CEC on the night of 23/24 February, where proponents of immediate peace led by Lenin won an extremely close vote. To be sure, a major hurdle on the road to withdrawing from the war had been overcome. However, with German forces moving ever closer to Petrograd, and with significant segments of the Bolshevik and Left SR parties still adamantly opposed to a separate peace, more obstacles lay ahead.

7

An Obscene Peace

DISPATCHING HIS acceptance of harsher peace terms to Berlin in the early morning of 24 February, Lenin hoped to head off the occupation of Petrograd by rapidly advancing German forces. He was, of course, unaware that the Germans planned to stop short of the city. His fears that the Germans intended to capture the Russian capital and crush the revolution were reawakened, therefore, by news he received later that day—first about the capture of Pskov, roughly 150 miles southwest of Petrograd and on a direct rail line to the capital; second, the German high command's rejection of Krylenko's request for an immediate cease-fire; and, finally, reports that enemy troops were moving beyond Pskov. Simultaneously, German forces were moving deep into what is now Belarus and Ukraine. The formal signing of the treaty ending Russia's participation in the world war was to take place in Brest on 3 March. At that time, the Presidium of the CEC would schedule the opening of the Fourth All-Russian Congress of Soviets for 12 March in Moscow to ratify the accord.[1] Meanwhile, with German forces continuing to advance, the Leninist government and party leadership had to prepare for evacuation, if that became necessary, and at the same time direct the defense of Petrograd and combat both the counterrevolution and fierce Left Communist and Left SR opposition to a separate, "obscene" peace.

* * *

The question of evacuating the national government to Moscow had been discussed by the Sovnarkom on 26 February, and a formal resolution to proceed with a move was adopted.[2] Several crises had occurred in the days preceding this decision. For example, as German troops occupied Pskov on 24 February, Russian forces fled helter-skelter from what seemed to be a broad German offensive aimed at Petrograd. At the same time, the universal mobilization of Petrograd workers for dispatch to the front greatly increased the government's vulnerability to domestic conspiracies. On 22 February, the Sovnarkom began to prepare for a move by creating an Emergency Commission for the Evacuation of Petrograd.[3] Even earlier, on 20 February, the Sovnarkom had formed the Provisional Executive Committee to act in the Sovnarkom's name during the rapidly escalating military crisis. By the next evening (21/22 February), the capital was declared under a state of siege, and the Petrograd Soviet created the Committee for the Revolutionary Defense of Petrograd that would direct defense-related functions.[4]

During its first hours of operation, the Sovnarkom's Provisional Executive Committee issued a spate of proclamations calling the Russian people to arms. The most important among these was "The Socialist Fatherland Is in Danger!"

> In order to save our exhausted and depleted country from the miseries of a new war we made the supreme sacrifice and notified the Germans of our readiness to accept their conditions for peace.... [However,] German generals are bent on establishing their own kind of "order" in Petrograd and Kiev.... The Socialist Republic of Soviets is in the gravest danger. Until the German proletariat rises and is victorious, it is the sacred duty of the workers and peasants of Russia to defend the Republic of Soviets against the bourgeois-imperialist German hordes.

Written by Trotsky and approved by Lenin, this proclamation informed Russian citizens that the Sovnarkom had decreed that all the country's forces and resources should be devoted wholly to revolutionary defense; that all soviets and other revolutionary organizations should defend every position to the last drop of blood; and that everything possible should be done both to prevent German use of Russian railway lines and equipment, and to keep Russian food supplies and other valuable property from falling into German hands. It also authorized the immediate shutdown of the counter-revolutionary press and the shooting, "on the spot," of "enemy agents, speculators, burglars, thieves, hooligans, counterrevolutionary agitators, and German spies." "The Socialist Fatherland Is in Danger" was telegraphed the next day to soviets throughout Russia and published in *Pravda* and *Izvestiia* in the name of the Sovnarkom.[5]

By the time the CEC met on the night of 21/22 February and agreed on the need to prepare for a united defense, efforts to hold back "the German hordes" had already begun. However, organizing an adequate defense was difficult regardless of the strength of German forces. The demoralized state of troops in the old front army indicated the hopelessness of trying to utilize them. Then, too, as Krylenko made plain to the Petrograd Soviet on 21 February, units of the Petrograd garrison were also in an advanced state of disintegration.

The unreliability of garrison troops became obvious on 25 February, when the Bolshevik commander of the Petrograd Military District and a member of the Committee for the Revolutionary Defense of Petrograd, Konstantin Eremeev, tried to move forces under his nominal command to the Northern front. Apart from a Latvian Rifle Regiment, garrison units slated for transfer out of the capital to meet the Germans refused to do so.[6] To be sure, on the night of 24/25 February, the so-called night of the factory sirens, when the fall of Pskov was interpreted by government authorities and citizens generally to mean that a German attack on the capital was imminent, mass meetings in most garrison units pledged to defend the capital to the death. In practice, however, they all stayed put. Some units rejected going into battle unless guaranteed increased rations and pay, but more typical was the behavior of the Petrogradskii and Izmailovskii regiments: with great effort, Bolsheviks in these units managed to get the men out of their barracks and into formation, but just a few scraggly groups of soldiers proved willing to march to trains awaiting them at the Warsaw station, and, ultimately, even these groups refused to board. Only individual Bolsheviks from these units got on.[7]

Mobilization of factory workers for defense was more complex. The relationship between the Petrograd proletariat and the Bolsheviks, in February and March 1918, had already cooled compared to what it had been when Kerensky advanced on the capital in late October 1917, and this hampered recruitment efforts. This change was partly a result of popular disenchantment with the economic consequences of the October revolution, above all food shortages and spiraling unemployment. Other factors impeding the recruitment of workers for defense at the end of February and in March 1918 included general demoralization; the large number of party members and unaffiliated factory workers already transferred from their jobs to serve with Red Guard detachments supporting consolidation of the revolution around the country or fighting counterrevolutionary forces on the Don; the startling suddenness of the resumption of German military operations; and the utterly confused military and political situation. Ever since 10 February Petrograd workers essentially had been led to believe that the war was *over*. Because Germany's announcement of 16 February that military operations would resume at midday on 18 February was not made public until after operations had actually begun, literally overnight workers were asked to speed to the front for a life-and-death struggle to defend the revolution. The order for mobilization, moreover, came at the time of Antonov-Ovseenko's first military triumph over the "Kornilov-Kaledin"–led counterrevolution in the South (Rostov had fallen to the Reds on 23 February). The public debate over war or peace with the Central Powers was still raging, and it appeared that the Soviet government allowed for the possibility that acceptable peace terms would be agreed on. Thus, workers often reacted to initial mobilization and recruitment appeals with bewilderment, even panic.[8]

Historians in Russia during the Soviet era invariably emphasized that Bolshevik party organizations effectively organized Petrograd's defenses at this time.[9] This is clearly misleading.[10] In response to the expanding military disaster following the resumption of the German offensive, the Petersburg Committee had appealed to party district committees to send personnel for dispatch to the front, and they had responded as best they could.[11] However, on 24 February the Petersburg Committee had issued blanket instructions to active party workers to make themselves available to district soviets, and this had further depleted the resources of district party committees.[12] Although the military function of Bolshevik party organizations in Petrograd during the German occupation scare of February 1918 was diminished in favor of having local institutions such as district soviets become more active militarily, the Left SRs formed independent party-controlled combat squads that the Bolsheviks encouraged to play an important role in defense. On 26 February, the barracks of the Litovskii Regiment and its inventory of weapons were turned over to these squads. That same day, at the instruction of Bolshevik authorities, the Left SRs seized all weapons in the Pages School (Pazhskii korpus), a former military academy in the center of Petrograd and, with the Bolsheviks' blessing, used it for their headquarters. For the duration of this crisis, the Left SR Mikhail Levinson was deputy chair of the Committee for the Revolutionary Defense of Petrograd, and Left SR combat squads were among the Committee's more reliable military forces.[13]

Apart from the Left SRs and their combat squads, the Committee for the Revolutionary Defense of Petrograd could draw on district soviets, in which opposition to acceptance of Germany's peace terms was initially high. This helps explain the Petersburg Committee's decision to put available cadres at their disposal. On their own, many district soviets, taking their cue from such proclamations as "The Socialist Fatherland Is in Danger," had stepped up defense preparations. The soviet in the Petrograd district resolved to form its own Committee for Revolutionary Defense. The resolution was implemented at a gathering of local factory committee and garrison unit representatives.[14] The Vasilii Island district soviet also swung into action, asserting the right to assign to military duty all its deputies, members of local factory committees, and revolutionary parties, as defense needs required. It also resolved to halt layoffs of factory workers between the ages of eighteen and fifty; and it mandated a six-hour work day so that workers would have the remaining two hours for obligatory military training. Female workers in the district were encouraged to spend two hours training for sanitation and medical duties. The soviet of the Vasilii Island district also agreed to form trench-digging brigades comprised of middle-class citizens.[15]

The Rozhdestvenskii district soviet called on factory committees to implement round-the-clock watches at local factories, to register everyone capable of bearing arms or digging trenches, and to intensify Red Army recruitment,[16] which was then just beginning. The Peterhof district soviet, having discussed problems pertaining to Red Army recruitment, resolved to form its own military section to work closely with local Red Guard headquarters on military recruitment.[17] Other district soviets simultaneously dispatched especially effective deputies to the front to try to bring order among troops of the old army. This was the case with the soviet in the outlying Novoderevenskii district.[18]

By the evening of 22 February, the Committee for the Revolutionary Defense of Petrograd began trying to coordinate these activities. In a cryptic phone message, it made district soviets and garrison regimental committees responsible for the immediate recruitment of personnel for Red Army detachments to be transferred out of Petrograd no later than the twenty-fourth.[19] However, district soviets jealously guarded their freedom of action, and their responses to directives from above were usually guided by their own independent assessments of the developing situation.

Trade unions were also potentially valuable for mobilizing workers. On 22 February, the Petrograd Trade Union Council, still headed by the Left Communist Riazanov, met in an emergency session to discuss the issue of war or peace.[20] Among participants in this meeting were representatives of twenty of Petrograd's largest and most active trade unions. Following a rousing speech by Riazanov calling on trade unions to alert workers to the need for maximum discipline, energy, and self-sacrifice in the interest of saving the revolution, and to utilize their organizational structure to help build a powerful, socialist Red Army, the Council appealed to the unions to rally their forces around the CEC and Sovnarkom for a do-or-die defense of the revolution. Trade unions that became actively involved in defense preparations at this time included the Union of Metal Workers, the Union of Transport Workers, the Food Processors Union, and the Union of Wood Workers.[21]

On a broader front, the Executive Committee of the Petrograd Soviet began planning a blitz of recruitment rallies for the afternoon and early evening of 23 February in theaters and meeting halls around the capital. Among featured speakers were Bukharin, Zinoviev, Lunacharskii, Volodarskii, Raskolnikov, and Slutskii for the Bolsheviks, and Kamkov, Shteinberg, and Trutovskii for the Left SRs. Press reports on the mood of Petrograd workers at these gatherings suggested that "momentary panic had been dissolved in an upsurge of feelings about revolutionary duty."[22] Yet revolutionary enthusiasm did not translate into a willingness to fight. These rallies yielded relatively few Red Army recruits, and the same can be said about the efforts of district soviets.[23] Instructions from the Committee for the Revolutionary Defense of Petrograd to all mass organizations on the night of 24/25 February, immediately following the occupation of Pskov by German forces, hinted of panic; they called on "all soviets, everybody, everybody" to declare the universal mobilization of all workers and soldiers and to rush them to Smolny, to make an inventory of all shovels, and to seize all automobiles and also deliver them to Smolny. All residents of Petrograd were ordered to prepare immediately for enemy air raids and gas attacks.[24]

* * *

Bolshevik authorities tried to overcome popular resistance to recruitment, justify crackdowns on counterrevolutionary activity in Petrograd, and enhance the powers of security agencies by attempting to link the German offensive in the popular mind with expanded efforts by the Russian bourgeoisie, the SRs, and even the Mensheviks to overthrow Soviet power from within. In the Bolshevik view, moderate socialists called for united struggle against German imperialism, as they had in the CEC the night of 23/24 February, only because they hoped that Bolshevism would be destroyed in a war that could not be won. The claim that Mensheviks were linked to domestic conspiracies to exploit the advance of the foreign foe to overthrow the Soviet government was particularly misleading, inasmuch as the Menshevik party actively opposed such action. Still and all, numerous documents of the time show that counterrevolutionary groups in Petrograd were indeed energized by the dissolution of the Constituent Assembly at the beginning of January 1918 and, subsequently, by the Sovnarkom's peace negotiations culminating in the acceptance of the Brest treaty.

As early as the second half of January, Smolny was plagued by a rash of bomb scares.[25] The VCheka, toward the end of the month, successfully broke up a conspiracy to overthrow the Soviet government in which it was alleged that several thousand well-armed officers, quite possibly with British support, participated. Ivan Polukarov, head of the VCheka's section on combating counterrevolution, later pointed to this conspiracy as the most dangerous faced by the VCheka during the first six months of its existence, because, as he explained, "its agents were everywhere."[26] Unpublished contemporary documents that shed light on this counterrevolutionary activity include an urgent message from Dzerzhinskii to Petrograd district soviets on 27 January, as well as protocols of emergency meetings of the Executive Committee of the Vasilii Island district soviet on 28 January and of the Peterhof district soviet and its Executive Committee on 28 and 29 January. These documents indicate that the VCheka held a citywide crisis meeting with representatives of district soviets the night of the 27th to issue an SOS for personnel and to discuss directives connected with suppressing the conspiracy.[27] All Petrograd district soviets were directed to go on twenty-four-hour alert, mobilize their resources, report on the progress of efforts to suppress the movement in their areas, and form district Chekas.[28]

A few weeks later, the resumption of the German offensive and the fear that it was aimed at the occupation of Petrograd led to a significant enhancement of the VCheka's arbitrary powers. One of the most militant proclamations published following the start of the enemy advance, "The Socialist Fatherland Is in Danger," as noted above, encouraged shooting common criminals and counterrevolutionaries at the scene of their crime. It had been issued by the Provisional Executive Committee without discussion by the full Sovnarkom.[29] Consequently, on 22 February, at a meeting of the Sovnarkom, a debate erupted between Left SRs and Bolsheviks over this blank check for summary executions. The Left SRs demanded that this precedent-setting provision be annulled, but, predictably, they were outvoted.[30] Shteinberg would later point to the provision in this first official document sanctioning arbitrary shooting of alleged political enemies as "clearing the way for Cheka terror."[31] The VCheka immediately seized upon this mandate, announcing on 22 February that "at a time when the hydra of counterrevolution is getting more brazen by the day," it had "no other means of combating counterrevolutionaries, speculators, thugs, hooligans, saboteurs, and other parasites than through their merciless execution at the scene of their crimes."[32]

Other agencies besides the Cheka, including Petrograd district soviets and the Emergency Headquarters for the Petrograd Military District, drew on the proclamation to legitimate execution at crime scenes.[33] On 22 February, the latter had followed the Cheka's lead and authorized shootings "on the spot" by Red Army troops, a mandate that was soon withdrawn. Nonetheless, from then on hastily recruited Red Army soldiers became the scourge of Petrograd.

In a message circulated on 23 February, the VCheka announced it had uncovered yet another nationwide plot by the Russian bourgeoisie to help the Germans and to stab Soviet power in the back by organizing armed insurrections in Petrograd, Moscow, and other Russian cities. The VCheka warned Petrograd district soviets and other worker institutions that many counterrevolutionary bands had ensconced themselves in such ostensibly humanitarian groups as organizations for aid to officers wounded in the war. This placed virtually all civic organizations not controlled by the government under a cloud. Soviets were to seek out, arrest, and shoot all participants in counterrevolutionary conspiracies. Counterrevolutionary organizations referred to in this message were the Organization for Struggle against the Bolsheviks and the Dispatch of Troops to Kaledin, All For the Fatherland, The White Cross, and The Black Dot. Around this time, some officers and cadets who opposed Brest gained a foothold in the recently reactivated Mikhailovskii Artillery Academy. From there, they conducted anti-Soviet agitation among soldiers and workers, and acquired arms for their supporters. This group was led by Right SRs, among them one Vladimir Perel'tsveig, about whom more will be said.[34]

The VCheka's announcement on 22 February of its intention to shoot counterrevolutionaries "on the spot" was published in the press. It can fairly be viewed as an example of preemptive state terror. That Soviet security agencies were genuinely concerned about the "hydra of counterrevolution" is attested by unpublished documents never intended for public consumption. In a memo of 24 February, marked "secret" and "extremely urgent," the Committee for the Revolutionary Defense of Petrograd ordered district soviets to form mobile [letuchie] detachments to combat internal counterrevolution at the same time that they formed detachments for transfer to the front.[35] On 26 February, district soviets were ordered immediately to organize searches of suspicious organizations, establishments, and individual bourgeois homes for weapons.[36] Another emergency, secret message to district soviets, dated 27 February, reflected the Committee's angst as German forces moved beyond Pskov. It read: "Take immediate measures to destroy typewritten proclamations posted around the city headed 'Russia has been sold to the Germans.' Anyone caught pasting up these posters should be shot on the spot."[37] To representatives of district soviets in the Interdistrict Conference, this was going too far. It circulated a directive to its constituent soviets limiting all "shootings on the spot" to cases in which suspects offered armed resistance.[38] This directive may fairly be viewed as a grass-roots attempt to stop excesses triggered by the Provisional Executive Committee's proclamation of 21 February.

* * *

Meanwhile, the popular response to mobilization efforts after the fall of Pskov on 24 February resulted in a brief up-tick in military recruitment among workers. This modest progress was reflected in reports from the Vyborg, Narva, Okhtinskii, First City, Second City, and Rozhdestvenskii districts regarding Red Army recruitment, the provisioning of recruits, and the political mood of workers locally from 23 to 26 February.[39] Although incomplete, these reports, taken together, comprise a roughly representative cross-section of Petrograd.

The report of the Vyborg district soviet is particularly interesting because of the district's historical importance as the citadel of Bolshevism in 1917, and also because it was now an area of industrial blight. It revealed that, as of 26 February, thirty-six hundred volunteers had signed up for the Red Army, almost all of them workers. The district soviet was able to supply these recruits with arms and ammunition. Provisions were a significantly more serious problem. Yet the report reflected confidence that this difficulty also could be overcome. The general mood of workers was deemed as "revolutionary as it could possibly be." Counterrevolutionary activity in the district was being "nipped at the roots." Orientation meetings for workers were being held and these were "well attended." By and large, life on the streets was "normal."[40]

The reporter from the economically and politically mixed Narva district, south of the city center, indicated that providing a precise tally of Red Army recruits was complicated because there were several area recruiting stations in the district. However, he expressed certainty that the figure was "more than two thousand." There were enough weapons to go around [but] no provisions. An inventory of "bourgeois" residents had been made, and they would receive defense-related work assignments "at the first call." This reporter warned that although the mood among workers was upbeat, it would be misleading to say it reflected eagerness to fight. Among residents, generally, the spirit was "counterrevolutionary" and anti-Soviet agitation was growing.[41]

Information from the right-bank, partially industrialized Okhtinskii district was that one thousand Red Army recruits had already been signed up (most of them workers, with a "sprinkling" of veteran soldiers). The mood of local workers was characterized as "brave," whereas that of better-

Red Army recruitment center. David King Collection.

off residents [*obivateli*] was interpreted as "cowardly." This report concluded that "life was proceeding normally—there were no signs of either panic or counterrevolutionary activity."[42]

Reports from smaller, less industrialized, "better" commercial, governmental, and residential districts in the center of the city were less encouraging than those from areas with higher concentrations of workers. For example, the message from the First City district soviet, which contained a few large, recently shut-down, state-owned defense plants, indicated that Red Army recruitment there was "quite lively" and that the mood in worker circles was "brave," even "uplifted." At the same time, as a result of counterrevolutionary agitation, the mood of residents generally was "lost . . . confused." The author of this report claimed that it was difficult to be exact about overall Red Army recruitment figures. Still, he recorded 250 recruits as having been sent to the front that morning (26 February) and another 250 as projected for dispatch in the evening.[43] The overall situation in the Second City district was the same as that in the First City district, although the report from there did not provide numbers.[44] Predictably, the situation in the Rozhdestvenskii district, a relatively very small, centrally located area strategically important because both Smolny and the Taurida Palace were located there, was even less promising. According to the report of its district soviet, enlistment in the Red Army was "very listless."[45]

A detachment of worker Red Guards poses for a photograph before departing for the front. Photograph by Ia. Shteinberg. David King Collection.

The total number of recorded Red Army recruits in these six districts for the three-day reporting period (23–26 February) was 10,320—not an especially impressive figure given the apparent immediacy of the enemy threat to Petrograd. However, this may not be the whole story. Available evidence suggests that even factory workers willing to fight preferred to enroll in ad hoc partisan detachments organized at their factories or by labor organizations rather than accept the longer-term, more rigorous obligations entailed by Red Army enlistment.[46] Moreover, Red Army recruitment figures did not include new members of Left SR combat squads.

When all is said and done, evaluating the attitudes of workers toward defending the revolution from German forces remains complicated. In memoirs published in 1927 Fedor Dingel'shtedt, a member of the Bolshevik Petersburg Committee, Left Communist, and Bolshevik agitator in factories on the Petrograd side, suggested that, in assessing responses to recruitment appeals during the Brest crisis, distinction must be made between local party leaders and "worker activists," on the one hand, and rank-and-file workers, on the other. According to Dingel'shtedt, although they were already beginning to rethink their positions at the time that the German advance was especially threatening, most of the activists were still sympathetic to revolutionary war and genuinely keen to combat the Germans. Rank-and-file workers, on the other hand, were reluctant to fight almost from the start.

Dingel'shtedt's recollections are particularly valuable, because they are based on a diary he kept during this period. Also, as a Left Communist he was unlikely to exaggerate labor passivity with respect to combating the Germans. To illustrate his argument, he describes two rallies at the large Pipe Factory which he addressed on 23 February. The first was an assembly of the Bolshevik collective in the factory which, Dingel'shtedt recalls, exhibited "marvelous" enthusiasm. The second was a mass workers meeting; according to him, it reflected just the opposite—a sharp drop in the mood of the politically unaffiliated masses, expressed by grumbling and dissatisfaction caused by the worsening economic situation and the threat of a new war. "Evidently such a picture can be considered more or less characteristic of a broad stratum of Petersburg workers during these days," he concluded. To further document his point, he described a meeting at the wagon works in the Aleksandr Machine Building Plant on 27 February, where he encountered an analogous situation.[47]

In contrast to Dingel'shtedt, most contemporaries who wrote on the subject saw a relatively quick swing away from initial support of revolutionary war to demands for immediate peace among both district-level party activists *and* factory workers generally. In a speech at the Seventh All-Russian Bolshevik Party Congress, on 7 March, Kiril Shelavin, among the few members of the Petersburg Committee who supported peace early on, pointed out that popular attitudes toward revolutionary war made a 180-degree turn the moment the German offensive became a matter of life or death.

> Two weeks ago workers supported revolutionary war. . . . [But] after they saw that the enemy was not merely White Guardists but terrifying [troops] armed with late model weapons . . . all collectives, one after the other, began passing resolutions regarding the impossibility of conducting a revolutionary war and about [the necessity of] concluding peace. . . . The time has passed when Petersburg workers, responding to factory sirens, came to the defense of revolutionary Petersburg.[48]

Under the pressure of their mass constituencies, precisely the kind of shift described by Shelavin seems to have occurred in trade unions and district soviets. As noted earlier, at an emergency meeting on 22 February, the Petrograd Trade Union Council had passed a resolution introduced by Riazanov pledging full support for revolutionary war. At a meeting on 28 February, after the Sovnarkom's acceptance of Germany's second, more devastating peace terms, the Council again adopted a Left Communist resolution presented by Riazanov, but that was his last success.[49] On 9 March, at a conference convened by the Council to sound out the views of member unions, Riazanov's position was defeated. A majority of the five hundred trade union representatives present voted in favor of ratification.[50]

An analogous swing away from support of revolutionary war can be observed among Petrograd district soviets. If most of them tended toward Left Communism at the beginning of the German advance, as appears to have been the case, this was no longer true in March. The mood in the Vyborg district, where Red Army recruitment had initially been relatively successful, and where the local soviet had characterized the mood among factory workers toward the end of February as being as "revolutionary as it could possibly be," reflected this change.[51] In early March, with an unstoppable German attack on Petrograd seemingly a foregone conclusion, the Vyborg district soviet focused attention on practical measures for evacuation, destruction of immovable property, house-by-house defense, if that became necessary, and plans for dealing with the bourgeoisie in the developing circumstances.

Such issues seemed to be on everyone's mind at a meeting of the Vyborg district soviet's executive committee on 4 March, a day after the peace signing at Brest-Litovsk, but at a point when the German advance still showed no sign of abating and efforts to strengthen Petrograd's defenses by the Committee for the Revolutionary Defense of Petrograd were continuing. Aleksandr Kuklin, a former member of the Petersburg Committee who chaired the meeting, urged that, in view of German brutalities toward factory workers at Pskov and Narva, all means of transport should be made ready and all workers organized into Red Guards. Clearly, he was thinking about defense in case workers could not get away in time. But accomplishing this systematically, without stirring panic, was a concern, as another speaker put it, since "waiting for directives from the center is pointless inasmuch as the center leans on us." Serious consideration was given to isolating all opponents of Soviet power "from shopkeepers to professors" in one location where they could be controlled. In the end, it was decided to introduce resolutions in the full soviet providing for such steps as mobilization of all workers aged eighteen to fifty without regard to political affiliation, blowing up everything that might be of value to the Germans, and executing all counter-revolutionaries if they made any kind of move.[52] A plenary meeting of the soviet added evacuation of worker families to this list.[53]

*   *   *

During this time of flux in popular sentiment about combat, a majority of the Petersburg Committee, true to its radical, independent tradition, steadfastly supported revolutionary war. On 25 February, the day after the new Germany peace terms were accepted, it convened a meeting with representatives of district party committees. Adopted at this meeting was a resolution condemning the government's action, insisting that it would not deter the German advance, and expressing certainty that there was no alternative to self-defense "with arms in hand."[54] The Fourth Petrograd Bolshevik City Conference had been suspended on 20 February, after demanding that the acceptance of Germany's peace terms be rescinded.[55] The conference reassembled on 1 March to reassess its position on war and peace and to select Petrograd's representatives to the Seventh All-Russian Bolshevik Party Congress, scheduled to convene in a week.[56]

At the time of this gathering, both the fear of an advance on Petrograd and the Sovnarkom's frantic efforts to defend it had, if anything, momentarily intensified. The circumstances of this renewed scare at the beginning of March border on the comic. It seems that, on 1 March, the new secretary of Russia's peace delegation at Brest, Lev Karakhan, dispatched two telegrams to the Sovnarkom in Petrograd: the first, written in code, described diplomatic issues relating to signing the peace; the second, sent in clear text, requested that a train be sent to pick up the delegation. It reflected the delegation's desire to escape the hostile environment behind the German lines as soon as the peace was signed. Unfortunately, it was the second telegram that reached Lenin first, and he jumped to the conclusion, which was announced in *Pravda* on 2 March, that the negotiations had broken down. In the announcement, Lenin issued an alert "to all soviets, to everyone" to prepare for an imminent German assault on Petrograd.[57] *Pravda*'s editors went a step further with a front-page headline that read: "Our Peace Delegation Is Returning to Petrograd. The Question of War Has Been Decided. War! . . . The Old Capitalist World Is Assaulting Us with All Its Might."[58] It is probably no coincidence that precisely at this time Lenin signed a decree centralizing command of all Soviet military forces in a new body, the Supreme Military Council.

This intensified occupation scare erupted the morning *after* the discussion of war and peace at the continuation of the Fourth Petrograd Bolshevik City Conference (1 March) and therefore could not have influenced the conference deliberations. Moreover, because conference delegates had all been elected in mid February, it is also unlikely that delegates' views would have reflected recent changes in worker attitudes regarding peace. Making the major speeches at the conference were prominent national leaders—Radek and Bukharin for the Left Communists, Sverdlov and Zinoviev for the Leninists. In stating the case for revolutionary war, Radek's main point was that the idea of a breathing space was "nonsense," as the realities of the situation were such that Russia would be forced to make "concession after concession or start a new war in two or three weeks." "There is no third way," he insisted. Sverdlov's argument, on the other hand, was just the opposite. His main point was that fighting now was not a practical possibility—that "when detachments for dispatch to the front were needed, we couldn't count on a single person." "After we conclude peace, we will organize a Red Army," he said. "To all the people we are announcing that we are signing this infamous peace [solely] for a brief respite." Sverdlov was adamant that the Left Communist repudiation of peace "contained the seeds of a [party] split," and he appealed to the conferees to reject this course.[59]

Sverdlov's suggestion that Left Communists were setting the stage for a split antagonized Bukharin. He made the perfectly valid point that Lenin had initiated a split by threatening to resign when a majority of the Central Committee favored revolutionary war.[60] Zinoviev, speaking last, based his argument in favor of ratification on his interpretation of labor sentiment as expressed in the Petrograd Soviet. After listening to the "revolutionary phrases" of Left Communists, its representatives had remained firm that signing the peace was a necessity. Although not completely discounting Left Communist claims that revolutionary enthusiasm could be detected among workers, he argued that "the dispatch of workers and all Bolsheviks to the front . . . would result in the physical destruction of the party and of the flower of the proletariat."[61] By this time, Left Communists in Petrograd were preparing to publish their own newspaper, *Kommunist*.[62] Zinoviev closed with an appeal to desist from this step. However, the arguments of Sverdlov and Zinoviev made no impact on most conferees. Endorsing the position of the Left Communists, they selected a delegation to the Seventh Party Congress, and a new Petersburg Committee, in which Left Communists had majorities.[63] The first issue of *Kommunist* appeared on 5 March.

At this point, Left Communists in Petrograd believed that they still had the support of district party committees and significant numbers of rank-and-file workers. However, by the time the Seventh Party Congress opened on 8 March, this confidence was shaken, as Left Communists candidly acknowledged. Thus, after recounting the negative impact of factory closings and Red Army mobilization on party structures and activity in Petrograd, especially in heavily industrialized districts such as Vyborg, a writer in the 14 March issue of *Kommunist* commented that "opinions in the districts on the question of war and peace have shifted. If, earlier, representatives of the districts, reflecting the attitudes of the latter, advocated revolutionary war, the predominant view now favors ratification of the peace treaty."[64] Records of Bolshevik district committees in mid March confirm this shift.[65]

A plenary session of the Petrograd Soviet had discussed the peace on 5 March; after a head-on clash between Zinoviev and Kamkov, a resolution to oppose Brest, supported by the Mensheviks, SRs, and Left SRs, was rejected in favor of a Bolshevik motion endorsing its ratification—this despite the Petersburg Committee's enduring support of revolutionary war. Indeed, under Zinoviev's direction, a meeting of the Bolshevik Petrograd Soviet fraction preceding the plenum had passed a resolution condemning the editors of *Kommunist* and demanding election of a new Petersburg Committee.[66] According to *Krasnaia gazeta,* the vote on this highly improper resolution was "a few hundred to one."[67] This was further evidence of a major grassroots shift in favor of ratification and against the Left Communists.

* * *

At the beginning of March, the apparently imminent German occupation of Petrograd prompted an appeal from the Petersburg Committee to the Central Committee for the transfer to Moscow of the Seventh All-Russian Bolshevik Party Congress, which was scheduled to convene on the fifth.[68] At the Petersburg Committee's instigation, Zinoviev also expedited an urgent request to the Central Committee for an emergency subsidy of several hundred thousand rubles to support the city party organization's continued operation in the event it was forced underground by an enemy occupation.[69] By this time, Bolshevik district committees had already begun preparations to go into hiding. Despite the fact that plans for the government's flight to Moscow were then well advanced, both requests were denied. It is fair to speculate that the Central Committee's coolness to the Petersburg Committee's concerns was influenced by the latter's open and fierce opposition to ratification of the Brest treaty. Symptomatic of this attitude was the fact that on 9 March, at its last Petrograd meeting, the Central Committee voted to *dissolve* the Petersburg Committee. Zinoviev, Smilga, and Lashevich, who had led the rebellion against the Petersburg Committee in the Bolshevik Petrograd Soviet fraction, were appointed to implement this decision and, presumably, to oversee formation of a more pliant, pro-Brest Petersburg Committee.[70]

What may have been the most noteworthy aspect of the Seventh All-Russian Bolshevik Party Congress, whose primary purpose was to adopt a position on ratification of the Brest treaty in advance of the Fourth All-Russian Congress of Soviets, was that it was held at all. Because of difficulties in traveling to Petrograd—the Germans were, after all, literally "at the gates" and rail transport was chaotic—the Bolshevik Central Committee had agreed in advance that this party congress would be considered legitimate if attendance exceeded half the number of delegates to the Sixth All-Russian Bolshevik Party Congress held in early August 1917.[71] Of those participating in that congress, 157 had full voting rights and 110 had "consultative rights." It follows, then, that at least 79 voting delegates were required for a quorum at the Seventh Congress, even if delegates with consultative rights were left out of the equation. Only 17 voting delegates were present on 5 March, when the congress was due to begin. The next day, 36 voting delegates were on hand, and a few additional delegates were reportedly in transit.[72] With still less than half the number required for a quorum, the congress was nevertheless allowed to proceed. The likely explanation for this departure from the procedure agreed upon is that Lenin was unwilling to tolerate further delay; he needed to neutralize the Left Communists and get the party's mandate for ratification of the Brest treaty, if he was to overcome strong opposition to the treaty by the Left SRs and moderate socialists at the fast approaching Fourth All-Russian Congress of Soviets. Also, the Germans appeared poised to begin an assault on Petrograd at any moment.

Lenin exploited his position as reporter for the Central Committee to start the debate on the ratification and to set its parameters. Primarily emphasizing the degree to which the unmitigated debacle at the front had validated his pleas for immediate peace beginning in January, and treating the Left Communists like rambunctious youngsters, he scolded them for the significantly more onerous peace terms now forced upon the revolution. Lenin also laid a significant share of the blame for Soviet Russia's predicament at Trotsky's feet. Although Trotsky's initial efforts to utilize the negotiations at Brest to further revolutions abroad had been magnificent, his failure to accept Germany's initial terms when presented as an ultimatum and, instead, to declare his strategy of "no war, no peace," had been an indefensible mistake, and, Lenin suggested, a violation of a firm understanding between them. Yet even though all Lenin's predictions regarding Russia's military weakness had come true and Russia had been vanquished by puny enemy forces in eleven days, all was not yet lost. To be sure, it seemed that Petrograd was doomed. Lenin was certain of that and, we now know, acted on this assumption. However, ratification of the treaty even in its existing form would provide a breathing space of at least a few days, and possibly more, which could be used to continue evacuating the capital, create a new army, establish domestic order, organize economic life, repair railroads, and make other essential defense preparations. In sum, Lenin made it clear that, as costly and painful as it was, ratification of the treaty was the necessary price of survival.[73]

Bukharin's measured reply for the Left Communists contrasted sharply with Lenin's opening salvo. In response to Lenin's repeated assertions that the Left Communists had persistently refused to face reality and the necessity of retreat, he reminded Lenin that, to the contrary, the Left Communists had consistently held to the principle that the Russian revolution would either be saved by revolutions abroad or would be crushed by the capitalist powers. Left Communists, moreover, had always assumed that Russia's conflict with imperialism would begin with defeats. To Bukharin, the fundamental difference between the two sides was that the Left Communists believed in the imminence of an international workers' revolution. Unlike the Leninists' pessimistic assessment of prospects for decisive immediate revolutions abroad, to Left Communists the worldwide workers' movement was just then in the process of a significant shift in the direction of revolution, which validated their proposed course.

Bukharin also rejected Lenin's claim that only a few days' breathing space was needed to facilitate defense preparations on the scale and character he envisioned—a point echoed especially powerfully by Uritskii later in this debate. As far as Bukharin and Uritskii were concerned, a very brief respite in the war with Germany would not be enough to make any major improvements in Russia's military capabilities. How could the revolution optimize its possibilities of survival? Lenin's answer was the breathing space, which he now presented as an elaborate theory. Bukharin's answer was revolutionary war; as German forces drove deeper into Russia, ever increasing numbers of workers and peasants, battered and oppressed by the invaders, would rise. At the outset, inexperienced partisan detachments would suffer setbacks, but in this struggle the working class, which was disintegrating in the face of economic chaos, would unite behind the slogan of a holy war against militarism and imperialism. Workers and peasants would learn to use weapons, they would build an army, and, ultimately, they would triumph.[74] To Bukharin, the fate of the Russian revolution and of the revolution internationally depended on adopting this strategy.

The fierce debate over Brest at the Seventh Party Congress lasted twelve hours and was spread over two days. In addition to Lenin and Bukharin, 17 delegates spoke out on the issue—10 in favor of ratification and 7 opposed. The result of a roll vote on ratification was 30 for, 12 against, and 4 abstentions.[75] This outcome was the last straw for Riazanov, for whom the betrayal of the international proletariat embodied in Lenin's resolution endorsing the Brest peace violated his most deeply felt revolutionary principles. He now demonstratively announced his resignation from the party.[76] Krestinskii, spurred by Lenin's vehement criticism of Trotsky for his "no war, no peace" strategy, offered a resolution lauding it. As he rightly pointed out, Trotsky's position had been embraced by the vast majority of the party leadership. Nonetheless, Krestinskii's resolution was defeated. Trotsky took umbrage at this affront, understandably concluding that he was being made a scapegoat for the impossible circumstances in which the party found itself, and that rejection of Krestinskii's resolution amounted to a vote of no confidence in him. He responded by resigning from all his positions in government.[77]

Zinoviev attempted to mollify Trotsky. A host of resolutions regarding Brest was proposed and voted on, at least some of which Lenin interpreted as veiled attempts to reopen the possibility of party members supporting revolutionary war at the Soviet Congress. He naturally opposed that. Ultimately, a proposal by Zinoviev praising the overall strategy of the Soviet delegation at Brest, but implicitly criticizing its failure to accept Germany's terms framed as an ultimatum, received the largest number of votes.[78]

At the last session of the congress the night of 8 March, the delegates accepted Lenin's argument that the party's formal name, the Russian Social Democratic Party (Bolshevik), was outdated and should be changed to the Russian Communist Party (Bolshevik), abbreviated to RKP (b).[79] How Trotsky was persuaded to withdraw his resignation is uncertain. In elections to the Central Committee, at the close of the congress, only he and Lenin received the maximum 34 votes, 5 of the 39 voting delegates present having abstained.[80] Perhaps, this strong endorsement helped heal the bruises from the criticism of his failed strategy at Brest. Be that as it may, even as delegates to the Bolshevik Seventh Party Congress finished their deliberations, some national government agencies were already establishing themselves in Moscow, and clandestine arrangements were well advanced for the immediate relocation there of the Sovnarkom, the CEC, and the Bolshevik and Left SR Central Committees.

∗   ∗   ∗

On 26 February, the day of its decision to flee Petrograd, the Sovnarkom ordered the immediate evacuation of the Government Printing Office and the gold stored in the treasury.[81] Hurried preparations for flight were now made by key government commissariats and foreign embassies. National departments considered of secondary importance, such as Lunacharskii's People's Commissariat for Enlightenment, were to remain in Petrograd for as long as possible. The American Embassy, headed by David Francis, was evacuated to the town of Vologda, 350 miles east of Petrograd, on the direct rail line to the northern port of Archangel. The British and French embassy staffs attempted to depart Russia via Finland, but only the British succeeded.

The French ambassador, Joseph Noulins, and his associates soon joined the Americans and smaller allied contingents in Vologda.[82] All these developments, coupled with the anticipation in business circles that German forces would stifle the revolution, caused prices on the deflated Petrograd stock market to soar.[83]

At the end of February, Zinoviev led a high-level delegation to Moscow to begin making arrangements for accommodating the national government there.[84] In order to free up office and living space for the newcomers, orders were issued for the immediate evacuation from Moscow of nonessential institutions and citizens. Even before Zinoviev returned to Petrograd on 4 March, some government agencies had entrained for the new capital. Although an operation of this magnitude could not be kept secret, and, indeed, the non-Soviet press reported it in accurate detail, on 1 March the Presidium of the CEC announced that all rumors about the flight of the Sovnarkom and CEC from Petrograd were completely false; that both the Sovnarkom and CEC were remaining in the city and preparing the most energetic defense of the capital possible; and that the question of evacuation could only be raised at the last minute, should Petrograd's safety come under the most dire, immediate threat, which was not yet the case.[85] Such denials persisted for another week.[86]

Behind the scenes, local Bolsheviks were worried about the negative impact the government's flight would have on Petrograd factory workers. This concern emerged at a meeting of the Petersburg Committee on 6 March 1918.[87] Fenigshtein reported that the evacuation had already begun and that it was being carried out in an inappropriate way, with government institutions first in line for departure. The masses were threatened with being left leaderless, and, if this occurred, the danger of a successful counterrevolution would be greatly enhanced.

By this time, Germany's acceptance of the Soviet government's capitulation had been received, and with this in mind Stanislav Kossior expressed confidence that the evacuation plan then being implemented would be revised. But even he protested the "panicked character of evacuation." Shelavin, not a Left Communist like Fenigshtein and Kossior, nonetheless shared their misgivings. He proposed that the evacuation should be carried out according to the following principles: (1) priority should be given to valuable factory equipment, not institutions of the government; (2) the evacuation of soviets was impermissible, because it would strip the city of agencies responsible for managing the economy, and a rushed evacuation of government institutions was inadvisable; (3) the party's evacuation must be prepared gradually; and (4) when the need arose, priority should be given to evacuating the CEC and the Bolshevik Petersburg Committee. These principles were accepted with the provision that the population would be prepared for any evacuation in advance, and that an evacuation would not be carried out in a panicked, sudden way. They were forwarded to the Central Committee but had no discernible effect on the character of the evacuation, even though, by now, the threat of an immediate German assault on Petrograd had receded.

On 7 March even *Krasnaia gazeta,* which had insisted a day earlier that no government officials "had or were planning to go anywhere," suddenly acknowledged that the transfer of government agencies was under way. This step was justified on the grounds that it would be impossible to rebuild political and economic institutions and to govern the Russian state with the enemy so close; the announcement was sweetened by the disclosure that Petrograd would be declared a free city, and that this status promised limitless economic benefits. According to *Novye vedomosti,* even some industrialists now looked forward to Petrograd's becoming a "second New York."[88] By the next day, Friday, 8 March, *Krasnaia gazeta* reported that the People's Commissariat for Justice was moving to Moscow on that day and would reopen in Moscow on the following Monday. It is worth noting that the VCheka tried to take advantage of Shteinberg's preoccupation with the transfer to execute some political prisoners. Apprised of this intention a couple of hours before his departure for Moscow, Shteinberg scribbled an order to his deputy, Aleksandr Shreider, to halt the shootings.[89]

The Sovnarkom's original decision to evacuate the government had specified that the move to Moscow should include minimal numbers of officials and their families from the central administration, and, implicitly, only critically important files and equipment.[90] In practice, most commissariats took advantage of the opportunity to escape the Germans and dispatched to Moscow large numbers of functionaries along with their families, from top officials to clerks, as well as enormous quantities of furniture and equipment, literally "down to the kitchen sink." This mass move imposed a heavy burden on Russia's already wildly overtaxed railway cars and lines, not to speak of housing in Moscow, and it contradicted the Sovnarkom's announcements that the evacuation was temporary and, in any case, subject to the approval of the Fourth All-Russian Congress of Soviets. Long lists of items shipped to Moscow illustrate this phenomenon. Included among 1,806 items on the Naval General Staff's list, for instance, were files, maps, office equipment, and furniture, as well as icons (at the top of the list of most offices), curtains, rugs, mirrors, ash trays, stoves, kitchen appliances, dishes, flatware, samovars, dining room furniture, towels, blankets, and numerous other accoutrements. Some fifty rooms were stripped bare.[91] To ship his own large library and other personal property, Bonch-Bruevich diverted two freight cars designated for transferring party literature to Moscow.[92] The VCheka also cleaned out its offices, after its leadership resolved on 8 March to evacuate the entire commission and its staff, "not leaving anyone behind."[93] Shipping all its Petrograd case files to Moscow, the VCheka left hundreds of its prisoners stranded at Gorokhovaia 2 and in the Crosses (Kresty) Prison, with no documentation of the reasons for their arrest.[94] Beyond greatly complicating and extending the national government's evacuation well into the late spring, all this added to the already horrendous problems facing Soviet authorities remaining in Petrograd. Not surprisingly, toward the end of March, the Petrograd Bolshevik leadership sent the party Central Committee a letter protesting the condition in which the national government had left the city. It was especially indignant about the behavior of the VCheka, which "took away the documentation [and] the investigators but left the prisoners."[95]

The top government institutions—the Sovnarkom and the CEC—and the Bolshevik and Left SR Central Committees fled Petrograd under cover of darkness the night of 10/11 March. Meticulous arrangements for the trip were made by Vladimir Bonch-Bruevich. According to top-secret instructions, government and party officials, with their families and personal baggage, would depart for Moscow promptly on a secluded spur of the Nikolaevskii railway line linking Petersburg and Moscow. At least three separate trains, guarded by Latvian Riflemen, had been assembled for the journey. Lenin, Krupskaia, Lenin's sister Maria Il'ichna, and other members of the Sovnarkom and their families rode in the lead train. It was followed at several minute intervals by trains carrying the CEC and the Central Committees of the governing parties.

All went smoothly until the convoy reached the small railway station of Malaia Vishera, approximately seventy-five miles southeast of Petrograd. There the convoy was stopped by the unexpected presence of a freight train loaded with unruly, armed Baltic Fleet sailors. The sailors were subdued in a few hours, and the government was able to proceed without further incident. Accounts published in Russia in the Soviet era dismissed the incident at Malaia Vishera as the work of anarchic sailors who were flocking home without authorization and happened to be in the area.[96] Roving bands of marauding soldiers and sailors were common on Russian railways at the time, and so that may have been true. The convoy arrived safely in Moscow the evening of 11/12 March. However, the possibility cannot be excluded that the sailors had been bent on stopping the government's evacuation.

As a group, Kronstadt sailors tended to be particularly enthusiastic and enduring supporters of revolutionary war. Their independence and radicalism were reflected in the strong influence that Left SRs (allied with the smaller, radical SR splinter group, the SR Maksimalists) attained in the Kronstadt Soviet during the first months of 1918. Typical of mass sentiment in Kronstadt at this time was a letter prominently featured in the 2 March issue of *Izvestiia Kronshtadtskogo soveta*.[97] "Did we overthrow Russian tsarism and the bourgeoisie to bow before German stranglers without a fight?" the writer of this letter asked, and then answered: "No, and a thousand times no! . . . Shame on the cowards who flee Red Petrograd!" The Kronstadt Soviet continued to call for the rejection of the Sovnarkom's peace policy and the resumption of war against Germany well after popular opinion, and the opinion of most soviets in Petrograd, had swung to support ratification. Consequently, as the Kronstadt Left SR Aleksandr Brushvit observed at the second Left SR national congress in April, "in Bolshevik circles Kronstadt has become suspect; they [the Bolsheviks] no longer brag about it being the glory and pride of the revolution."[98]

* * *

The Fourth All-Russian Congress of Soviets convened in Moscow on the evening of 15 March, three days after the main body of national officials arrived there. Congress delegates were faced with a fait accompli with respect to the main issues on the congress's agenda, namely, ratification of the Brest peace and transfer of the capital from Petrograd to Moscow. According to the official tally of the credentials committee, 814 of the 1,172 voting delegates who participated were Bolsheviks (most of whom came to the congress pledged to support ratification), 238 were Left SRs, and 114 belonged to smaller parties or were unaffiliated.[99] Representation from individual soviets was capricious, owing primarily to the lack of firmly enforced regulations for election of delegates, poor communications, and transport difficulties. Yet, at least concerning the proportion between "Leninist," Left Communist, and Left SR representatives, it does not appear that the composition of the congress had been corrupted. A pre-congress public pledge by Shteinberg to screen all delegations for "dead souls" notwithstanding, the credentials of only 14 Bolshevik voting delegates were challenged.[100] Not during the congress nor after did the Left SRs or Left Communists question the congress's legitimacy.

Published tabulations of questionnaires about attitudes toward war and peace that the Sovnarkom and CEC had solicited from soviets around the country revealed much stronger support for revolutionary war than was evident among congress delegates; however, these data were largely invalidated as indicators of sentiment in mid March, as a high percentage of them predated the preliminary peace agreement between Soviet Russia and Germany signed on 3 March, and also predated subsequent pre-congress regional and local assemblies at which delegates to the Fourth Congress of Soviets were elected.[101] Probably of greatest influence on the vote of Bolshevik fractions at these pre-congress gatherings was the strong endorsement of ratification at the Seventh All-Russian Bolshevik Party Congress, as well as news of the continuing debacle at the front.

The overwhelming support for ratification among Bolshevik delegates to the national soviet congress emerged at initial fraction meetings on 13 and 14 March; at these meetings, after Lenin presented the case for ratification and provincial party organizations delivered their reports, it was decided that Lenin would present the party's position on the question at the congress. The Left Communists, having been defeated again, later met separately to decide on their strategy.[102] It was agreed, at this gathering, that the Left Communists' opposition to the Brest peace, and their future tactics, would be outlined in a formal declaration to the congress. In the interest of maintaining party discipline, however, Left Communists would not participate in the congress debate over ratification and they would abstain from voting on the issue.

The Left SR congress fraction, meeting simultaneously, heard reports from their representatives in local soviets, a majority of whom rejected the peace. Kamkov and Shteinberg made fervent appeals for continued opposition to ratification and, after a lengthy debate, the fraction adopted this position. Arguments among Left SRs at this time centered less on whether to oppose ratification than on the decision of the Left SR Central Committee to require its representatives in the Sovnarkom to resign their posts if the Brest treaty was approved so that the party would be free to lead continued "uprisings" against German imperialism.

In view of all this, the proceedings of the Fourth All-Russian Congress of Soviets were, predictably, perfunctory. Most of the first session on 15 March was taken up by a long, elliptical presentation by Lenin in favor of ratification. The battle against opponents of ratification having already been won, Lenin avoided unnecessarily offending the Left Communists in the hope of restoring a measure of party unity as quickly as possible. A central theme of his remarks was that the onslaught of imperialism and finance capital on the Russian revolution had begun with Germany's mid-February offensive, and that, helpless to combat it, the further development of the Russian revolution depended on a successful uprising of the European proletariat.[103]

With the Left Communists remaining silent, the main speeches for the opponents of ratification were made by Kamkov and Shteinberg. Kamkov ridiculed the very idea that the congress was being asked to ratify peace, pointing to areas of the former Russian Empire, such as Ukraine, where German advances were being met with spirited resistance. To him, Soviet Russia was still at war with Germany; Germany would continue to make crippling demands on Russia irrespective of ratification, and, consequently, ratification would inevitably lead to the total suffocation of the Russian revolution and the complete defeat of everything the laboring classes had achieved in the preceding year.

In his speech, Lenin had not elaborated on the idea of the "breathing space" that was central to his argument for peace at the Seventh Party Congress and in his writings of this period. This did not deter Kamkov, however. He made it plain that, to him, the notion that a "peace" on the terms the Germans offered could be of any strategic value whatsoever was ludicrous. Building an army, for one, would be impossible under Germany's terms. From whatever angle it was approached, stressed Kamkov, ratification would not solve anything. Yet he did not exaggerate the prospects for a successful defense by the Russian army, placing considerably less emphasis on traditional military combat than on the efficacy of partisan warfare and on the probability that imminent decisive socialist revolutions abroad would come to revolutionary Russia's rescue unless they were undermined by her capitulation to German imperialism. By ratifying the Brest treaty, Soviet Russia would not only destroy itself, it would commit a profoundly treacherous act toward the revolutionary proletariat abroad. It would suppress the popular international upsurge that would ensue at the sight of a struggling, perhaps dying, but undefeated revolutionary Russia rather than the defeated, suppressed, groveling, and trampled one that would be the inevitable result of the capitulation Lenin proposed.[104]

In concluding remarks, Kamkov sketched out the strategy of the Left SRs in the event the peace with Germany was ratified. They would do everything they could to insure that the peace terms would not be fulfilled, and they would transfer their forces to wherever Russian workers and peasants were continuing to fight against the Germans, confident that, eventually, the international revolutionary movement would come to their rescue.[105] Shteinberg also heaped scorn on Lenin and insisted that the aspirations of the Germans left Soviet Russia with no choice but to fight and, by example, stimulate worldwide revolutionary uprisings. If the peace was ratified, he warned, Left SRs would withdraw from the Sovnarkom, following which the best elements of the laboring classes led by Left SRs, arm in arm with healthy elements in the Bolshevik party, would fight on.[106] This comment by Shteinberg was the only mention by Left SRs at the congress of their hopes for collaboration with Left Communists.

Interspersed with the speeches of Lenin, Kamkov, Shteinberg, and Zinoviev, the Soviet Congress heard remarks by Martov for the Mensheviks, Mikhail Likhach representing Right and Centrist SRs, Aleksandr Ge representing the Anarchist-Communists, Grigorii Rivkin for the SR Maksimalists, and Valerian Pletnev for the United Social-Democratic Internationalists. All of the latter fiercely opposed ratification and proposed resolutions reflecting this position. Except for the Anarchist-Communists and the SR Maksimalists, these resolutions also called for removing the Bolsheviks from power through re-convocation of the Constituent Assembly, election of a new government on the basis of universal suffrage, or a fundamental restructuring of the existing Soviet system. The overwhelming vote in favor of ratification was anticlimactic, as the result was apparent from the outset. Only after it was registered did Sverdlov permit the Left Communists to make public their continued opposition to the Brest treaty. On the last day of the congress (16 March), in a formal statement obviously prepared for presentation before the vote, the Left Communists declared that the treaty should not be ratified but, instead, be replaced by an appeal for the holy defense of the socialist revolution. The declaration, signed by fifty-eight Left Communist voting delegates and nine additional Left Communist members of the CEC, ended by explaining that, although its supporters felt obligated to openly express their views, a [formal] split in the Bolshevik party would be dangerous to the revolutionary cause and therefore, having read their declaration, they would abstain from the vote on ratification. In sum, while distancing themselves from ratification and backing away from openly splitting the party, the Left Communists made it clear that they would continue to oppose the separate peace and work to mobilize revolutionary Russia's defenses.[107]

The decision on ratification having been made, the congress turned to a similarly perfunctory consideration of transferring the capital to Moscow. It fell to Zinoviev, still chairman of the Petrograd Soviet, to present the Bolshevik position on this issue. According to him, transfer of the capital was dictated by the fact that, strategically, Petrograd was in an extremely critical situation (at which point a delegate on the right screamed out: "What, you mean you don't have enough suitcases?"). Acknowledging that relocation of the capital was not a matter of "weeks or months," Zinoviev insisted that it would be relatively short. The resolution he presented, which was adopted by a near unanimous vote, simply stipulated that, pending a change in Petrograd's military situation, the capital of the Russian Socialist Federated Soviet Republic would "temporarily" move from Petrograd to Moscow.[108]

*   *   *

The Left Communists and Left SRs carried through on their threat to withdraw from the Sovnarkom if the Brest Treaty was ratified. A couple of days after the Fourth All-Russian Congress of Soviets closed, at the first Moscow meeting of the Sovnarkom on 18 March, the main item on the agenda was the "general ministerial crisis" caused by the resignations from the government of the Left SRs and the Left Communists Aleksandra Kollontai, Vladimir Smirnov, Valerian Obolenskii (Osinskii), and Pavel Dybenko. In hastily scribbled notes, virtually all the departing Left SRs grounded their resignations on the decision of their Central Committee.[109]

Observers could be pardoned if their heads spun from the speed of the ensuing change in the Bolshevik–Left SR relationship at the national level. During the Third All-Russian Congress of Soviets, in January, Lenin had beamed with enthusiasm about the Bolshevik–Left SR alliance, declaring that it was growing stronger not by days but by hours, that in the Sovnarkom most questions were resolved by unanimous vote.[110] Little more than two months later, following the Fourth All-Russian Congress of Soviets, he dismissed the union of the two parties as "love without joy, separation from which would be devoid of sadness."[111]

After withdrawing from the Sovnarkom, both Left Communists and Left SRs remained engaged in lower-level and local soviet institutions and continued their struggle against the Brest treaty. The Left SRs also stepped up their guerrilla warfare against the Germans in the Baltic region and Ukraine. Moreover, they initiated steps to implement a program of terrorism against high-level German officials.[112]

Meanwhile, the struggle for political leadership between Leninists and Left Communists had played out in Petrograd. On 9 March, the Bolshevik Petersburg Committee had voted to convene an emergency city party conference on 20 March, the Emergency Fifth City Congress of Petrograd Bolsheviks. Ostensibly, the purpose of this conference was to assess the attitudes of the local party organization's rank and file toward the decision of the Seventh All-Russian Bolshevik Party Congress the day before to endorse ratification of the Treaty of Brest-Litovsk.[113] Apparently, the Petersburg Committee first discussed the hostile resolution adopted by the party's Soviet fraction at a meeting on 12 March, during the brief interval between the Seventh Party Congress in Petrograd and the Fourth All-Russian Congress of Soviets in Moscow. Its response to the fraction's attack on *Kommunist,* and its unprecedented demand for the election of a new Petersburg Committee, was remarkably restrained, no doubt owing in part to its own loss of confidence. The committee simply reaffirmed its scheduling of an emergency city party conference to consider all controversial issues, and pointedly reminded the Soviet fraction that its Left Communist theses had been adopted at the continuation of the Fourth Conference of Petrograd Bolsheviks on 1 March.[114]

An announcement to this effect appeared in *Kommunist* on 14 March.[115] The Left Communist majority of the Petersburg Committee undoubtedly hoped that, upon reflection and discussion, and with the help of *Kommunist,* Bolsheviks "in the districts" would ignore the Seventh Party Congress's vote to support the Brest treaty, as well as its formal ratification by the Fourth All-Russian Congress of Soviets, if that was the decision made there. In short, their hope was that Bolsheviks at lower levels of the Petrograd party organization would remain true to revolutionary principles as Left Communists defined them and that they would vote accordingly in the election of delegates to the city conference. But this was not to be. In the debate over peace and war at the Emergency Fifth City Conference of Petrograd Bolsheviks on 20 March, Radek, for the Left Communist Petersburg Committee, blasted the Brest peace as a grave setback for the socialist revolution and appealed for an end to concessions to Germany. Zinoviev, speaking for supporters of ratification, heaped criticism on the Left Communists, insisted that *Kommunist* be shut down, and demanded that the Left Communists work harmoniously in common party organizations. The result of this clash was a complete reversal of voting on 1 March. A resolution opposing Brest proposed by Radek received seven votes, whereas Zinoviev's resolution in favor of ratification garnered fifty-seven.[116]

* * *

In the days immediately following the resumption of Germany's military operations on 18 February, Soviet authorities in Petrograd had begun a frantic effort to shore up the city's defenses. They were impeded, however, by the profound demoralization of garrison troops and the instability of factory workers, disenchanted by the economic results of the October revolution, ravaged by transfers out of the city, and disoriented by the unexpectedness of the German assault. Neither the best efforts of Petrograd district soviets, where many of the Bolsheviks' most experienced local-level leaders were increasingly concentrated, nor appeals by the Bolsheviks' and the Left SRs' most prominent national figures yielded significant numbers of Red Army recruits. Moreover, further complicating the crisis of Soviet power in Petrograd at this time was the expansion of subversive activity by domestic counterrevolutionary groups, despite intensified efforts by security agencies to suppress them. The occupation of Pskov by German forces on 24 February stimulated a modest improvement in military recruitment, especially when additions to ad hoc partisan detachments and Left SR combat squads were combined with those for the Red Army. But as the gravity of the Russian debacle at the front became widely known, and workers concluded that trying to combat the Germans meant certain death, the modest surge in recruitment evaporated.

During this time, the Left Communist leadership of the Bolshevik party organization in Petrograd remained fiercely opposed to the Brest peace and steadfastly supportive of revolutionary war, as shown by its position upon resumption of the Fourth City Conference of Petrograd Bolsheviks on 1 March, and the publication of the first issue of *Kommunist* on 5 March. Yet, very quickly, Petrograd Left Communists were forced to recognize the weakness of popular support for their views. Also, the Petersburg Committee's independent stance triggered the rebellion against it by the Leninist party fraction in the Petrograd Soviet and the Central Committee's decision to replace the committee. The end of an independent Left Communist movement in Petrograd was marked by the Emergency Fifth City Conference of Petrograd Bolsheviks on 20 March, at which the Left Communists led by Radek were routed by Leninists led by Zinoviev.

Meanwhile, the Brest peace had been ratified by the skeletal Seventh All-Russian Bolshevik Party Congress, held in Petrograd, after which the Soviet government had fled to Moscow. Although the treaty was also confirmed by the Fourth All-Russian Congress of Soviets, controversy over the treaty raged on, as did its negative impact. At the national level, both the Left Communists and Left SRs withdrew from the Sovnarkom, and many of them adopted an independent course. Moreover, if after the relocation of the national government Petrograd's primary importance to Lenin lay in the human and industrial resources that could be saved from the Germans for use elsewhere, this view was most certainly not shared by Bolshevik leaders left behind. For them, "Red Petrograd" still had pride of place as the headquarters and standard bearer of the approaching world revolution. Most important, they were faced with the daunting task of directing the survival of Soviet power in Petrograd in an ever more hostile and complex environment.

PART THREE

SOVIET POWER ON THE BRINK

8

A Turbulent Spring

THE SOVNARKOM's flight to Moscow coincided with deepening food and fuel shortages and skyrocketing social problems. Bolshevik leaders staying in Petrograd were also faced with the emerging opposition of Petrograd workers, the social class most responsible for their rise to power in 1917. In the late spring and early summer of 1918, these problems worsened and new ones emerged, among them military moves toward Petrograd by Finnish Whites supported by the Germans, endangering the still formidable Russian Baltic Fleet; a rebellion by disgruntled workers from the large Obukhov plant, supported by Baltic Fleet personnel; and a devastating cholera epidemic. On top of all this, civil war exploded from the Volga to the Pacific and on the Don, and Red Army and armed worker detachments were mobilized to squeeze grain from the peasantry by force, imposing new pressures for the ever dwindling human resources still at the disposal of Bolshevik authorities in Petrograd. In its struggle to overcome these crises, the Council of Commissars of the Petrograd Labor Commune (SK PTK) initially adopted a relatively moderate political course. Although it later turned to tougher measures, it resisted using the extreme forms of repression Moscow was pressing. During this period of deepening turmoil, the ability of Soviet power in Petrograd to survive was in no small part the result of effective collaboration between the Bolsheviks and Left SRs in governing the region.

* * *

The Soviet central government and Bolshevik Central Committee fled Petrograd on the night of 10 March 1918, believing that German forces would soon occupy the city. At the Seventh Party Congress two days earlier, Lenin acknowledged that signing the peace would probably only spare Piter for a few days, although he immediately instructed stenographers not to "even think about recording my remark."[1] Because the Sovnarkom assumed that Soviet power in Petrograd was doomed and because it was preoccupied with preparations for evacuation, it did not devote any attention to Petrograd's future government or security prior to its departure. At its second to last Petrograd meeting, on 8 March, the Sovnarkom discussed preparations for an unimpeded escape. The next day it took account of potential problems related to the transfer of critical industrial plants and personnel from Petrograd. Members of the Emergency Commission for the Evacuation of Petrograd were instructed to stay at their posts "until the last."[2] Beyond this, the Sovnarkom apparently assumed that, until the capital fell, the Petrograd Soviet and its Executive Committee would be responsible for directing local administration according to directives from Moscow. It did not consider that the move necessitated any major structural change in the Petrograd government.

About the time of the Sovnarkom's final Petrograd meeting (9 March), the Executive Committee of the Petrograd Soviet summoned district soviet representatives to form a Petrograd Cheka (PCheka). District soviets were urged, as usual, to appoint "their most energetic people" who would be available for full-time duty.[3] Named head of the PCheka was Uritskii, the former ardent Left Communist. Although, later, Bolshevik opponents often referred to him as the "Robespierre of Petrograd," in practice he had a far more moderate approach to combating counterrevolution compared to the VCheka in Moscow under Dzerzhinskii.[4]

According to Zinoviev, not until the night of the national government's departure did it occur to Bolshevik officials remaining behind that it would be sensible to form an authoritative local government structurally analogous to the central Sovnarkom.[5] What is indisputable is that on the day after the dash to Moscow the Petrograd Soviet's Executive Committee formed the Council of Commissars of the Petrograd Labor Commune (SK PTK), thus associating the abandoned "Red Petrograd" in the popular mind with the heroic myth of the Paris Commune. According to its "constitution," the SK PTK would be responsible to the Petrograd Soviet; the authority of its individual commissariats, merged with corresponding departments of the Petrograd Soviet, would supersede that of local agencies of the national government; and sections of district soviets would be transformed into local agencies of corresponding commissariats of the SK PTK.[6] Although never fully implemented, this "constitution" was a limited declaration of Petrograd's independence from Moscow and of the "Commune" government's ultimate goal of vertically integrating district soviet sections.

Several years later, Aleksandr Il'in-Zhenevskii (the Bolshevik military leader whose wife had committed suicide a few weeks earlier, upon learning that the Germans had resumed their advance on Petrograd) would recall

Leaders of the PCheka. Seated: Uritskii and Bokii; standing: Borizevskii and Ioselevich. State Museum of the Political History of Russia, St. Petersburg.

his exhilaration when he went out into the street after the formation of the Petrograd Labor Commune was announced:

> It seemed strange to find the usual scene. Snow was falling. Pedestrians were hurrying along the pavements. From time to time a horse-drawn cab ambled by. All just as on any other day. Yet we now had a commune! A commune, we could only read about until then. . . . It made one feel giddy just to think of it, and raised ones spirits to unprecedented heights.[7]

Petrograd Bolsheviks, from the beginning, hoped that the new local government would include Left SRs. Zinoviev approached Aleksei Ustinov, for one, about a cabinet appointment. But with most top Left SR leaders already in Moscow for the Fourth All-Russian Congress of Soviets, he was noncommittal. Only Bolsheviks, therefore, were included in the SK PTK, which was confirmed at a plenary session of the Petrograd Soviet on 12 March. The government was to be chaired by Zinoviev, and appointed to head commissariats were Lunacharskii (enlightenment);[8] Viacheslav Menzhinskii (finance); the former mayor Mikhail Kalinin (municipal services); Mikhail

Lashevich (food supply), Petr Stuchka (justice); Viacheslav Molotov [Skriabin] (economy); Adolf Ioffe (social welfare); Miron Vladimirov (transportation); and Ivar Smilga (Petrograd Military District).[9] The most powerful figure in the new government was to be Trotsky, as head of a unique Military-Revolutionary Commissariat with unlimited powers to defend Petrograd from foreign and domestic enemies.[10]

Trotsky held this post only for a few days, just long enough to issue a few tough sounding proclamations.[11] He was pressured out of the government by a majority of the Petrograd Bureau of the Bolshevik Central Committee, composed of Central Committee members who were kept behind in Petrograd, because of his insistence that party commissars not be allowed to meddle in strategic and technical directives of so-called military specialists, or *spetsy*—former tsarist officers now serving as commanders in the new Red Army and Navy. Upon the recommendation of his closest party comrades, Trotsky was hurriedly transferred to Moscow to serve as people's commissar for war.[12] Another member of the original SK PTK, Stuchka, was soon called to Moscow to replace Shteinberg.[13] In short order, Nikolai Krestinskii was appointed commissar for justice, and Uritskii, Boris Pozern, and Adolf Ioffe were named to head commissariats for internal, military, and foreign affairs, respectively. Evgenii Pervukhin, a physician, was placed in charge of the Commissariat for Public Health.

Neither the Petrograd Bureau of the Bolshevik Central Committee nor the Bolshevik Petersburg Committee appears to have played a role in these appointments (apart from the involvement of the former in Trotsky's ouster). When it needed advice on government matters, the SK PTK turned to soviet organs and not to those of the party.[14] This was still a fluid time in the relationship between soviet and party agencies in Petrograd. Local party bodies, stripped of many of their most experienced members, were now beginning to consider broader political and economic issues. However, they still shied away from direct involvement in government. This was because of their overall deference to Bolshevik leaders in soviets and to prevailing attitudes about the appropriate relationship of party to soviet work. In his memoir/study of the Petrograd Bolsheviks in 1918, Kiril Shelavin, the Petersburg Committee's authority on organizational issues, explained that among Petrograd Bolsheviks two views on this issue had emerged. Some leaders were infused with an exclusively "soviet" spirit and looked down on party work as relatively unimportant in building the socialist state. This outlook, along with the many burdens of Bolsheviks in government, helps explain their nearly total separation from party work. Others, "preservers of old traditions," as they were referred to at the time, looked at government service as somehow "dirty" in contrast to "clean" party activity. However, both groups viewed party work simply as agitation and propaganda, according to Shelavin.[15]

At a meeting on 6 March, several days before the central government's departure but after the evacuation had begun, the Petersburg Committee's agenda included preliminary preparations to go underground in case of German occupation, internal party matters such as arrangements connected with the Seventh All-Russian Party Congress, the publication of *Kommunist*,[16] and problems with how the evacuation was being handled.[17] On 12 March, the day after the government's flight, the Petersburg Committee discussed the attack by the Bolshevik fraction in the Petrograd Soviet on its opposition to the Brest peace, as well as preparations for the Emergency Fifth City Conference of Petrograd Bolsheviks.[18] The same meeting also addressed the recruitment of party members for the Cheka. After issuing levies to district party committees, the city party leadership, as was then customary, abdicated further responsibility for a government institution (in this case the PCheka). Also on the Petersburg Committee's agenda on the twelfth were such nongovernmental matters as the provision of firearms to party members (it was decided that this was "desirable" and that the committee's embryonic military detachment should provide instructors in the use of weapons) and preparations for a "triumphant" meeting of the Petrograd Soviet that evening to commemorate the first anniversary of the February revolution.[19] Selection of a comrade to represent the party organization in the Petrograd Soviet was tabled. However, nothing was said on the sixth or the twelfth about how Petrograd should be governed in the absence of the Sovnarkom and the CEC.

On 25 and 27 March, initial meetings of the Assembly of Organizers created by the Fourth City Conference of Petrograd Bolsheviks revealed that party work was paralyzed in most districts after the transfer of seasoned Bolshevik leaders from party to government and military work, and following plant shutdowns, massive unemployment, and the debilitating impact of intraparty conflict over the Brest treaty. In textile mills, which were among the relatively very few industrial enterprises still operating, a particular problem appeared to be the great difficulty in even getting a hearing from their largely female workforce.[20]

On 26 March the Petersburg Committee rescinded its decision of 24 February to encourage party activists to give priority to soviet work over party work.[21] On 6 April, the First Northern Oblast [Bolshevik] Party Conference agreed on the importance of enhancing the authority of party agencies over soviets, and, finally, on 8 April, the Petersburg Committee adopted measures to facilitate the influence of district committees, if not their control, over district soviets.[22] For example, the organization of district soviet fractions nominally subordinate to party committees was now instituted. Although such measures represented implicit recognition of the primacy of party bodies over soviets, which Lenin and the central party leadership in Moscow were emphasizing at this time, they were ineffective as a result of continuing drains on the personnel of district committees and the continued concentration of the party's most senior and most competent members in soviets. As Stasova wrote, on 22 May, "Party work is in terrible decline because all our forces have gone into soviets."[23]

Also reflecting this state of affairs was a remarkably candid report that the Bolshevik party committee in the Second City district submitted to the Sixth City Conference of Petrograd Bolsheviks in June 1918. As the report put it, "the majority of [our] party members who have gone to work in soviets or [other] municipal agencies have lost all touch with the district [party committee] and any kind of control over their work is beyond the realm of possibility. . . . [Moreover,] as a result of our own isolation from the worker masses . . . our activity has been limited to regular weekly meetings. . . . [Even] efforts to influence the activity of the [district] soviet have failed. . . . Decisions on upgrading party work exist only on paper."[24]

*   *   *

During this initial transition period from capital to "second city," municipal government in Petrograd was reminiscent of the first chaotic weeks after October; a major difference was that rotting, uncollected refuse and the carcasses of dead animals were now hidden under mountains of unshoveled snow. Meanwhile, 205 new cases of typhus were recorded in Petrograd during the week preceding the government's flight, and medical specialists practically guaranteed that warmer weather would bring a devastating cholera epidemic. "I have been in China, Persia, and all of Asia," a worried epidemiologist attached to the Military Medical Academy told a newspaper reporter at the beginning of April, "but I have never seen anything like what I am now seeing in Petrograd."[25]

As it strove somehow to establish a functioning government and overcome mounting problems, the SK PTK received precious little support from Moscow. From the start, Petrograd authorities were strapped for funds. Resources at the disposal of the national government were also very limited. Still, records of the central Sovnarkom reveal that requests for emergency financial allocations from the SK PTK, however urgent, were invariably received with striking callousness. For example, after one of its earliest meetings, the SK PTK sent an urgent appeal to Moscow for a maintenance subsidy of one hundred million rubles. The Sovnarkom's response, which was adopted at only its third Moscow meeting on 21 March, but that would become typical, was to put off a decision pending clarifications.[26] Also, the requested funds were labeled as an advance against budgeted expenses. This frustrating response notwithstanding, clarifications followed quickly. This time, on 28 March, the Sovnarkom approved an allocation of twenty million rubles on the condition that all expenditures would be controlled by the state comptroller and that, in the future, the Petrograd government would present a budget for advances against expenses ahead of time. At Trotsky's suggestion, it was also stipulated that the government of Petrograd should inventory available reserves of materials and food supplies, and ship all possible surpluses out of the city; and that, subject to [prior] approval by the central government, all marketable military and other surpluses that could not be evacuated from Petrograd should be sold. The division of proceeds from such sales would be the prerogative of the central government.[27]

On 11 April, Zinoviev sent an urgent emergency funding request to Moscow by courier. In this case, he based a plea for an additional one hundred million rubles on the unemployment and food supply crises, which had reached new highs and were providing fertile ground for agitation among workers by opposition groups and antisemitic, right-wing extremists. Zinoviev correctly perceived that this posed a dangerous new threat to Soviet power: "Unemployment in Petrograd . . . has taken an especially sharp [upward] turn," he wrote. "Every day delegations come from our factories in the Vyborg and other [worker districts] and tell us . . . it is impossible to live like this any longer. . . . [It is] vital that a workers' government not allow workers to die of hunger . . . An *immediate* allocation of one hundred million [rubles] is essential or else [Soviet power] in Petrograd will find itself in the most critical situation imaginable."[28] In a separate message to the party leadership in Moscow, the Petrograd Bureau of the Bolshevik Central Committee declared bluntly that it would be unable to accept responsibility for party work in the former capital if Zinoviev's request was rejected.[29] On 12 April, upon Sverdlov's recommendation, the Sovnarkom approved the one hundred million ruble allocation. However, release of this sum, minus the twenty million approved on 28 March, was predicated on the issuance of guarantees regarding the correct and sensible use of the funds according to a plan developed by an ad hoc commission of the central Sovnarkom.[30]

These provocative responses may have reflected attempts by Moscow to force Petrograd to make efficient use of its own resources, institute accountability in budgetary matters, and assert its authority over Petrograd. However, they also betrayed a coolness toward Petrograd's needs, a sense that Petrograd no longer mattered, which was profoundly resented in the former capital. In a similar spirit, Moscow felt completely free to direct matters relating to Petrograd that would have been better handled by consultation. For example, the Sovnarkom unilaterally assigned Petrograd Bolsheviks to positions elsewhere at will. On 9 April, after several key Petrograd personnel were unexpectedly assigned to Moscow, the SK PTK resolved to inform the central government that no more "responsible figures in the Petrograd Labor Commune could be torn from their work without its approval."[31] There is no evidence that this injunction had any effect.

The Sovnarkom also attempted to control matters central to Petrograd's internal affairs, such as industrial evacuation, which local authorities wished to coordinate. In a blunt letter to Moscow dated 23 March, Zinoviev conveyed Petrograd's decision to take control of evacuation, because, as he explained, evacuation was proceeding without prior planning, with the result that Petrograd industries slated for evacuation and those plants already in the provinces were idle.[32] Relevant sources suggest that unilateral administrative reorganization, whether emanating from Moscow or Petrograd, only served to make evacuation a bigger mess than it already was. In any case, minutes of meetings of the central Sovnarkom and the SK PTK, as well as correspondence between the Petrograd Bureau of the Central Committee and the Central Committee, leave no doubt: relations between Petrograd and Moscow at this time were greatly complicated by provocative exchanges over budget, personnel, evacuation, and other less weighty but symbolically significant matters. Chaotic evacuation policies and practices also contributed mightily to deepening unrest among Petrograd's factory workers.

* * *

In trying to overcome Moscow's coldness to Petrograd's needs and to strengthen popular support for Soviet power in the Petrograd region, which had been undermined by the Sovnarkom's "panicked" flight to Moscow, deepening food shortages, expanding unemployment, and chaotic evacuation policies, the SK PTK initially adopted a moderate political tack with mixed results. This policy shift can be seen in the contrast between the Moscow and Petrograd governments in the area of political repression. As soon as it was on its feet, the PCheka began to arrest suspected counterrevolutionaries, speculators, and thieves.[33] However, many of these suspects, especially political detainees, were released soon after being deposed.[34] The shooting of prisoners in Petrograd by authorized agencies other than the PCheka continued, primarily for particularly heinous common crimes (the VCheka had begun conducting such shootings in late February). Also, theft and killings by criminals, many of them members of gangs, with an extraordinarily high percentage posing as Chekists, skyrocketed. So did wild shootings, often by newly recruited Red Army soldiers, Red Guards, and anarchists.[35] Every night, Petrograd's hospitals received piles of bodies picked up on the street. Frequently, the killers made off with the victims' clothing. Most corpses remained in morgues for weeks unidentified and then were buried by the truckload.[36] Yet Uritskii, as head of the PCheka, steadfastly refused to sanction shootings. His emphasis was less on the restoration of order through terror than by concrete measures aimed at halting violence, economic crimes, and abuses of power.

This orientation, which differed markedly from that of the VCheka in Moscow,[37] was reflected in Uritskii's earliest directives. On 15 March, he issued preliminary guidelines aimed at strict regulation of searches and at catching fake and corrupt Chekists.[38] Conspicuously missing from agencies authorized to conduct searches were Red Army personnel.[39] One week later, Uritskii issued a widely circulated order giving citizens three days to turn in unauthorized arms, bombs, grenades, and explosives. Individuals violating this order were to be sent to the Revolutionary Tribunal for trial but were not threatened with shooting. Simultaneously, district soviets were directed to intensify street patrols to confiscate weapons from citizens who did not have permits for them.[40]

Nikolai Krestinskii was named commissar for justice in the SK PTK on 4 April. Like Uritskii, he had a degree in law and a long history of revolutionary activity, was a Left Communist in the dispute over the signing of the Treaty of Brest-Litovsk, and was also against extreme repression of political foes. His appointment, along with pressure from Uritskii, appears to have prodded the SK PTK, then concerned with regaining popular support by displaying a "human face," to speed up judicial proceedings against jailed political figures. Apparently this decision was also influenced by the need to reduce Petrograd's burgeoning prison population, if only because feeding, housing, and controlling the spread of infectious disease among prisoners was prohibitive (typhus, for one, was then rampant in jails). Also, sailors at the Kronstadt naval base were balking at accepting Petrograd's prison overflow, a position that had been expressed in an *Izvestiia Kronshtadtskogo soveta* editorial of 10 March:

> Individuals and whole groups of people are being sent to Kronstadt. . . . What is more, most of them arrive without documentation on what is to be done with them. . . . Such an ugly understanding of Kronstadt's role must

stop. Great Kronstadt is neither a warehouse for counterrevolutionaries, a universal prison, nor a scaffold. . . . It cannot and does not want to be a kind of revolutionary Sakhalin: it does not want its name to become synonymous with prison and executioner.[41]

Only a few days after his appointment, Krestinskii was authorized to take all necessary measures to speed up the investigation, trial, and disposition of prisoners.[42] A May Day amnesty for broad categories of common criminals charged with minor offenses, political prisoners, and prisoners older than seventy, as well as a 50 percent reduction in the sentences of common criminals guilty of more serious offenses, initiated by the SK PTK on 27 April, extended this effort.[43] In comments at a meeting of the Bolshevik fraction in the First Northern Oblast Congress of Soviets which endorsed it, Zinoviev took pains to emphasize the amnesty's political significance; he argued that "it was necessary for Soviet power to renounce its previous methods of struggle against political opponents, [that] Soviet power had become so strong that individual political opponents no longer constituted a threat, [and that] workers and soldiers . . . having vanquished them [their enemies] in economic and political combat, did not want to treat them in ways that were customary in all imperialist and monarchist states."[44] To the Petrograd Soviet, which also endorsed the amnesty, Zinoviev boasted that the question of a May Day amnesty arose in Petrograd independently of Moscow.[45]

Simultaneously, the PCheka's self-imposed ban on shootings was broadened. On 16 April, the SK PTK received a report from Uritskii on limiting, to investigations, the Committee for the Revolutionary Security of Petrograd in the Commissariat for Internal Affairs. The report apparently led to a comprehensive discussion of shootings by city agencies. At this time, the Committee for the Revolutionary Security of Petrograd was the main city-level police agency still carrying out summary executions after the VCheka's departure and Uritskii's prohibition of PCheka shootings. Charged with developing guidelines for the prohibition of shootings, and situations in which resort to arms was permissible,[46] Krestinskii presented his guidelines a week later, and the SK PTK then issued a public announcement stipulating that, henceforth, "no institutions in the city of Petrograd had the right to conduct shootings."[47] This absolute ban applied to the PCheka, the Committee for the Revolutionary Security of Petrograd, Revolutionary Tribunals, Red Guards, Red Army troops, and district soviets, thus officially annulling the authorization for shootings proclaimed during the German advance in late February. Although conspiratorial political activity and major crime in

Moscow at this time resulted in unofficial "Red Terror," the SK PTK's prohibition of extreme repression lasted through the summer.

* * *

The growing disenchantment of Petrograd workers with Bolshevik/Soviet power, in the spring of 1918, was reflected in the formation of the Extraordinary Assembly of Delegates from Petrograd Factories and Plants (EAD), a citywide opposition movement of moderate socialists and unaffiliated factory workers that subsequently spread to other industrial areas. The primary driving force for this movement was horrendous food supply shortages. In mid January 1918, the already alarming food supply situation in Petrograd suddenly worsened, then eased a bit in February, but rose more sharply than ever in the early spring. Some of the many factors causing these shortages were related to the effects of the Brest treaty. In 1917 more than half of Russia's grain reserves had come from Ukraine (350 million of 650 million puds),[48] with another 110 million puds from the North Caucasus, 143 million from the steppe borderlands and Western Siberia, and the remainder from the Central black earth region. After consummation of the Brest treaty, grain from Ukraine was lost altogether. Moreover, German occupation of the provinces of Kursk and Voronezh blocked grain shipments from the North Caucasus. The best Soviet Russia could then hope for was around 150 million puds of grain, mostly from Western Siberia.[49]

Grain procurement problems affecting Petrograd were also worsened by the dreadful conditions of railway cars and lines necessary for grain shipments from Western Siberia. Further, with the Germans and Ukrainians controlling the Donets Basin, coal supplies to power trains fell by more than 25 percent. Owing to the prevailing disorganization, the sowing of grain dropped by an estimated 40–70 percent. Unable to furnish peasants with manufactured goods, the Soviet government had resorted to printing increasingly worthless paper money, causing peasants to lose incentive to produce for the market. And, as if this were not enough, traditional mechanisms for buying and selling grain were in chaos as a result of mutual hostility and mistrust between holdover institutions and personnel, and inexperienced, competing soviet food procurement organs and officials.[50]

A second major element contributing to disaffection with Bolshevik/Soviet power among Petrograd workers and to the creation of the EAD was mass unemployment, partially caused, and greatly exacerbated, by inefficient demobilization and evacuation policies. The industrial crisis in Petrograd had begun long before the October revolution, primarily because of shortages of fuel and raw materials. It worsened further toward the end of

1917 and the beginning of 1918, after factories engaged in war-related production were ordered to move eastward or adapt production to peacetime needs or shut down altogether.

Early Soviet economic policies contributed to the deepening of the industrial crisis in other ways. "Workers' control" in factories was a prominent Bolshevik slogan before the October revolution, and, in its immediate aftermath, workers naturally strove to implement it. Efforts by the Sovnarkom to impose some order into the process of giving workers a voice in plant management through supervisory councils of workers' control failed to stop Bolshevized workers, led by their factory committees, from frequently intervening in running their plants. Toward the end of 1917, and in the first months of 1918, clashes between workers and management led to the Soviet government's nationalization of individual Petrograd enterprises to prevent frustrated owners from shutting them down.[51] At the beginning of December, moreover, efforts to create councils of workers' control were dropped and the Sovnarkom established the Supreme Council of the National Economy (VSNKh) to direct the entire economy. Over the next few years, the VSNKh and a nationwide network of regional, provincial, and local SNKhs developed into the Soviet government's primary institutions for the centralization and administration of industry. In the short run, however, spontaneous workers' control, coupled with these institutional zigzags, only caused the further disintegration of Petrograd industry.[52]

A few statistics illustrate the magnitude of the resulting economic and social catastrophe: between January 1 and the beginning of April 1918, approximately 134,000 workers, or 46 percent of Petrograd's industrial labor force, joined the ranks of the unemployed,[53] and an estimated 265 Petrograd factories sat idle. Hardest hit by this economic and social calamity were workers in larger metalworking and chemical plants and in parts of Petrograd such as the "Red" Vyborg workers' district, which had been at the forefront of mass support for the Bolsheviks and Soviet power throughout 1917.[54] As food shortages became increasingly acute, a significant percentage of unemployed workers fled Petrograd for the countryside.

The emergence of the EAD was also stimulated by the widespread view that trade unions, factory committees, and soviets, perhaps especially district soviets, were no longer representative, democratically run working-class institutions; instead, they had been transformed into arbitrary, bureaucratic government agencies. There was ample reason for this concern. At this point, virtually all the functions of former, sub-district duma boards and agencies had in fact been transferred or were in the process of being shifted to district soviets, thus transforming them into self-proclaimed masters in their neighborhoods. They now jealously guarded their independent authority over all aspects of local rule, not only horizontally, from encroachments by local Bolshevik committees, but also vertically, from direction of their sections "from above" by corresponding departments of the SK PTK.[55]

Laying claim to the supreme authority of district soviets was one thing; finding loyal, qualified personnel to meet rapidly expanding obligations efficiently was quite another. Before the October revolution, a handful of unpaid volunteers easily recruited from among elected deputies were all the staff that district soviets required to carry on their operations and maintain contact with working-class constituents. For a brief time after October, Bolshevik and Left SR party committees could be counted on to provide additional personnel as needed. By the first quarter of 1918, however, many Bolshevik and Left SR district soviet leaders were no longer available. Large numbers of them had been transferred out of Petrograd. The continuing flow of Bolsheviks from party work into government did not compensate for these losses. Indeed, the personnel pool at the disposal of district party committees was already so thin and untested that frequently the committees themselves quickly regretted their appointments to district soviets and complained about their bureaucratization.[56] At the same time, dedicated veterans who remained in the district soviets filled two and sometimes more full-time positions, for which they were, in any case, unprepared. In these circumstances, to an ever increasing degree, a good part of district soviet work was perforce in the hands of hastily recruited, sometimes corrupt, paid administrators, clerks, militiamen, agitators, foremen, and technical personnel. With committed deputies trying to do so much, and given the many vacancies at any one time because of transfers, plenary meetings of district soviets were convened less and less frequently, and were poorly attended. Even decisions on important matters were often decided by whoever happened to be on hand. As in the case of Bolshevik district committees, links between local soviets and factory workers, critical for leftist success in 1917, were broken. Who had time for meetings and agitation among constituents with the Germans at the gates?

The Soviet government's seemingly frantic retreat to Moscow after weeks of denying that a move was being considered gave another boost to the EAD. In many factories the surreptitious move, in the dead of night, triggered resentment, even panic. "[Workers] are referring to 12 March as the day the revolution died," lamented a representative of a locomotive maintenance shop at the first EAD plenary meeting on 13 March.[57] "Last year, we were screaming 'Down with Nicholas!'" recalled a delegate from the Staryi Lessner machine-building plant. "Now the workers are shouting 'Down with the Bolsheviks!'" A representative of the Rechkina railcar factory added that workers there were "devastated," that it seemed to them that everything was rotting. According to a report by the Izhorskii shipbuilding and armaments plant representative at the next plenary meeting of the EAD, on 15 March, workers had been so angry about the government's flight that they proposed blowing up the trains carrying government personnel to Moscow.[58]

Some sources trace the origins of the EAD to discussions in Right Menshevik circles in mid January, following the dissolution of the Constituent Assembly.[59] Iurii Denike specifically pointed to his Menshevik comrade, Boris Bogdanov, a participant in these discussions, as the progenitor of the movement.[60] At the first plenary meeting of the EAD, on 13 March, in a report on behalf of its organizational bureau, Bogdanov himself credited "a group of [Menshevik] party workers" with the original idea for the movement. It was then picked up by factory workers in the southwestern, heavily industrialized Nevskii district, among whom Mensheviks and SRs continued to have a strong influence. An initial organizational meeting attended by moderate socialist and unaffiliated workers was held there on 3 March, and the next day they began organizing the election of delegates to the EAD and stimulating the formation of organizational bureaus to conduct elections in other districts.[61]

It seems clear, then, that Mensheviks had a hand in founding the EAD and that elected factory delegates, Mensheviks, SRs, and unaffiliated skilled workers among them, played key roles in its organization, orientation, and direction. Many had led their fellow workers into the streets during the February revolution. Moreover, they had facilitated moderate socialist domination of the Petrograd Soviet through the spring and summer of 1917, before being overwhelmed by the Bolsheviks in the fall. Increasingly influential in their factories, they now presented the EAD fairly and with considerable success as a citywide movement of workers, for workers. At the first plenary meeting of the EAD, official representatives of political parties, as such, were expressly prohibited from membership.[62] This policy reflected widespread disenchantment not only with the Bolsheviks but with all political parties, and a corresponding desire by the movement's leadership to at least appear to rise above factional interests.

The majority of delegates to the EAD, who together represented a significant portion of Petrograd's most important factories and plants, at first hoped to work within the Soviet system to bring about a renewal of the revolution and the reconvocation of the Constituent Assembly. In this spirit, one of the EAD's first acts was to send a delegation to the Fourth All-Russian Congress of Soviets in Moscow. However, the congress's Bolshevik–Left SR leadership refused to give the delegation a hearing.[63] Such rebuffs notwith-standing, at this early stage, between March and the end of April, the EAD continued to focus primarily on studying and formulating positions on the critical question of food supply, on unemployment, and on evacuation, as well as on strengthening itself organizationally. This was done openly and publicly. EAD leaders rejected secrecy on principle. Even when threats of government reprisals became most strident, they made no plans to go under-ground. Reporters were welcome at their plenary meetings, and full and can-did accounts of the sessions were featured in the non-Soviet press.[64]

During this initial period, the Assembly's goals were sufficiently am-biguous that a typographer, K. F. Grigoriev, who identified himself as "un-affiliated" when registering in the EAD but who later owned up to being a Bolshevik, and possibly other Bolsheviks participated in it.[65] Further, the Bolshevik party committee in at least one key district of Petrograd, the Vy-borg district, circulated EAD recruitment materials to factory collectives.[66] Moreover, for months Soviet authorities in Petrograd held back from taking decisive action against the movement, perhaps because it sprang from the Bolsheviks' own constituency, namely, factory workers; it operated in the open and was a popular response to drastic emergencies that the Bolsheviks were unable to ease; its relative strength and explosiveness were difficult to gauge; and Soviet institutions in Petrograd were unstable in the aftermath of the central government's flight to Moscow.

Less than two weeks after the EAD's first session, *Petrogradskaia pravda* launched an attack against it.[67] A band of Red Guards, on 31 March, raided the offices of the EAD's leadership bureau.[68] For the time being, however, that was about all. Privately, Petrograd officials were worried about the ex-panding worker unrest and the EAD's early success. This was one of the fac-tors that motivated Zinoviev's pleas to the Sovnarkom in late March and early April for immediate, emergency financial aid to combat hunger among Petrograd workers. Riazanov, no longer a Bolshevik but at this time still head of the Petrograd Trade Union Council, appealed to his colleagues to rejuve-nate dormant, docile trade unions. The emergence of the EAD, he warned, indicated that "trade unions are no longer responsive to the issues most on the minds of Petrograd workers."[69]

By the beginning of April, it was becoming clear to EAD leaders that efforts to change the existing system "from within" were not working. At the same time, all the major problems that had spawned their movement were becoming more acute. Indeed, just then a new source of concern was that frustrated workers, in increasing numbers, were succumbing to right-ist propaganda and, among other things, venting their desperation in antisemitic pogroms. For their part, Soviet authorities in Petrograd now seemed prepared to take whatever steps were necessary to curb labor protest, including arresting workers.[70] This, in turn, led to the intimidation, apathy, and passivity of other segments of the Petrograd working class.

In the EAD's earliest weeks, a majority of delegates seemed agreed that, in the initial months after October and through the dispersal of the Constituent Assembly, most Petrograd workers still supported the Bolsheviks. A significant transformation in the existing popular mood, they felt, began during the second half of January and in February. However, contradictory developments in early April led to splits within the EAD between "optimists" and "pessimists."[71] The pessimists had strong doubts about the possibility of mobilizing workers and winning out in any open clash with the government. In the existing circumstances, "engaging in experiments is out of the question," declared Grabovskii, a pessimist from the Cartridge factory, at a plenary meeting of the EAD on 3 April. "At a time when [popular attitudes] are in transition but when change is not yet decisive, it is essential to proceed very carefully to avoid a bloodbath," he said. For their part, the optimists demanded more, not less, aggressive action against the government. Declared Kossirskii, an optimist representing the Otto Kirkhner office supply factory: "the prevailing ruin is being consciously fostered to send away workers. Grabovskii's fears are groundless."[72]

These divisions first emerged strongly during preparations for a May Day demonstration on behalf of the EAD's program that began in mid April. During the run-up to the demonstration, the pessimists worried about their ability to mobilize active support and about the possibility of bloody clashes with government-sponsored celebrations. Still, they considered this a necessary risk. On the other hand, the optimists viewed a potential confrontation as salutary. The government would be scandalized by any bloodshed on May Day, and the EAD would be strengthened commensurately. In any case, Aleksei Smirnov, a veteran Menshevik also from the Cartridge factory and a prominent figure in the leadership bureau of the EAD, undoubtedly spoke for virtually everyone present at a plenary meeting on 17 April, when he declared: "Russia is at the edge of an abyss—to stand aside now would be criminal."[73]

Between 17 and 24 April, a special May Day Commission, along with EAD delegates generally, worked feverishly on demonstration preparations despite Zinoviev's threats to block their march, ostensibly because it conflicted with a demonstration and other May Day festivities planned by the Petrograd Soviet. Meanwhile, Metropolitan Veniamin also issued a prohibition on all political activities during Lent, which encompassed May Day. At an EAD plenary meeting on the twenty-fourth, some delegates conveyed the news that workers were unresponsive to their appeals and would not march because they were confused, intimidated, reactionary, or religious. Influenced by such reports, and by a drop in attendance at EAD meetings, some pessimists talked of canceling the demonstration altogether. In the end, however, in the spirit articulated by Smirnov on 17 April, everyone agreed that they were obliged to proceed with preparations, come what may. "So we must die if necessary," intoned one brave soul.[74]

By the time an emergency EAD meeting was held on 29 April, a combative mood dissipated following a litany of dismal reports about prospects for worker participation in the planned demonstration. An SR from the still sizable Obukhov plant, where SR influence remained dominant, described the workers' mood there as deflated, and concluded that if his fellow workers appeared on May Day it would only be in small groups that would impress no one. Reporting on the situation at the sprawling Putilov metalworking and machine-building plant,[75] Nikolai Glebov, a longtime Menshevik metalworker and advocate for labor solidarity and independence, announced that the spirit among his fellows was "indifferent," that no one had the slightest interest in the first of May.

Smirnov belatedly revealed that at an earlier emergency meeting of representatives from worker organizations called by the May Day Commission it had been agreed that the circumstances called for a reconsideration of the decision to demonstrate. He observed that fear of Soviet authorities was not the only cause of passivity among workers; other contributing factors were the danger from nearby German forces and the generally dismal situation of the working class. A worker at one organizational meeting Smirnov attended asked, "If not today then tomorrow the Germans will occupy the city, and we are going to take part in a triumphal march?" The Bureau, in turn, had concluded that, rather than staging a citywide demonstration, May Day events should be limited to district meetings and assemblies. Only a few optimists argued against this retreat, and the Bureau's position was accepted with the proviso that district parades should be organized where feasible.[76] Official Soviet-sponsored demonstrations and other events, although modest in scale and worker participation, dominated the celebration of May Day, 1918, in Petrograd.

This setback for the EAD did not last long. In early May it was both invigorated and radicalized by a new series of frightening events: yet another steep drop in food supply; the shooting of protesting housewives and workers in the suburb of Kolpino; the arbitrary arrest and abuse of workers in another suburb, Sestroretsk; the closure of newspapers and arrests of individuals who protested the Kolpino and Sestroretsk events; and the resumption of labor unrest and conflict with authorities in other Petrograd factories. The incidents at Kolpino and Sestroretsk were a direct result of food shortages. According to the testimony of eyewitnesses, the trouble in Kolpino had begun with bread scarcities during the Easter holidays. On the morning of 9 May, a crowd of women, finding no food in the local grocery, descended on the Kolpino soviet. There they took their fury out on soviet officials, who were accompanied by several Red Army soldiers. Evidently wishing to rouse local residents, the women demanded that the town siren be sounded. When one of the officials, Commissar Trofimov, refused, a woman swung a handbag at him, and a youngster set the siren off. Trofimov pulled out his revolver and began firing and then the soldiers started shooting. A few of the women and some bystanders were wounded in this first incident.

That evening, workers in the Izhorskii plant, the main industrial enterprise in Kolpino, gathered at the plant to discuss a response to the morning shootings and were met by Red Guards and Red Army troops positioned in a yard across from the plant, as though preparing for military action. Soviet officials at the gathering vehemently denied responsibility for the morning's shootings and explained that the Red Guards and soldiers outside were only on "maneuvers." The workers present passed a resolution censuring the soviet for its behavior and calling for an immediate reelection. They also protested the presence of Red Guards and Red Army troops around the plant and demanded that they be disarmed. When the meeting ended and the workers went outside, they were fired on by the troops. Several workers were wounded and an official of the local electrician's union was killed in this second incident.[77]

In Sestroretsk, around the same time, a crowd of housewives and workers from the Sestroretsk weapons factory, angered that they had been given a quarter pound of oats instead of an expected ration of bread, beat up a representative of the local soviet. In retaliation, local authorities arrested several workers, after which their comrades demanded their release on bail and the appointment of a commission to investigate the affair. When these requests were denied, the Sestroretsk workers went on strike for three days and brought their case to the EAD.[78] At this time, violent incidents against hungry workers and their families demanding bread occurred with increasing regularity.

Stenographic records of plenary meetings during this period reveal that a turning point in the EAD's strategic orientation was reached in mid May, in response to the critical dip in food supply and resulting violence. If the EAD leadership had previously hoped to work within the existing system to stimulate change, now it first began to talk directly about overthrowing the Soviet government and the need to coordinate an attack on the existing regime with likeminded groups around the country, especially in Moscow. At a meeting on 18 May, only the Bolshevik Grigoriev opposed sending a delegation to Moscow; he appealed to fellow delegates to forego party rivalries and, instead, to work with Soviet authorities in dealing with the food emergency, but the rest of the EAD would have none of that. Without argument, the EAD approved resolutions condemning the government's food procurement and distribution policies, and endorsing the dispatch of a delegation to Moscow.[79]

Meanwhile, rumors spread that Petrograd authorities were about to suppress the EAD. (As it turned out, the leadership of the Petrograd Soviet had tabled the question.) For the rest of May and June, then, the EAD concentrated on expanding nationally and preparing Petrograd factory workers to respond to an attack with a one-day general strike. The EAD's leaders assumed that a citywide strike would reveal the strong support they enjoyed among workers and force the authorities to pull back.

Whipping up spirit for a coordinated strike, while holding labor protest in check until the government attacked, proved difficult. Throughout this period, increasingly desperate workers intensified pressure on the EAD to act without delay, and fierce arguments over how to react to this pressure now arose at virtually all plenary meetings. At the end of May and beginning of June, a wave of strikes to protest the lack of bread swept Nevskii district factories, the birthplace of the EAD. But a majority of delegates concerned about ambiguous reports on the mood of workers elsewhere in the city, resolved to call on striking workers to return to work and continue preparations for a general strike.[80] On 26 June, at what was destined to be their final plenary meeting, the EAD learned that members of its delegation to Moscow had been arrested, and that strikes followed by bloody clashes between workers and Soviet authorities had erupted in scattered parts of central Russia. This worrisome news was coupled with the suppression of rebelling workers from the Obukhov plant and sailors from a minelaying flotilla moored on the Neva, as well as word of the Bolshevik "victory" in rigged elections to the Petrograd Soviet.[81] At this point, with little to lose, even the pessimists voted in favor of organizing a citywide general strike for 2 July.[82]

* * *

The growing disenchantment of Petrograd workers with economic conditions and the evolving structure and operation of Soviet political institutions, as reflected in the emergence and growth of the EAD, naturally worried Bolshevik authorities in Petrograd. This was true of representatives of Petrograd district soviets in the Interdistrict Conference no less than of government officials at the highest level. To be sure, representatives of district soviets were proud of their efforts to govern their neighborhoods, and staunchly protective of their independent power. However, they were deeply concerned about their increasing isolation. At the end of March, acting on their own despite the fact that most were Bolsheviks, they resolved to convene successive nonparty workers' conferences in each of the city's districts, in part to undercut the EAD by strengthening ties between district soviets and workers. Moreover, they issued instructions to govern their organization and operation.[83]

Amid unmistakable signs of the widening rift between Bolshevik-dominated political institutions and ordinary factory workers, such popular soviet-sponsored conferences attracted the attention of the leadership of the Petrograd Soviet. Petrograd authorities now were under increasing pressure to hold long delayed elections to both the Petrograd Soviet and district soviets. However, Zinoviev, for one, was profoundly uneasy about the outcome of early soviet elections in view of the negative impact on workers of ever more dire food shortages and the degree to which it seemed to him that existing Bolshevik–Left SR-controlled soviets had become isolated from their constituencies. He declared bluntly that district soviets had become "Houses of Lords."[84] In Zinoviev's view, nonparty workers' conferences under the aegis of district soviets composed of workers elected directly in factories and Red Army units could provide a means of rebuilding grass-roots support for Bolshevik-dominated Soviet power. Beyond this, when elections to the Petrograd Soviet could no longer be put off, it might be possible to draw on conference delegates for a core of loyal deputies to supplement Petrograd Soviet deputies elected directly in factories and military units. At Zinoviev's urging, the Presidium of the Petrograd Soviet endorsed the Interdistrict Conference's initiative.

Zinoviev's closest party comrades in the Petrograd Bureau of the Central Committee were dismayed by his thinking. Although sharing his unease about Bolshevik fortunes in early soviet elections in the workplace, they rebelled against his ideas for radical changes in the way the Petrograd Soviet would be composed.[85] Worth noting is that communications between the Bureau and the Petersburg Committee at this time were so haphazard that, initially, the latter was oblivious to Zinoviev's thinking on nonparty workers' conferences and their relationship to the future structure of the Petrograd Soviet. The Petersburg Committee's reaction to the idea of nonparty workers' conferences, when it was first formally raised on 14 May, was to try to delay convocation of the conferences until food shortages had eased.[86] However, three days later, after it became apparent that such conferences organized by district soviets either had been held or were already scheduled, the city party leadership was left with no alternative but to go along.[87]

On 20 May, before the high-level intraparty debate over nonparty workers' conferences and their relationship to soviets was settled, Zinoviev, who had heretofore shunned personal involvement with grass-roots party organizations, popped up at a weekly meeting of the Petersburg Committee's Assembly of Organizers.[88] There he overcame intense opposition by veteran Bolsheviks loyal to the principle of democratic, popularly rooted Soviet power and lobbied successfully for the earliest possible convocation of nonparty workers' conferences in districts where they had not been held as a means of restoring linkages to labor. At this meeting, he also implicitly favored ignoring any instructions the Interdistrict Conference issued concerning nonparty district workers' conferences that impeded the strongest possible Bolshevik representation in them and obliquely linked them to the future composition of soviets.[89]

In the late spring and early summer, nonparty workers' conferences were held in most districts of Petrograd.[90] The comprehensive, published proceedings of the conference in the First City District provides an extraordinarily valuable picture that is in many ways illustrative of these conferences generally.[91] The workers' conference in the First City District opened on 25 May and ended on 5 June.[92] From the start, at least some Bolshevik and Left SR district soviet leaders viewed it not just as a one-time means of helping to deal with an extraordinary crisis but as the first of periodic assemblies at which they would have to account for their policies to working-class constituents and seek their advice on future programs. In short, in their view, this conference was to be a more or less permanent institution to legitimize the district soviet's work and to provide it with a new, much-needed conduit to the masses (hence its "official" title, "The *First* Conference of Workers' and Red Army Deputies in the First City District").

Although Bolsheviks and Left SRs had a clear majority in the First City District Soviet, the initial First City District Workers' Conference was not their exclusive enterprise. All political groups in the First City District Soviet were represented in the organizing and credentials commissions of the conference (this was not the case in all district nonparty workers conferences). Among the voting delegates were representatives from local factories and Red Army units, the First City District Soviet, district trade unions, united cooperatives, the unemployed, and factory health care funds, as well as Bolshevik, Left SR, Menshevik-Internationalist, Menshevik, and SR committees in the First City District.[93] A majority of participants were elected at special factory and office assemblies and at meetings of the unemployed, according to specified norms.[94] An estimated twenty-three thousand to twenty-five thousand "working citizens" were represented. Although Bolsheviks and Left SRs had advantages in the election of delegates,[95] even Bolshevik opponents seemed to concede at the conference's close that, on the whole, it had been fairly organized and run. All told, the 201 voting delegates included 134 Bolsheviks (67 percent), 13 Left SRs (6 percent), 30 Mensheviks and Menshevik-Internationalists (15 percent), and 24 SRs (12 percent).[96]

The conference agenda included separate, lengthy considerations of the unemployment problem, the food-supply crisis, the formation and organization of the Red Army (then still a contentious issue), the structure and operation of the district soviet, and assessment of the "current moment." In the present context, the most important agenda items were the reports of some fifty rank-and-file delegates on the conditions and prevailing mood in their workplaces, with which the conference began,[97] and a review and critique of the First City District Soviet's development and activities after October, with which it closed.[98]

The delegate reports revealed that some district workers felt they had fared well after October, and support for Soviet power remained strong among them. Also positively disposed toward Soviet power were representatives of lower-ranking civil servants who, in the words of one of their delegates, considered themselves not so much employees as "faithful servants of the revolution" and, ironically, spokesmen for some five thousand organized unemployed. The most enthusiastic supporters of Soviet power at the First City district workers' conference were delegates from locally based Red Army units. Implicitly referring to the efforts of the EAD, one of these military delegates pledged that, "regardless of who the enemies of Soviet power were, whether they hid behind nonparty labels or were Mensheviks or SRs," his unit would respond, ready to shoot, as soon as the Soviet ordered. Such fervent expressions of support were probably small comfort to district soviet leaders, however, because of the lack of discipline habitually exhibited by Red Army troops and because they were submerged in a flood of worker complaints about post-October economic conditions and practices, and demands for fundamental political change—often for convocation of the Constituent Assembly and creation of a more broadly based democratic authority as a replacement for the Soviet government. Apparent trouble spots for the Bolsheviks and Left SRs included larger enterprises in the district, such as the Westinghouse machine plant and the San Gali iron foundry and machine-building factory, as well as the shell casing section of the Cartridge factory.

Workers at the Westinghouse plant were mainly agitated by the food supply crisis. "Earlier there was inflation," one of its representatives explained, "but somehow we managed to scrape up enough food for ourselves . . . now there have been cases of workers collapsing [from hunger] at their benches." The San Gali factory had been an island of relative calm between management and labor in the revolutionary period; apparently not until December 1917, when management felt compelled to reduce the labor force by half, was there a serious labor conflict there. During subsequent tensions, ending with the layoff of even more workers than had initially been envisioned, the San Gali workers became deeply disillusioned with the existing government. It appeared to them that they had been left to the mercy of fate. The San Gali representative ended his report by reading an "instruction" which the workers had furnished him. It directed him to demand bread for the hungry, work for the unemployed, and assurance that planned food procurement expeditions to the countryside would be peaceful.

The report of a Cartridge factory delegate was similarly disquieting. Before October, he declared, virtually all the plant's workers had been sympathetic to the Bolsheviks, but the Soviet government's arbitrary, utterly chaotic evacuation policies had a negative impact on their outlook. In fact, as a result of their experience, the mood of Cartridge factory workers was, in this delegate's words, "one of utter despondency. . . . [The workers] have lost confidence in the [Bolshevik] government." He also concluded with an "instruction" given him by his coworkers upon dispatching him to the conference—"to fight staunchly for a democratic system, for the convocation of a Constituent Assembly, for a democratic government elected on the basis of secret and equal suffrage."

The review of the First City District Soviet's development and activities began with reports by its Bolshevik chairman, Anton Korsak, a holdover from 1917 and a leader in the Interdistrict Conference, and several of his section heads. Korsak and his colleagues acknowledged that some of the soviet's policies were ill advised, and its endeavors were continually impeded by the absence of qualified personnel. For the most part, however, the reports concluded that the preceding seven months saw considerable achievement, with the hard-pressed Bolshevik–Left SR leadership of the soviet successfully fending off the counterrevolution, assuming responsibility for all aspects of local government, and surviving to participate in the coming world revolution and local socialist development. During discussions of key issues earlier in the conference, spokesmen for the Socialist Revolutionaries and Mensheviks bitterly criticized almost everything about the development of the district soviet after October. The conclusion of reports by Korsak and his colleagues offered a final opportunity for them to enlarge on their complaints, which focused on three main themes: Korsak and his associates had deluged the conference with details about soviet activities but had done almost nothing to explain basic policy formation and goals; officials and staff of the soviet were totally unequipped to deal with the complex tasks they had taken on, thereby contributing mightily to existing crises; and the character of the soviet had fundamentally changed for the worse after October, having transformed from an institution for furthering working-class interests, which was its proper function, into a bloated, isolated, bureaucracy composed of incompetent, paid *chinovniki* (bureaucrats).

Korsak took offense, most of all at the suggestion that, in accepting pay for work, soviet officials had become *chinovniki*. "I myself receive money from the soviet," he insisted, "but I am not a *chinovnik* and see nothing scandalous in receiving support for myself and my family." Yet, his subsequent remarks, and the resolution the conference adopted on the past and future of the soviet, tacitly acknowledged that at least some of the opposition's charges were justified. At the same time, the resolution reflected the Bolshevik–Left SR soviet leadership's conviction that the district soviet would fend off both the opposition and the proclivities of higher authorities to centralize power, and would continue to play the primary role in local political and administrative affairs.

Although Soviet power and the operation of district soviets were subject to similarly harsh criticism at other nonparty district conferences for which records have been preserved, most had sizable Bolshevik–Left SR majorities. Thus, as Zinoviev had suggested, when necessary they could shore up Bolshevik strength in elections to the Petrograd Soviet.

9

Continuing Crises

ON TOP OF the mounting unrest among workers, throughout the spring and early summer of 1918 Petrograd remained threatened by German occupation. The military danger was heightened by German troops who had come ashore at the southwestern tip of Finland on 3 March and joined Finnish White forces that had been sweeping eastward, scoring decisive victories over the Reds. The enemy advance soon jeopardized ships of the Russian Baltic Fleet in the Helsingfors harbor and threatened Petrograd from the northwest.

Seizure of the Baltic Fleet was of particular concern to the British. In late January and February Captain Francis Cromie, the British naval attaché in Petrograd, had been engaged in preparations to sink his own flotilla of submarines stranded in the Gulf of Finland; in efforts to prevent the Russian Baltic Fleet from falling into German hands; and in coordinating the evacuation from Petrograd of precious metals and allied military stores (which was his initial charge). At the end of January he participated in discussions with the Central Committee of the Baltic Fleet about the possibility of Britain's financing the fleet as a means of securing allied control over it.[1] The subsequent negotiation of the Brest treaty made these discussions moot. During the second half of February, when German seizure of Petrograd appeared inevitable, Cromie hoped to organize the destruction of the fleet with the aid of its commander-in-chief, Admiral Aleksandr Rozvozov.[2] In March, however, Rozvozov, who insisted on complete autonomy in fleet operations,[3] was removed for refusing to pledge loyalty to Soviet power. Ultimately, the fleet was saved from the Germans by the heroism of Captain First Rank Aleksei Shchastny, Rozvozov's successor.

Elsewhere, I have described in detail Shchastny's heroic action and tragic fate.[4] Shchastny first captured national attention at the end of February 1918, when he directed the transfer of sixty-two ships from Revel (Tallinn) across the frozen waters of the Gulf of Finland to the Baltic Fleet's main base in Helsingfors to prevent their seizure by German forces sweeping through Estonia. This achievement was dwarfed, however, by what he did in mid March and April, when the occupation of Helsingfors by German and Finnish White forces threatened the bulk of the Baltic Fleet with capture. Article VI of the Brest treaty specifically obligated the Soviet government to clear Finland and the Aaland Islands of Russian troops and Red Guards, and to remove Russian naval ships and forces from Finnish ports.[5] On 20 March, the Naval General Staff issued instructions to move the ships from Helsingfors to Kronstadt—as many ships as could make it through the thick ice—and to prepare the entire fleet for demolition. However distasteful to Shchastny, the latter directive was duly implemented.[6] Three weeks later, the German government gave the Sovnarkom until 12 April to comply with its obligations regarding the Baltic Fleet. Shchastny was now instructed by the Commissariat for Naval Affairs headed by Trotsky to disarm all ships of the fleet still in Helsingfors on 11 April. At the same time, he was authorized to continue moving as many of them as possible to Kronstadt.[7] Meanwhile, with no hope now of saving his cherished flotilla of British submarines trapped off the Finnish coast from the Germans, Captain Cromie had them sunk.[8]

Between 12 March and 11 April, when German and Finnish White forces entered Helsingfors, Shchastny superintended the transfer to Kronstadt of three naval convoys, including the biggest dreadnoughts in the fleet. The ships could move only during daylight, and each morning ice breakers had to work them free. This unprecedented journey, the celebrated "Ice March of the Baltic Fleet," was further hampered as transfers and demobilization had sharply reduced ships' crews, and as the ships had to maneuver through narrow channels close to the shoreline while facing fire from Finnish coastal batteries. Nonetheless, by the end of April, the core of the fleet, more than two hundred vessels, had made it safely to Kronstadt.[9] Most of the ships dropped anchor there, although some were deployed at the mouth of the Neva, off Petrograd. With Trotsky's permission, others, including a large division of minelayers, were moved slowly through the Neva bridges into the heart of the former capital, in the expectation that they would soon steam upriver to Lake Ladoga.[10] Following this feat, the Russian public dubbed Shchastny "Admiral," although he was still a captain first rank. He was now a popular hero, revered by rank-and-file sailors as much as by his officers.

The "Ice March," however sensational, did not significantly reduce the military threat to the Baltic Fleet, Kronstadt, or Petrograd. The German navy controlled the Gulf of Finland, which was rapidly becoming fully navigable. More ominously, German and Finnish forces were advancing toward the Russian border. The most significant and revealing incident, in a series of threatening enemy moves in the Baltic at this time, involved the fate of Fort Ino, located on the Finnish coast slightly northwest of Petrograd. Fort Ino was built shortly before World War I as part of a system of naval fortifications for the defense of Petrograd. In the spring of 1918, Germany's control of the Gulf of Finland and its occupation of Estonia, and domination of Finland, put these fortifications in immediate peril. By the third week of April 1918, the coast adjoining Fort Ino was occupied by Finnish White forces, and on 24 April the Finns, supervised by German officers, demanded its surrender.[11]

Even before receipt of this demand, when the Finnish threat was already apparent, the SK PTK proceeded with unprecedented alacrity to implement a CEC decree ordering obligatory military training for all citizens who did not exploit others' labor. Whereas the SK PTK decree was restricted to workers, the CEC decree applied to workers *and* peasants. Also, district soviets and factory committees were pushed to facilitate recruitment of their best personnel into the Red Army, if only temporarily.[12] The SK PTK, upon receiving the demand on 25 April, vowed to "defend Fort Ino at any cost."[13] The Executive Committee of the Petrograd Soviet immediately ordered district soviets and trade unions to provide workers between the ages of eighteen and forty capable of fighting; and both the Military Section of the Petrograd Soviet and the Executive Committee of the Petrograd Province Soviet put all forces at their disposal on highest alert. The Kronstadt Soviet declared an end to the "breathing space" with Germany, and ordered ships and detachments of sailors to defend Fort Ino. Endorsing this directive, Shchastny declared that "Fort Ino cannot be surrendered and must be defended from attacks of any kind."[14]

It is noteworthy that Fort Ino was not mentioned at meetings of the Bolshevik Petersburg Committee on 26 and 30 April nor on 3, 5, 7, and 10 May.[15] The reason for the omission is that, true to its customary practice, even decision making on life-and-death matters was left to Soviet authorities despite adoption of the principle that party bodies should control government policies. Nonetheless, the 26 April issue of the party's *Petrogradskaia pravda,* reflecting the fundamental shift in the position of the Petrograd Soviet's Bolshevik majority, announced that the Brest "breathing space" was nearing an end, that the Soviet government could make no further concessions to Germany, and that a decisive struggle for Petrograd's survival was at hand.[16]

If government authorities in Petrograd (not to speak of Shchastny and his colleagues in the Baltic Fleet) were determined to defend Fort Ino even if it meant the end of Brest, in Moscow Lenin and Trotsky did not agree. Quite

Petrograd workers drill on Palace Square. State Museum of the Political History of Russia, St. Petersburg.

apart from the crisis surrounding Ino, Berlin was then peppering them with complaints and ultimatums regarding Soviet compliance with provisions of the Brest treaty. At the same time, Soviet naval intelligence was reporting that German military forces were massed on Russia's new, compressed borders, often encroaching on Russian territory, and seizing or sinking Russian ships. With the formation of the Red Army still at a very early stage, it seemed clear to the two top Bolshevik leaders that extending the fragile peace with Germany would require new concessions. They certainly were in no mood to let the Fort Ino emergency escalate into the resumption of a full-scale war. This difference in outlook between the authorities in Petrograd and those in Moscow emerged sharply at a tense meeting of Shchastny, Trotsky, and the Supreme Military Council in Moscow on 25 April.

Unlike the Petrograd Bureau of the Bolshevik Central Committee and the party's Petersburg Committee, the Bolshevik Central Committee was by then closely involved in government decision making. Late the night of 6 May, the Central Committee met in an emergency session to consider late-breaking foreign-policy issues, among them German demands for the surrender of Fort Ino, the expanding allied intervention in Murmansk and Archangel, and British threats to support Japanese encroachments in the Far East.[17] The meeting ended with the adoption of a resolution by Lenin that

endorsed "yielding to the German ultimatum." As a footnote to this stipulation, Lenin scrawled: "Immediately start evacuating everything [in Petro-
grad] to the Urals, and especially the Government Printing Office."[18] This
was another clear indication of Lenin's enduring assumption that Petrograd
was doomed.

Although the Central Committee's deliberations were top secret, during the second week in May the few non-Bolshevik papers in Moscow and
Petrograd still publishing were filled with sensational reports of new demands by the German government and the imminent German occupation
of both cities.[19] Around this time, copies of letters allegedly from German
officials that seemed to support the widely held belief that Soviet policies in
the Baltic were being dictated by the German General Staff in accordance
with secret clauses of the Treaty of Brest-Litovsk were circulated in Petrograd.[20] The combination of rumors relating to an imminent German attack
and Soviet subservience to Germany caused such a stir that Bolshevik authorities in Petrograd were forced to issue a declaration that such talk was a
"total fabrication."[21]

This declaration had no impact. At this point, even Stasova betrayed
concern about an early German occupation of Petrograd by trying to ship
the party's printing press to Ekaterinburg. Captain Cromie, for his part,
greatly intensified his efforts to prevent the Baltic Fleet from falling into
German hands. At one time or another, his plans included sinking British steamers at the approaches to Kronstadt, demolition of the fleet, and
an elaborate and substantial program of payments to Russian naval officers to render their vessels inoperable. Provision was also made for resettling
Cromie's Russian accomplices in England.[22] Beginning in the second half
of May, the British Foreign Office and the Admiralty gave top priority to re-
allocating their funds in Russia for rapid financing of one or another variant
of Cromie's schemes.[23] Cromie himself was fully cognizant of the dangerous
game he was now engaged in and of the likely need for a quick departure
from Russia.[24] Although he opposed allied intervention through most of
May and tried to work with Trotsky, his efforts to assure the timely destruction of the fleet also necessitated collaboration with anti-Soviet individuals
and groups. Thus they paved the way for activities he would undertake in the
summer to overthrow the Bolsheviks.[25]

On 9 May, deepening anxiety about the intentions of the Germans and
Finns, as well as about the German-Soviet relationship, prompted Petrograd
civil authorities to meet with top military commissars and spetsy.[26] The spetsy
presented alarming reports on a recent buildup of German troop strength
on the borders of Petrograd Province and, consequently, on the necessity of

promptly mobilizing the *entire* population in defense of the "fatherland . . . not Soviet power." Some of the top-ranking Petrograd Bolsheviks present regarded the nationalistic, patriotic fervor of the spetsy, some of whom were in touch with Cromie, as anti-Soviet "treachery." Nonetheless, Zinoviev declared it essential to "put everything on the scales" in defense of the city. At the same time he hinted that a final decision had not been made on whether Petrograd would be defended. His lack of clarity reflected differences on this question between Petrograd leaders committed to their city's defense and officials in Moscow, such as Lenin and Trotsky, for whom Petrograd (not to speak of the Baltic Fleet) was a secondary priority. Ultimately, with the two sides at the 9 May meeting so far apart, no agreement was reached on steps to strengthen Petrograd's defenses.

The determination of Lenin and Trotsky to avoid a renewal of war with Germany in May 1918 was not only a consequence of their enduring assumptions about the hopelessness of successfully defending Petrograd. Also weighing heavily on their thinking was that Russia's civil war fronts were beginning to heat up precisely at that time. On 6 May, General Krasnov's Cossacks managed to retake Novocherkassk, their capital, and very quickly the Don territory again became a center of active resistance to Soviet rule. During this same time, the Volunteer Army under Generals Denikin and Alekseev (Kornilov having been killed by a chance artillery shell in April) was building up its strength in the Kuban. Most immediately threatening, however, was a rebellion of the powerful Czech Legion.

The Czech Legion was composed of more than forty thousand well-armed and disciplined Czechs and Slovaks, many of them former prisoners of war or deserters who were dedicated to the creation of an independent Czechoslovak republic after the war. Originally formed in 1916 to fight alongside Russian forces on the Eastern front, in March 1918, with the approval of Soviet authorities, the Legion boarded trains in Kursk in the hope of crossing Siberia and leaving Russia by way of Vladivostok in order to join Czech forces fighting in France. During the second half of May and early June 1918, at a time when most of the Legion was strung out aboard seventy trains along the Trans-Siberian Railway from west of Samara to Irkutsk, a series of catastrophic misjudgments, misunderstandings, and unfortunate incidents culminated in the Legion's rebellion, its seizure of major cities and railway junctions along more than twenty-five hundred miles of the railway, and its collaboration with anti-Soviet movements in this huge area.

This expansion of the civil war began just as the latent conflict between Shchastny and Trotsky, which stemmed from their tense meeting on 25 April, was coming to a head. During the first weeks of May, several factors had further poisoned Trotsky's already jaundiced view of Shchastny. The most important of these, or rather Trotsky's interpretation of them, included Shchastny's failure to move the flotilla of minelayers to Lake Ladoga; his continuing reluctance to prepare the fleet and naval installations for demolition; and, perhaps most significant, Shchastny's efforts to discredit Trotsky by improperly disseminating his secret orders about the destruction of the Baltic Fleet. Information in Cheka and Naval archives indicates that Shchastny was largely or wholly blameless in these matters, most importantly that he himself had prepared the fleet for demolition in the event of necessity, and that his dissemination of Trotsky's orders was less an effort to undermine Trotsky than a reflection of his close collaboration with Baltic Fleet officer and sailor committees. Be that as it may, on 22 May, Shchastny, frustrated by Trotsky's policies and lack of trust in him, submitted his resignation. Trotsky rejected it, ordered him to Moscow, set him up for arrest, and single-handedly organized an investigation, sham trial, and death sentence on the spurious charge of attempting to overthrow the Petrograd Commune with the longer-term goal of fighting the Soviet republic.[27]

*   *   *

In revolutionary Petrograd, distrust of spetsy in command positions was so great that they were routinely arrested and beaten up for no good reason.[28] Shchastny had been a major exception. At the end of May, news of his arrest provoked a firestorm of protest in the Baltic Fleet. His execution on the night of 21/22 June 1918 caused an even greater furor. Indeed, it was a major factor in stirring a failed insurrection in late June against Soviet power in Petrograd in late June. In addition to popular upset over Shchastny's fate, two main elements were at the root of this unsuccessful rebellion. The first was escalating concern on the part of Baltic Fleet personnel about aggressive German actions in the Baltic and passive Soviet responses to them. The extent of this anxiety had been reflected at opening sessions of the Third Congress of Baltic Fleet Delegates (29 April–24 May 1918). Even though a majority of participants in the congress were Bolsheviks, they dismissed a telegraphed greeting from Trotsky, pointedly requesting that he appear to explain the government's position on the future of the fleet. Equally telling, the delegates had cheered Shchastny when he stood before them to declare that the moment had come for the central government to stand up and fight the Germans.[29]

A couple of weeks later, officers and men of the powerful flotilla of minelayers that had moved from Helsingfors during the "Ice March," and was still anchored along the Neva in the heart of Petrograd, issued a more direct challenge to the city's civil authorities.[30] On 11 May, informed of extraordinary efforts by Trotsky to insure the timely demolition of the fleet, they adopted a resolution calling for dissolution of the Petrograd Commune and the creation of a dictatorship of the Baltic Fleet that could be entrusted with defense and government in the Petrograd region.[31] Although this demand caused an uproar at the time and was hopelessly naïve, the minelayers' main concern was to somehow overcome the Bolshevik government's reluctance to contest the Germans. At a meeting of ship committees in the flotilla the next day, two staunchly anti-Bolshevik officers who had helped organize the previous day's protest meeting, Feodosii Zasimuch and Grigorii Lisanevich, clashed with Lunacharskii and Fedor Raskolnikov over the government's military and foreign policies. The assembly cheered Zasimuch and Lisanevich, and hooted down Lunacharskii and Raskolnikov. The hostility of the minelayers to the existing Soviet government, as shown by their earlier demand to dissolve the Petrograd Commune, had the unintended effect of alienating a majority of delegates at the Third Congress of Baltic Fleet Delegates. Although concerned about the fleet's survival, the delegates were loyal to Soviet power. On 13 May, they condemned the minelayers for their attack on the government, blamed their actions on "the agitation of criminals," and vowed to oust Lisanevich and Zasimuch from the navy.[32] However, their hope that ships' crews would turn in Lisanevich and Zasimuch was quickly dashed, largely because their men supported them and Soviet authorities shied away from forcing the issue. Moreover, such developments as the demolition of Fort Ino on 14 May, which was erroneously assumed to prove Bolshevik subservience to Germany, reinforced their stature.[33]

On 25 May, a plenary meeting of delegates from the minelayers' flotilla vowed to protect Lisanevich and Zasimuch "by all possible means." This meeting also adopted a resolution supporting the ideal of Soviet power as the embodiment of government by the people but condemned the existing repressive Bolshevik-dominated government as essentially counterrevolutionary and disastrous for the motherland.[34] At another rally two days later (27 May), the delegates again registered their independence by rejecting the authority of Ivan Flerovskii, Trotsky's appointee as chief commissar of the Baltic Fleet. That was the day Trotsky arrested Shchastny, further roiling the minelayers.

The second element at the root of the late June rebellion against Soviet power in Petrograd consisted of workers at the Obukhov plant, who had participated in the mass demonstrations on behalf of the Constituent Assembly on 28 November and 5 January. Representatives of the plant later were active in the EAD. One of Russia's largest producers of artillery, mines, shells, steel, and iron for military purposes, Obukhov was hit hard by the sudden halt in defense orders following demobilization in December 1917. The efforts of management to switch to peacetime production were thwarted by fuel shortages; as a result, the plant was shut down and its 14,500 workers were laid off. Those who were able joined the swelling migration out of Petrograd. The following spring, the plant somehow managed to obtain enough fuel and production orders to be able to recall some four thousand workers.[35]

The partial reopening of the plant coincided with the deepening of food shortages and the sharp rise in discontent among Petrograd workers that led to the formation of the EAD. Beginning in April, production at the plant was continually interrupted by mass rallies to protest the increasingly dire food crisis. Like workers from most of the other Petrograd industrial enterprises represented in the EAD, Obukhov workers were too deflated to march on May Day. But matters began to crystallize on 8 May when the Bolshevik Obukhov factory committee, under pressure from workers, tried unsuccessfully to obtain an increase in bread rations, which were then down to an eighth of a pound per day.[36] At a mass rally at the plant that evening, attended by three thousand workers, SRs and Mensheviks heaped criticism on the government for the policies that led to the food emergency. A resolution was adopted demanding an increase in the bread ration and other food supplies commensurate with workers' needs, the immediate convocation of the Constituent Assembly, and an end to civil war.[37] Another resolution adopted at a plant rally on 12 April put the demand for bread in the form of an ultimatum: either the commune government raised food supplies to an adequate level or it would face a mass rebellion. The antigovernment mood at this rally became especially inflamed by reports of bloody confrontations that pitted women seeking bread for the Easter holidays and unarmed Izhorskii plant workers in Kolpino against local soviet officials and trigger-happy Red Guards and Red Army soldiers.[38] Obukhov plant representatives were sent to the Putilov factory, where tension over food shortages was also high, to sound out workers there about a move against the government.[39] Toward the end of May, Petrograd authorities tried to cool the Obukhov workers by shutting down the plant for several days but to no avail. At the same time technical problems thwarted efforts to move the minelaying division to Lake Ladoga.[40] As ships of the flotilla were moored near the Obukhov plant, during the second half of May and in June disgruntled sailors and angry workers continually intermingled and at mass rallies discussed joint political action. In this way, the two main elements in the abortive rebellion that erupted on 22 June merged. At an especially heated rally at the Obukhov plant on 16 June, the day after elections for a new Petrograd Soviet were announced, workers vowed to use the elections to transform soviets into a voice for the reestablishment of universal voting rights and for convening the Constituent Assembly. They also called on the EAD to commit itself to a struggle for power, and on the minelayers to join in it.[41]

At their meeting on 16 June, the Obukhov plant workers also voted to send a delegation to Zinoviev to request the expansion of the government to include representatives of all left political groups pending convocation of the Constituent Assembly. Naturally, this request was rejected, on the grounds that the coming Petrograd Soviet elections would be a referendum on the people's will. Nonetheless, under pressure from the Obukhov delegation, Zinoviev agreed to address a mass meeting at the plant on 20 June. At this meeting, the speeches of Zinoviev and Lunacharskii were drowned out by waves of heckling. Lunacharskii could not even complete his remarks, and he drove off well before the Obukhov plant workers adopted yet another resolution demanding the convocation of a Constituent Assembly.[42]

On 20 June, at roughly the time of this raucous mass meeting, Volodarskii was assassinated in the Nevskii district not far from the Obukhov plant.[43] Approximately fifteen residents were arrested during a search of neighborhood buildings surrounding the crime scene. After interrogation, all were released but three: Grigorii Eremeev and two comrades, all SRs. Grigorii Eremeev, like his brother Aleksei, was one of the Obukhov plant's most popular leaders. More to the point, he had no connection to Volodarskii's killing. PCheka documents suggest that Soviet authorities used the sweep of the district, prompted by the search for Volodarskii's killer, to arrest him and other "troublemakers," and also to press the PCheka to keep them under lock and key.[44]

A general meeting of Obukhov workers the next day, 21 June, declared an "Italian strike"[45]—the workers threw out management and seized control of the plant, pending Eremeev's release. On 22 June, another mass meeting at the plant resolved to demand that the EAD should declare political strikes in all Petrograd plants and factories for 25 June to protest the political repression of workers. The Obukhov workers also resolved to continue their "occupation" until Eremeev was let go, and to send a joint delegation of workers and minelayers to Smolny demanding his release by 10:00 that evening, and to reassemble again at that time, obviously to adopt more drastic, antigovernment measures if Eremeev was not freed.[46] Meanwhile, news that Shchastny had been executed further angered the minelayers. Lisanevich, commander of the destroyer *Kapitan Izyl'met'ev,* in an especially blatant demonstration of solidarity with the rebelling Obukhov workers, docked his ship alongside their plant.

On 21 and 22 June, Petrograd authorities led by Zinoviev were trapped between two fires. On one side were workers such as those at the Obukhov plant and lower-ranking military personnel, such as the minelayers, who were poised for a decisive clash with the government over food shortages, repression of workers, and frustration with Soviet timidity in relations with Germany at the expense of the Baltic Fleet. On the other side were pro-Soviet hotheads bent on revenge for the assassination of their hero, Volodarskii. In these circumstances, under pressure from Uritskii, Zinoviev restrained the hotheads.[47] As regards the workers and minelayers, after weighing the situation, he adopted a hard line. Thus, his initial response to the delegation of workers and sailors seeking Eremeev's release was to send their demand to Gorokhovaia 2 with the promise that Uritskii would arrange it, which he did. At the same time, he sent an emissary to the Putilov plant to find out whether workers there would join the Obukhov workers' strike. News of Volodarskii's assassination had caused an immediate, if temporary, softening of dissatisfaction with Soviet power there. After this became clear, direction of the incipient rebellion's suppression was placed in the hands of an inter-government troika. Orders were issued to shut down the Obukhov plant, and the next day, 23 June, the neighborhood surrounding the plant was placed under martial law, leading local-level SRs were arrested, and the SR club was shut down, as were SR party headquarters in the Nevskii and Obukhov districts.[48]

On 22 June, the Bolsheviks and Left SRs transformed Volodarskii's funeral into a mass demonstration of support for Soviet power. In this atmosphere, the popular mood swung against the minelayers, and they were easily suppressed with the help of some five hundred Kronstadt sailors who had marched in Volodarskii's funeral procession.[49] Volodarskii's assassination muted the sailors' upset over Shchastny's execution and helped turn them against the minelayers, just as it had softened the Putilov workers. Gorky's *Novaia zhizn'*, which had staunchly supported political protest earlier, captured this swing. A lead editorial, on 23 June, grieved at the loss of Volodarskii, "an indefatigable agitator . . . [and] leader of socialism who had given his soul to the working class" and condemned his killing as "madness." The editorial also expressed concern lest his death set off a chain of bloodshed.[50]

The Kronstadters were supported by three gunboats, which blocked the *Kapitan Izyl'met'ev* when it tried to escape. After a brief negotiation its crew was disarmed, and several officers and sailors were arrested without incident. Lisanevich managed to slip away. Three other destroyers raised anchor, moved upstream, and prepared to fight, but their surrender was also negotiated without bloodshed. Some officers and crewmen were arrested, but Zasimuch, like Lisanevich, evaded capture.[51] The minelayers suffered a fate similar to that of the Obukhov workers in the immediate aftermath. Flerovskii superintended a thorough purge of the flotilla, arresting as many of those who had helped mobilize the fleet against the Petrograd government as he could get his hands on.

* * *

On 8–10 June, Petrograd Bolsheviks had gathered for their sixth quarterly city conference. Zinoviev, in an opening address, put a positive spin on the results of the Brest treaty, but he did not try to hide Soviet Russia's difficult international situation, the negative impact of dire food shortages on Petrograd workers, or the catastrophic state of local party organizations. Bolshevik membership had dropped from 36,000 in February 1918 to 13,472;[52] a high percentage of members were fully engaged in government or military work, and had lost all contact with their party organizations. Even worse, Zinoviev estimated that "hundreds and even thousands" of newcomers included in this measly total were out-and-out criminals. Subsequent discussion of various aspects of the state of the party reinforced this horrific picture. Pressure from the Bolshevik Central Committee to end the conflict between party committees and soviet fractions, and to strengthen local party work and discipline, prompted the delegates to adopt strong measures to rebuild district party committees and factory collectives, and to designate the enhancement of party work as the primary task of all Bolsheviks in all positions.[53]

At this time, demands from below for the immediate reelection of the Petrograd Soviet were intensifying.[54] Although there seems to have been a consensus at the city conference that elections needed to be delayed until spiraling food shortages eased, a few days later (13 June) the leadership of the Petrograd Soviet announced that voting would be held during a seven-day period beginning 17 June.[55] A number of factors besides popular pressure prompted this step: the CEC's decision in Moscow to convene an early All-Russian Congress of Soviets and to encourage a purge of moderate socialists from all soviets;[56] a desire to counteract the self-proclaimed right of the EAD to represent workers; and Bolshevik success in gaining control of nonparty district workers' conferences, thus offering a way to help offset possible weaknesses in the governing parties' electoral strength in factories.

New regulations governing the elections were confirmed at a plenary meeting of the Petrograd Soviet on 15 June.[57] Perhaps the most significant change in the makeup of the new soviet was that numerically decisive representation was given to agencies in which the Bolsheviks had overwhelming strength, among them the Petrograd Trade Union Council, individual trade unions, factory committees in closed enterprises, district soviets, and district nonparty workers' conferences.[58] The Left SRs requested that representation from trade unions be reduced and that representatives of district nonparty workers' conferences be eliminated, to no avail.[59]

The revised system's advantage for the Bolsheviks is illustrated by the representation accorded the nonparty workers' conference in the First City district. The conference was reconvened for one short session, on 22 June, and by majority vote, with the Bolsheviks and Left SRs joining forces, the conference agreed on a "winner take all" rather than a proportional representation system for election of soviet deputies. As a result, all twenty-eight individuals elected to the Petrograd Soviet by the conference were either Bolsheviks or Left SRs. The sizable Menshevik/SR minority in the conference (27 percent) received no representation at all.[60] An analogous procedure produced the same result in the Narva district.[61] Relevant archival documents suggest that the same scenario emerged in elections at *most* district worker conferences and in *most* district soviets. Winning seats in district soviets were either two Bolsheviks and a Left SR or three Bolsheviks. Finally, Red Army forces, which essentially excluded Mensheviks and SRs, were given representation equal to workers (i.e., one deputy per five hundred soldiers).[62]

Only about 260 of roughly 700 deputies in the new soviet were to be elected in factories, which guaranteed a large Bolshevik majority in advance.[63] As the voting began, Zinoviev took no risk in declaring that "the fate of the Bolsheviks in Petrograd depends on the electoral results," and that "if the election does not yield the desired result, obviously the Bolsheviks will give up power."[64] It was similarly disingenuous to imply, as the Bolsheviks' campaign manager Volodarskii did a few days before his assassination, that retention of a Bolshevik majority would serve as a mandate for repression of such opposition movements as the EAD.[65] Still, Bolshevik leaders realistically understood that the party's failure to do well among Soviet delegates elected directly in factories would potentially be very damaging.

On the first day of voting, the leadership of the Bolshevik Petersburg Committee stipulated that workers should vote only for candidates who staunchly supported Soviet power, who would be merciless in fighting all enemies of laboring people, and who would uphold the principle that *all minorities in the new soviet should be bound to obey decisions of the majority.*[66] The Petersburg Committee leadership also arranged a meeting of the Assembly of Organizers for the night of the seventeenth at which Volodarskii, in what was fated to be his last appearance in a party forum, explained Bolshevik electoral strategy. A resolution adopted after his presentation reflected how seriously the party viewed elections in factories, and the acute shortage of experienced cadres for the campaign. Thus, the resolution sanctioned the formation of blocs with Left SRs in cases where this was necessary to thwart the opposition, and it encouraged shuttling the very limited number of experienced agitators available for the campaign around districts to maximize coverage of the entire city.[67]

Volodarskii envisioned that electoral commissions formed by district party committees and the committees themselves would coordinate the Bolshevik campaign at the local level, and some district party committees managed to form such agencies.[68] But the narrow time frame of the contest, as well as the paralysis of most party committees, prevented the committees from playing significant roles. As it was, a heavy load of campaigning fell to the chief figures in the Petrograd Bolshevik and Left SR hierarchy. At the behest of Volodarskii and Zinoviev, indefatigable campaigners themselves, "politically conscious" sailors were rushed from Kronstadt to help.[69] In the space of a few days, by means of an intensive "blitz," advocates for the existing regime attempted to gain back the popular support that had severely eroded in the preceding weeks and months during which "party work" in factories practically stopped. Their central theme, trumpeted daily in the Bolshevik and Left SR press, and at endless factory assemblies and political rallies, was that only the Bolsheviks and Left SRs, among the contending parties, stood for the realization of revolutionary goals. The enemy was the Mensheviks and SRs, who stood for the capitalists' return to power and early restoration of the hated ways of the old regime. As in the Bolshevik campaign in elections to the Constituent Assembly, a vote for the opposition was deemed a vote for counterrevolution. There was no middle ground.[70]

The Bolsheviks and Left SRs took the elections seriously from the start, but only after some hesitation did the Mensheviks and SRs campaign in earnest. Whereas the Bolsheviks sought to shift popular attention away from immediate economic troubles to long-term revolutionary goals, and argued that opposition demands to reconvene the Constituent Assembly were merely pretexts for restoring traditional injustices, the Mensheviks and SRs did the reverse—they played on popular anxieties over the threat of famine, the likelihood of German occupation, the spread of disease, and the horror of an expanding, bloody civil war so as to underscore the bankruptcy of the Soviet experiment and the importance of the Constituent Assembly as the only means of averting total catastrophe.[71]

By 26 June, when the EAD set 2 July for a general strike, elections to the Petrograd Soviet were nearing completion. The selection process created by the Bolsheviks achieved its goal, delivering an overwhelming majority for the party.[72] Yet, although it is now possible to document how the Bolsheviks contrived a majority in the new Petrograd Soviet, it remains difficult to evaluate the election results on the shop floor in terms of the workers' political sentiment. Judging by official tabulations, the Bolsheviks had modest success in direct elections at the workplace, electing 127 of 260 factory delegates. The Left SRs received the second largest number of delegates elected by workers, roughly 75. Together, the governing parties received a 3 to 1 majority among workers. SRs, Mensheviks, and unaffiliated candidates fared well in several larger enterprises, among them the Putilov, Obukhov, Cartridge, Nevskii, Baltiiskii, and Arsenal plants, in printing establishments, and among Petrograd factory women, many of them employed in tobacco firms and textile mills. Perhaps primarily because of food shortages and threatened layoffs,[73] long gone was the time when the Bolsheviks attracted strong support from female workers, as in the elections to the Constituent Assembly. After the election, Konkordia Samoilova, leader of the Bolshevik campaign among factory women, conceded that it had been a disaster, that factory women would not even give Bolsheviks a hearing.[74] Still, a post-election editorial in *Novaia zhizn'*, while taking note of Bolshevik defeats, SR and Menshevik successes, and the intimidation of voters, concluded that "many workers have not yet rid themselves of Bolshevik 'Communism,' [as they] still consider Soviet power . . . representative of their interests, [and] associate their fate and the fate of their movement with it."[75]

Undoubtedly that was true. One is still left, however, with the nagging question of how many Bolshevik deputies from factories were elected instead of the opposition because of press restrictions, voter intimidation, vote fraud, or the short duration of the campaign. In individual districts, factory elections were administered by election commissions that were selected by local soviets and excluded the opposition. Elections at the factories were implemented by Bolshevik-dominated factory committees, many of which had not been reelected since 1917. Factory committees from closed factories could and did elect soviet deputies (the so-called dead souls), one deputy for each factory with more than one thousand workers at the time of their shutdown. Even unemployed workers were accorded representation roughly equal to employed workers. Their electoral assemblies were organized through Bolshevik-dominated trade union election commissions.[76] On 15 June, Volodarskii had "magnanimously" authorized the reopening of some opposition newspapers, among them the SRs' *Delo naroda* and the Mensheviks' *Luch*. However, this was only a couple of days before the start of voting. Before then, most of the moderate socialist press remained muzzled.

On the eve of the decisive split between Bolsheviks and Left SRs in early

July,[77] Left SRs candidly acknowledged Bolshevik abuses in the elections. At the third Left SR national congress in Moscow (28 June to 1 July), Spiridonova claimed that three hundred of the four hundred Bolshevik deputies in the newly elected soviet had illegitimate credentials. "We did not speak or resist this [fraud] because the counterrevolution [and] defensist party is so strong in Petrograd that defeat of the Bolsheviks would have meant . . . the destruction of Soviet power and put Petrograd into the hands of the black reaction. We had to be silent about it despite the fact that the indignation of workers . . . was enormous."[78] Where, then, does this leave us? Perhaps the least that can now be said is that the Bolshevik "victory" in the June 1918 elections to the Petrograd Soviet, elections that would have significant political consequences, was highly suspect, even on the shop floor.

On 25 June, the Bolshevik Petersburg Committee took steps to organize and assert control over the party's fraction in the new soviet, which was scheduled to hold its first meeting two days later.[79] Although this attempt to implement the principle that soviet fractions were subordinate to party committees failed, it was a noteworthy, potentially precedent-setting initiative. Around this time, efforts were intensified to establish Bolshevik fractions and collectives nominally responsible to local party committees in all district soviets and other civic agencies that lacked them.

Concurrent efforts were started to rejuvenate party work among female workers. With the shutdown of *Rabotnitsa* at the end of January,[80] the leading Petrograd Bolshevik women who had been associated with it focused their energy on general party work, either in the Petersburg Committee or district party committees. A notable exception was Aleksandra Kollontai, who moved to Moscow as a member of the SNK in mid March. In June, the need to replace party cadres that had transferred out of Petrograd, coupled with the disastrous results of elections to the Petrograd Soviet among factory women, underscored the importance of acquiring greater support among them. The necessity of upgrading party work among factory women had first been raised and approved by the Petersburg Committee on the eve of the elections. On 14 June, the Petersburg Committee had, in fact, charged Samoilova to organize a special section for agitation and propaganda among factory women.[81] At a meeting of the Assembly of Organizers on 26 June, Samoilova presented her views on the importance and complexities of gaining a hearing among angry factory women threatened by starvation and loss of work, after which she made a proposal to establish special sections attached to the Petersburg Committee and district party committees for communicating with the factory women. Some of the assembled district organizers criticized these proposals, either because they considered that winning over "dark, reactionary" female workers was hopeless, or because they were already so overloaded that establishing yet another section seemed, as one of her listeners put it, an "utter illusion."

Even Zheniia Egorova, organizer for the Vyborg district Bolshevik Committee and a member of the Petersburg Committee, who shared Samoilova's views about the critical importance of party work among factory women, felt that primary leadership in this endeavor had to come from "above," from a women's section attached to the Petersburg Committee. Anna Itkina, organizer for the Narva district Bolshevik Committee, came to Samoilova's defense, arguing that the chief weakness of earlier Bolshevik party work among factory women was precisely that it did not have an organizational base at the grass-roots level. The Assembly of Organizers decided to form sections for party work among women at the city and district levels *concurrently.* Such sections were established by all Bolshevik district party committees.[82] Most of them did not accomplish much, however, largely because of continuing economic crises affecting women and their families, as well as the traditional, denigrating attitudes of most male Bolsheviks toward women generally and particularly toward party work among female factory workers. Samoilova stressed the negative impact of gender discrimination among male comrades during this period in a speech to the Eighth City Conference of Petrograd Bolsheviks in December 1918. As an illustration, she lamented that, when women at one of Petrograd's largest industrial enterprises selected one of their own to represent them on the plant's worker committee, they were rebuffed on the grounds that if representation was granted to female workers, it would be necessary also to give representation to children.[83]

At the Assembly of Organizers meeting, on 26 June, Samoilova also raised the question of resuming publication of *Rabotnitsa,* making it clear that while she hoped it would be revived she was ambivalent about whether it should be published in Petrograd or Moscow, as the capital's resources would be advantageous. Egorova demonstrated no such ambivalence. Apparently even more hostile to feminism than Samoilova, she declared unequivocally that transferring the periodical to Moscow, where its contents would be shaped by the arch feminist Kollontai, was absolutely "impermissible!"[84] Because of this lack of unanimity, a final decision on this issue was left to the Petersburg Committee.[85] Two days later, on 28 June, and again on 2 July, the Petersburg Committee considered the question and agreed to publish *Rabotnitsa* itself, as soon as district sections for party work among factory women had been established. Samoilova, Nikolaeva, and Praskovia Kudelli, who had comprised *Rabotnitsa's* editorial board in 1917, were again appointed to the editorial board for the magazine's reincarnation.[86] A few weeks later, however, on 19 July, this decision was reversed during a general consolidation of the party and government press brought on by financial and personnel shortages. The Petersburg Committee resolved to forgo publication of *Rabotnitsa* for the time being, and instead to offer its editorial board weekly columns in the Petrograd Soviet's *Krasnaia gazeta*.[87]

The first of these weekly "Rabotnitsa" columns in *Krasnaia gazeta* appeared on 4 August, and from the outset the members of its editorial board strove to distance themselves from any hint of separatism or of "Kollontai's feminism." Thus, in an initial introductory message, they expressed satisfaction that common work in the same newspaper would strengthen the bond uniting female and male workers in the struggle for the great cause of freeing all laborers from the decay of capitalism. Just as the earlier *Rabotnitsa* had only focused on the lives of female workers as they related to the common tasks of the working class, so the new column would deal with factory women as one of the detachments of the great labor army.[88] To be sure, subsequent columns emphasized issues of particular concern to women such as food shortages and the bloody civil war. The most consistent theme, however, which was often highlighted in a bold-face side bar, called on factory women not to lag behind men in dealing with common tasks.

* * *

Meanwhile, Bolshevik leaders in the Petrograd Soviet elected in June had wasted no time in drawing on their dubious "mandate" to justify suppressing the EAD and head off the EAD-led general strike set for 2 July. A resolution condemning the EAD as an element of the domestic and foreign counterrevolution was adopted at the first plenary session of the new soviet on 27 June, several days before the elections were finished.[89] All Petrograd newspapers were obliged to feature this condemnation on their front pages. Factories were admonished that if they participated in the general strike they would face immediate shutdown, and individual strikers were threatened with fines or loss of work. Agitators and members of strike committees were subject to immediate arrest, and these warnings were later made good.[90]

On the afternoon of the thirtieth, the Executive Committee of the Petrograd Soviet held a hurried emergency meeting with representatives from district soviets and district Bolshevik and Left SR party committees to devise additional anti-strike measures.[91] Beginning on 1 July, printing plants suspected of opposition sympathies were sealed, the offices of hostile trade unions were raided, martial law on lines in the Petrograd rail hub was declared, and armed patrols with authority to prevent work stoppages were formed and put on twenty-four-hour duty at key points around the city.

Taking note of these tough measures, a writer in *Novaia zhizn'* concluded that "never, even during the severest repression of the Bolsheviks under Kerensky following the July uprising, was the freedom and will of workers so inhibited as it is under the terrorist stewardship of the present worker-peasant government."[92] The Bureau of the EAD dug further back in time, declaring in a broadsheet that "no government in Russia of the Romanovs had taken such extreme measures to thwart a strike as the Soviet government had."[93]

At least partly because of these strong countermeasures, the response to the EAD's strike call was limited to a very few factories and printing plants. In the repressive atmosphere prevailing in Petrograd in the aftermath of the failed strike (made worse by the reaction to the "conspiracy" of the Left SRs a few days later),[94] the EAD was doomed. Its Bureau met for the last time on 19 July. Notes from this meeting, obviously scratched out in great haste, indicate that it dealt exclusively with vacating the Assembly's headquarters, and paying and releasing staff.[95]

Subsequent developments relating to the EAD took place in Moscow and were exclusively concerned with organizing a national workers' congress aimed at giving representatives of labor from all over the country an opportunity to seek solutions to Russia's problems. At its last meetings, in addition to issuing a call for a general strike, the EAD had agreed to organize a congress of workers from industrial centers, primarily in the Northern and Central oblasts, to plan an early national workers' congress. Moreover, immediately following its meeting on 26 June, it dispatched two key leaders, Aleksei Smirnov and N. K. Borisenko, to Moscow to help prepare the regional congress. A preliminary meeting for it was held in Moscow on 28 June. With delegates from Petrograd, Moscow, Tula, Iaroslavl, Nizhnii Novogorod, Sormovo, Vladimir, Kolomna, the Mal'tsev region, Briansk, and Tver, it formed an organizing committee and scheduled convocation of the regional congress for 20 July in Moscow.[96]

The organizing committee began operating immediately, developing a draft agenda that made no allowance for the obvious determination of the Soviet government to retain power at practically any price. The regional congress was still to openly consider and prepare draft resolutions on the most critical political and economic problems of the day. The subsequent All-Russian Workers' Congress, with the support of a reunited working class, was to act on them. This agenda ignored the fact that the organizing committee's efforts were undermined from the start by the disintegration of the EAD in Petrograd and by the stifling political conditions prevailing in Moscow and other industrial centers. Indeed, so few delegates had managed to get to the capital on 20 July that the opening of the regional congress was postponed until 22 July. On 21 July, the number of delegates in Moscow was still so small that, assembling informally, they were left with no choice but to scale down the designation of the next day's talks, as well as the agenda for the talks. Barring a sudden jump in the number of arriving delegates, the gathering was now to be called a meeting (*soveshchanie*) rather than a congress or even a conference. Also, instead of drafting positions on critical political, economic, and foreign policy issues for a national workers' congress, the "meeting" was to be limited to hearing reports on conditions locally and dealing with questions regarding the purpose and organization of the national congress (rather than with broad policy issues).[97]

The roughly thirty-five participants in this "meeting" on 22–23 July had barely begun to address this constricted program when their deliberations were broken up by Red Guards, rifles at the ready.[98] All the participants were treated roughly, arrested, and bundled off to VCheka headquarters for interrogation and transfer to the infamous Taganka Prison. Among those seized, in addition to elected worker delegates, were four prominent nonvoting representatives of socialist parties: Raphael Abramovich, Aleksandr Beilin, and Aleksandr Volanen from the central committees of the Menshevik, SR, and Edinstvo parties, respectively, and Aleksandr Alt'er from the Bund.[99]

Documentation of this meeting, however incomplete, is of considerable interest because it provides insights into the behavior of government and labor under the impact of civil war, unemployment, disease, and hunger. The value of organizing a national workers' congress was not disputed during sessions of the meeting, and the relationship of this congress to Soviet power as it then existed was barely mentioned, thus complicating the VCheka's future case against the participants. The only substantive issue that triggered argument was the feasibility of forming a single, powerful national workers' "union" or "party," free of influence from the intelligentsia. The emergence of this question, like the idea of a national workers' congress partly reflected the same disenchantment with all existing political parties that had contributed to the formation of the EAD in the first place.

*   *   *

The first sign of the terrible cholera outbreak that epidemiologists had warned of in the spring appeared on 1 July, when government authorities in Petrograd were focused on preventing the next day's general strike. On that date, seven suspected cases of the dreaded disease were registered in city hospitals. Typical of cholera, the number of cases rose very quickly but its peak did not last long, after which the decline in cases was steady but stretched over a significantly longer period of time. The figures for the first week (1–

7 July) were 456 confirmed and suspected cases, with 59 resulting in death. The epidemic peaked during the second week (8–14 July), when the figure was a staggering 4,247 cases, with 1,264 resulting in death. The third week (15–21 July) saw 2,304 cases, with 1,044 resulting in death, and, during the fourth week (22–28 July), the number of cases and deaths dropped another 50 percent to 1,219 cases, 507 of them fatal. The number of cases and deaths, although still worrisome, dropped steadily in August and September; the figures for all of August were 2,331 cases, leading to 861 deaths, and, for September, 1,091 cases leading to 372 deaths. Hit hardest by the epidemic, not surprisingly, were districts and neighborhoods of Petrograd populated by the poor and uneducated, the least able to resist infection, with a high percentage of unskilled and unemployed workers.[100]

The total number of registered cases between July and September was 12,047, of which 8,223 were confirmed and 4,305 deaths were recorded. These totals do not include large numbers of victims who died at home or in the streets. Nonetheless, the sheer number of registered cases made it the largest outbreak of cholera in the city's history. It was three times larger than a major cholera epidemic in Petrograd (then Petersburg), in 1892, and one and a half times larger than one that ravaged the city in 1902.[101] A report on the peak of the epidemic at a Bolshevik Petersburg Committee meeting on 10 July suggested that an extraordinarily high percentage of victims were factory women.[102]

Framed against the backdrop of fierce class warfare during the period already described, the battle to bring the Petrograd cholera epidemic of 1918 under control appears as a kind of brief, limited armistice, during which customarily hostile political elements of the population collaborated for the common good. The quickest to respond to the outbreak were Bolshevik and Left SR representatives of district soviet medical sections assembled in the Interdistrict Conference. For the duration of the emergency, local efforts to educate the public about avoiding infection were headed by medical sections of individual district soviets or hastily formed district soviet "troikas" to combat cholera, supported by epidemiologists, staffs of local hospitals, and pharmacists. The medical sections also established multiple neighborhood cholera first-aid stations and vaccination centers, which functioned around-the-clock, and strove mightily to eradicate sources of contamination.[103] The Commissariat for Public Health SK SO formed an Emergency Commission for the Struggle against Cholera which became a citywide coordinating center for anti-cholera efforts.

At an initial meeting on 9 July the Emergency Commission, headed by Pervukhin, the Bolshevik commissar for public health, developed a plan to establish independent district medical/sanitation centers to fight cholera.[104] But the Emergency Commission's records suggest that it ended up channeling many of its efforts at the local level through district soviet medical sections and troikas. The Emergency Commission also appears to have worked well with a Central Workers' Committee to Combat Cholera that had been formed by the Petrograd Soviet. Although representatives of district soviets were belatedly added to the Emergency Commission, serving alongside the city's leading medical experts, the Central Workers' Committee claimed the right to coordinate district-level efforts to combat cholera.[105] The committee often served as a conduit between the labor organizations generally and the Emergency Commission and district soviets. Even the Bolshevik Petersburg Committee became involved. At the peak of the crisis, it took steps to stop the sale of fruit by street vendors, facilitate the quick adoption of emergency preventative health measures by workers, and mobilize workers to bury a huge backlog of coffins at the city's cemeteries.[106] Labor conflict associated with the epidemic was minimal and understandable. Grossly overworked grave diggers at the Uspenskii Cemetery demanded an increase in their miserly bread ration. The same was true of employees at the city's waterworks, especially stokers who themselves became victims of the disease in inordinately high percentages; they insisted on a supplemental ration equal to that granted personnel carrying out high-risk medical duties. These demands were forwarded to the Emergency Commission and, presumably, were met.[107]

*   *   *

Petrograd's political, economic, and social problems worsened immeasurably during the first half of 1918. The SK PTK, which initially was left largely to fend for itself by the Sovnarkom in Moscow, tried to cope with these problems with a measure of moderation but to no avail. The rapid expansion of the EAD was partly a reflection of this failure. Even now, when the EAD's voluminous files are available for study, it is impossible to quantify its following. However, these records leave no doubt that in the spring of 1918 the EAD had the support of significant numbers of workers from a broad cross-section of Petrograd factories and plants. It is also clear that at the start, in mid March, when the EAD was attempting to work within the existing political system to bring about change, this support was driven primarily by bread-and-butter issues—food shortages, unemployment, chaotic evacuation, and the like—coupled with the apparent unwillingness of existing labor organizations and institutions of self-government to help resolve them. By mid May, however, as all these problems deepened, the EAD's goals, and popular support for the EAD, became more overtly political and anti-Soviet.[108]

Petrograd district soviets attempted to respond by restoring their following among workers through their own nonparty workers' conferences. Despite Bolshevik-Left SR majorities in them, these conferences, like plenary sessions of the EAD, revealed the growing desperation of a Petrograd labor force crushed by devastating food shortages and catastrophic unemployment. Meanwhile, the Treaty of Brest-Litovsk had not ended the threat that the Germans would seize the Russian Baltic Fleet, forcing its treacherous "Ice March" from Helsingfors to Kronstadt led by Aleksei Shchastny, or that Petrograd would be occupied, symbolized by the renewed war scare at the time of the crisis surrounding the fate of Fort Ino.

More than this, Moscow's never-ending demands for personnel stripped the Bolshevik party organization of its already limited cadres, undermining all attempts to strengthen the party so that it could resume political activity in workplaces and play a leading role in Petrograd's government (after initial ambiguity about the party's proper tasks). Symptomatic of the profound crisis of Soviet power in Petrograd at this point were the rebellion of the minelaying flotilla and Obukhov workers, the need that Petrograd Bolsheviks obviously felt to assure a victory in the June elections to the Petrograd Soviet by corrupting the electoral process, and the brutal suppression of the EAD's general strike.

The population of Petrograd, at the beginning of 1917, was conservatively estimated at approximately 2.3 million, but a census in early June 1918, the first since 1910, revealed a decline of almost a million to just under 1.5 million.[109] During the last half of May and the first half of June alone, roughly 150,000 citizens, a high percentage of them workers, fled the former capital, streaming to the countryside to escape hunger.[110] Ever more frightening food shortages, the increasing threat of Red Terror, and the unprecedented cholera epidemic drove the mass exodus into mid summer. It is not surprising that in August, in a letter to Novgorodsteva in Moscow, even Stasova lamented that "Piter is empty, it is sad to look at her."[111]

In coping with these myriad emergencies, the Petrograd Bolsheviks were aided by collaboration with the Left SRs. The critical importance of the Bolshevik-Left SR alliance for the survival of Soviet power in the Petrograd region in the spring and early summer of 1918 is illustrated by the history of the so-called Northern Commune.

10

The Northern Commune and
the Bolshevik–Left SR Alliance

ZINOVIEV, IN March 1918, had opposed the relocation of the national government to Moscow—the pre-Petrine Russian capital—because he recognized that moving it there instead of to a less central and less important city reduced the likelihood of its ever returning to Petrograd (Zinoviev's choice was Nizhnii Novgorod). Once the move was made, Zinoviev stressed that because the Russian people still viewed Petrograd as the capital, in the short term Soviet authorities in Petrograd and Moscow would need to share national government functions.[1] Stasova was among other prominent Petrograd Bolsheviks who held this view.[2] In early April, Zinoviev, Lashevich, and Ioffe had come away from a chaotic Central Committee plenum in Moscow convinced that the central party leadership was paralyzed and sorely needed reinforcement from Petrograd. Dysfunctional central leadership at this point was a result of continuing, bitter conflict between the Leninist Central Committee and Sovnarkom, on the one hand, and the Left Communist–controlled Moscow Oblast Bureau and oblast government, on the other.[3] Based on their experience, Zinoviev, Lashevich, and Ioffe were increasingly uneasy about Moscow, and suspicious that, especially in foreign affairs, the Moscow party leadership was taking steps behind their backs that they would not approve.[4] Also, military, food procurement, and public health concerns dictated stronger regional, if not national, direction from Petrograd.

Creation of a regional Bolshevik organization to coordinate the party's activities in the Northern Oblast (or region) preceded establishment of an oblast government. The Petrograd Bureau of the Bolshevik Central Committee, on 20 March, resolved to integrate provincial party committees in northwest Russia into a regional Northern Oblast party organization. For this purpose, on 3–6 April, the Bureau convened a conference of party representatives from the neighboring provinces of Petrograd, Archangel, Vologda, Novgorod, Olonets, and Pskov.[5] This conference, the First Northern Oblast [Bolshevik] Party Conference, formed a representative committee, the Northern Oblast Committee (SOK) to direct party work in the Northern Oblast.[6]

Concurrently, the Sovkom of the Petrograd Labor Commune (the SK PTK) began planning for a congress of soviets in the Northern Oblast,[7] which ultimately met in Petrograd on 26–29 April. Inasmuch as its outcome (establishment of an oblast government) was a foregone conclusion, its primary historical interest lies in the revealing arguments that broke out there between Zinoviev and the prominent Petrograd Left SR Iakov Fishman over Left SR participation in the new government and over the government's structure.

On 23 March, the SK PTK had responded to feelers from the Left SRs by sanctioning negotiations to include the Left SRs in an oblast government.[8] These talks evidently went well. The SK PTK, after listening to a report by Zinoviev on 11 April, reconfirmed its interest in forming a coalition with the Left SRs and designated the government portfolios that could be offered to them: "Agriculture, transportation, and internal affairs, but not military affairs, under any circumstances."[9] A week before the opening of the First Northern Oblast Congress of Soviets, Zinoviev had led negotiations along these lines with the Petrograd Left SR leadership.[10]

A day or two before the start of the congress, however, a majority of delegates to the Second All-Russian Left SR Party Congress (held in Moscow on 17–23 April),[11] following a week of acrimonious debate about whether to withdraw from the Sovnarkom because it had ratified the Brest treaty, endorsed withdrawal. At the same time, the delegates recommended active participation of Left SRs in other national and regional government agencies.[12] The opening of the First Northern Oblast Congress of Soviets also coincided with the major new war scare surrounding Fort Ino.[13] As we have seen, government authorities in Petrograd feared that this threat was the prelude to an attack on their city and had fervently proclaimed their determination to defend Petrograd "at any cost."[14] Naturally, then, on the first day of the congress, Zinoviev began a report on the SK PTK with a ringing reaffirmation of this pledge to defend the city. Foreshadowing a central theme of Lenin's "Immediate Tasks of Soviet Power,"[15] Zinoviev listed Petrograd's grave problems, concluding that they could be resolved only by the institution of a strong, oblast-wide dictatorship, discipline, unconditional obedience, and revolutionary unity.

The continued Left SR boycott of the Sovnarkom together with this concern about unconditional obedience and revolutionary unity were apparently the catalyst for the ferocious attack on the Left SRs which Zinoviev launched next. Then, too, he may have been trying to move in tandem with Lenin's freshly articulated disdain for the Left SRs. In any case, Zinoviev accused the Left SRs of hypocrisy, deception, and sabotage. As a consequence of their "fatal error" in not supporting the ratification of the Brest treaty, the Left SRs had squandered their popular following. They also erred in thinking that they could withdraw from the Sovnarkom and continue their engagement in Soviet government elsewhere. Under existing circumstances, the basis for effective political collaboration in government between Bolsheviks and Left SRs had been undermined. Petrograd Left SRs had the choice either of working with the Bolsheviks [at all levels] or leaving the soviets entirely and joining the counterrevolution in their effort to overthrow the Bolsheviks. Repeatedly, Zinoviev contended that continuing lack of clarity in the policies of the Left SRs was intolerable. Yet, somewhat contradictorily, he also declared that if the Left SRs wanted to participate in the oblast government they would be welcome, provided their intent was not to "sabotage" the Bolsheviks' policies but to work closely with them and support the decrees of the central government and the Fourth All-Russian Congress of Soviets (in other words, implementation of the Brest treaty).[16]

Because the Bolshevik majority rejected Left SR requests that Zinoviev's speech be discussed at once,[17] it was not until the last day of the congress on 29 April that Iakov Fishman, spokesman for the Left SRs, was able to rebut him. In the interim, cooler heads, recognizing the importance of help from the Left SRs if Soviet power in the Northwest was to survive, worked out an understanding on their participation in the government.[18] Nonetheless, Fishman, well known for his fiery oratory, did not mince words in responding to Zinoviev.[19] Seizing upon Zinoviev's fervent pledge to combat the advance of German forces at Fort Ino to the last, Fishman declared that insofar as the Petrograd Commune remained true to this commitment, the Bolsheviks and Left SRs were united. On this central question in the Bolshevik–Left SR conflict, Bolshevik authorities in Petrograd might have a quarrel with the Sovnarkom in Moscow, but most certainly not with the Left SRs. To Fishman, in fact, a common determination to defend Petrograd at all costs provided Bolsheviks and Left SRs in the Northern Oblast with a solid basis for collaboration.

Fishman wondered just how the Bolsheviks expected Left SR "sabotage" would be manifested. If Bolsheviks thought that the Left SRs would demand socialization of land instead of [urban] "gardening," and genuine workers' control rather than invitations to representatives of commercial-industrial circles, then they would be saboteurs. Here Fishman was referring to the Bolsheviks' promotion of planting vegetables in open spaces in and around Petrograd as a means of easing the food shortages crisis, and to the use of bourgeois specialists as paid advisors on military and industrial projects.

Responding to Zinoviev's inference that staying out of an oblast government followed naturally from the withdrawal of the Left SRs from the Sovnarkom, Fishman explained that there was only one reason for this act—the Fourth All-Russian Congress of Soviets had adopted a resolution (ratification of the Brest treaty) that the Left SRs were convinced had placed the October revolution in an utterly hopeless position. Consequently, the Left SRs, by allowing their representatives to participate in the Sovnarkom, would be actively collaborating in policies they were certain would lead to the smothering of the revolution. The Sovnarkom in Moscow would be forced to implement the Brest treaty, Fishman continued. So be it. This did not mean the Left SRs had to abandon the Bolsheviks. They had not lost faith in them. The Bolsheviks had said that Soviet Russia would get a breathing space of a week or two, and if it was faced with intolerable conditions, the treaty would be torn up. If that was true, the Left SRs could participate in oblast governments with clear consciences. "You won't be implementing the peace treaty here, you will just be exchanging notes with German representatives and we will leave that happy chore to you," Fishman chuckled. To the degree that you don't retreat from revolutionary measures to which we both subscribe, he declared, "we will gladly work together."

Fishman went on to describe Petrograd Left SR thinking on Soviet government, in general, and on the structure of a future oblast political system, in particular. Here the contrast was significant between Fishman, representing the dominant Petrograd Left SR point of view, and Zinoviev, who, in step with Lenin, was now contemptuous of democratic scruples and determined that strict party discipline and centralized government were the keys to saving the revolution. The core of the Left SR view on government, as Fishman elaborated it, was an abiding faith in the ability of workers and peasants, organized around democratic soviets, to develop the revolution. Genuine Soviet power and a revolutionary democracy necessarily had to be based on healthy social forces, meaning those toiling elements of the urban and rural population. Because the urban proletariat was then in the process of migrating to the countryside, the main social base of revolutionary government would have to be Russia's still enormous, healthy, and politically able class of laboring peasants: middle and poorer peasants working their own modest plots, as opposed to wealthier landowners who employed hired labor. Because this class was alive and well, there was no justification for introducing purely bureaucratic institutions or the dictatorship of party commissars into the soviet system. This malignancy of bureaucracy and commissars had developed into an epidemic as a result of the fact that the Bolsheviks' natural social base among factory workers was disintegrating. To compensate for this, the *diktat* of party officials was being substituted for class-based democracy exercised through freely elected, representative soviets. To Fishman, it was essential that this process be reversed. Privately, of course, Bolshevik authorities in Petrograd led by Zinoviev were themselves concerned about the isolation of soviets from their labor constituency and looked to mitigate it through district nonparty workers' conferences.[20]

The proposals that Fishman presented on behalf of the Left SRs for structuring an oblast government flowed from a deep belief that government should be implemented primarily through popularly controlled, democratically operated, representative soviets. Thus, Fishman proposed that, essentially, the SK PTK should be abolished and that the main government body in the Northern Oblast should be a flexible and elastic Soviet Executive Committee, whose members should be subject to recall whenever the masses wished so that it would always reflect the popular will. The Executive Committee should have sections, corresponding to existing commissariats, with each section headed by a member of the Executive Committee so that the entire system would be under the Executive Committee's complete control. Section heads would not meet as a body. (Presumably, similarly structured executive committees, subject to control by popularly elected soviets, would be responsible for government at lower levels.) If all this were done, Fishman concluded, executive committees would not be the fiction that the CEC in Moscow had become, and the masses would be re-engaged in the political life of the country and of the revolution.[21]

Subsequently, two resolutions on the structure of a government for the Northern Oblast Union of Communes, as the Northern Oblast was commonly referred to (Northern Commune, for short), were voted on by the delegates. One incorporated the radical (some would say quixotic) innovations Fishman proposed. The other, presented by the Bolsheviks, essentially conformed to existing Soviet structural models. The Bolshevik resolution also pledged that the new government would follow the line adopted at the Fourth All-Russian Congress of Soviets, implementing the decisions of all previous national congresses of soviets (whatever that meant) and closely collaborating with the central Sovnarkom and the CEC. The vote was 45 for the Left SR resolution and 82 for the Bolshevik resolution.[22]

Bolsheviks selected for the Sovkom of the Northern Oblast or Northern Commune (SK SO) on 29 April were Zinoviev (chair); Sheiman (finance);

Lunacharskii (enlightenment); Krestinskii (justice); Uritskii (internal affairs); Zalutskii (labor); Volodarskii (press); Malyshev (economy); Lilina (social welfare); Anvel't (nationalities); Pervukhin (public health); Pozern (military affairs); and Voskov (food supply).[23] In early May, four Left SRs joined this group: Proshian replaced Uritskii as head of the Commissariat for Internal Affairs and of the Committee for the Revolutionary Security of Petrograd (Uritskii retained his post as head of the PCheka); M. D. Samokhvalov (oblast control); Nikolai Kornilov [Kirill Korenev] (agriculture); and Leonid Bekleshov (post and telegraph).[24]

The Bolsheviks not only conceded four posts in the new government to the Left SRs, rather than the three originally projected for them, but they appeared to be forthcoming on the relationship between institutions of the new oblast government. According to a resolution adopted by the Central Executive Committee of the Northern Oblast on 14 May, in the interim between Northern Oblast congresses of soviets, the Central Executive Committee, composed of twenty-five Bolsheviks and fourteen Left SRs, was to be the "directing and controlling organ" in the region. The SK SO was to be its Executive Committee. All members of the Central Executive Committee were to be distributed among commissariats, and the committee was to meet as a body no less than once every two weeks. Members of the SK SO who were not also members of the Central Executive Committee would be limited to consultative voting rights.[25] On the surface, this design seems to have represented an effort to respond to Left SR concerns about the arbitrary power of commissars, and the primacy of the Central Executive Committee over the SK SO. In any case, in practice it quickly fell by the wayside; as in the central government, the Central Executive Committee of the Northern Oblast was subordinate to the SK SO, and the latter, headquartered in Smolny, essentially adopted and issued decrees pertaining to Petrograd and the surrounding region at will. At the same time, creation of the SK SO and the Central Executive Committee of the Northern Oblast Congress of Soviets further confused governance in Petrograd by adding another layer of institutions with claims to authority in the city. This state of affairs was mitigated, but not eliminated, by the fact that high officials of the SK SO, the SK PTK, and the Presidium and Executive Committee of the Petrograd Soviet, were often one and the same, and Zinoviev chaired them all.[26]

The debate between Zinoviev and Fishman at the First Northern Oblast Congress of Soviets, which in retrospect had been the central feature of the congress, graphically illustrated the ties that bound the Bolsheviks and Left SRs, as well as the profound differences between the two parties. For the Petrograd Bolsheviks, starved for cadres, the Left SRs were a source of energetic, competent personnel who were often infinitely more dedicated to the revolution than hastily and indiscriminately recruited new Bolshevik party members. In the aftermath of the Northern Oblast congress, Left SRs in Petrograd remained active and even expanded their roles in individual commissariats, in the PCheka, and in such institutions of municipal government as the Petrograd Soviet and district soviets.

Future events would demonstrate that, at bottom, Fishman's claim that the Left SRs still had faith in the Bolsheviks was not spurious. To be sure, most Petrograd Left SR leaders viewed the Treaty of Brest-Litovsk as a shameful betrayal of the international socialist revolution. Nonetheless, to them the Bolsheviks were still the heroic architects of "October." They still had a healthy core—the Left Communists—with whom Left SRs felt an especially strong kinship. It seemed inevitable that under pressure from them, the Bolshevik party as a whole would return to the revolutionary path from which it had strayed, and together the two parties would work to further world revolution. The alternatives for Petrograd Left SRs—either turning against the Bolsheviks and, in effect, aiding the counterrevolution, or going it alone—were out of the question. It was, after all, only yesterday, at the second Left SR national party congress, that the new and still weakly organized Left SR party nearly imploded.

At the same time, the debate between Zinoviev and Fishman revealed the many major programmatic principles that differentiated the Bolsheviks from the Left SRs. To the Bolshevik leadership, the solution to the continuing disintegration of economic and political life, and to the threats posed by foreign and domestic enemies, lay in dictatorship, institutional centralization, utilization of the technical expertise of the bourgeoisie and of former officers, and extension of the "breathing space" in hostilities with Germany provided by the Brest treaty at virtually any price. To the Left SRs, who were committed to the ideal of worker and peasant empowerment exercised through democratic soviets, and who viewed a worldwide popular uprising as the Russian revolution's only hope for survival, these policies were an abomination.

*   *   *

Two related developments soon after the creation of the Northern Commune reinforced Left SR concerns about the direction of Bolshevik policies. One was Lenin's major new programmatic statement, "Immediate Tasks of Soviet Power," published in *Pravda* and as a special supplement to *Izvestiia*, on 28 April, and summarized in a speech to the CEC, on 29 April (the last day of the Oblast Congress).[27] The statement was Lenin's detailed response to Left Communist theses presented in a discussion with the Leninist majority of the Central Committee and leading Left Communists on 4 April and published in *Kommunist* on April 20.[28] It was also Lenin's detailed rebuttal to Left SR attacks on his foreign and domestic policies at the Second Left SR Party Congress. On the assumption that the destructive stage of the revolution, in which the power of the richest bourgeoisie and big landowners needed to be broken, was largely completed, Lenin defined the more important "immediate tasks of Soviet power" to be suspending the offensive against capitalism and putting an end to economic chaos so as to revive Russia's economic strength and military capabilities. These tasks necessitated the unquestioning implementation of government directives, obedience to individual dictators (commissars), utilization of paid "bourgeois specialists" in economic management, the re-imposition of one-man managerial authority and labor discipline, and other such "capitalist" measures in industry as restoration of wage incentives to workers. Lenin referred to this mixed economic system as "state capitalism" and readily acknowledged that it was consciously modeled after Germany's wartime economy. All these positions were anathema to Left SRs, as Karelin made clear to the CEC on 29 April. Also, in the CEC Lenin devoted considerably more attention to assailing the Left SRs for not understanding the needs of the moment than he had in written versions of the statement, a fact that Karelin studiously ignored, focusing, instead, on challenging Lenin's fundamental assumptions and policies.[29]

Lenin's "Immediate Tasks of Soviet Power" caused a great stir among Petrograd Left SRs. At the Seventh City Conference of Petrograd Left SRs, on 3 May, the delegates passed a resolution endorsing the Second All-Russian Left SR Party Congress's opposition to the Brest peace and withdrawing from the central government. They also seconded participation in the Northern Oblast government "until such time as it retreated completely from the slogans of the October revolution." In addition, they endorsed the "theses" against Lenin's "new course" that were originally adopted by the Left SR fraction in the CEC, and that emphasized in particular Lenin's intention to develop a "businesslike" relationship with the bourgeoisie and to foster dictatorships in politics and economic management. Echoing Karelin's rebuttal to Lenin in the CEC, on 29 April, the theses attacked Lenin's new program as a systematic retreat from the basic principles underlying October, and a conscious retreat from social revolution that stemmed from a faulty evaluation of the social role of the laboring peasantry and a lack of faith in the creative power of the urban proletariat. Instead of dictatorships and compromise with the domestic and foreign counterrevolution, the theses embodied the view that the resolution of Russia's economic problems was inseparable from the world revolution. Thus they called for an immediate offensive against German imperialism and the fullest possible participation of workers and peasants in revolutionary construction and struggle through the expansion and strengthening of democratic soviets.[30]

The second development that reinforced Left SR concerns about the direction of Bolshevik policy soon after the creation of the Northern Commune was Lenin's use of armed force to solve the ever more urgent problem of urban hunger. On 23 March, the Sovnarkom had issued a decree proposed by Lenin endowing the people's commissar for transportation, and a hierarchy of regional dictators subordinate to him, with unlimited powers to restore and direct the operation of railways throughout the country. The decree also mandated the formation of extraordinary armed security detachments to maintain strict order on railways.[31] Judging by the situation of the Petrograd railway hub, these orders, apart from creating another layer of inexperienced, often corrupt security forces, had little, if any, practical impact. In any case, the food supply crisis in Petrograd worsened in the late spring and early summer. In March, workers in Petrograd already were allocated a daily ration amounting to only 1,082 calories (the norm was 3,600 calories). The figures for April, May, and June were 1,013, 899, and 714 calories per day, respectively. Yet even these allocations do not reflect the actual state of affairs, because available food supplies often were insufficient to meet even these minimal allocations. In memoirs written years later a Vyborg district Bolshevik, Vasilii Kaiurov, recalled that in May, workers ate significant numbers of the city's horses, and that beginning then, for weeks at a time, the most workers could get for their ration cards were sunflower seeds and nuts.[32]

At a meeting of the Petrograd Soviet on 9 May, both Bolsheviks and Left SRs still looked to peaceful measures to deal with the food emergency,[33] which was also on the agenda of a Bolshevik Delegates Soviet meeting on 17 May.[34] Only a small percentage of district committee delegates showed up for this meeting. But because the situation was already so threatening, and because of the presence of A. I. Puchkov, a Bolshevik representative on the Central Food Supply Board, the delegates agreed to declare the meeting "unofficial" and just to listen to what Puchkov had to say. Explaining the causes of the food supply crisis, he pointed to the unwillingness of peasants to part with grain for worthless paper money as well as transportation problems and obstructionism by anti-Soviet elements at all levels of food procurement, shipment, and distribution. He rejected, as a "delusion," the notion that the crisis could be solved by eliminating restrictions on free trade or forcibly squeezing grain from kulaks (richer peasants who used hired labor). Puchkov especially emphasized the critical importance of producing the manufactured goods required by peasants, creating a reliable barter system between town and country, improving transportation facilities and administration, and establishing a uniform class-based, food-rationing system throughout the country.

Some of Puchkov's listeners were completely demoralized by his remarks, if only because existing fuel shortages and widespread hunger appeared to preclude production of manufactured goods required for barter. Other delegates were less pessimistic about the possibility of easing the crisis through Puchkov's nonviolent measures as well as by finding the resources required to improve shipping; evacuating the unemployed to areas where food shortages were less acute than in Petrograd; increasing the exploitation of fishing resources in the North; encouraging the planting of vegetable gardens in the city and its environs; and appointing significant numbers of workers to watch over saboteurs in food supply agencies until reliable replacements could be trained.

Virtually everyone was opposed to "provoking panic" and playing into the hands of the counterrevolution by making the extent of the crisis generally known. Implicit in Puchkov's report, as well as in the subsequent discussion, was that the survival of Soviet power in Petrograd depended on somehow improving or, at any rate, avoiding further deterioration in the food situation. Nonetheless, no one questioned Puchkov's exclusive emphasis on nonviolent methods of dealing with the crisis.[35]

Puchkov's approach, however, conflicted with the plan of using coercion that was laid out by Lenin and the Sovnarkom. On 9 May, operating on the premise that despite starvation in the consumer provinces, "kulaks and the rich people" in grain-producing provinces were holding back significant grain surpluses in order to force the government to pay dearly for them, the Sovnarkom agreed to "respond to coercion against the starving poor by those possessing grain with coercion against the bourgeoisie." In this spirit, it adopted a decree ordering that all grain surpluses in the hands of those with grain beyond the minimum amount needed to sow their fields and feed their families until the next harvest had to be turned in at designated collecting points within a week.

All peasants with grain surpluses after this period would be declared "enemies of the people." Those arrested would be turned over to revolutionary tribunals, sentenced to no fewer than ten years of hard labor in prison, deprived of all property, and permanently banished from their communes. The people's commissar for food supply, Aleksandr Tsiurupa, and his deputies were empowered to use armed force to seize grain surpluses. They could dissolve any local food supply bodies that defied their orders, and they could fire and submit for trial all individuals from government or private agencies who interfered with them.[36] During discussions of this decree in the CEC on the same day (9 May), Karelin spoke for the Left SRs and raised strong objections.[37] However, they were ignored. On 13 May, the decree was confirmed by the Presidium of the CEC.[38]

* * *

Lenin's policy of squeezing the peasantry to feed starving workers, and the resulting creation of a virtual state of war between town and country, was implemented on a large scale in the late spring and summer. At that time, armed worker and Red Army units, the so-called food procurement detachments (*prodotriady*), were dispatched to farming regions to seize "surpluses" from peasants at gunpoint. Subsequently, Committees of the Village Poor (*kombedy*), from which kulaks and rural residents who owned commercial or industrial enterprises were excluded, were formed in agricultural regions.[39] The primary purpose of the *kombedy* was to help food supply detachments locate grain surpluses and generally assist in implementing the food supply dictatorship.

The decree on the formation of *kombedy* was adopted by the Sovnarkom on 8 June and came before the CEC for confirmation on 11 June. There Karelin bitterly criticized it for undermining "the entire structure of Soviet power in the countryside." As he saw it, elective peasant soviets, which were already developing food supply sections, were to be subordinated to entirely new, "isolated" institutions. Also, a whole new category of small landholders, guilty only of trying to save minimal amounts of grain needed to obtain the industrial goods they required for survival, were to be defined as class enemies and their meager grain surpluses confiscated. Peasants were to supply grain at fixed prices, but the prices of manufactured goods they required were not fixed. To Karelin, these were all signs of Bolshevik bias toward workers and an affinity for bureaucratic centralization.

Lenin, from the start, sought to maximize the recruitment of Petrograd Bolsheviks and ordinary workers for dispatch to the countryside without regard to the effect this would have on the stability of Soviet power in the city. Thus, on 10 May, the day after the Sovnarkom adopted the decree authorizing the forceful seizure of surplus grain from peasants, he asked a Putilov plant representative to convey an appeal to Petrograd workers to participate in food procurement detachments on a mass scale. Reinforced with a written authorization from Aleksandr Tsiurupa to use all necessary force to obtain bread, the appeal called for recruitment in Petrograd alone of twenty thousand "select" workers for "a merciless armed assault on the rural bourgeoisie."[40] On 21 May, Lenin also telegraphed to Zinoviev and the Bolshevik Petersburg Committee the text of an open letter to Petrograd workers regarding the mobilization of food procurement detachments. Published the next day, the letter called for the immediate mobilization of tens of thousands of advanced Petrograd workers to obtain grain from the peasantry by force of arms in order to escape "the outstretched bony hand of hunger."[41]

Just a day later (22 May), Lenin penned a second "Letter to Workers in Piter," following another stormy session of the CEC where Bolshevik attitudes toward the peasantry and the indiscriminate grain procurement policies were attacked by the Left SRs Karelin and Trutovskii, also a leading Left SR. Baiting workers to join in a holy procession to the countryside, Lenin's second letter was more brash and, if anything, more alarmist and reckless than the preceding one. Perhaps the most significant difference between the two was this letter's ferocious attack on the Left SRs, for it charged that they were now the party of the weak-willed, apt to defend kulaks, undermine absolutely essential forced grain procurement policies, and, overall, subvert Soviet power to the same degree as the domestic and international counter-revolution.[42]

Lenin's second letter appeared on the front page of *Krasnaia gazeta* on 26 May. Petrograd Left SRs, who were then working closely with Bolsheviks in the coalition government established after the First Northern Oblast Congress of Soviets, were again incensed. The timing of Lenin's assault was especially awkward in the former capital, because it coincided with a further decline in the local food supply; the rising tide of labor unrest that led to increased support for the EAD; the antisemitic outbursts among workers and other disturbing signs of activity by rightist elements; and the fresh German occupation scare accompanying the threat to Fort Ino—all of which underscored the critical need for unity among government forces if Soviet power in the Northwest was to survive.

A blistering front-page editorial in the Petrograd Left SRs' *Znamia bor'by* on 28 May began and ended with fierce criticism of Lenin's indiscriminate assault on the Left SRs. Two days earlier (26 May), leading Petrograd Left SRs and representatives of district party committees had gathered for their Eighth City Conference, where Lenin's second letter, which had appeared in the morning papers, triggered an understandable explosion. "Lenin has finally exceeded all bounds," one participant apparently roared. "He doesn't shy away from anything, even [the grossest] distortion of fact," bemoaned another. "It is essential to restrain the dictator gone berserk," shouted a third.

The conference adopted a resolution declaring that Lenin's demagoguery had "exceeded all bounds" and calling on the Left SR Central Committee to request the Bolshevik party to immediately express its opinion on Lenin's position.[43]

I have found no record of any response to this request. Under Zinoviev, the Presidium of the Petrograd Soviet wasted no time in responding to Lenin's appeals. On 23 May, even before the publication of Lenin's second letter, it called on district soviets to form grain procurement detachments "no later than 27 May." Lists of the composition of these units were to be delivered to the Food Supply Commission of the Petrograd Soviet by 28 May. As a start, each district soviet was assigned a quota of recruits ranging from 20 to 50, for a total of 515 recruits. The Presidium obligated itself to instruct and arm the detachments.[44] On 29 May an emergency plenary meeting of the Petrograd Soviet endorsed this plan, and on 2 June the Presidium of the Petrograd Soviet announced that the first detachments, numbering four hundred workers, had departed Petrograd.[45]

On 31 May, the Petrograd Bureau of the Bolshevik Central Committee convened a rare meeting of party leaders from the SK SO, SOK, the Petersburg Committee, district party committees, trade unions, and the like. A primary purpose of this meeting appears to have been to consider directives from the Central Committee to "restore" strict intraparty discipline and, once again, to enhance party work over soviet work.[46] The most immediate task at the meeting was to discuss how to respond to Lenin's insistence on significantly more of the Petrograd party organization's "finest" for service with worker grain procurement detachments (which destroyed any possibility of enhancing party work). In an effort to resolve these conflicting goals, the meeting confirmed the appointment of a commission of three (Zinoviev, Stasova, and Sarah Ravich) with "dictatorial powers" to direct the appointment and distribution of cadres, and resolved to assign 25 percent of the party's membership locally to grain procurement detachments.[47]

The Bolshevik Petersburg Committee's Assembly of Organizers discussed the proposed dispatch from Petrograd of 25 percent of its most effective members on 5 June. The organizers focused on the negative impact that this huge outflow of experienced personnel would have on their efforts to rebuild factory collectives. Although clearly receptive to the formation of food procurement detachments, they also concluded that letting go of 25 percent of party members was unrealistic but that district party committees ought to do everything possible to maximize the number of comrades who could be spared for food procurement brigades.[48]

The recruitment of the brigades was on the agenda of the Bolshevik Petersburg Committee on 19 July, after Lenin gave a third open letter addressing Petrograd workers to Kaiurov, the Vyborg district Bolshevik, for dissemination in Petrograd.[49] In this letter, Lenin called for the dispatch of an additional ten thousand workers to the countryside. By then some twenty-five hundred comrades had been sent to the provinces, at the same time that conscription and party mobilizations for the Red Army were also drawing large numbers of available personnel from Petrograd.[50] The committee members ignored the scope of Lenin's demand, which, if fulfilled, would have veritably wiped out the party organization and its most reliable supporters. However, they treated his directive seriously because, as they put it, "the fate of the revolution depends on it," and busied themselves with procedures to improve the quality of participants in food procurement brigades but leaving enough competent personnel behind in Petrograd so that essential party organizational work could continue.

Simultaneously, Kaiurov presented Lenin's message to a meeting of the Executive Committee of the Vyborg district soviet, which responded by assigning some of its key leaders to duty with food procurement detachments. However, a row was caused in the Executive Committee of the Petrograd Soviet by the selection procedures initiated by the Petersburg Committee and by Lenin's dispatch of his letter with Kaiurov, thus by-passing both the Central Committee in Moscow and Petrograd party authorities. This prompted the Petrograd Bureau of the Central Committee to convene a joint meeting with the Petersburg Committee on 22 July. Adopted there was a resolution making confirmation of participants in food procurement detachments the joint responsibility of the Petersburg Committee and the Presidium of the Petrograd Soviet, and censuring both Lenin and Zinoviev—Lenin for violating organizational procedures by giving his letter directly to Kaiurov, and Zinoviev for publicly attacking the Petersburg Committee in the Executive Committee of the Petrograd Soviet.[51]

The Left SR Central Committee, meanwhile, prohibited party members from joining "punishment units," their term for the food procurement detachments,[52] and the ban was observed in Petrograd. True to their practice of avoiding damaging conflicts with the Bolsheviks, however, Petrograd Left SRs did not make an issue of Bolshevik food procurement policy. Thus, at a session of the Petrograd Soviet that endorsed the policy, their spokesman limited himself to recommending that agitators also be sent to the countryside to justify what was being done, and then spent the balance of his time bashing the Mensheviks and SRs.[53]

By a decree of 10 June, the SK SO dissolved the existing food supply bureaucracy and established a centralized food supply dictatorship for the city of Petrograd. Management of the procurement and distribution of food supplies was to be the responsibility of the People's Commissariat for Food Supply in Moscow *and* the Petrograd Soviet. Moreover, district soviets were encouraged to nominate food supply authorities for their districts.[54] Both of these departures from Moscow's directives appear to have been a response to the concerns of local Bolsheviks and Left SRs. Indeed, one of the most striking aspects of this whole episode is the extent to which it demonstrates that Petrograd Left SRs and Bolsheviks avoided harsh polemics, despite their fundamental differences on political, social, and economic issues, in order to address problems critical to the survival of Soviet power in the Northwest.

* * *

Partly as a result of the moderating influence of the Left SRs, especially Proshian, the commissar for internal affairs, Bolshevik authorities in Petrograd resisted pressures in June to institute "Red Terror" as a means of suppressing counterrevolutionary activity.[55] More than this, by mid June Proshian, who had been openly hostile to the Cheka as an institution from the start, had developed a comprehensive draft plan for policing Petrograd with a trained security "guard" of the Committee for the Revolutionary Security of Petrograd at the city and district levels, and ordinary citizens who would carry out periodic mandatory police duties in their neighborhoods. The latter would be organized into unarmed patrols that were to maintain twenty-four-hour watches throughout the city. The primary task of these patrols would be to report all signs of criminal activity, including suspicious political activity, to the professional police for appropriate action. However unrealistic, this draft plan would seem to have obviated the need for such ad hoc agencies as the PCheka.[56]

There is good reason to believe that at this time Uritskii's views on the PCheka coincided with Proshian's. For one thing, the PCheka had become infested by speculators—middlemen who enriched themselves by the illegal sale of essential goods such as food and fuel at inflated prices. On 20 April, Elena Stasova, in a letter to Novgorodsteva in Moscow, responded to a complaint from the Central Committee regarding negative attitudes toward the Cheka in Petrograd with the comment that "if we believed that the two commissions [Dzerzhinskii's and Uritskii's] had no positive value at all, we would launch an immediate campaign against them and get them liquidated . . . criticism of what exists is always necessary." "I don't know about Dzerzhinskii," she continued, "but Uritskii says quite definitely that, with respect to combating speculation, they [PCheka leaders] are constantly confronted by the fact that tracks lead back precisely to them at Gorokhovaia, which is thus the center for speculation."[57]

Uritskii probably would not have opposed dissolution of the PCheka for two other reasons: he found that directing it was distasteful, and, more important, he had a badly strained relationship with Dzerzhinskii, his superior. The problem between the two was initially complicated by the impossible situation left by the VCheka following its flight to Moscow. Dzerzhinskii had ignored repeated requests from Uritskii for the return of case files pertaining to Cheka prisoners in Petrograd. More basic still, Uritskii saw the VCheka shootings as counterproductive and its methods of interrogation as egregious.[58]

Dzerzhinskii, on the other hand, was outraged by Uritskii's arrest in early June of Aleksei Filippov, one of the VCheka's first foreign intelligence agents and Dzerzhinskii's associate, on suspicion of involvement with a counterrevolutionary organization, the "Comorra for Vengeance of the Russian People."[59] Dzerzhinskii also knew of the PCheka's shift toward moderation after the VCheka's flight from Petrograd, and he considered Uritskii both insubordinate and too soft for his position. In mid April, for example, Dzherzhinskii was appalled to learn that the PCheka had released some prisoners he had ordered to be permanently exiled from Russia on suspicion of espionage.[60] His concerns about Uritskii were reflected in the decisions of a meeting on 12 June of the Bolshevik fraction in the First All-Russian Conference of Chekas, which met in Moscow from 11 to 14 June to discuss particularly sensitive policy and organizational issues.[61] The fraction adopted a resolution calling for the use of secret agents; the incarceration of prominent and active monarchist-Kadet, Right SR, and Menshevik leaders; the shadowing of generals and officers and surveillance of the Red army—its commanders, clubs, circles, schools, and so on; and the summary shooting of prominent and clearly guilty counterrevolutionaries, speculators, thieves, and [officials] guilty of accepting bribes. In this same hard-line spirit, the fraction voted to propose to the party Central Committee that it recall Uritskii from his post as head of the PCheka and replace him with a "stronger and more decisive comrade, capable of firmly, unswervingly, [and] mercilessly rooting out and combating hostile elements that were ruinous to Soviet power and the revolution."[62] The chair of this meeting was Ivan Polukarov, a central figure in the VCheka by virtue of his position as head of the section for fighting counterrevolution. It is most unlikely that Polukarov would have shepherded *any* major recommendations through the conference's Bolshevik fraction, let alone a call for Uritskii's ouster, without Dzerzhinskii's prior approval.

The problem was not just Proshian and Uritskii, however. There are indications that their attitudes on the future of the PCheka were shared by a majority in the Petrograd Bureau of the Bolshevik Central Committee as well as by some Petrograd district soviets, and also Krestinskii, commissar for justice in the SK SO. As early as 13 April, the Petrograd Bureau of the Bolshevik Central Committee had considered a resolution proposed by Adolf Ioffe to recommend that the Central Committee in Moscow abolish the VCheka and PCheka, because "they were more dangerous than useful." Ultimately, only Ioffe voted for his resolution. Most revealing, however, is that the Bureau went on to adopt a motion "to *temporarily* refrain from making a case against the continued existence of Dzerzhinskii's and Uritskii's commissions, because [at that time] it would only be a pointless gesture."[63]

Opposition to the PCheka by some district soviets emerged during a discussion of a plan for the security of Petrograd at a meeting of the Interdistrict Conference on 22 May.[64] During this period, Petrograd district soviets generally were concerned most of all with maintaining their own authority over their territory. Therefore, they were hostile to the hierarchical PCheka and developed draft schemes for restructuring the Committee for the Revolutionary Security of Petrograd that would have given this committee and its district agencies primary responsibility for combating counterrevolution, speculation, and crime locally.[65]

Press reports on a meeting of high officials in the Commissariat for Justice on 20 June provide a strong clue to Krestinskii's thinking about the PCheka. According to these reports, which were not denied, the meeting was convened to consider the work of "Uritskii's Commission" and the reform of the Justice Commissariat's criminal investigation agency. However, the meeting was devoted mainly to discussing problems connected with the PCheka. At its close, the assembled officials adopted a resolution to "*liquidate* the PCheka."[66]

These press reports reached Dzerzhinskii two days later, and one can well imagine his upset about them. His grand vision of the supreme importance of the Cheka vis-à-vis other security organs was reflected in a decision by the mid-June national conference of chekas to assume the full burden of the merciless struggle against counterrevolution, speculation, and corruption in government throughout Russia. It was also reflected in the conference's unilateral dissolution of all other security organs, and its declaration that chekas were the supreme organs of administrative power throughout

Soviet Russia. Yet, in spite of this assertion that the VCheka was the exclusive guardian of Russia's domestic security, and that it should have the strictly hierarchical, independent chain of authority also approved at the conference, the Cheka in Russia's second city appeared poised to disband unilaterally.[67] After discussing this situation with his colleagues, Dzerzhinskii sent a telegram to Zinoviev making his opposition to the dissolution of the PCheka crystal clear. As he put it:

> There is information in the papers that the Commissariat for Justice is trying to dissolve Uritskii's Emergency Commission. The Cheka considers that, in the present especially aggravated moment, dissolving an agency of this kind is impermissible; to the contrary, after listening to local reports on the political situation of the country, the All-Russian Conference of Chekas reached the firm conclusion that it is necessary to strengthen these organs through the centralization and coordination of their work. The Cheka requests that you inform Comrade Uritskii of the above.[68]

As indicated below, at the beginning of July, in the wake of Volodarskii's assassination and signs of expanding popular unrest, Soviet authorities in Petrograd sent Dzerzhinskii a denial of press accounts relating to the PCheka's dissolution.[69]

* * *

Left SR influence in the SK SO far exceeded their numbers (four of thirteen commissars). An example of their importance is the independent-minded and impulsive Prosh Proshian. As a people's commissar in the national Sovnarkom between December 1917 and mid March 1918, Proshian had fought Lenin and his party colleagues more fiercely than anyone when Bolshevik policies and practices clashed with Left SR principles. Following ratification of the Brest treaty, he consistently supported and defended the withdrawal of Left SRs from the Sovnarkom as an absolutely essential aspect of international revolutionary strategy. Upon assuming his post as commissar for internal affairs in the government of the Northern Commune, second in importance only to Zinoviev, Proshian found that his commissariat was not yet functional.[70] Yet, during his brief tenure, he devoted enormous energy to developing the commissariat as a region-wide, genuinely collaborative administrative institution. A major step in this direction was his organization, in early June, of a congress of representatives from internal affairs sections of provincial soviets in the Northern Oblast.[71] That congress endorsed an organizational structure for the Commissariat for Internal Affairs and for internal affairs sections in the provinces down to the *volost* level.[72]

On 15 June, the Central Executive Committee of the Northern Oblast accepted his organizational plan,[73] and the new organizational structure was put into place during Proshian's incumbency and retained after his departure. As he did during his tenure as people's commissar for post and telegraph in the Sovnarkom, in his internal affairs post he replaced hostile staff with personnel loyal to Soviet power, many of them Left SRs. That some key decrees of the time were issued over his and Zinoviev's signatures showed his importance in the Northern Commune. His appointment, in early June, to an emergency, all-powerful, high-level intra-government troika also indicated his stature. The troika was formed to combat counterrevolutionary pogromist activity conducted among workers by right-wing groups, which was just then becoming a serious problem, as well as the threat posed to the retention of Soviet power by such emerging opposition forces as the EAD.[74]

As commissar for agriculture, the Left SR Nikolai Kornilov was similarly resourceful, energetic, and ambitious. Although he was also forced to build his department from scratch, his work may have been facilitated by a special commission established under the auspices of the SK SO, several weeks before his appointment, to develop a plan for organizing a Commissariat for Agriculture, SK SO.[75] On 23 May, soon after assuming his post, he dispatched a carefully framed programmatic memorandum to soviet agricultural sections throughout the Northern Oblast. Apart from announcing the formation of his commissariat and trying to establish a mutually fruitful relationship with the sections, his aim in this initial communication was to set forth his primary purpose, namely, to work closely with them in preparing to implement the Left SR fundamental land reform program. In this connection, he targeted such related tasks as reorganizing plant, animal, and forest husbandry; improving land; rural resettlement and education; and gathering information and records pertinent to addressing these tasks. He also announced that he would immediately form, and be the director of, a "temporary land council"; it would be composed of Kornilov's collegium and particularly competent elected representatives of provincial soviet land sections under his jurisdiction, to help develop reform plans responsive to local realities.[76] Comprehensive regulations governing the organization and operation of the Commissariat for Agriculture and its local agencies were prepared during his tenure,[77] and he developed planning and budgetary procedures for immediate implementation. Clearly envisioning an extended stay in his position, he ordered the preparation of detailed budgets for the entire 1918–19 fiscal year.[78] Moreover, his internal instructions reveal that he managed his commissariat meticulously and with an iron hand.[79]

Bolsheviks and Left SRs also worked arm in arm in such institutions as the Petrograd Soviet and district soviets. By this time Bolsheviks, supported by Left SRs, had majorities in all but one Petrograd district soviet. The exception was the Rozhdestvenskii district soviet, where Left SRs had a majority. This mutual support endured well into the summer. Thus, at a session of a nonparty workers conference in the Porokhovskii district, on 3 July, a Left SR fended off criticism of the Bolsheviks by Mensheviks and SRs.[80] Although in his opinion the Bolsheviks had been wrong in accepting the Brest peace, he immediately added that "only those who don't do anything, don't make mistakes." Typifying *public* Petrograd Left SR attitudes toward relations with the Bolsheviks in Petrograd, he went on to say that "we might have temporary differences with the Bolsheviks; however, we are marching forward bound together."[81]

At the beginning of May, the Petrograd Soviet's daily, *Izvestiia,* was renamed *Severnaia kommuna* (Northern Commune); its editorial board included two Bolsheviks and one Left SR. The relatively tranquil working relationship between Bolsheviks and Left SRs in Petrograd during the emergencies of the spring and early summer of 1918 contrasts strikingly with the situation prevailing in Moscow. To be sure, in Moscow the Left SRs remained active in the collegiums of individual commissariats, in the city and district soviets, and in the VCheka. However, while Bolshevik domestic and foreign policy was subject to daily, hard-hitting criticism in the Moscow Left SRs' *Znamia truda,* with the exception of attacks on the Brest treaty and forced food procurement, criticism of Bolshevik policies in *Znamia bor'by* was relatively muted, cautious, and benign. Significantly less attention was devoted to berating Bolsheviks than to attacking common domestic and foreign enemies, especially the EAD.

When prominent national Left SR leaders traveled from Moscow to Petrograd, they devoted less attention to finding fault with the Bolsheviks than to defending Soviet power and, at times, even the Bolsheviks. Maria Spiridonova spent several days in Petrograd at the beginning of June, primarily to participate in the First Northern Oblast Left SR Party Congress. A few weeks later, along with Boris Kamkov, she campaigned for the Left SR-Bolshevik bloc in elections to the Petrograd Soviet.[82] It is apparent from her comments at sessions of the Peasant Section of the CEC and at meetings of the Left SR Central Committee prior to these trips, that she had become profoundly disillusioned with the Brest treaty and was a fierce critic of Bolshevik grain procurement policies, primarily because of their devastating effect on peasants. Yet, while in Petrograd, during endless rounds of speech making, she kept her growing rage over Bolshevik policies and practices largely to herself. Instead, she appealed to her listeners, usually workers, to ignore demands by Mensheviks and SRs to reconvene the Constituent Assembly; to rouse themselves from their political lethargy; and to focus on the critical task of restoring industrial production and continuing the struggle against the bourgeoisie. The Mensheviks and SRs were cruelly exploiting hunger to mobilize the masses against Soviet power and the Bolshevik party, "which was shouldering the impossibly difficult burdens of government and fighting to the last to defend the triumph of the people."[83] A Constituent Assembly would give the people nothing but renewed enslavement. Soviet power, on the other hand, represented the first experience in history of workers and peasants governing themselves in their own interests, and its survival demanded great discipline and a long period of suffering and sacrifice. But, in the end, the outcome would be altogether glorious.[84]

A red thread running through Spiridonova's speeches of this period was that all of Europe was on the verge of a monumental revolutionary explosion and that tolerance of German imperialism had reached the breaking point. However, with German forces threatening Petrograd, it is doubtful that many of her listeners caught the distinction between her message and the appeals of Bolshevik authorities in the former capital to strengthen the city's defenses. In some of her speeches, she strongly opposed collaboration with capitalists in any form.[85] Yet despite Lenin's fresh assaults on the Left SRs, she did not link this criticism to him.

The Left SR national leadership in Moscow was generally much more supportive of the SK SO than their Bolshevik counterparts. Following its establishment, the central Sovnarkom remained as cool as ever to appeals for financial aid from Petrograd. Beyond this, the people's commissar for internal affairs, Grigorii Petrovskii, stubbornly refused even to recognize the Northern Commune's existence. Thus, on 22 May, Martin Latsis, Petrovskii's deputy, wrote provocatively that, since "all the central government knew about the establishment of the Northern Oblast [government] was what it read in newspapers and chance documents, the central government could not take account of the Northern Commune, nor could it take any steps to regularize relations with it."[86] Before Zinoviev even had an opportunity to respond to this missive, Petrovskii circulated similar messages to the six provinces in the Northern Oblast.[87] This kind of sniping went on for months.

Zinoviev was not the only one who had problems with Petrovskii. Provincial soviets and heads of individual commissariats in Petrograd did also. Proshian, as both commissar for internal affairs and a Left SR, had particularly great difficulties. Upon assuming his post, Proshian requested Petrovskii to route through him all correspondence with provincial soviets and other institutions in the Northern Oblast. In the telegram, Proshian also asked Petrovskii to send him whatever files he had relating to provincial soviets in the Northern Oblast.[88] A short time later, Proshian followed this telegram with a letter in which he raised critical budgetary issues and insisted that "not a single item of business or financial allocation to provincial soviets be directed straight to them, bypassing him." He also requested copies of all information dealing with the Northern Oblast, and of all Petrovskii's decrees and directives concerning the granting of pensions and the establishment of internal security forces.[89] I have not been able to find responses to either of these messages.

Petrovskii used various pretexts to justify his position on the Northern Commune. When one was eliminated, he would find another. At first his justification was that the CEC had to approve regional governments before he could recognize them.[90] After the Northern Commune received the required approval, he insisted that his hands were tied until he received certification from each of its constituent provincial soviets of a desire to join the Northern Commune.[91] Clearly, this conflict reflected the central government's aversion, particularly Lenin's, to semi-autonomous regional associations, as well as Lenin's increasing predilection for extreme centralization. By contrast, the Left SR Central Committee's advocacy of decentralized government helps account for its strong support of the Northern Commune.

* * *

The SK SO, the Bolshevik-Left SR coalition government established by the First Northern Oblast Congress of Soviets, functioned effectively and relatively harmoniously despite the Left SRs' enduring antipathy to the Treaty of Brest-Litovsk and several subsequent, potentially crippling developments: the Left SRs' profound aversion to "state capitalism" as articulated by Lenin in "Immediate Tasks of Soviet Power"; Lenin's brutal approach to grain procurement and the upset of Left SRs over Lenin's notoriously ill-timed public assaults on them, and the refusal of Petrovskii even to recognize the existence of the Northern Commune.

The success of the coalition is partly explained by Bolshevik cadre shortages, which were made infinitely worse by Lenin's ever larger and shriller demands for personnel to serve in the armed forces and in grain procurement detachments sent to the provinces. The Petrograd Bolsheviks needed the Left SRs. However, the main reason for the coalition's durability was the common ground the Petrograd Bolsheviks and the Left SRs shared on such matters as the distaste of Proshian, Uritskii, and Krestinskii for the Cheka; the contributions that such Left SRs as Proshian and Kornilov made to the improvement of government at the highest level; and their shared commitment to the survival of Soviet power in the northwest.

For Soviet power in the region, the period between mid March and July 1918 was a time of continuing crises. That it survived without resort to terror was due in no small part to effective collaboration between Petrograd Bolsheviks and Left SRs, and their mutual restraint in dealing with each other. However, the collaboration was not to last. The breakdown of the Bolshevik–Left SR bond in Petrograd and in the Northern Commune would soon be triggered by events and directives from Moscow.

11

The Suicide of the Left SRs

DURING THE TIME that Petrograd Bolsheviks and Left SRs were suppressing their differences and working together to preserve Soviet power in Petrograd, divisions between the national Communist and Left SR leadership in Moscow widened precipitously. Their "honeymoon" had come to an abrupt halt during the second half of March, after ratification of the Brest treaty by the Fourth All-Russian Congress of Soviets and the withdrawal of Left SRs from the Sovnarkom. Between April and June, the relationship between national Left SR leaders and Lenin and his colleagues in the Sovnarkom deteriorated as a result of the latter's continuing concessions to the Germans and the on-going pursuit of authoritarian domestic policies. Most national Left SR leaders were opposed to the creation of the food supply dictatorship; the utilization of worker food procurement detachments and Committees of the Village Poor to forcefully seize grain from peasants; the reliance on paid spetsy in industrial management and technical leadership of the armed forces; and the reinstitution of judicial capital punishment symbolized by the execution of "Admiral" Shchastny. In their eyes, these measures were incompatible with revolutionary ethics, the international character of social revolution, definitions of class and class struggle, and the democratic-populist principles underlying Soviet power.

At the same time, Lenin and the national Bolshevik leadership saw that the fragile peace with Germany and their tenuous hold on power were being threatened by the Left SRs' strident attacks on their policies and aggressive efforts to undermine them, and also by the sharply increasing support for the Left SRs, especially among peasants in the provinces.[1] Lenin's response included harshly worded attacks on the Left SRs in the CEC and in his second "Open Letter to Workers in Piter."[2] Thus, as spring turned to summer, Left SR and Bolshevik national leaders were on a collision course that would have serious implications for Bolshevik–Left SR collaboration in Petrograd.

* * *

Protocols of meetings of the Left SR Central Committee in May and early June, although fragmentary, document this deterioration of the Bolshevik–Left SR relationship at the highest level from the Left SR point of view.[3] The conflict was also played out in the pages of *Znamia truda* and *Pravda* and, as we have seen, at plenary sessions of the CEC. The growing antagonism between Bolsheviks and Left SRs over policies toward the peasantry and grain procurement had an especially adverse impact on the CEC Peasant Section, a Left SR bastion headed by the legendary Spiridonova.

The Peasant Section, created as an autonomous department of the CEC in January 1918, had its own large Executive Committee and party fractions, and it published an independent, nationally circulated daily newspaper, *Golos trudovogo krest'ianstva*. It is fair to say that during the first months of 1918 the Peasant Section was Soviet Russia's primary coordinating institution for organizing and preparing peasants for land reform, mobilizing them in support of Soviet power, establishing soviets in outlying regions where they did not yet exist, and identifying, articulating, and defending peasant interests. As Spiridonova explained, an additional purpose of the Peasant Section was to "unite peasants and workers into one integrated whole . . . to unite city and country" under the Soviet banner.[4]

Between January and April 1918, the Peasant Section launched numerous initiatives to lay the groundwork for land reform and, more generally, to build support for Soviet power in rural Russia. It implemented intensive training programs for rural agitators on issues connected with implementation of the Left SR land reform program and developed courses of study for rural schoolteachers on agronomic and social problems (in both cases, it recruited and subsidized participants from the areas to which they were later assigned). It also prepared mountains of brochures and pamphlets on agrarian, social, and political issues for distribution among peasants.[5] The section carried on a lively correspondence with rural soviets, peasant cooperatives, and individual peasants, and, using carefully developed questionnaires, gathered systematic information on political, economic, and social aspects of peasant life.[6] In this and other ways, the Peasant Section developed a rich database on conditions in rural Russia. Thanks to the myth surrounding Spiridonova's name among peasants, the section became a national center to which peasants looked for advice and help.

In a report on the Peasant Section at the Second Left SR Party Congress, on 17 April 1918, Spiridonova stressed that Bolshevik benevolence toward the section had ended in mid March 1918, in the wake of the Left SRs' resignations from the Sovnarkom. According to Spiridonova, an ongoing struggle developed after that between the Bolshevik leadership of the CEC and the Left SR leadership of the Peasant Section over the latter's "separatism." Funds for budgeted expenses had not been received from the CEC, and so the Peasant Section was nearing the point at which it could no longer function.[7]

In fairness to the Bolsheviks, antagonism toward the Peasant Section for "separatism" undoubtedly seemed justified. After the CEC voted to accept Germany's new peace terms, the section became enmeshed in Left SR attempts to scuttle the peace. Spiridonova acknowledged as much at the Second Left SR Party Congress when she reported that significant numbers of the section's agitators were already then being sent to regions bordering the German front.[8] Clearly, their task was less to gather data and spread socialism than to organize resistance to German occupation forces. This is documented in a telegram of late June from a Bolshevik official protesting the disorganizing activity of Peasant Section agitators in the Pskov region.[9]

On 16 June, after the CEC endorsed the Sovnarkom's decree on Committees of the Village Poor, Karelin publicly announced that Left SRs would do everything they could to prevent its implementation. Printed materials which the Peasant Section dispatched to the countryside in January and February had included a balance of Left SR and Bolshevik texts. This was no longer true by the late spring, after Bolshevik and Left SR peasant policies diverged. In the ensuing battle between town and country, Left SR representatives of the Peasant Section naturally took the side of the peasantry against the Bolsheviks. There is also ample evidence that, in food-producing regions, Left SRs from local soviets deliberately impeded Bolshevik food procurement efforts, especially the attempt to form local Committees of the Village Poor that would facilitate forced seizures of grain.[10]

Because of the Peasant Section's close ties with the peasants and its ability to gather information from them, after armed food procurement detachments, such as those from Petrograd, began their forays into grain-producing regions in early June, the section was flooded with data and graphic personal accounts about the atrocities the detachments had wrought. Many of these accounts have been preserved in the archives of the Federal Security Service (FSB), the present-day successor to the VCheka, in files pertaining to Spiridonova's work in the Peasant Section.[11] In an open letter to the Bolshevik Central Committee, Spiridonova quoted extensively from letters graphically recording the brutalities of food procurement brigades, aided by Committees of the Village Poor, against starving peasants and the resulting state of war in the countryside. As one letter writer put it:

We didn't hide any grain. As was decreed, we left ourselves nine puds a person for a year. Then we were sent a decree to keep seven puds, and to turn over two. We did that. [But] Bolsheviks came with detachments. They made a total wreck of everything [*razzorili v konets*].

We rose up. [Now,] it's bad in Iukhnovskii County. We have been battered by artillery. Whole villages are on fire. Our homes have been burned to the ground. We gave up everything—we wanted things to be good. We knew cities were hungry, [so] we didn't spare ourselves.[12]

By mid June, protests against the violence of Bolshevik-led food procurement detachments from Petrograd began to reach the Bolshevik Petersburg Committee. At a meeting on 18 June, Egorova complained that the "detachments were being badly organized" and were "composed of undesirable elements that deserved to be arrested." Looking to the future, she insisted that it was essential to be very selective in recruitment. No one challenged the legitimacy of her concerns and recommendations; as a leader of the Vyborg district Bolsheviks, she obviously knew what she was talking about. Rather, it was agreed that a special memorandum embodying her concerns be prepared for the CEC in Moscow.[13] I have found no evidence of this memorandum's fate. But on 6 August the Sovnarkom, gripped by the initial panic triggered by the Allied interventions,[14] adopted a resolution confirming all past decrees on using violence against class enemies, including peasants who resisted grain seizures with firearms.[15]

Less than a year later, in a report on the work of the Central Committee delivered at the Eighth Communist Party Congress in March 1919, Lenin conceded that the Bolsheviks had made "terrible errors" in their approach to the peasantry. "Because of the inexperience of our workers, [and] the complexity of the problem," he said then, "blows meant for kulaks struck the middle peasantry."[16] But why was the problem so complex, one wonders? And who more than Lenin was responsible for the "terrible errors"?

* * *

The Bolsheviks' gradual strangulation of the Peasant Section prompted some Left SR members to call for convocation of a separate All-Russian Congress of Soviets of Peasants' Deputies. For the time being, however, Spiridonova and her colleagues in the Left SR Central Committee resisted those demands, preferring to step up pressure for an early All-Russian Congress of Soviets of Workers' *and* Peasants' Deputies.[17] Their hope was to unite peasants and force fundamental policy changes by subjecting the government's domestic and especially foreign policies to criticism by the broadest possible popular forum. Naturally, top Bolsheviks also opposed a separate national congress of soviets of peasants' deputies. A separate congress would have destroyed the de facto consolidation of national soviet institutions under Bolshevik control that had been achieved in January and would further empower the Left SRs. Although a Bolshevik majority in a legitimately elected *combined* national soviet congress was by no means assured, it was preferable to a separate peasant congress controlled by the Left SRs. Lenin was forced to yield. The CEC decided, on 10 June, to convene the Fifth All-Russian Congress of Workers', Peasants', Soldiers', and Cossacks' Deputies in Moscow on 28 June.[18]

The intraparty conflict between Leninists and Left Communists at the national level had festered into May and June, encouraging Left SR leaders that perhaps Left Communists would side with them at the national congress of soviets in the event of a clash over the Sovnarkom's foreign policy. The rift in the Bolshevik leadership was essentially over by the end of June, however, and Lenin emphasized this, on 1 July, in a long interview with a reporter from the Swedish newspaper *Folkets daglad politiken*. "The opposition within the Bolshevik party has calmed down," he observed early in the interview. "Bukharin, Radek, and the others are once again participating in party work."[19] This circumstance may also help explain the Bolsheviks' willingness to risk convocation of a national congress of soviets. No longer did Lenin have to fear a Left Communist–Left SR alliance at the congress or inevitable demands by the Left Communists to convene a party congress to settle disputed issues prior to the congress of soviets. Rather, the Left SRs would face an outwardly united Bolshevik party, determined to whittle down the Peasant Section's independent power and, more important for the Bolsheviks, to neutralize the Left SRs.

* * *

Following the decision to schedule the opening of the Fifth All-Russian Congress of Soviets for 28 June, both the Bolsheviks and Left SRs turned their attention to winning a majority in that assembly. With good reason, Lenin was by no means sanguine about the outcome. He recognized that electoral regulations that strongly privileged workers over peasants might not be enough to offset likely Left SR domination of the vote in rural areas.[20] At a CEC meeting on 14 June, upon the initiative of the Bolshevik leadership, the Mensheviks and SRs were expelled from that body, and soviets throughout the country were encouraged to follow suit. There seems little doubt that the timing of this sudden move, which was justified by the argument that the Mensheviks and SRs had become part of the counterrevolution, was driven by the goal of undermining these two contenders for congress delegates.[21]

Elections to the Fifth All-Russian Congress of Soviets, to my knowledge, have never been independently investigated, and it is probably impossible to do so now. The preliminary breakdown of delegates by party announced at the opening session was Bolsheviks, 678, and Left SRs, 269. The remaining 88 delegates were divided among [SR] Maximalists (roughly 30), Social-Democratic Internationalists (5–6), and unaffiliated delegates (about 48), for a total of 1,035 delegates with full voting rights.[22] Recalling this unexpected, huge preponderance of Bolshevik delegates, an unidentified Left SR delegate, most likely Aleksandra Izmailovich, a member of the Left SR Central Committee, later wrote that "the Left SRs failed to consider the Bolsheviks' capacity to work miracles." "The Bible tells us," this Left SR continued, "that God created the heavens and the Earth from nothing . . . In the twentieth century the Bolsheviks are capable of no lesser miracles: out of nothing, they create legitimate credentials."[23]

There is, in fact, substantial circumstantial evidence that the huge Bolshevik majority in the congress was fabricated, and that the number of legitimately elected Left SR delegates was roughly equal to that of the Bolsheviks. Sharp increases in support for the Left SRs in peasant soviets on the eve of the Fifth All-Russian Congress of Soviets had given Left SR leaders confidence that they would have a majority at the national congress. At the end of June, Left SR delegates at the Third Left SR Party Congress in Moscow had also been encouraged by reports on voting results in district and province soviet congresses at which delegates to the national congress were elected.[24] Preliminary tallies of arriving delegates published by *Znamia truda* during the week preceding the opening of the congress indicated that the Left SRs would have near parity with the Bolsheviks. On the eve of the congress, the independent Moscow dailies *Novosti dnia*, *Nashe slovo*, and *Zhizn'* conveyed the same impression.[25]

Unfortunately for the Left SRs, these tallies did not include roughly 399 Bolshevik delegates whose right to be seated was challenged by the Left SR minority in the congress's credentials commission.[26] Around 25 June, at the same time that Sverdlov had postponed the opening of the congress from 28 June to 3 July (further delayed until the fourth), urgent calls had gone out to the party's leaders in soviets around the country to immediately send additional Bolshevik delegates to Moscow. The legitimacy of these delegates was challenged by the Left SR minority in the credentials commission and by Left SRs in the institutions from which they came. At the start of the congress, Left SRs insisted on parity with the Bolsheviks on the credentials commission in order to expose these manipulations, but these demands were rejected in a straight party-line vote, strongly suggesting a cover-up.[27] Archival documents for Mogilev Province, much of which was occupied by the Germans, clearly illustrate this fraud.[28]

The Bolshoi Theater in Moscow during the Fifth All-Russian Congress of Soviets. State Museum of the Political History of Russia, St. Petersburg.

It is not surprising that the first sessions of the congress, which was held in the Bolshoi Theater, exploded into a no-holds-barred verbal free-for-all.[29] With Sverdlov, who was anything but evenhanded, as chair, the Left SRs were at an enormous disadvantage. On 4 July, the day the congress opened, Trotsky, in effect, requested authorization to shoot anybody, "on the spot," who was resisting arrest for opposing German occupation forces in Ukraine.[30] Spiridonova, responding for the Left SRs, reasonably interpreted this as a direct threat.[31] After Trotsky's request was adopted as a formal resolution, there could be no doubt that it was part of a preemptive strike against the Left SRs. The next day (5 July), Lenin repeatedly baited the Left SRs to withdraw from the congress. Thus, early on, in a report on the policies of the Sovnarkom, he referred to Spiridonova's failure to take account of the Bolsheviks' huge congress majority and declared without ceremony that "if these people [the Left SRs] prefer walking out of the congress, good riddance."[32] Lenin later declared that "if there are Left SRs like the previous orator [Spiridonova], who say . . . 'we can't work with Bolsheviks, we are leaving,' we will not regret that for a minute. Socialists who abandon us at such a [critical] time . . . are enemies of the people."[33]

Karelin and Kamkov who, in addition to Spiridonova, were the main speakers for the Left SRs at the congress, stood their ground. They fiercely attacked the Bolsheviks and German imperialism, to the angry glares of a

Leading Left SRs. Top row: Kamkov and Karelin. Bottom row: Shteinberg, Spiridonova, and Proshian. Drawings by Iu. K. Artsybushev.

high-level German delegation that occupied a front box. The main point, however, is that, at the end of this first day, the Left SR leaders' hope that they could use the combined congress to reshape Sovnarkom policies was shattered. As a result, they felt pressed to turn to a traditional SR weapon, individual terror, specifically the assassination of the German Ambassador to Moscow, Count Wilhelm Mirbach. The decision was taken hastily, out of fear that Left SR leaders were in immediate physical danger and in the belief that killing Mirbach would save them by provoking the resumption of war with Germany.

*   *   *

The use of terror against foreign "imperialist" leaders in order to undermine Brest was first discussed and approved at a closed session of the Second All-Russian Left SR Party Congress in April. Those identified as potential targets included General Eikhord, commander of German occupation forces in Ukraine; Count Mirbach; and Kaiser Wilhelm. In May, Grigorii Smolianskii, secretary of the CEC and a member of the Left SR Battle Organization, made a secret trip to Berlin to sound out German Social Democrats about assassinating the Kaiser. Their dismay at the idea caused it to be shelved.[34] On 24 June, when Sverdlov postponed the opening of the Fifth All-Russian Congress of Soviets from 28 June to 3 July, and it appeared possible that the congress might not be held at all, the Left SR Central Committee revisited the idea of assassinations. It thereupon adopted a resolution providing for the organization of a series of terrorist acts against top representatives of German imperialism.[35] Although this resolution did not name Count Mirbach or any specific targets for assassination, one may safely assume he was still a prime target, as he was the leading symbol of German imperialism in Soviet Russia and had been high on the Left SR hit list in April.

The text of the Left SR Central Committee's resolution of 24 June indicates that the committee envisioned that some time would be needed to mobilize military forces and prepare the masses and local party organizations for terrorist acts, and that their purpose was to undermine the policy of the Leninist Sovnarkom, not to fight the Bolsheviks unless this was required for self defense. These measures, therefore, would have been unnecessary had the Fifth All-Russian Congress of Soviets voted to revoke the Brest peace. The Left SR Central Committee's resolution of 24 June was, in short, a contingency option. In any case, the resolution was approved, in veiled form, by the Third All-Russian Left SR Party Congress.[36]

Serious preparations for the assassination of Count Mirbach began late on the night of 4/5 July, after the opening session of the Congress of Soviets. Initially, the murder was scheduled for the next day (5 July),[37] but when it became clear that more time was needed for preparations, the act was postponed until the following afternoon (6 July). The assassination was carried out by two Left SR Chekists, Iakov Blumkin and Nikolai Andreev, in a drawing room at the German Embassy. Meanwhile, virtually the entire Left SR Central Committee assembled in the military headquarters of the VCheka, where the formidable military forces there were commanded by a former Black Sea Fleet sailor, the Left SR Dmitri Popov.

In the early afternoon of 6 July, Lenin received news of a major uprising against Soviet power in Yaroslavl, a provincial city on the Volga roughly 150 miles northeast of Moscow, necessitating the deployment there of more of Moscow's dwindling troops.[38] Coming hard on the heels of major transfers of military personnel to the Murmansk and Czech fronts, this left Moscow's security largely in the hands of relatively small Latvian Rifle and VCheka forces, and a motley array of undisciplined Red Guard and Red Army units, most of them still being formed and trained.

A short time later, Vladimir Bonch-Bruevich phoned Lenin with the first word of an attempt on Mirbach's life. Initially, the extent of the ambassador's injuries was unclear, but word of his death soon came. In these first frenzied moments it did not occur to Lenin that the Left SRs might be responsible for the assassination.[39] Lenin first learned from Dzerzhinskii that Mirbach had been killed by Blumkin and Andreev when he paid a condolence call at the German Embassy in the late afternoon. Lenin also was told that Blumkin was under the protection of the VCheka's main military force and that the unit was led by Left SRs. Further disturbing news came from the people's commissar for foreign affairs, Georgii Chicherin, who informed Lenin that the German government would be pressing for German troops to be stationed in Moscow.

Dzerzhinskii, accompanied by two assistants, went directly from the German Embassy to his military headquarters, now the Left SR command center, to arrest Blumkin and Andreev. At this point, Dzerzhinskii seems to have assumed that the two had acted on their own.[40] He was quickly disabused of this idea. While searching VCheka military headquarters for the assassins, he happened upon many of the top Left SR leaders, including Donat Cherepanov, Georgii Sablin, Spiridonova, Kamkov, Proshian, Karelin, Trutovskii, Fishman, and his own senior deputy, Aleksandrovich. They informed him that Mirbach had been killed on orders of the Left SR Central Committee, which took full responsibility for the act. Dzerzhinskii immediately arrested Proshian and Karelin and threatened to shoot Popov if he did not turn over Blumkin and Andreev. Dzerzhinskii later testified that some sailors had then forcibly disarmed him. Spiridonova explained that Dzerzhinskii and his assistants were being detained, "because they were with Mirbach," and Cherepanov added that "the Bolsheviks would have to face up to the fact that the peace was in shambles, that the Left SRs did not seek power," and, indeed, that it would be fine with them "if the situation in Ukraine . . . [i.e., where a partisan war against German occupation forces was in full swing] was duplicated in Moscow."[41]

Back in the Kremlin, Lenin did not learn of the extent of Left SR involvement in Mirbach's killing until early evening. Bonch-Bruevich, who was with Lenin at the time, recalled that he was stunned and momentarily unnerved by the news, and that "he turned white as he typically did when he was enraged or shocked by a dangerous, unexpected turn of events."[42] However, still convinced that all-out war with Germany would be an unmitigated disaster for the revolutionary cause, Lenin quickly recovered and focused on showing the Germans that the Bolsheviks were quite capable of easily handling the Left SRs. The catch was that it was by no means clear that the organized military forces immediately available to him were a match for those at the disposal of the Left SRs. His main security agency, the VCheka, was riddled with Left SRs.

Nonetheless, the stakes were obviously extraordinarily high, and subsequent developments showed that Lenin was prepared to accept the risk. Branding Mirbach's assassination as part of an all-out effort by the Left SRs to overthrow Soviet power, Lenin entrusted its suppression to Trotsky, who, in turn, appointed Ivar Smilga to command the units involved in this task.[43] Colonel Ioakim Vatsetis (commander of the Latvian Rifles Division), Podvoiskii (then a member of the Supreme Military Council), and Nikolai Muralov (commissar of the Moscow Military District) were to coordinate an immediate assault on Popov's headquarters.[44] Lenin also ordered Uritskii and Petr Zaslavskii, secretary of the Bolshevik Petersburg Committee, to return to Petrograd at once to head off possible Left SR moves there. Unofficial telephone and telegraph services within the city of Moscow, and between Moscow and the rest of the country, were cut, and strict controls were imposed on motor traffic within Moscow as well as on rail services in and out of the capital.

At 8:00 PM the entire Left SR Fifth Congress fraction was detained in the foyer of the Bolshoi Theater. Members of the fraction and their guests, numbering more than four hundred, had assembled for the scheduled start of the late afternoon session of the congress, unaware that their own Central Committee was planning to assassinate Mirbach, let alone that he had actually been killed.[45]

The Soviet government's first official statement about Count Mirbach's assassination was soon telegraphed around the country. Condemning the "scoundrel Left SRs" for bringing Russia to the brink of war with Germany and launching an uprising against Soviet power, the government announced that all Left SR delegates to the Fifth Congress of Soviets were being detained as hostages, and that all necessary measures were being taken to liquidate "the rebellion of the new servants of White Guard schemes immediately." It called on "everyone" to take up arms in defense of the revolution.[46]

Unfortunately for Lenin, who hoped to quell the "rebellion" of the Left SRs without delay, a military assault on Popov's headquarters planned by Vatsetis for 2:00 AM encountered a major snag. The day of the planned assault was July 7, a Sunday and also a religious holiday, St. John the Baptist's Day, and not one unit of the Red Guards, Red Army, or Latvian Rifles ordered to participate in the attack (and among these only the Latvian Rifles were truly operational) showed up on schedule at jumping off points. Consequently, as Podvoiskii and Muralov sheepishly acknowledged in a report to Lenin a few days later, "The nighttime character of the operation was lost and it necessarily became a daylight raid."[47] The government's attack finally began at noon, when heavy artillery shells were lobbed, from a distance of "two hundred steps," at Popov's headquarters and two neighboring buildings, badly damaging them. An exchange of fire from rifles and machine guns followed, causing Popov's forces and the Left SR leadership to scatter, leaving Dzerzhinskii behind.

By the night of 6 July, the actions of the Left SRs, beginning with Count Mirbach's assassination, were already being defined by the Soviet government as "an uprising against Soviet power," and historians have often depicted the episode that way. But is this characterization valid? Having sifted through the available published and unpublished evidence, I conclude that it was not. Upon investigation, with the possible exception of Prosh Proshian's brief occupation of the Central Telegraph Office and his behavior there, which may well have been unauthorized,[48] all of the Moscow Left SRs' actions following Mirbach's assassination were consistent with the objective of reshaping the policies of the Leninist Sovnarkom but not with forcibly seizing power or even fighting the Bolsheviks except in self-defense.

* * *

Lenin and Grigorii Petrovskii acted decisively to eliminate the Left SRs as a political factor to be reckoned with, now that they were on the run. Blumkin and Andreev managed to evade capture. So did eleven of fourteen other Left SR leaders later indicted in connection with Mirbach's assassination. However, more than four hundred Left SRs, mostly rank-and-file members, were caught and an uncertain number were summarily shot (Aleksandrovich among them).[49]

Members of the Left SR Fifth Congress fraction were sandwiched into two upstairs rooms of the Bolshoi for a few days, after which thirteen "main culprits" were sent to cells in the Kremlin, one hundred were released, and the remainder were held in barracks at the Aleksandrovskii Military Academy and gradually freed. Significantly, among the main culprits were Left SR members of the credentials commission. They were not released until after the congress ended, at which point their challenges of Bolshevik delegates no longer mattered. Left SRs from the Peasant Section who were not congress delegates were also arrested and held in the Kremlin.[50] Spiridonova, who was arrested when she showed up at the Bolshoi to explain the Left SRs' action, was held in a Kremlin cell until the end of November.

The Left SRs' two central newspapers, *Znamia truda* and *Golos trudovogo krest'ianstva,* which had been shut down on 7 July, were not permitted to reopen. On 9 July, the Fifth Congress of Soviets resumed, minus the Left SRs. It passed a resolution condemning the events of 6–7 July as a brazen attempt by the Left SRs to seize power, endorsed the actions of the Soviet government in quashing the rebellion, and banned all Left SRs unwilling to disavow the actions of their Central Committee from membership in soviets.[51] Implementing this policy, Petrovskii, people's commissar for internal affairs, went a step further. He ordered local soviets to expel all Left SRs from responsible positions in government regardless of their attitudes toward the actions of their Central Committee.[52] Moreover, the Peasant Section was now essentially gutted.

Shortly before the Fifth Congress closed on 10 July, it adopted the first Soviet constitution. Iurii Steklov, a member of the commission that drafted the constitution, acknowledged when he presented the document to the congress that, although its distinguishing feature was to demonstrate the accession of workers and peasants to state power and articulate their goal of creating an egalitarian, democratic, socialist society free of economic exploitation and political domination, the struggle against the domestic and international bourgeoisie necessitated the formation of a strong, centralized dictatorship during the transition from capitalism to socialism.[53] Thus, the constitution perpetuated the fiction that the elective All-Russian Congress of Soviets was the highest organ of state authority, and that between its convocations, except in dire emergencies, the Sovnarkom was subordinate to the CEC which was the supreme legislative, administrative, and controlling organ of government; in practice, however, the opposite prevailed. Between the Fifth Congress in July 1918 and the Sixth Congress the following November, the CEC assembled only eight times (as a rule, the Sovnarkom met daily), and, with the Mensheviks, SRs, and Left SRs effectively excluded, its meetings were largely ceremonial.[54]

The right to vote was given to all male and female citizens over eighteen who gained their livelihood by their own production or socially useful labor, and to soldiers and the disabled. Persons employing hired labor, or receiving income from industrial or business enterprises—in sum the former middle and upper classes—were disenfranchised. A provision apparently limiting the voting rights of working women in a late draft of the constitution was omitted in the version presented and approved by the congress.[55] However, the privileged position of workers over peasants in Soviet elections, which had facilitated though not assured the building of a huge Bolshevik majority at the Fifth All-Russian Congress of Soviets, was also firmly cemented in the constitution. In future elections to congresses, city soviets were to be allotted 1 deputy for each 25,000 electors, and representatives of provincial congresses of soviets were to be allowed 1 deputy for each 125,000 electors.[56]

Two days after the Congress of Soviets dispersed (14 July), Lenin's worst fear was realized. Acting German Ambassador Kurt Riezler formally requested that a battalion of German troops armed with machine guns, mortars, and flame throwers be allowed into Moscow to protect his embassy. The request presented Lenin with a seemingly hopeless dilemma. An affirmative response was incompatible with Soviet Russia's sovereignty. For practical purposes, it would have made the Sovnarkom hostage to the whim of the German High Command. On the other hand, rejecting Riezler's request appeared to guarantee the resumption of the all-out war with Germany which Lenin still believed would be suicidal.

Lenin could breathe more easily, however, when the second Battle of the Marne began at midnight 14 July, tying up German forces in a major offensive in the West. Chicherin quickly rejected Riezler's demand, promising to do everything possible to provide security for the German Embassy.[57] Lenin echoed Chicherin's message in a formal statement at a hastily assembled first meeting of the new CEC.[58] The immediate crisis in Soviet-German relations ended with an understanding that one thousand Red Guards would be assigned to protect the German Embassy in Moscow, and that this force could be augmented by three hundred unarmed German soldiers in civilian dress.

* * *

Developments in Petrograd following Count Mirbach's assassination confirm that this ill-conceived act was precisely what the Left SRs claimed it to be and not part of a failed Left SR conspiracy to seize power. The day of 7 July 1918, St. John the Baptist's day in Petrograd, was sunny and hot. By noon, the streets in the former capital were filled with holiday strollers. The only mention of events in Moscow in the morning papers was a two-line official bulletin, phoned out of the capital just after Mirbach's death, before regular telephone and telegraph communications in the capital were cut: "The German ambassador Mirbach has been assassinated. Two bombs were thrown at him." Significantly, this was the only indication of an emergency in Moscow to appear in the Left SR *Znamia bor'by.* The day's banner headline, as had been the case for several days, was still aimed at building pressure for a change in foreign policy by the Fifth All-Russian Congress of Soviets: "Down with the Brest Noose, Which Is Stifling the Revolution!"

The night before, the few top Bolshevik officials in the Petrograd Soviet who were not at the Soviet congress received directives from Moscow to head off a Left SR rising locally. They immediately formed a Military-Revolutionary Committee with unlimited authority to deal with the perceived emergency. The committee quickly began preparations to disarm the main Left SR detachment at Left SR military headquarters in the centrally located Pages School. It also decided to shut down *Znamia bor'by* and to try to capture the Petrograd Left SR City Party Committee, both of which were located in the former Pertsov mansion on Ligovskaia Street, not far from the Pages School. Moreover, the committee directed that military-revolutionary troikas, also with extraordinary powers, be immediately established by Bolshevik officials in district soviets to keep a close watch on influential local-level Left SRs, and to coordinate preemptive strikes against district Left SR agencies. District soviet troikas were formed in most districts of Petrograd late on the night of 6 July and on 7 July.[59] They took charge of removing Left SRs from key positions, reinforcing security, and disarming Left SR detachments in their neighborhoods.

It is noteworthy that even now Bolshevik party organizations played secondary roles in these decisions and in their implementation. At the end of a report on economic administration in the Northern Commune at an evening meeting of the Bolshevik Delegates Soviet on 6 July, the Petersburg Committee's Sergei Gessen rushed in and read an announcement about Mirbach's assassination and the Military-Revolutionary Committee's directive to district soviets. That was all. Despite the fact that delegates from all major districts of Petrograd were present (twenty-seven delegates in all), Gessen's news does not appear to have been discussed, nor were the delegates called on to help organize suppression of the Left SRs.[60] Moreover, the Bolshevik Petersburg Committee was not called into special session. It held regular meetings on 5 and 10 July, and, seemingly, none in between.[61] In response to the apparent emergency, at least three Bolshevik district party committees (those in the Rozhdestvenskii, Okhtinskii, and Vasilii Island districts), acting on their own, formed or activated emergency troikas on 7 July.[62] Except for the Rozhdestvenskii district, where Left SRs had a majority in the local soviet, however, the work of party troikas appears to have been quickly superseded by the military-revolutionary troikas established by district soviets.

Abundant evidence demonstrates that Bolshevik authorities in Petrograd learned of the Left SR role in Mirbach's assassination well before Petrograd Left SRs were aware of it. In an interview with a reporter on 10 July, N. Krasikov, a Left SR in the Press Commissariat, reported that "news of the [Left SRs'] armed action in Moscow was greeted by the party's Petrograd Committee with amazement and disbelief. For us this was completely unexpected," he explained. Krasikov received the news upon being denied access to his office in Smolny on 7 July. At that time, he heard the Bolshevik view of the Left SRs' actions.[63]

Krasikov's experience underscores an important point. With *Znamia bor'by* shut down, and telephone and telegraph communications to Moscow cut, any assessment of the reaction of Petrograd Left SRs to news of Mirbach's assassination must consider that the information they received about it for several days came from Bolshevik sources, and this was even true of reports in the non-Bolshevik press. In ever more lurid and damning terms, these sources conveyed the news not only that the Left SR Central Committee was responsible for Mirbach's killing but that the Left SRs had embarked on a number of steps aimed at overthrowing Soviet power. This must have seemed completely incomprehensible to Left SRs, as the heart of the Left SR credo included the hegemony of democratic, revolutionary soviets.

Uritskii returned to Petrograd at around 3:00 PM on 7 July and assumed direction of the Military-Revolutionary Committee. The replacement of Left SR heads of commissariats and other party members in prominent government positions by Bolsheviks, which began earlier in the day, was now intensified. Uritskii retained chairmanship of the Petrograd Cheka and reclaimed the post of commissar for internal affairs from Proshian. Even before that, Left SR offices in the Aleksandr wing of Smolny were isolated by forces loyal to the Bolsheviks, trapping unsuspecting Left SR functionaries. At around 2:00 PM these offices were shut down. Simultaneously, the Left SR fraction in the Petrograd Soviet was arrested and taken to Gorokhovaia 2.[64] Soon after, the Left SR Petrograd Committee learned of government preparations to disarm the party's military detachments, and it immediately alerted its military headquarters and district committees and detachments, warning them of likely Bolshevik attacks and instructing them to go into hiding.[65] The committee members themselves then went underground.

Information reaching the Military-Revolutionary Committee later in the afternoon indicated that Left SRs at all levels reacted to this alert with shock and bewilderment. Authoritative local leaders reportedly asked one another: "Why are we being urged to make preparations to operate illegally?"[66] In the late afternoon a *Vechernye ogni* reporter looking for a story in the offices of the Left SR Petrograd Committee and *Znamia bor'by* found them empty except for a forlorn paperboy and a Left SR from the nearby Aleksandr-Nevskii district who was trying to find out what was going on. In response to a query from the reporter, the Left SR replied, "The only thing we Petrograd Left SRs know is that our Central Committee has been arrested. We are not aware of any offensive action by Left SRs. The message we received from our Petrograd Committee has left us all baffled. Why are we being disarmed? Why is the Petrograd Committee telling us to go underground? Apparently, something has happened."[67]

A Bolshevik Putilov worker later recalled that on the morning of 7 July everything was quiet in his district. "Left SRs and their families strolled in the sun. They were oblivious to what was occurring, even though the more important of them were already under close surveillance."[68] Representatives of Bolshevik district committees canvassed at a Bolshevik Petersburg Committee meeting on 10 July reported similar confusion among local Left SRs on 7 July. "The escapade caught Left SRs [in our area] completely unaware. They assumed it must be a provocation," the representative of the First City District reported.[69] In short, from the start Soviet authorities in Petrograd knew full well that Left SRs in the former capital were not party to whatever "conspiracy against Soviet power" had occurred in Moscow. Rank-and-file Petrograd Left SRs were, in fact, so disoriented that nowhere did they resist confiscation of weapons. The only known casualties during disarmament of Left SR detachments in the districts were the result of an accident. As Latvian riflemen were seizing weapons from Left SRs near the Obukhov plant, a grenade fell to the ground killing four and wounding fourteen.[70]

*   *   *

The main stage upon which the "Left SR uprising" of 7 July 1918 in Petrograd and its suppression was played out was the area around the Pages School. What took place there was less a drama than a tragicomedy. Commanded by a sailor named Sandurov, the main Left SR detachment in the Pages School was a shadow of what it had been in February and March 1918, when, with the encouragement of the Bolsheviks, it had been formed to help defend Petrograd from the Germans.[71] As was the case with Bolshevik forces, when the civil war expanded in the late spring and early summer, the most experienced personnel in the detachment had been rushed to the front. The result was that by early July most of the roughly 350–380 soldiers in the Pages School were mercenaries, mostly teenagers, with little training and no party allegiances. A significant proportion had only very recently been lured away from Red Army and naval units by promises of higher pay and better working conditions.[72]

On the morning of 7 July, members of the detachment were denied passes into the city, informed of Mirbach's assassination, and alerted to the possibility of an attack by German or Finnish White Guard forces. They were not told about Left SR complicity in the murder or the possibility of an attack by Red Army forces.[73] At 5:00 PM, telephone service to the Pages

School was cut. From then on, the unit had no communications, either with the Left SR political leadership or with district detachments. An hour later, Red Army soldiers on horseback began patrolling Nevskii Prospekt and other strategically important streets and government buildings. Pickets were established at the main approaches to the area around the Pages School, evening performances at the nearby Mariinskii, Aleksandrinskii, and Malyi theaters were canceled, readers at the adjoining Imperial Public Library were rushed out the door, and a medical facility was set up in the City Duma building (also nearby). The Military-Revolutionary Committee, which was to direct the disarmament of the Left SR detachment, established itself in the southwest wing of the Gostiny Dvor, a two-story labyrinth of shops on Nevskii Prospekt, a main wing of which faced the Pages School. Light artillery pieces were positioned along Bankers Lane (behind the State Bank), on the corner of Nevskii Prospekt and Sadovaia Street, and on Chernyshevskii Lane.[74]

Just before these last preparatory moves, Uritskii sent Zalutskii and another party colleague, Nikolai Kuzmin, into the Pages School to try to negotiate the surrender and disarmament of the Left SR detachment.[75] Their proposal was rejected. Following this, an attempted sneak attack by Bolshevik-led loyalist troops was turned back by grenades tossed from windows of the Pages School. One more attempt was made to negotiate a surrender. Negotiations were evidently still in progress when individuals on both sides resumed fighting. Meanwhile, rumors of "an event" had drawn thousands of curious onlookers to the area around the Pages School. It was still very light, and would be for hours, and so the onlookers strained against police pickets, trying to get a glimpse of the action.

At around 7:00 PM, the crowd watched as soldiers, some of them carrying machine guns, established a perimeter around the Pages School. An hour or so later, government forces launched their main assault, pounding the school with artillery shells and rifle and machine gun fire. The defenders answered back, sporadically battering the facade of the Gostiny Dvor and ripping away windows. The ear-splitting boom of artillery shattered windows in the public library and terrified unsuspecting strollers, many of them children, in the Anichkov Palace Park. The gaping crowds scurried for cover when the firing became heavy and surged back each time it subsided, unperturbed by the acrid, dense smoke now filling the air. Moura Benckendorff, the probable Cheka informer, and Captain Cromie, who had destroyed all his records as soon as he found out what was happening, were among the onlookers.[76]

Once the artillery bombardment of the Pages School began, the stream of soldiers fleeing the building and surrendering to loyalist troops became a flood. Toward the end of the battle, some sailors were observed scampering across neighboring rooftops. Finally, at around 9:00 PM, onlookers spotted a white towel hanging from a window of the Pages School. The firing stopped while an agreement was arranged providing for the surrender and disarmament of the Left SR detachment in exchange for a guarantee of the personal safety of its personnel. Moments later, attacking troops entered the building, disarmed and arrested the 150 or so members of the detachment still inside, and took them to Gorokhovaia 2.

PCheka documents indicate that the assault on the Pages School was an unprovoked preemptive strike. Most of those arrested attested in depositions that they had joined the Left SR detachment to defend Soviet power and, not wishing to fight it, had not participated in the shooting that occurred at the school. The PCheka was unable to find any evidence that the Left SR leadership had authorized the detachment to resist government forces or had done anything other than instruct it to go underground. Judging by a State Political Administration (GPU) tabulation made in July 1935 (and corroborating PCheka file documents), of the 161 suspects arrested in the case of the "Armed Resistance of Left SRs in Petrograd," 36 appear to have been set free the same evening. The GPU was unable to ascertain the outcome of proceedings against the remaining 125, suggesting that they were also quickly released for lack of incriminating evidence.[77] On 10 December 1918, the PCheka's investigation was officially closed and files relating to it were put in storage, because, in the words of a secret PCheka resolution, "all suspects in the case had been freed and no further inquiry was conducted."[78] Nonetheless, the battle at the Pages School became an important element of the official myth surrounding the Left SR conspiracy against Soviet power nationally and was used to justify the repression of the Left SRs.[79]

* * *

The 9 July resolutions of the Fifth Congress, not to speak of Petrovskii's harsher follow-up directive, obliged Bolshevik authorities in Petrograd to expel Left SRs who were unwilling to disavow their Central Committee from membership in soviets.[80] On 10 July, by which time Zinoviev had returned from Moscow, the Petrograd Soviet endorsed this principle. In practice, however, the Petrograd Soviet limited itself to banning Left SRs who were unwilling to repudiate their Central Committee from its Executive Committee and, by extension, banning them from leadership posts in district soviets. The removal of Left SRs from the soviet altogether was left to recall elections.[81] This restraint, which was characteristic of Bolshevik officials in the Petrograd Soviet amid continuing instability among workers, was belatedly endorsed by the Bolshevik Petersburg Committee on 19 July, which was the first time the "Left SR problem" came up for discussion in that forum.[82]

At its meeting on 10 July, the Petrograd Soviet had also resolved that the armed forces should be purged of Left SRs who did not disassociate themselves from the Left SR Central Committee. In this connection, the sailors of the nearby Kronstadt naval base were cause for special concern. In March 1918, the strong influence of Left SRs on Kronstadt's revolutionary politics had been reflected in the Kronstadt Soviet's fierce opposition to the Brest peace. In May, at the time of the crisis over the fate of Fort Ino, the Kronstadt Soviet and its executive committee had adopted a spate of resolutions proclaiming the Brest "breathing space" all but over.[83] Most recently, on the eve of the Fifth All-Russian Congress of Soviets, by which time the Left SRs, in alliance with SR Maximalists, had a majority in the Kronstadt Soviet, it had adopted a resolution expressing aversion to centralized dictatorial government as a violation of the principle "All Power to the Soviets" and a throwback to bourgeois systems of government.[84]

In contrast to the situation prevailing in Petrograd, where Left SRs do not appear to have constituted a security risk during the July events in Moscow, the danger was very real that thousands of armed, independent-minded Kronstadters led by Left SRs might respond to news of the Left SR "rebellion" against the Bolsheviks in Moscow with a rising of their own. Bolshevik authorities in Petrograd were alert to this risk. Taking advantage of the momentary disorientation of the Kronstadt Left SR leadership, they formed a Revolutionary Committee at the naval base on 7 July composed of the entire Kronstadt Bolshevik party committee that successfully assumed strict political control at the base.[85] Bolshevik apprehensions were confirmed when Kronstadt Left SRs, to a man, refused to sign a pledge obligating them to obey the Revolutionary Committee. On 9 July Bolshevik officials in Petrograd responded by dissolving the Kronstadt Soviet and establishing a puppet committee in its place. This committee shut down *Izvestiia Kronshtadtskogo Soveta*, the voice of revolutionary Kronstadt ever since March 1917, ordered the disarmament of Kronstadt Left SRs and Maximalists, and banned political meetings of any kind at the base.[86] The committee also decreed regulations for the election of a new soviet that effectively excluded Left SRs. For practical purposes, the Left SRs were outlawed.[87] The Bolsheviks justified all these moves on the basis of the Kronstadt Soviet's "criminal indecisiveness and inability to defend Soviet power" and on "the need for a strong revolutionary dictatorship in order to prevent the triumph of the schemes of imperialist agents."[88]

As for Petrograd Left SRs, on the first day or so after the announcement of "the Left SR rebellion against Soviet power," some district-level Left SR leaders were so stunned by seemingly irrefutable evidence of their national leadership's effort to overthrow Soviet power that they repudiated their own leadership.[89] At factories, Bolsheviks tried to take advantage of this disorientation to wean Left SR workers from the party.[90] Subsequently, under the pressure of a continuing barrage of hostile Bolshevik propaganda, some Petrograd Left SRs remained alienated from their party leadership and either joined the Bolshevik party or the Popular Communists (*Narodniki kommunisti*), a Left SR splinter group organized in September 1918.

Desertions from the Left SRs were not the typical response, however. Images of the "Left SR conspiracy against Soviet power" in Petrograd, trumpeted in the local Bolshevik and Soviet press, differed so drastically from what Petrograd Left SRs *knew* to have occurred that most of them quickly became skeptical of the government's version of events in Moscow. These reservations hardened after protest leaflets from comrades in Moscow reached Petrograd.[91] The leaflets provided compelling information on the fabrication of a Bolshevik majority at the Fifth Congress of Soviets, on the motivation behind Mirbach's assassination, on the scope of repressions of Left SRs in Moscow, and on Bolshevik abuses of power generally. As a result, Petrograd Left SRs increasingly resisted demands that they disavow the actions of their Central Committee as the price of keeping "responsible positions" or even of retaining their elective seats in soviets. Occasionally, they blamed the Bolsheviks for attacking them, rather than the other way around, and demanded an end to Bolshevik attacks.

Miraculously, given the extreme harassment to which they were now subjected, Petrograd Left SRs were able to convene the Tenth City Conference of Petrograd Left SRs in mid July. There a resolution was adopted approving the actions of the Left SR Central Committee and demanding the immediate liberation of imprisoned Left SR leaders.[92] Even earlier, at the meeting of the Petrograd Soviet on 10 July, a majority of the Left SR fraction refused to condemn the actions of their Central Committee.[93] The fraction stubbornly held its ground at a meeting of the Petrograd Soviet on 16 July, when the Bolshevik leadership, in effect, gave the Left SRs a last chance to back down, and then formed a new Executive Committee without them.[94] From then on, regardless of the gravity of the crisis, Left SRs were frozen out of the central Soviet leadership. During policy discussions at Petrograd Soviet plenary meetings, Left SRs were treated as pariahs whether the issue was military mobilization, labor unrest, or even public health.[95]

The tendency of Petrograd Left SRs, at the grassroots level, to rally around their Central Committee, and pay dearly for it, is well reflected in their behavior in district soviets. In the Peterhof District Soviet, for instance, the Executive Committee minus Left SRs, on 9 July, officially substituted Bolsheviks for Left SRs in leadership positions. At the same time, the Executive Committee also banned Left SRs from their offices and required them to relinquish their weapons.[96] The full soviet did not get around to discussing relationships with Left SRs until 14 July. A couple of days earlier hundreds of workers at the Putilov wharf, within the district, had adopted and circulated a resolution protesting Bolshevik repression of the Left SRs, "a party truly protective of workers and peasants." The resolution demanded the release of jailed Left SRs so that they would have an opportunity to explain themselves to workers, and the reopening of *Znamia truda* and *Znamia bor'by* as well as an impartial investigation of the matter.[97] However, Bolsheviks in the Peterhof District Soviet ignored this resolution by an important segment of their constituency. At the meeting of the soviet on the 14th, they demanded that Left SR deputies in attendance declare whether they were with the Bolsheviks or against them, and whether they approved of the actions of the SR Central Committee. "If you approve," they stated, "we will count you among our enemies. If you do not, our formerly friendly association can continue."

The Left SR response was that, as a Soviet party, they stood and would stand for Soviet power. However, they would fight the dictatorship of individuals. They did not condemn the action against Mirbach, as such, and would not break with their Central Committee until the Left SR press was reopened and there was definitive clarification of whether the Left SR Central Committee had attempted to overthrow Soviet power. The spokesman for the Left SR fraction rejected the accusation that Petrograd Left SRs had participated in a conspiracy. He suggested that the order to disarm Left SRs in the district had come from above and that local Bolshevik comrades had not, in fact, lost trust in the Left SRs, nor, for that matter, lost interest in working together in the future. He urged the Bolsheviks to state openly whether this was so. The question was answered by a Bolshevik resolution passed at the meeting. It endorsed the measures taken by the Executive Committee "against a party that had betrayed the revolutionary cause" and called on "workers to give a merciless rebuff to adventurers [read: the Left SRs] . . . seeking to drag Russia into war."[98] A roughly analogous process took place in the Vyborg and Narva district soviets.[99]

As nearly as I have been able to tell, local Bolshevik party committees, as such, did not figure in the decisions of the Peterhof, Vyborg, and Narva district soviets to purge Left SRs from leadership positions. Rather, they acted on a general signal from the Petrograd Soviet. By contrast, the Vasilii Island Bolshevik district committee took the initiative in demanding reelection of the local soviet executive committee, the restructuring of the soviet, and the ouster of suspicious Left SRs from all leadership posts.[100] These decisions were made and implemented through Bolshevik district soviet leaders at meetings of the district soviet executive committee on 16 July and of the full soviet on 18 July.[101]

The situation in the Rozhdestvenskii district was more complex. In the aftermath of the events of early July, the transfer of exclusive authority to Bolsheviks in the district soviet there took on special importance because of the close proximity of both Smolny and the Taurida Palace. However, accomplishing this was complicated by the great strength of Left SRs locally. At meetings of the district soviet on 8, 11, 12, and 15 July, Bolsheviks heaped abuse on Left SRs, and the latter, supported by SR Maximalists, vigorously defended themselves, exclaiming, for example, how dare the Bolsheviks attack a party that included individuals like Spiridonova, who had suffered so much for the revolution. Whatever action the Moscow Left SRs had taken, they insisted, was a move against compromises with imperialism and the dictatorship of individuals, not against Soviet power. Indeed, in Petrograd, it had been the Bolsheviks, not the Left SRs, who were the aggressors. The Left SR Petrograd Committee, in fact, had issued express instructions prohibiting offensive steps by forces loyal to it. By what right had Bolsheviks in the district created an all-powerful troika, usurped the authority of the district soviet, and arbitrarily ravaged local Left SR personnel and agencies? You, not we, have explaining to do, Left SR deputies in the Rozhdestvenskii District Soviet insisted, adding that they would be willing to continue work in the soviet but only on equal terms with the Bolsheviks.

Such defiance so rattled Bolsheviks in the Rozhdestvenskii District Soviet that their chief spokesman declared that Admiral Shchastny sank the Black Sea Feet to please the Left SRs (!). At another point, this spokesman insisted that, since Petrograd Left SRs justified the actions of their Central Committee, it followed that they had been apprised of its actions in advance. Nonetheless, under the impact of the fierce Left SR rebuttal, after initially excluding Left SRs from the Executive Committee, the district soviet Bolshevik fraction reversed itself and selected an Executive Committee in which Left SRs had parity with Bolsheviks.[102] This act so incensed the Bolshevik party committee in the district that it scheduled an immediate meeting of the fraction to force an agreement to remove Left SRs from the Executive Committee and from all other leadership positions in the soviet.[103] This direct intervention in the operation of the district soviet by the local Bolshevik party committee, along the lines pursued in the Vasilii Island district, achieved its aim. A resolution to exclude Left SRs from the Executive Committee was adopted at a meeting of the full Rozhdestvenskii District Soviet on 18 July, with the provision that three of sixteen places on the committee would be reserved for Left SRs who formally condemned their Central Committee.[104] Within three days, Left SRs had been removed from the Executive Committee, and Bolsheviks had been installed as heads of all the district soviet's administrative sections.[105]

The First City District Soviet was among a minority of Petrograd district soviets in which Left SRs bowed to intense Bolshevik pressure and repudiated their Central Committee.[106] However, even in Petrograd district soviets in which Left SR fractions distanced themselves from their Central Committee as well as in district soviets in which they remained defiant, Left SRs were never able to regain their previous status as genuine partners in local government.

This is not to suggest that Left SRs disappeared from government agencies entirely. The Petrograd Bolsheviks were so strapped for cadres that for some time they had no choice but to continue to rely on Left SRs for staff. As late as the end of August 1918 Stasova, in a plea for personnel from district soviets on behalf of the Northern Oblast Bolshevik Committee (SOK), complained that "of 117 people on the staff of the politically critical Commissariat for Internal Affairs, only 4 were Bolsheviks. As a result," she wrote, "despite our strong desire to send Bolsheviks to investigate local conflicts [in rural areas outside Petrograd], this is impractical. Comrade Uritskii is forced to send out Left SRs."[107] Nonetheless, as Stasova's frustration implies, Petrograd Left SRs were now regarded, at best, as a necessary evil. Collectively, they were hounded along with all moderate socialist, liberal, and conservative parties and groups.

*　*　*

The end of the Bolshevik–Left SR alliance marked the decisive turn to one-party government in Soviet Russia. Around this same time, government centralization in Petrograd was advanced by the abrogation of the taxing powers of district soviets and by the undermining of the autonomy of some of their more important sections. For example, the Soviet of the Economy for the Northern Region (SNKhSR), since its formation in late March, had been trying to overcome what Molotov, its chair, referred to as the "parochialism" of district soviet economic sections so as to impose control over them.[108] Now it tried a diplomatic approach. It issued guidelines for economic sections setting forth their goals and tasks; it attempted to systematize their organization; and it established their relation to the SNKhSR. Yet the guidelines were sufficiently ambiguous and attuned to the sensibilities of district soviets to make them mutually acceptable. Thus, although district economic sections were supposedly responsible for controlling and organizing the local economy under the direction of the SNKhSR, the sections were expressly identified as agencies of the district soviet, not the SNKhSR. Permanent contact between the SNKhSR and district soviets was to be maintained through the mutual exchange of delegates. This was deemed especially important during the period of socialist construction; after that, implicitly, district soviets might be more, not less, independent. Representatives of economic sections, one per district, were given the right to participate in plenary meetings of the SNKhSR but without voting rights. Moreover, a specific role was identified for interdistrict conferences of economic section representatives that were to be convened no less than twice a month to discuss and coordinate activities.[109]

These guidelines enabled the SNKhSR and district soviet sections to develop a stable relationship in the short run, and provided a model for centralization in other areas that was more acceptable than the ultra-centralized dictatorships Lenin promoted. However, economic administration in Petrograd remained inefficient. Both city and districts maintained substantial bureaucracies with overlapping functions and responsibilities. Not until military emergencies in 1919 would districts soviets tacitly acknowledge the need for significantly more rigorous centralization. During the late summer of 1918, their modus vivendi with the SNKhSR notwithstanding, district soviets remained fiercely protective of their prerogatives.

* * *

The collapse of the Bolshevik–Left SR alliance in Petrograd should not hide its vital importance to the creation of a viable Soviet government in the Petrograd region after the Sovnarkom's flight to Moscow, and to the survival of Soviet power there during the severe economic, political, and military crises of late spring and early summer 1918. Nor should it obscure the immense historical significance of the alliance's destruction nationally.

In view of this, the decision of the Left SR Central Committee to exercise "the terror option" following its defeat in the struggle over credentials at the Fifth All-Russian Congress of Soviets seems particularly unfortunate. At the Fourth All-Russian Left SR Party Congress in October 1918, Left SR leaders consoled themselves with the idea that, by assassinating Mirbach, they had served the long-term cause of international socialist revolution.

That is debatable but, in any case, does not alter the fact that following Mirbach's killing, all the Left SRs' plans and expectations went awry. The Left SR leadership had assumed that the assassination of Mirbach would provoke an immediate German military attack. But Lenin's government, aided by fortuitous developments on the Western front, successfully averted that. The Left SRs also hoped that the Left Communists were still sympathetic to their concerns and would ultimately support their action. Together with this Bolshevik core, they would lead the revolutionary struggle. But with the Bolsheviks' hold on Soviet power hanging by a thread, even the most ardent Left Communists maintained party discipline.

Worst of all, for the Left SRs the Bolsheviks' successful fabrication of a large majority in the Fifth All-Russian Congress of Soviets had come as such a shock, and the July events had developed so quickly, that the Left SR Central Committee had not even begun to prepare the party as a whole for a possible radical change in tactics. With quixotic faith in the power of revolutionary spontaneity, Left SR leaders, belatedly charged with implementing the "terror option," did not give this problem a second thought, leaving powerful Left SR organizations in Petrograd, Kronstadt, and elsewhere unprepared for a Bolshevik attack. Spiridonova, from her Kremlin cell, acknowledged this fatal error. In an anguished letter to the Fourth Left SR Party Congress, she tried to help her Central Committee colleagues fend off a relentless barrage of intraparty criticism: "The Mirbach act," she wrote, "was the whole party's doing—the result of its Third Congress's resolution regarding 'abrogation' of the Brest treaty, of its mood . . . and of its international and revolutionary spirit." At the same time, she admitted, "the Central Committee and I in particular are to blame for shortsightedness—for not having had the foresight to envision the possible consequences of our act and to neutralize them in advance." "Our party's lack of preparation technically and psychologically was gigantic," she lamented. "Our biggest mistake was hurrying too much. . . . If only it were possible, I would quarter myself for my personal blame."[110]

The Soviet government's first official announcement about Mirbach's assassination accused the Left SRs of giving the Germans the best possible excuse to attack Russia. But by the same token, the Left SRs' act, however understandable framed against the fraudulent composition of the Fifth All-Russian Congress of Soviets and the ominous developments at the congress's start, offered Lenin a better excuse than he could possibly have hoped for to eliminate the Left SRs as a significant political rival. He took full advantage of the opportunity in Moscow and also pressed leaders in key political centers such as Petrograd, where the Bolshevik–Left SR partnership endured, to launch preemptive strikes against the Left SRs and to neutralize them for good as a significant political force. Despite their skyrocketing strength in the countryside before Mirbach's assassination, the Left SRs never recovered from the battering they received at the hands of the Bolsheviks following their impetuous act.

PART FOUR

CELEBRATION AMID TERROR

12

The Road to "Red Terror"

THE SUMMER OF 1918 saw a hardening of policies toward real and potential counterrevolution in Petrograd. Volodarskii's assassination, the removal of the moderating influence of the Left SRs on Petrograd government, an upsurge of anti-Bolshevik activity involving Allied secret agents, the increased danger of German occupation after Count Mirbach's assassination, and the constantly growing threat of famine and epidemic diseases all threatened the survival of Soviet power. In addition, Moscow stepped up its pressure on cadre-starved Petrograd for more and more personnel—from party leaders to unskilled workers—either to serve with armed detachments foraging for grain in the countryside or to join Red Army units on Soviet Russia's civil war fronts.

These threats grew with astounding speed. In early May Krasnov's Cossacks had begun to reestablish themselves as the predominant power in the Don region, which remained a hotbed of rebellion and opposition to Soviet rule through the summer. Further south the Volunteer Army of Denikin and Alekseev consolidated power in the Kuban and North Caucasus, while landings by Allied interventionist forces in the northwest, in Murmansk and Archangel, reawakened the danger of an early occupation of Petrograd, either by the Allies or the Germans. Perhaps the greatest threat to the survival of Soviet power came from the East—from rebelling elements of the Czech Legion, then collaborating with White, anti-Soviet movements in vast expanses along the Trans-Siberian railway. On 8 June the western-most elements of the Legion bolstered military forces loyal to the SRs, the future "People's Army," when they captured the Volga city of Samara. There delegates to the Constituent Assembly led by SRs formed a rival national government, the "Committee of Members of the Constituent Assembly," or Komuch, which assumed the mantle of the Constituent Assembly.

We need not be detained by the tangled, at times bloody battle for hegemony in the East during the rest of the summer and fall, primarily between

SRs associated with Komuch and conservative former SRs and White officers centered in the Western Siberian city of Omsk, culminating in the establishment of a reactionary government headed by Admiral Aleksandr Kolchak in the winter.[1] Suffice it simply to note that before the advance of the People's Army, supported by the Czechs, along the Volga was finally reversed in September 1918, it had captured Kazan, no more than five hundred miles southeast of Moscow; that at the peak of its power, Komuch controlled the provinces of Samara, Simbirsk, Kazan, and Ufa, and part of Saratov province; and that, roughly concurrently, a linkup of Allied forces with the Czechs, and their simultaneous march on Moscow and Petrograd, appeared to be a real possibility. This prospect energized the counterrevolution in Petrograd, roiled the Germans, and badly frightened gravely weakened Bolshevik authorities in the former capital. The drift to Red Terror in Petrograd and other Russian cities during the late summer of 1918 grew out of the insecurity caused by these ominous developments. Factors often cited for causing the Terror, such as pressure from Lenin, the assassinations of Volodarskii and Uritskii, and the unsuccessful attempt to kill Lenin, played a less significant role.[2]

*   *   *

In the spring and early summer of 1918 Volodarskii had been commissar for the press, agitation, and propaganda in the SK PTK and later in the SK SO. In these posts he directed repression of the opposition press. In mid June he was also the chief Bolshevik organizer of rigged elections to the Petrograd Soviet and editor of the Petrograd Soviet's radical popular tabloid, *Krasnaia gazeta*. All this made him a high-profile object of derision by enemies of Bolshevism, on a par with Zinoviev and Uritskii. On the other hand, to rank-and-file factory workers who still supported the Bolsheviks as guardians of worker empowerment, Volodarskii was one of the most popular spokesmen for the Petrograd party organization.

Volodarskii was assassinated on 20 June.[3] If his murder by an unknown assailant was intended to further anti-Bolshevik sentiment among disgruntled factory workers, the tactic may have had some success, coinciding as it did with the angry response of Baltic Fleet sailors to Shchastny's execution and Obukhov workers to the arrest of their leaders. The abortive rebellion of the Baltic Fleet minelayers and the Obukhov factory workers occurred within days of Volodarskii's assassination. However, increased hostility to Soviet power at a popular level does not appear to have been the most common reaction to the sensational killing. Judging by *Novaia zhizn'*, which was then highly critical of the Bolsheviks, word of Volodarskii's death shocked

Volodarskii lying in state at the Taurida Palace. State Museum of the Political History of Russia, St. Petersburg.

most workers in neighboring factories and increased the danger of mob violence.[4]

Volodarskii's colleagues on *Krasnaia gazeta*'s editorial board demanded quick vengeance in the form of immediate mass terror for the murder of their leader.[5] Simultaneously some district-level Bolsheviks formally registered concern about intensified activity by enemies of Soviet power and expressed a desire to settle scores with them.[6] Also, on the morning of 21 June a stream of worker delegations showed up at Zinoviev's office in Smolny to demand immediate repression as retaliation for Volodarskii's killing so that "revolutionary leaders would not be cut down, one at a time." Zinoviev asserted, however, that "we opposed this mood . . . we insisted that there be no excesses."[7] The Executive Committee of the Petrograd Soviet met in emergency session the same day (21 June) to discuss the greatly inflamed mood. According to *Novye vedomosti,* the meeting's general sentiment was that lynch justice should be opposed.[8]

Several days later Lenin learned of Petrograd's restraint and was plainly infuriated by the news. He immediately cabled a tongue lashing to Zinoviev, Lashevich, and other members of the Petrograd Bureau of the Central Committee and the Petersburg Committee: "We heard only today that in Piter, workers wanted to respond to the killing of Volodarskii with mass terror and that you held them back," he scolded. "This is in-tol-er-able!"[9] Nonetheless, Uritskii was able to prevent excesses for the time being. At the same time Volodarskii's assassination, followed by the actions of the minelayers and Obukhov workers, appeared to demonstrate the continued need for such potentially powerful, ad hoc security organs as the PCheka. The killing quashed the movement to abolish the PCheka, which had been picking up steam.[10] It was left to the virtually moribund Presidium of the SK PTK to respond to Dzerzhinskii's message of 24 June regarding the impermissibility of abolishing the PCheka. On 2 July the Presidium informed the VCheka that information about the liquidation of the PCheka was false.[11]

* * *

Volodarskii's replacement as commissar for the press, agitation, and propaganda was Nikolai Kuzmin, previously an editor of *Petrogradskaia pravda*. Toward the end of June, at the time Kuzmin assumed his post, the SK SO enhanced his powers to combat the opposition press.[12] Precisely at that time the Petersburg Committee began to assert itself, however gingerly, on key government matters. The committee had not been consulted about Kuzmin's appointment, was unhappy with *Petrogradskaia pravda* during his tenure there, and was apparently fearful that he was not tough enough to fully utilize the prerogatives of his office.[13] At a meeting on 12 July, after discussing the work of the Press Commissariat, the Petersburg Committee passed a resolution declaring that, although the new press commissar had made hardline pronouncements, he had taken no concrete steps against hostile papers; the resolution demanded more energetic measures. In something of a landmark in its relationship with local government authorities, the Petersburg Committee nominated one of its most respected members, Moisei Kharitonov, for the post of press commissar, on the condition that he work under the committee's constant control. In this connection, the Petersburg Committee assigned Samoilova and Zalutskii to conduct negotiations with Zinoviev regarding Kharitonov's appointment and to discuss the shutdown of bourgeois newspapers with Kuzmin.[14]

At the start of the Petersburg Committee's next meeting on 18 July, Kuzmin presented a plan of work for his commissariat.[15] Because a majority of members wanted to shut down all bourgeois papers at once, whereas Kuzmin visualized a more gradual, piecemeal approach, the response to his report was a resolution calling for a discussion and a decision on curbing the bourgeois press at an early meeting of the Petrograd Soviet's Executive Committee. The resolution envisioned that, at this meeting, a representative of the Petersburg Committee would "insist on the most decisive measures possible against the bourgeois press . . . as the [voice of the] most evil class enemy of the proletariat." At the same time assemblies [of party members] in the districts would be convened to explain the necessity of suppressing the bourgeois press entirely and to demand that this be done. The Petersburg Committee's resolution included the unprecedented provision that "Kuzmin could stay on as commissar but that he would be obligated to make weekly reports to it and to change his tactics toward the bourgeois press."[16] Kuzmin subsequently stiffened his policies.[17]

* * *

Following the murder of Volodarskii, despite expanding arrests of suspected oppositionists, Uritskii successfully resisted pressure for PCheka shootings, as well as the practice, instituted by the VCheka in Moscow, of holding high-profile political prisoners as hostages to be shot in the event of further killings of prominent Soviet leaders. Among well-known figures arrested by the PCheka at this time was Nikolai Kutler, a former tsarist official, leading Kadet, and deputy from Petersburg in the second and third state dumas. Picked up on 23 June, he was released two days later. Press reports suggest that intercepted letters he wrote to a colleague abroad had aroused the suspicions of PCheka investigators; however, upon reviewing the letters, Uritskii found nothing incriminating in them and ordered Kutler's release.[18]

A week after Kutler's arrest, the former Russian prime minister Vladimir Kokovtsev was roused in the middle of the night, arrested, and hauled off to Gorokhovaia 2, where he spent about a week. His arrest, like Kutler's, was triggered by suspicious mail intercepts, in Kokovtsev's case, letters between counterrevolutionaries who, unbeknownst to him, had discussed the possibility of his becoming prime minister in a post-Soviet government. Uritskii's trip to Moscow for the Fifth Congress of Soviets delayed consideration of Kokovtsev's release. He deposed Kokovtsev on 7 July and let him go the same day. In his memoirs, Kokovtsev depicted his interrogation by Uritskii as a long and civil discussion that dealt as much with his resignation as prime minister in 1914, and his impressions of Nicholas II, as with questions relating to his arrest.[19] Aleksandr Amfiteatrov, a prominent prose writer, literary critic, and fiercely anti-Bolshevik journalist who was arrested by the PCheka on 24 June, had a similar experience. Held at Gorokhovaia 2, he was discharged two days later. In *Novye vedomosti,* the paper he was then working for, he characterized his deposition by Uritskii as a political conversation rather than an interrogation. Uritskii was interested in such topics as his relations with Grigorii Aleksinskii and other "Plekhanovites,"[20] whether his orientation was toward Germany or the Entente, his literary and newspaper work, and the source of *Novye vedomosti*'s funding. After they had discussed these subjects, Uritskii said Amfiteatrov was free to go.

None of this is to suggest that detention at Gorokhovaia 2 in mid summer 1918 was not a demeaning and trying experience or that hundreds of other, often lower-profile political prisoners were as fortunate as Kutler, Kokovtsev, and Amfiteatrov. Their descriptions leave little doubt about that. And there is also no question that conditions in Petrograd's even more over-crowded and unsanitary prisons were far worse than in the makeshift cells at Gorokhovaia 2.[21] It is simply to say that Uritskii still resisted the extrem-ist tide at a time when the Cheka in Moscow was already arbitrarily shooting class enemies and when, for practical purposes, unofficial Red Terror was in full sway there and in other Russian cities.[22]

To be sure, Petrograd authorities adopted various repressive measures to prevent the general strike scheduled by the EAD and to suppress the orga-nization for good. However, I have found no evidence that the PCheka ar-rested leaders of the EAD, as the VCheka in Moscow had done in early June when it incarcerated several members of an EAD delegation in Moscow, and again on 22 July, after its suppression of the regional workers' congress.[23] Similarly, following Mirbach's assassination, Uritskii tried to avoid unnec-essary bloodshed in Petrograd, despite the official endorsement of mass ter-ror by the Fifth All-Russian Congress of Soviets.[24] Rather, he focused on the suppression of specific counterrevolutionary conspiracies. This was the case with the anti-Soviet conspiracy in the Mikhailovskii Artillery Academy.[25] Its leaders were left alone, under close watch, until 11 July, when they intensi-fied preparations for violent action against the government. Not until then were twelve of them arrested.[26]

*   *   *

During the first three months of 1918, while the Treaty of Brest-Litovsk was being negotiated and the battle over its ratification raged, the British, French, and American governments had worked to dissuade the Soviet leader-ship from withdrawing from the war. This was the motivation behind Bruce Lockhart's appointment as Britain's special envoy to Petrograd in January.[27] Moreover, for some time after the treaty was ratified, the Allied powers played on the apprehensions of the Soviet government about the extent of German ambitions in Russia to try to entice it into some kind of collabora-tion that would result in the resumption of hostilities on the Eastern front. This was a policy dictated by fears, naturally strongest among the French, that a protracted lull in the east would undermine the Allied war effort in the west, resulting in a successful German drive on Paris.

By the late spring of 1918, as Bolshevik concessions to Germany mounted, renewed Soviet resistance to the Germans was no longer a prospect. At this point the Western allies, especially the British and French, began to support various anti-Bolshevik movements friendly to the cause of pursuing the war against Germany to victory, at first primarily with large infusions of money. Lockhart, through an old friend, had opened a channel to Boris Savinkov, who, he knew, intended to murder the top Bolshevik leadership on the night of the planned Allied landing in Archangel, and to take advantage of popular discontent over famine conditions to establish a military dictatorship.[28] By July, moreover, Lockhart had joined the French in funneling substantial funds to General Alekseev, director of the Volunteer Army's political arm and a leading candidate to head a military dictatorship.[29]

Roughly 170 British marines had landed in Murmansk, in early March, to guard allied military supplies before ratification of the Brest treaty and the hardening of Soviet attitudes toward the Allies. At the beginning of June the marines were augmented by an additional six hundred British troops. Skirmishes soon broke out between the British and Red Army forces. Still, among the Allies the issue of military intervention in Russia was complex and controversial. This was especially true in Washington, where, on principle, Woodrow Wilson opposed furnishing American troops for action in Russia. But even the French, desperate to repel Germany's offensive in the West, could ill afford to divert significant forces for a joint expeditionary force in Russia. Thus the number of military personnel the Western allies could commit to intervention in Russia was relatively very small. On 2 August, by which time President Wilson had grudgingly agreed to furnish troops for limited operations in the Russian North, some twelve hundred British and French troops, and a smattering of American soldiers, went ashore in Archangel.[30] Richard Ullman, whose study of early Anglo-Soviet relations remains the most reliable on the subject, concluded that the occupation of Archangel on 2 August marked the real beginning of Allied intervention in Russia. The Allied troops, under the overall command of General Frederick Poole, helped establish an anti-Bolshevik government headed by the venerable populist Nikolai Chaikovskii in Archangel.[31] Nonetheless, because their forces were puny, the Allies looked to link up with elements of the Czech Legion to realize their goals in northwest Russia, but this was never achieved.

Especially after the troop landing in Archangel, the Allies encouraged use of their beachheads in Murmansk and in Archangel as staging areas for the buildup and training of indigenous Russian, anti-Bolshevik, anti-German forces. In connection with the latter, the British subsidized a project to recruit unemployed former officers in the Russian Imperial Army and Navy, and technical specialists (pilots, engineers, railroaders, demolition experts, and the like) for service with the military units being assembled in the north. Clandestine operations connected with this project, dubbed by the PCheka "The Case of Recruitment of White Guardists for Murmansk," were carried out in Moscow, Vologda, Petrograd, and other locations in western Russia throughout the summer. Petrograd was a natural center for these activities, and Captain Cromie, who had by now become a strong advocate of unilateral Allied military intervention in force, helped finance them.[32] A significant number of recruits came from oppositionists in Soviet administrative institutions, and Red Army units in the city of Petrograd, and even recruits from the South, were processed in Petrograd.[33]

Even with the addition of indigenous recruits, the Allied expeditionary force was too small to launch significant offensive operations. However, for some time the Soviet leaders overestimated its strength. With the fledgling Red Army already stretched thin by campaigns against the Czechs in the east, Krasnov's Cossacks on the Don, and Denikin's and Alekseev's Volunteer Army in the Kuban, they feared early, unstoppable Allied advances on Vologda, Moscow, and Petrograd. In his memoirs Arkadii Borman, son of the Kadet leader Ariadna Tyrkova-Williams, who was then an undercover White intelligence agent in the Soviet government, recalled the utter panic that seized even Lenin in the first days after the occupation of Archangel.[34] In Petrograd, popular anxiety over an imminent enemy advance on the city, either by Allied interventionists or the Germans, reached levels not seen since the occupation of Pskov in February or the crisis over Fort Ino in May.[35]

In June and July 1918 the threat to the revolution posed by the successes of the Whites and Czechs had rekindled efforts begun by Petrograd authorities during the "Ino crisis" to enroll Bolsheviks, and workers generally, in crash military training courses.[36] At the end of June this threat also prompted Moscow to begin conscription into the Red Army of Moscow and Petrograd workers born in 1896 and 1897 (expanded to include workers born in 1893–1895 a month later).[37] The negative impact of these drafts on the Petrograd Bolshevik party organization, and on the security of Soviet power in Petrograd, was made infinitely worse by a separate Central Committee directive mandating mass mobilization into the Red Army of party members with combat experience. Among high-level Petrograd Bolsheviks now ordered into the Red Army were Lashevich, Ivan Bakaev, and Petr Zalutskii, a member of the Petrograd Bureau of the Central Committee, Secretary of the Executive Committee of the Petrograd Soviet, and commissar for labor in the SK SO, respectively. Conscription and party mobilizations for the Red Army came on top of levies for grain procurement detachments.[38] By the beginning of August the Bolshevik Petersburg Committee was balking at releasing any more "responsible" party members for Red Army service.[39] This resistance was solidified by anxiety over the threat to Petrograd posed by the Allied landing in Archangel, by a sudden move of the German Embassy from Moscow to Petrograd, and by ominous German naval movements in the Gulf of Finland.

During the rest of August and well into September a network of new minefields was laid at the approaches to Kronstadt and Petrograd, and elements of the Baltic Fleet were placed on full alert with instructions to engage the enemy.[40] Moreover, Petrograd authorities, following Moscow's example, sought protection by launching a new round-up of former officers and some prominent civilians thought to be sympathetic to the Allies. A few days after the Allied landing in Archangel, Cromie cabled the Admiralty that in Petrograd seven thousand officers and civilians had been arrested in the previous two days and that he was trying to negotiate the release of the officers for cash.[41] Cromie himself managed to evade capture by clambering "over roofs before they got up the stairs."[42]

* * *

In short order, Cromie's activities had branched out from coordinating the evacuation of military supplies from Petrograd, trying to arrange the timely destruction of the Baltic Fleet, and facilitating the movement of Russian officers to supplement Allied forces in the north, to winning over Latvian units that had previously served as a Soviet praetorian guard and funding and "uniting three large anti-Bolshevik groups," with the evident aim of overthrowing the Soviet government in Petrograd.[43] After the killing of Mirbach, Cromie had destroyed his ciphers, thus disrupting the possibility of effective communications with London.[44] He had assumed that General Poole, the overall commander of Allied interventionist forces, would provide him with some direction, but this did not happen.[45] Making matters worse, the compartmentalization of covert activities by agents from different intelligence agencies represented in the British Embassy meant that Cromie had to rely largely on his own devices and judgment. Soviet authorities had already demonstrated their disdain for the niceties of diplomatic immunity, so that Cromie now felt it necessary to lead a fugitive existence, moving from one safe house to another.[46] His close association with members of the former nobility at this time may have strengthened his attraction to restoring the monarchy or to a military dictatorship in Russia.[47] Other factors that might have pushed Cromie in a counterrevolutionary direction included his personal observations of the chaos associated with Bolshevik rule, his growing conviction not only that the Bolsheviks were controlled by the Germans but that "the Hun" would soon occupy Petrograd, and his constantly expanding interactions with active counterrevolutionaries generally. There is no reason to doubt, as others have noted, that he was primarily motivated by patriotism, in Richard Ullman's apt phrase, "keeping Russia non-German."[48] He was, after all, a dedicated professional military officer, and Britain *was* at war with Germany. In the conditions prevailing in Petrograd during the late summer of 1918, however, his patriotic goals came to include the overthrow of the Soviet government.

By then, Cromie was intensifying his conspiratorial activities. Among "White" conspirators he appears to have been collaborating with in August were two undercover Cheka agents, Steckelman and Sabir. Steckelman had persuaded Cromie that he had sixty thousand Finnish White Guards, plus twenty-five thousand Latvian troops at his disposal, and that he had the means to control rail, telegraph, and telephone services for support of Allied expeditionary forces in the North, the neutralization of German forces in Finland, and, if desired, a powerful joint march on Petrograd. At the same time Sabir was reported to have assured Cromie that the soldiers guarding all the Bolsheviks' armored cars at night were in his pay. With their help and the aid of a battalion of White officers loyal to him, he would be able to take responsibility for "arrangements" inside Petrograd (that is, for a coup timed to coincide with an Allied advance from the north).[49]

Cromie was sufficiently satisfied that Steckelman and Sabir were reliable that he attempted to arrange meetings between them and representatives of the other counterrevolutionary groups which he was subsidizing. Moreover, he made Sabir responsible for blowing up a key bridge over the Neva in the event of a German advance on Petrograd from Finland.[50] Lockhart, who was then providing large sums of money to the infamous Sidney Reilly, the top operative of the British Secret Intelligence Service (SIS) inside Russia who was bent on single-handedly masterminding the liquidation of the Soviet national government,[51] had at least a general sense of these activities. In a "Secret and Confidential Memorandum on the Alleged Allied Conspiracy in Russia" which Lockhart submitted to the Foreign Office shortly after his return to London in November 1918, he emphasized his warm relations with Cromie and that he was aware that both Cromie and Commander Ernst Boyce, nominal director of the SIS in Russia, were involved with several counterrevolutionary organizations in Petrograd and were spending considerable sums of money on them.[52]

* * *

In *British Agent,* Lockhart conceded that the Allied intervention was an indirect cause of the Red Terror.[53] There is a kernel of truth in that, at least in so far as Petrograd is concerned. Toward the end of June, when the proclamation of Red Terror was first pressed by radical Petrograd workers, Uritskii had already publicly linked Volodarskii's assassination to the collaboration between the Allies and the Right SRs.[54] Subsequently, as Allied agents such as Cromie and Lockhart increased their aid to counterrevolutionary organizations and Allied intervention became a reality, amid fears of an early attack on Petrograd by the Allies or by Germany, official propaganda against the imperialists, especially the British and French, became a drumbeat that further fueled popular anxieties. Records of Bolshevik district committees leave no doubt that fear of an enemy attack and the occupation of Petrograd at this time was genuine. Moreover, the readiness of even party members to serve at the front was moderated by the belief that it was first necessary to safeguard the survival of the revolution in the rear by crushing domestic foes.[55]

At its regular meeting on 23 July the Petersburg Committee had put its weight behind the significant expansion of political repression. Foreshadowed by its hard-line position on treatment of the opposition press a week earlier, this move was triggered by an ominous warning of massive counterrevolutionary activity in the Vasilii Island district reported by Aleksandr Sergeev and Sergei Rapoport, chairman of the Vasilii Island district soviet and head of its trial and investigation section, respectively. According to them, an estimated seventeen thousand officers in their district, many of whom defined themselves as monarchists, were then organizing a counterrevolutionary conspiracy. Their report was taken very seriously. The Petersburg Committee responded to it by adopting a resolution protesting the laxness of the government's security policies and affirming the necessity of "employing Red Terror against the very real efforts of counterrevolutionaries to organize rebellions."[56]

With the aim of lobbying for implementation of a systematic program of mass terror, the Petersburg Committee arranged a meeting with the Petrograd Bureau of the Central Committee and Sergeev and Rapoport for ten o'clock that evening (specifically identifying, as essential participants, Zinoviev, Zorin, Uritskii, and Pozern, representing the Petrograd Soviet, the Revolutionary Tribunal, the PCheka, and the military, respectively).[57] The meeting was held at the Astoria Hotel, the residence of most top party leaders, and often referred to as the "Cheka hotel" because it was close to Gorokhovaia 2. The Petersburg Committee seems to have been unsuccessful in persuading a majority of the necessity of implementing a program of "Red Terror" or even of lifting the ban on summary shootings adopted by the SK PTK in April. However, arrests of suspected counterrevolutionaries, some of whom were soon designated as hostages, were now expanded.[58]

During the war scare of early August, signs increased that Uritskii was losing ground to advocates of "Red Terror" in the SK SO, as well as his colleagues in the PCheka leadership. These signs included the detention, as hostages, of former officers and civilians. The class antagonism pressed by Bolshevik zealots, such as those on the editorial board of *Krasnaia gazeta,* party members in the districts, and a majority of the Petersburg Committee, was also reflected at the Second Northern Oblast Congress of Soviets held in Smolny on 1–2 August. The contrast with the First Northern Oblast Congress of Soviets in late April is striking. The first congress had been a relatively free forum where Bolsheviks and Left SRs debated fundamental issues.[59] The Second Northern Oblast Congress was less a meaningful dialogue on key issues than a political rally, similar to what plenary sessions of the Petrograd Soviet had become by then. Congress delegates were outnumbered by the entire Petrograd and Kronstadt soviets, as well as delegates to district soviet conferences, members of the Petrograd Trade Union Council, Red Army and Navy committees, and central and district railroad worker committees. Whipped to fever pitch after rousing speeches by Sverdlov and Trotsky, who were in Petrograd at this time, congress participants adopted a Bolshevik resolution "On the Current Moment," which set the stage for a program of mass terror. "Soviet power must insure the safety of the rear [by] maintaining a close watch over the bourgeoisie [and] . . . instituting a policy of mass terror toward it," read the resolution. Henceforth, "our motto is mass armament of workers and the concentration of all forces for a life or death military attack on the counterrevolutionary bourgeoisie."[60]

Implicit in this resolution was the reintroduction of the summary shooting of counterrevolutionaries that had been practiced and encouraged by the VCheka since February. At least some Petrograd district soviets immediately endorsed this call for mass terror.[61] By his own admission, Zinoviev, now referred to as "boss" of Petrograd, became an advocate of "Red Terror" in the wake of Volodarskii's killing but was restrained from trying to put this new orientation into practice by Uritskii and, in all probability, by Proshian and Krestinskii as well. As noted earlier, the moderating influence of Proshian and of Petrograd Left SRs generally was eliminated following the assassination of Count Mirbach in July. In mid August Krestinskii was transferred to

Presidium of the Second Northern Oblast Congress of Soviets, 1 August 1918. Seated: Uritskii, Trotsky, Sverdlov, Zinoviev, and Lashevich. Standing: Kharitonov, Lisovskii, Korsak, Voskov, Gusev, Ravich, Bakaev, and Kuzmin. St. Petersburg Institute of History, Russian Academy of Sciences.

Moscow to become the people's commissar for finance. As a result, Uritskii had become increasingly isolated within the SK SKSO and the leadership of the PCheka.

The impact of this weakened position was soon apparent. At a meeting on 17 August the SK SO issued a decree authorizing the PCheka, at its discretion, to shoot persons guilty of counterrevolutionary agitation and of a broad range of other political and economic crimes.[62] The best Uritskii could get was a stipulation that decisions on shootings would require the unanimous vote of the PCheka Collegium.[63]

The decision actually to proceed with the shootings was taken at a PCheka Collegium meeting on 19 August. Uritskii argued long and hard against it. One of the most illuminating accounts of Uritskii's difficulties with his colleagues in the PCheka leadership at this time was written by S. G. Uralov during the Khrushchev era; it is undocumented but purports to be based on the unpublished memoir of an unnamed younger PCheka firebrand who was a member of the PCheka Collegium. In his recollections, this firebrand alluded to continuing pressures on Uritskii to approve the shootings during the run-up to the 19 August Collegium meeting. "With ever increasing frequency there was talk of the need for shootings," he is quoted as having written. "During official meetings and private conversations, several comrades persistently raised the issue of [instituting] Red Terror." According to his account, as conveyed by Uralov, after the SK SO's decision forced a vote on shootings in the PCheka Collegium, only Uritskii opposed them. He did so on practical grounds. But after the Collegium soundly rejected his argument that shootings would be counterproductive, he abstained from a vote on the fate of twenty-one political prisoners and common criminals so that the will of the majority would prevail.[64] Two days later (21 August), the twenty-one prisoners were shot. The makeup of this first batch of PCheka victims is instructive: nine were shot for common crimes; four of the nine were former PCheka commissars. The remaining twelve were political prisoners, most of them alleged to have conducted counterrevolutionary agitation among Red Army soldiers. Included in the latter were six of twelve conspirators from the Mikhailovskii Artillery Academy arrested in July. Among them was the former officer Vladimir Perel'tsveig whose execution was to have serious consequences, primarily for Uritskii.[65]

The night of the PCheka's first shootings (21 August), the prevailing spirit of using violence against political opposition was captured in a resolution adopted by the Fifth Petrograd Province Congress of Soviets. "In every village and county we must carry out a radical purge," the resolution declared. "Counterrevolutionary officers, and indeed all White Guardists who even think about returning power to the rich, must be mercilessly liquidated."[66] A week later (28 August) a plenary meeting of the Petrograd Soviet moved the official proclamation of Red Terror a step closer in response to an alleged attempt on Zinoviev's life. Provoked by unsubstantiated rumors that an unidentified individual behaving suspiciously had sought out Zinoviev at the Astoria Hotel two nights earlier in order to kill him, the Soviet passed a resolution declaring its determination "to liquidate all the White Guardists in our hands should a hair fall from the head of one of our leaders" and "to annihilate all leaders of the counterrevolution to a man."[67] This resolution was similar to the one passed by the Petrograd Soviet on 22 June, following Volodarskii's killing. However, the resolution adopted by the Petrograd Soviet at that time was explicitly a warning, whereas in the conditions prevailing at the end of August 1918 there could be little doubt that it was a statement of policy.

* * *

On the morning of 30 August 1918 Uritskii was shot and killed on the way to his office at the Commissariat for Internal Affairs on Palace

Leonid Kannegisser. Author's personal collection.

Square. The details of his murder and the dramatic capture of his assassin emerge with clarity from voluminous Cheka files on the case.[68] Uritskii was shot by Leonid Kannegisser, a twenty-two-year-old former cadet in the Mikhailovskii Artillery Academy who was a talented poet well known in Petrograd literary circles (among his friends were Maria Tsvetaeva and Sergei Esenin).[69] Although Kannegisser appears to have been a Popular Socialist and an enthusiastic supporter of Kerensky in 1917, in repeated interrogations by PCheka investigators he refused to divulge his political affiliation, if indeed he had one, in 1918, and steadfastly insisted he had acted alone. The PCheka established that following the October revolution he had some connections to counterrevolutionary conspiratorial groups.[70] However, its conclusion that Uritskii's killing was part of one grand domestic and international conspiracy against Soviet power is not substantiated by any evidence in the PCheka's hands. Perel'tsveig, who had been among those executed by

Uritskii's funeral, 1 September 1918. Zinoviev is standing second from right. Molotov is fourth from right wearing a raincoat. State Museum of the Political History of Russia, St. Petersburg.

the PCheka on 21 August, was Kannegisser's close friend. Kannegisser had no way of knowing that, in general, Uritskii had been steadfastly opposed to shootings, and, in particular, that he had made last-ditch efforts to stop the executions of Perel'tsveig and his comrades. Uritskii's name appeared on execution orders published in the press, and Kannegisser, by his own admission, had acted to avenge his friend's death.[71] In Mark Aldanov's words, "the death of a friend turned him into a terrorist."[72] Kannegisser was executed for his act. To the consternation of PCheka investigators, 144 other individuals arrested in the case, including Kannegisser's mother, father, sisters, and a large number of his friends and acquaintances who were listed in his address book somehow survived the Red Terror and were released.[73]

Informed promptly of Uritskii's assassination, Lenin responded by ordering Dzerzhinskii to go to Petrograd without delay to direct an investigation. Prior to Dzerzhinskii's departure, Lenin sent him documents relating to counterrevolutionary activity that were to be published the next day. In a cover note to them that has been published, Lenin asked whether Dzerzhinskii thought it would be wise to carry out arrests at a location specified in the documents. In this connection, he suggested that these arrests might enable the VCheka to "find the threads and links among counter-revolutionaries." Apparently referring to Uritskii's killing, he stressed that now "for possibly the first time, there is 'official' confirmation of ties between those who did the shooting and the SR party."[74]

In two subsequent speeches to factory workers on 30 August, however, Lenin did not mention Uritskii's murder, the possible arrest of SRs, or official implementation of state terror.[75] After the second speech, at the Mikhelson iron foundry, machine-building, and weapons plant, he narrowly escaped a second assassination attempt (the first had occurred the previous January).[76] He was shot at several times. One bullet struck him in the chest, and another passed through his left arm and lodged in his neck. Lenin's condition appeared to be critical. While medical experts worked to stabilize him, his party held its collective breath.

13

The Red Terror in Petrograd

THE ASSASSINATION OF Moisei Uritskii on the morning of 30 August and the attempt on Lenin's life that night have usually been viewed as the direct cause of the Red Terror. Actually, undeclared Red Terror in all its forms had been under way in Moscow and other Russian cities for months. In Petrograd the practice of taking political hostages had begun in late July. Uritskii's ban on shootings had been reversed by the PCheka on 19 August (after which the shootings of the twenty-one prisoners had been carried out), and Red Terror had been all but officially declared at a plenary session of the Petrograd Soviet on 28 August. However, it is certainly true that in the former capital the murder of Uritskii, coupled with the failed attempt on Lenin's life, unleashed a wave of arrests and an orgy of politically motivated seizures of hostages and shootings by the PCheka, district security agencies, and worker and soldier bands that far exceeded anything that had come before, even in Moscow.

The fundamental aim of the Red Terror in Petrograd, in the fall of 1918, was to ensure political stability at a time when the city was being stripped of security forces. Nonetheless, responsibility for its proclamation is murky. It does not appear to have originated from the top, as has been commonly assumed. The national Sovnarkom did not issue a green light for mass terror beyond what was contained in the resolution of the Fifth All-Russian Congress of Soviets until the second of two meetings on 4 September.[1] By then, the Red Terror in Petrograd was already raging. Not until 6 September did the SK SO and an expanded plenary session of the Petrograd Soviet consider official responses to Uritskii's assassination. The SK SO reconfirmed its decree of 17 August which authorized shootings by the PCheka for various political crimes.[2] Amid the wave of arrests and shootings then cresting in Petrograd, revalidation of this decree may well have been an attempt to reassert the Cheka's control over summary executions. Simultaneously, at a plenary meeting of the Petrograd Soviet that began with eulogies of Uritskii, the deputies adopted a resolution branding "Right SRs, Mensheviks, Black

Hundred officers, priests, and kulaks" as outlaws, proclaiming martial law, and pledging to answer "White Terror by bourgeois killers with Red Terror."[3] Yet on this very day, a PCheka progress report published in the government and party press revealed that, during the *preceding* week, 512 counterrevolutionaries had already been shot. The report also included the first of several lists of individuals arrested as hostages to be executed in the event of another terrorist attack on a Bolshevik leader (120 hostages were on this list).[4] Where, then, did official authorization for a program of mass terror in Petrograd originate?

*   *   *

Less than two hours after Uritskii's assassination on 30 August, the Presidium of the Petrograd Soviet dispatched a "highly urgent" message to all district soviets, district offices of the Red Army, and stations of the Committee for the Revolutionary Security of Petrograd. Besides announcing Kanegissar's capture and identifying him as a Right SR, and implicating the British and French in Uritskii's killing, it ordered that guard posts be strengthened, barricades be erected at strategically important locations, and "all forces" be readied for battle. In the first hours after the killing of the PCheka chief, the Petrograd Soviet leadership feared that this killing might be the start of the long-expected, full-scale domestic and Allied attack on Soviet power in Petrograd. The message authorized immediate, unlimited searches and arrests of the bourgeoisie, Imperial officers, suspicious elements among students, civil servants, and the British and French.[5] Together with the PCheka's conditional authorization for shooting counterrevolutionaries that was adopted by the SK SO on 19 August, the message can be properly viewed as another major step toward the proclamation of Red Terror in Petrograd.

Upon careful examination, however, it is apparent that the initiative for implementing an official program of full-scale Red Terror in Petrograd, including mass summary executions, came from the Bolshevik Petersburg Committee. Immediately after the news of Uritskii's assassination was received, the committee convened a meeting of appropriate members of the SK SO and the party leadership that afternoon (30 August)—again in the Astoria Hotel. Significantly, this took place before the attempt on Lenin's life that evening. Elena Stasova described this gathering in her memoirs.[6] Early in the meeting Zinoviev, harking back to the party's restraint following Volodarskii's killing, demanded that, this time, "appropriate" measures be adopted without delay. Among the measures he advocated was "letting workers deal with the intelligentsia as they wished, on the street."

Stasova claims that participating "comrades" listened to Zinoviev's extreme pronouncements with "embarrassment." After she took the floor to oppose him, he stormed out of the room in a rage. Among those siding with her was Gleb Bokii, representing the PCheka.[7] Ultimately the gathering agreed to form special troikas to go to the districts to hunt down "counterrevolutionary elements." Other steps decided upon at this meeting, or shortly after it, included the immediate execution of the sizable number of political hostages already in the hands of the PCheka, and the assignment of Stasova to the PCheka's presidium to review lists of individuals to be executed. Slogans adopted at this meeting and published the next day in the name of the Bolshevik Petersburg Committee included "In response to the White Terror of Counterrevolutionaries, we respond with Red Revolutionary Terror!" "White Guardists have gone unpunished too long—the hour for settling scores has arrived!"[8]

A high percentage of PCheka arrests and shootings during the Red Terror of 1918 in Petrograd occurred during the first few days after the decision by the expanded meeting of the Petersburg Committee on 30 August. The night of 30/31 August, in the Admiralteiskii district alone, the Cheka arrested roughly forty people in raids, most of them former officers and Right SRs.[9] Contemporary newspaper reports suggest that particularly large numbers of "counterrevolutionaries" were shot the night of 31 August/1 September.[10]

Many of the initial victims had languished in prison for months. This was the case with Vasilii Mukhin, a wealthy, by all accounts unusually benevolent former landowner who, according to PCheka records, was arrested in May on hearsay evidence connected with the "Case of the Comorra for the Vengeance of the Russian People."[11] Representatives of the EAD from Petrograd who had been arrested in Moscow in mid July, during the government's raid on the regional workers' congress, were more fortunate than Mukhin. As they were still incarcerated at the start of the Red Terror, their execution seemed certain. However, the Menshevik leadership had mobilized foreign socialists in their support. The Soviet government was leery of antagonizing them further, and Riazanov, working through Sverdlov and Chicherin, was able to get several of them released into his custody.[12]

On 2 September, in the Moscow Soviet, deputy Voznesenskii, who had just returned from Petrograd, reported that five hundred "representatives of the bourgeoisie" had already been shot there.[13] If accurate, this figure represents the number of political prisoners shot by the PCheka the nights of 30/31 August and 31 August/1 September.[14] This number also accounts for all but twelve of the executions announced in the press on 6 September and more than two-thirds of the "up to" eight hundred PCheka shootings during the entire period of the Red Terror in Petrograd that Bokii reported to a Northern Commune Cheka congress in mid October.[15] The latter number also corresponds to the combined total of people shot during the Red Terror listed in comprehensive, year-end statistical tables for the PCheka and the Petrograd Province Cheka that were prepared for internal use.[16] Additionally, about five hundred out of roughly one thousand hostages were shot by the Kronstadt Cheka during the Red Terror.[17]

This said, the precise count of Red Terror victims in the Petrograd region will probably never be known, as available figures do not include executions carried out by district-level security agencies and roving worker bands, some of them loosely directed by the PCheka. In an unpublished memoir written in the late 1920s or early 1930s, S. P. Petrov described the activities of one such worker band. In 1918 Petrov, a Bolshevik, was employed in the Novyi Lessner machine-building plant. He recalled that, right after the assassinations of Volodarskii and Uritskii, he and his comrades feared that they might be the next targets of bomb-throwing SRs. "We led all workers in our plant on anti-SR demonstrations," Petrov explained. "We [also] proclaimed and carried out responses [in kind]. . . . We weren't shy then—we drowned inveterate enemies in barges off Lisyi Nos'. . . . On the evening of an operation, the guys would gather [and] I would let them know what had to be done."[18]

Such lynch justice was fed by the Petrograd party and government press, especially by *Krasnaia gazeta*. From the time of Volodarskii's slaying, it had surpassed all other Petrograd papers in the virulence of its demands for immediate "Red Terror." Thus it is not surprising that its advocacy of vengeance in the aftermath of Uritskii's killing was also more strident and lasted longer than coverage in other papers. The lead editorial in *Krasnaia gazeta* on 31 August, titled "Blood for Blood," captures the paper's tone throughout the Terror. It called on workers to steel their hearts so they would not feel pity when their enemies were slaughtered and would not waver at the sight of oceans of their blood. The editorial ended: "Let the blood of the bourgeoisie and its servants flow—more blood!"[19]

Another *Krasnaia gazeta* editorial on the first day of Red Terror in Petrograd, this one entitled "To the Wall!" drew a parallel between France during the Great Terror of 1793 and the situation prevailing in Russia. After the French people had rebelled against the power of the aristocracy, priests, and kings, victory had not come easily, contended the author of this editorial. The old order had put up stiff resistance but through superhuman effort the French had overcome all obstacles. First, the French revolutionaries decided to deal with the internal enemy, and thus proclaimed the Terror to be directed against all enemies of the revolution! Their slogan was "All aristocrats, to the lamp posts!" In the course of dealing with counterrevolutionaries, the revolution gradually strengthened itself militarily and, ultimately, the French began to defeat their external enemies. We are going through a phase that is similar to this moment in the Great French Revolution, the writer went on. And now we, too, must first conquer the internal counter-revolution. French revolutionaries carried rebellious aristocrats "to the lamp posts," they hung enemies of the people by the thousands. The Russian revolution stands its enemies against the wall and shoots them, he concluded. "To the wall with the bourgeoisie!"

To the editors of *Krasnaia gazeta*, the scale of shootings during the first days of Red Terror in Petrograd was a disappointment. Their featured opinion piece on the morning of 4 September acknowledged that executions since Uritskii's assassination and the attempt on Lenin's life were a start but no more than that. The party had not yet rid itself of criminal softness; instead of the several thousand shootings that had been promised, no more than a few hundred representatives of the bourgeoisie had actually been shot.[20]

The Red Terror in Petrograd was backed by a massive campaign aimed at bringing the workers' hostility toward domestic and foreign enemies to a boiling point, and at linking the two enemies together. During the first week of September 1918, news articles and editorials only slightly less inflammatory than those in *Krasnaia gazeta* appeared in all Petrograd newspapers. Daily rallies in factories, worker clubs, and meeting halls throughout the city, featuring the party's most prominent figures speaking on the subject "Who We Are Fighting Against," were also used to reinforce popular support for the Terror.[21]

By September 2 it was apparent that Lenin's medical condition was no longer life-threatening and that he was recovering. Nonetheless, the major Petrograd newspapers featured front-page medical bulletins detailing his condition well after that. The bulletins appeared alongside myriad resolutions from factories, labor organizations, and Red Army units expressing hope that Lenin would survive, condemning the attack on him, and demanding vengeance; essays describing Lenin's seminal importance to the Russian and international labor movements; and descriptions of Uritskii's killing, updates on the PCheka's investigation of it, and eulogies of Uritskii as the ideal party leader.

The centerpiece of the concerted effort to link domestic and foreign enemies revolved around the so-called Lockhart Plot, allegedly a joint Al-

Moura Benckendorff in 1918.
Sir Robert Hamilton Bruce
Lockhart Collection, Hoover
Institution Archives.

lied conspiracy directed by Bruce Lockhart, under way in both capitals, to overthrow Soviet power.[22] At the beginning of August a member of the VCheka leadership in Moscow, Varvara Iakovleva, had been assigned to co-ordinate the investigation of the case in Petrograd. While she was in the former capital, Lockhart, Sidney Reilly, and Colonel Henri de Verthamon, co-ordinator of the extensive French anti-Bolshevik sabotage operations and one of Reilly's chief co-conspirators, were unmasked in Moscow by Dzerzhinskii's agents, if not by Moura Benckendorff then by Colonel Eduard Berzin, commander of a Latvian rifle regiment and a Dzerzhinskii operative, who had fooled Lockhart and Reilly into believing that his men were ripe to turn against the Soviet regime. Evidence in the PCheka's hands indicated that the British Embassy in Petrograd was at the center of Allied planning to overthrow Soviet power there. In view of this, toward the end of August additional Cheka investigators were dispatched from Moscow to Petrograd, and Dzerzhinskii himself was scheduled to go there soon.[23] Lenin's first action upon learning of Uritskii's killing, as we have seen, was to send Dzerzhinskii to Petrograd.

In Soviet accounts, an assault on the British Embassy by the PCheka the evening of 31 August is pictured as a magnificently successful operation to capture participants in the Lockhart Plot—a domestic and international conspiracy against Soviet power that included the murder of Uritskii. Although British archival sources indicate that there were solid grounds for linking the embassy with domestic counterrevolutionary conspiracies, there is no evidence that the subversive activities of Lockhart and Cromie were coordinated. In a debriefing shortly afterward, Harold Trevenen Hall, a civilian SIS employee who worked closely with Cromie in Petrograd, concluded that the two undercover agents Sabir and Steckelman, who had been collaborating with Cromie in August, were agents provocateurs. He testified that, around midday on 31 August, he met with them at their request. Sabir and Steckelman maintained that the time for action had come, and they proposed a planning meeting at the nearby Hotel France as soon as possible with them and other representatives of anti-Bolshevik organizations working with Cromie.[24]

On 31 August the Red Terror was already in high gear. On the night of 30/31 August the British Consul, Arthur Woodhouse, as well Cromie's closest associate, Le Page, had been arrested. So Sabir's and Steckelmann's impatience did not arouse Hall's suspicions. It was Hall's idea to schedule the meeting later that very afternoon, and to hold it at the embassy rather than the Hotel France. If Sabir and Stecklemann had their way, the trap they were setting for Cromie and his fellow conspirators would have been sprung at the Hotel France, not the embassy. After hearing from Hall about what Sabir and Steckelmann had to say, Cromie began arranging the requested meeting. The only counterrevolutionary leader Hall mentioned by name was General Yudenich and a car was sent to fetch him.[25] Subsequently the Soviet press reported that Savinkov and Maksimilian Filonenko (a close associate of Savinkov's and one of Lockhart's counterrevolutionary contacts) were among prominent enemies of the revolution that the PCheka had expected to be at the embassy meeting.[26] Whatever the case, it turned out that Yudenich was hiding out at the Dutch Embassy, and none of Cromie's other Russian contacts except for Sabir and Steckelmann showed up at the appointed hour.[27]

Meanwhile, Dzerzhinskii had arrived in Petrograd toward evening on 31 August,[28] where he learned of the attempt to assassinate Lenin in Moscow and, presumably, of the trap set by Sabir and Steckelmann. Before hurrying back to Moscow to take charge of the emergency there, he approved the raid on the British Embassy. Semen Geller of the PCheka was assigned to lead it.[29] Participants in the early evening raid were Geller's deputy, Ia. Sheinkman; one of the investigators from Moscow, Bronislav Bortnovskii; and several other Cheka commissars and intelligence agents. In his debriefing, Hall indicated that shortly before the raid began, Sabir went downstairs to the street level of the embassy, explaining that he was going to order his "detectives to keep a sharp lookout." In retrospect, Hall assumed Sabir's purpose was to issue a go-ahead for the ensuing attack. Because the expected counterrevolutionary leaders of interest to the PCheka were absent, it may have been that Sabir tried and failed to abort it.

Minutes after Sabir returned, Geller and his comrades, pistols drawn, broke into the embassy. They were making their way toward Le Page's office on the second floor, where Cromie, Hall, Sabir, Steckelmann, and perhaps others were gathered, when shooting erupted. In the confused gun battle at close quarters that followed, a Cheka intelligence specialist, Robert Ionson, and Cromie, pistol blazing, were killed. Sheinkman and Bortnovskii were seriously wounded. Geller later admitted to having fired the shot that hit Bortnovskii.[30] Approximately forty people in the embassy at the time of the attack were arrested and led off to Gorokhovaia 2. Apart from Sabir, Steckelmann, and one Prince Shakhovskii, the captured were Russian or British embassy employees. It was payday, and most were caught in "Paymaster" Ernst Boyce's office.[31] That Sabir and Steckelmann were seized but, unlike Shakhovskii, not listed among those arrested supports Hall's retrospective conclusion that they were agents-provocateurs.

News reports in all the Petrograd newspapers during the days immediately following the incident proclaimed that compromising material gathered in the raid, combined with knowledge provided by unnamed informants, indicated that the PCheka had successfully liquidated a "grandiose conspiracy" involving domestic "party organizations and foreign agents of Anglo-French capital." The embassy attack probably was a success insofar as it linked "Anglo-French capital" to domestic conspiracies against Soviet power in the popular mind. The image of the arrested British officials as a dangerous threat was enhanced by the fact that they were held in the infamous Trubetskoi Bastion of the Fortress of Peter and Paul, in cells that had been reserved for particularly dangerous political prisoners during the tsarist era. Yet, in important ways, the raid was a failure. The most likely primary architect of the Lockhart Plot, Sidney Reilly, who actually was in Petrograd on 31 August, was not caught. Also, John Merritt, a British businessman turned clandestine agent who had worked closely with Cromie during the preceding summer, kept up the flow of money to at least some anti-Bolshevik individuals and groups he had been subsidizing. Merritt became so adept at spiriting British officials who were not swept up in the embassy raid, as well as compromised Russian contacts, across the border to Finland that he became known as a modern day "Scarlet Pimpernel."[32] Moreover, British agents,

such as Paul Dukes, soon picked up the pieces of the subversive network established by Cromie.[33] Although the British government was initially ap-
prehensive about what the documents seized in the raid might reveal, their
importance turned out to be minimized by Cromie's destruction of incriminating records and ciphers in July. From the point of view of Soviet authorities, the raid was probably disappointing and unfortunate in yet another way. It prompted the VCheka in Moscow to move prematurely on the
conspirators there.[34] Mass arrests of British and French consular personnel
in Moscow were conducted the night of 31 August/1 September. Among
those caught in this roundup were Lockhart, his mistress Moura Benckendorff
dorff (the likely Cheka informer), Captain W. L. Hicks (Lockhart's closest associate), and Xenophon Kalamatiano, head of an American espionage
ring in Russia, and many of his key Russian agents. Escaping, along with
Sidney Reilly, was de Verthamon, the leading French collaborator in Reilly's
schemes.

Lockhart and his British and French partners incarcerated in Moscow,
as well as Cromie's associates imprisoned in Petrograd, were released after
several weeks in exchange for Maxim Litvinov, the Soviet Union's future
people's commissar for foreign affairs, and his entourage. Litvinov, the Soviet government's provisional plenipotentiary to Great Britain, had been interned in London's Brixton Prison following Lockhart's arrest. Thus Kalamatiano was the lone Allied defendant present for the public "Lockhart trial,"
heard by the Supreme Revolutionary Tribunal from 28 November to 3 December 1918. Along with Kalamatiano and roughly fifteen alleged members of his spy network and five of Reilly's, Allied defendants in the case,
all tried in absentia, were Lockhart, the French Consul-General Colonel
Ferdinand Grenard, and de Verthamon.[35] None of the Petrograd-based Allied secret agents was among the accused, perhaps because the most important of them, Cromie, had been killed. Under the circumstances, dredging
up what was known about Cromie's subversive activities and trying his colleagues would only have further inflamed anti-Soviet passions in London.
Nor was any significant effort made to link anti-Soviet conspiracies in Petrograd with those in Moscow.

Among Russian defendants tried, only Colonel Aleksandr Fride, found
guilty of being Kalamatiano's chief agent, was sentenced to death and shot.
Several of Kalamatiano's operatives received relatively light prison sentences.
Try as he might, chairman of the Supreme Revolutionary Tribunal Krylenko was unable to demonstrate that Russian defendants connected to Allied agents other than Kalamatiano were more than minor figures. Charges
against some of them were dropped; other defendants were acquitted or received very light sentences. Kalamatiano was sentenced to death but the exe-

cution was delayed, and he was released in August 1921, as a condition of emergency food deliveries to Soviet Russia by the American Relief Administration. Lockhart, Reilly, Grenard, and de Verthamon were declared "enemies of labor" and "outlaws," and were to be shot if ever found on Russian territory.

The PCheka's storming of the British Embassy and the shooting of Cromie, coupled with the brutality of the Red Terror in Petrograd, triggered an international outcry. Dzerzhinskii and authorities in Petrograd tried as best they could to mute this criticism and especially its impact on workers internationally. In a radio broadcast abroad, on 2 September, they charged that Anglo-French agents and domestic counterrevolutionaries had joined together to reverse the revolution and restore the tsarist regime, which was at least partly true, and that these agents were personally and directly responsible for the murders of Volodarskii and Uritskii, and the attempted assassinations of Lenin and Zinoviev, which was not true. Significantly this accusation was not leveled at the Lockhart trial. The September broadcast, the text of which was published, had this to say about the results of the embassy raid:

> On 31 August, at 6:00 PM, our Commission for Struggle against Counterrevolution was able to catch one of the main English conspiratorial groups red-handed in the British Embassy. . . . A huge amount of correspondence was seized, which will be published. It incriminates the English conspirators completely . . . The eyewitness testimony of some of those detained has established that [Allied agents] . . . planned to arrest the Soviet of People's Commissars. . . . [In normal circumstances,] we would never have resorted to a search of a [foreign] embassy. But we cannot be silent when one is transformed into a conspiratorial headquarters for plotters and killers.[36]

The response of the British Foreign Office to these accusations, and, more generally, to the embassy raid, Cromie's death, and the arrest of its personnel in Petrograd and Moscow, was remarkably restrained, probably because the British knew that some of the charges were valid and were uneasy that hard evidence relating to these might come to light.[37] In reality, the "huge amount" of incriminating evidence supposedly seized in the British Embassy was never published, suggesting that Geller and his men came away from their raid empty-handed.

* * *

On 2 September, when the indiscriminate character and broad scope of arrests and shootings in Petrograd were already clear, local representatives of Ukraine, Poland, Georgia, and Lithuania sent a joint letter to Zinoviev asserting the unacceptablity of applying such measures to their countrymen who were then in Petrograd.[38] The response to their appeal reflected the chaotic nature of the Red Terror of 1918 in the city. Predictably large numbers of individuals from these countries, then under German occupation, were arrested. The German Consul in Petrograd reacted by bombarding Bokii with letters demanding the release of most of them on the grounds that they were under German protection.[39] Attached to each letter was a list of persons arrested since the previous letter, their nationalities, and their places of detention—all told, almost a thousand individuals.[40] On 10 September Bokii sent the German Consul the text of a message he had dispatched to district soviets ordering that they release all imprisoned citizens of nations under German protection against whom they had no specific evidence to support charges of counterrevolution or speculation. Bokii also ordered that individuals of these nations against whom specific charges could not be lodged not be arrested in the future.[41] Subsequent letters and lists from the German Consul to Bokii reveal that these orders were ignored. Arrests of citizens of nations under "German protection" continued. By the end of September, only about two hundred had been released out of the roughly one thousand prisoners identified on the German consul's lists.[42]

In mid September the Bolshevik-led Petrograd Trade Union Council became alarmed by the indiscriminate character of the Red Terror. On 14 September, "in order to avoid fatal and irreparable errors," the council appealed to Zinoviev and Bokii to institute strict controls and safeguards on shootings generally, on arrests and searches at trade union offices, and on arrests of trade union officials.[43] At the same council meeting that issued the appeal, Riazanov proposed an amendment calling for an end to outlawing entire parties and taking political hostages. However, it was defeated.[44] Ironically, during the Red Terror, even Zinoviev who, as we have seen, advocated allowing workers free reign to deal with the bourgeoisie "as they wished," became exasperated by the difficulty he encountered in getting information about PCheka prisoners. After repeated failed attempts to find out the status of this or that individual purportedly in the PCheka's hands, in a memo to Iakovleva he directed the PCheka to immediately form an "information bureau." However, evidently realizing the futility of this demand in the prevailing circumstances, he ended his message by pleading that, if nothing else, the PCheka should respond to his queries about individuals as quickly as possible.[45]

Zinoviev, as head of the SK SO and the Petrograd Soviet, seems to have been at least temporarily concerned about inadvertent arrests and shootings of Bolsheviks, Bolshevik sympathizers, or unaffiliated individuals of special importance to the government. S. P. Petrov, the Novyi Lessner plant worker who described his nocturnal forays to hunt down political enemies, recalled saving the lives of honest revolutionaries on the brink of execution.[46] Stasova, in her memoirs, indicated that there was good reason to worry about "fatal and irreparable errors." She recalled checking arrest lists and freeing those who were "accidentally" on the list. Arrests were "frequently incorrect because they were based on incidental information," she remembered. "Among those arrested were people who were sympathetic to us, who worked with us, and so forth."[47]

During these frightening days, large numbers of professionals identified as popular representatives of the bourgeoisie were arrested, among them prominent figures in theater and music.[48] Also netted were individuals of importance to Petrograd's survival, such as technical specialists in soviets and on ships of the Baltic Fleet, further crippling them,[49] and physicians, who were attempting to cope with epidemic diseases not only in the Northern Commune but nationally. The People's Commissariat for Health alerted the People's Commissariat for Internal Affairs to this problem toward the end of September, and Petrovskii, who had earlier strongly advocated the blanket roundup of hostages from among the bourgeoisie and officers,[50] hurriedly dispatched a letter to soviets around the country prohibiting the arrest of doctors and other health personnel "only because they were popular."[51] At the beginning of October Petrovskii broadened his caution, complaining that according to his data not enough had been done to assure the security of the rear, primarily because some soviets had directed Red Terror at the petty bourgeoisie and the intelligentsia generally rather than at politically influential representatives of the grande bourgeoisie and the old regime (this was plainly the case in Petrograd). Petrovskii ordered that hostage lists be reviewed with an eye to releasing prisoners unsuitable as hostages because of their low political visibility.[52]

In a speech opening the Seventh City Conference of Petrograd Bolsheviks on 17 September, Zinoviev made no such distinctions. Contradicting his earlier concern about groundless, potentially debilitating shootings, he now interpreted unwavering Red Terror as a necessary response to White Terror at a moment when, according to him, civil war in Russia was nearing its apogee. At this time the advance of the People's Army was reversed, but this success was clouded by the advances of Krasnov's Cossacks and the Volunteer Army. Pointing to areas of the country where Red Terror had already resulted in particularly large numbers of arrests and shootings, Zinoviev concluded approvingly that "if we continue at this pace, we will [significantly] reduce the bourgeois population of Russia."[53] The resolution on the "current moment" adopted by the Seventh City Conference embodied Zinoviev's new extremist bent and pointed to the connection between the Red Terror in Petrograd and the need to mobilize human resources for the front:

> The civil war in Russia is peaking. The necessity of adopting Red Terror in response to White Terror is a reflection of this fact. . . . The working class must finally implement a dictatorship of steel and settle scores with all its enemies coarsely. Security in the rear must be assured and all forces devoted to the front . . . It is essential to teach male and female workers that they are all employees of the Cheka, that all of us are participants in the great struggle with the counterrevolution [now] breathing its last.[54]

According to a late Soviet-era biography of Bokii, in mid September Zinoviev still favored issuing arms to Petrograd workers generally and giving them the go-ahead to mete out "lynch justice" at their discretion.[55] Bokii's opposition to such extremism prompted Zinoviev to replace him before the month was out. Stasova, for one, feared for his life if he remained in Petrograd without protection, to such an extent that she appealed to Sverdlov to have Bokii transferred to a government post in the safety of the Kremlin.[56]

Additional insights into Zinoviev's attitude toward Red Terror generally and to the importance of the Cheka in particular are provided by the stenographic record of a plenary session of the Petrograd Soviet on 24 September, one of the purposes of which was to mobilize workers for participation in preparations for a triumphal celebration of the first anniversary of "October." After Maria Andreeva, the well-known actress and Gorky's common law wife who was then deputy commissar for the arts in the People's Commissariat for Enlightenment, described the work of a special "Central Bureau" formed to organize the "October" celebration, a fierce argument erupted between Riazanov and Zinoviev. Riazanov had returned to Petrograd a couple of weeks earlier, after having obtained the release of several participants in the regional workers' congress who had been incarcerated in Moscow.[57] In Petrograd, he was appalled by the indiscriminate, chaotic way that Red Terror was being implemented, and he tried unsuccessfully to mobilize his colleagues in the Petrograd trade union leadership to push for changes.[58] He was also deeply disturbed by the inhuman conditions prevailing in Petrograd's wildly overcrowded prisons. In an impassioned address, he argued that the Petrograd proletariat could not celebrate "October" as a holiday of joy, as Andreeva had proposed, unless the red banners to be carried that day were free of the blood stains of guiltless proletarians. Riazanov expressed the opinion that Petrograd authorities had to form a commission to help the PCheka liberate all innocent victims of the Red Terror during the coming month in order to create the "psychological prerequisite" for the holiday—in his words "so that on 25 October [o.s.] we can declare with clean hearts, honor, and enthusiasm that only those whose individual guilt can be established are still suffering in our jails."[59]

Surely Andreeva was sympathetic to Riazanov's plea. She herself had lobbied for the release of innocent theatrical performers caught up in the Terror.[60] Indeed, most of Riazanov's listeners responded to his ideas with applause—until Zinoviev indignantly attacked him. According to Zinoviev, if anything critical was to be said about the revolution, it was that it was too "soft and fainthearted." He was particularly offended by Riazanov's implicit criticism of the Cheka. Only our finest are sent to the Cheka, he averred, and their work is the most difficult that we have to assign, because imprisoning even enemies is stressful and agonizing. "Honor and glory to comrades who carry this burden!" he thundered. "We have arrested representatives of the bourgeoisie, not proletarians, and Comrade Riazanov knows it," he added. Immediately contradicting himself, however, Zinoviev suggested that if workers followed such "bandits" as Right SRs, the revolution had no choice but to make war on them. "Long Live Red Terror," he declaimed. Riazanov's efforts to respond were drowned out by a wave of catcalls directed toward him and stormy applause for Zinoviev.[61]

* * *

At the Seventh Conference of Petrograd Bolsheviks held on 17–21 September, the drastic decline in local Bolshevik party membership that had been a major impetus to the launching of the Red Terror was starkly revealed. Just since the previous city conference in June, it had dropped by nearly 50 percent, from 13,472 to 6,000. This figure amounted to less than 2 percent of organized factory workers in the city.[62] Declining membership was not the only problem the party faced. A detailed questionnaire that the Petersburg Committee circulated to its members at the end of August reveals the dramatic change in the complexion and competence of the local party. The Petersburg Committee received 3,559 responses to its questionnaire, or better than 60 percent of those sent. Tabulated by the leading Soviet economist and statistician Stanislav Strumilin, the questionnaires provide a valuable picture of the Petrograd party organization in the fall of 1918. They reveal, for example, that 40 percent of the current members had joined the party after the October revolution (1,419 respondents), indeed that the vast majority of these green "October" Bolsheviks had come into the party during the preceding eight months.[63] Clearly, then, mobilization of experienced Bolsheviks for positions in the Red Army and food procurement detachments, following earlier outflows, had drastically altered the proportion of party veterans to newcomers to the detriment of the party organization.[64] Soviet officials, from Zinoviev down, continually repeated the refrain first articulated in June, that new recruits included many corrupt profiteers who belonged in jail.[65] The deterioration of the party organization in Petrograd explains why, at this point, responsible members of district party committees were forced to devote significant portions of their time to weeding out rotten apples, often through party trials; why the Petersburg Committee now systematized such proceedings and also developed an appeals process for them;[66] and why, despite critical shortages of cadres, rules for membership were tightened.

A second trend that emerges from Strumilin's tabulations is the high percentage of Petrograd Bolsheviks working full-time in Petrograd soviets, municipal agencies, educational or other cultural bodies, trade unions, cooperatives, the Red Army, and domestic security agencies compared to those working in party organizations (58 percent, or 2,071 of 3,559).[67] Indeed, even these figures do not give a true picture of the party's declining fortunes inasmuch as only a small proportion of those still working in party organizations were qualified to hold responsible positions. For one thing, a high proportion of university-educated Bolsheviks took advantage of opportunities to move to Moscow in mid March or soon after. The result was that only 87 of the 3,559 respondents had university degrees or some form of higher education.[68] It is likely that a high proportion of this group were not engaged in party work.

Nor were the Bolsheviks successful in recruiting Petrograd women into the party. Despite initiatives to attract female workers such as *Krasnaia gazeta*'s weekly "Rabotnitsa" columns and the efforts of women's sections now attached to the Petersburg Committee and district party committees, less than 10 percent of the Petrograd Bolshevik membership, or roughly 700 members, were women. Of this already small percentage of women, only 7 percent, or around fifty, were factory workers, this at a time when 39 percent of Petrograd's employed factory workers were women (44,629 of 113,346 employed workers).[69] Strumilin attributed this low percentage of female worker–Bolsheviks to the fact that factory women "belonged to relatively backward elements of the worker masses, culturally and politically, that were primarily prevalent among textile workers, workers in tobacco and candy factories, house maids, and the like."[70]

To help compensate for the dearth of a critical mass of personnel serving in party organizations, the Seventh City Conference elected to follow Moscow's lead and create a special category of Bolshevik "sympathizers": factory workers who would actively support the party, especially in times of crisis, but who would not be subject to the admission requirements, often burdensome responsibilities, and susceptibility to mandatory transfer out of Petrograd of full-fledged party members.[71] It also resolved to press all "responsible" Bolsheviks in nonparty agencies to become involved in some form of active party work. Reflecting this emphasis on obligatory party work for everyone, the chief slogan of the day, "No Party Members without Party Responsibilities!" was substituted for the milder "Strengthen Party Work!" that had been adopted at the Sixth City Conference of Petrograd Bolsheviks.

In spite of the weaknesses of party organizations compared to soviets, as well as the often contentious relations between them, the Seventh Conference's resolution on the work of the Petersburg Committee emphasized the need to strengthen control of the Petrograd Soviet and its agencies. By extension, it was deemed equally important for party committees to exert control over soviets at the district level.[72] The enhanced importance of the policy setting role of party organizations in local government was reflected in the fact that now, for the first time, Zinoviev, who headed the government in Petrograd, became a member of the Petersburg Party Committee.[73] That for some time he continued to direct city and regional government as though the Petersburg Committee did not exist testifies to the difficulties party committees continued to encounter in imposing controls over soviets.

Participants in the Seventh City Conference of Petrograd Bolsheviks enacted another, notable organizational change. In February the Fourth City Conference of Petrograd Bolsheviks had created the broadly representative "Delegates Soviet" which was to be the most authoritative party body for the city of Petrograd. The Delegates Soviet was supposed to counterbalance a diminished Petersburg Committee. Because of the limited availability of experienced leaders for party work, the Petersburg Committee had been reduced from forty or more representatives elected by district committees to nine members picked at large. In practice, however, the Delegates Soviet did not replace the Petersburg Committee as the party's top local leadership body. Never more than a sounding board, it was rarely convened and, even so, its meetings were poorly attended, especially during the late spring and early summer, as the shortage of local party veterans became progressively more acute. In fact, virtually from the start, the Assembly of Organizers, although not even mentioned in the party's statutes, played a more important practical role than the Delegates Soviet in the Petrograd party organization. The Assembly of Organizers, an appointive body, developed into the chief citywide conduit through which the Petersburg Committee learned about problems facing the districts and its primary forum for discussion and dissemination of new organizational policies. The Delegates Soviet seems to have met for the last time on 6 July.[74] It was formally abolished by the Seventh Conference of Petrograd Bolsheviks in September.[75] In this haphazard way, the drastic shortage of experienced cadres led to the failure of the effort by the Fourth City Conference of Petrograd Bolsheviks to retain the party organization's relatively democratic operation.[76]

*   *   *

During the Red Terror, the powers of the Cheka were inevitably enhanced. To be sure, in Moscow Bolshevik leaders such as Mikhail Ol'minskii, an editor of *Sotsial demokrat* and a member of the Bolshevik Moscow Committee, publicly attacked the Cheka for the indiscriminate manner in which the terror was conducted, for its lack of accountability, and for its exalted pretensions vis-à-vis other soviet institutions. Ol'minskii took special aim at the VCheka's official periodical, *Ezhenedel'nik chrezvychainykh komissii po bor'be s kontr-revoliutsiei i spekulatstii* (*Cheka Weekly*), which glorified chekas and their excesses throughout Russia.[77] His salvo was the tip of a bitter intra-party debate over the operations of chekas during the terror. Although the *Cheka Weekly* was shut down at the end of October after only six issues were published, this was less the result of criticism by moderates such as Ol'minskii than because its extreme fanaticism was unacceptable even for Lenin. For practical purposes, the VCheka emerged from the attacks against it essentially unscathed precisely because of the support of Lenin, Trotsky, and a majority of the party Central Committee in Moscow, and of Zinoviev and the Bolshevik Petersburg Committee in Petrograd.

Beginning a few days after Uritskii's killing and the attempt on Lenin's life, the leadership of the VCheka had made use of the prevailing crisis atmosphere to speed up formation of identically structured local chekas responsible for combating counterrevolution and speculation throughout the country. One of the main purposes of the *Cheka Weekly* was to propagate the ideas and methods promoted by the VCheka so that, in the words of its opening issue, chekas everywhere in the country would conduct their work of liquidating the "ideologues, organizers, and leaders of hostile classes in an identical, well planned, and methodical manner."[78]

In this spirit, the purpose of a mid-October congress of Cheka representatives from the Northern Commune was to develop a common plan of work and establish effective communications and relationships among them, and also assess the results of the Red Terror. The Cheka congress of the Northern Commune opened in Smolny on 15 October with seventy-two delegates representing all eight provinces. It began with local reports revealing that most district and even province chekas had been created by party committees after the events of late August, not so much in response to instructions from above than as a means of implementing Red Terror on the ground. Judging by these reports, many district and province chekas, some of them working in tandem with Committees of the Village Poor, had arrested significant numbers of hostages. A few chekas had already conducted shootings, but most of those that had pronounced death sentences were waiting for sanction from the center before carrying them out.[79]

Bokii, by now no longer head of the PCheka, summarized its work during the preceding seven months. He announced that the PCheka had made a total of 6,229 arrests. Between 15 August and 15 October the PCheka had begun to process 1,101 cases of counterrevolution, of which 364 were completed, and during the Red Terror, it had shot as many as 800 prisoners. Presumably those executed included the 512 Bokii announced in the press on 6 September and an additional 288 or so shot between 6 September and 15 October.[80]

Zinoviev was the keynote speaker for the congress's discussion of the role of chekas in the prevailing situation. Concerning domestic issues, his long address adhered closely to his speech at the recent Seventh City Conference of Petrograd Bolsheviks and his rebuttal to Riazanov's plea for the liberation of innocent hostages before the first anniversary of the October revolution in the Petrograd Soviet. After first praising the Cheka as the "vanguard of worker collectives recruited to defend the revolution," he warned that "although the bourgeoisie had been badly beaten and reduced, and here and there even liquidated, it could recover." The rebellion of the Second Fleet Detachment three days earlier (about which more is said below) demonstrated that the revolution was still threatened and that only the Communist party could be tolerated. Lauding Red Terror as it had been implemented in Petrograd, he cautioned against any slackening of the squeeze on political opposition. Toward the close of his speech, he criticized "objectionable discussions within the Cheka about who was supreme." The Cheka, like the Red Army, was an arm of the Bolshevik party and discussions about seniority ignored the principle of internal discipline that was its foundation.[81]

Not long after Zinoviev finished, a debate erupted at the congress over the seniority question or, more precisely, over the hotly contested structural issue of whether local chekas would be responsible to the Cheka hierarchy or to administrative sections of corresponding soviets. The issue had first become the focus of controversy in the late spring and summer, when a network of regional and local chekas accountable solely to the VCheka began to emerge, and as the VCheka's pretensions vis-à-vis all other government institutions escalated. The response of local soviets to these pretensions had come at the First Congress of Representatives of Province Soviets and Chairs of Province [Soviet] Administrative Sections, which was convened in Moscow by the People's Commissariat for Internal Affairs at the end of July. Attended by fifty-nine delegates, all of them Bolsheviks, the congress firmly and unanimously rejected Cheka autonomy. In a resolution, "On Chekas," delegates declared that the unification of administration was the primary organizational task of local government, and that the previous practice of isolation and separatism on the part of chekas, which had led to constant tensions and conflicts with the otherwise unified elements of local administration, had demonstrated that the situation was abnormal. Therefore, it was essential to restructure local chekas into subsections of the administrative sections of corresponding local soviets.[82]

Coincidentally, a congress of administrative-section representatives from soviets in the Northern Commune was meeting in Petrograd at the time of the regional Cheka congress. The congress of administrative sections' representatives was chaired by Sarra Ravich, Uritskii's replacement as commissar for internal affairs in the SK SO, who happened to be a strong supporter of Cheka independence. However, her position on the issue was not shared by most congress delegates. On 17 October, just before a scheduled discussion of the organizational status of local chekas that appeared certain to end in the endorsement of the plan to make chekas subordinate agencies of soviets, she announced that the Cheka conference "had agreed" to discuss the issue together.[83] At a joint meeting, after lengthy, often acrimonious debate, the views of administrative-section representatives seeking to rein in chekas were overwhelmed by the arguments of PCheka representatives, strongly supported by Ravich and her staff, who emphasized that the Cheka needed autonomy in the life-and-death struggle for survival in which Soviet power was then engaged. The resolution adopted by the joint meeting specified that, structurally, local chekas should be sections of local soviets, "responsible to them for political direction." For practical purposes, however, this stipulation was canceled out by the significantly more important provision that in their "internal operation" chekas were to be "absolutely autonomous and directly [and solely] responsible to the next highest authority [in the cheka chain of command]."[84]

At the same the time that the PCheka was establishing cheka autonomy vis-à-vis soviets, it successfully overcame local party efforts to bring it under its wing. As in the case of the Petrograd Soviet and district soviets, this effort had intensified in the wake of the Sixth Conference of Petrograd Bolsheviks in June.[85] At the end of July some forty-five Bolsheviks in the PCheka organized themselves into a collective headed by an activist leadership Bureau, which aspired to a meaningful voice in all matters involving the PCheka. This corresponded to the principle then being promoted by the top party leadership that by working through subordinate Bolshevik fractions in soviets, and collectives in other government agencies, party committees should assert systematic oversight on policy-making and strict party discipline in them. However, Uritskii would have none of that. He interpreted the collective's aspirations as an expression of lack of confidence in the PCheka's leadership.[86]

During negotiations that dragged on into the fall, and acrimonious charges and countercharges, the PCheka collective scaled down its ambitions, agreeing to stay out of operational matters and limiting its role to internal personnel issues, including key appointments and the protection of employee rights. However, even this was unacceptable. The PCheka Presidium insisted that the collective confine itself to such mundane, purely internal party matters as confirming new party members, collecting dues, distributing Bolshevik literature, and arranging lectures. Following this dismissal, the PCheka collective, reluctant to consider a strike against the PCheka leadership, backed away from a decisive confrontation and elected to present its case to the Petersburg Committee and request its formal recognition before proceeding further.[87] At least for now, the powers of the PCheka's leadership remained intact.

* * *

The Red Terror in Petrograd was unleashed to eliminate subversive political opposition in the former capital, but in this respect its effect was limited. Domestic conspiracies against the government continued during the last quarter of 1918. A case in point was the failed rebellion of the Petrograd-based Second Baltic Fleet Detachment, a reflection of the Petrograd Left SRs' rejuvenated political opposition, and of the alienation from Bolshevik rule of demobilized sailors, recalled to service following the Red Army's setbacks in the south and on the Volga. Their failed insurrection foreshadowed the Kronstadt revolt of March 1921.

With the demobilization of the old Russian navy and the creation of a new "Red Navy," service in the fleet had become voluntary and contractual. At that point, tens of thousands of sailors drafted into the tsarist navy during the war took the opportunity to return home, either to factory jobs in the cities or to the countryside. This process was intensified in May 1918, when the destruction of much of the huge Russian Black Sea Fleet resulted in an intensified flow of naval personnel into civilian life. However, the voluntary principle governing naval service proved unworkable largely because a high percentage of technically qualified, veteran sailors loyal to the revolution were transferred to civil war fronts and because many experienced specialists were unwilling to serve for the low pay specified in contracts. This left less-qualified newcomers in their places, and by the summer of 1918 the Baltic Fleet, for one, suffered an acute shortage of capable specialists without whom ships could not operate. At that time, its ships were interned in Kronstadt, outside Petrograd, or along the Neva. This being the case, the recall of experienced sailors for the Baltic Fleet was less an attempt to overcome personnel shortages aboard ships than a way of generating a pool of veterans from which troops desperately needed for service on civil war fronts could be drawn. Only individual mobilized sailors with specifically required skills were to receive shipboard assignments.[88]

In September 1918 demobilized sailors conscripted in 1915, 1916, and 1917 were recalled. Authorities in Moscow and Petrograd were divided as to how they should be deployed. Moscow wanted to assign them directly to the Red Army, whereas proprietary naval authorities in Petrograd were determined to organize them into units under their control. Since these were naval personnel, Baltic Fleet commissars viewed them as replacements for naval units already at the front.[89] The naval authorities prevailed. Upon recall, thousands of these newly mobilized sailors were sent to Petrograd and Kronstadt for orientation and dispatch to the front. As a Baltic Fleet commissar acknowledged at the time, "Our hope was that in each sailor there existed a revolutionary spark which we would always be able to fire up."[90]

It quickly became apparent that Moscow's expectations regarding the military value of mobilized sailors and the hopes of Baltic Fleet commissars for them were equally unrealistic. In retrospect, it is difficult to see how it could have been otherwise. Many of the mobilized sailors came from rural villages where Left SR influence still predominated. During the preceding summer they had witnessed the horrors imposed on the peasantry by armed, Bolshevik-led grain procurement detachments and Committees of the Village Poor. Other sailors came from industrial centers, where they had found their factories shut down and had observed the misery inflicted on workers by unemployment, hunger, and epidemic disease.

Moreover, arrangements for the settlement of mobilized sailors were chaotic. The number of sailors who showed up was double the number expected (ten thousand rather than five or six thousand).[91] Because it was immediately clear that it would be politically unwise to settle them onboard ships, where their antagonism to the Bolsheviks could most easily be spread to existing skeleton crews (and, furthermore, where hostility of mobilized veterans toward fledgling volunteers was likely to cause friction), many were assigned to barracks and make-shift housing in Kronstadt and Petrograd. Very quickly every facility of this kind was overwhelmed. Living conditions in all of them were uniformly horrid—none more so than in the ramshackle barracks of the Second Baltic Fleet Detachment, where a few thousand mobilized sailors were settled. The barracks were filthy, gloomy, and terribly overcrowded. Windows were broken and doors did not have locks. Toilets were ghastly. Asphalt floors in the barracks were covered with sticky mud; they were not swept, let alone washed. Excrement festered in corners. Bunks were old, with iron springs, many of them broken. A majority of bunks had nothing on them—no mattresses, blankets, or pillows. There were no bowls, tea kettles, or mugs. The sailors ate from common slop buckets, of which there was a shortage. Some water pipes were broken. There was neither soap nor linen, the sailors lacked uniforms, and more than half did not have shoes.[92]

It is not surprising, then, that newly mobilized sailors were ripe for rebellion. At a gathering of the Petersburg Committee, on 26 September, Zinoviev voiced alarm about mobilized sailors—about the "intolerable" conditions in their barracks and the urgency of political work among them.[93] A week and a half later, the Bolshevik-dominated Executive Committee of the Kronstadt Soviet took note of "anti-Soviet attitudes" among a majority of mobilized sailors, blamed them on "undesirable and dangerous elements," and resolved to take steps to eliminate them.[94] But neither the absence of party work nor the presence of undesirables was at the root of the problems among mobilized sailors, and, in any case, nothing was done about either one. And so the sailors gravitated more closely to the Left SRs, whose influence among them was strong from the start, and who demonstrated interest in their plight. Political resolutions adopted by the mobilized sailors of the Second Baltic Fleet Detachment prior to their rebellion reflected natural synergy between them and the Left SRs.

Initial signs of political unrest among mobilized sailors were observed in Kronstadt.[95] The first mass protest meeting of mobilized sailors in the Second Baltic Fleet detachment quartered in Petrograd took place on 4 October, not long after most of them had arrived. The resolutions passed at this meeting, by unanimous vote, blended personal concerns with positions on broader issues propagated by the Military Naval Organization attached to the Left SR Petrograd Committee.[96] Concern about personal safety and survival was reflected in resolutions stipulating that all companies of the detachment should be armed (subsequently, the detachment was only able to secure some revolvers). All issues related to food supply, and its improvement, were to be entrusted to an elected committee, and the sailors were to get uniforms without delay. Broader concerns were reflected in two resolutions: one to rid the fleet of all incompetent volunteers and replace them with qualified mobilized personnel[97] and a second to undertake the release of sailors unjustly imprisoned by the Bolsheviks.[98]

Petrograd authorities were well aware of the hostility toward them of the mobilized sailors, especially those from the former Black Sea Fleet, but they were helpless to improve the sailors' material situation. They concluded that severe repression was required to establish order among the sailors but were loathe to take repressive action without justification. In the words of Ivan Flerovskii, the chief Baltic Fleet commissar who had been one of the leading proponents of stationing mobilized sailors in Petrograd, "serious repression requires a serious excuse."[99] And so security units were readied for action against the mobilized sailors—at the appropriate moment.

During the second week of October a newly arrived former Black Sea Fleet sailor, Yakov Shashkov, emerged as a leader of disgruntled mobilized sailors in the Second Fleet Detachment. Shashkov was a Left SR activist. Around the same time (no later than 12 October) the Left SR military-naval organization issued a fiery revolutionary appeal to the sailors. Although every phrase of the appeal was a condemnation of Bolshevik practice and a call to sailors to assume the role of revolutionary vanguard they had played in 1917, tactically its emphasis was less on immediate action than on steadfastness, organization, and self-discipline.[100] But, by then, the sailors were holding daily rallies, each more incendiary than the last.

The final straw for the detachment appears to have been attempts by Flerovskii and Il'ya Fruntov, his deputy, to pacify the unit at a rally on 13 October. The sailors shouted down Flerovskii. They were even rougher with Fruntov, pulling him off the speakers' platform and screaming "get rid of them, damn it!" glaring at both him and Flerovskii.[101] Before dispersing, they selected representatives to go to Kronstadt to win support for revolutionary action, but Bolshevik authorities there prevented them from entering the naval base. At another mass rally that evening Shashkov, acknowledged as a powerful orator even by Bolsheviks, electrified the sailors with a fierce condemnation of Bolshevik rule and the demand for a return to government by liberated, democratic soviets—that is, 1917-type soviets, free of domination by one party. The sailors adopted a resolution by acclamation that testifies better than anything else to their rejection of Bolshevik practice, as well as to the influence of Left SRs on their behavior:

We demand the immediate nullification of the Brest treaty, which has shamed the revolutionary people. We demand rejection of payments [to the Germans] . . . [H]aving just returned from fields [*poluga*] and work benches, we cannot remain silent about the moans of toiling people everywhere suffering under the weight of arbitrary rule and the violence of hired bureaucrats–commissars. We ourselves have experienced the breakup and arrest of congresses of worker and peasant soviets. We have witnessed the beating and shooting of often innocent workers, peasants, and sailors. . . .

We demand the reestablishment of genuine Soviet power! . . .

Down with the Brest noose!

Long live the International Socialist Revolution![102]

The PCheka subsequently charged that this resolution was drafted and reproduced on a duplicating machine in Petrograd Left SR headquarters.[103]

The next day, October 14, the mobilized sailors were still defiant at another mass rally, where they demonstrated their independence by electing one among themselves, Georgii Shanin, to replace Flerovskii's appointee, Avgust Kulberg, as their commissar. They also picked a staff to assist Shanin. In an Order No. 1, announcing these changes, Shanin annulled all orders of Bolshevik commissars as of noon that day (14 October). A follow-up, Order No. 2, closed the detachment's premises to anyone without permission from the new authorities.[104]

After taking these steps the sailors, many armed with revolvers, marched to the nearby parade ground of the First Naval Coastal Detachment, They staged a protest rally there and, in company with an unspecified number of sailors from that unit, marched to the square in front of the Mariinskii Theater and held another rally. By then it was 7:00 PM. Several sailors led by Shashkov entered the theater, stopped a performance of Wagner's opera *Die Walkyrie* in the middle of the first act, and commandeered the brass section of the orchestra. Accompanied by their new marching band and shouting anti-Bolshevik slogans, they set off for the nearby Neva quay to try to persuade crews of naval vessels anchored there to join them.

Simultaneously Flerovskii tried to round up forces on these same vessels to suppress the increasingly embarrassing and potentially threatening rebellion of the Second Baltic Fleet Detachment.[105] Riding in an automobile along an embankment, he suddenly found his way blocked by the marchers. He was immediately recognized, pulled out of the car, and forced to accompany them. According to Flerovskii, Shashkov then led the demonstrators toward Nevskii Prospekt, the main stage for countless political demonstrations in 1917. When Flerovskii tried to break away, he was severely beaten. Indeed, it appears that only a chance rifle shot in the distance, which prompted the mobilized sailors to scatter, saved him from being torn limb from limb. In the ensuing confusion, he managed to escape.[106]

The rebellion of the Second Fleet Detachment ended a few hours later, when the mobilized sailors, tired and frustrated by their largely unsuccessful efforts to attract support from ships' crews, straggled back to their barracks. While they rested, Shashkov went in search of rifles. A truck in which he was riding was soon stopped, and he was arrested.[107] The barracks of the Second Fleet Detachment were surrounded by security forces, and roughly fifty members of the unit were arrested.[108] Efforts by the Petrograd and Northern Oblast Left SR committees to stimulate popular support for them were unsuccessful.[109]

Meanwhile, Zinoviev viewed the failed rebellion as an excellent opportunity to rid Petrograd of Left SRs, once and for all. As he expressed it in a report on the abortive insurrection to an emergency meeting of the Petrograd Soviet on 15 October, "The Petrograd proletariat must finally hammer the last stake into the heart of the White Guardist party of Kamkov." Much of this meeting was devoted to denouncing the rebellion of the Second Baltic Fleet Detachment, after which the deputies passed a resolution condemning it as the work of a "shady gang of Left SR intriguers and conscious agents of Anglo-French capital," "a pathetic copy of the July uprising of Left SRs in Moscow."[110] Thus the resolution further criminalized the Left SRs.

In this same spirit, the Executive Committee of the Petrograd Soviet centralized suppression of similar counterrevolutionary outbursts in the future and authorized "the most decisive measures to combat the Left SRs, including liquidation of their organizations in the districts."[111] Concurrently the Presidium of the Petrograd Soviet appointed an emergency commission to inspect the barracks of the Second Fleet Detachment. The intolerable living conditions recorded in the commission's report of October 18, as described above, underscored the legitimacy of some of the mobilized sailors' most serious personal grievances. On 21 October Fruntov cabled the People's Commissariat for Military Affairs in Moscow to halt the shipment of mobilized sailors to Petrograd.[112]

On 15 October the PCheka raided Petrograd Left SR headquarters, ransacked files there, and arrested nine party members on the premises.[113] During the next few days the PCheka interrogated all those arrested in the case, and, on 21 October, recommended to the PCheka Presidium that thirteen leaders of the rebellion, two of whom were not yet in custody and six of whom were Left SRs, be shot and that the rest be freed.[114] The Presidium endorsed the recommendation the next day, and that night the eleven condemned sailors in the PCheka's hands were marched to the Fortress of Peter and Paul and shot.[115]

Following the rebellion, the Petrograd Soviet initiated a program, mandatory for members of the Second Fleet Detachment, to indoctrinate Baltic Fleet sailors with a better understanding of their revolutionary duty.[116] Naval commissars addressed mass meetings of ships' crews that inevitably ended with the passage of resolutions condemning the rebellion of the Second Baltic Fleet Detachment and pledging loyalty to Soviet power in its existing form. The resolutions were duly published in the Petrograd press.[117] The shooting of the eleven prisoners deemed guilty of leading the rebellion of the Second Fleet Detachment on the night of 22/23 October was not made public for a week.[118] Significantly, the day after the shootings were announced, the crew of the battleship *Petropavlovsk,* whose condemnation of the mobilized sailors' rebellion had been among those published in its immediate aftermath,[119] boldly protested what it termed the "brutal massacre . . . of genuine proletarians who, because of genuine, truly terrible hunger, participated in nothing more than a hunger riot which was later dubbed an anti-Soviet insurrection." The protest of the *Petropavlovsk* sailors was not published. Forwarded to the PCheka for action, it was preserved in the case file on the rebellion.[120]

*   *   *

The initiation of the Red Terror by the Bolshevik Petersburg Committee marked a major enhancement of its role in Petrograd government. The committee's attraction to mass terror was rooted in its radicalism during the October revolution and in genuine anxiety about losing out, at a time of extreme organizational weakness, to the domestic counterrevolution supported by Allied agents. In the aftermath of Uritskii's assassination and the failed attempt on Lenin's life, *Krasnaia gazeta*'s rallying cry, "Blood for Blood," captured the sentiments of the Bolshevik Petersburg Committee as well as those of the young firebrands in the PCheka and such party zealots on the shop floor as S. P. Petrov. That the Red Terror in Petrograd exploded with greater fury, expanded more quickly, and was ultimately more chaotic than in Moscow and other urban centers was partly due to Zinoviev's violent reaction to Uritskii's assassination and, ironically, also to the impatience of a segment of Petrograd workers to settle scores with their perceived enemies that had been building during Uritskii's tenure as head of the PCheka.

14

Celebrating "The Greatest Event in the History of the World"

AGAINST THE BACKDROP of the Red Terror in Petrograd, Bolsheviks in the former capital were preparing to celebrate the first anniversary of the October revolution. The history of the organization and staging of this premier Soviet holiday sheds light on broader political and social issues confronting the Petrograd Bolsheviks and Soviet power a year after "October." These issues include the redefinition of Petrograd's identity from the perspective of Petrograd Bolsheviks, the relationship between Petrograd and Moscow, the institutional locus and structure of power and authority, and the extent of popular support for Soviet power in the Petrograd region.

Considering the previous months of continuing crises, in the fall of 1918 Petrograd workers could still legitimately ask, as many had on the eve of May Day, "What do we have to celebrate?" Nonetheless, many Petrograd Bolsheviks saw ample reasons to rejoice as the anniversary approached. In west central Russia, the advance of the Czechs and Whites had been reversed. Kazan had been recaptured on 10 September. Most important, German forces in Western Europe were in full retreat. In October and early November, the German war effort collapsed completely, the Habsburg Empire disintegrated, and democratic revolutions toppled the old order in Central Europe. Although Lenin was deeply troubled by the possibility that the Entente powers would unite with defeated Germany and attempt to stamp out the threat to capitalism posed by Bolshevism in Russia, his reading of the significantly enhanced threat to the survival of Soviet power caused by Germany's impending defeat was taken with a grain of salt by leading Petrograd Bolsheviks.

"What we are seeing now exceeds our loftiest expectations," gushed the popular Bolshevik Petersburg Committee member Moisei Kharitonov at a plenary meeting of the First City District Soviet in mid September. "Just recall that last October the fondest dream of almost all of us was to somehow survive until the Constituent Assembly. . . . At that time, very few of us agreed with Lenin's confidence in the permanence of Soviet power. Now it is an accomplished fact." At a meeting of the same district soviet a month later, Ivan Pashkevich, a highly educated former member of the German Social Democratic Party,[1] speaking on behalf of the soviet's leadership, dismissed both foreign and domestic threats out of hand. "Recently, events have been developing with the speed of a moving picture," he observed. "Each new day brings more news than one could previously expect in a year, and that which recently seemed out of reach is now achieved easily and quickly. We are gradually growing accustomed to considering our situation stable." To hear Pashkevich tell it, the Czechs were retreating in panic. Once German forces left the Don region and Ukraine, those areas would quickly come under Soviet control. Whatever meager [new] interventionist forces the Allies might muster would quickly become as demoralized as were the Allied units then in North Russia. Dismissing Lenin's concerns, Pashkevich insisted that "fear of [further] foreign intervention is unjustified."[2]

In the fall of 1918, euphoria over revolutionary triumphs on the Volga and in Central Europe was reflected in the Petrograd press, in reports and resolutions at Petrograd Soviet meetings,[3] as well as in speeches by Petrograd Bolshevik leaders at weekly Sunday rallies[4] and in the proceedings of the Seventh City Conference of Petrograd Bolsheviks and the First Petrograd Province Bolshevik Conference (7–11 October).[5] To be sure, in these forums Petrograd Bolshevik leaders echoed Lenin's call for continued sacrifice and the building of a three-million-man army. But, in contrast to Lenin, they considered a huge military buildup, universal military training, and the like, necessary not so much to defend Soviet Russia from White forces and an inevitable attack by a coalition of imperialist powers as to prepare for the Red Army's role in bringing about the triumph of socialist revolutions in Central Europe. They drew strength from the fact that Soviet power in Russia had survived for a full year (significantly longer than the legendary Paris Commune), and from the firm belief that they were the vanguard at the dawn of the global socialist millennium. This, in broadest outline, was the mood among Petrograd Bolsheviks as they prepared for a grand festival to mark what the future prominent Soviet historian Vadim Bystranskii referred to at the time as "the greatest event in the history of the world."[6]

* * *

Early planning for the October holiday in Petrograd was begun by the Commissariat for Enlightenment of the SK SO, in August 1918.[7] At the beginning of September, the leadership of the Petrograd Soviet assumed direction of holiday preparations. Despite steps taken to enhance the political power of party organs vis-à-vis soviets, the party's enduring weakness insured that the Petrograd Soviet would need to take the lead in organizing a massive oblast-wide celebration to do justice to the seminal, global significance of the October revolution and to Petrograd as its source. The Bolshevik Petersburg Committee does not appear to have played a particularly significant role in organizing the holiday, and district party committees mostly coordinated their own participation in holiday events.

A ten-member Central Bureau for Organization of the October Festivities, the ad hoc agency designated to direct arrangements for the holiday, was formed at a conference convened by the Presidium of the Petrograd Soviet on 15 September.[8] Initially headed by Maria Andreeva and later by Naum Antselovich, a trade union leader and member of the Executive Committee of the Petrograd Soviet, the Central Bureau reported to the Presidium of the Petrograd Soviet. It was empowered to issue mandatory decrees and requisition supplies at will, and each of its nearly dozen sections had similar authority. The authority of the Central Bureau was strongly buttressed by the fact that its multi-million-ruble budget, extraordinarily large for the time, was intended to provide not only for its own expenditures but for district soviet holiday commissions which had few other funding sources. This top-down administrative structure, which conformed to the centralized institutional models that Moscow had pressed on national, regional, and local governments for months with only marginal success, gave the Central Bureau control over spending on most activities connected with the holiday.

During the second half of September, the Central Bureau developed its internal structure and hired personnel, forming separate, largely autonomous sections for arts and decoration, theater, music, cinema, construction, economic matters, route of march, lighting, and auto transport. It also established a "front section" to deliver gifts and entertainment to Red Army troops on the northwestern fronts during the holiday. The preliminary design for the grand holiday in Petrograd was developed by the Central Bureau at meetings on 17 and 19 September. The commemoration was initially envisioned as a day-long memorial to fallen revolutionary heroes and a celebration of "October." A. F. Oksiuz, secretary of the Central Bureau, was delegated to prepare a report on the character and organization of the holiday, as a basis for launching arrangements for it.[9] The Central Bureau's meeting on the nineteenth was chaired by Lunacharskii himself. At the beginning of the meeting Oksiuz summarized his report. The holiday's start would be signaled by a salute from cannons at the Fortress of Peter and Paul. Later, celebrants would assemble in their districts and proceed to the Field of Mars in a "carnivalesque manner." Mobile side shows along the way would foster the desired gaiety. The separate processions would meet at the communal graves of fallen revolutionary heroes, which would be decorated with palm fronds. There the columns of marchers would be met by a "mighty" state orchestra playing the *Internationale*. Platforms would be erected alongside the graves from which orators would address the crowds. At dusk, the columns would reassemble for a torchlight parade through the city. All Petrograd would be ablaze with fire and lights. At set intervals, spectacular fireworks would be set off from rooftops. Simultaneously, revelers would be entertained by a variety of nighttime spectacles. All theaters would be open and would stage free plays and concerts throughout the night.[10]

Lunacharskii suggested dividing the festival into three distinct parts and enhancing the joyous atmosphere by "creating nonstop noise by youth equipped with whistles, rattles, metal pipes, and the like."[11] In a plan for the October festivities that he had submitted to the Moscow soviet, he proposed "repeating the emotional experience of the October revolution." The festival would be "split into three parts: struggle, victory, the intoxication of victory . . . Initially the mood culminates, then attains its high point, and ends in general gaiety."[12] Very likely, this is what Lunacharskii also had in mind for Petrograd.

Following Lunacharskii's remarks, Antselovich proposed extending the October festivities to two days. The first day would be taken up by political rallies and a show of the proletariat's military strength. He suggested that the central focus of this first day be Smolny, as the main symbol of the proletarian revolution in the consciousness of the popular masses. A triumphal plenary session of the Petrograd Soviet would be followed by an imposing mass march. Festive, universal gaiety would be the hallmark of the second day. The population would be awakened by loud bells and trumpets. Warships, big and small, would ply the Neva. A gigantic red banner would be lifted into the sky over the Field of Mars by a helium balloon. Revelers in the streets would be showered by revolutionary literature tossed from automobiles.

Antselovich suggested that either the headquarters of the Proletarian Cultural Association (Proletkult) or the Palace of Labor should be the central focus on the second day and that, for this occasion, a celebration of labor, all trade unions should be called upon to prepare fancy banners. Unlike the conceptions of Oksiuz and Lunacharskii, Antselovich's plan eliminated the Field of Mars as a central focus of festivities. As Antselovich explained, the holiday should not be a memorial (although fallen heroes should receive their due), but a forward-looking celebration of revolutionary triumphs, either achieved or imminent. Toward the end of this meeting, it was agreed that the main event on the first day (7 November) would be a political demonstration and that the center of events would be Smolny. The second day (8 November) would be a time for rejoicing. On that day, monuments to revolutionary heroes would be unveiled, and a festive ceremony would be organized to mark the official opening of the Palace of Labor, originally the Nikolaevskii Palace and later the Kseshiinskii Institute, primarily for daughters of the nobility. Because Moscow had by then decreed a three-day holiday, Thursday–Saturday (7–9 November), and participants in the meeting felt overwhelmed by the task of organizing such a long program, it was agreed that, on the ninth, citizens would be free to do as they wished.[13]

On 24 September, Andreeva delivered a progress report to a plenary meeting of the Petrograd Soviet,[14] revealing that the Central Bureau had drawn on Lunacharskii's structural scheme within a conceptual framework combining ideas put forth on the nineteenth by him, Oksiuz, and Antselovich. At the outset, Andreeva stressed that, although a major purpose of celebrating the anniversary was to instill the proletariat with confidence in the ultimate success of its cause, a bloody struggle for the triumph of the revolution was still in progress, and therefore the October festivities had to have a "serious and solemn aspect." The theme of the first day of the holiday would be to assess and demonstrate the strength and power of the revolution. The Petrograd masses would be awakened by the thunderous and joyous sounds of music—either from orchestras or choruses or maybe even bells (though definitely not church bells). Processions of workers and Red Army troops, organized by district, would march to the Field of Mars, participate in a brief tribute to fallen heroes buried there, and continue on to Smolny. As the preeminent center and symbol of the October revolution, Smolny was to be the focus of events on that day. A commemorative session of the Petrograd Soviet would be held there, and a new monument to "our great teacher" Marx, mounted on a pedestal in front of the building, would be unveiled and dedicated. The remainder of the afternoon would be reserved for rallies throughout the city. In the evening, all theaters would be open.

The theme of the second day of festivities would be the celebration of workers. The government would officially present the Palace of Labor to the city's workers, and commemorative meetings would be held in its spacious halls. A highlight of the events there would be the unveiling of a mammoth statue of a metalworker, standing tall and mighty before the entryway into the palace. This would be followed by public merrymaking along the Neva and other open spaces along Petrograd's many waterways. Newly created monuments to revolutionary heroes would be unveiled in the city's parks and squares. In the evening, special lighting effects, theater programs, and other popular spectacles would carry through the central themes of the day.[15] Subsequently, the elements of the October festivities that Andreeva outlined would be refined and juggled, some new elements would be added, but much of Andreeva's basic concept would endure.

* * *

During the second half of September commissions for the October holiday, attached to district soviets, were organized at the instigation of the Central Bureau. District Bolshevik party committees were allowed to elect one representative each to serve on these commissions. For district soviets, a magnificent holiday celebration would be not only a means of celebrating the triumph of the Russian people but also a way of highlighting their own achievements and restoring connections with workers. The response of the Rozhdestvenskii District Soviet to the idea of a grand celebration was typical. On 30 September, it accepted with alacrity a proposal by its commission for the October festivities to develop a plan for the holiday together with representatives of neighboring factories, with the proviso that the plan should be ready "no later than the next week." The district soviet specified that workers should be encouraged to organize festivities in their places of work and that three workers from each factory should be elected to help develop a district-wide plan for the holiday.[16]

Three days later, in a similarly enthusiastic and populist spirit, the executive committee of the Peterhof District Soviet formed a three-person commission to familiarize itself with the plan for the holiday developed by "the center" and to design a plan of its own for consideration at the next soviet plenary meeting.[17] At this meeting, on 6 October, a member of the commission complained that, in their district, the Central Bureau was only planning to decorate the Narva gates and the headquarters of the district soviet. Plainly unimpressed by the Central Bureau's plans, he declared that the historical significance of the first anniversary of October simply "had to leave a [significant] mark in the hearts of the revolutionary proletariat." Sharing his misgivings, a commission colleague insisted that the *entire* district be decorated so that, "at least on this one great day, the unsightliness of our living conditions will be completely obscured." He urged that decorating be put in the hands of proletarians who, he felt, could easily handle the task with but five hundred thousand of the ten million rubles that he alleged had been allocated to the Central Bureau. His recommendation was approved, as was that of another deputy who asked that workers be furnished free meals during the holiday. For this purpose, an official of the soviet was empowered to requisition food from a local market and to hoard provisions confiscated from speculators.[18] Among district soviets and workers generally, a penchant for decorating *everything*, and for broad worker involvement in the development and staging of holiday events, was widely shared.

District soviets undoubtedly recognized that their independence on matters relating to holiday planning would clash with the predilections of the Central Bureau. The position of the Central Bureau had been articulated in the earliest published bulletins of its sections. Thus, a proclamation from the Music Section published on 9 October informed all government institutions, district soviets, party organizations, educational institutions, and musicians that the arrangement of all [festival] concerts and [musical] shows belonged *exclusively* to it.[19] On 14 October, after the holiday planning of some district soviets was well advanced, the Central Bureau convened a conference with district soviet representatives. The chairman of the Rozhdestvenskii district soviet suggested, at a plenary meeting of his soviet later the same day, that the Central Bureau had deluged the district soviet representatives with the originality and colossal variety of holiday events it had planned, the imposing numbers of experts and other resources it already had at its disposal, and, at least implicitly, the enormous advantages that would accrue to district soviets if they worked in accordance with the holiday arrangement procedures it had established.[20]

The message that these opportunities would be closed to district soviets if they did not accede to the Central Bureau's control appears, at the very least, to have been understood. All the district soviet representatives who participated in this conference, including those from the Rozhdestvenskii and Peterhof districts, voted to accept procedures presented by the Central Bureau which gave it the final say in all critical matters pertaining to the holiday arrangements. Under these procedures, direction of all aspects of organizing the holiday was to be transferred to the Central Bureau; unapproved, separate projects by individual districts were prohibited; district soviets were also forbidden to produce placards or to issue slogans without clearance from the Central Bureau; and all decorating projects in districts had to be conducted under the Central Bureau's supervision. Individual factories, other places of work, and civic organizations were required to submit cost estimates for holiday projects to their district soviet. District soviets, in turn, were obligated to prepare comprehensive district-wide budget estimates for the Central Bureau's approval. Nobody at the meeting of the Rozhdestvenskii district soviet on 14 October raised questions about accepting these strictures, and the chairman closed by urging his colleagues to press district factories to submit their project designs and budgets as quickly as possible.[21]

Although the formal mandate of the Central Bureau, as an agency of the Petrograd Soviet, did not extend outside Petrograd, it was budgeted to support the celebration of the first anniversary of "October" in all Northern Commune provinces and among Red Army troops facing the Germans. In practice, its main effort outside Petrograd was focused on preparations for festivities at the front. After Oksiuz, on behalf of the Central Bureau, described the Central Bureau's design for the holiday at a meeting of the Petrograd Province Commission for Preparation of the October Festivities attended by representatives of rural soviets on 5 October, the representatives presented plans that seemed to satisfy him. They envisioned a four-day celebration. During the first two days delegates from local soviets would come to Petrograd to participate in festivities there. On the next two days, all "active forces" in Petrograd would fan out into the province to take part in celebrations in even the smallest villages.[22]

Between 5 October and a follow-up meeting on 11 October, the Commission for Preparation of the October Holiday in Petrograd Province scaled down, to one day (9 November), the holiday festivities among peasants in which Petrograders would participate. At the meeting on the eleventh, a commission member explained that celebrants in Petrograd would be on their own on the ninth because, on that day, all "active forces" in Petrograd would go into the countryside to clarify the momentous meaning of the holiday to peasants and to demonstrate the strength of the revolution to political enemies.[23]

As it turned out, holiday celebrations, some of them quite elaborate, were staged in towns and villages throughout Petrograd Province and in other provinces in the Northern Commune but without help from Petrograd's "active forces."[24] The Central Bureau furnished outlying areas with instructions, miles of red bunting, mountains of leaflets, and busts and portraits of soviet leaders in various sizes.[25] Beyond that, the main emphasis of Petrograd authorities involved in planning the commemoration for the region was to bring the "countryside" to see the wonders of the holiday in Petrograd. First, peasant soviets everywhere in the Northern Commune were invited to elect delegates to participate in holiday festivities in "the red capital." These delegates were guaranteed free travel, housing, meals, and entertainment, as well as participation in what was promoted as a uniquely magnificent, seminal historical event.[26] Second, Soviet authorities scheduled the Northern Oblast Congress of Committees of the Village Poor to be held in Petrograd on 3–6 November, so that the projected five thousand or so peasants expected to attend would participate in the holiday festivities there beginning on the seventh.

According to the official bulletin announcing this congress, radioed to the furthest reaches of the Northern Commune on 17 October, congress delegates would be housed in the Winter Palace, congress sessions would meet there, and all their expenses would be fully covered.[27] To be sure, convocation of this congress was justified as a means of forging links with the peasantry, better defining and coordinating the work of Committees of the Village Poor and their relationship to local soviets in the countryside, and facilitating the mobilization of peasants for mandatory service in the Red Army. At the beginning of September, military conscription was extended to include peasants in the Petrograd region, necessitating a more sensitive and forthcoming approach to them. Beyond that, however, like invitations to peasant soviets, the timing of the congress represented a conscious effort by Petrograd authorities to bring peasants and workers together for what they were determined would be the grandest mass spectacle ever. Peasant representatives would then become conduits for spreading word of the October revolution's great triumphs and prospects to the backward countryside. As Zinoviev explained, "most important is that several thousand peasants live in Petrograd for about a week, see our organizations, breathe the air of the red capital along with the revolutionary proletariat, form friendly ties with Petersburg workers, hear our best orators, and depart with a bag of literature for [their] villages . . . they will be a living bridge between city and countryside."[28]

The Central Bureau's policy about involving personnel from Petrograd in holiday activities at the front contrasted with its position on dispatching party cadres to rural areas. Unlike peasants, soldiers in battle zones could not leave their posts for the holiday. In the wake of their first major military triumphs, Red Army troops that previously were reviled as the scourge of Petrograd were now hailed as heroes. As we shall see, the Central Bureau spared nothing in its efforts to bring the joys of the October holiday to the soldiers.

* * *

Meetings of the Central Bureau on 17 and 19 September and Andreeva's report in the Petrograd Soviet on 24 September had established broad parameters for the first two days of the October festivities in Petrograd. Planning and organization continued through October and the first days of November, growing exponentially in response to pressures from district soviets and the seemingly decisive revolutionary upsurge unfolding in Central Europe. On 19 October, the press published a list of seventy-one prominent sites in Petrograd designated for major decoration projects and the artists whose designs were selected. More projects and artists were later added to the list. Among sites to be decorated according to designs by many of the city's best-known artists were main public buildings, rail stations and bridges, central squares, prominent thoroughfares and street corners, and the headquarters of district soviets.[29] Beginning in early October, all Petrograd was dotted by holiday construction sites. Arrangements for the October festivities by the theater, music, and film sections were similarly ambitious.[30]

Ships and personnel of the Baltic Fleet based in Kronstadt and in and around Petrograd since the late Shchastny's "ice march" were designated to play prominent roles in the festivities. The prize battleships would be moved to the mouth of the Neva, cruisers would be positioned on the Neva south of the Nikolaevskii Bridge, and an armada of destroyers would lay anchor between the Nikolaevskii and Liteinyi bridges in the heart of Petrograd. All these ships would be decorated with brightly colored flags and furnished with material for spectacular lighting effects and fireworks. The main naval shows were scheduled to begin at 6:00 PM. From then until midnight, search lights, rockets, and other fireworks would light up the night sky.[31] Similar, albeit more modest lighting and firework displays would be put on by military vessels anchored near provincial towns along the Neva between Petrograd and Lake Ladoga.[32]

Featured plays, concerts, films, firework and light shows, and naval demonstrations were just the tip of the iceberg. Among other forms of entertainment planned by the Central Bureau and its sections were roving street variety shows;[33] band ensembles playing on decorated trucks and balconies around the city;[34] improvisations depicting scenes from the revolutionary past (heralds, either on horseback or on foot, would announce what was taking place at different locations);[35] and mobile cinemas showing films "under the opens skies" after outdoor concerts. In addition to a film based on a screenplay by Lunacharskii, "on moving into bourgeois apartments," a cinematic chronology of the revolution was scheduled for outdoor viewing.[36]

Then, too, varied programs of rallies, theatricals, concerts, and poetry readings were planned by all Petrograd district soviets despite stresses connected with obtaining approval and budget authorizations from the Central Bureau. The centerpiece of most district-level celebrations was a gala concert/plenary meeting of the local soviet, with its headquarters festively decorated. Despite the rich talent promised by the Central Bureau, district soviets often preferred to use their own resources for entertainment at local holiday events. The Central Bureau does not appear to have tried to stop them probably because of its own dependence on district soviets to complete holiday projects as the holiday drew closer. Thus, soviets in both the Narva and Moscow Gate districts formed their own "proletarian" choruses. Belatedly, sections of the Central Bureau furnished instructors to help district soviets prepare concerts and theatricals.[37] Only the First City district soviet had its own newspaper, the *Vestnik soveta 1-ogo gorodskogo raiona*. For the October holiday, its editors prepared a double issue, with photographs, year-end reports on the work of district soviet sections, and reminiscences. At least one other district soviet, the Second City district soviet, produced a commemorative history glorifying its activities during the previous twelve months.[38]

In order to bring the October holiday to Red Army troops at the front, the Central Bureau's section for holiday celebrations in battle zones coordinated the collection of gifts for soldiers, formed delegations to deliver them, and recruited and organized groups of entertainers for holiday performances among frontline soldiers. On the road, however, these traveling ensembles had to fend for themselves. One of the first groups to leave was the so-called First People's Great Russian Orchestra. It departed Petrograd for a two-week tour of the Northern front on 2 November.[39] The next day, a group of entertainers, including a twenty-four-man brass band, left for the Karelian front. Its tour began inauspiciously in Petrozavodsk, where it was given accommodations in train carriages, only to be thrown out during the night by hostile railway administrators. On 7 November, the group led a holiday demonstration in Petrozavodsk, and between the eighth and the twenty-fourth, traveling by train, boat, sleigh, and horseback, it put on variety shows for soldiers in garrison towns in central Karelia.[40]

Both Lunacharskii and Zinoviev attached special importance to the October festivities and played energetic roles in holiday preparations. One of Zinoviev's major concerns was to promote Red Petrograd, "where the first and decisive battles [of the October revolution] were played out," as the center of the worldwide revolutionary socialist movement. He outlined an ambitious publications program aimed at furthering this objective. A key work in this program was to be a compendium of memoirs by participants in the October seizure of power who had remained in Petrograd when the national government fled to Moscow and who could illuminate the city's leading role in the first socialist revolution. Zinoviev urged that the model set by the bourgeoisie of revolutionary Paris be followed. "Just look at how the French bourgeoisie managed to learn about and sing praises to its revolution . . . and how every corner of Paris in which events of any consequence took place has been immortalized. . . . We must not forget that, in Petrograd, every stone [also] belongs to history . . . we [also] walk on hallowed ground." An essential element of the holiday, according to Zinoviev, was to record revolutionary events everywhere in Petrograd, "so that they will be preserved for our brothers [and] for future generations." "The one hundred to two hundred stories in this book," he concluded, "will become the golden book of worldwide socialism."[41]

Most citywide holiday activities were initiated by Lunacharskii, Zinoviev, the Central Bureau, or one of its sections. A significant exception was a program for children of the poor, which became a last-minute feature of the third day of festivities. During the second half of October, a number of separate projects aimed at involving children in the jubilee had begun to be organized, several of them initiated at the neighborhood level. The children's department of the Central Bureau's Theater Section planned a children's march and special theatrical presentations for 9 November.[42] Concurrently, the music section, in collaboration with the theater section, put together variety shows for children;[43] the Petrograd district soviet planned a "grandiose" children's parade, accompanied by a marching band;[44] a group of employees in the Commissariat for Enlightenment was involved in organizing choruses in schools and teaching them revolutionary songs;[45] the Irinovskii railway organized an outing for children featuring rides on brightly decorated trains, holiday refreshments, and children's shows;[46] and railway workers in the Nevskii district prepared to offer a production of "Sleeping Beauty" for their children.[47] On 2 November, the social welfare section of the Spasskii district soviet announced that it was organizing the first proletarian holiday for children of the district's poor and invited other institutions to contact it and join forces to organize a broader children's festival.[48] Each of these activities was developed independently. Not until the very eve of the October celebrations were they combined.

It is notable that nothing had been said about events for children at an expanded plenary meeting of the Petrograd Soviet on 1 November at which Antselovich gave a comprehensive "final" report on the program for the October festivities that had been developed by the Central Bureau. There was no mention of children's events, even in holiday programs published in the Petrograd daily press as late as 6 November. The first public announcement that during the third day of the holiday "everything had to be put at the disposal of children, [including] orchestras, automobiles, flowers, performers, managers, etc.," appeared in instructions for holiday organizers published and circulated late in the day of 6 November. The instructions included a detailed plan for a children's march, a rally and concert for children on Palace Square, and concerts and film showings in the Winter Palace. The thirty thousand children expected to participate were promised such treats as white bread and apples.[49] Apparently the all-day children's festival was among the few citywide elements of the holiday generated largely "from below."

The plenary meeting of the Petrograd Soviet on 1 November had begun with effusive comments by Zinoviev on the huge number of peasant delegates streaming into Petrograd for the regional Congress of Committees of the Village Poor, which Zinoviev interpreted as a clear sign that the Bolshevik campaign to win the support of the peasantry was making headway, and on popular eruptions in Central Europe, which Zinoviev viewed as decisive steps toward the triumph of socialist revolution on the Russian model on a global scale. In general, the scheme presented by Antselovich conformed to the broad plan for a two-day celebration set forth by Andreeva in the Petrograd Soviet on 24 September.[50] Better than any other source, Antselovich's presentation conveys the significance the Central Bureau attached to the holiday as a whole and to its separate elements. As Antselovich put it, the socialist revolution in Russia had immediate relevance to the momentous developments then taking place in the West. By implication, the celebration of "October" in Petrograd had to embody a vital international message. At the same time, even without the revolutions then erupting in the West, the survival of worker power in Russia for an *entire* year merited a festival surpassing any other. Not only did the commemoration need to be constructed in a way that would enable the masses to rest from their heavy burdens, it was essential that they get a full sense of the colossal import of their epoch-making achievement.

For Antselovich, during the first day it was crucial that all of Petrograd's military and proletarian forces be mobilized to show the bourgeoisie, "ourselves," and the world the strength of the city's working class. Smolny had been selected as the center of festivities on the first day, because the resolutions adopted there marked the beginning of a new era not only in the life of the Russian proletariat but in the experience of all mankind. The Field of Mars had been rejected as a focal point, because, as Antselovich put it, "a year has passed and we don't have only corpses, we [still] have proletarian power."

If the first day was intended to represent the triumphant struggle for a proletarian dictatorship, the second day was intended to symbolize what had been achieved thanks to the efforts of the working class. Its central focus would be the opening of the first proletarian palace of labor in Russia. Clarifying the symbolism of the gigantic statue of a metalworker that would be unveiled there, he explained that it was to be the counterpoint to the work of a famous Belgian sculptor depicting a metalworker deep in thought. The Belgian statue represented the state of the working class under the Second International. The image of the metalworker in front of the Palace of Labor symbolized workers in the new era. "The metalworker has awakened, he is standing, and in his hands is a hammer with which he crushes all violence in the country." The organization of workers by trade for citywide demonstrations on the second day "symbolizes those worker ranks that are building a [new] life, a [new] economy—that are building palaces of labor." On this second day, workers would demonstrate on Nevskii Prospekt and inundate the bourgeois quarter. "The proletariat has not yet had time to settle there," Antselovich explained. "But it owns the street[s] and the entire bourgeois quarter. . . . [It] must show who is boss there."Toward the close of his report, Antselovich reemphasized the domestic educational function of the holiday:

> Every one of us must try to involve our wives and sisters [in the festivities] so that all of our poor are in the streets. We will come out of the worker districts to the center of the city. Each of us must go so that the demonstration will be grandiose, so that the masses, even the most backward, take part. . . . [F]or us a demonstration is not just a time for exercise . . . It is a great school that educates and gives birth to Communists. Each worker in a column of demonstrators will sense his strength . . . and the most timid will feel the great power of workers collectively.[51]

Zinoviev, paraphrasing the comment of a peasant who had referred to the October revolution as "the Easter of the working class and poorer peasantry," expressed the hope that the celebration of "Red Easter" would be glorious and, declaring that Antselovich's report was only informational, cut off discussion of it.[52]

* * *

Participation in the October holiday in Petrograd was "by invitation." The festivities were designed for officials and delegates from soviets, the Bolshevik/Communist party, trade unions, and other approved institutions; civic bodies; honored foreign guests; and Bolshevik and unaffiliated workers, peasants, Red Army soldiers, and Baltic Fleet sailors. Members of the former upper and middle classes engaged in mandatory labor, except those unloading food supplies, were excused for the holidays. Specifically excluded from holiday events were "byvshie liudi" ("former people," the declassé) and members of opposition parties (especially Left SRs), as well as worker and peasant "bandits" who supported them.

This policy became apparent in early October when the Executive Committee of the Petrograd Soviet banned the Menshevik-dominated printers' union from participation in holiday parades.[53] During the immediate run-up to the anniversary, Soviet authorities in Petrograd hurriedly superintended the creation of a Bolshevik-controlled "Union of Red Printers," which was to represent printing plant workers in the festivities.[54] The detailed order of march for parades drawn up by the Central Bureau's route of march section, in which each participating element had a precisely designated location at five-minute intervals, was partly intended to prevent intrusion by unauthorized individuals and groups.[55]

The Central Bureau tried hard to insure that free tickets to theater performances and concerts would reach ordinary workers and peasants to give them a rare glimpse of elite culture, offer plenty for them to see and do, and the opportunity, above all, to enjoy themselves.[56] In contrast, only a hierarchy of government and party officials, foreign guests, and a smattering of elected delegates from mass organizations could attend the most prestigious functions, including the unveiling of the monument to Marx on the morning of the seventh, the ceremonial concert and meeting of the Petrograd Soviet that evening, and the grand opening of the Palace of Labor on the night of the 8th.[57]

In view of the ambitiousness of the Central Bureau's plans, and the difficulties in Petrograd at the time, it is not surprising that the completion of all construction projects turned out to be impossible. Petty crime plagued the Central Bureau—most commonly, the unauthorized requisitioning of building materials by fake agents of the Central Bureau during the day and theft from building sites at night. Criminals caught posing as agents of the bureau or stealing from construction sites were threatened with "punishment according to the law in wartime."[58] At the local level, district soviet holiday commissions encountered snags in receiving budgetary appropriations from the Central Bureau, sometimes forcing them to seek out alternate sources of support or to rely on their creativity.[59]

A major worry of holiday planners was food supply during the festivities, but that fear was laid to rest at a meeting of the Central Bureau on 19 October. The report of an official from the Commissariat for Food Supply of the SK SO revealed that it had been laying away provisions for the holiday during the most difficult days of the summer and early fall. Suddenly, as if by magic, the Commissariat was able to guarantee ample supplies of meat, fats, even French rolls.[60]

* * *

From the start, Petrograd authorities viewed the celebration of the first anniversary of the October revolution as an opportunity to assert Red Petrograd's aspiration to leadership of the worldwide socialist revolution over Moscow's competing claim. This thinking was partly an extension of the age-old rivalry between Petrograd and Moscow that, since mid March, had been shaped by the national government's frenzied flight from Petrograd. Later, it was fueled by ongoing conflict between the governments of the two "capital cities." At an early stage of holiday preparations in Petrograd, it became public that Petrovskii and Zinoviev were in continual conflict over the unwillingness of the former to officially recognize the Union of Northern Communes. The conflict escalated after Petrovskii, in an *Izvestiia* interview of 10 October, described the Northern Commune as the epitome of the kind of autonomous, self-appointed regional government that violated the Soviet constitution and the principles of Soviet state building. Occurring at precisely the time when Petrograd was working feverishly to establish its preeminence as the revolutionary capital in connection with the holiday, Petrovskii's onslaught begged for a strong response. It came in the form of a blunt open letter to him from Ravich, Commissar for Internal Affairs, SK SO, published on 17 October. Depicting the formation of the Northern Oblast government as a mandatory response to pressures from the population for leadership and a need to fill a power vacuum, Ravich accused Petrovskii of ignorance, deceit, and self-serving narrow-mindedness.[61]

Less than a week later, the Bolshevik Central Committee in Moscow put a severe crimp in Petrograd's plans to assert its primacy during the holiday by scheduling the opening, in Moscow, of the Emergency Sixth All-Russian Congress of Soviets for 5 November (later changed to 6 November). A primary purpose of this hastily called congress was to provide a national forum for discussing Lenin's views on the impact of the impending sudden end of the world war on Soviet Russia's international situation and, in that connection, on its urgent military tasks. A secondary purpose was to consider the reform of Soviet institutions in the countryside. However, Sverdlov made plain to the CEC on 22 October that the emergency congress was timed so that the celebration of the first anniversary of the October revolution would begin in Moscow. Reflecting this aim, the first item on the projected agenda of the congress was a speech by Lenin on "The First Anniversary of Soviet Power."[62]

Zinoviev was on a tour of the Urals front when the convocation of the emergency congress was announced. Upon his return, he and Lunacharskii attempted to counter Moscow's "trump" by attracting provincial representatives from all over Russia to join in holiday festivities in Petrograd. Their invitation, published on the front page of three successive issues of *Severnaia kommuna*, read:

> The Petrograd Soviet . . . and the [SK SO] . . . invite the Moscow soviet and all city, province, county, and village soviets [around the country] to send their delegates to the celebration of the October revolution in Petrograd. The revolution of 25 October (7 November) took place in Petrograd; the leading role in our entire socialist revolution belonged to the proletariat of Petrograd; [and] the victims of our October battles are buried in Petrograd. The holiday in Petrograd must have a Russian-wide character. Therefore, we ask that our soviets send one or two people for the two to three days of the holiday at the same time they send delegates to the All-Russian Congress of Soviets.
>
> Zinoviev, Lunacharskii[63]

* * *

As the October holiday drew closer, the primary concerns of all Soviet authorities in Petrograd were focused on completing major construction projects, hiding or eliminating symbols of the old regime, maximizing popular participation in holiday events, and insuring that Bolshevik opponents would not disrupt them. The biggest impediment to finishing the enormous number of decorating projects was the difficulty in recruiting enough construction workers for the task even after large numbers of laborers were brought in from the provinces. At the beginning of November, supervisors of all building and renovation projects in the city of Petrograd unrelated to the holiday were ordered to immediately release all carpenters, joiners, painters, and unskilled laborers in their employ and send them to the Central Bureau for assignment. Construction workers who did not report for duty at once were again threatened with dire punishment.[64]

Efforts to hide or eliminate symbols of the old regime took a number of forms. Smaller statues, paintings, and similar artifacts were destroyed or hidden away. Large monuments, Imperial emblems on buildings, and so on, were draped with red bunting or decorative panels. This was the case with the huge equestrian statue of Alexander III on Znamenskii Square. In his report to the Petrograd Soviet on 1 November, Antselovich pledged to rename all streets and squares that "remind us of the time of damnation."[65]

Most new names of streets and squares, as well as bridges and buildings, honored revolutionary heroes, events, or institutions. For instance, Nevskii Prospekt became 25 October Prospekt, Liteinyi Prospekt became Volodarskii Prospekt, Suvorovskii Prospekt became Soviet Prospekt, Ivan Street became Socialist Street, Palace Square became Uritskii Square, Znamenskii Square became Uprising Square, the Taurida Palace became the Uritskii Palace, Nobles' Bridge became Republican Bridge, and Police Bridge became People's Bridge.[66]

During the second half of October, press reports on holiday preparations proliferated. On 24 October, *Severnaia kommuna* carried a detailed, enthusiastic description of how the Field of Mars was being decorated and, from then on, similarly effusive advertisements for other major holiday construction sites were published daily.[67] It was then customary for Petrograd's political leaders to give speeches on critical issues at weekly Sunday afternoon mobilization rallies. On Sunday 27 October, the theme of these mass meetings was "The Great Anniversary." Accounts of the speeches in the press indicate that Petrograd's top Bolsheviks fanned out across the city to whip up enthusiasm for the domestic and international triumphs of the October revolution and for the approaching jubilee as a celebration of the Petrograd proletariat as the vanguard of international revolution.

Daily press bulletins informed Petrograders of unusually large supplies of grain and even delicacies being shipped from distant food-producing regions to the revolutionary capital, as gifts to "Red Petrograd" for the October festivities. Thus, on 1 November, it was announced that in Orlovskii Province ten thousand geese were being shipped to Petrograd for the holiday tables of the revolutionary proletariat.[68] It was also reported that unusually large quantities of grain had already been received by the city's bakeries; and half pound loaves of bread were to be baked the night of 5–6 November for distribution to shops on the night of the sixth.[69] What better news to put a starving city into a festive spirit?

A major issue with implications for the popular mood during the October festivities was settled on 2 November, when the Executive Committee of the Petrograd Soviet responded to workers' anxieties by publishing a decree that factory workers and white collar employees would be paid in full during the holidays. According to this decree, all those who could not be given the holidays off were to receive double pay.[70] Attitudes of female workers were of particular concern to holiday planners, as factory women often seemed cool, if not openly hostile, to the celebration. A *Krasnaia gazeta* editorial on 20 October declared that it was high time for factory women to come to their senses and finally rid themselves of their habitual political passivity. In an adjacent article, "Why the Working Class Cele-brates the October Revolution," Samoilova singled out women employed in textile mills and tobacco factories for special criticism. Clearly, however, the fundamental problem she voiced, namely, the unwillingness of factory women to support Bolshevism, was in fact widespread. After enumerating the epoch-making gains wrought by the October revolution, Samoilova criticized female workers who, she wrote, were refusing to participate in cele-brating "October" and, worse yet, were insisting on working during the fes-tivities because they considered the celebration "a Jewish holiday." "The face of every conscious female worker is covered with shame when she reads these words," Samoilova lamented.[71]

To undermine attempts by their opponents to disrupt the holidays, the Bolsheviks in Petrograd arrested hundreds of prominent and middle-level potential troublemakers still at liberty. This new crackdown began the night of 4/5 November. Two of the jailed were the Obukhov plant SRs Grigorii and Aleksei Eremeev; the former had been arrested and briefly detained the previous June, following Volodarskii's assassination.[72] Also rounded up was Aleksandr Izgoev, a member of the Kadet Central Committee, who had been marked for arrest as a hostage at the start of the Red Terror but had been among opposition political leaders who were overlooked in the fren-zied waves of arrests back then. He recalled in his memoirs that, on the night of 4/5 November, a group of soldiers and sailors conducted a lengthy search of his apartment, seized heaps of his writings, and hauled him off to the lo-cal police station. There he was held in a makeshift basement cell with forty other victims of the pre-holiday roundup. It soon became clear that the only common thread uniting Izgoev and his cellmates was that they had all been on candidate lists for elections to district dumas in the spring of 1917; these lists for the first truly democratic elections in Russian history were thus used to determine the identities and addresses of those subject to arrest.[73]

On 6 November, the Central Bureau issued instructions governing speeches at post-parade rallies and other public events aimed at preventing them from being turned into forums for free discussion. Orators at outdoor rallies were instructed to speak only from designated locations, either plat-forms or movable rostrums; rallies could last no more than an hour; open-ing greetings had to be delivered by agitators selected by district soviets; and all speakers had to be accredited. Each district soviet was responsible for pro-viding agitators at local theatrical and musical performances who were re-stricted to short greetings conforming to guidelines furnished by the Central Bureau. Similarly, designated representatives of the Petrograd Soviet were to deliver brief, scripted greetings at large communal theaters.[74]

At the same time, the military commissar for Petrograd and Petrograd Province put all locally based Red Army forces on full alert. Leaves for Red Army personnel were canceled. Fifty-man cavalry units were ordered to patrol central areas of the city nightly, and all suspicious elements on the streets, not to mention anybody agitating against Soviet power, were to be arrested at once. Security was tightened at government buildings, the State Bank, the Fortress of Peter and Paul, key bridges, telephone and telegraph stations, and post offices. Combat-ready security forces were ordered to duty at police stations.[75] Also, district soviets formed "troikas" with unlimited powers in case of an emergency during the holidays.[76]

Significantly, on this occasion, Baltic Fleet sailors were not drawn on for protection because city authorities were particularly wary about possible holiday disturbances by angry sailors. This concern mounted after the belated public announcement on 30 October that eleven seamen judged to have been ringleaders of the abortive insurrection on 14 October had been executed. On 2 November, the Executive Committee of the Petrograd Soviet privately acknowledged the failure of its Military Section to conduct organizational work among sailors or to improve their living conditions.[77] So, at the same time that it rebuked and reorganized the section, it issued a spate of warnings about disruptions planned by Bolshevik enemies. Typical was an appeal by the Petrograd Soviet to ships' crews and mobilized sailors claiming that Left and Right SRs had joined forces and were planning action against Soviet power during the approaching holiday. "For some reason, these White Guardists are counting on you most of all, comrade sailors," this appeal read. "If 'Left' and/or Right SR provocateurs, [or] Black Hundred officers dressed up as sailors, appear [among you], escort them to Gorokhovaia 2 immediately."[78] Another appeal of this period warned that "information has been received from many sources that counterrevolutionary bands . . . have set themselves the task of preventing the celebration of the first anniversary of the October revolution." "The proletariat of the entire world, led by Russian workers and peasants, is engaged in the final decisive battle against the bourgeoisie, and therefore our holiday is being transformed into a great worldwide celebration of the triumph of revolutionary socialism," concluded the appeal. "We cannot allow these days to be clouded by any acts hostile to worker-peasant power."[79]

* * *

The primary themes of the October holiday were vividly reflected in editorials and reports in the only newspaper that appeared in Petrograd on 7–9 November, *God proletarskoi revoliutsii* (*A Year of Proletarian Revolution*), a combined publication of *Petrogradskaia pravda, Severnaia kommuna, Krasnaia gazeta, Vooruzhennyi narod,* and Petrograd news agencies. Perhaps the most important of these themes was that, largely as a result of the revolutionary fire started in Petrograd in October 1917, all Europe was on the edge or already in the throes of decisive revolutionary explosions, and that the anniversary coincided with a decisive turning point in the struggle for survival of Soviet power in Russia. The agonizing wait for the eruption of world revolution, during which revolutionary Russia was forced to battle for survival alone, was all but over.

In speeches on 7 November, both Lunacharskii and Zinoviev pointed to Petrograd and Smolny as "the cradle of the worldwide socialist revolution,"[80] and A. Naglovskii, in the 7 November issue of *A Year of Proletarian Revolution,* concluded confidently that "the most difficult moments and stages [in the consolidation of the October revolution] have been overcome."[81] In an essay, "The Great Anniversary," which appeared in his journal *Plamia* that same day, Lunacharskii expressed certainty that all Europe would celebrate the second anniversary of the October revolution in 1919. Nonetheless, nowhere would it be feted as it would in Petrograd, because Petrograd would retain its place as the capital of the worldwide socialist revolution and be the natural meeting place of congresses of soviets of workers' and peasants' deputies from all over the globe.[82]

This Petrograd-centered, exhilarated mood was typical of most Petrograd officials at this juncture. "Our predecessors, the Paris Communards, held power for only a few weeks. Russian workers have held it for a year," crowed Zinoviev in a lead editorial, also in the first issue of *A Year of Proletarian Revolution.* Paris workers succumbed, because, he continued, unlike us, they were not supported by the rest of the country. Conceding that the triumph of the October revolution would not be stable if the working class in the rest of the world remained aloof from Russia's struggle, he expressed absolute certainty that that would not happen.

In this editorial, Zinoviev forecast the course of revolutionary events around the world in the near term:

> Republics in Austria and Hungary will be established in the next few days . . . In Vienna, Budapest, and Prague, state power will be transferred to Soviets of workers and soldiers deputies. Shortly, the revolution will pass from Austria to Italy . . . The moment when we will see soviets in Milan and Rome is close. . . . The [early] triumph of the German working class is inevitable . . . [and] when a red flag is permanently raised over Berlin, it will signify that the hour when that same red flag is raised over Paris is not far off . . . It is possible that English capital will survive for a few years alongside socialist regimes

in the rest of Europe. But from the moment when socialism in Russia, Austria, Germany, France, and Italy becomes a fact, English capitalism will have reached its end.[83]

Another primary holiday theme was the growing invincibility of Red Army troops. Already, they had begun to replace Baltic Fleet sailors as the praetorian guard and pride of the revolution. A prominently featured essay by one L. Vyborgskaia in *A Year of Proletarian Revolution* on 8 November put the matter this way:

> Anybody who was in the street and squares of Piter today [7 November] would have to concede that all the beauty of the decorations and floats notwithstanding . . . the most gorgeous sight of the day was surely our Red Army . . . A year ago, all we had was a small group of courageous worker Red Guards. . . . Now we have an army that even Imperial Europe would have to praise.

*   *   *

At midnight on 6 November, the pounding booms of a twenty-five-gun salute from cannons at the Fortress of Peter and Paul signaled the start of the first anniversary celebration of the October revolution in Petrograd. Carpenters and artists at construction sites racing to finish holiday projects were drenched by a cold driving rain that would last through the next day. At 7:30 AM, crowds from the Second City district, the lead marchers in the grand parade that day, began to assemble in front of the local soviet's headquarters. While they formed, women circulated among them collecting funds to buy presents for Red Army troops at the front. Promptly at 8:00, after seven more blasts from cannon at the Fortress of Peter and Paul, trucks loaded with holiday literature, placards, pins, and a trumpeter to signal the start of the march sped from the Palace of Labor to the Second City district soviet building and to each of ten other district assembly points around Petrograd. Somewhat later, led by the chairman carrying the banner of the Second City district soviet, accompanied by a marching band, and followed by the local Red Army unit, the Second City district soviet leadership, members of the district Bolshevik party committee and of sundry local civic and labor organizations, along with contingents of workers and their families, all singing the *Internationale,* began to slog through the rain and mud along a circuitous route to Smolny. This routine was repeated at other district assembly points around Petrograd at set intervals for the rest of the day.[84]

There are no reliable estimates of the number of participants in the holiday marches in Petrograd on 7 and 8 November. Most of the foreign press, absorbed by Germany's defeat and the expanding revolutionary outbreaks

Celebrants at the Field of Mars, 7 November 1918. *Krasnyi Petrograd,* 1919.

in central Europe, ignored the Bolshevik festival altogether. If one were to judge by *A Year of Proletarian Revolution,* the turnout on 7 November exceeded all expectations (and the same was also true the next day). Among opponents of Soviet power, an announcement in the Soviet press the evening of 6 November that the Germans had broken relations with the Soviet government,[85] allegedly because it was behind revolutionary eruptions in Germany and had not punished Mirbach's killers, gave rise to rumors that German forces would finally occupy Petrograd and stifle Bolshevism. Along with fear of being attacked by revelers, this prospect seems to have kept such observant anti-Soviet notables as Ziniada Gippius off the streets during the holiday. From her windows on Sergievskaia Street near the Uritskii (Taurida) Palace, she could see "long red calico rags and a gigantic portrait of a disheveled Marx" hanging on the fence surrounding the palace gardens and could hear the blaring horns of marchers on their way to Smolny but could not see them.[86] Still, there is little reason to doubt the large number of participants, mobilized by a mixture of carrots and sticks, energized by Germany's imminent surrender and the eruption of social revolutions in Central Europe, and bolstered by many thousands of guests from the provinces, military personnel, and peasant-delegates to the Northern Oblast Congress

Representatives of Committees of the Village Poor in Petrograd during a celebration of the first anniversary of the October revolution. State Museum of the Political History of Russia, St. Petersburg.

of Committees of the Village Poor, even after allowance is made for huge population losses in the preceding year.

By noon, lead elements of the procession from the Second City district, joined by representatives from the Congress of Committees of the Village Poor, reached Dictatorship of the Proletariat (Lafonskaia) Square in front of Smolny. Distributing themselves at designated points around the veiled statue of Marx, they listened as Lunacharskii, standing on a makeshift podium atop an automobile decorated with red bunting, hailed the meeting place of the Petrograd Soviet as the "cradle of the revolution," paid homage to Marx, and announced the most recent joyous tidings about the spread of social revolution in Germany. Then they watched as the statue was unveiled, and, after listening to several more renditions of the *Internationale,* they marched back to their starting points. The rest of the processions from "the districts," arriving at the square at several-minute intervals, slowed at the monument to Marx where they were "saluted" by the strains of the *Internationale* and responded with cheers, after which they paraded through the center of Petrograd and returned "home." This procedure was scripted to the minute and, despite the rain, seems to have proceeded without a hitch.[87]

The holiday session of the Petrograd Soviet, attended by distinguished

Commissars of the Northern Commune after the unveiling of a memorial to Karl Marx: (1) Zinoviev; (2) Lunacharskii; (3) (behind Lunacharskii) Pozern; (4) (extreme right) Evdokimov; (6) Lilina; (7) (behind Lilina) Lisovskii; (8) Voskov; (9) Ravich. Boris Sokoloff Collection, Hoover Institution Archives.

foreign socialists, officials of the government and party, and selected representatives of soviet and labor organizations, was scheduled to begin at 7:00 PM. But not until 8:00 did the orchestras and lead soloists of the state operas and the Smolny cathedral choir file onstage for a concert of classical music which began the session. The concert ended with a performance of Mozart's *Requiem*. Zinoviev, the keynote speaker, took this as a cue to pay homage to Volodarskii, Uritskii, and "hundreds" of other former members of the Petrograd Soviet who had given their lives for the revolutionary cause. This was one of the few solemn moments in Zinoviev's speech. Another came when, in a rare moment of candor, he apologized that so little had been accomplished for labor during a year of Soviet power. "It has turned out to be impossible to clothe workers," he acknowledged. "They are in tatters, hunger is imprinted on their faces, and life is difficult for their wives and children." Nonetheless, the great achievement of Soviet power in Russia had been to wake up "brother-proletarians" around the world.[88]

Forgotten was Zinoviev's own strong opposition to the Bolshevik seizure of power in October. Essentially, this was Zinoviev's victory speech. Although he repeated Lenin's warning that the Allies, victorious in the West, might well pounce on Soviet Russia, he seemed to dismiss this as a serious threat to the survival of the revolution, in as much as the new Red Army was quickly becoming strong enough to repel any foe. Moreover, recalling the run-up to October, he scoffed at moderate socialists who had rejected the possibility of a socialist revolution in backward Russia; at the time, it had been easy and clear to see that the exploited were ripe to rise against the exploiters. "We took that into account a year ago. And a year of social revolution has proven the accuracy of our prophecies to everyone," he declared triumphantly.

Repeatedly, Zinoviev exulted in the sheer joy of the holiday. "Waiting for the moment when the working class in the West would become conscious of its role was long and painful," he declaimed. "But surely it is impossible to conceive a sweeter moment than the one we are living through." "The sun has never been as close to us as it is now. We will definitely live to see the moment when not only we but the French, English, and Americans have their own Smolny . . . [yet even then] the proletariat of all countries will view [our] Smolny as the holiest of holies." Zinoviev's closing toasts—"Long live the best of the best, the Petrograd proletariat!" "Long live the revolutions that are approaching and those that have already arrived!" "Long live dear Smolny!"—were drowned out by the combined sounds of the assembled musical ensembles playing the *Internationale* and the boom of fireworks exploding in the black sky over the nearby Neva. At the conclusion of his speech, Zinoviev was driven the short distance to the Nikolaevskii Station, where a train was waiting to take him to Moscow and the Sixth All-Russian Congress of Soviets.[89]

As Zinoviev spoke the rain stopped. Ignoring the winter chill, contingents of workers and soldiers and their families, interspersed with groups of peasants, crowded the Neva embankments to watch the light and fireworks show. By the standards of the time, it must have been quite a sight. To one observer, toward evening on 7 November the Neva took on a "magical appearance." Hydroplanes skimmed over the water toward the Field of Mars and back again. Garlands of brightly colored lights were strung on ships, linking them together, while searchlights crisscrossed the sky and swept the tightly packed, cheering spectators on the embankments. On cue, a rocket on one of the ships shot into the heavens and dissolved into a huge waterfall of sparks, after which rockets and blue signal flares from all the ships let loose a barrage that lasted several hours. The spectacular light show continued well into the night, while free film showings, "under the skies," and musical and theatrical performances attracted large crowds of ordinary people all over the city.[90] Richard Stites, a leading American historian of Russian and Soviet culture, vividly described the elaborate decorations that formed the setting for these activities:

[T]he decor for November 7 in Petrograd was brilliant, having been executed by major artists such as Mstislav Dobuzhinsky, Natan Altman, K. S. Petrov-Vodkin, and Boris Kustodiev. Dobuzhinskii retained the classical beauties of Zakharin's Admiralty, augmenting its thematic with maritime pennants, flaglets, and anchors, and hiding the ugly structures . . . along the Neva River. Altman, on the other hand, sought to destroy utterly the monumentality of autocratic architecture in Palace Square . . . behind modernist designs. The result was festive richness but also a diminution of Petrograd's appearance as a center of unambiguous power.[91]

By all accounts, it was a mass festival unlike any Petrograd had ever witnessed.

The next day's celebration of labor was no less spectacular, as the central focus shifted from Smolny to the Palace of Labor. Participants in mass marches that day were deliberately routed through the elite neighborhoods adjacent to Nevskii Prospekt, effectively occupying them for several hours. The starting point for the most prominent marchers—top trade union officials, members of the government, high-ranking Bolsheviks, and officials from the Commissariat for Labor and from the SNKh SR—was at the foot of 25 October (Nevskii) Prospekt at the corner of Bolshaia Morskaia Street. They were followed by more than one hundred thousand workers, many of them unemployed, grouped by trade union. Led by metalworkers, the trade unionists, joined by sundry bands and choruses, stretched past Uprising (Znamenskii) Square at the end of 25 October Prospekt and spilled over into every side street adjoining it.

At noon, following another cannon salute, thousands of marchers began moving toward the Admiralty and the Palace of Labor. A podium had been erected across from the palace and the veiled statue of the metalworker. After about an hour, by which time the open space in front of the palace was crammed with notables and ordinary citizens, Lunacharskii climbed to the podium and dedicated the statue.[92]

The main event of the second day of the October holiday in Petrograd was the ceremonial opening of the Palace of Labor itself. Antselovich began this proceeding with a pledge that in the future all of Petrograd's palaces would be palaces of labor, because, as he put it, "we are strong and can do anything we wish." Lunacharskii, filling in for Zinoviev, was the featured speaker. He began with some platitudes about the evolution of trade unions and the modern workers' movement, and ended with similarly bland comments on the role of labor and labor unions during the transition to socialism as reflected in Russia's experience during the preceding year.[93]

Following Lunacharskii, Riazanov, representing the Petrograd Trade

Dedication of monument, "The Metal Worker," at ceremonial opening of the Palace of Labor, 8 March 1918. Photo by Ia. Shteinberg. State Museum of the Political History of Russia, St. Petersburg.

Union Council, was given the floor. Earlier, as the oldest revolutionary present, he had been invited to join the presidium. The festival organizers undoubtedly were wary about what he might say and his remarks were given only passing mention in *A Year of Proletarian Revolution.* The stenographic account reveals that he was as independent-minded as ever. Rejecting Lunacharskii's hyperbole, he attempted to moderate what seemed to him to be wildly misplaced optimism regarding the development of revolutions abroad. Declaring that it was necessary to look truth in the eye, even during the celebration of "October," he insisted that, just as Left Communists had predicted, the capitulation at Brest had delayed eruption of a "real international revolution." Thanks to Germany's defeat, the shameful peace had been annulled. However, the triumph of Allied imperialism had created more dangerous conditions than ever. With as much certainty as Lenin, Riazanov took it for granted that the victorious Allies would soon seek to stifle the Russian revolution. For Red Petrograd, there was no alternative to resistance at any price. On the other hand, if "the cradle of the revolution" found the will to defend itself, in tandem with the Austrian and German proletariat, it would ultimately survive until the outbreak of decisive social-ist revolutions in Western Europe.[94]

In the prevailing atmosphere, Riazanov's "wet blanket" was coolly re-ceived. Much more popular were the messages of Viacheslav Molotov, for the SNKh SR, and Sergei Zorin, on behalf of the SK SO. Molotov confi-dently predicted that the Palace of Labor would become the center for the Petrograd proletariat's final suppression of the bourgeoisie, and Zorin ex-pressed hope that the October holiday and the opening of the Palace of La-bor would become worldwide symbols of the great power of the working class. Zorin exhorted: "We are saying to them [workers of the world], look, we are stifling our bourgeoisie, stifle yours."[95]

Meanwhile, the plans to devote the next day (9 November) to a celebra-tion of "proletarian children" were about to get under way. The program was crafted to mimic the previous days' adult marches. Participants, now pro-jected to number fifty thousand, all children of workers or, in any case, of the poor, were drawn from factory children's organizations, public primary schools, and orphanages. Beginning at 10:00 AM, carrying red banners, flags, and placards (some obviously of their own creation), the "little proletari-ans" gathered at assembly points all over Petrograd at two-hour intervals under the watchful eyes of their teachers and volunteer coordinators from trade unions. The children then clambered aboard decorated streetcars, the youngest ones riding the entire way to the headquarters of the General Staff adjoining Uritskii (Palace) Square, across from the Winter Palace. Older children alighted several blocks away, formed columns led by girls in red ker-chiefs carrying white chrysanthemums or multicolored flags, and paraded down 25 October Prospekt to Uritskii Square singing the *Internationale*. To a *Petrogradskaia pravda* reporter, "the sound of their anthem coming from the mouths of youthful proletarians warmed the hearts of workers lining the streets and watching with delight as the younger, developing generation of future citizens and builders of socialism on earth moved passed."[96]

The crowds of children formed a giant quadrangle on the vast square be-fore the Winter Palace. The day was blustery, but the sky was a clear blue. Shivering, the children listened to a military band playing the *Internationale* and to Lunacharskii describing the altogether glorious future that awaited them thanks to their elders' struggle for freedom, equality, and brotherhood. In the Winter Palace, short skits, motion pictures, and concerts were pre-sented for them. The children were treated to hot tea and snacks, and then, accompanied by military bands and costumed clowns, they paraded up Nev-skii Prospekt to Uprising Square, where they boarded streetcars and returned to their assembly points. To *Krasnaia gazeta*'s editors the next day, this event

Children of the poor celebrate the first anniversary of the October revolution, 9 November 1918. State Museum of the Political History of Russia, St. Petersburg.

proved that now no one could abuse Petrograd's orphaned, homeless children, because in the Soviet government they had a loving mother.[97] More soberly, Samoilova was as realistic about the situation of poor and orphaned children as she had been in public comments about the political backwardness of female workers.[98] Lauding the fact that children of the working poor were given a chance to feel that they were part of the October holiday, she stressed that, fundamentally, almost nothing had been done to improve their lot. To her, 9 November was less a children's celebration than a celebration of children, and an expression of the need to address their continuing plight.[99]

* * *

Devoting 9 November to a grand "proletarian children's day" eliminated the possibility that, on that day, "all forces from Petrograd" would disperse into the surrounding province to take part in holiday festivities there. Soviets from some regional centers provided holiday speakers but, for the most part, outlying towns and villages had to arrange their own holiday events. A report sent to the Petrograd Telegraph Agency by a proud Bolshevik from Kotel'skii county (*volost'*) in the Iamburg district (*uezd*) southwest of Petrograd, provides the fullest description I have been able to find of the holiday celebration in a remote corner of Petrograd Province.[100] Torrential rains on the night of 6/7 November and the following day had caused major flooding, according to this report, but in the early morning local peasants, undeterred, had decorated their huts and waded through ankle-deep mud to village assemblies (*skhody*). For purposes of the celebration, the county, which embraced fifty-six villages and several small factories, was divided into four districts. Around midday, the inhabitants of villages in each of these districts, many of them carrying red banners and flags, gathered together. At these assemblies, a local Bolshevik gave a speech about the international significance of the seizure of power by the proletariat and the village poor in Russia, and the future course of the struggle for socialism abroad. After these remarks, the villagers, singing revolutionary songs, set off for Kotly, the county seat.

During the previous night the residents of Kotly, the center of one of the four districts, had built a "peasant-style" triumphal arch designed by a "local builder" and finished equipping a so-called Worker-Peasant University Named after Lenin. Its grand opening was to be a highlight of the local festivities. Peasants from surrounding villages arrived carrying banners. Gathering at the "university," they were formed into columns. At the front were children from the Kotel'skii school carrying two crimson silk banners decorated with golden tassels and cords. Behind them was a group of local Bolsheviks carrying a banner that read "Death to Kulaks—The Poor Are Coming." The crowd listened to a representative of the Iamburg Soviet speak on the international significance of unity between the proletariat and the multimillion poorer peasantry in Russia, and then to cheers and revolutionary songs by the county's theater circle, the throng marched through surrounding villages, many of them decorated with greenery, red flags, and arches covered with green pine boughs, and back to Kotly. There, they merged with the other three district processions at the triumphal arch, and proceeded to the "university" for an official opening by representatives of the Iamburg Soviet. A red flag was raised on the flagpole of the "university," and the Kotel'skii military detachment fired several blank rounds from their rifles in salute. The assembled marchers shouted rousing cheers, after which they were invited into the building for tea and candy (free for children and official delegates, and at a "nominal fee below cost" for everyone else).

In the early evening, the crowd gathered around a "bonfire of the revolution" to witness the burning of effigies of tormentors and servants of the old regime, including "Albert," an especially hated local former landowner. To the author of this account, an unforgettable sight was the gray-bearded men who had learned about the torment of serfs imposed by landowners from their fathers and grandfathers dancing in childlike merriment around the bonfire as flames lapped at an effigy of Albert. At that moment, he wrote, it seemed as if everybody was welded together by the complete destruction of the old system and the blaze of world revolution that was spreading socialism to Europe. Following the celebration around the bonfire, a dance for young people was held at the "university"; rooms were also set aside for those who wanted to sing. The gaiety lasted well into the night, and space was found for inhabitants of distant villages who wanted to spend the night.[101]

*   *   *

The organization of the commemoration of the first anniversary of the October revolution in Petrograd sheds light on several key questions relating to the Bolsheviks and Soviet power in the former capital a year after "October." First is the issue of the institutional locus of power and authority at that time. Putting aside for a moment the relationship between Bolshevik party committees and local soviets, the position of higher Soviet authorities in Petrograd with respect to district soviets had changed significantly since the mid summer. To be sure, district soviets still jealously guarded their independence, but, in practice, it was now clear that they were fighting a losing battle. Testifying to this reality was the dominating role in festival arrangements of the Central Bureau for Organization of the October Festivities, formed under the aegis of the Presidium of the Petrograd Soviet, and the strictly subordinate position of organizing commissions attached to district soviets in preparations at the local level.

Especially at the start, district soviets had strong, independent ideas about the organization of the holiday in their neighborhoods, including concern for involving representatives of local factories in holiday planning as a way of reestablishing connections with workers generally. At the same time, these soviets exhibited their customary disdain for higher-ups. However, the fact that the Central Bureau controlled funding for the holiday forced district holiday commissions to suppress their distaste for supervision and accept comprehensive direction from above. The only major element of the holiday generated largely "from below" was the festival for children. Although still a long way from realization, by the fall of 1918 the kind of centralized, strict, exclusively Bolshevik hierarchical power structure fostered by the Central Bureau and its separate sections was already being aggressively promoted as the model for all government institutions, from the SK SO and its commissariats, as well as the Petrograd Soviet, down to district soviets and their sections.

Concurrently, in district soviets to a greater extent than in the SK SO and the Petrograd Soviet, not to speak of the PCheka, the direct influence of party agencies was no longer limited to token representation, as it had been for much of the year. The modest involvement of party agencies in organizing the holiday was less a measure of relative power than of utility. More commonly, in ways that differed significantly from district to district, the party's influence was now exerted through nominations to soviet leadership posts, mandatory periodic reports by soviet officials and criticism of them at local party meetings, and organized district soviet Bolshevik fractions. Yet, even in districts where these mechanisms were best developed, they indicated growing influence rather than control over district soviet policies. As a result, acrimony between district party committees and soviets, as well as between district soviets and city-level government agencies, was still the norm. The structural relationship of party bodies to soviets remained unsettled.

15

Price of Survival

DURING THE culminating stage of the October revolution in Petrograd, Lenin's demand that power be seized at once won out over the Bolshevik moderates' more patient and cautious plan of undermining the Provisional Government gradually and linking its formal removal to the action of the Second All-Russian Congress of Soviets. Yet, despite this initial, seemingly decisive setback, the moderates continued to fight for their goals which, it should be reemphasized, were enshrined in the Bolsheviks' pre-October political program. Firmly convinced that for the Bolsheviks to maintain an independent, ultra-radical course, as Lenin and Trotsky demanded, would be suicidal for the revolution, they sought support for broadening the government at meetings of the Bolshevik Central Committee and Petersburg Committee, and in the party's CEC fraction. Moreover, together with the Left SRs, the Menshevik-Internationalists, and smaller left socialist parties, they stood firmly for the preservation of civil liberties and for the accountability of the Sovnarkom to the more broadly representative CEC, as stipulated by the soviet congress, at CEC plenary sessions, and, most important, at the emergency talks on the formation of a broad socialist coalition government sponsored by Vikzhel.

At first, the efforts of moderate Bolsheviks at the Vikzhel talks were impeded by the determination of the Mensheviks and SRs to exclude Lenin and Trotsky from any future government, if not to reverse the October revolution entirely. Subsequently, they were undercut by popular enthusiasm for the program of the soviets, the early military successes of revolutionary forces, and the defection of the Left SRs to the Leninists. Indisputably, as well, the moderates were outmaneuvered by Lenin at every turn. Their ouster from control of the Bolshevik fraction in the Constituent Assembly in December 1917 marked the end of their collective fight against the Leninists, and an end to their existence as an influential, intraparty national grouping.

Historians generally have been dismissive of the moderate Bolsheviks, emphasizing their opposition to Lenin's triumphant radicalism before and after the Bolshevik seizure of power and ignoring their critically important role as stewards of the party during Lenin's extended absence from Petrograd in the summer and early fall of 1917. Undeniably, however, without the moderate Bolsheviks' forceful and clever *political* strategy during the run-up to the October days, which was supported by Trotsky and other radical Bolshevik leaders who shared Lenin's theoretical views and goals but were wary of his violent tactics, Lenin's belated *military* moves against the Provisional Government on 25 October would not have been feasible. Then, too, the moderates were certainly not the small minority depicted in Soviet accounts. Their views on revolutionary strategy and goals were widely shared inside and outside the party. In retrospect, their thinking about the long-term dangers of an exclusively Bolshevik assumption of power in backward Russia appears very wise. In line with their assumptions, the decisive uprisings of the European proletariat that Lenin and Trotsky believed were the precondition for building socialism in Russia failed to materialize.

The Bolsheviks' struggles for survival during the first year of Soviet power in Petrograd provide valuable insights into the dynamics of the earliest stage in the process leading to the consolidation of the highly centralized, ultra-authoritarian Bolshevik political system in Soviet Russia. The answer to the central historiographical question posed at the start of this book is clear. Neither revolutionary ideology nor an established pattern of dictatorial behavior are of much help to explain fundamental changes in the character and political role of the Bolshevik party, or of soviets in Petrograd, between November 1917 and November 1918, although the impact of both cannot be entirely discounted. The fact is that the Petrograd Bolsheviks had to transform themselves from rebels into rulers without benefit of an advance plan or even a concept. Most significant in shaping the earliest evolution of party and soviet bodies, their relationship to each other, and the Soviet political system generally, were the realities the Bolsheviks faced in their often seemingly hopeless struggle for survival.

So it was that, in the aftermath of "October," ignoring the principle that all government power should be transferred to local soviets, Petrograd's new authorities did not dissolve the Petrograd City Duma until it became apparent that it had become a national center for opposing them. Moreover, not until forced to act because of the dissolution of the Military Revolutionary Committee (MRC) and strikes by civil servants did the Bolshevik-dominated Petrograd Soviet take power into its own hands, and, even then, it sought to retain much of the city duma's administrative infrastructure and professional personnel. Similarly, toward the end of 1917, district soviets were also left with no choice but to dissolve antagonistic district dumas. Although forgoing the election of new ones, district soviet leaders tried their best to staff newly created administrative sections with experienced personnel from corresponding duma boards. Precisely because all this was done without any plan or central direction, the structure of local soviets and the locus of power within them varied significantly. They tended to operate on their own and, in large measure, to define their constantly expanding roles in response to emerging needs and concerns. Relatively quickly, they became politically powerful and staunchly protective of their autonomy and independence from interference both by national and citywide government agencies and by higher and parallel party bodies. In these circumstances, each of Petrograd's districts became rather like neighborhood fiefdoms headed by the local district soviet.

Yet, because district soviets quickly became so important for police protection, food distribution, schooling, housing, public health, peoples' courts, social welfare, military recruitment, and local administration generally, the Petrograd Soviet, the SK PTK, the SK SO, and even the PCheka relied on them and, in this way, contributed immeasurably to their aggrandizement. They became the new regime's primary institutions of local government. Party bodies assigned their most capable personnel to work in district soviets. Nonetheless, during the first half of 1918, they took no further interest in them. This was as true of the relationship of the Bolshevik Petersburg Committee to the Petrograd Soviet as it was of the association between district party committees and district soviets.

Three factors explain the relatively weak leadership role of the Petrograd Bolshevik party organization during the first months of Soviet rule. Initially, the most important of these was the lack of any special concern on the part of most veteran Bolsheviks with the institutionalization of an authoritative and exclusive directing role for party organs in government. Most historians of Soviet Russia have assumed that the development of a highly centralized, party-directed authoritarian political system was one of the keys to the ability of the Bolsheviks to survive their early crises, and that this organizational model was envisioned and pursued from the start. However, the large body of relevant sources now available leaves no room for doubt that for some time the need for a highly structured, all-powerful, centralized party dictatorship was by no means apparent to most Petrograd Bolsheviks. In 1917, the Bolsheviks had called for transfer of all power to independent, representative, and democratic soviets. In the aftermath of the October revolution, although initially hesitant, Bolshevik leaders in the Petrograd Soviet and in district soviets enthusiastically embraced this ideal.

A second factor that helps explain the weak leadership of the Petrograd Bolshevik organization in these earliest months was that, between January and April 1918, it was a participant in, and on occasion paralyzed by, the bitter intraparty conflict over ratification of the Brest treaty. Until mid March, Left Communists dominated the Petersburg Committee and most district committees, and a state of war existed between them and the Leninist leadership of the Petrograd Soviet headed by Zinoviev. The debilitating effects of the controversy on the party and on local government were not eased until late March when, at the emergency Fifth Conference of Petrograd Bolsheviks, the Left Communists were defeated.

A final factor contributing to the ineffectiveness of the Petrograd Bolshevik organization at this juncture was the colossal attrition of its most reliable and qualified personnel. It cannot be emphasized enough that, during the culminating stage of the struggle for power during the October 1917 revolution in Petrograd, the Bolsheviks drew great strength from their party's representative character, and its close ties and continuing interaction with factory workers, lower ranking military personnel, and a myriad of mass organizations. Another advantage was that party membership in the city totaled roughly fifty thousand, headed by the cream of veteran leaders at all levels of the Bolshevik organization. Then, too, tens of thousands of additional workers, including significant numbers of factory women, soldiers of the Petrograd garrison, and Baltic Fleet sailors were enthusiastic supporters of the Bolshevik revolutionary political platform.

The organizational dynamism stemming from the party's relatively large number of dedicated members began to evaporate as soon as the Bolsheviks came to power. In the aftermath of the October days in Petrograd, thousands of party members were sent off either to help consolidate the revolution around the country or to enter full-time government service with the MRC, Petrograd soviets, or other municipal agencies. Virtually overnight, the political work of Bolshevik district committees, the lifeblood of the party in 1917, slowed precipitously.

The Bolsheviks retained sufficient organizational strength to mount a vigorous, compelling, and ultimately successful campaign in elections to the Constituent Assembly in Petrograd and the surrounding region. And this, in turn, helped them to overcome organizational weaknesses and to neutralize the threat to Soviet power posed by the Constituent Assembly, in which the SRs had a majority. However, the impact of the initial enthusiasm for Soviet power was bound to wane, especially as the state of the Petrograd party organization deteriorated. During the first months of 1918, fresh demands for party members to fight the counterrevolution on the Don, to join the newly forming Red Army, and to defend the approaches to Petrograd from the advancing Germans continued to drain party bodies, frequently leading to the complete breakdown of their agitation and organizational work. Ongoing recruitment efforts of new party members and crash training courses for them could not compensate for these losses. The close, interactive linkages between the Petrograd party organization and factory workers, soldiers, and sailors that had been key to the development of popular political programs and successful military strategies in 1917 were shattered. Despite the Bolsheviks' efforts, district soviets were crippled by personnel shortages just as their responsibilities for municipal government escalated. Participatory democracy in district soviets fell victim to this pinch. In the late winter and spring, drastic food shortages, expanding unemployment, and general disenchantment with the results of the October revolution accelerated these processes and significantly reduced the Bolsheviks' social base, as hungry and jobless workers fled Petrograd in search of food and employment.

By mid February, Bolshevik party membership in the capital had dropped from the estimated fifty thousand in October 1917 to around thirty-six thousand. Yet even these figures are deceptive, as a high percentage of the party's "finest" were engaged in full-time government, security, or military service and were completely divorced from party work. Moreover, large numbers of Bolsheviks nominally involved in the party (and local soviets, as well) were inexperienced new recruits and, even worse, many of the newcomers were outright criminals or simply self-serving individuals with no commitment to the party.

Political partnership with the Left SRs helped ease the difficulties caused by the early attrition of experienced Bolshevik personnel in terms of defending and deepening the revolution in Petrograd. Along with educated, intellectually lively, seasoned, independent-minded revolutionary leaders, the Left SRs were a source of dedicated rank-and-file cadres who were often more capable and reliable than hastily, indiscriminately recruited new Bolsheviks. Then, too, the Fourth City Conference of Petrograd Bolsheviks in mid February 1918 took steps to ease intraparty leadership problems arising from the loss of their most effective personnel. The size of the Petersburg Committee was drastically reduced, and it was replaced as the party's primary policy-making body for the city of Petrograd by the new, authoritative, and representative Delegates' Soviet. The creation of the Delegates' Soviet was an attempt to offset the potential blow to informed decision making caused by the shrinking of the Petersburg Committee. However, the Delegates' Soviet was plagued by the same exhausting pressures on party leaders that had prompted the restructuring of the Petersburg Committee, and it ceased to function during the endless crises of mid summer. The result was that, instead of helping retain the Petrograd Bolshevik organization's democratic norms and practices, the structural reforms undertaken by the Fourth City Conference of Petrograd Bolsheviks appear in retrospect to have been a major step toward their elimination.

At the time of the German advance toward Petrograd in the second half of February, the Bolshevik organization was battered by the loss of party members to the Red Army or irregular forces, and by the policy of encouraging government work over party work that was officially declared at that time and not rescinded for more than a month. The flight of the national government to Moscow in mid March to escape German forces dealt another major blow to Soviet power in Petrograd. The problem was not simply that the chief heroes of "October" slunk off to Moscow in apparent panic, naturally demoralizing factory workers. Equally important is that Lenin seems to have considered Petrograd doomed long after the immediate threat of occupation had eased. This helps explain his enduring tendency to ignore Petrograd's personnel needs and to treat the former capital as an unlimited source of manpower for service elsewhere.

In the spring of 1918, the Petrograd Bolsheviks were also weakened by the attraction of the Extraordinary Assembly of Delegates from Petrograd Factories and Plants to suffering factory workers. The history of the EAD has been of interest to historians primarily as the most important organized worker opposition movement outside the Bolshevik party to emerge in Russia during the Soviet era. But in the context of the critical problems that spawned the movement, as well as the depleted state of the Bolshevik party and the soviets, the history of the EAD merits attention as a gauge of the weakness and instability of Soviet power in the northwest. The need of top Petrograd Bolshevik leaders to manipulate elections to the Petrograd Soviet to assure their dominance of it is another measure of this weakness. Following the elections, government authorities in Petrograd took long delayed steps against the EAD. Yet, if anything, the extraordinary measures they took to prevent the EAD's general strike of 2 July revealed a lack of confidence rather than new-found strength.

By the time of the Sixth City Conference of Petrograd Bolsheviks in mid June, party membership had dropped another 63 percent to 13,472. Again, the full impact of this huge decline on the effectiveness of the party cannot be evaluated without considering the large percentage of Bolsheviks fully engaged in government service and the low quality of many of those still involved in party work in terms of experience, discipline, and commitment to the revolution. These realities impelled the Sixth City Conference to order that all Bolsheviks in government service become involved in some form of party activity. This admonition fell on deaf ears because of the impossibly heavy, unfamiliar burdens Bolsheviks carried in local government and because of the Bolsheviks' tendency, when engaged in soviets, to wholly dismiss the significance of party work and the authority of party bodies. At the same time, Moscow's insistent demands for party members to serve with food procurement detachments in grain-producing regions and to serve in the Red Army continued apace.

The impact of Bolshevik cadre shortages on attempts to revitalize party work, and on soviets, was also weakened immeasurably by the Soviet national government's treatment of the Left SRs. Between November 1917 and March 1918, Bolsheviks and Left SRs managed to collaborate productively despite fundamental differences on key issues. By the spring of 1918, however, the constructive stage in the Bolshevik–Left SR relationship at the national level was derailed by unbridgeable differences over the Brest treaty at the same time that the growing strength of the Left SRs in rural Russia threatened the Bolsheviks' continued hegemony over the revolution. For a majority of Left SRs, ratification of the Brest treaty was the last straw. In mid March, they withdrew from the Sovnarkom, and, from then on, the deterioration of their relationship with the Bolsheviks nationally accelerated. Concurrently, however, in Petrograd the Bolshevik–Left SR partnership thrived. Nikolai Kornilov's enlightened record as commissar of agriculture in the SK SO, though brief, provided an intriguing glimpse of the great potential value of collaboration with the Left SRs in developing the revolution in the countryside. The important, enduring steps of Prosh Proshian, second in importance only to Zinoviev, toward refashioning the Commissariat for Internal Affairs into an oblast-wide entity, and also working harmoniously with the Bolsheviks in the SK SO, are a similarly important indicator of the partnership's longer-term potential.

More often than not, Petrograd Left SRs focused on helping to cope with endless political and economic emergencies and, above all, not contributing to the instability of the Northern Commune. Thus, they suppressed their differences with the Bolsheviks over continuing concessions to the Germans, the reinstitution of juridical capital punishment as reflected in the execution of the "hero of the Baltic Fleet" Aleksandr Shchastny, and violent grain procurement policies. They turned a blind eye to the manipulation of the Bolsheviks' "victory" in the June elections to the Petrograd Soviet, and they collaborated in the suppression of the EAD. The conclusion is inescapable: from the time the Northern Commune was formed in May until the Left SRs were criminalized in July, cooperation between Bolsheviks and Left SRs at all levels of Petrograd government was one of the main keys to the survival of Soviet power in the northwest.

The critically important alliance between Bolsheviks and Left SRs in Petrograd was shattered by events in Moscow. Confident of their strength, national Left SR leaders had looked to the Fifth All-Russian Congress of Soviets as a vehicle for reshaping Soviet policies that they opposed. Only after electoral fraud gave the Bolsheviks a huge majority of congress delegates did they implement their ill-conceived, as yet undeveloped contingency option, the assassination of the German Ambassador to Moscow Count Wilhelm Mirbach. Their hope was that his killing would bring a quick end to the Brest peace by provoking Germany to resume military operations against Russia. The start of the second Battle of the Marne, which put German forces in the west on the defensive, and quick action by Lenin, destroyed this hope. Lenin orchestrated the brutal repression of Left SRs in the capital. Even though Soviet authorities in Petrograd knew that Mirbach's assassination caught Petrograd Left SRs by complete surprise, in a rare act of obedience to counterproductive instructions from Moscow, they forced the Petrograd Left SR leadership into hiding, launched a successful violent strike against Left SR military forces that they had previously counted on for help, and superintended the ouster of Left SRs from responsible positions in Petrograd government from top to bottom. From then on, Petrograd Left SRs, like their counterparts in Moscow, were essentially relegated to the ranks of the enemy.

Looking back on the development of the Bolshevik–Left SR partnership nationally, it is fair to conclude that its breakup had historical ramifications beyond marking the moment when the Soviet political system became a one-party dictatorship. The Left SRs provided Soviet power with a critically important link to the countryside. Had the Bolshevik–Left SR alliance survived, it seems likely that the Russian civil war would have been significantly less torturous. To be sure, once the Left SRs became a threat to the Bolsheviks' hold on power, as was the case in June and early July 1918, a decisive break with them may have been inevitable. It is also true, however, that in Petrograd the Bolshevik–Left SR alliance at all levels of city and regional government operated reasonably well and had not exhausted its potential when it was shattered by events in Moscow.

With respect to the structural evolution of the Soviet system, the political and economic crises of the late spring and early summer of 1918 in

Petrograd reflected the continued primacy of soviets, and the evolving role of party organizations in government. More precisely, although it is still difficult at this point to discern efforts by the SOK or the Bolshevik Petersburg Committee to exert systematic control over the policies of the SK SO or the Petrograd Soviet, a harbinger of the future relationship of party and soviets was the alacrity with which the Petersburg Committee acted to organize the party's fraction in the Petrograd Soviet following the elections in late June. At the same time, the events of this period showed that the relationship between the Petrograd Soviet and district soviets was then still fluid. From time to time the Petrograd Soviet and its leadership bodies attempted to direct district soviets. But, for the most part, district soviets successfully guarded their independence, and retained the possibility of accepting or rejecting directives from above, and creating institutions and pursuing policies of their own making. Not until the fall of 1918, amid preparations to celebrate the first anniversary of the October revolution, did this situation begin to change.

Despite the negative effects of the Petrograd Bolsheviks' break with the Left SRs, during the rest of the summer Lenin's demands for the participation of party members and unaffiliated workers in food procurement detachments not only continued but significantly increased. At the same time, the mandatory Red Army service for workers and for Bolsheviks with military experience, which had been instituted in connection with the expansion of the civil war and the beginning of the Allied interventions, also contributed to the Petrograd Bolsheviks' emasculation. And all this came when the Bolshevik Central Committee was pressing for the imposition of a system of controls over government policy decision making through party fractions and collectives in soviets and other government agencies. Although implementation of systematic control was totally unrealistic in the prevailing environment, the Bolshevik Petersburg Committee, for one, now began to consider public policy and attempted to intervene in government issues about which it felt strongly. Moreover, under these strains, amid fears that nearby German forces were preparing to finally occupy Petrograd, as well as signs of increased counterrevolutionary activity, the Petrograd Bolsheviks developed a siege mentality.

This mind-set was reinforced by the continued free fall of party membership, from 13,472 in June to a paltry 6,000 in September. The qualitative implications of this decline were captured in Strumilin's statistical survey of party members in Petrograd which suggested that more than 50 percent of the membership held full-time positions outside the party; almost as high a percentage of the membership were newcomers who had joined the party in 1918; and, overall, only a tiny proportion of members who were engaged in party work were qualified to hold responsible positions, either by experience or education. This explains why increased emphasis was now placed on party schools, as well as crash training in the use of weapons for all Petrograd Bolsheviks who needed it. The siege mentality of Petrograd Bolsheviks was reflected most significantly in the Petersburg Committee's increasing attraction for immediate mass Red Terror against perceived enemies as an essential security measure.

Contrary to conventional wisdom, the Red Terror that exploded in Petrograd on 30 August was not the consequence of a nationwide political crackdown inspired by Lenin and orchestrated by the VCheka, nor was it a spontaneous, popular response to the assassination of Uritskii on 30 August and the failed attempt on Lenin's life that evening. The burden of existing evidence indicates that these events can best be understood as the culmination of a gradual process during which the moderating influence of such key individuals as Uritskii, Krestinskii, and Proshian was replaced by pressure for systematic Red Terror, in part "from below."

The process leading to this outcome had begun in earnest during the second half of June, following Volodarskii's assassination. A month later, after hearing a disturbing report on the rejuvenation of the counterrevolution, the Bolshevik Petersburg Committee pushed for the immediate proclamation of a program of mass terror against class enemies. On this occasion, Petrograd government and military leaders resisted the Petersburg's Committee's pressure. Thereafter, however, signs of the degree to which Uritskii's moderation was losing ground to proponents of mass terror as a means of safeguarding the rear mounted week by week.

The start of the Red Terror in Petrograd can be traced to a meeting of top government and party officials convened by the Bolshevik Petersburg Committee on 30 August, a few hours after Uritskii's assassination but well before the failed attempt on Lenin's life. Fed by unsubstantiated allegations that the killing was part of a coordinated domestic and international conspiracy to overthrow Soviet power in northwest Russia, its primary motivation was to safeguard the home front in order to maximize the personnel that could be spared for service with food procurement detachments and the Red Army. Not until the initial wave of arrests and executions in Petrograd had subsided did national government bodies in Moscow, as well the SK SO and the Petrograd Soviet, endorse the proclamation of Red Terror.

That the Red Terror in Petrograd was initiated by the Bolshevik Petersburg Committee reflected the increasing willingness of party bodies to intervene in government. Subsequently, popular hostility toward domestic and foreign enemies was fueled by a concerted campaign in the press and at mass meetings and rallies. A centerpiece of this campaign was the "Lockhart Case," which was intended to demonstrate the close ties between domestic and foreign conspirators in Moscow and Petrograd aimed at crushing Bolshevism. Yet, after initially justifying the raid on the British Embassy in Petrograd, during which Cromie was killed, on the grounds that a counterrevolutionary plot was being hatched there, and pledging to publish incriminating correspondence seized in the attack, little more was said about it. The near silence about Cromie and his colleagues amid the storm of attacks on Allied secret agents during much of the Red Terror in Petrograd may have been because little of value was seized in the raid. Also, although British archival sources provide solid documentation of Cromie's extensive efforts to engineer the Petrograd Bolsheviks' overthrow and leave no doubt that Soviet agents had infiltrated Cromie's operation, focusing attention on him following his death would only have further discredited the Soviet government internationally.

Be that as it may, once rolling, the Red Terror in Petrograd developed a momentum of its own, ensnaring popular figures with no political value, critically important professionals, trade unionists, and even individuals who worked with the Bolsheviks. The precise PCheka tabulations of shooting victims in the former KGB archive tell only part of the story, as they do not include Cheka hostages and large numbers of executions carried out by district-level security agencies and roving worker bands. Nonetheless, the Red Terror failed in its objective of halting conspiracies against the Bolsheviks, as evidenced by the abortive rebellion of the Second Baltic Fleet Detachment in mid October.

The beginning of preparations for the first anniversary of the October revolution in Petrograd coincided not only with the Red Terror but with promising news from battle fronts in west central Russia and the intensification of revolutionary explosions in Central Europe. To Petrograd Bolsheviks at all levels, the latter appeared to be certain harbingers of the long-awaited worldwide socialist revolution that would inevitably bring desperately needed aid from abroad to long-suffering Russia—after which the Bolshevized workers of Petrograd and other Russian urban centers, alongside their foreign comrades, would join in an inexorable march to consolidate the socialist revolution internationally. A magnificent jubilee unlike any other in history in terms of content and popular participation was intended to give a strong fillip to revolutionary explosions abroad and to put the "Imperialist powers," including their subversive agents in Russia, on the defensive.

Closely related to this was the Petrograd Bolsheviks' self-perception or, better, their perception of Red Petrograd, as the universally recognized capital and vanguard of the worldwide proletarian revolution. Virtually all the plans for the holiday celebration were aimed at demonstrating and furthering Petrograd's past and future glory under Bolshevik hegemony. Consequently, Moscow's scheduling of the Sixth All-Russian Congress of Soviets, intended to establish its pride of place as revolutionary headquarters, was a bitter blow to the Petrograd Bolsheviks. At a time of great political difficulty and unprecedented scarcity, they spared nothing to counter it.

On the night of 9/10 November, as the spectacular celebration marking the first anniversary of October ended, word reached Petrograd that Kaiser Wilhelm had abdicated and that a Soviet government on the Russian model had taken power in Berlin. Il'in-Zhenevskii, then an official at the Commissariat for Military Affairs, was at the theater taking in a holiday offering when he heard the joyous news:

> Everything was normal. . . . Before one of the acts was about to begin, a man in a jacket and high boots came on to the stage and said, "Comrades! We have just had news from Germany. There has been a revolution . . . Wilhelm has been overthrown. A Soviet of workers' deputies has been formed in Berlin and has sent us a greeting." It is hard to convey what followed. . . . The announcement was met with a kind of roar, and frenzied applause shook the theater for several minutes . . . Here it was, it had come, support from the proletariat of Western Europe. . . . It seemed that everything would develop differently from now on. All interest in what was happening on the stage vanished . . . There they were still speaking their lines . . . but our thoughts were far away, over there in Berlin, where red flags were flying in the streets, where a soviet of workers' deputies was in session, where another knot had been tied in the world proletarian revolution.[1]

Sailors of the Baltic Fleet immediately radioed fraternal greetings to their counterparts in "free Germany":

> We knew that you, sailors of Kiel, are our brothers and would be with us. . . . We salute you in these great days . . . Comrades, use our experience—we are happy to help you . . . Long live the international Red Fleet.[2]

Bolsheviks at the Government Printing Office hurriedly organized German-language courses for party members in their plant, clearly to facilitate close interaction with revolutionary German masses.[3] Even Lenin, in a telegram for immediate circulation in Petrograd announcing the "triumph of the revolution in Germany," suddenly sounded euphoric.[4] To members of the Executive Committee of the Vyborg district soviet, the change in the situation of Petrograd brought about by the late-breaking developments in Germany seemed so decisive that they immediately resolved to send an appeal to the Sovnarkom to return to Red Petrograd, because, as they put it, "the political situation has changed drastically and unfolding developments indicate that the time has come for Petersburg to resurrect itself as the center [of international revolution] and to play a commanding role in the European revolution."[5]

The assumptions underlying the appeal of the Executive Committee of the Vyborg district soviet were dashed so quickly that it is unlikely that the call to return to Petrograd was even considered. In contrast to the situation in Russia on the eve of the 1917 revolutions, in the fall of 1918 decisive military defeats and economic difficulties, rather than a fundamental repudiation of the existing social and political order, dictated the democratization of Germany's government, the formation of a left liberal-moderate socialist cabinet, and its request for the armistice that was to end the world war even before Kaiser Wilhelm's formal abdication on 9 November. During the first week and a half of November, worker and soldier soviets on the Russian model had been formed by sailors in Kiel, and later by workers and soldiers in Munich, Berlin, and other major German cities. However, a majority of radical Independent Socialists agreed to join a new national government controlled by the moderate Majority Socialists.

For a short while, a kind of dual power existed in Germany, with workers' and soldiers' soviets operating alongside a new provisional government. But the vast majority of these soviets were controlled by the moderates. Committed to a Western-type parliamentary democracy, they consolidated their power and restored relative calm. Ironically, the creation of soviets by rebelling German workers, soldiers, and sailors demanding bread and an end to the war was a conscious replication of the Russian revolutionary experience. By the same token, aversion to Bolshevik extremism was a significant factor in shaping the moderate outcome of the 1918 German revolution. Following their joyous celebration of the first anniversary of the October revolution, in the absence of unification with their revolutionary German brethren, the Petrograd Bolsheviks remained on their own. Their lonely, costly struggle for survival resumed with scarcely a pause.

CHRONOLOGY OF KEY EVENTS

1917

October

25–27	Second All-Russian Congress of Soviets
29	Military Revolutionary Committee (MRC) suppresses anti-Soviet uprising in Petrograd
29–5 November	Vikzhel-sponsored talks on broadening government
30	Red forces repulse General Krasnov's Cossacks supporting Kerensky at Pulkovo

November

3–4	Bolshevik moderates resign from party Central Committee and the Sovnarkom
12–14	Elections to the Constituent Assembly in Petrograd
13	Zinoviev becomes chair of Petrograd Soviet
15	All-Russian Executive Committee of Peasants' Soviets merges with the CEC
17–9 December	Negotiations between Bolsheviks and Left SRs result in the formation of a coalition
19–28	First Left SR National Congress
22	Armistice between Russia and the Central Powers
28	Original opening date for the Constituent Assembly; arrests of Kadets begin

December

1	Bolshevik moderates gain control of the party's Constituent Assembly fraction
5	MRC abolished
7	Sovnarkom creates All-Russian Extraordinary Commission for Combating Counterrevolution, Speculation, and Sabotage (VCheka)
9	Formal peace negotiations with the Central Powers begin in Brest-Litovsk
12	Bolshevik moderates purged from leadership of party's Constituent Assembly fraction
16	Arrests and harassment of moderate socialist delegates to the Constituent Assembly intensify

1918

January

1	Failed attempt to assassinate Lenin
3–4	Martial law declared in Petrograd
5	Soviet security forces fire on mass demonstrations supporting Constituent Assembly
5–6	Constituent Assembly meets and is forcibly dispersed
8	Start of a bitter two-month conflict within Bolshevik leadership and between Leninists and Left SRs over separate peace
10–18	Third All-Russian Congress of Soviets of Workers' and Soldiers' Deputies
12–21	Major wave of political strikes in Western and Central Europe
13	Third All-Russian Congress of Soviets of Peasants' Deputies merges with Third All-Russian Congress of Workers' and Soldiers' Deputies
15	Formation of Red Army begins
28	Trotsky refuses to sign "obscene" peace, and Soviet delegation leaves Brest-Litovsk

February

1/14	Russia switches from Julian calendar to the Western Gregorian calendar
17–20	Fourth City Conference of Petrograd Bolsheviks
18	Germans resume offensive on Eastern Front, meeting little resistance
18/19	Germany's annexationist peace terms accepted, but its attack continues
20	Sovnarkom issues proclamation, "The Socialist Fatherland Is in Danger!"
21/22	Petrograd declared under siege
24	New, harsher German peace terms accepted by Soviet goverment German forces continue unimpeded advance—Petrograd appears threatened
26	Sovnarkom resolves to move capital to Moscow

March

3	Treaty of Brest-Litovsk signed
6–8	Seventh All-Russian Bolshevik Party Congress approves Brest treaty
10/11	Soviet government and Bolshevik and Left SR leadership flee Petrograd for Moscow
11	Sovkom of the Petrograd Labor Commune (SK PTK) formed
13	Extraordinary Assembly of Delegates from Petrograd Factories and Plants (EAD) holds first of nineteen plenary meetings
15–16	Fourth All-Russian Congress of Soviets meets; ratifies Brest treaty

18	Left SRs and Left Communists resign from Sovnarkom
20	Emergency Fifth City Conference of Petrograd Bolsheviks

April

17–25	Second All-Russian Left SR Party Congress meets; endorses withdrawal of Left SRs from Sovnarkom
24–14 May	Crisis over fate of Fort Ino
26–29	First Northern Oblast Congress of Soviets meets; creates "Northern Commune" with Bolshevik–Left SR coalition government, the Sovkom of the Northern Oblast (SK SO)

May

8–12	Unrest among Petrograd workers over drastic food shortages reaches new highs
9	German occupation of Petrograd again appears imminent
	Policy of forming food procurement detachments to seize surplus grain from peasants by force instituted
10	Lenin issues the first of several appeals for Petrograd to furnish thousands of workers for food procurement detachments
25	Rebellion of Czech Legion along Trans-Siberian railway erupts

June

8	Decree on Committees of the Village Poor (*kombedy*) adopted
8–10	Sixth City Conference of Petrograd Bolsheviks
10	Fifth All-Russian Congress of Soviets scheduled to convene on 28 June
14	Mensheviks and SRs expelled from CEC
17–28	Elections to Petrograd Soviet
20	Volodarskii assassinated
22	Failed rebellion of Obukhov workers and mine-laying flotilla
24	Left SR Central Committee adopts contingency plan to assassinate German officials in Russia to provoke resumption of war with Germany
26–2 July	EAD plans general strike but is suppressed by government; movement shut down
29	Red Army draft begins

July

4–10	Fifth All-Russian Congress of Soviets in Moscow
6	Count Mirbach assassinated by Left SRs
7	Bolshevik authorities in Moscow and Petrograd suppress Left SRs
8–14	Record cholera epidemic in Petrograd peaks
10	Fifth All-Russian Congress of Soviets adopts first Soviet constitution
14/15	Germans begin last offensive on Western Front
16	Nicholas II and his family executed in Ekaterinburg

18–22	German offensive in West is stopped and tide turns decisively against Central Powers
22	EAD's planning meeting for national workers' congress broken up by Soviet authorities
23	Bolshevik Petersburg Committee protests security lapses; exerts pressure for Red Terror

August

1–2	Second Northern Oblast Congress of Soviets calls for mass terror toward the bourgeoisie as a means of securing the rear
2	Allied intervention begins in earnest with occupation of Archangel
21	PCheka begins shooting prisoners
26	Alleged attempt to kill Zinoviev
28	Petrograd Soviet proclaims intention of liquidating all political prisoners in the event of further attempts to assassinate Bolshevik leaders
30	Uritskii shot and killed Red Terror in Petrograd begins Lenin seriously wounded in failed assassination attempt
31	PCheka raids British Embassy; Cromie, leader of anti-Soviet conspiracy, killed in shootout

September

4	Sovnarkom authorizes shooting of all persons belonging to counter-revolutionary organizations or involved in antigovernment plots Main American interventionist forces come ashore at Archangel
6	Shooting of 512 political prisoners in Petrograd during preceding week announced First of several hostage lists published Petrograd Soviet resolves to answer White Terror with Red Terror
15	Central Bureau for the organization of festivities to celebrate the first anniversary of the October revolution formed
17–21	Seventh Conference of Petrograd Bolsheviks
24	Progress report on preparations for October holiday presented to Petrograd Soviet

October

3	Lenin calls for formation of three-million-man Red Army
14	Failed rebellion of the Second Baltic Fleet Detachment
15–18	Conference of Chekas in Northern Oblast
30	Revolt of sailors at Kiel, Germany's chief naval base

November

1	Final report on preparations for the October holiday presented to Petrograd Soviet
2	Kiel sailors, joined by workers and soldiers, form soviet on Russian

model; movement spreads to most other naval bases and major German cities

3–6	Congress of *kombedy* in the Northern Oblast
6–9	Emergency Sixth All-Russian Congress of Soviets in Moscow
7–9	First anniversary of the October revolution celebrated in Petrograd
8–9	Mass protest demonstrations break out in Berlin
	Workers' and soldiers' soviet is formed in Berlin
9/10	Kaiser Wilhelm abdicates
	German Republic proclaimed

NOTES

Prologue

1. The Left SRs, the main radical wing of the Socialist Revolutionary Party, opposed the war effort and coalition with the liberals, and called for creation of an exclusively socialist coalition government under the aegis of the soviets. Led by Iulii Martov, the Menshevik-Internationalists were an analogous left group within the Menshevik movement. Martov and like-minded Mensheviks demanded immediate peace without annexations or indemnities. In the spring of 1917, they opposed socialist participation in the Provisional Government and, by mid-summer, they advocated the formation of an exclusively socialist government. Both the Left SRs and the Menshevik-Internationalists were particularly strong in the SR and Menshevik organizations in Petrograd.

2. RGASPI, f. 60, op. 1, d. 26, l. 4, 4 ob.

3. V. I. Lenin, *Polnoe sobranie sochineniia,* 5th ed., vol. 34 (Moscow, 1962), pp. 239–247.

4. RGASPI, f. 17, op. 1, d. 81, l. 1. Institut marksizma-leninizma pri TsK KPSS, *Perepiska sekretariata TsK RSDRP (b)-RKP (b) s mestnymi partiinymi organizatsiami,* vol. 1 (Moscow, 1957), pp. 52–53.

5. Lenin, *Polnoe sobranie sochinenii,* 34:281.

6. According to a preliminary report by the Credentials Committee, 300 of the 670 delegates to the congress were Bolsheviks, 193 were SRs (of whom more than half were Left SRs), 68 were Mensheviks, 16 were United Social-Democratic Internationalists, 14 were Menshevik-Internationalists, and the remainder either were affiliated with one of a number of smaller political groups or did not belong to any formal organization. An overwhelming number of delegates, some 505 of them, were firmly committed to the transfer of "All Power to the Soviets," that is, to the creation of a Soviet government that reflected the party composition of the congress (M. N. Pokrovskii and Ia. A. Iakovleva, eds., *Vtoroi vserossiiskii s"ezd sovetov R. i S. D.* [Moscow-Leningrad, 1928], pp. 144–153).

7. Ibid., pp. 4, 34.

8. The United Social-Democratic Internationalist Party was formed in mid-October 1917 by left Mensheviks, several of whom were associated with *Novaia zhizn',* Maksim Gorky's daily.

9. Pokrovskii and Iakovleva, *Vtoroi vserossiiskii s"ezd sovetov,* pp. 4, 35.

10. Ibid., pp. 4–7, 35–38.

11. N. N. Sukhanov, *Zapiski o revoliutsii,* vol. 3 (Moscow, 1992), p. 307.

12. Pokrovskii and Iakovleva, *Vtoroi vserossiiskii s"ezd sovetov,* pp. 7–8, 42–44.

13. B. I. Nikolaevskii, "Stranitsy proshlogo: K 80-letiiu L. O. Tsederbaum-Dan," *Sotsialisticheskii vestnik,* 1958, no. 7/8:150.

14. Pokrovskii and Iakovleva, *Vtoroi vserossiiskii s"ezd sovetov,* pp. 8–9, 45.

1. Forming a Government

1. Institut marksizma-leninizma pri TsKPSS, *Protokoly tsentral'nogo komiteta RSDRP (b), avgust 1917–fevral' 1918* (Moscow, 1958), p. 120.

2. A. I. Razgon, "Zabytye imena," in *Pervoe Sovetskoe pravitel'stvo* (Moscow, 1991), p. 455.

3. *Znamia truda,* October 27, 1917, p. 4. See also S. Mstislavskii, *Five Days Which Transformed Russia* (Bloomington, 1988), p. 130.

4. A. I. Razgon, "Pravitel'stvennyi blok," *Istoricheskie zapiski,* vol. 117, 1989, p. 108. See also R. M. Savitskaia, "Istochniki o V. I. Lenine po podgotovke i provedenii II vserossiiskogo s"ezda sovetov," in *Velikii Oktiabr': Istoriia, istoriografiia, istochnikovedenie* (Moscow, 1978), p. 263; Pokrovskii and Iakovleva, *Vtoroi vserossiiskii s"ezd sovetov,* pp. 26, 83. For Kamkov's retrospective explanation of the rationale behind this rejection, see *Protokoly pervogo s"ezda partii levykh sotsialistov-revoliutsionerov internatsionalistov* (Petrograd, 1918), p. 43.

5. Pokrovskii and Iakovleva, *Vtoroi vserossiiskii s"ezd sovetov,* pp. 13, 56–57.

6. Ibid., pp. 15–16, 59–62.

7. Ibid., pp. 29, 86–87.

8. Ibid., pp. 15–21, 59–68.

9. Ibid., pp. 21–25, 69–77.

10. Lenin, *Polnoe sobranie sochinenii,* 35:28–29.

11. Apart from Lenin and Trotsky, nominees for posts in the government were Aleksei Rykov, internal affairs; Ivan Teodorovich, food supply; Vladimir Miliutin, agriculture; Aleksandr Shliapnikov, labor; Vladimir Antonov-Ovseenko, Nikolai Krylenko, and Pavel Dybenko, army and naval affairs; Viktor Nogin, commerce and industry; Anatolii Lunacharskii, education; Ivan Skvortsov-Stepanov, finance; Georgii Lomov, justice; Nikolai Avilov, post and telegraph; and Iosif Stalin, nationalities.

12. Pokrovskii and Iakovleva, *Vtoroi vserossiiskii s"ezd sovetov,* pp. 25, 80–82.

13. Ibid., pp. 25–26, 82–83.

14. Ibid., pp. 26–30, 83–87.

15. Ibid., pp. 30, 87–89.

16. Ibid., pp. 30–31, 89–90.

17. Sukhanov, *Zapiski o revoliutsii,* 3:361.

18. Pokrovskii and Iakovleva, *Vtoroi vserossiiskii s"ezd sovetov,* pp. 90–92.

19. L. Trotsky, *Lenin* (New York, 1959), p. 110.

20. Institut marksizma-leninizma pri TsK KPSS, *Dekrety Sovetskoi vlasti,* vol. 1 (Moscow, 1957), pp. 25–26.

21. Formed the night of 25–26 October, the ACS was made up of representatives of the Petrograd City Duma, the former Pre-parliament, the "old" All-Russian Central Executive Committee of Workers' and Soldiers' Deputies, and the Executive Committee of the All-Russian Congress of Peasants' Deputies, as well as of the Menshevik and SR fractions in the Second Congress of Soviets.

22. RGASPI, f. 5, op. 1, d. 2857, l. 1.

23. The Sovnarkom first met as a body on 3 November and did not meet again until 15 November (RGASPI, f. 19, op. 1, dd. 1, 1a). In this connection, see the unpublished memoirs of N. P. Gorbunov, the secretary of the Sovnarkom (TsGAIPD, f. 4000, op. 5, d. 2220, l. 8).

24. *Dekrety Sovetskoi vlasti,* 1:24–25.

25. See the record of a meeting of representatives of garrison units arranged by Bolsheviks on 29 October at which Lenin, Trotsky, and the Marxist historian Mikhail Pokrovskii, presenting himself as a specialist in partisan warfare, made a successful appeal for support ("Soveshchanie polkovykh predstavitelei Petrogradskogo garnizona, 29 oktiabria 1917 g.," *Krasnaia letopis',* 1927, no. 2 (23): 220–225.

26. TsGAIPD, f. 1, op. 1, d. 26, ll. 19, 26.

27. *Novaia zhizn',* October 31, 1917, p. 3.

28. RNB SPb RO, "Stenograficheskie otchety Petrogradskoi tsentral'noi gorodskoi dumy sozyva 20 avgusta 1917 g.," 1:368–369.

29. *Izvestiia,* November 2, 1917, pp. 1–2.

30. John L. H. Keep, trans. and ed., *The Debate on Soviet Power: Minutes of the All-Russian*

Central Executive Committee, Second Convocation (Oxford, 1979), pp. 44–45; *Protokoly zasedanii Ispolnitel'nogo Komiteta Sovetov R., S., Kr., i Kaz. Deputatov II sozyva* (Moscow, 1918), pp. 9–10. The documentary reconstruction of the new CEC's sessions produced by Keep is much fuller than the latter. See, also, P. Vompe, *Dni Oktiabr'skoi revoliutsii i zheleznodorozhniki* (Moscow, 1924), pp. 21–22.

31. A. Anskii, ed., *Protokoly Petrogradskogo soveta professional'nykh soiuzov za 1917 g.* (Leningrad, 1928), pp. 128–129; P. A. Garvi, *Professional'nye soiuzy v Rossii* (New York, 1981), pp. 29, 128–129 n. 1.

32. *Protokoly tsentral'nogo komiteta RSDRP (b),* pp. 122–123, 269–270.

33. Keep, *The Debate,* p. 46; *Protokoly zasedanii Ispolnitel'nogo Komiteta Sovetov R., S., Kr., i Kaz. Deputatov II sozyva,* p. 10.

34. *Protokoly tsentral'nogo komiteta RSDRP (b),* p. 127.

35. A. Bubnov, "Oktiabr'skie biulleteny TsK bol'shevikov," *Proletarskaia revoliutsia,* 1921, no. 1:10–11.

36. Z. Galili and A. Nenarokov, eds., *Mensheviki v 1917 godu,* vol. 3, pt. 2 (Moscow, 1994), pp. 261–262; S. V. Tiutiukin, *Menshevizm: Stranitsy istorii* (Moscow, 2002), p. 435.

37. For a detailed record of these proceedings, see GARF, f. 5498, op. 1, d. 67, ll. 1–31. A copy of this record from RGASPI, f. 275, op. 1, d. 43, is published in Galili and Nenarokov, *Mensheviki v 1917 godu,* vol. 3, pt. 2, pp. 602–628. See also Tiutiukin, *Menshevizm,* pp. 437–440.

38. See, for example, Dan's opening salvos in GARF, f. 5498, op. 1, d. 67, ll. 6–7, 10.

39. GARF, f. 5498, op. 1, d. 67, ll. 1–2, 11.

40. Ibid., ll. 8–9. See also GARF, f. 5498, op. 1, d. 56, ll. 7–8, for the diary entry of an unidentified Vikzhel representative describing these discussions.

41. On Riazanov's desperation, because of his extreme sense of urgency about the need for an immediate agreement among all socialist groups at this time, see S. Anskii, "Posle perevorota 25-ogo Oktiabria 1917 g., *Arkhiv russkoi revoliutsii,* 8:47.

42. GARF, f. 5498, op. 1, d. 1, ll. 11–12.

43. RNB SPb RO, "Stenograficheskie otchety Petrogradskoi gorodskoi dumy, 1:369–405.

44. GARF, f. 5498, op. 1, d. 67, ll. 3–4.

45. Ibid., ll. 4–6.

46. Ibid., l. 9.

47. On the significance of this factor for the Mensheviks, see R. Abramovich, "Stranitsy istorii: Vikzhel (noiabr' 1917)," *Sotsialisticheskii vestnik,* May 1960, p. 99, and June 1960, pp. 118–119; and B. I. Nikolaevskii, *Mensheviki v dni Oktiabr'skogo perevorota* (New York, 1962), pp. 5–9. See also GARF, f. 5498, op. 1, d. 56, l. 9.

48. GARF, f. 5498, op. 1, d. 67, ll. 24–25, 29; Nikolaevskii, *Mensheviki,* pp. 6–7.

49. Galili and Nenarokov, *Mensheviki v 1917 godu,* vol. 3, pt. 2, p. 271; Nikolaevskii, *Mensheviki,* p. 4; Abramovich, "Stranitsy istorii," p. 119; Tiutiukin, *Menshevizm,* p. 439.

50. GARF, f. 5498, op. 1, d. 67; ll. 24–29; f. 5498, op. 1, d. 57, l. 31; RNB SPb OR, Stenograficheskie otchety Petrogradskoi gorodskoi dumy, 1:456–458; *Izvestiia,* November 3, 1917, p. 4. See also A. Razgon, *VTsIK Sovetov v pervye mesiatsy diktatury proletariata* (Moscow, 1977), p. 130; and Vompe, *Dni Oktiabr'skoi revoliutsii,* p. 37.

51. A resolution embodying these demands was adopted by a mass meeting of Obukhov workers on 31 October. The resolution appears to have reflected the sentiments of a broad section of plant workers (GARF, f. 5498, op. 1, d. 70, l. 3.).

52. RNB SPb RO, Stenograficheskie otchety Petrogradskoi gorodskoi dumy, 1:463–464.

53. A. L. Fraiman, *Forpost sotsialisticheskoi revoliutsii: Petrograd v pervye mesiatsy sovetskoi vlasti* (Leningrad, 1969), pp. 86–87, citing a stenogram of this meeting and a report in *Izvestiia Gelsingforsskogo soveta,* 2 November 1917 (Extra). I have been unable to locate either of these sources. A draft list of prospective ministers close to Fraiman's is contained in GARF, f. 5498, op. 1, d. 57, l. 31. A description of the meeting that dovetails with Fraiman's account is contained in an oral report delivered to the Petrograd City Duma a few hours later (RNB SPb RO,

"Stenograficheskie otchety Petrogradskoi gorodskoi dumy," 1:456–473). See also K. V. Gusev, *V. M. Chernov, Shtrikhi k politicheskomu portretu* (Moscow, 1999), p. 104.

54. Abramovich, "Stranitsy istorii," *Sotsialisticheskii vestnik,* June 1960, p. 119.

55. RGASPI, f. 275, op. 1, d. 208, ll. 46–47.

56. For example, see the optimistic report of A. Malitskii, chair of the Vikzhel talks, regarding prospects for a quick agreement on the morning of 1 November in GARF, f. 5598, op. 1, d. 57, l. 40.

57. T. A. Abrosimova et al., eds., *Peterburgskii komitet RSDRP (b): Protokoly i materialy zasedanii* (St. Petersburg, 2003), pp. 523–534. This marvelously annotated post-Soviet compendium of the Petersburg Committee's protocols for 1917 is more complete and accurate than the original Ispart edition, P. F. Kudelli, ed., *Pervyi legal'nyi Peterburgskii komitet bol'shevikov v 1917 g.* (Moscow–Leningrad, 1927).

58. TsGAIPD, f. 1, op. 4, d. 92, ll. 6 ob., 10–15, 22–25.

59. *Peterburgskii komitet,* pp. 523–530.

60. Ibid, pp. 535–550; L. Trotsky, *The Stalin School of Falsification* (New York, 1972), pp. 107–123; *Protokoly tsentral'nogo komiteta RSDRP (b),* pp. 124–130.

61. *Peterburgskii komitet,* pp. 533–538; Trotsky, *The Stalin School,* pp. 108–111.

62. *Peterburgskii komitet,* pp. 538–540; Trotsky, *The Stalin School,* pp. 112–115.

63. *Peterburgskii komitet,* pp. 540–544; Trotsky, *The Stalin School,* pp. 112–115.

64. RGASPI, f. 19, op. 1, d. 1, l. 1. See also N. P. Gorbunov, "Kak sozdalsia v Oktiabr'skie dni rabochii apparat soveta narodnykh komissarov," in *Utro strany sovetov,* ed. M. P. Iroshnikov (Leningrad, 1988), pp. 149–150.

65. *Peterburgskii komitet,* pp. 543–544; Trotsky, *The Stalin School,* p. 120.

66. *Peterburgskii komitet,* pp. 544–545; Trotsky, *The Stalin School,* pp. 121–122.

67. *Protokoly tsentral'nogo komiteta RSDRP (b),* p. 125.

68. See, for example, RGASPI, f. 67, op. 1, d. 46, l. 175.

69. *Protokoly tsentral'nogo komiteta RSDRP (b),* p. 126.

70. *Protokoly Petrogradskogo soveta professionalnykh soiuzov za 1917 g.,* p. 136.

71. *Protokoly tsentral'nogo komiteta RSDRP (b),* p. 128.

72. Ibid., pp. 124–129.

73. Ibid., p. 126.

74. Ibid., pp. 130, 274–275.

75. See Rabinowitch, *The Bolsheviks Come to Power,* pp. 197–198.

76. Keep, *The Debate,* pp. 51–53; *Protokoly zasedanii Ispolnitel'nogo Komiteta Sovetov R., S., Kr., i Kaz. Deputatov II sozyva,* pp. 12–13.

77. Keep, *The Debate,* pp. 53–58; *Protokoly zasedanii Ispolnitel'nogo Komiteta Sovetov R., S., Kr., i Kaz. Deputatov II sozyva,* pp. 13, 15.

78. *Izvestiia TsK KPSS,* 1989, no. 1:231–232, reconfirms that meetings of the Central Committee dealing with the leadership struggle were held on those days.

79. *Protokoly tsentral'nogo komiteta RSDRP (b),* pp. 131–132.

80. Ibid., p. 275

81. *Peterburgskii komitet,* pp. 555, 560.

82. Ibid., pp. 556–559.

83. Keep, *The Debate,* pp. 59–67; *Protokoly zasedanii Ispolnitel'nogo Komiteta Sovetov R., S., Kr., i Kaz. Deputatov II sozyva,* pp. 17–22.

84. Keep, *The Debate,* pp. 60–61; *Protokoly zasedanii Ispolnitel'nogo Komiteta Sovetov R., S., Kr., i Kaz. Deputatov II sozyva,* pp. 20–21.

85. *Protokoly pervogo s'ezda partii levykh sotsialistov-revoliutsionerov,* p. 44.

86. Keep, *The Debate,* pp. 62–63; *Protokoly zasedanii Ispolnitel'nogo Komiteta Sovetov R., S., Kr., i Kaz. Deputatov II sozyva,* pp. 21–22.

87. *Protokoly zasedanii Ispolnitel'nogo Komiteta Sovetov R., S., Kr., i Kaz. Deputatov II sozyva,* p. 22

88. Ibid. See also *Protokoly tsentral'nogo komiteta RSDRP (b),* pp. 275–276 n. 176.

89. GARF, f. 5498, op. 1, d. 67, ll. 34–39; RGASPI, f. 71, op. 34, d. 88, l. 2.

90. *Protokoly tsentral'nogo komiteta RSDRP (b),* pp. 133–134, 275 n. 175.

91. Ibid., p. 134.

92. Ibid., pp. 135–136. See also A. L. Fraiman, *Forpost sotsialisticheskoi revoliutsii,* p. 94; R. Abramovich, "Stranitsy istorii," p. 123.

93. See Institut marksizma-leninizma pri TsK KPSS, *Perepiska sekretariata TsK RSDRP(b) s mestnymi partiinymi organizatsiiami,* vol. 2 (Moscow, 1957), p. 27; B. Elov, "O partiinykh konferenstiiakh RKP Petrogradskoi organizatsii," in *Spravochnik Petrogradskogo agitatora,* 1921, no. 10:96; RGASPI, f. 60, op. 1, d. 26, l. 31.

94. See, for example, "Protokoly zasedanii TsIK i Biuro TsIK S. R. i S. D. 1-go sozyva posle Oktiabria," *Krasnyi arkhiv,* 1925, vol. 10, p. 99.

95. In mid-November, in an effort to rekindle the talks, Vikzhel convened a two-day conference of rail line representatives in Moscow. The conference endorsed this effort but it got nowhere (RGASPI, f. 71, op. 34, d. 88, ll. 49–79).

96. RGASPI, f. 67, op. 1, d. 46, ll. 173–175; Institut marksizma-leninizma pri TsK KPSS, *Vladimir Il'ich Lenin, Biograficheskaia khronika,* vol. 5 (Moscow, 1974), p. 32.

97. *Rabochii i soldat,* November 6, 1917, p. 4.

98. *Rabotnitsa* was a Bolshevik tabloid periodical for women workers edited by several female party leaders. Initially published in February 1914, it was interrupted by tsarist authorities the following June, after the publication of seven issues. It resumed publication in May 1917, becoming the centerpiece of Bolshevik work among Petrograd factory women during the run-up to the party's seizure of power. In January 1918, however, a shortage of newsprint and ink forced its closure. See Barbara Evans Clements, *Bolshevik Women* (Cambridge, 1997), pp. 131–132.

99. *Novaia zhizn',* November 7, 1918, p. 4; *Izvestiia,* November 7, 1918, p. 3; Elizabeth A. Wood, *The Baba and the Comrade: Gender and Politics in Revolutionary Russia* (Bloomington, 1997), pp. 69–70.

100. *Izvestiia,* November 7, 1918, p. 7.

101. *Protokoly Petrogradskogo soveta professional'nykh soiuzov za 1917,* pp. 129–130.

102. Ibid., pp. 134–135.

103. Ibid., p. 137.

104. Keep, *The Debate,* pp. 91–94; *Protokoly zasedanii Ispolnitel'nogo Komiteta Sovetov R., S., Kr., i Kaz. Deputatov II sozyva,* p. 35.

105. For Kamkov's elaboration of this position, see *Protokoly pervogo s"ezda partii levykh sotsialistov-revoliutsionerov,* p. 46.

106. See below, chapter 3.

107. See above.

108. *Izvestiia TsK KPSS,* 1989, no. 1:229.

109. Institut marksizma-leninizma pri TsK KPSS. *Shestoi s"ezd RSDRP (bol'shevikov), avgust 1917 goda: Protokoly* (Moscow, 1958), pp. 69–70.

110. *Izvestiia,* November 2, 1918, p. 1. See above.

111. Keep, *The Debate,* pp. 59–60; *Protokoly zasedanii Ispolnitel'nogo Komiteta Sovetov R., S., Kr., i Kaz. Deputatov II sozyva, p.* 18.

112. See above.

113. Keep, *The Debate,* p. 68; *Protokoly zasedanii Ispolnitel'nogo Komiteta Sovetov R., S., Kr., i Kaz. Deputatov II sozyva,* p. 23.

114. Keep, *The Debate,* p. 69.

115. Ibid., pp. 69–70; *Protokoly zasedanii Ispolnitel'nogo Komiteta Sovetov R., S., Kr., i Kaz. Deputatov II sozyva,* pp. 23–24.

116. Keep, *The Debate,* p. 77; *Protokoly zasedanii Ispolnitel'nogo Komiteta Sovetov R., S., Kr., i Kaz. Deputatov II sozyva,* p. 27.

117. Keep, *The Debate,* pp. 77–78; *Protokoly zasedanii Ispolnitel'nogo Komiteta Sovetov R., S., Kr., i Kaz. Deputatov II sozyva,* pp. 27–28. In addition to Shliapnikov, the other Bolshevik

officials included Nikolai Derbyshev (Commissar for Press Affairs), S. V. Arbuzov (Commissar for Government Printing Presses), Il'ia Yurenev (Commissar for the Red Guards), Georgii Fedorov (Head of the Conflict Section in the Commissariat for Labor), Larin, and Riazanov.

118. *Novaia zhizn',* November 6, 1917, pp. 1–2.

119. Keep, *The Debate,* pp. 78–79; *Protokoly zasedanii Ispolnitel'nogo Komiteta Sovetov R., S., Kr., i Kaz. Deputatov II sozyva,* p. 28.

120. Keep, *The Debate,* pp. 80–81; *Protokoly zasedanii Ispolnitel'nogo Komiteta Sovetov R., S., Kr., i Kaz. Deputatov II sozyva,* pp. 28–29.

121. Keep, *The Debate,* p. 86; *Protokoly zasedanii Ispolnitel'nogo Komiteta Sovetov R., S., Kr., i Kaz. Deputatov II sozyva,* pp. 31–32; Razgon, *VTsIK Sovetov,* p. 162.

122. Keep, *The Debate,* p. 86; *Protokoly zasedanii Ispolnitel'nogo Komiteta Sovetov R., S., Kr., i Kaz. Deputatov II sozyva,* p. 32. See Razgon, *VTsIK Sovetov,* p. 155, for an analysis of voting strength at this meeting. It is noteworthy that the Leninists lost a procedural vote earlier in the meeting when the People's Commissars did not vote.

123. Keep, *The Debate,* p. 86; *Protokoly zasedanii Ispolnitel'nogo Komiteta Sovetov R., S., Kr., i Kaz. Deputatov II sozyva,* p. 32.

124. This threat was contained in a formal note to the four written by Lenin on 5 or 6 November. *Protokoly tsentral'nogo komiteta RSDRP (b),* p. 137.

125. Ibid., p. 142.

126. V. Bonch-Bruevich, *Na boevykh postakh fevral'skoi i oktiabr'skoi revoliutsii* (Moscow, 1931), p. 164; *Protokoly tsentral'nogo komiteta RSDRP (b),* p. 146.

127. See below.

128. This is Elena Stasova's characterization (RGASPI, f. 17, op. 4, d. 11, ll. 24–26).

129. Of 330 delegates, 195 were Left SRs, 65 were Right SRs, 37 were Bolsheviks, 14 were unaffiliated, 7 were Maximalists, 4 were Popular Socialists, 3 were left Mensheviks, and 2 were Anarchists (V. M. Lavrov, *"Krest'ianskii parlament" Rossii* [*Vserossiiskie s"ezdy sovetov krest'ianskikh deputatov v 1917–1918 godakh*], [Moscow, 1996], p. 130).

130. Ibid., pp. 169, 172–176. See also *Izvestiia TsK KPSS,* 1989, no. 1:234.

131. *Protokoly pervogo s"ezda partii levykh sotsialistov-revoliutsionerov,* p. 46.

132. On this point, see Allan K. Wildman, *The End of the Russian Imperial Army: The Road to Soviet Power and Peace* (Princeton, N.J., 1987), esp. chap. 9.

133. RGASPI, f. 564, op. 1, d. 5, ll. 74–75.

134. *Izvestia TsK KPSS,* 1989, no. 1:234; *Lenin, Biograficheskaia khronika,* 5:59.

135. See above.

136. A compelling analysis and interpretation of the genesis and development of the mythology surrounding Spiridonova's name is contained in Sally Boniece, "Maria Spiridonova, 1894–1918: Feminine Martyrdom and Revolutionary Mythmaking" (Ph.D. diss., Indiana University, 1995).

137. *Protokoly pervogo s"ezda partii levykh sotsialistov-revoliutsionerov,* p. 36.

138. RGASPI, f. 564, op. 1, d. 4, l. 280.

139. *Protokoly zasedanii Ispolnitel'nogo Komiteta Sovetov R., S., Kr., i Kaz. Deputatov II sozyva,* p. 71.

140. *Znamia truda,* November 18, 1918, p. 3; Keep, *The Debate,* pp. 141–142; *Protokoly zasedanii Ispolnitel'nogo Komiteta Sovetov R., S., Kr., i Kaz. Deputatov II sozyva,* p. 71.

141. *Protokoly pervogo s"ezda partii levykh sotsialistov-revoliutsionerov,* p. 46; See also Razgon, *VTsIK Sovetov,* pp. 203–204.

142. See, for example, Keep, *The Debate,* pp. 100–108.

2. Rebels into Rulers

1. TsGA SPb, f. 9618, op. 1, d. 185, ll. 1–42.

2. For an insightful sketch of Zinoviev as political boss of Petrograd, see A. N. Chis-

tikov, "U kormila vlasti," in *Petrograd na perelome epokh,* ed. V. A. Shishkin (St. Petersburg, 2000), pp. 35–42.

3. On this point, see ibid., p. 11.

4. D. A. Chugaev, ed., *Petrogradskii voenno-revoliutsionnyi komitet: Dokumenty i materialy,* vol. 1 (Moscow, 1966), p. 277.

5. RGASPI, f. 19, op. 1, d. 2, l. 2.

6. *Izvestiia,* November 18, 1917, pp. 4–5.

7. TsGAIPD, f. 1, op. 1, d. 12, l. 8 ob.–13 ob.

8. Ibid.

9. For a record of this procedure in the Kolpinskii district, see TSGAIPD, f. 2315, op. 1, d. 2, ll. 19–20 and d. 3, l. 48 ; for the Petersburg district, f. 6, op. 1. 1, d. 1, ll. 31 ob., 32 ob, 39–39 ob., and 40–41; and for the Okhtinskii district, f. 10, op. 1, d. 12, ll. 4–5.

10. See, for example, the minutes of a general party meeting of Novoderevenskii Bolsheviks on 11 December 1917. After a barrage of criticism of the district committee's work, the meeting registered its independent authority by rejecting the former's selections for the Novoderevenskii district soviet (TsGAIPD, f. 13, op. 1, d. 1, l. 21 ob.).

11. On this point, see Chistikov, "U kormila vlasti," p. 43.

12. Commonly, district committee positions on key political issues were formed following a report on them from an authoritative local leader, sometimes the district's representative in the Petersburg Committee, and reports on popular sentiment from local factory representatives. See, for example, the debate over the Vikzhel negotiations in the Second City district Bolshevik committee (TsGAIPD, f. 1817, op. 1, d. 3, ll. 56–57) and, in the Okhtinskii district Bolshevik committee, over the convocation and role of the Constituent Assembly, and over peace negotiations (TsGAIPD, f. 10, op. 1, d. 12, ll. 1–10).

13. *Peterburgskii komitet,* pp. 523–524.

14. TsGAIPD, f. 2315, op. 1, d. 2, l. 18, d. 3, l. 41, and d. 4, l. 3.

15. Ibid., d. 2, l. 19 and d. 3, l. 42.

16. *Peterburgskii komitet,* pp. 571–572. See also TsGAIPD, f. 6, op. 1, d. 1, l. 39.

17. In this connection, see the district committee's report and discussion of cadre losses at a general meeting of Bolsheviks in the Petersburg district on 11 December (TsGAIPD, f. 6, op. 1, d. 1, ll. 29 ob.–30 ob.).

18. TsGAIPD, f. 1, op. 4, d. 84, ll. 20–25; f. 2315, op. 1, d. 4, l. 3; f. 6, op. 1, d. 33.

19. See the prologue to this volume.

20. The best published source on the MRC, though incomplete, is Chugaev, *Petrogradskii voenno-revoliutsionnyi komitet,* vols. 1–3 (Moscow, 1966–67).

21. Ibid., 3:270.

22. RGASPI, f. 19, op. 1, d. 11, l. 2; and see below, chapter 3.

23. See Chistikov, "U kormila vlasti," pp. 10–11. Also see the report on the MRC of Vladimir Algasov, one of its members, at the first Left SR national congress (*Protokoly pervogo s"ezda partii levykh sotsialistov-revoliutsionerov,* p. 47).

24. The most illuminating and comprehensive study of the electoral campaign for the Constituent Assembly, its results, and its fate is L. G. Protasov, *Vserossiiskoe uchreditel'noe sobranie: Istoriia rozhdeniia i gibeli* (Moscow, 1997).

25. See O. N. Radkey, *Russia Goes to the Polls: The Election to the All-Russian Constituent Assembly* (Ithaca, N.Y., 1989), esp. pp. 87–135. On this point, see also M. V. Vishniak, *Vserossiiskoe uchreditel'noe sobranie* (Paris, 1932), p. 92.

26. RGASPI, f. 19, op. 1, d. 11, l. 10 ob.

27. P. F. Kudelli, ed., *Vtoraia i tret'ia Petrogradskie obshchegorodskie konferentsii bol'shevikov v iiule i oktiabre 1917: Protokoly* (Moscow-Leningrad, 1927), pp. 115–117.

28. Protasov, *Vserossiiskoe uchreditel'noe sobranie,* p. 266.

29. *Peterburgskii komitet,* p. 564.

30. GOPB, Leaflet collection.

31. *Pravda,* November 13, 1917, p. 1. These elections, as was the case for most others

in Russia at this time, were determined by the party list. The number of seats each party won in a given electoral district depended on the number of votes cast for its list. Party committees ranked individual candidates on each party's list, and this ranking could significantly affect each candidate's prospects for election.

32. See above, chapter 1.

33. *Rabotnitsa,* December 8, 1917, pp. 10–11.

34. Ibid., January 26, 1918, pp. 10–11.

35. Ibid., pp. 11–12. On differences between the two sides at the conference, see Wood, *The Baba and the Comrade,* pp. 69–70.

36. *Rabotnitsa,* October 18, 1917, pp. 5–7.

37. Quoted in O. N. Znamenskii, *Vserossiiskoe uchreditel'noe sobranie: Istoriia sozyva i politicheskogo krusheniia* (Leningrad, 1976), p. 257.

38. James Bunyan and H. H. Fisher, *The Bolshevik Revolution, 1917–1918: Documents and Materials* (Stanford, 1965), pp. 345–346.

39. *Rabochaia gazeta,* November 12, 1917, p. 1; November 13, 1917, p. 1.

40. *Delo naroda,* November, 12, 1917, p. 2.

41. Ibid.

42. See, for example, the leaflet, "Women, Vote in Elections to the Constituent Assembly!" in GOPB, Leaflet collection.

43. Radkey, *Russia Goes to the Polls,* p. 36.

44. Znamenskii, *Vserossiiskoe uchreditel'noe sobranie,* end table 1.

45. Radkey, *Russia Goes to the Polls,* p. 36.

46. Znamenskii, *Vserossiiskoe uchreditel'noe sobranie,* p. 277 and end table; Akademiia nauk SSSR, Institut istorii, Leningradskoe otdelenie, *Oktiabr'skoe vooruzhennoe vosstanie: Semnadtsatyi god v Petrograde,* vol. 2 (Leningrad, 1967), p. 491.

47. RGASPI, f. 19, op. 1, d. 15, ll. 2, 30.

48. *Novaia zhizn',* November 16, 1917, p. 1.

49. Keep, *The Debate,* pp. 144–146.

50. T. V. Osipova, *Rossiiskoe krest'ianstvo v revoliutsii i grazhdanskoi voine* (Moscow, 2001), p. 66. Osipova shows that, since the decree on land was already being implemented, many peasants no longer cared about the Constituent Assembly and, in their resolutions, insisted that if it did not confirm the decrees of the Soviet government, it should be dissolved. Based on data from peasant meetings in 415 rural districts (*volosts*), she concludes that a majority of peasants in 53.5 percent of these districts opted for Soviet power, 30 percent still favored transfer of authority to the Constituent Assembly, and 16.5 percent wavered between these alternatives.

51. On the linkage between dissolution of the Petrograd City Duma and concerns about counterrevolutionary activity connected with the Constituent Assembly, see Razgon, *VTsIK Sovetov,* p. 250.

52. *Zhurnal Petrogradskoi gorodskoi dumy* (Petrograd, 1917), no. 123, session of November 20, 1917, pp. 1–24.

53. Ibid., pp. 3–5; RNB SPb RO, "Stenograficheskie otchety Petrogradskoi tsentral'noi gorodskoi dumy," 3:21.

54. RNB SPb RO, "Stenograficheskie otchety Petrogradskoi tsentral'noi gorodoskoi dumy," vol. 3.

55. Boris Sokolov, "Zashchita vserossiiskogo uchreditel'nogo sobraniia," *Arkhiv russkoi revoliutsii,* vol. 13 (Berlin, 1924), p. 30.

56. Institut marksizma-leninizma pri TsK KPSS, *Dekrety Sovetskoi vlasti,* vol. 1 (Moscow, 1957), pp. 167–168.

57. GARF, f. 130, op. 1, d. 10a, l. 30. See also Znamenskii, *Vserossiiskoe uchreditel'noe sobranie,* pp. 301–302.

58. *Dekrety sovetskoi vlasti,* 1:167.

59. Ibid., 3:159.

60. I. I. Liubimov, *Revoliutsiia 1917 goda: Khronika sobytii,* vol. 6, *Oktiabr'–dekabr'* (Moscow, 1930), p. 222.

61. *Pravda,* November 27, 1917, p. 1; *Rabochii i soldat,* November 27, 1917, p. 1.

62. *Peterburgskii komitet,* pp. 596–600.

63. A discussion of the Constituent Assembly was also on the agenda of a meeting of the Petersburg Committee on 2 December, the minutes of which are missing. Its stance as developed on 2 December was recounted at a meeting of the Okhtinskii district party committee on 4 December. This account also left no doubt of the Assembly's lack of legitimacy vis-à-vis Soviet power in the eyes of the Petersburg Committee (TsGAIPD, f. 10, op. 1, d. 12, ll. 1–4).

64. *Protokoly pervogo s"ezda partii levykh sotsialistov-revoliutsionerov,* pp. 65–66, 108.

65. Ibid., pp. 87, 91–92, 111.

66. Znamenskii, *Vserossiiskoe uchreditel'noe sobranie,* pp. 301–302. Demonstrations supporting the Constituent Assembly were held in many Russian cities on 28 November.

67. William G. Rosenberg, *Liberals in the Russian Revolution: The Constitutional Democratic Party, 1917–1921* (Princeton, N.J., 1974), pp. 277–278; N. G. Dumova, *Kadetskaia kontrrevoliutsiia i ee razgrom* (Moscow, 1982), p. 54; E. N. Gorodetskii, *Rozhdenie sovetskogo gosudarstva, 1917–1918 gg.* (Moscow, 1965), p. 276.

68. Lev Protasov, the leading contemporary Russian specialist on the Constituent Assembly, concludes that the estimate of one hundred thousand marchers by pro–Constituent Assembly journalists was probably inflated but much closer to the actual figure than the ten thousand procession participants cited in Soviet accounts (Protasov, *Vserossiiskoe uchreditel'noe sobranie,* p. 271).

69. Znamenskii, *Vserossiiskoe uchreditel'noe sobranie,* p. 308; Liubimov, *Revoliutsiia 1917 goda: Khronika sobytii,* 6:225.

70. Znamenskii, *Vserossiiskoe uchreditel'noe sobranie,* p. 309; Vishniak, *Vserossiiskoe uchreditel'noe sobranie,* p. 95.

71. RGASPI, f. 19, op. 1, d. 13, l. 2.

72. Bonch-Bruevich, *Na boevykh postakh fevral'skoi i oktiabr'skoi revoliutsii,* pp. 187–189.

73. V. V. Shelokhaev, project director, *Protokoly tsentral'nogo komiteta konstitutsionno-demokraticheskoi partii, 1915–1920* (Moscow, 1998), pp. 6, 412.

74. RGASPI, f. 19, op. 1, d. 13, ll. 6–7; *Dekrety sovetskoi vlasti,* 1:165–166. Kolegaev had joined the cabinet a few days earlier.

75. RGASPI, f. 19, op. 1, d. 13, l. 2; *Dekrety sovetskoi vlasti,* 1:161–162.

76. *Novaia zhizn',* November 30, 1917, p. 1.

77. *Znamia truda,* November 30, 1917, p. 1.

78. Keep, *The Debate,* pp. 172–173; *Protokoly zasedanii Ispolnitel'nogo Komiteta Sovetov R., S., Kr., i Kaz. Deputatov II sozyva,* p. 124; Razgon, *VTsIK Sovetov,* p. 300.

79. Keep, *The Debate,* pp. 172–173, 354.

80. Ibid., pp. 175–176.

81. Ibid., p. 177.

82. Ibid., pp. 177–178, 356.

83. Ibid., pp. 177–179.

84. See above, chapter 1.

85. Keep, *The Debate,* p. 181; *Protokoly zasedanii Ispolnitel'nogo Komiteta Sovetov R., S., Kr., i Kaz. Deputatov II sozyva,* pp. 121–122.

3. Gathering Forces

1. See, for example, George Leggett, *The Cheka: Lenin's Political Police: The All-Russian Extraordinary Commission for Combating Counterrevolution and Sabotage* (Oxford and New York, 1986), pp. 15–18; and V. A. Kutuzov, V. F. Lepetiukhin, V. F. Sedov, and O. N. Stepanov, *Chekisti Petrograda na strazhe revoliutsii* (Leningrad, 1987), pp. 53–56.

2. See above, chapter 1.

3. Until then, Left SRs accounted for only 20 percent of the MRC's membership.

4. GARF, f. 130, op. 1, d. 1, l. 10 ob.

5. Chugaev, *Petrogradskii voenno-revoliutsionnyi komitet,* 3:232, 259.

6. Ibid., p. 285.

7. RGASPI, f. 19, op.1, d. 11, l. 2.

8. See above, chapter 2.

9. GARF, f. 1236, op. 1, d. 3, l. 149. By then, tension between the MRC and Sovnarkom had intensified to such a degree that word of it leaked to the non-socialist press. On 1 December 1917, *Nash vek* reported that a left faction within the MRC, unhappy with Lenin's efforts to steer Bolshevik domestic policies into a legal framework, had gained the upper hand and that the MRC was operating "absolutely autonomously and making its decisions without regard to advice from people's commissars" (p. 3).

10. TsGA SPb, f. 9618, op. 1, d. 186, l. 11.

11. M. Latsis, *Otchet vserossiiskoi chrezvychainoi komissii za chetyre goda ee deiatel'nosti (20 dekabria 1917–20 dekabria 1921 g.): 1. Organizatsionnaia chast'* (Moscow, 1922), p. 8.

12. RGASPI, f. 19, op. 1, d. 2, l. 13 ob.; Razgon, "Pravitel'svennyi blok," p. 121.

13. Razgon, "Pravitel'svennyi blok," p. 128.

14. See, for example, the resolution on the government adopted at a meeting of garrison units in mid November. After listening to presentations by representatives of the CECs, the City Duma, and all the socialist parties, the soldiers adopted a resolution expressing confidence in the Soviet government and declaring that the entry of Left SR representatives into the government is "essential" (TsGA SPb, f. 9618, op. 1, d. 53, l. 376).

15. N. N. Smirnov, *Tret'ii vserossiiskii s"ezd sovetov* (Leningrad, 1988), p. 111.

16. They included Prosh Proshian (post and telegraph); Vladimir Trutovskii (local self-government); Aleksandra Izmailovich (palaces of the republic); Vladimir Karelin (co-people's commissar for military and naval affairs and people's commissar for protection of property of the republic); Vladimir Algasov (internal affairs without portfolio).

17. *Izvestiia,* December 10, 1917, p. 7.

18. *Znamia truda,* December 16, 1917, p. 2.

19. Ibid., p. 3.

20. Ibid., December 19, 1917, p. 3.

21. Latsis, *Otchet,* p. 14.

22. Ibid.

23. Galili and Nenarokov, *Mensheviki v 1917 godu,* vol. 3, pt. 2, p. 559.

24. *Nash vek,* December 19, 1917, p. 3.

25. RGASPI, f. 5, op. 1, d. 2565, l. 1.

26. *Vladimir Il'ich Lenin, Biograficheskaia khronika,* 5:142.

27. RGASPI, f. 5, op. 1, d. 2565, l. 1 ob.

28. RGASPI, f. 19, op. 1, d. 30, l. 2.

29. I. N. Steinberg, *Als ich Volkskommissar war: Episoden aus der russischen Oktoberrevolution* (Munich, 1929), pp. 35–37.

30. RGASPI, f. 19, op. 1, d. 30.

31. Steinberg, *Als ich Volkskommissar war,* pp. 35–37.

32. RGASPI, f. 19, op. 1, d. 30, l. 2 ob.

33. V. V. Shelokhaev, project director, Ia. V. Leontiev, ed., *Partiia levykh sotsialistov-revoliutsionerov: Dokumenty i materialy,* vol. 1 (Moscow, 2000), p. 179.

34. This is Razgon's count (Razgon, "Pravitel'svennyi blok," p. 135).

35. TsA FSB RF, f. 1, op. 10, d. 52, ll. 5–6.

36. RGASPI, f. 19, op. 1, d. 42, l. 1 ob.

37. Ibid.

38. *Protokoly tsentral'nogo komiteta RSDRP (b),* p. 154. See also *Izvestiia TsK KPSS,* 1989, no. 1:236.

39. Rabinowitch, *The Bolsheviks Come to Power,* p. 188.

40. E. Gorodetskii and Iu. Shaparov, *Sverdlov* (Moscow, 1971), pp. 233–234; V. I. Lenin, *Sochineniia,* 3rd ed., vol. 22 (Moscow, 1931), pp. 130, 593 n. 62; *Izvestiia TsK KPSS,* 1989, no. 1:236; *Novaia zhizn',* December 2, 1917, p. 3; *Nash vek,* December 2, 1917, p. 3.

41. *Protokoly tsentral'nogo komiteta RSDRP (b)*, pp. 160–161, 279 n. 192; *Izvestiia TsK KPSS*, 1989, no. 1:237; Lenin, *Polnoe sobranie sochinenii*, 35:469 n. 70; *Lenin, Biograficheskaia khronika*, 5:125.

42. *Protokoly tsentral'nogo komiteta RSDRP (b)*, pp. 160–161; *Izvestiia TsK KPSS*, 1989, no. 1:237– 238.

43. Lenin, *Polnoe sobranie sochinenii*, 35:162–166.

44. *Protokoly tsentral'nogo komiteta RSDRP (b)*, p. 161.

45. A. Bystrova, "Bor'ba za ukreplenie diktatury proletariata: Pervye shagi diktatury proletariata," in O. A. Lidak, ed., *Oktiabr' v Petrograde* (Leningrad, 1933), p. 325.

46. Gorodetskii and Sharapov, *Sverdlov*, p. 234. For brief press reports of this meeting, see *Delo naroda*, December 14, 1917, p. 2; and *Sotsial demokrat*, December 14, 1917, p. 2.

47. *Protokoly tsentral'nogo komiteta RSDRP (b)*, p. 161.

48. Ibid., p. 280.

49. *Oktiabr'skoe vooruzhennoe vosstanie*, 2:493.

50. RGASPI, f. 19, op. 1, d. 31, l. 2 ob.

51. Keep, *The Debate*, p. 247.

52. RGASPI, f. 19, op. 1, d. 39, l. 1; *Znamia truda*, January 4, 1918, p. 3; *Izvestiia TsK KPSS*, 1989, no. 2:176.

53. Keep, *The Debate*, pp. 257–258; Lenin, *Polnoe sobranie sochinenii*, 35:221–224.

54. Bakhmetiev Archive, Columbia University, Zenzinov Collection (protocols of the SR Central Committee), p. 19.

55. See above, chapter 2.

56. V. V. Shelokhaev, project director, D. B. Pavlov, ed., *Partiia sotsialistov-revoliutsionerov: Dokumenty i materialy*, vol. 3, pt. 2 (Moscow, 2000), p. 197.

57. RGASPI, f. 274, op. 1, d. 45, ll. 1–340; N. Sviatitskii, "Fraktsiia partii S. R., uchreditel'noe sobranie i ee deiatel'nost'," *Partiinye izvestiia*, 1918, no. 5:32–42; N. Oganovskii, "Dnevnik chlena uchreditel'nogo sobraniia," *Golos minuvshego*, 1918, nos. 4–6:145–148; Sokolov, "Zashchita vserossiiskogo uchreditel'nogo sobraniia," pp. 33–34, 58.

58. RGASPI, f. 274, op. 1, d. 45, ll. 15, 45–46.

59. *Partiia sotsialistov-revoliutsionerov*, vol. 3, pt. 2, p. 197.

60. Ibid., pp. 271–274.

61. Oganovskii, "Dnevnik chlena uchreditel'nogo sobraniia," pp. 113, 151.

62. N. Sviatitskii, "5–6 ianvaria 1918 goda: Iz vospominanii byvshego esera," *Novyi mir*, 1928, no. 2:220–221; Sokolov, "Zashchita vserossiiskogo uchreditel'nogo sobraniia," pp. 31, 35.

63. Bakhmetev Archive, Columbia University, Zenzinov collection (protocols of the SR Central Committee), pp. 18–19.

64. TsA FSB RF, f. 1, op. 1, d. 5, l. 144.

65. Sokolov, "Zashchita vserossiiskogo uchreditel'nogo sobraniia," pp. 31, 35. See also Sviatitskii, "5–6 ianvaria 1918 goda," p. 222.

66. N. Ia. Bykovskii, *Vserossiiskii sovet krest'ianskikh deputatov 1917 g.* (Moscow, 1929), p. 34.

67. Sokolov, "Zashchita vserossiiskogo uchreditel'nogo sobraniia," p. 48. Whether the 1 January attempt on Lenin's life was connected to Onipko's plans is uncertain.

68. Bakhmetev Archive, Columbia University, Zenzinov collection (protocols of the SR Central Committee), p. 19.

69. TsA FSB RF, f. 1, op. 2, d. 7, l. 42.

70. Sokolov, "Zashchita vserossiiskogo uchreditel'nogo sobraniia," p. 42.

71. *Biulleten' vserossiiskogo soiuza zashchity uchreditel'nogo sobraniia*, January 3, 1918, p. 2.

72. Sokolov, "Zashchita vserossiiskogo uchreditel'nogo sobraniia," p. 44; G. Semenev, *Voennaia i boevaia rabota partii sotsialistov-revoliutsionerov* (Moscow, 1922), p. 13.

73. Sokolov, "Zashchita vserossiiskogo uchreditel'nogo sobraniia," pp. 41, 44. See also V. Vladimirova, *God sluzhby 'sotsialistov' kapitalistam* (Moscow–Leningrad, 1927), p. 106; and Semenev, *Voennaia i boevaia rabota partii sotsialistov-revoliutsionerov*, pp. 10–11.

74. *Biulletin' vserossiiskogo soiuza zashchity uchreditel'nogo sobraniia*, December 31, 1918,

p. 2; January 5, 1918, p. 2. See also Bykovskii, *Vserossiiskii sovet krestianskikh deputatov, 1917,* p. 349.

75. Sokolov, "Zashchita vserossiiskogo uchreditel'nogo sobraniia," p. 50.

76. Ibid., p. 60. A slightly different version of these events is given in Semenev, *Voennaia i boevaia rabota partii sotsialistov-revoliutsionerov,* p. 13. See also Vladimirova, *God sluzhby 'sotsialistov' kapitalistam,* pp. 109–110.

77. Thus, meetings of the Petersburg Committee during the last two weeks of December appear to have been devoted largely to this issue (*Peterburgskii komitet,* pp. 607–623).

78. TsGA SPb, f. 143, op. 1, d. 52, ll. 29–29 ob.

79. The Investigating Commission of the Petrograd Soviet's Revolutionary Tribunal was established on 24 November. Two other bodies—the Emergency Commission for the Security of Petrograd and the Committee to Combat Pogroms—were created in early December.

80. Latsis, *Otchet vserossiiskoi chrezvychainoi komissii,* p. 11. See also, S. V. Leonov, *Rozhdenie Sovetskoi imperii* (Moscow, 1997), pp. 248–249.

81. Ia. Kh. Peters, "Vospominaniia o rabote v VChK v pervyi god revoliutsii," *Proletarskaia revoliutsiia,* 1924, no. 10 (33): 10.

82. TsA FSB RF, f. 1, op. 2, d. 25, l. 1.

83. TsGA SPb, f. 9618, op. 1, d. 185, ll. 1–26.

84. Ibid., l. 19; "Prezidium Petrogradskogo soveta rabochikh i soldatskikh deputatov, dekabr' 1917 g.," *Krasnaia letopis',* 1932, no. 1–2 (46–47): 111.

85. GARF, f. 337, op. 1, d. 4, ll. 1, 13, 17.

86. TsA FSB RF, No. N-972, vol. 8, l. 23.

87. Ibid.

88. Ibid., vol. 1, ll. 1–2; vol. 2, l. 30; vol. 8, ll. 24–25; vol. 10, ll. 169–176.

89. TsGAIPD, f. 1, op. 1, d. 273, l. 2.

90. *Znamia truda,* January 4, 1918, p. 3; *Izvestiia TsK KPSS,* 1989, no. 2:176.

91. *Znamia truda,* January 4, 1918, p. 3.

92. GARF, f. 9618, op. 1, d. 185, l. 20.

93. *Izvestiia,* January 5, 1918, p. 3. See *Oktiabr'skoe vooruzhennoe vosstanie,* 2:496–500, for a detailed account of security measures adopted by Petrograd authorities during the run-up to the Constituent Assembly.

94. *Izvestiia,* January 5, 1918, p. 3.

95. Ibid.

96. Ibid., January 4, 1918, p. 1.

97. Ibid. This proclamation was widely published and otherwise disseminated on 4 and 5 January.

98. *Biulleten' vserossiiskago soiuza zashchity uchreditel'nogo sobraniia,* January 4 and 5, 1918, p. 1.

99. *Petrogradskoe ekho,* January 5, 1918, p. 1.

100. TsGA SPb, f. 9618, op. 1, d. 185, ll. 26–30; TsGAIPD, f. 1, op. 4, d. 121, ll. 1–4.

101. TsGAIPD, f. 1, op. 4, d. 121, l. 1.

102. Ibid., ll. 2–4.

103. Ibid.

104. Ibid, l. 4. See also, "Pervye shagi bol'shevistskogo Petrogradskogo soveta v 1917 godu: Protokoly zasedanii," *Krasnaia letopis',* 1927, no. 3 (24): 80–82.

105. *Izvestiia,* January 5, 1918, p. 1; *Znamia truda,* January 5, 1918, p. 4; A. F. Ilyin-Zhenevsky, *The Bolsheviks in Power: Reminiscences of the Year 1918,* translated and annotated by Brian Pearce (London, 1984), pp. 18–19.

106. *Izvestiia,* January 5, 1918, p. 1.

4. The Fate of the Constituent Assembly

1. *Novaia zhizn',* January 6, 1918, p. 2.

2. TsGAIPD, f. 4000, op. 5, d. 2365, ll. 1–12.

3. Protasov, *Vserossiiskoe uchreditel'noe sobranie*, p. 306.

4. *Nash vek,* January 6, 1918, p. 3.

5. *Novaia zhizn',* January 6, 1918, p. 2.

6. Ibid.

7. Louis de Robien, *The Diary of a Diplomat in Russia, 1917–1918* (New York and Washington, D.C., 1969), p. 196.

8. V. Shklovskii, *Sentimental'noe puteshestvie* (Moscow, 1990), pp. 144–145.

9. *Novaia zhizn',* January 6, 1918, p. 2.

10. See above, chapter 3.

11. *Nash vek,* January 6, 1918, p. 3.

12. *Novaia zhizn',* January 6, 1918, p. 2.

13. Ibid.

14. *Nash vek,* January 6, 1918, p. 2.

15. M. N. Pokrovskii and Ia. A. Iakovleva, eds., *Vserossiiskoe uchreditel'noe sobranie* (Moscow–Leningrad, 1930), p. 68.

16. *Novaia zhizn',* January 6, 1918, p. 2.

17. M. V. Vishniak, *Vserossiiskoe uchreditel'noe sobranie* (Paris, 1932), p. 99.

18. N. Sviatitskii, "5–6 ianvaria 1918 goda: Iz vospominaniia byvshego esera," *Novyi mir,* 1928, no. 2:223.

19. V. L. Zenzinov, *Iz zhizny revoliutsionera* (Paris, 1919), p. 99. See also Vishniak, *Vserossiiskoe uchreditel'noe sobranie,* p. 100.

20. Oganovskii, "Dnevnik chlena uchreditel'nogo sobraniia," p. 148.

21. F. F. Raskolnikov, *Tales of Sub-Lieutenant Ilyin,* translated and annotated by Brian Pearce (London, 1982), p. 2.

22. *Sotsial demokrat,* January 6, 1918, p. 3.

23. In an unpublished memoir written in the 1920s, Podvoiskii indicated that most Bolshevik delegates from the provinces were unaware of Lenin's most recent thinking about the Constituent Assembly (RGASPI, f. 146, op. 1, d. 47, ll. 12–14).

24. Raskolnikov, *Tales of Sub-Lieutenant Ilyin,* pp. 2–5.

25. On this point, see O. N. Znamenskii, *Vserossiiskoe uchreditel'noe sobranie: Istoriia sozyva i politicheskogo krusheniia* (Leningrad, 1976), p. 339.

26. Ibid. See also Pokrovskii and Iakovleva, *Vserossiiskoe uchreditel'noe sobranie*, p. 203.

27. Bonch-Bruevich, *Na boevykh postakh,* p. 248.

28. Ibid. See also F. Raskolnikov, "Rasskaz o poteriannom dne," *Novyi mir,* 1933, no. 12:97–98; Mstislavskii, *Five Days Which Transformed Russia,* pp. 141–142; Oganovskii, "Dnevnik chlena uchreditel'nogo sobrania," pp. 154–155; Sviatitskii, "5–6 ianvaria 1918 goda," p. 225.

29. Pokrovskii and Iakovleva, *Vserossiiskoe uchreditel'noe sobranie,* pp. 4–5.

30. Sviatitskii, "5–6 ianvaria 1918 goda," p. 225. Idealizing this incident, Sviatitskii writes, "This was a momentous scene. The entire Constituent Assembly, without regard to fractional divisions, joined in the singing of the revolutionary socialist hymn."

31. Pokrovskii and Iakovleva, *Vserossiiskoe uchreditel'noe sobranie,* p. 9.

32. Ibid., p. 17. For highly critical assessments of Chernov's speech, see Oganovskii, "Dnevnik chlena uchreditel'nogo sobraniia," pp. 156–171; Vishniak, *Vserossiiskoe uchreditel'noe sobranie,* pp. 108–109; and Mstislavskii, *Five Days Which Transformed Russia,* p. 146.

33. Oganovskii, "Dnevnik chlena uchreditel'nogo sobraniia," p. 157.

34. Pokrovskii and Iakovleva, *Vserossiiskoe uchreditel'noe sobranie,* pp. 9–23; V. M. Chernov, *Pered burei* (New York, 1953), pp. 362–380.

35. Mstislavskii, *Five Days Which Transformed Russia,* p. 146.

36. O. N. Radkey, *The Sickle under the Hammer: The Russian Socialist Revolutionaries in the Earliest Months of Soviet Rule* (New York, 1963), p. 394.

37. TsGA SPb, f. 1,000, op. 1, d. 7, l. 27.

38. For an illuminating study of Bukharin and his role in Bolshevik and Soviet history, see Stephen F. Cohen, *Bukharin and the Bolshevik Revolution: A Political Biography* (New York, 1973).

39. Pokrovskii and Iakovleva, *Vserossiiskoe uchreditel'noe sobranie,* pp. 25–31.
40. Ibid., pp 32–34.
41. Ibid., pp. 35–36.
42. Mstislavskii, *Five Days Which Transformed Russia,* p. 147.
43. Pokrovskii and Iakovleva, *Vserossiiskoe uchreditel'noe sobranie,* p. 36.
44. Oganovskii, "Dnevnik chlena uchreditel'nogo sobraniia," p. 150.
45. Pokrovskii and Iakovleva, *Vserossiiskoe uchreditel'noe sobranie,* p. 38.
46. Ibid., pp. 41–44.
47. Ibid., p. 45.
48. Ibid., pp. 50–53.
49. Mstislavskii, *Five Days Which Transformed Russia,* p. 148; Oganovskii, "Dnevnik chlena uchreditel'nogo sobraniia," p. 158; Albert Rhys Williams, *Journey into Revolution: Petrograd, 1917–1918* (Chicago, 1969), p. 200. See also Vishniak, *Vserossiiskoe uchreditel'noe sobranie,* p. 152; and Leopold Haimson, "The Mensheviks after the October Revolution," pt. 3, *Russian Review* (July 1980): 467–469.
50. Iu. P. Denike, "I. G. Tsereteli," *Novyi zhurnal,* 1959, no. 57:284.
51. This Sorokin is not to be confused with Pitirim Sorokin, who was then still incarcerated.
52. Pokrovskii and Iakovleva, *Vserossiiskoe uchreditelnoe sobranie,* pp. 61–64; Oganovskii, "Dnevnik chlena uchreditel'nogo sobraniia," p. 158.
53. Pokrovskii and Iakovleva, *Vserossiiskoe uchreditelnoe sobranie,* pp. 62–63.
54. Ibid., pp. 63–64.
55. Oganovskii, "Dnevnik chlena uchreditel'nogo sobraniia," p. 158.
56. *Znamia truda,* January 7, 1918, p. 4.
57. Pokrovskii and Iakovleva, *Vserossiiskoe uchreditel'noe sobranie,* p. 64.
58. Mstislavskii, *Five Days Which Transformed Russia,* p. 148.
59. *Novaia zhizn',* January 7, 1918, p. 2.
60. Raskolnikov, *Tales of Sub-Lieutenant Ilyin,* p. 16.
61. *Novaia zhizn',* January 7, 1918, p. 2.
62. Raskolnikov, *Tales of Sub-Lieutenant Ilyin,* p. 16; Vishniak, *Vserossiiskoe uchreditel'noe sobranie,* pp. 112–113.
63. Raskolnikov, *Tales of Sub-Lieutenant Ilyin,* p. 17; Sviatitskii, "5–6 ianvaria 1918 goda," p. 227.
64. Pokrovskii and Iakovleva, *Vserossiiskoe uchreditel'noe sobranie,* pp. 85–90.
65. Ibid., pp. 88–90.
66. Ibid., p. 89.
67. Raskolnikov, *Tales of Sub-Lieutenant Ilyin,* p. 18.
68. Pokrovskii and Iakovleva, *Vserossiiskoe uchreditel'noe sobranie,* p. 90; Mstislavskii, *Five Days Which Transformed Russia,* pp. 149–150.
69. Pokrovskii and Iakovleva, *Vserossiiskoe uchreditel'noe sobranie,* pp. 90–91.
70. Ibid., pp. 91–94.
71. Ibid., pp. 108–109.
72. Ibid., p. 110. See also Mstislavskii, *Five Days Which Transformed Russia,* pp. 152–154; Oganovskii, "Dnevnik chlena uchreditel'nogo sobraniia," p. 160; Vishniak, *Vserossiiskoe uchreditel'noe sobranie,* p. 115.
73. Pokrovskii and Iakovleva, *Vserossiiskoe uchreditel'noe sobranie,* p. 110.
74. Ibid., pp. 110–113.
75. Vishniak, *Vserossiiskoe uchreditel'noe sobranie,* p. 105.
76. Sviatitskii, "5–6 ianvaria 1918 goda," p. 228.
77. RGASPI, f. 19, op. 1, d. 41, l. 1; GARF, f. 130, op 2, d. 1, ll. 9–10. See also Razgon, *VTsIK Sovetov,* p. 287.
78. Keep, *The Debate,* p. 260; *Znamia truda,* January 7, 1918, p. 4.
79. Lenin, *Polnoe sobranie sochinenii,* 3:238–242; Keep, *The Debate,* pp. 260–264.
80. Keep, *The Debate,* p. 264.

81. Ibid., pp. 265–266.

82. *Znamia truda,* January 9, 1918, p. 3.

83. *Tret'ii vserossiiskii s"ezd sovetov rabochikh, soldatskikh, i krest'ianskikh deputatov* (St. Petersburg, 1918), pp. 43–34, 87.

84. Ibid., 93–94.

85. *Partiia levykh sotsialistov-revoliutsionerov: Dokumenty i materialy,* 1:235–237.

86. Ibid. On the Peasant Section, also see below, chapter 11; T. A. Sivokhina, "Obrazovanie i deiatel'nost' krest'ianskoi sektsii VTsIK, *Vestnik Moskovskogo universiteta,* 1969, no. 2:14–16; and Spiridonova's report on the Peasant Section at the Fifth All-Russian Congress of Soviets (*Piatyi vserossiiskii s"ezd sovetov rabochikh, krest'ianskikh, soldatskikh i kazach'ikh deputatov: Stenograficheskii otchet* [Moscow, 1918], pp. 50–59).

87. *Tret'ii vserossiiskii s"ezd,* pp. 87, 94. The CEC formed by the Third All-Russian Congress of Soviets was composed of 160 Bolsheviks, 125 Left SRs, 2 Menshevik-Internationalists, 3 Anarchist-Communists, 7 SR Maximalists, 7 Right SRs, and 2 Mensheviks.

5. Fighting Lenin

1. See Lenin, *Polnoe sobranie sochinenii,* 35:253.

2. *Peterburgskii komitet,* pp. 571–576.

3. Ibid., pp. 579–593.

4. Ibid., pp. 581–587.

5. For a perceptive analysis of these negotiations, see Richard K. Debo, *Revolution and Survival: The Foreign Policy of Soviet Russia, 1917–1918* (Toronto, 1979), pp. 45–112.

6. Keep, *The Debate,* pp. 213–217; *Protokoly zasedanii Ispolnitel'nogo Komiteta Sovetov R., S., Kr., i Kaz. Deputatov II sozyva,* pp. 152–155.

7. RGASPI, f. 19, op. 1, d. 28, l. 2.

8. Keep, *The Debate,* pp. 223–239.

9. Ibid., p. 228; *Protokoly zasedanii Ispolnitel'nogo Komiteta Sovetov R., S., Kr., i Kaz. Deputatov II sozyva,* p. 164.

10. RGASPI, f. 19, op. 1, d. 28, l. 2.

11. See above, chapter 2.

12. M.Kedrov, "Iz krasnoi tetradi ob Il'iche," in *Vospominaniia o Vladimire Il'iche Lenine,* vol. 2 (Moscow, 1957), p. 97; N. I. Podvoiskii, "Ot krasnoi gvardii k krasnoi armii," *Istorik marksist,* 1938, no. 1:16–34. The text of Lenin's questionnaire is contained in Lenin, *Polnoe sobranie sochinenii,* 35:179–180, 472.

13. See Debo, *Revolution and Survival,* p. 60; and E. N. Gorodetskii, "Demobilizatsiia armii v 1917–1918 gg.," *Istoriia SSSR,* 1958, no. 1:15–19.

14. *Vechernyi chas,* December 18, 1917, p. 2.

15. RGASPI, f. 19, op. 1, d. 29, l. 2.

16. RGASPI, f. 19, d. 29, l. 2; f. 5, op. 1, d. 2424, l. 19; M. N. Simonian, *Ego professiia revoliutsiia: Dokumental'nyi ocherk o zhizni i deiatel'nosti N. V. Krylenko* (Moscow, 1985), pp. 93–94. In a letter to Istpart in the 1920s, Krylenko indicated that, following the meeting of military representatives, he submitted a special written report to Lenin in which he emphasized the utter hopelessness of relying on any fighting by the old army, since it had interpreted the armistice and the beginning of peace talks as indicating that the war was over (Istpart, *Protokoly s"ezdov i konferentsii vsesoiuznoi kommunisticheskoi partii (b): Sed'moi s"ezd, mart 1918 goda* [Moscow-Leningrad, 1928], pp. 261–262 n. 48).

17. Lenin, *Polnoe sobranie sochinenii,* 35:472; A. Chubarian, *Brestskii mir* (Moscow, 1964), p. 106.

18. RGASPI, f. 19, op. 1, d. 29, l. 28; Lenin, *Polnoe sobranie sochinenii,* 35:181.

19. RGASPI, f. 5, op. 1, d. 2423, l. 19 ob.

20. *Peterburgskii komitet,* pp. 607, 608.

21. Ibid., pp. 609–611, 621–622.

22. Ibid., pp. 611–618.

23. Ibid., pp. 615–616.

24. Ibid., p. 619.

25. *Vladimir Il'ich Lenin, Biograficheskaia khronika,* 5:156–157.

26. See, for example, Dmitri Volkogonov, *Lenin: A New Biography* (New York, 1994), pp. 109–128; Richard Pipes, *Three "Whys" of the Russian Revolution* (New York, 1995), pp. 45–46; Richard Pipes, *The Russian Revolution* (New York, 1994), pp. 410–412, 431–438, and 612–624; and Richard Pipes, ed., *The Unknown Lenin: From the Secret Archive* (New Haven, 1996), pp. 6, 15–16.

27. L. Trotskii, *Sochineniia,* vol. 17, pt. 1 (Moscow–Leningrad, 1926), p. 631 n. 38.

28. Lenin, *Polnoe sobranie sochinenii,* 35:225.

29. Ibid., 35:243–252.

30. Institut marksizma-leninizma pri TsK KPSS, *Leninskii sbornik,* vol. 11 (Moscow, 1929), pp. 43–44; Institut marksizma-leninizma pri TsK KPSS, *Sed'moi ekstrennyi s"ezd RKP (b), mart 1918 goda: Stenograficheskii otchet* (Moscow, 1962), pp. 216–218.

31. Ibid.

32. L. Trotsky, *My Life* (New York, 1970), pp. 382–383.

33. Kedrov, "Iz krasnoi tetradi ob Il'iche," p. 10.

34. *Protokoly tsentral'nogo komiteta RSDRP (b),* p. 168. See also N. N. Smirnov, *Tret'ii vserossiiskii s"ezd sovetov* (Leningrad, 1988), p. 98.

35. On this point, see Debo, *Revolution and Survival,* p. 79.

36. *Protokoly tsentral'nogo komiteta RSDRP (b),* pp. 168–169.

37. Ibid., pp. 169–170.

38. Ibid., p. 170.

39. Ibid., p. 172. Lenin's notes on this meeting are contained in *V. I. Lenin. Neizvestnye dokumenty, 1891–1922* (Moscow, 1999), pp. 223–224.

40. For example, such a shift occurred among Okhtinskii district Bolsheviks (TsGAIPD, f. 10, op. 1, d. 11, ll. 1 ob.–2 ob.).

41. *Protokoly tsentral'nogo komiteta RSDRP (b),* p. 173.

42. *Petrogradskoe ekho,* January 12, 1918, p. 2; *Nashi vedomosti,* January 13, 1918, p. 2.

43. *Tret'ii vserossiiskii s"ezd sovetov rabochikh, soldatskikh, i krest'ianskih deputatov,* pp. 21–34.

44. Ibid., pp. 48–55; Trotskii, *Sochineniia,* vol. 17, pt. 1, pp. 53–69.

45. *Tret'ii vserossiiskii s"ezd sovetov rabochikh, soldatskikh, i krest'ianskih deputatov,* pp. 56–58.

46. Ibid., pp. 71, 92–93.

47. See the statement of the Executive Commission in *Protokoly tsentral'nogo komiteta RSDRP (b),* pp. 180–183.

48. See GARF, f. 1235, op. 18, d. 7, l. 31.

49. *Tret'ii vserossiiskii s"ezd sovetov rabochikh, soldatskikh, i krest'ianskih deputatov,* p. 52.

50. Ibid., p. 64.

51. Ibid. p. 59.

52. *Krasnaia gazeta,* January 13, 1918, p. 1.

53. Ibid., January 17, 1918, p. 1.

54. Ibid., January 19, 1918, p. 1.

55. Ibid., January 21, 1918, p. 1.

56. RGASPI, f. 19, op. 1, d. 47.

57. *Protokoly tsentral'nogo komiteta RSDRP (b),* p. 181.

58. Ibid., pp. 182–183.

59. Ibid., p. 176; see, esp., theses 5 through 8.

60. Ibid., pp. 183–184.

61. Ibid., pp. 174–180.

62. Ibid., pp. 175–176, 283–284 n. 207.

63. Ibid., pp. 175, 283 n. 206.

64. In this connection, see the twenty-second thesis which Lenin added to his "Theses on the War" on 21 January (Lenin, *Polnoe sobranie sochinenii,* 35:251–252).

65. *Protokoly tsentral'nogo komiteta RSDRP (b),* pp. 190–191. See also *V. I. Lenin. Neizvestnye dokumenty,* pp. 225–227.

66. Trotskii, *Sochineniia,* vol. 17, pt. 1, pp. 103–104, 106; Max Hoffman, *War Diaries and Other Papers,* trans. Eric Sutton, vol. 2 (London, 1939), pp. 218–219.

67. Hoffman, *War Diaries,* 2:219; John W. Wheeler-Bennett, *Brest-Litovsk: The Forgotten Peace, March 1918* (London, 1963), p. 229.

68. Trotsky, *My Life,* p. 386.

6. "The Socialist Fatherland Is in Danger"

1. *Novye vedomosti,* January 29, 1918, p. 2.
2. I. N. Steinberg, *In the Workshop of the Revolution* (New York, 1953), p. 237.
3. *Sotsial demokrat,* February 13, 1918, p. 2.
4. *Izvestiia,* January 31, 1918, p. 3.
5. GARF, f. 1235, op. 18, d. 4, l. 1.
6. *Krasnaia gazeta,* January 31, 1918, p. 1.
7. *Znamia truda,* January 30, 1918, p. 1.
8. For a recent biography of Cromie, see Roy Bainton, *Honored by Strangers: The Life of Captain Francis Cromie CB DSO RN—1882–1918* (Shrewsbury, 2002).
9. Nina Berberova's classic *Zheleznaia zhenshchina, 1892–1974* (New York, 1991), although somewhat dated, remains the best study of Moura Benkendorf. For an excellent, abridged English translation of this work, see Marian Schwartz and Richard D. Sylvester, trans., *Moura: The Dangerous Life of Moura Budberg* (New York, 2005).
10. Hoover Institution, Lockhart Collection, Box 6, Sidney Reilly.
11. Fortunately, a comprehensive record of the special CEC meeting, prepared for printing in 1918 but never published, has been preserved (see GARF, f. 1235, op. 18, d. 5, ll. 1–25). My reconstruction of the 1/14 February session is based on this archival record, supplemented by accounts in *Novaia zhizn',* February 15, 1918, p. 2; *Nash vek,* February 15, 1918, p. 2; and *Znamia truda,* February 15, 1918, p. 4.
12. Russia switched from the Julian calendar to the Gregorian calender on this day (1/14 February). Unless identified as "old style" [o.s.], dates from here on correspond to the "new style" Gregorian calendar used in the West.
13. GARF, f. 1235, op. 18, d. 5, ll. 1–4.
14. See above, chapter 1; *Dekrety sovetskoi vlasti,* 1:39–41; and *Tret'ii vserossiiskii s'ezd Sovetov,* pp. 43–44.
15. GARF, f. 1235, op. 18, d. 5, ll. 4–11.
16. Ibid., ll. 11–21, 23.
17. Kamenev's mission failed miserably. Deported from Great Britain not long after his arrival, he was arrested trying to slip back into Russia by Finnish Whites and held in isolation on the Aaland Islands until August 1918.
18. *Izvestiia,* February 19, 1918, p. 2.
19. According to Sverdlov, many members of the government, not just Trotsky, felt that after a three-month armistice fighting would be impossible for *both* German and Russian soldiers (GARF, f. 1235, op. 18, d. 7, l. 32).
20. Debo, *Revolution and Survival,* pp. 116–120; Z. A. B. Zeman, ed., *Germany and the Revolution in Russia: Documents from the Archives of the German Foreign Ministry* (London, 1958), pp. 274–275; Wheeler-Bennett, *Brest-Litovsk,* pp. 229–232; Gordon Craig, *Germany, 1866–1945* (New York, 1959), p. 391; Trotsky, *My Life,* p. 386.
21. Ministerstvo inostrannykh del SSSR, *Dokumenty vneshnoi politiki SSSR,* vol. 1 (Moscow, 1957), p. 105; S. M. Maiorov, *Bor'ba Sovetskoi Rossii za vykhod iz imperialisticheskoi voiny* (Moscow, 1959), p. 217; A. Samoilo *Dve zhizni* (Moscow, 1958).

22. Trotsky, *My Life*, pp. 387–388.

23. There was nothing in the Petrograd papers about the renewal of hostilities until the 19th, by which time the German advance was already in full sway.

24. This is apparent from contingency military directives issued during the day, 17 February (RGA VMF, f. r-342, op. 1, d. 144, l. 1). Regarding the Sovnarkom, Samoilo's message may have arrived after a Sovnarkom meeting on 16 February, and, judging by archival records, a cabinet meeting scheduled for the 17th was canceled.

25. See RGA VMF, f. r-342, op. 1, d. 20, l. 14.

26. *Protokoly tsentral'nogo komiteta RSDRP (b)*, pp. 194–195.

27. Ibid., pp. 197–199.

28. Information on this meeting is sketchy and contradictory. My reconstruction is based on a very brief protocol in RGASPI, f. 19, op. 1, d. 64, and on reports in *Novaia zhizn'*, February 20, 1918, p. 3, *Vechernaia zvezda*, February 19, 1918, p. 1; *Novyi den'*, February 20, 1918, p. 3; *Novyi vechernyi chas*, February 20, 1918, p. 1; *Novyi luch*, February 20, 1918, p. 1; *Novye vedomosti*, February 19, 1918, p. 1; *Petrogradskoe ekho*, February 19, 1918, p. 1 and February 20, 1918, p. 1; and *Krasnaia gazeta*, February 20, 1918, p. 1.

29. *Protokoly tsentral'nogo komiteta RSDRP (b)*, pp. 200–205. See also *Petrogradskii golos*, February 21, 1918, p. 2; and *Vladimir Il'ich Lenin, Biograficheskaia khronika*, 5:263.

30. *Novaia zhizn'*, February 20, 1918, p. 3.

31. *Russkie vedomosti*, February 21, 1918, p. 2; *Petrogradskoe ekho*, February 19, 1918, p. 1.

32. *Novaia zhizn'*, February 21, 1918, p. 3; *Novy den'*, February 20, 1918, p. 3; *Nashi vedomosti*, February 20, 1918, p. 2; *Russkie vedomosti*, February 21, 1918, p. 2; *Petrogradskii golos*, February 21, 1918, p. 2.

33. *Petrogradskii golos*, February 21, 1918, p. 2.

34. Ibid.; and *Novyi den'*, February 21, 1918, p. 3.

35. *Sotsial demokrat*, February 20, 1918, p. 2; *Petrogradskoe ekho*, February 19, 1918, p. 1.

36. GARF, f. 1235, op. 33, d. 10, l. 1.

37. Records for Bolshevik and Left SR CEC fraction meetings and for joint Bolshevik–Left SR fraction meetings during this period are not available in Russian archives. The best press accounts that I have seen for meetings on 19–20 February include those in *Nash vek*, February 21, 1918, p. 2; *Novyi den'*, February 21, 1918, p. 3; *Novaia zhizn'*, February 20, 1918, p. 3, and February 21, 1918, p. 2; and *Sotsial demokrat*, February 21, 1918, pp. 2–3.

38. *Kommunist*, March 14, 1918, p. 2.

39. This was the figure used by Sverdlov at the seventh national party congress in early March 1918. *Sed'moi ekstrennyi s"ezd RKP (b)*, p. 4.

40. TsGAIPD, f. 4000, op. 7, d. 814, ll. 12–17; *Kommunist*, March 5, 1918, p. 4.

41. For a compelling study of key female Bolsheviks, among them several Petrograd responsible organizers, see Barbara Evans Clements, *Bolshevik Women* (Cambridge, 1997).

42. For minutes of Assembly of Organizers meetings in March, April, and June, see TsGAIPD, f. 1, op. 1, d. 66, ll. 1–25, 50–33; and f. 4000, op. 7, d. 814, ll. 1–81. The Assembly of Organizers continued to meet at least until 25 December, 1918, the last date for which a protocol of its meeting has been found.

43. For minutes of meetings of the Delegates Soviet between April and July 1918, see TsGAIPD, f. 4000, op. 7, d. 820.

44. *Kommunist*, March 5, 1918, p. 4; *Pravda*, February 19, 1918, p. 4.

45. TsGAIPD, f. 12, op. 1, d. 4, l. 1 ob.; *Kommunist*, March 5, 1918, p. 4; *Nash vek*, February 21, 1918, p. 2; *Russkie vedomosti*, February 21, 1918, p. 2.

46. *Protokoly tsentral'nogo komiteta RSDRP (b)*, pp. 209–210.

47. *Novaia zhizn'*, February 21, 1918, p. 2. The Third Conference of Petrograd Left SRs quickly endorsed this switch (*Znamia truda*, February 26, 1918, p. 1).

48. *Nash vek*, February 21, 1918, p. 2.

49. Ibid. See, also, D. V. Oznobishin, *Ot Bresta do Iur'eva* (Moscow, 1966), p. 88.

50. Ilyin-Zhenevsky, *The Bolsheviks in Power*, p. 22.

51. RGASPI, f. 19, op. 1, d. 65, l. 1.

52. *Novaia zhizn',* February 23, 1918, p. 3.

53. RGASPI, f. 19, op. 1, d. 66, ll. 1 ob.–2; *Nash vek,* February 22, 1918, p. 2.

54. *Izvestiia,* February 22, 1918, pp. 2–3; *Novyi vechernyi chas,* February 22, 1918, p. 2; *Nash vek,* February 22, 1918, p. 3.

55. L. Stupochenko, *V Brestskie dni* (Moscow, 1926), pp. 10–12.

56. *Nash vek,* February 22, 1918, p. 3; *Izvestiia,* February 22, 1918, p. 3; *Novyi vechernyi chas,* February 22, 1918, p. 2.

57. For a remarkably graphic description of the near total chaos prevailing among these troops, see the report of a Red Army commissar in RGASPI, f. 146, op. 1, d. 169, l. 30.

58. *Izvestiia,* February 22, 1918, p. 3. According to Sverdlov, this committee was to have unlimited powers (GARF, 1235, op. 18, d. 8, l. 40).

59. On this point, see A. L. Fraiman, *Revoliutsionnaia zashchita Petrograda v fevrale-marte 1918 g.* (Moscow–Leningrad, 1964), p. 82. Original members of the Committee for the Revolutionary Defense of Petrograd were the Bolsheviks Zinoviev, Sverdlov, Lashevich, Volodarskii, and Zalutskii, and the Left SRs Iakov Fishman and Mikhail Levinson. Its membership was later expanded to include one representative from the People's Commissariat for Military Affairs, all five members of an Emergency Headquarters for the Petrograd Military District formed earlier that day (21 February), five representatives of the CEC, and two members each from the Bolshevik and Left SR parties (*Pravda,* February 23, 1918, p. 2).

60. GARF, f. 1235, op. 18, d. 7, ll. 32–41; RGASPI, f. 86, op. 1, d. 76, ll. 1–15.

61. GARF, f. 1235, op. 18, d. 7, ll. 30–32.

62. Ibid., l. 39.

63. Ibid., l. 37.

64. Ibid., ll. 34–38.

65. Ibid., l. 38.

66. *Nash vek,* February 24, 1918, p. 2.

67. Debo, *Revolution and Survival,* p. 142; Wheeler-Bennett, *Brest-Litovsk,* pp. 255–257.

68. *Protokoly tsentral'nogo komiteta RSDRP (b),* pp. 211–218.

69. Ibid., p. 216.

70. Ibid.

71. *Vladimir Il'ich Lenin, Biograficheskaia khronika,* 5:274. The note itself is published in *Leninskii sbornik,* 11:27.

72. Stupochenko, *V Brestskie dni,* pp. 18–19.

73. A summary of Lenin's speech is in Lenin, *Polnoe sobranie sochinenii,* 35:372.

74. Stupochenko, *V Brestskie dni,* p. 24.

75. *Nash vek,* February 26, 1918, p. 2.

76. Stupochenko, *V Brestskie dni,* p. 27.

77. GARF, f. 1235, op. 18, d. 8, ll. 91–110; *Nash vek,* February 26, 1918, p. 2.

78. GARF, f. 1235, op. 18, d. 8, l. 98, l. 101.

79. Ibid., ll. 99, 102.

80. Ibid., ll. 95–97.

81. Ibid., ll. 97–98, 103–104; *Nash vek,* February 26, 1918, p. 2.

82. Figures on the numbers of participants at this meeting vary. The number of votes cast approximates 230. There is no doubt that the Bolsheviks did not have a majority. See the totals of participants by fraction and the official breakdown of voters identified by party in GARF, f. 1235, op. 18, d. 8, ll. 70, 109–110.

83. In 1924, several former Left Communists acknowledged that Kamkov had approached Bukharin and Piatakov with the idea that they should break with Lenin, exercise the Left Communist majority in their Central Committee, and join with the Left SRs to form a new anti-Brest government. The former Left Communists claimed that Kamkov's proposal was casual and they did not take it seriously (*Pravda,* January 3, 1924, p. 5). Although this may well be true, there is no reason to doubt the earnestness of Kamkov's proposal.

84. *Nash vek,* February 26, 1918, pp. 2–3.

85. K. T. Sverdlova, *Iakob Mikhailovich Sverdlov* (Moscow, 1960), p. 350.
86. GARF, f. 1235, op. 18, d. 8, ll. 109–110.
87. Lenin, *Polnoe sobranie sochinenii,* 35:381.

7. An Obscene Peace

1. *Dekrety sovetskoi vlasti,* 1:512; *Izvestiia,* March 3, 1918, p. 1.
2. RGASPI, f. 19, op. 1, d. 70, l. 1.
3. Ibid., d. 68, ll. 1–1 ob.
4. See above, chapter 6.
5. *Izvestiia,* February 22, 1918, p. 1; RGASPI, f. 19, op. 1, d. 67.
6. Fraiman, *Revoliutsionnaia zashchita Petrograda,* p. 132.
7. TsGAIPD, f. 4000, op. 5, d. 212, l. 148.
8. See, for example, *Znamia truda,* February 24, 1918, p. 3.
9. For example, see Fraiman, *Revoliustionnaia zashchita Petrograda,* p. 122.
10. The Bolshevik Military Organization, which had prepared units of the Petrograd garrison for revolutionary action in 1917, and which had furnished the first military leaders and political commissars for Red forces, Podvoiskii, Krylenko, Antonov-Ovseenko, and Eremeev among them, was now moribund. It was formally dissolved toward the end of March 1918. See *Petrogradskaia pravda,* March 26, 1918, p. 1.
11. See, for example, TsGAIPD, f. 10, op. 1, d. 12, ll. 5–6, for the positive response to this appeal at a general meeting of Bolsheviks and Bolshevik sympathizers in the Okhtinskii district on 24 February.
12. TsGAIPD, f. 4000, op. 7, d. 814, l. 91.
13. See, for instance, TsGASP, f. 9618, op. 1, d. 229, l. 83. At the end of March, the Bolshevik Petersburg Committee belatedly began organizing similar party detachments. However, for some time their development was stunted by organizational bickering and by the recruitment of their personnel into the Red Army and, later, into food procurement detachments (TsGAIPD, f. 4000, op. 7, d. 64, ll. 5, 6–6 ob., 12, 23, 37, 58–60, 215–218).
14. Fraiman, *Revoliutsionnaia zashchita Petrograda,* p. 91.
15. *Izvestiia,* February 26, 1918, p. 3; and Fraiman, *Revoliutsionnaia zashchita Petrograda,* p. 91.
16. *Izvestiia,* February 23, 1918, p. 3.
17. TsGA SPb, f. 101, op. 1, d. 38, l. 120.
18. TsGA SPb, f. 150, op. 1, d. 3, l. 121.
19. TsGA SPb, f. 9618, op. 1, d. 240, l. 19.
20. For minutes of this meeting, see TsGA SPb, f. 6276, op. 3, d. 163, l. 5–6.
21. Fraiman, *Revoliutsionnaia zashchita Petrograda,* p. 93. For the metal workers, see A. L. Fraiman, comp., *Krakh germanskoi okkupatsii na Pskovshchine: Sbornik dokumentov* (Leningrad, 1939), p. 73; for transport workers, TsGA SPb, f. 6276, op. 3, d. 123, ll. 6–7; for food processors, f. 6261, op. 2, d. 2, l. 29; and for wood workers, f. 5937, op. 2, d. 4, l. 49.
22. *Izvestiia,* February 23, 1918, p. 1; February 26, 1918, p. 6.
23. See, for example, Fraiman, *Revoliutsionnaia zashchita Petrograda,* pp. 88–89.
24. TsGA SPb, f. 9618, op. 1, d. 240, l. 30; f. 2421, op. 1, d. 4, ll. 18–19.
25. GARF, f. 130, op. 2, d. 1098, l. 8.
26. See Polukarov's statement to this effect at the opening session of the First All-Russian Conference of Chekas on 11 June 1918 (TsA FSB, f. 1, op. 3, d. 11, l. 4).
27. TsGA SPb, f. 9618, op. 1, d. 266, l. 6; TsGA SPb, f. 47, op. 1, d. 28, ll. 32–32 ob.; f. 101, d. 30, l. 119; d. 38, ll. 2–3 ob.
28. The Vasilii Island and Peterhof district soviets created Chekas at this time (TGA SPb, f. 47, op. 1, d. 28, ll. 32–32 ob.; f. 101, op. 1, d. 38, ll. 2–3 ob.), and other Petrograd district soviets may also have done so.
29. See RGASPI, f. 19, op. 1, d. 67.

30. RGASPI, f. 19, op. 1, d. 68, l. 2.

31. Shteinberg, *In the Workshop,* p. 146.

32. *Iz istorii VChK* (Moscow, 1958), pp. 95–96.

33. *Pravda,* February 22, 1918, p. 2.

34. AU FSB SPb i LO, No. N-47037. On Perel'tsveig, see chapter 12.

35. TsGA SPb, f. 9618, op. 1, d. 226, l. 43.

36. TsGA SPb, f. 101, op. 1, d. 53, l. 14; d. 226, l. 39.

37. TsGA SPb, f. 9618, op. 1, d. 240, l. 59. Although shootings at the scene do not appear to have actually been carried out, many individuals were arrested and brought before the Revolutionary Tribunal of the Petrograd Soviet for spreading anti-Soviet propaganda during this crisis. See GARF, f. 336, op. 1, dd. 69, 149, 216.

38. TsGA SPb, f. 47, op. 1, d. 44, l. 85.

39. For a compilation of these reports, see GARF, f. 393, op. 2, d. 70, ll. 137–138 ob.

40. GARF, f. 393, op. 2, d. 70, l. 138 ob.

41. Ibid., l. 137 ob.

42. Ibid., ll. 137 ob–138.

43. Ibid., l. 137.

44. Ibid.

45. Ibid.

46. V. I. Startsev, *Ocherki po istorii Petrogradskoi krasnoi gvardii i rabochei militsii* (Moscow–Leningrad, 1965), pp. 244–246.

47. F. Dingel'shtedt, "Iz vospominanii agitatora Petrogradskogo komiteta RSDRP (b) (s sentiabria 1917 g. po mart 1918 g.)," *Krasnaia letopis',* 1927, no. 1 (22): 65–68.

48. *Sed'moi ekstrennyi s"ezd,* p. 90.

49. The resolution Riazanov presented is in TsGA SPb, f. 6276, op. 3, d. 6, l. 12.

50. Ibid., l. 14 ob.

51. TsGA SPb, f. 9618, op. 1, d. 191, ll. 44–64.

52. Ibid., ll. 45–47.

53. Ibid., ll. 57–58.

54. RGASPI, f. 17, op. 65, d. 57, l. 35.

55. See above, chapter 6.

56. TsGAIPD, f. 1, op. 4, d.113, ll. 7–9 ob.; see also f. 1, op. 1, d. 67.

57. *Pravda,* March 2, 1918, p. 1.

58. Ibid.

59. TsGAIPD, f. 1, op. 4, d. 113, ll. 7–8 ob.

60. Ibid., l. 9. Bukharin had in mind the 23 February Central Committee meeting described in chapter 6.

61. Ibid., l. 9 ob.

62. Not to be confused with the theoretical journal of the same name published by the Bolshevik Moscow Oblast Bureau between April and June 1918.

63. *Kommunist,* March 5, 1918, p. 4. See also *Kommunist,* March 14, 1918, p. 2.

64. *Kommunist,* March 14, 1918, p. 3. There were exceptions. At a meeting of the Narva district party committee on 14 March, a majority voted for revolutionary war. See *Kommunist,* March 15, 1918, p. 4; March 17, 1918, p. 4.

65. See, for examples, TsGAIPD, f. 2315, op. 1, d. 3, l. 83 and f. 8, op. 1, d. 2, ll. 1–1 ob.

66. TsGA SPb, f. 9618, op. 1, d. 201, l. 3.

67. *Krasnaia gazeta,* March 6, 1918, p. 2.

68. TsGAIPD, f. 1, op. 4, d. 128, l. 3.

69. TsGAIPD, f. 1, op. 1, d. 3, l. 2. Independently, the Petersburg Committee sent the Central Committee an analogous request (TsGAIPD, f. 1, op. 1, d. 105, l. 1).

70. *Protokoly tsentral'nogo komiteta RSDRP (b),* p. 165. The minutes of this meeting were added to the edition of the Central Committee's records for 1917–1918, published in 1958. However, they were dated 19 January which, as the Soviet historian E. V. Klopov first argued in

1966, was obviously an error. The French historian Eva Berar contends that 19 January was the correct date of this meeting. Although she makes a persuasive argument for the importance of escaping continuing counterrevolutionary conspiracies in Petrograd as a factor influencing the government's evacuation, it is apparent that the meeting indeed took place on 9 March. For the competing arguments, see E. V. Klopov, "Daty zasedanii TsK RKP (b) neobkhodimo utochnit' (9 marta 1918)," *Voprosy istorii KPSS*, 1966, no. 11:118–119; and Eva Berar, "Pochemu bolsh'eviki pokinuli Petrograd?" *Minuvshee: Istoricheskii al'manakh*, 1993, no. 14:226–250.

71. *Sed'moi ekstrennyi s"ezd*, p. 1.

72. Ibid.

73. Ibid., pp. 7–24.

74. Ibid., pp. 24–40.

75. Ibid., pp. 127–128.

76. Ibid., p. 128.

77. Ibid., p. 129.

78. Ibid., p. 137.

79. Ibid., pp. 176–177.

80. Ibid., p. 170.

81. RGASPI, f. 19, op. 1, d. 70, l. 1.

82. On Vologda as the diplomatic capital of Russia, see A. Bykov and L. Panov, *Diplomaticheskaia stolitsa Rossii* (Vologda, 1998).

83. *Izvestiia*, February 27, 1918, p. 2.

84. *Nashe vremia* (Moscow), March 7, 1918, p. 3; *Krasnaia gazeta*, March 6, 1918, p. 4.

85. *Znamia truda*, March 1, 1918, p. 3.

86. As late as 6 March, the Presidium of the Petrograd Soviet ordered that individuals spreading false rumors regarding the government's flight be arrested (TsGA SPb, f. 9618, op. 1, d. 240, l. 80). See also TsGA SPb, f. 47, op. 1, d. 42, l. 49.

87. TsGAIPD, f. 1, op. 2, d. 3, ll. 1–5.

88. *Novye vedomosti*, March 21, 1918, p. 4.

89. GARF, f. 6148, op. 1, d. 2. Published in *Puti revoliutsii (stat'i, materialy, vospominaniia)* (Berlin, 1923), p. 357.

90. RGASPI, f. 19, op. 1, d. 70, l. 1.

91. TsA VMF, f. r-342, op. 1, d. 116, ll. 34–56 ob.

92. Iz perepiski E. D. Stasovoi i K. T. Novgorodtsevoi (Sverdlovoi), mart–dekabr' 1918 g.," *Voprosy istorii*, 1956, no. 10:91–92.

93. A. L. Litvin, *Levye esery i VCheka: Sbornik dokumentov* (Kazan, 1996), pp. 51–52.

94. *Novaia zhizn'*, March 14, 1918, p. 1. The VCheka fled Petrograd at noon on 9 March.

95. RGASPI, f. 446, op. 1, d. 1, ll. 2–2 ob.

96. For examples, see V. D. Bonch-Bruevich, *Pereezd Sovetskogo pravitel'stva iz Petrograda v Moskvu (po lichnym vospominaniiam)* (Moscow, 1926), pp. 16–18; and V. Iakovlev, "Malo-Visherskii epizod (Pereezd Sovnarkoma v Moskvu v 1918 g.)," *Krasnaia letopis'*, 1934, no. 1 (58): 94–102.

97. *Izvestiia Kronshtadtskogo soveta*, March 2, 1918, p. 3.

98. *Partiia levykh sotsialistov-revoliutsionerov: Dokumenty i materialy*, p. 261.

99. *Stenograficheskii otchet 4-go chrezvychainogo s"ezda sovetov rabochikh, soldatskikh, krest'ianskikh i kazach'ikh deputatov* (Moscow, 1920), p. 83.

100. Ibid., p. 82. For Shteinberg's pledge, see *Novyi vechernyi chas*, March 14, 1918, p. 1.

101. See, for example, D. V. Oznobishin, "Leninskii svod otvetov mestnykh sovetov na zapros SNK o zakliuchenii Brestskogo mira," in *Istochnikovedenie istorii sovetskogo obshchestva*, issue 2 (Moscow, 1968), pp. 189–243.

102. *Sotsial demokrat*, March 15, 1918, p. 2.

103. *Stenograficheskii otchet 4-go chrezvychainogo s"ezda sovetov rabochikh, soldatskikh, krest'ianskikh i kazach'ikh deputatov*, pp. 18–22.

104. Ibid., pp. 23–31.

105. Ibid., pp. 48–51.

106. Ibid., pp. 40–43.

107. Ibid., pp. 64–65.

108. Ibid., pp. 70–73.

109. RGASPI, f. 19, op.1, d. 77, ll. 9–14. Among Left Communist People's Commissars who now resigned, only Aleksandra Kollontai, People's Commissar for State Welfare, elaborated on the reasons for her action in writing. She explained that her support for revolutionary war, and her conviction that ratification of the understanding with "Austro-German imperialists" weakened the revolutionary thrust of the world proletariat and undermined the stability of Soviet power in Russia, left her no alternative but to resign (RGASPI, f.19, op.1, d. 79, l. 10).

110. *Tret'ii vserossiiskii s"ezd,* p. 23.

111. *Vechernye vedomosti,* March 18, 1918, p. 4.

112. See below, chapter 11.

113. See *Kommunist,* March 10, 1918, p. 1 for the Petersburg Committee's announcement of this conference and its purposes.

114. TsGAIPD, f. 4000, op. 7, d. 814, ll. 82–83.

115. *Kommunist,* March 14, 1918, p. 2.

116. TsGAIPD, f. 1, op. 1, d. 69, ll. 2ob.–8; M. Lur'e, "Iz istorii bor'by s 'levymi' kommunistami v Petrogradskoi organizatsii bol'shevikov," *Krasnaia letopis',* 1934, no. 2 (59): 105–111.

8. A Turbulent Spring

1. *Sed'moi ekstrennyi s"ezd,* p. 113.

2. RGASPI, f. 19, op.1, d. 76, l. 2.

3. TsGA SPb, f. 9618, op. 1, d. 226, l. 55.

4. For an examination of Uritskii as head of the PCheka, see Aleksandr Rabinovich, "Moisei Uritskii: Robesp'er revoliutsionnogo Petrograda?" *Otechestvennaia istoriia,* 2003, no. 1:3–21.

5. See excerpts from Zinoviev's speech to the Petrograd Soviet on 12 March explaining this step in *Gazeta kopeika,* March 14, 1918, p. 3; and his report on the subject at the First Congress of Northern Oblast Soviets on 25 April in TsGA SPb, f. 143, op. 1, d. 3, l. 5.

6. *Sbornik dekretov i postanovlenii po soiuzu kommun severnoi oblasti,* issue 1, pt. 1 (Petrograd, 1919), p. 23.

7. Il'in-Zhenevskii, *The Bolsheviks in Power,* p. 26.

8. Luncharskii was to direct the Commissariat for Enlightenment in the SK PTK and the national Commissariat for Enlightenment.

9. *Novaia zhizn',* March 14, 1918, p. 1.

10. *Krasnaia gazeta,* March 12, 1918, p. 1. Both the Cheka and the Red Army were to report to Trotsky.

11. See, for example, Trotsky's initial proclamation in *Krasnaia gazeta,* March 12, 1918, p. 1.

12. RGASPI, f. 5, op. 1, d. 1032, ll. 6–7. After Trotsky's departure, the Petrograd Bureau of the Central Committee consisted of Zinoviev, Stasova, Krestinskii, Lashevich, Smilga, and Ioffe.

13. A. P. Nenarokov, ed., *Pervoe Sovetskoe pravitel'stvo: Oktiabr' 1917–iiul' 1918* (Moscow, 1991), p. 426.

14. Thus, when it needed someone to head a Commissariat for Nationalities, the SK PTK requested that the Presidium of the Petrograd Soviet identify a suitable candidate (TsGA SPb, f. 144, op. 1, d. 1, l. 30).

15. K. I. Shelavin, "Iz istorii Peterburgskogo komiteta bol'shevikov v 1918," *Krasnaia letopis',* 1928, no. 2 (26): 110–111.

16. TsGAIPD, f. 1, op. 2, d. 3, l. 1.

17. TsGAIPD, f. 1, op. 1, d. 3, ll. 1–2; and see above, chapter 7.

18. TsGAIPD, f. 4000, op. 7, d. 814, ll. 82–85.

19. TsGAIPD, f. 4000, op. 4, d. 814, l. 82.

20. TsGAIPD, f. 1, op. 1, d. 66, ll. 1–3. On the creation of the Assembly of Organizers, see above, chapter 6.

21. TsGAIPD, f. 4000, op. 7, d. 814, l. 91.

22. *Petrogradskaia pravda,* April 9, 1918, p. 3; TsGAIPD. f. 1, op. 1, d. 64, ll. 6–6 ob. On the First Northern Oblast [Bolshevik] Party Conference, see below, chapter 9.

23. RGASPI, f. 17, op. 4, d. 10, l. 38.

24. TsGAIPD, f. 1817, op. 1, d. 29, ll. 1–30.

25. *Strana,* April 5, 1918, p. 4; See also *Novye vedomosti,* March 21, 1918, p. 7.

26. RGASPI, f. 19, op.1, d. 79, l. 3.

27. RGASPI, f. 19, op.1, d. 84, l. 3.

28. RGASPI, f. 19, op.1, d. 94, ll.13–13 ob.; emphasis in original.

29. RGASPI, f. 82, op. 2, d. 7, ll. 107–110.

30. RGASPI, f. 19, op. 1, d. 94, ll. 2–3.

31. TsGA SPb, f. 144, op.1, d. 1, l. 1.

32. RGASPI, f. 5, op.1, d. 2858, ll. 6–6 ob.

33. *Nash vek,* March 17, 1918, p. 4; *Krasnaia gazeta,* March 30, 1918, p. 3.

34. See, for example, a report on the release of six PCheka prisoners in *Novye vedomosti,* March 18, 1918, p. 5.

35. The protocols of the Vyborg district soviet during this period reflect this phenomenon particularly well (see TsGA SPb, f. 148, op. 1, d. 51).

36. For descriptions of these conditions by morgue personnel, see "Uzhasy vremeni," in *Novye vedomosti,* April 13, 1918, p. 7.

37. The Kazan historian Alter Litvin has published fragmentary protocols for fourteen meetings of the VCheka between January and May 1918. They reflect a clear pattern of support for summary shooting as a means of controlling crime and political subversion by a majority of the VCheka leadership (see Litvin, *Levye esery i VCheka,* pp. 48–65).

38. *Nash vek,* March 16, 1918, p. 1.

39. *Sbornik dekretov i postanovlenii po kommun severnoi oblasti,* issue 1, pt. 1, p. 97.

40. TsGA SPb, f. 2421, op. 1, d. 1, l. 142.

41. *Izvestiia Kronshtadtskogo soveta,* March 10, 1918, p. 2.

42. TsGA SPb, f. 143, op. 1, d. 31, l. 126.

43. GARF, f. 130, op. 2, d. 342, l. 27; TsGA SPb, f. 143, op. 1, d. 3, l. 32; *Sbornik dekretov i postanovlenii,* issue 1, pt. 1, pp. 539–540.

44. *Novye vedomosti,* April 29, 1918, p. 6.

45. *Nash vek,* May 1, 1918, p. 3.

46. TsGA SPb, f. 144, op. 1, d. 1, l. 13 ob.

47. TsGA SPb, f. 143, op. 1, d. 31, l. 163; f. 144, op. 1, d. 1, l. 32.

48. A pud equals approximately thirty-six pounds.

49. See the report of S. S. Zagorskii to the EAD on 18 May (TsGA SPb, f. 3390, op. 1, d. 13, l. 119). See also Hoover Institution archives, Isaac Steinberg Collection, XX692–10V, "The Events of July 1918," pp. 5–9.

50. TsGA SPb, f. 3390, op. 1, d. 13, ll. 119–121.

51. For examples of early nationalization decrees, see M. P. Iroshnikov, ed., *Dekrety Sovetskoi vlasti o Petrograde, 1917–1918* (Leningrad, 1986), pp. 76–79, 87–89, 94–96, 98, 111–112.

52. On the connection between problems caused by "workers' control," the earliest nationalization of industry, and the creation of the VSNKh, see E. H. Carr, *The Bolshevik Revolution, 1917–1923,* vol. 2 (Baltimore, 1966), pp. 72–90.

53. TsGA SPb, f. 9618, op.1, d. 185, ll. 50–51.

54. By March roughly thirty thousand workers had been laid off in the Vyborg district

(*Novaia zhizn'*, March 27, 1918, p. 3). At that time, only four factories were still in operation there (TsGA SPb, f. 9618, op. 1, d. 191, l. 46).

55. For an examination of this phenomenon in one Petrograd district soviet, see Alexander Rabinowitch, "The Evolution of Local Soviets in Petrograd, November 1917–June 1918: The Case of the First City District Soviet," *Slavic Review* 46, no. 1 (1987): 20–37.

56. This situation was reflected in a remarkably candid, top-secret letter protesting the bureaucratic behavior of Vyborg district soviet personnel circulated among local Bolsheviks in the late spring by the Vyborg district party committee (TsGAIPD, f. 2, op. 1, d. 7a, l. 1).

57. TsGA SPb, f. 3390, op. 1, d. 13, l. 4 ob.

58. TsGA SPb, f. 3390, op.1, d.13, ll. 2 ob., 11.

59. See, for example, G. Ia. Aronson, "Dvizheniia upolnomochennykh ot fabrik i zavodov v 1918 godu" (New York, 1960); see also Dmitrii Churakov, *Revoliutsiia, gosudarstvo, rabochii protest: Formy, dinamika i priroda massovykh vystuplenii rabochikh v Sovetskoi Rossii 1917–1918 godu* (Moscow, 2004), pp. 124–128.

60. Iu. Denike, "B. O. Bogdanov v nachale 1918," *Sotsialisticheskii vestnik,* January 1960, p. 48; idem, "From the Dissolution of the Constituent Assembly to the Outbreak of the Civil War," in *The Mensheviks from the Revolution of 1917 to the Second World War,* ed. Leopold H. Haimson (Chicago and London, 1974), pp. 115–116. There appears to be no direct connection between Bogdanov's initiative and the UDCA's worker conferences which continued to assemble through early March.

61. TsGA SPb, f. 3390, op. 1, d. 13, ll. 1 ob.–2.

62. TsGA SPb, f. 3390, op. 1, d. 13, l. 2. This was the case notwithstanding that more than half the elected delegates present were either Mensheviks or SRs, and also that representatives of the moderate socialist leadership were expressly invited to provide advice at a pivotal strategy session.

63. TsGA SPb, f. 3390, op.1, d. 13, l. 72.

64. Actually, the EAD published full and accurate accounts of its first meetings in its own journal until it was banned (See *Chrezvychainoe sobranie upolnomochennykh fabrik i zavodov g. Petrograda,* nos. 1–2, March 18, 1918, and nos. 3–4, April 16, 1918).

65. TsGA SPb, f. 3390, op. 1, d. 13, l. 137; d. 9, l. 16.

66. TsGAIPD, f. 4000, op.1, d. 4, l. 3.

67. *Petrogradskaia pravda,* March 24, 1918, p. 1; March 27, 1918, p. 1.

68. See reports on these developments in TsGA SPb, f. 3390, d. 13, l. 60.

69. TsGA SPb, f. 6276, op.3, d.163, l. 14.

70. This changed situation is documented by arrest lists for this period (see, for example, TsGA SPb, f. 506, op. 1, d. 1a, ll. 1–4, 7 ob.–9, 13–32, 34–41, 44–45, 46 ob.).

71. These terms were used at the time to distinguish between the two viewpoints. See, for example, TsGA SPb, f. 3390, op. 1, d. 13, l. 149.

72. TsGA SPb, f. 3390, op. 1, d.13, ll. 65–66.

73. TsGA SPb, f. 3390, op. 1, d.13, l. 89.

74. TsGA SPb, f. 3390, op. 1, d.13, ll. 98–102.

75. At this time, 11,400 workers were still employed at the Putilov plant, and another 500 at the Putilov shipyard (TsGA SPb, f. 3390, op. 1, d. 11, l. 14).

76. TsGA SPb, f. 3390, op.1, d.13, ll. 105–113.

77. TsGA SPb, f. 3390, op.1, d. 2, ll. 1–31; d. 13, ll. 115–117; f. 9672, op. 1, d. 246, l. 20.

78. TsGA SPb, f. 3390, op.1, d. 13, l. 124.

79. TsGA SPb, f. 3390, op.1, d. 13, ll. 133–140; d. 17, ll. 16, 16ob., 38–38 ob.

80. TsGA SPb, f. 3390, op.1, d. 13, ll. 156–169, 172, 181.

81. See below, chapter 9.

82. TsGA SPb, f. 3390, op. 1, d. 13, ll. 219–225.

83. For these instructions, see TsGA SPb, f. 101, op. 1, d. 68, ll. 14–14 ob.

84. TsGAIPD, f. 1, op. 1, d. 66, l. 18.

85. RGASPI, f. 466, op. 1, d. 1, l. 15 ob.

86. TsGAIPD, f. 4000, op. 7, d. 814, ll. 135–137.

87. TsGAIPD, f. 4000, op. 7, d. 814, l. 139; K. Shelavin, "Iz istorii Peterburgskogo komiteta," *Krasnaia letopis',* 1928, no. 2 (26): 110; 1928, no. 3 (27): 162–164.

88. On the formation of the Assembly of Organizers in mid-February 1918, see above, chapter 6.

89. TsGAIPD, f. 1, op. 1, d. 66, ll. 18–19.

90. TsGAIPD, f. 1, op. 1, d. 66, l. 18–19; f. 4000, op. 7, d. 820, ll. 94 –99; f. 4000, op. 4, d. 814, l. 142.

91. *Pervaia konferentsiia rabochikh i krasonarmeiskikh deputatov 1-ogo gorodskogo raiona (stenograficheskie otchety 25 maia–5 iiunia)* (Petrograd, 1918). For protocols of nonparty workers' conferences in the Vasilii Island and Porokhovskii districts, respectively, see TsGA SPb, f. 47, op. 1, d. 27, ll. 1–9, and f. 511, op. 1, d. 1, ll. 1–14.

92. For a comprehensive account of this conference, see Rabinowitch, "The Evolution of Local Soviets in Petrograd," pp. 20–30.

93. *Pervaia konferentsiia,* p. ix.

94. Ibid., pp. viii–xv.

95. For one thing, the Bolsheviks controlled most factory committees which, as a rule, organized the factory electoral assemblies at which many delegates were selected. Also, the Bolshevik–Left SR leadership had a bloc of some forty-five Red Army representatives whose loyalty to the existing regime was a condition of service.

96. *Pervaia konferentsiia,* pp. xv, 269–274.

97. Ibid., pp. 19–85.

98. Ibid., pp. 300–361.

9. Continuing Crises

1. The National Archives of the UK (TNA): Public Records Office (PRO), FO 371/3315/34853.

2. Ibid.

3. TNA: PRO, ADM 137/1731/82.

4. See A. Rabinovich, "Dos'e Shchastnogo: Trotskii i delo geroia Baltiiskogo flota," *Otechestvennaia istoriia,* 2001, no. 1:61–81. For an abridged English language version of this essay, see Alexander Rabinowitch, "The Shchastny File: Trotsky and the Case of the Hero of the Baltic Fleet," *Russian Review* 58, no. 4 (October 1999): 37–47.

5. Ministerstvo inostrannykh del SSSR, *Sovetsko-Germanskie otnosheniia: Ot peregovorov v Brest-Litovske do podpisaniia Rapal'skogo dogovora,* vol. 1 (Moscow, 1968), p. 368.

6. AU FSB SPb i LO, No. 3614, l. 50; A. L. Fraiman, ed., *Baltiiskie moriaki v bor'be za vlast' sovetov (noiabr' 1917–dekabr' 1918)* (Leningrad, 1968), pp. 51, 126, 131.

7. *Krasnaia armiia i flot,* April 9, 1918, p. 2; A. K. Drezen, ed., *Baltiiskii flot v Oktiabr'skoi revoliutsii i grazhdanskoi voine* (Leningrad, 1932), p. 81.

8. F. N. A. Cromie, *Letters [on Russian Affairs] from Captain Cromie RN* (n.p., 1919), pp. 118–189.

9. RGA VMF, f. r-92, op. 1, d. 135, ll. 27–30; P. Stashevich, "Ledovyi pokhod Baltiiskogo flota," in *Oktiabr'skii shkval: Moriaki Baltiiskogo flota v 1917 goda* (Leningrad, 1927), pp. 129–144; A. I. Muranov and V. E. Zviagintsev, *Dos'e na marshala: Iz istorii zakrytykh sudebnykh protsessov* (Moscow, 1996), pp. 14–78.

10. A proposal by Shchastny to move ships of the fleet to Lake Ladoga was approved by Trotsky on 22 April (AU FSB SPb i LO, No. 3614, l. 55).

11. RGA VMF, f. r-52, op. 5, d. 1, l. 44. On the Fort Ino crisis, see A. I. Rupasov and A. N. Chistikov, *Sovetsko-finliandskaia granitsa, 1918–1938* (St. Petersburg, 2000), pp. 13–14.

12. TsGA SPb, f. 144, op. 1, d. 1, ll. 30–32. On the CEC's decree, see *Protokoly zaseda-*

nii vserossiiskogo tsentral'nogo ispolnitel'nogo komiteta 4-ogo sozyva (Moscow, 1920), pp. 10–13, 169–193.

13. TsGA SPb, f. 144, op. 1, d. 1, l. 41. See also GARF, f. 130, op. 1, d. 342, l. 25.

14. TsGA SPb, f. 47, op. 1, d. 42, l. 93; f. 9618, op. 1, d. 240, l. 99; f. 1000, op. 79, d. 12, ll. 48–48 ob.; RGA VMF, f. r-661, op. 1, d. 138, l. 23; f. r-52, op. 1, d. 4, l. 1; f. r-852, op. 1, d. 25, l. 32.

15. TsGAIPD, f. 4000, op. 4, d. 815, ll. 108–134.

16. *Petrogradskaia pravda,* April 26, 1918, p. 1.

17. On the Allied interventions, see below, chapter 12.

18. *Izvestiia TsK KPSS,* 1989, no. 4:141–142, 155 n. 1; Lenin, *Polnoe sobranie sochinenii,* vol. 36, pp. 315, 607 n. 122.

19. See, for example, *Novye vedomosti,* May 9, 1918. The entire front page of this issue was devoted to reports on German demands and the imminent occupation of Petrograd and Moscow.

20. In a careful analysis of similar "German letters," the late George F. Kennan concluded that they were forgeries. See George F. Kennan, "The Sisson Documents," *Journal of Modern History* 28, no. 2 (1956): 130–154.

21. *Novye vedomosti,* May 10, 1918, p. 3.

22. TNA: PRO, ADM 137/1731, pp. 53–54, 59–60.

23. TNA: PRO, ADM 137/1731, pp. 51, 77; ADM 137/1773, p. 7; FO 371/3329/86376.

24. *Letters [on Russian Affairs] from Captain Cromie RN,* p. 136.

25. See above, chapter 9.

26. For a detailed record of this meeting, see AU FSB SPb i LO, No. 3614, ll. 286–300.

27. For example, Trotsky was the sole witness allowed to testify at Shchastny's trial, possibly the first Soviet "show trial." In 1995, Shchastny was cleared posthumously of all charges against him and officially rehabilitated (RGA VMF, f. r-2244, op. 1, d. 14, l. 1).

28. TsGAIPD, f. 1, op. 1, d. 109, l. 13. See also TsGAIPD, f. 1817, op. 1, d. 24, l. 15.

29. RGA VMF, f. r-96, op. 1, d. 72, l. 6.

30. Included in the division were roughly twenty-five ships, seventeen of them destroyers. Between 14 and 16 May, the ships, earmarked for transfer to Lake Ladoga, were moved through the Neva bridges and deployed close to the Obukhov plant, in the southwest Nevskii district of Petrograd.

31. AU FSB SPb i LO, No. N–3614, l. 170.

32. AU FSB SPb i LO, No. N–3614, l. 21. See also, RGA VMF, f. r-96, op. 1, d. 72, ll. 27–29.

33. Actually, the demolition of Fort Ino was directed by the commandant of Kronstadt, Konstantin Artamonov, who acted on his own out of concern that the fort was in immediate danger of being overwhelmed by Finnish forces or of being turned over to the Germans intact. In hostile hands, Artamonov reasoned, Kronstadt and the Baltic Fleet's most valuable ships would be imperiled by Ino's big guns (RGA VMF, f. r-52, op. 1, d. 1a, ll. 3–6).

34. Drezen, *Baltiiskii flot v Oktiabr'skoi revoliutstii i grazhdanskoi voine,* p. 121.

35. RGA VMF, f. r-5, op. 1, d. 93, ll. 117–118 ob.

36. TsGA SPb, f. 9672, op. 1, d. 200, l. 20.

37. TsGA SPb, f. 9672, op. 1, d. 200, l. 19.

38. On the Kolpino incident, see above, chapter 8.

39. Mikhail Shkarovskii, "Beskrovnyi miatezh," p. 3 (unpublished manuscript).

40. RGA VMF, f. r-342, op. 1, d, 111, l. 19.

41. TsGA SPb, f. 9672, op. 1, d. 246, l. 29.

42. TsGA SPb, f. 9672, op. 1, d. 246, ll. 30–31. Shkarovskii, "Beskrovnyi miatezh," pp. 8–9.

43. On Volodarskii, his assassination, and its political impact, see below, chapter 11.

44. See, for example, TsA FSB, No. N-199, ll. 112, 118, 125.

45. *Nash vek,* June 26, 1918, p. 3.

46. TsGA SPb, f. 143, op. 1, d. 31, l. 235.

47. See below, chapter 12.

48. *Nash vek,* June 26, 1918, p. 3.

49. E. N. Shoshkov, *Namorsi A. M. Shchastnyi* (St. Petersburg, 2001), p. 299.

50. *Novaia zhizn',* June 22, 1918, p. 1.

51. RGA VMF, f. r-342, op. 1, d. 115, l. 16.

52. TsGAIPD, f. 1, op. 4, d. 116, ll. 1, 6–13; and *Den' velikoi revoliutsii,* November 7, 1921.

53. TsGAIPD, f, 1, op. 4, d. 116, l. 18; *Petrogradskaia pravda,* June 14, 1918, p. 4; *Krasnaia gazeta,* June 18, 1918, p. 4.

54. Reflecting this increased pressure was a resolution adopted at a mass meeting of Putilov workers convened on 28 May, primarily to discuss how best to deal with the hunger problem. The resolution recalled the plant's representatives in the Petrograd Soviet and authorized the immediate election of replacements (TsGA SPb, f. 1788, op. 23, d. 5a, l. 4). This action by Petrograd's largest plant raised the specter that an uncontrolled recall movement based on dissatisfaction with food procurement policies would quickly spread to other enterprises.

55. *Severnaia kommuna,* June 13, 1918, p. 1.

56. See below, chapter 10.

57. *Severnaia kommuna,* June 16, 1918, pp. 2–3.

58. Each district worker's conference was allotted one deputy per one thousand workers and Red Army soldiers represented in the conference. Moreover, each district soviet, regardless of size, was allowed three deputies (*Severnaia kommuna,* June 18, 1918, p. 1).

59. *Krasnaia gazeta,* June 16, 1918, p. 3.

60. *Vestnik soveta 1-go gorodskogo raiona,* July 4, 1918, no. 16–17, pp. 8–9.

61. TsGA SPb, f. 100, op. 1, d. 10, l. 22; *Narodnoe delo,* June 27, 1918, p. 2.

62. *Severnaia kommuna,* June 18, 1918, p. 1.

63. Ibid., July 5, 1918, p. 3.

64. *Gazeta-kopeika,* June 19, 1918, p. 3.

65. Ibid., June 16, 1918, p. 2; *Petrogradskaia pravda,* June 16, 1918, p. 2.

66. *Petrogradskaia pravda,* June 18, 1918, p. 1.

67. TsGAIPD, f. 4000, op. 7, d. 814, l. 25.

68. This was the case, for example, in the Okhtinskii and Vyborg districts (TsGAIPD, f. 10, op. 1, d. 12, l. 23 ob., and f. 2, op. 1, d. 4, l. 6).

69. RGA VMF, f. r-661, op. 1, d. 1, l. 30.

70. See above, chapter 2. These were among the main themes of campaign editorials in the major Bolshevik dailies, *Petrogradskaia pravda* and *Krasnaia gazeta,* in the Petrograd Soviet's *Severnaia kommuna,* and in the Left SR's *Znamia bor'by.*

71. *Novaia zhizn'* (Petrograd), June 18, 1918, p. 2.

72. The final published results were as follows: Bolsheviks and their sympathizers, 474; Left SRs and their sympathizers, 87; Right SRs and their sympathizers, 44; Mensheviks and their sympathizers, 35; other parties, 2; no affiliation, 35 (*Severnaia kommuna,* July 6, 1918, p. 3).

73. Many female factory workers were then being replaced by demobilized male workers returning to their old jobs. Also, thousands of women employed in textile plants were threatened by layoffs because of a blockage of cotton shipments from Turkestan.

74. TsGAIPD, f. 1, op. 1, d. 66, ll. 28–29.

75. *Novaia zhizn',* July 2, 1918, p. 1.

76. *Severnaia kommuna,* June 18, 1918, p. 1.

77. See below, chapters 10 and 11.

78. RGASPI, f. 564, op. 1, d. 4, l. 201.

79. TsGAIPD, f. 4000, op. 7, d. 814, ll. 166–174, 183–184.

80. See above, chapter 1 n. 98.

81. TSGAIPD, f. 1, op. 1, d. 66, l. 30.

82. TsGAIPD, f. 1, op. 1, d. 66, ll. 30–33; f. 2, op. 3, d. 4, ll. 8–8 ob. Sections for party

work among women were formed by the Petersburg, Vasilii Island, and Vyborg district committees in July (TsGAIPD, f. 6, op. 6, d. 6, l. 67; f. 4, op. 1, d. 1, l. 16; f. 2, op. 1, d. 4, ll. 7–8 ob.; f. 2, op. 1, d. 1, l. 6), and by the Second City and Narva district committees in early August (f. 1817, op. 1, d. 24, ll. 26–26 ob.; *Krasnaia gazeta,* August 7, 1918, p. 3). On 31 August, the Petersburg Committee announced that their formation had been completed (*Krasnaia gazeta,* September 1, 1918, p. 3).

83. TsGAIPD, f. 1, op. 1, d. 75, ll. 144–145.

84. TsGAIPD, f. 1, op. 1, d. 66, l. 33.

85. TsGAIPD, f. 1, op. 1, d. 66, ll. 29–33.

86. TsGAIPD, f. 1, op. 1, d. 64, ll. 24, 26 ob.

87. TsGAIPD, f. 1, op. 1, d. 64, ll. 32–32 ob.

88. *Krasnaia gazeta,* August, 4, 1918, p. 3.

89. Ibid. (evening), June 28, 1918, p. 3.

90. Numerous documents relating to reprisals against the relatively few enterprises and individuals participating in the strike can be found in Petersburg archives. For example, after management, employees, and workers at the still sizable Government Printing Office struck, sixteen supervisory personnel were immediately fired with loss of pensions and government housing. Participating workers were fined (TsGAIPD, f. 1949, op. 1, d. 11, ll. 70–71; d. 7, l. 4; and TsGA SPb, f. 143, op. 1, d. 31, l. 257).

91. *Novaia zhizn',* June 30, 1918, p. 1.

92. Ibid., July 2, 1918, p. 1.

93. TsGA SPb, f. 3390, op. 1, d. 17, l. 34.

94. See below, chapter 11.

95. TsGA SPb, f. 3390, op. 1, d. 12, ll. 33–33 ob.

96. TsGA SPb, f. 3390, op. 1, d. 4, ll. 3–4.

97. TsA FSB RF, f. 1, op. 2, d. 126, ll. 87–87 ob.

98. My brief summary of this "meeting" is based on rough, incomplete notes kept by a participant, a substantial description contained in a letter written soon after the event by Aleksei Smirnov, and data from VCheka depositions (TsGA SPb, f. 3390, op. 1, d. 4, ll. 5–18; TsA FSB, RF, f. 1, op. 2, d. 126, v. 1, ll. 114–119, 135–174; v. 2, ll. 16, 18, 58, 76, 83, 90, 104, 123).

99. On the subsequent proceedings against those arrested, see below, chapter 12.

100. I. G. Fedorov, "Epidemiia kholery v Petrograde v 1918 g.," *Izvestiia komissariata zdravookhraneniia soiuza kommun severnoi oblasti,* 1918, no. 1:82–88.

101. Ibid., pp. 84–85.

102. TsGAIPD, f. 4000, op. 7, d. 814, ll. 160–162.

103. The efforts of the Vyborg District Soviet are particularly well documented (see TsGA SPb, f. 148, op. 1, d. 43, ll. 76 ob.–77 ob.; d. 51, ll. 143, 145 ob.), as are those of the First City District Soviet (see *Vestnik soveta 1-go gorodskogo raiona,* July 17, 1918, p. 2; July 20, 1918, p. 5; July 27, 1918, pp. 5–6; November 7, 1918, pp. 7–8). A representative collection of printed materials produced by district soviets during the cholera emergency—posters, leaflets, brochures, announcements of lectures, and the like—has been preserved in files of the Commissariat for Public Health SK SO (see TsGA SPb, f. 2815, op. 1, d. 342).

104. For the protocols of the commission's meetings, see TsGA SPb, f. 2815, op. 1, dd. 337, 338.

105. Fedorov, "Epidemiia kholery v Petrograde v 1918 g.," p. 14.

106. TsGAIPD, f. 1, op. 1, d. 109, l. 15.

107. TsGA SPb, f. 2815, op. 1, d. 344, l. 78; d. 388, l. 24 ob.; d. 337, l. 26.

108. For differing points of view on the sources and limits of unrest among Petrograd workers and their support for the EAD in the spring of 1918, see William G. Rosenberg, "Russian Labor and Bolshevik Power after October," *Slavic Review* 44, no. 2 (1985): 227–238; Moshe Lewin, "More Than One Piece of the Puzzle Is Missing," *Slavic Review* 44, no. 2 (1985): 239–243; and Vladimir Brovkin, "Politics, Not Economics, Was the Key," *Slavic Review* 44, no. 2 (1985): 244–250.

109. *Nash vek,* July 10, 1918, p. 4; *Materialy po statistike Petrograda,* issue 2, p. 113.

110. *Novye vedomosti,* June 17, 1918, p. 4.
111. RGASPI, f. 17, op. 4, d. 10, l. 33.

10. The Northern Commune and the Bolshevik–Left SR Alliance

1. TsGA SPb, f. 143, op.1, d. 3, ll. 5–6.
2. RGASPI, f. 17, op. 4, d. 11, ll. 24–26. As Stasova put it in a letter to Novgorodtseva in Moscow, "It's not enough to say that Piter is no longer the capital. The people will not become accustomed to Moscow being the capital in a month or two and 'probably not even in a year!' Think how long it took Moscow to yield preeminence to Piter!" (ibid.).
3. The Bureau's minutes for a meeting on 13 April reveal that after listening to the reports of Lashvich, Zinoviev, and Ioffe on the plenum, it was concluded that the trip had been a waste, that there really had not been a plenum because Lenin and Stalin were absent and Trotsky only stopped by, and that not only the party leadership but even the government in Moscow was in disarray. In view of this, the Bureau adopted a resolution declaring that, "because of the absence of party work in Moscow, and the necessity . . . of preserving and strengthening the party *apparat,* it is necessary for the Petrograd Bureau of the Central Committee to conduct work throughout Russia" (RGASPI, f. 466, op.1, d.1, l. 10).
4. RGASPI, f. 466, op. 1, d. 1, ll. 2–2 ob.
5. TsGAIPD, f. 1, op. 1, d. 107, l. 3. See V. P. Khmelevskii, *Severnyi oblastnyi komitet RKP (b)* (Leningrad, 1972), pp. 32–35.
6. Khmelevskii, *Severnyi oblastnoi komitet,* pp. 36–38. For notes on this conference, see RGASPI, f. 67, op. 1, d. 1.
7. M. Roliakov, "Soiuz kommun Severnoi oblasti," *Khoziaistvo Severo-zapadnogo kraia,* 1927, no.9:13.
8. GARF, f. 130, op.2, d. 342, l. 4.
9. TsGA SPb, f. 144, op.1, d.1, l. 7. Zinoviev *informed* his colleagues in the Petrograd Bureau of the Central Committee of this decision. No one in the Bureau questioned the government's prerogative to make such key political decisions without consulting the leading party body (RGASPI, f. 466, op.1, d.1, l. 10 ob.)
10. TsGA SPb, f.143, op.1, d.3, l. 11.
11. For the stenogram of the Second Left SR Party Congress, see RGASPI, f. 564, op. 1, dd. 1–3; it is published in *Partiia levykh sotsialistov-revoliutsionerov: Dokumenty i materialy,* 1:210–672.
12. *Partiia levykh sotsialistov-revoliutsionerov,* pp. 241–242.
13. See above, chapter 9.
14. TsGA SPb, f. 144, op. 1, d. 1, l. 41; GARF, f. 130, op. 2, d. 342, l. 25.
15. This essay by Lenin was first discussed in the Bolshevik Central Committee on 26 April, the day *after* Zinoviev's speech at the Northern Oblast Congress. However, its main themes reflected the thrust of Lenin's thinking and central government policies since the Fourth All-Russian Congress of Soviets.
16. TsGA SPb, f. 143, op.1, d. 3, ll. 8–12.
17. RGASPI, f. 67, op.1, d. 106, ll. 58–59.
18. The admission of the Left SRs into the government was formally accepted by the SK PTK on 27 April (TsGA SPb, f. 144, op. 1, d. 1, l. 41).
19. TsGA SPb, f. 143, op. 1, d. 3, ll. 43–48.
20. See above, chapter 8.
21. TsGA SPb, f. 143, op.1, d. 3, ll. 47–48. As we have seen, the whittling down of the Sovnarkom's policy-making power and the primacy in governance of the CEC, and of soviets and their executive committees down to the lowest levels of government, had been a Left SR goal since November 1917. This structure reflected the Left SR leadership's views on the seminal role of the CEC in achieving Soviet democracy since "October," and was embodied

in the draft for a Soviet constitution adopted by the third Left SR party congress at the end of June 1918 (RGASPI, f. 71, op. 34, d. 224, l. 75).

22. TsGA SPb, f. 143, op.1, d. 3, l. 52.

23. *Novaia zhizn'*, April 30, 1918, p. 3.

24. *Izvestiia Petrogradskogo Soveta*, May 11, 1918, p. 1. For a recent critical view of the creation of the SK SO, see Chistikov, "U kormila vlasti," pp. 29–31.

25. TsGA SPb, f. 142, op. 1, "Spravka," l. 5; f. 143, op.1, d. 2, l. 6.

26. On this point, see A. V. Gogolevskii, *Petrogradskii sovet v gody grazhdanskoi voiny* (Leningrad 1982), p. 60.

27. *Protokoly zasedanii vserossiiskogo tsentral'nogo ispolnitel'nogo komiteta 4-go sozyva*, pp. 206–219.

28. For a succinct analysis of differences between Lenin's views and those of Left Communists on domestic issues, which were analogous to differences between Lenin and the Left SRs, see Cohen, *Bukharin and the Bolshevik Revolution*, pp. 69–78.

29. *Protokoly zasedanii vserossiiskogo tsentral'nogo ispolnitel'nogo komiteta 4-go sozyva*, pp. 222–223.

30. *Znamia bor'by*, May 8, 1918, p. 4.

31. *Dekrety Sovetskoi vlasti*, 2:18–21.

32. *Dekrety Sovetskoi vlasti o Petrograde, 1917–1918*, p. 171.

33. *Izvestiia Petrogradskogo Soveta*, May 10, 1918, pp. 2–3; May 11, 1918, pp. 2–3.

34. On the creation of the Delegates Soviet, see above, chapter 6.

35. TsGAIPD, f. 4000, op. 7, d. 820, ll. 68–88.

36. RGASPI, f. 19, op. 1, d., 112.

37. *Protokoly zasedanii vserossiiskogo tsentral'nogo ispolnitel'nogo komiteta 4-go sozyva*, pp. 254–256.

38. *Dekrety Sovetskoi vlasti*, 2:264–266.

39. Because peasants were reluctant to join *kombedy*, they included a large numbers of migrant laborers, army deserters, demobilized soldiers, and workers recently arrived from the city.

40. *Vladimir Il'ich Lenin, Biograficheskaia khronika*, 5:442; A. V. Ivanov, "Putilovskii rabochii na prieme u Il'icha," *Vospominaniia o V. I. Lenine*, vol. 2 (Moscow, 1957), pp. 336–338.

41. *Krasnaia gazeta*, May 22, 1918, p. 1.

42. Ibid., May 26, 1918, p. 1.

43. *Znamia bor'by*, May 28, 1918, p. 4.

44. *Krasnaia gazeta*, May 23, 1918, p. 2.

45. *Izvestiia Petrogradskogo soveta*, May 30, 1918, p. 2; May 31, 1918, p. 3.

46. These directives were contained in two circular letters which the Central Committee sent to all party organizations during the second half of May (*Perepiska sekretariata TsK RSDRP(b)-RKP (b) s mestnymi partiinymi organizatsiiami*, 3:72–74, 81–83).

47. RGASPI, f. 17, op. 4, d. 11, l. 52 ob.

48. TsGAIPD, f.1, op.1, d.66, ll. 21–21 ob.; f. 4000, op. 7, d. 814, ll. 67–70.

49. TsGAIPD, f. 4000, op. 7, d. 814, ll. 175–178, 202; f. 1, op. 1, d. 54, l. 32. For the text of Lenin's letter, see Lenin, *Polnoe sobranie sochinenii*, 36:521–522.

50. See below, chapter 12.

51. TsGAIPD, f. 1, op. 1, d. 54, l. 33; RGASPI, f. 17, op. 4, d. 59, l. 15.

52. RGASPI, f. 564, op.1, d. 11, ll. 17 ob.–18.

53. *Izvestiia Petrogradskogo soveta*, May 31, 1918, p. 2.

54. *Sbornik dekretov i postanovlenii po soiuzu kommun severnoi oblasti*, issue 1, pt. 1, p. 319.

55. On this point, see below, chapter 12; and Rabinovich, "Moisei Uritskii: Robesp'er revoliutsionnogo Petrograda?" pp. 8–9.

56. See Proshian's comments on his plan in *Novye vedomosti*, June 18, 1918, p. 7. Records of meetings of the Presidium of the Committee for the Revolutionary Security of Petrograd re-

veal that it shared Proshian's contempt for the PCheka (see, for example, TsGA SPb, f. 73, op. 1, d. 4, ll. 16, 17, 20–20 ob., 25).

At first, leaders of the VCheka, on principle, also eschewed "Okhrana methods"—the use of secret agents, agent provocateurs, and the like. Their hope, like Proshian's, was that vigilant workers, serving as the VCheka's "eyes and ears," would suffice for intelligence (Latsis, *Otchet vserossiiskoi chrezvychainoi komissii za chetyre goda ee deiatel'nosti,* p. 11). On this point, see also Leonov, *Rozhdenie Sovetskoi imperii,* pp. 248–249.

57. RGASPI, f. 17, op. 4, d. 11, ll. 24–26. At least some listeners who heard a speech by Uritskii on security matters in Petrograd toward the end of May concluded that he was attempting to justify dissolution of the PCheka. See, for example, Sergeev's observation at a meeting of the Presidium of the Committee for the Revolutionary Security of Petrograd on 23 May (TsA SPb, f. 73, op. 1, d. 3, l. 35).

58. Uritskii's sense of outrage at the Cheka's methods of interrogation is reflected in an undated letter he sent to Dzerzhinskii. The letter was prompted by Uritskii's deposition of a fourteen-year-old, Vsevolod Anosov, who had been brutally terrorized during several interrogations by VCheka investigators in Moscow. Uritskii protested the incident, demanding that Dzerzhinskii investigate it and call to account the agents Anosov named (RGASPI, f. 76, op. 3, d. 10, ll. 1–1 ob.).

59. For a summary of the "Case of the Comorra for Vengeance by the People" based on Cheka files, see Rabinovich, "Moisei Uritskii: Robesp'er revoliutsionogo Petrograda," pp. 7–8. On Filippov, see "Bankir iz VChK," in *Ocherki istorii vneshnoi razvedki,* ed. E. M. Primakov, vol. 2 (Moscow, 1997), pp. 19–24.

60. TsGA SPb, f. 142, op. 9, d. 1, l. 34.

61. Judging by the records of the conference, neither Uritskii nor any representative of the PCheka attended it (see TsA FSB RF, f. 1, op. 3, d. 11).

62. RGASPI, f. 17, op. 4, d. 194, ll. 3–3 ob.

63. RGASPI, f. 466, op. 1, d. 1, ll. 9–10.

64. TsGA SPb, f. 73, op. 1, d. 1, l. 150; *Novaia zhizn'* (Petrograd), May 23, 1918, p. 3.

65. See, for example, TsA FSB SPb i LO, no. 30377, vol. 3, ll. 310–320.

66. *Novaia zhizn'* (Petrograd), June 22, 1918, p. 3; *Novye vedomosti,* June 22, 1918, p. 3.

67. TsA FSB RF, f. 1, op. 3, d. 11, ll. 77–78.

68. TsGA SPb, f. 143, op. 1, d. 49, l. 50.

69. See below, chapter 12.

70. See an account of Proshian's report on his commissariat at the Eighth City Conference of Petrograd Left SRs on 26 May in *Znamia bor'by,* May 28, 1918, p. 4.

71. *Znamia bor'by,* June 8, 1918, p. 3. Without referring to Proshian, the key role of this conference in the development of the Commissariat for Internal Affairs, SK SO, was acknowledged in a report of 20 October 1918 by one of his successors (TsGA SPb, f.143, op. 4, d. 4, l. 2). On the importance of the Commissariat for Internal Affairs in Petrograd government under Proshian, see the report of a delegate from Petrograd, Kasparian, at the third Left SR national congress at the end of June 1918 (RGASPI, f. 564, op. 1, d. 4, l. 166).

72. *Znamia bor'by,* June 12, 1918, p. 3; *Severnaia kommuna,* June 13, 1918, p. 6.

73. TsGA SPb, f. 143, op. 3, d. 6, ll. 5 ob–6.

74. *Severnaia kommuna,* June 5, 1918, p. 1; and *Znamia bor'by,* June 4, 1918, p. 3; June 5, 1918, p. 1. In addition to Proshian, other members of the troika were Uritskii and the Chief Commissar for the Petrograd Military District, the Bolshevik Mikhail Lashevich.

75. On the appointment of this commission, see the guide to the files of the Commissariat for Agriculture, SK SO (TsGA SPb, f. 8957).

76. TsGA SPb, f. 8957, op. 1, d. 3, l. 1, 1 ob.

77. TsGA SPb, f. 143, op. 1, d. 40, ll. 4–15.

78. TsGA SPb, f. 8957, op. 3, d. 13, ll. 3–3 ob.

79. Ibid., op. 1, d. 10, l. 16.

80. Moderate socialists had especially significant strength in the nonparty conference in the Porokhovskii district.

81. TsGA SPb, f. 511, op. 1, d. 1, l. 13 ob.

82. A. L. Milshtein, "Rabochie Petrograda v borbe za ukreplenie sovetov (Perevybory Petrogradskogo soveta v iiune 1918 g." in *Rabochie Leningrada v bor'be za pobedu sotsializma* (Moscow–Leningrad, 1963), p. 152.

83. *Pervaia konferentsiia rabochikh i krasnoarmeiskikh deputatov 1-ogo gorodskogo raiona*, p. 255.

84. Ibid., p. 258.

85. See, for example, *Znamia bor'by*, June 7, 1918, p. 4.

86. GARF, f. 393, op. 2, d. 70, ll. 185–185 ob.

87. GARF, f. 393, op.1, d. 58, l. 150.

88. GARF, f. 393, op.1, d. 58, l. 90.

89. GARF, f. 393, op.1, d. 58, l. 45.

90. TsGA SPb, f. 142, op. 1, d. 9, l. 245.

91. TsGA SPb, f. 142, op. 1, d. 9, ll. 232, 234.

11. The Suicide of the Left SRs

1. See Osipova, *Rossiiskoe krest'ianstvo v revoliutsii i grazhdanskoi voine,* pp. 144–145, for suggestive statistics on the growth of support for Left SRs in provincial soviets during the spring of 1918.

2. See above, chapter 10.

3. RGASPI, f. 564, op.1, d.11, ll. 3–21. Unfortunately a similar reconstruction of the Bolshevik side is impossible. No protocols for Bolshevik Central Committee meetings between 19 May and 26 September 1918 have been published or are available for study in Russian archives.

4. *Piatyi vserossiiskii s"ezd sovetov rabochikh, krest'ianskikh, soldatskikh, i kazach'ikh deputatov: Stenograficheskii otchet* (Moscow, 1918), pp. 51–52.

5. *Doklad o deiatel'nosti krest'ianskogo otdela vserossiiskogo tsentral'nogo ispolnitel'nogo komiteta sovetov* (Moscow, 1918), p. 10.

6. TsA FSB RF, No. N-685, v.10, ll. 230–230 ob.

7. RGASPI, f. 564, op.1, d. 1, ll. 33–39. Even personal appeals from Spiridonova to Lenin did not help. See, for example, RGASPI, f. 5, op. 1, d. 1381, ll. 1–1 ob.

8. Ibid., ll. 31–32. See also *Znamia bor'by*, April 21, 1918, p. 2.

9. GARF, f. 1235, op. 92, d. 2, l. 309.

10. See, for instance, the record of a conference in May of rural land reform sections in Voronezh Province (TsA FSB RF, No. N-685, vol. 10, ll. 175–184).

11. For examples, see TsA FSB RF, No. N-685, vol. 10.

12. RGASPI, f. 274, op. 1, d. 30, l. 60.

13. TsGAIPD, f. 4000, op. 4, d. 814, l. 174; f. 1, op. 2, d. 4, l. 62.

14. See below, chapter 12.

15. RGASPI, f. 19, op. 1, d. 174, l. 23.

16. *Vos'moi s"ezd Rossiiskoi kommunisticheskoi partii (bol'shevikov): Stenograficheskii otchet* (Moscow, 1919), p. 20.

17. RGASPI, f. 564, op.1, d. 11, ll. 11–12 ob.

18. *Protokoly zasedanii vserossiiskogo tsentral'nogo ispolnitel'nogo komiteta 4-go sozyva,* p. 398.

19. Lenin, *Polnoe sobranie sochinenii,* 36:482–483.

20. According to these regulations, each rural district (*uezd*), regardless of size, was allowed two elected representatives, whereas workers were allotted one representative per twenty-five thousand workers. The result was that in a district with three hundred thousand peasants, for example, six peasants would have representation equal to that of one worker (*Znamia truda,* July 6, 1918, p. 1).

21. *Protokoly zasedanii vserossiiskogo tsentral'nogo ispolnitel'nogo komiteta 4-go sozyva,* pp. 419–439.

22. *Piatyi vserossiiskii s"ezd,* p. 5.

23. RGASPI, f. 564, op.1, d. 19, ll. 1–1 ob. ("Doklad [chernovik] neizvestnoi o IV s"ezde partii levykh eserov i period deiatel'nosti partii mezhdu III i IV s"ezdami").

24. Ibid.

25. *Novosti dnia,* July 3, 1918, p. 3; *Nashe slovo,* July 3, 1918, p. 2; *Zhizn',* July 2, 1918, p. 2, and July 3, p. 1.

26. According to leaflets published by the Left SR Moscow Oblast Party Committee around 8 July 1918, 399 was the number of challenged delegates cited in a report by Left SR members of the credentials commission (TsA FSB RF, No. N-8, v. 12, l. 331a; see also, RGASPI, f. 564, op.1, d. 18, l. 31). A valuable account by Dmitrii Shliapnikov, a Left SR congress delegate from Kazan, published in Kazan in mid-July 1918, put the number of protested Bolshevik delegates at "around 300." Shliapnikov wrote that an additional 90 legitimate Left SR delegates were unfairly denied voting rights (see Shliapnikov's report in *Za zemliu i voliu* [Kazan], July 16–18, 1918; republished in A. L. Litvin, *Levye esery i VChK,* pp. 211–213). If Sverdlov's delegate count is revised in accordance with Shliapnikov's figures for protested Bolshevik delegates and Left SRs wrongly denied voting rights, the overall tally of delegates with full voting rights would be Bolsheviks, 378; Left SRs, 379; and SR Maximalists, 30—giving the Left SR–SR Maximalist bloc a 30-vote plurality.

27. *Piatyi vserossiiskii s"ezd,* p. 18.

28. GARF, f. 393, op. 3, d. 210, ll. 51, 55–58. These documents reveal that, at a plenary meeting of the Executive Committee of the Mogilev Province Soviet on 21 June, in response to an initial call for delegates, the chair of the committee, a Left SR, proposed that one Left SR and one Bolshevik be sent. In turn, Vainshtein, a Bolshevik, urged the committee to limit itself to the dispatch of one Bolshevik because Left SRs were "obviously opponents of Soviet power." However, by a vote of 13 to 12, it was agreed to send a Bolshevik and a Left SR. Then, on 1 July, the Bolshevik soviet fraction in the Executive Committee received a telegram from its delegate to the congress who was already in Moscow requesting the dispatch of five additional congress delegates from the Executive Committee and two additional delegates from each district soviet in the province. Without informing the Left SRs of this request, the fraction hurriedly selected five additional delegates, all Bolsheviks, and sent them off on the first train to Moscow. When the Left SRs protested this action in the Executive Committee, they were brushed off with the explanation that "the struggle for the survival of Soviet power was then under way" and that the "honor and duty" of socialists necessitated this step. After bitter recriminations, the Bolsheviks simply left the hall, after which the Left SRs sent a protest to Moscow. The five additional Bolshevik delegates were among the Bolshevik delegates challenged by the Left SRs on the Credentials Commission, to no avail. At the Fifth Congress, Karelin cited the Mogilev case to show how the huge Bolshevik majority had been attained (*Piatyi vserossiiskii s"ezd,* pp. 16–17).

29. *Piatyi vserossiiskii s"ezd,* pp. 4–102.

30. Ibid., pp. 22–23.

31. Ibid., p. 30.

32. Ibid., p. 63.

33. Ibid., p. 69.

34. *Partiia levykh sotsialistov-revoliutsionerov,* pp. 676, 845 n. 555; I. K. Kakhovskaia, "Delo Eikhorda i Denikina (Iz vospominanii)," in *Puti revoliutsii* (Berlin, 1923), pp. 192–193; L. M. Ovrutskii and A. I. Razgon, "Poniat' dukh 6 iiulia," *Otechestvennaia istoriia,* 1992, no. 3:54; G. Smolianskii, *Obrechennye* (Moscow, 1927), pp. 11–17; S. D. Mstislavskii, "Vospominaniia S. D. Mstislavskogo," in Litvin, *Levye esery i VCheka,* p. 181.

35. For the text of this resolution, see P. Makintsian and M. Ia. Latsis, eds., *Krasnaia kniga VCheka,* 2nd ed., vol. 1 (Moscow, 1989), pp. 185–186.

36. The Third All-Russian Left SR Party Congress lasted from 28 June to 1 July (RGASPI, f. 564, op. 1, d. 4).

37. On this point, see "Vospominaniia S. D. Mstislavskogo," in Litvin, *Levye esery i VCheka,* pp. 164–168.

38. The uprising in Yaroslavl was the work of Boris Savinkov and his "Union for the Defense of the Homeland and Freedom" and was not connected to the action of the Left SRs in Moscow.

39. *Dekrety Sovetskoi vlasti,* 3:529–530; TsA FSB RF, f. 1, vol.1, op. 2, d. 215, l. 30.

40. *Krasnaia kniga VChK,* 1:257.

41. Ibid., 1:258–259. For Proshian's version of these acts a few hours after they occurred, see TsGALI SPb, f. 63, op. 1, d. 4, l. 155.

42. V. D. Bonch-Bruevich, *Ubiistvo germanskogo posla Mirbakha i vosstanie levykh eserov (po lichnym vospominaniiam)* (Moscow, 1927), p. 27.

43. RGASPI, f. 326, op. 2, d. 10, l. 232.

44. For an interesting view of Vatsetis's role in this event, see G. Swain, "Vacietis: The Enigma of the Red Army's First Commander," *Revolutionary Russia,* June, 2003, pp. 68–86.

45. TsA FSB RF, f. 1, op. 2, d. 2, ll. 6–7. See also "Vospominaniia S. D. Mstislavskogo," and the untitled observations of D. Shliapnikov, a Kazan Left SR, of the events of July 1918 in Moscow from the Kazan newspaper *Za zemliu i voliu,* both reprinted in Litvin, *Levye esery i VCheka,* pp. 163–233.

46. *Dekrety Sovetskoi vlasti,* 2:530–531.

47. GARF, f. 130, op. 2, d. 1098, l. 2.

48. The ever impulsive and combative Proshian, accompanied by ten sailors, occupied the telegraph office at midnight, 6 July. Allegedly announcing that "we killed Mirbach, the Sovnarkom is under arrest," he seems to have directed dispatch of a cable instructing telegraphers around the country to hold up "all telegrams signed by Lenin, Trotsky, and Sverdlov, and also by Right SRs and Mensheviks, as dangerous to Soviet power in general and to the *presently governing party, in particular the Left SRs*" (TsA FSB RF, No. N-8, vol. 1a, l. 58; emphasis added).

49. *Krasnaia kniga VChK,* 1:247. In her "Last Testament," written in 1937, Spiridonova put the number of executed at more than two hundred, which seems high (TsA FSB RF, No. N-13266, vol. 3, l. 74). The "official" count of Left SRs summarily shot by the VCheka the night of 7/8 July was thirteen, which is clearly low (*Krasnaia kniga VChK,* 1:242).

50. TsA FSB RF, No. N-685, vol. 6, ll. 46 ob.–47.

51. *Piatyi vserossiiskii s"ezd,* pp. 208–209.

52. GARF, f. 393, op. 2, d. 3, l. 46.

53. *Piatyi vserossiiskii s"ezd,* pp. 184–185.

54. See *Piatyi sozyv vserossiiskogo tsentral'nogo ispolnitel'nogo komiteta: Stenograficheskii otchet* (Moscow, 1919).

55. In this connection, see the vehement protest against the form and substance of the constitution as it stood on 4 July signed by five prominent members of the drafting commission (GARF, f. 1235, op. 140, d. 4, ll. 1–3).

56. *Piatyi vserossiiskii s"ezd,* pp. 183–184, 200–201; *Dekrety Sovetskoi vlasti,* 2:550–564.

57. Ministerstvo inostrannykh del SSSR, *Sovetsko-Germanskie otnosheniia: Ot peregovorov v Brest-Litovske do podpisaniia Rapallskogo dogovora,* vol. 1 (Moscow, 1968), p. 585.

58. *Piatyi sozyv vserossiiskogo tsentral'nogo ispolnitel'nogo komiteta,* pp. 55–56.

59. Thus, for example, after this directive was presented at an emergency meeting of the Executive Committee of the Vyborg District Soviet on the afternoon of 7 July, it immediately formed a troika (TsGA SPb, f. 9618, op. 1, d. 260, l. 3.).

60. TsGAIPD, f. 4000, op. 3, d. 820, l. 118.

61. Ibid., f. 4000, op. 4, d. 814, ll. 193–196, 153–163.

62. TsGAIPD, f. 165, op. 1, d. 3, ll. 9 ob., 23 ob., 24; f. 10, op. 1, d. 12, l. 27 ob.; f. 4, op. 1, d. 1, l. 20 ob.

63. *Vechernye ogni,* July 11, 1918, p. 2.

64. *Nash vek,* July 9, 1918, p. 3; *Vechernye ogni,* July 8, 1918, p. 2; *Novyi vechernyi chas,* July 8, 1918, p. 1. Members of the fraction were released after a day or two.

65. *Vechernye ogni,* July 8, 1918, p. 2.

66. Ibid.

67. Ibid.

68. A. Minichev, "V dni levo-eserskogo miatezha v Petrograde v 1918 g. (iz vospominanii)," *Krasnaia letopis'*, 1928, no.1 (25): 68.

69. TsGAIPD, f. 4000, op. 4, d. 814, ll. 153–156. Protocols of Petrograd district soviets corroborate the fact that the events of 6–7 July in Moscow came as a complete surprise to district level Left SRs in Petrograd. See, for example, the comments of Left SRs at an emergency meeting of the Vyborg District Soviet Executive Committee on 7 July (TsGA SPb, f. 9618, op. 1, d. 260, l. 4.), and of the Left SR spokesman at a meeting of the First City District Soviet on 18 July (*Vestnik soveta 1-go gorodskogo raiona,* July 24, 1918, p. 4).

70. TsGAIPD, f. 4000, op. 4, d. 814, l. 156.

71. See above, chapter 7.

72. This is attested to by depositions from soldiers in the detachment and Red Army officers. Thus, an officer from the Second Petrograd Composite Detachment who took part in the government's raid on the Pages School later testified that, during unrest over a proposed reorganization of his unit the day before, some Left SRs persuaded 38 of his men to join the Left SR detachment because they would be paid 300 rather than 250 rubles a month, receive good meals, table linen, and dishes, and maids would do their cleaning (TsA FSB RF, No. N-8, vol. 1, l. 11). Soldiers often emphasized in their depositions that politics was not a factor in their decisions to transfer, since both the Red Army and the Left SR forces defended Soviet power and they would be sent to the front in any case. (See, for example, the independent testimony of seven newly recruited members of the detachment, in TsA FSB RF, No. N-8, vol. 1, ll. 1–14).

73. TsA FSB RF, No. N-8, vol. 1, ll. 1–28.

74. My reconstruction of the attack on the Pages School is based on FSB documents on the case and reports in *Novaia zhizn'* (Petrograd), July 9, 1918, p. 3; *Novyi vechernyi chas,* July 8, 1918, p. 1; *Vechernye ogni,* July 8, 1918, p. 2; and *Nash vek,* July 9, 1918, p. 3.

75. TsGA SPb, f. 143, op. 1, d. 31, l. 255.

76. TNA: PRO, ADM 137/1731, unnumbered; Benckendorff to Lockhart, Lilly Library, Lockhart, R. mss., box 2, folder 8.

77. TsA FSB RF, No. N-8, vol. 1, ll. 1–35

78. Ibid., l. 8.

79. The outline of this myth was already reflected in a front-page account about the developments of the previous day in a *Krasnaia gazeta* (Extra) on 8 July. According to this report, a couple of hundred Left SRs, armed from head to foot with machine guns, cannons, hand grenades and various other weapons, having received instructions from their rebellious Central Committee in Moscow, *occupied* the former Pages School (emphasis mine—A.R.). The Military Revolutionary Committee, determined to suppress counterrevolutionary action of any kind, was left with no choice but to surround and disarm the Left SRs. Upon arriving at the school, Red Army soldiers were greeted by heavy rebel machine gun and artillery fire, following which it became necessary to subject the building to [return] fire, and, quickly, its occupiers tossed out a white flag (*Krasnaia gazeta,* July 8, 1918 [Extra], p. 1).

80. See above.

81. *Severnaia kommuna,* July 17, 1918, p. 3.

82. TsGAIPD, f. 4000, op. 4, d. 814, ll. 181, 202.

83. See *Znamia bor'by,* May 16, 1918, p. 3.

84. *Znamia truda,* July 6, 1918, p. 4.

85. TsGAIPD, f. 16, op. 1, d. 289, l. 13.

86. TsGA VMF, f. r-661, op. 1, d. 136, l. 3.

87. TsGAIPD, f. 15, op. 1, d. 1, ll. 6–6 ob.

88. *Novaia zhizn',* July 11, 1918, p. 3.

89. TsGAIPD, f. 4000, op. 4, d. 814, ll. 153–158.

90. TsGAIPD, f. 1, op. 1, d. 64, ll. 28–29.

91. In order of their probable date of publication, these included leaflets from the Peasant Section of the CEC (TsA FSB RF, No. N-685, vol. 9, l. 45); from the Left SR Fifth Congress

fraction, produced following its members' release from incarceration (GOBP, Leaflet Collection); from the Left SR fraction in the CEC, Fourth Convocation (GOBP, Leaflet Collection); from Left SR and SR Maximalist members of the Peasant Section, printed by hand and mimeographed (TsA FSB RF, No. N-685, vol. 10, ll. 272–272 ob.); and from the Left SR Moscow Oblast Committee (GOBP, Leaflet Collection).

92. Gogolevskii, *Petrogradskii sovet v gody grazhdanskoi voiny*, p. 170.

93. *Nash vek*, July 11, 1917.

94. *Severnaia kommuna*, July 17, 1918, p. 3.

95. For examples, see stenograms of plenary meetings of the Petrograd Soviet on 30 July and 7 August, during discussion of mobilizations for the Czech front; and on 15 August, during a discussion of worker unrest at the Putilov factory (TsGA SPb, f. 1000, op. 2, d. 3, ll. 16–26; d. 5, ll. 20–25; f. 1000, op. 53, d. 1. ll. 1–50).

96. TsGA SPb, f. 101, op. 1, d. 38, ll. 38 ob.–39.

97. *Novaia zhizn'*, July 13, 1918, p. 3.

98. TsGA SPb, f. 101, op. 1, d. 39, l. 117.

99. TsGA SPb, f. 148, op. 1, d. 43, ll. 66–71; f. 9618, op. 1, d. 260, ll. 6–10; f. 9618, op. 1, d. 229, ll. 61, 63.

100. TsGAIPD, f. 4, op. 1, d. 1, ll. 17 ob., 19 ob.–20 ob.

101. TsGA SPb, f. 47, op. 1, d. 26, l. 60 ob.

102. TsGA SPb, f. 3, op. 1, d. 1, ll. 73–89 ob.

103. TsGAIPD, f. 165, op. 1, d. 3, ll. 9, 16, 23 ob.

104. TsGA SPb, f. 3, op. 1, d. 1, l. 90.

105. TsGAIPD, f. 165, op. 1, d. 3, l. 16.

106. *Vestnik soveta 1-ogo gorodskogo raiona*, July 24, 1918, p. 4.

107. TsGAIPD, f. 1817, op. 1, d. 32, l. 15.

108. TsGAIPD, f. 2, op. 1, d. 4, l. 9 ob.

109. *Vestnik soveta 1-go gorodskogo raiona*, July, 24, 1918, no. 20–21, p. 6.

110. TsA FSB RF, No. N-685, vol. 6, l. 35 ob.

12. The Road to "Red Terror"

1. See Geoffrey Swain, *The Origins of the Russian Civil War* (London and New York, 1996), pp. 186–205, 219–246, for an insightful discussion of this battle and its outcome.

2. On Uritskii's assassination and the failed attempt on Lenin's life, see below.

3. See above, chapter 9.

4. *Novaia zhizn'* (Petrograd), June 21, 1918, p. 3.

5. Ilyin-Zhenevsky, *The Bolsheviks in Power*, p. 105. Il'in-Zhenevskii was then a member of *Krasnaia gazeta*'s editorial board.

6. For example, a general meeting of Bolsheviks in the Vyborg district, after listening to a report on Volodarskii's killing from Zhenia Egorova of the Petersburg Committee, pledged to answer "White Terror" with merciless class "Red Terror" (TsGAIPD, f. 2, op. 1, d. 1, l. 2).

7. *Novaia zhizn'* (Petrograd), June 23, 1918, p. 3; *Petrogradskaia pravda*, June 27, 1918, p. 2.

8. *Novye vedomosti*, June 22, 1918, p. 4.

9. Lenin, *Polnoe sobranie sochinenii*, 50:106.

10. See above, chapter 10.

11. TsGA SPb, f. 143, op. 1, d. 49, l. 49.

12. *Sbornik dekretov i postanovlenii po soiuzu kommun severnoi oblasti*, issue 1, pt. 1, p. 290.

13. Concern with the shortcomings of *Petrogradskaia pravda* was voiced at meetings of the Bolshevik Petersburg Committee on 7 May and the Delegates Soviet on 21 May (see, respectively, TsGAIPD, f. 1, op. 1, d. 64, l. 12; and f. 4000, op. 7, d. 820, ll. 101–102).

14. TsGAIPD, f. 4000, op. 4, d. 814, l. 198.

15. Ibid., l. 200.

16. Ibid.

17. In a progress report to the Second Congress of Soviets in the Northern Oblast Union of Communes, dated 1 August, Kuzmin listed fifteen opposition newspapers that he had shut down permanently and five editors or publishers whom he was holding as hostages (*Sbornik dekretov i postanovlenii po soiuzu kommun severnoi oblasti,* issue 1, pt. 1, p. 292).

18. See, for example, *Novyi vechernyi chas,* June 26, 1918, p. 1.

19. V. N. Kokovtsev, *Iz moego proshlogo: Vospominaniia 1903–1919 gg.* (Paris, 1933), pp. 445–462.

20. During the 1917 revolutions and in the months preceding his death in May 1918, Georgii Plekhanov, the "father of Russian Marxism," and Aleksinskii, a former Bolshevik, were allied in Plekhanov's right socialist Edinstvo group and were implacable foes of Bolshevism.

21. See *Novye vedomosti,* July 16, 1918, p. 7, for an informative, seemingly balanced description of jail life in Gorokhovaia 2 at this time. For an exposé of the ghastly conditions prevailing at the notorious Kresty prison by the Bolshevik chairman of the Vyborg district soviet, David Trilisser, see his "Nel'zia molchat'," *Severnaia kommuna,* December 4, 1918, p. 1.

22. VCheka shootings in Moscow were commonplace at this time.

23. See above, chapter 9.

24. TsGA SPb, f. 143, op. 1, d. 31, l. 57. The official endorsement of terror was contained in the Bolshevik resolution approving the policies of the CEC and Sovnarkom adopted by the Fifth All-Russian Congress of Soviets on 5 July (*Piatyi vserossiiskii s"ezd,* p. 98).

25. See above, chapter 7.

26. AU FSB SPb i LO, No. 47037, ll. 42–43, 44–46 ob., 64–70 ob.; TsGAIPD, f. 2, op. 1, d. 4, l. 9 ob.

27. See above, chapter 6.

28. TNA: PRO, FO 371/3332/92708; TNA: PRO, FO 337/3332/95780.

29. TNA: PRO, ADM 137/4183, unnumbered.

30. The main American force, some forty-five hundred men, did not land in Archangel until 4 September. See George F. Kennan, *Soviet-American Relations, 1917–1920,* Vol. 2, *The Decision to Intervene* (New York, 1967), p. 379.

31. Richard H. Ullman, *Anglo–Soviet Relations, 1917–1921,* Vol. 1, *Intervention and the War* (Princeton, N.J., 1961), pp. 235–237.

32. Cromie, *Letters [on Russian Affairs],* p. 129; TNA: PRO, FO 371/3307/137793. Cromie began to advocate "immediate intervention on a large scale" toward the end of May (TNA: PRO, ADM 137/1731, pp. 70–71). Subsequent events enhanced his sense of urgency in this respect. In a telegram dated 24 June conveying a plea for immediate intervention on behalf of one Vinogradeff, whom Cromie identified as "our chief agent," Cromie endorsed Vinogradeff's claim that "intervention on a thorough scale is the only thing that will save the situation [Russia's complete domination by Germany] . . . forces raised locally cannot be relied on unless each unit is stiffened by at least 25 percent Allied troops" (TNA: PRO, FO 371/3286, p 337).

33. See "Delo nabora belogvardeitsev na Murman," AU FSB SPb i LO, No. 10940, vols. 1–6; and N. Antipov, "Ocherki o deiatel'nosti Petrogradskoi chrezvychainoi komissii," *Petrogradskaia pravda,* January 5, 1919, pp. 2–3.

34. A. A. Borman, "Moskva–1918 (iz zapisok sekretnogo agenta v kremle)," *Russkoe proshloe,* book 1, 1991, pp. 138–139.

35. See, for example, TsGAIPD, f. 457, op.1, d. 1, l. 1. As Winfried Baumgart shows, there were ample reasons for this anxiety. See Winfried Baumgart, *Deutsche Ostpolitik 1918: Von Brest–Litowsk bis zum Ende des Erstein Weltkrieges* (Vienna and Munich, 1966), pp. 56–57.

36. For examples, see TsGAIPD, f. 4000, op. 7, d. 814, ll. 165, 183, 195, 196.

37. *Dekrety Sovetskoi vlasti,* 2:507.

38. See above, chapter 10.

39. Thus, at a meeting on 2 August, the Petersburg Committee resolved not to send any

more "responsible members" to the Czech front and to request its Assembly of Organizers to identify rank-and-file Bolsheviks not engaged in critical party or government work for military duty (TsGAIPD, f. 4000, op. 7, d. 814, l. 210).

40. Concern about German naval operations in the Gulf is reflected in urgent cable traffic between elements of the Baltic Fleet and between its headquarters in Petrograd and the Naval Command and People's Commissariat for Naval Affairs in Moscow (RGA VMF, f. r-852, op. 1, d. 28, l. 15; f. r-342, op. 1, d. 145, ll. 170, 179–180, 183, 187; f. r-2, op. 1, d. 161, ll. 109, 161; f. r-96, op. 1, d. 62, ll. 13–30; f. r-50, op. 1, d. 15, ll. 15, 24, 25, 32, 35, 41, 44, 48).

41. TNA: PRO, ADM 137/1731, p 121.

42. Cromie, *Letters [on Russian Affairs]*, p. 131.

43. TNA: PRO, FO 337/88/137.

44. Ibid. For numerous telegrams reflecting communications problems following the destruction of Cromie's ciphers, see TNA: PRO, FO 371/3330, pp. 157–267, passim. In a letter of 26 July to his superior Blinker Hall, Cromie explained that he had been unable to send or receive letters and telegrams, and he had considered it inadvisable to keep any records since the murder of Mirbach. "Our main scheme," presumably providing for destruction of the Baltic Fleet, "is in good order," he added. "There is some danger in having so many irons in the fire, but I think I have enough friends to get me out even if it comes to flying" (Cromie, *Letters [on Russian Affairs]*, pp. 128–129).

45. TNA: PRO, FO 337/88/137.

46. *Cromie, Letters [on Russian Affairs]*, pp. 131–133.

47. See, for example, ibid., p. 132.

48. Ullman, *Intervention and the War*, p. 186.

49. TNA: PRO ADM 223/637, p 83.

50. Ibid.

51. On Sidney Reilly's subversive activities at this time, see S. Reilly, *Britain's Master Spy: The Adventures of Sidney Reilly* (New York and London, 1933), pp. 1–63; and Richard Spence, *Trust No One: The Secret Life of Sidney Reilly* (Los Angeles, 2003), pp. 200–229.

52. TNA: PRO, FO 371/3348/190442.

53. Bruce R. H. Lockhart, *British Agent* (New York and London, 1933), p. 308.

54. *Novaia zhizn'* (Petrograd), June 23, 1918, p. 3; *Petrogradskaia pravda*, June 23, 1918, p. 3.

55. See, for example, the fiery resolution adopted at a general meeting of Bolsheviks in the Vasilii Island district on 9 August (TsGAIPD, f. 4, op. 1, d. 2, ll. 14 ob.–15).

56. TsGAIPD, f. 4000, op. 4, d. 814, l. 208.

57. TsGAIPD, f. 1, op. 1, d. 128, l. 7.

58. This greatly intensified wave of arrests is reflected in émigré memoirs. See, for example, Kokovtsev, *Iz moego proshlogo*, p. 463. Referring to these arrests, Kokovstev writes: "Before 21 July, everything was relatively tolerable but from that day on mass arrests began all around . . . everyday I heard of the seizure of one or another of my acquaintances."

59. See above, chapter 10.

60. *Severnaia kommuna*, August 2, 1918, p. 3. For a partial stenographic record of this congress, see TsGA SPb, f. 143, op. 1, d. 3.

61. See, for example, the resolution adopted by the soviet in the Vasilii Island district on 6 August (TsGA SPb, f. 47, op. 1, d. 26, l. 72 ob.).

62. *Sbornik deketrov i postanovlenii po soiuzu kommun severnoi oblasti*, issue 1, pt. 1, p. 132.

63. S. G. Uralov, *Moisei Uritskii: Biograficheskii ocherk* (Leningrad, 1962), p. 116.

64. Ibid.

65. *Krasnaia gazeta*, August 22, 1918, p. 1. On Perel'tsveig and the conspiracy in the Mikhailovskii Artillery Academy, see above, chapter 7. On the July arrests, see above.

66. *Stenograficheskii otchet o rabotakh piatogo s"ezda sovetov rabochikh i krest'ianskikh deputatov Peterburgskoi gubernii* (Petrograd, 1918), p. 112.

67. *Severnaia kommuna,* August 29, 1918, p. 2.

68. TsA FSB RF, No. N-196.

69. For a personal portrait of Kannegisser by Mark Aldanov, who knew him well, see M. Aldanov, *Kartiny Oktiabr'skoi revoliutsii, istoricheskie portrety, portrety sovremennikov, zagadka Tolstogo* (St. Petersburg, 1999), pp. 124–131, 140–144.

70. This is confirmed by Aldanov. He recalled that in the spring of 1918, in reaction to the signing of the Treaty of Brest-Litovsk, Kannegisser dabbled in amateurish conspiratorial work aimed at overthrowing the Bolsheviks (ibid., pp. 129–130).

71. TsA FSB RF, No. N-196, v. 1, ll. 45–49.

72. Aldanov, *Kartiny Oktiabr'skoi revoliutsii,* pp. 129, 141.

73. TsA FSB RF, No. N-196, vol. 1, ll. 3–6.

74. S. K. Tsvigun et al., eds., *V. I. Lenin i VChka: Sbornik dokumentov (1917–1922 gg.)* (Moscow, 1975), pp. 84–85.

75. Lenin, *Polnoe sobranie sochinenii,* 37:81–85.

76. See above, chapter 3.

13. The Red Terror in Petrograd

1. A resolution adopted at this meeting provided for safeguarding the Soviet republic by isolating class enemies in concentration and shooting all persons belonging to "Whiteguardist" organizations or involved in conspiracies or revolts (RGASPI, f. 19, op. 1, d. 192, l. 2, 10).

2. TsGA SPb, f. 143, op. 1, d. 66, ll. 115–116.

3. TsGA SPb, f. 1000, op. 2, d. 7, l. 17; *Severnaia kommuna,* September 7, 1918, p. 3.

4. *Petrogradskaia pravda,* September 6, 1918, p. 3; *Severnaia kommuna,* September 6, 1918, p. 3.

5. TsGA SPb, f. 9618, op. 1, d. 300, l. 2.

6. Elena Stasova, *Stranitsy zhizni i bor'by* (Moscow, 1988), pp. 154–155; idem, *Vospominaniia* (Moscow, 1969), p. 161.

7. Stasova referred to this clash with Zinoviev and Bokii's position in a letter of 28 September to Sverdlov in Moscow (RGASPI, f. 466, op. 1, d. 7, l. 80).

8. *Petrogradskaia pravda,* August 31, 1918, p. 1.

9. *Vooruzhennyi narod,* September 1, 1918, p. 1.

10. See, for example, ibid., September 3, 1918, p. 1.

11. The PCheka's case file on the "Comorra" indicates that it consisted primarily of one young antisemitic zealot, Luka Zlotnikov, rather than significant numbers of former members of the Union of the Russian People, as alleged at the time. He was also shot (AU FSB SPb i LO, No. 30377, vol. 3, l. 63; vol. 4, ll. 17, 53–53 ob.).

12. TsA FSB RF, f. 1, op. 2, d. 126, vol. 2, ll. 6 ob., 14, 163; A. L. Litvin, ed., *Mensheviki v Sovetskoi Rossii: Sbornik dokumentov* (Kazan, 1998), pp. 38–39; Nik. Begletsov, "V dni 'krasnogo' terrora," in *Che-Ka: Materialy po deiatel'nosti chrezvychainykh komissii* (Berlin, 1922), pp. 69–80. Those still held were given amnesty on 18 November (GARF, f. 1235, op. 36, d. 2, l. 2).

13. *Petrogradskaia pravda,* September 6, 1918, p. 2.

14. See, for example, *Vooruzhennyi narod,* September 3, 1918, p. 1.

15. *Ezhenedel'nik chrezvychainykh komissii po bor'be s kontre-revoliutsiei i spekulatsiei,* no. 6, October 27, 1918, p. 19. On the PCheka congress, see below.

16. AU FSB SPb i LO, f. 1, ll. 7, 8. The combined figure for shootings during the Red Terror in these tables is 841. For the entire period from 14 March 1918 to 1 January 1919, they show that 10,227 individuals accused of political and economic crimes were held in concentration camps; 13,742 in prisons; and 1,800 "by the PCheka," presumably in Gorokhovaia 2. An additional 6,106 individuals were held as "hostages." One assumes that a high percentage of the hostages were seized during the Red Terror. According to these tables, a total of 38,075

people were arrested by the PCheka and the Petrograd Province Cheka during the nine and a half months that the tables cover.

17. *Severnaia kommuna,* October 19, 1918, pp. 2–3.

18. TsGA SPb, f. 9672, op. 1, d. 566, ll. 13–14.

19. *Krasnaia gazeta,* August 31, 1918, p. 1.

20. Ibid., September 4, 1918, p. 1.

21. TsGALI, f. 63, op. 1, d. 62, ll. 135–149.

22. For a valuable analysis of the Lockhart Plot, which suggests that Lockhart was much more deeply involved in trying to overthrow the Soviet government than he admitted, see Debo, "Lockhart Plot or Dzerzhinskii Plot?" *Journal of Modern History* 43, no. 3 (1970): 413–439.

23. *Severnaia kommuna* (evening), September 2, 1918, p. 3.

24. See a top-secret memorandum dated 19 September 1918, evidently prepared by Major John Scale's office, if not by Scale himself. An experienced Russian hand, Scale was then an intelligence officer in Stockholm with authority over covert agents in Russia. The memorandum reported on the debriefing of Hall, who had just arrived in Stockholm from Petrograd (TNA: PRO ADM 223/637/ p. 83).

25. Ibid.

26. *Severnaia kommuna,* September 2, 1918, p. 3.

27. TNA: PRO, ADM 223/637/p. 83

28. V. A. Sobolev, ed., *Lubianka 2: Iz istorii otechestvennoi kontrrazvedki* (Moscow, 1999), p. 171.

29. P. G. Sofinov, *Ocherki istorii VChK* (Moscow, 1960), p. 101; V. I. Berezhkov, *Piterskie prokuratory: Rukovoditeli VChK-MGB* (Petersburg, 1998), p. 35.

30. Berezhkov, *Piterskie prokuratury,* p. 36.

31. "Paymaster" was the position Boyce, as head of the SIS in Russia, used as a cover.

32. TNA: PRO, FO 371/3975/206714.

33. Michael Hughs, *Inside the Enigma: British Officials in Russia, 1900–1930* (London, 1997), p. 176.

34. In memoirs on the Lockhart plot Iakov Peters, who superintended the investigation of the case in Moscow, conveyed a strong sense of annoyance at the PCheka for jumping the gun in arresting "Lockhart's agents." According to him, it necessitated a roundup of foreign agents in Moscow before the investigation of them was close to complete (Ia. Kh. Peters, "Vospominaniia o rabote v VChK v pervyi god revoliutsii," *Proletarskaia revoliutsiia,* 1924, no. 10 [33]: 25).

35. The fullest reports on the trial appeared in *Izvestiia* (Moscow), November 29, 1918, p. 3; November 30, 1918, p. 3; December 1, 1918, p. 2; December 3, 1918, p. 3; December 4, 1918, p. 2.

36. *Severnaia kommuna,* September 3, 1918, p. 1.

37. On this point, see Gordon Brook-Shepherd, *Iron Maze: The Western Secret Services and the Bolsheviks* (London, 1999), p. 90.

38. TsGA SPb, f. 8098, op. 1, d. 1a, l. ll. 164–164 ob.

39. Seven letters, each with an attached list, were sent to Bokii by the German Consul in September alone. For examples, see TsGA SPb, f. 8098, op. 1, d. 1a., ll. 11, 51, 172, 172 ob.

40. TsGA SPb, f. 8098, op. 1, d. 1a, l. 172 ob. This figure includes 218 prisoners arrested before the Red Terror.

41. Ibid., l. 71.

42. Ibid., l. 172 ob.

43. TsGA SPb, f. 143, op. 1, d. 48, l. 172.

44. TsGA SPb., f. 6276, op. 3, d. 5, ll. 46–46 ob.

45. TsGA SPb, f. 143, op. 1, d. 51, l. 183.

46. TsGA SPb, f. 9672, op. 1, d. 566, l. 13 ob.

47. E. D. Stasova, *Stranitsy zhizni i bor'by,* p. 155.

48. A batch of appeals from individual artists, musical and theater groups, and theater

directors for the release of colleagues and leading performers are in TsGA SPb, f. 2551, op. 1, d. 2266, ll. 1–11.

49. RGA VMF, f. r-5, op. 1, d. 265, ll. 54, 68, 69, 80, 90; f. r-342, op. 1, d. 116, l. 597; f. r-852, op. 1, d. 26, l. 313.

50. *Ezhenedel'nik chrezvychainykh komissii po bor'be s kontr-revolutsiei i spekulatsiei*, no. 1, September 22, 1918, p. 11.

51. *Sbornik dekretov i postanovlenii po soiuzu komun severnoi oblasti*, issue 1, pt. 1, p. 147.

52. TsGA SPb, f. 142, op. 1, d. 9, l. 308.

53. TsGA SPb, f. 1000, op. 1, d. 8, ll. 14–15.

54. TsGAIPD, f. 1, op. 1, d. 117, l. 11.

55. T. Alekseeva, and N. Matveev, *Dovereno zashchishchat' revoliutsiu: O G. I. Bokii* (Moscow, 1987), pp. 218–219.

56. RGASPI, f. 466, op. 1, d. 7, ll. 80–81.

57. See above.

58. TsGA SPb, f. 6276, op. 3, d. 5, l. 43 ob.

59. TsGA SPb, f. 1000, op. 2, d. 10, ll. 3–9.

60. TsGA SPb, f. 2551, op. 1, d. 2266, ll. 1–11.

61. TsGA SPb, f. 1000, op. 2, d. 10, l. 8.

62. TsGAIPD, f. 1, op. 1, d. 75, l. 154.

63. Ibid., f. 1, op. 1, d. 120, l. 44. Some data from these questionnaires were published by Strumilin at the end of 1918 (see [S.] Strumilin, "Sostav partii Kommunistov v Petrograde v sentiabre 1918 goda," *Petrogradskaia pravda*, December 12, 1918, p. 2).

64. On this point, see also the Petersburg Committee's "annual report" for 1918 (TsGAIPD, f. 1, op. 1, d. 64, l. 71).

65. See, for example, Zinoviev's speech at the Fifth Petrograd Province Congress of Soviets on 21 August (*Stenograficheskii otchet o rabotakh piatogo s"ezda sovetov rabochikh i krest'ianskikh deputatov Petrogradskoi gubernii*, p. 18), and above, chapter 9.

66. TsGAIPD, f. 4000, op. 7, d. 814, l. 239.

67. TsGAIPD, f. 1, op. 1, d. 120, l. 82.

68. TsGAIPD, f. 1, op. 1, d. 120, l. 80.

69. A. Rashin, "Demobilizatsiia promyshlennogo truda v Petrogradskoi gubernii za 1917–18 gg." in *Materialy po statistike truda*, ed. S. G. Strumilin, issue 5 (Petrograd, 1919), p. 48; *Petrogradskaia pravda*, December 12, 1918, p. 2.

70. TsGAIPD, f. 1, op. 1, d. 64, ll. 71 ob.–72; *Petrogradskaia pravda*, December, 12, 1918, p. 2.

71. TsGAIPD, f. 1, op. 1, d. 72, ll. 1–11; *Vooruzhennyi narod*, September 22, 1918, p. 2. For regulations governing "sympathizers," see *Ustav organizatsii sochuvstvuiushchikh Rossiiskoi kommunisticheskoi partii (bol'shevikov)* (Petrograd, 1918).

72. TsGAIPD, f. 1. op. 1, d. 117, l. 4.

73. Ibid.

74. TsGAIPD, f. 4000, op. 7, d. 814, l. 195–196; d. 820, l. 18, 104–118.

75. TsGAIPD, f. 1, op. 1, d. 64, l. 48.

76. See above, chapter 6.

77. See M. Ol'minskii, "O chrezvychainykh komissiiakh," *Pravda* (Moscow), October 8, 1918, p. 1.

78. *Ezhenedel'nik chrezvychainykh komissii po bor'be s kontr-revolutsiei i spekulatsiei*, no. 1, September 22, 1918, p. 1.

79. Ibid., no. 6, October 27, 1918, pp. 17–24.

80. Ibid., p. 19.

81. Ibid., pp. 20–22. Zinoviev claimed that, in one Cheka, the question had been raised about whether, if necessary, the Sovnarkom could be arrested.

82. *Protokoly 1-go s"ezda predstavitelei gub. sovdepov i zavedyvaiushchikh gubernskikh otdelami upravleniia* (Moscow, 1918), p. 78; See also TsGA SPb, f. 143, op. 1, d. 4, l. 72.

83. GARF, f. 393, op. 1, d. 58, ll. 272, 277–277 ob. See also *Vestnik oblastnogo komissariata vnutrennykh del (soiuza komun severnoi oblasti)*, 1918, no. 3:156–157.

84. GARF, f. 393, op. 1, d. 58, l. 278; *Ezhenedel'nik chrezvychainykh komissii po bor'be s kontr-revoliutsiei i spekulatsiei,* no. 6, October 27, 1918, p. 22.

85. See above, chapter 9.

86. TsGAIPD, f. 1817, op. 1, d. 107, ll. l–4 ob., 7–7 ob., 11–13.

87. TsGAIPD, f. 1817, op. 1, d. 107, ll. 4–4 ob., 11–13, 15, 18.

88. RGA VMF, f. r-342, op. 1, d. 145, l. 244.

89. *Severnaia kommuna,* October 16, 1918, p. 2.

90. Ibid.

91. I. Flerovskii, "Miatezh mobilizovannykh matrosov v Peterburge," *Proletarskaia revoliutsiia,* 1926, no. 8 (55): 220.

92. TSGA VMF, f. r-96, op. 1, d. 21, ll. 57–59.

93. TsGAIPD, f. 4000, op. 4, d. 814, l. 230.

94. RGA VMF, f. r-661, op. 1, d. 139, l. 24.

95. *Severnaia kommuna,* October 16, 1918, p. 2.

96. TsA FSB RF, No. N-2, vol. 3, l. 2.

97. Ibid. See also TsA FSB RF, No. N-2, vol. 3, l. 2; RGA VMF, f. r-96, op. 1, d. 7, l. 120.

98. TsA FSB RF, No. N-2, vol. 3, l. 2.

99. Flerovskii, "Miatezh mobilizovannykh matrosov v Peterburge," p. 225.

100. TsA FSB RF, No. N-2, vol. 3, l. 6.

101. *Severnaia kommuna,* October 16, 1918, p. 2.

102. TsA FSB RF, No. N-2, v. 3, ll. 3–3 ob.

103. TsA FSB RF, No. N-2, v. 2, l. 4.

104. These orders are published in Flerovskii, "Miatezh mobilizovannykh matrosov," pp. 226–227.

105. Ibid., p. 229.

106. TsA FSB, No. N-2, vol. 2, ll. 4 ob.–5; *Severnaia kommuna,* October 16, 1918, p. 2; Flerovskii, "Miatezh mobilizovannykh matrosov," pp. 229–231.

107. TsA FSB, No. 2, N-2, vol. 2, l. 5.

108. *Vooruzhennyi narod,* October 17, 1918, p. 2.

109. GOPB, fond listovok.

110. *Severnaia kommuna,* October 16, 1918, p. 2.

111. TsGA SPb, f. 9618, op. 1, d. 252, l. 53.

112. RGA VMF, f. r-342, op. 1, d. 245, l. 312.

113. TsA FSB, No. N-2, vol. 2, ll. 9–9 ob.

114. TsA FSB, No. N-2, vol. 2, ll. 4–6.

115. TsA FSB, No. N-2, vol. 2, ll. 10–11.

116. *Vooruzhennyi narod,* October 18, 1918, p. 2.

117. See, for example, *Vooruzhennyi narod,* October 17, 1918, p. 4; and October 18, 1918, p. 4.

118. *Petrogradskaia pravda,* October 30, 1918, p. 2.

119. *Vooruzhennyi narod,* October 18, 1918, p. 4.

120. RGA VMF, f. r-96, op. 1, d. 7, l. 126.

14. Celebrating "The Greatest Event in the History of the World"

1. TsGAIPD, f. 1728, op. 1, d. 48973, l. 7.

2. *Vestnik soveta 1-ogo gorodskogo raiona,* October 9, 1918, p. 3; October 30, 1918, p. 2.

3. See, for example, Zinoviev's speech and his resolution on foreign affairs adopted by

the Petrograd Soviet on 4 October (*Severnaia kommuna,* October 5, 1918, p. 2; October 6, 1918, pp. 2–3).

4. For examples, see accounts of speeches on the theme "Thrones Are Shaking" by Zinoviev and Lunacharskii at Sunday rallies on 6 October in *Severnaia kommuna,* October 8, 1918, p. 2.

5. TsGAIPD, f. 1, op. 1, d. 8, ll. 1–9; f. 1, op. 1, d. 117, l. 11; f. 1, op. 1, d. 72, l. 3; f. 16, op. 1, d. 293, l. 6 ob.

6. V. Bystranskii, "Oktiabr'skaia revoliutsiia—velichaishee sobytie v mirovoi istorii," *God proletarskoi revoliutsii,* November 7, 1918, p. 1.

7. TsGA SPb, f. 142, op. 1, d. 28, l. 307.

8. *Severnaia kommuna,* September 25, 1918, p. 2.

9. TsGALI, f. 63, op. 1, d. 62, l. 197.

10. *Severnaia kommuna,* September 21, 1918, p. 2.

11. Ibid.

12. James von Geldern, *Bolshevik Festivals, 1917–1920* (Berkeley, 1993), p. 62.

13. *Severnaia kommuna,* September 21, 1918, p. 2. The Kseshiinskii Institute, which was shut down in 1917, was located in the central Admiralteiskii district, near the Winter Palace. Labor organizations had established offices in the ornate building well before the October festivities. Still, its past association gave symbolic significance to its refurbishment in the fall of 1918 and its official opening as the Palace of Labor on 8 November.

14. This was the meeting that triggered the fierce argument between Riazanov and Zinoviev over the release of innocent political prisoners before the holiday. See above, chapter 12.

15. TsGA SPb, f. 1000, op. 2, d. 10, ll. 1–3; *Severnaia kommuna,* September 25, 1918, p. 2.

16. TsGA SPb, f. 3, op. 1, d. 2, ll. 31–31 ob.

17. Ibid., f. 101, op. 1, d. 38, l. 65.

18. Ibid., ll. 66 ob.–67. Similarly, after hearing a report on the Bureau's holiday plans, irate Bolshevik factory "organizers" in the First City district appealed to their soviet to decorate *all* buildings in their neighborhoods with red flags and greenery, and to organize choruses to learn revolutionary songs in *all* factories and military units (*Vestnik soveta 1-ogo gorodskogo raiona,* November 3, 1918, p. 3).

19. *Severnaia kommuna,* October 9, 1918, p. 1. In succeeding days, analogous pronouncements were issued by the cinema and by the theater sections (see *Severnaia kommuna,* October 15, 1918, p. 2; October 19, 1918, p. 1).

20. TsGA SPb, f. 3, op. 1, d. 2, ll. 41–41 ob.

21. TsGA SPb, f. 3, op. 1, d. 2, l. 41 ob.

22. TsGA SPb, f. 1000, op. 79, d. 40, ll. 1–2 ob.

23. TsGAIPD, f. 16, op. 1, d. 295, l. 12.

24. See below.

25. TsGA SPb, f. 1000, op. 2, d. 14, l. 62.

26. RGASPI, f. 67, op. 2, d. 4, l. 18.

27. *Krasnaia gazeta,* October 17, 1918, p. 1; M. Lur'e, "Pervyi s"ezd komitetov derevenskoi bednoty soiuza kommun severnoi oblasti," *Krasnaia letopis',* 1931, no. 4 (43): 8.

28. *Severnaia kommuna,* October, 25, 1918, p. 2.

29. Ibid., October 23, 1918, p. 3.

30. For the theater section's plans, see *Krasnaia gazeta,* October 22, 1918, p. 3; and *Severnaia kommuna,* October 24, 1918, p. 3; for the music section, *Severnaia kommuna,* October 24, 1918, p. 3; and for the film section, *Severnaia kommuna,* November 3, 1918, p. 1.

31. *Severnaia kommuna,* November 5, 1918, p. 2.

32. TsGA SPb, f. 1000, op. 80, d. 60, l. 8.

33. Ibid., op. 2, d. 14, l. 64.

34. *Severnaia kommuna,* October 24, 1918, p. 3.

35. TsGA SPb, f. 2551, op. 1, d. 2467, l. 2 ob.

36. *Krasnaia gazeta,* October 25, 1918, p. 3; November 5, 1918, p. 2.

37. See, for example, *Severnaia kommuna,* November 1, 1918, p. 4.

38. *Tvorchestvo revoliutsionnykh rabochikh 2-go gorodskogo raiona: Otchet o rabote sovdepa 2-go gor. raiona s pervykh dnei revoliutsii do godovshchiny velikoi oktiabr'skoi revoliutsii* (Petrograd, 1918).

39. *Severnaia kommuna,* November 1, 1918, p. 1.

40. TsGA SPb, f. 6276, op. 3, d. 27, ll. 41–42.

41. The fullest published account of Zinoviev's remarks appeared in *Severnaia kommuna,* October 26, 1918, p. 2, as an appeal to workers, sailors, and Red Army personnel. See also, TsGA SPb, f. 1000, op. 2, d. 10, l. 9.

42. TsGA SPb, f. 2551, op. 1, d. 2246, l. 10 ob.

43. *Severnaia kommuna,* October 24, 1918, p. 3.

44. Ibid., October 25, 1918, p. 3.

45. Ibid., October 24, 1918, p. 3.

46. Ibid., November 1, 1918, p. 4.

47. TsGA SPb, f. 2551, op. 1, d. 2246, l. 10.

48. *Krasnaia gazeta,* November 2, 1918, p. 3.

49. *Vestnik godovshchiny velikoi raboche-krest'ianskoi revoliutstii,* November 7–9, 1918, p. 4.

50. TsGA SPb, f. 1000, op. 2, d. 4, ll. 59–65; *Severnaia kommuna,* November 2, 1918, p. 3.

51. TsGA SPb, f. 1000, op. 2, d. 4, l. 65.

52. Ibid.

53. RGASPI, f. 324, op. 1, d. 13, l. 13.

54. *Severnaia kommuna,* November 3, 1918, p. 1.

55. Late on 6 November, the extraordinarily detailed march route was distributed in a special publication, *Vestnik godovshchiny velikoi raboche-krest'ianskoi sotsialisticheskoi revoliutsii.*

56. TsGA SPb, op. 2, d. 14, l. 64.

57. *Severnaia kommuna,* November 6, 1918, p. 5.

58. *Severnaia kommuna,* October 19, 1918, p. 2.

59. See, for example, in this connection, the final report of the holiday commission in Kolpino (TsGA SPb, f. 1000, op. 80, d. 61, ll. 47–49 ob.).

60. *Severnaia kommuna,* October 23, 1918, p. 3.

61. Ibid., October 17, 1918, p. 3.

62. *Piatyi sozyv vserossiiskogo tsentral'nogo ispolnitel'nogo komiteta,* p. 274; *Izvestiia TsK KPSS,* 1989, no. 6:162; *Vladimir Il'ich Lenin, Biograficheskaia khronika,* 6:176–177.

63. *Severnaia kommuna,* October 31, 1918, p. 1; reprinted on November 1 and 2, 1918.

64. *Severnaia kommuna,* November 1, 1918, p. 4.

65. TsA SPb, f. 1000, op. 2, d. 14, l. 65.

66. *Vestnik godovshchiny velikoi raboche-krest'ianskoi sotsialisticheskoi revoliutsii,* November 7–9, 1918, p. 4.

67. *Severnaia kommuna,* October 24, 1918, pp. 2–3.

68. *Vooruzhennyi narod,* November 1, 1918, p. 5.

69. Ibid.

70. TsGA SPb, f. 9618, op. 1, d. 252, ll. 57, 61.

71. *Krasnaia gazeta,* October 20, 1918, p. 3.

72. TsA FSB, RF No. N-199, vol. 1, l. 120; see above, chapter 9.

73. A. S. Izgoev, "Piat' let v Sovetskoi Rossii (obryvki vospominanii i zametki)," *Arkhiv russkoi revoliutsii,* vol. 10 (Berlin, 1923), pp. 30–34, 53.

74. *Krasnaia gazeta,* November 6, 1918, p. 3.

75. TsGA SPb, f. 100, op. 1, d. 47, l. 41.

76. A similar emergency troika was formed by the Executive Committee of the Vasilii Island District Soviet on 6 November (TsGA SPb, f. 47, op. 1, d. 28, l. 173).

77. TsGA SPb, f. 9618, op. 1, d. 252, l. 61.

78. *Severnaia kommuna,* November 5, 1918, p. 1.

79. Ibid.

80. *God proletarskoi revoliutsii,* November 8, 1918, p. 3; November 9, 1918, p. 4.

81. Ibid., November 7, 1918, p. 3.

82. *Plamia,* November 7, 1918, p. 433.

83. *God proletarskoi revoliutsii,* November 7, 1918, p. 1.

84. Ibid., November 7, 1918, p. 4; November 8, 1918, p. 3.

85. See, for example, *Krasnaia gazeta,* November 6, 1918, p. 1.

86. Zinaida Gippius, *Dnevniki,* vol. 2 (Moscow, 1999), p. 149.

87. TsGAIPD, f. 999, op. 1, d. 48, ll. 2–3; *God proletarskoi revoliutsii,* November 8, 1918, p. 3.

88. *God proletarskoi revoliutsii,* November 8, 1918, p. 2.

89. Ibid.

90. Ibid.

91. Richard Stites, *Revolutionary Dreams: Utopian Vision and Experimental Life in the Russian Revolution* (New York and Oxford, 1989), p. 93. On the art of the celebration in Petrograd, see also von Geldern, *Bolshevik Festivals, 1917–1920,* pp. 93–97.

92. *God proletarskoi revoliutsii,* November 9, 1918, p. 3.

93. Ibid.

94. TsGA SPb, f. 1000, op. 2, d. 17, l. 40.

95. *God proletarskoi revoliutsii,* November 9, 1918, p. 3.

96. *Petrogradskaia pravda,* November 10, 1918, p. 2.

97. *Krasnaia gazeta,* November 10, 1918, p. 4.

98. See above.

99. *God proletarskoi revoliutsii,* November 9, 1918, p. 2.

100. TsGALI, f. 63, op. 1, d. 62, ll. 74–76.

101. Ibid., l. 75.

15. Price of Survival

1. Ilyin-Zhenevsky, *The Bolsheviks in Power,* pp. 127–128.

2. RGA VMF, f. r-96, op. 1, d. 57, l. 286.

3. TsGAIPD, f. 1949, op. 1, d. 7, l. 36.

4. *Dekrety Sovetskoi vlasti,* vol. 4 (Moscow, 1968), pp. 9–10.

5. TsGA SPb, f. 148, op. 1, d. 51, l. 238 ob.

SELECTED BIBLIOGRAPHY

Archives

Russia

GARF, Gosudarstvennyi arkhiv Rossiiskoi federatsii
f. 130   Council of People's Commissars (SNK)
f. 336   Investigating Commission of the Petrograd Soviet's Revolutionary Tribunal
f. 337   Revolutionary Tribunal for the Press
f. 353   People's Commissariat for Justice
f. 393   People's Commissariat for Internal Affairs
f. 1074   Revolutionary Tribunal attached to the Petrograd Soviet
f. 1235   Central Executive Committee (CEC)
f. 1236   Military Revolutionary Committee (MRC)
f. 1810   All-Russian Commission on Elections to the Constituent Assembly
f. 5498   Executive Committee, All-Russian Rail Workers Union (Vikzhel)
f. 6148   Shreider, Aleksandr (Deputy People's Commissar for Justice)
f. 9462   Zinoviev, G. E.

RGASPI, Rossiiskii gosudarstvennyi arkhiv sotsial'no-politicheskoi istorii
f. 2   Lenin, V. I.
f. 5   V. I. Lenin's Secretariat
f. 17   Bolshevik Central Committee
f. 19   Council of People's Commissars (Sovnarkom)
f. 60   Bolshevik Moscow Oblast Bureau
f. 66   Bolshevik Petersburg Committee
f. 67   Bolshevik Northern Oblast Committee
f. 71   Institute of Marxism-Leninism attached to the Central Committee of the Communist Party
f. 76   Dzerzhinskii, F. E.
f. 82   Molotov, V. M.
f. 86   Sverdlov, Ia. M.
f. 131   Eremeev, K. S.
f. 146   Podvoiskii, N. I.
f. 274   SR Central Committee
f. 275   Menshevik Central Committee
f. 323   Kamenev, L. B.
f. 324   Zinoviev, G. E.
f. 325   Trotskii, L. D.
f. 326   Radek, K. B.
f. 329   Bukharin, N. I.
f. 356   Stasova, E. D.

f. 466   Petrograd Bureau of the Bolshevik Central Committee
f. 558   Stalin, I. V.
f. 564   Left SR Central Committee
f. 588   Lozovskii, A. S.
f. 670   Sokolnikov, G. Ia.

TsGA SPb, Tsentral'nyi gosudarstvennyi arkhiv Sankt-Peterburga
f. 1   Okhtinskii District Soviet
f. 2   Nevskii District Soviet
f. 3   Rozhdestvenskii District Soviet
f. 47   Vasilii Island District Soviet
f. 55   Second City District Soviet
f. 73   Committee for the Revolutionary Security of Petrograd
f. 83   Military Section of the Leningrad Soviet
f. 100   Narva District Soviet
f. 101   Peterhof District Soviet
f. 142   Commissariat for Internal Affairs, Union of Communes of the Northern
          Oblast
f. 143   Council of Commissars and Central Executive Committee, Union of
          Communes of the Northern Oblast (SK and CEC, SK SO)
f. 144   Council of Commissars, Petrograd Labor Commune (SK PTK)
f. 148   Vyborg District Soviet
f. 150   Novoderevenskii District Soviet
f. 153   Spasskii District Soviet
f. 506   Leningrad Oblast Section of the All-Russian Society of Political Prisoners
          and Exiles
f. 511   Porokhovskii District Soviet
f. 1000   Petrograd Province Soviet and Executive Committee
f. 1788   Putilov Plant
f. 2411   Petrograd and Petrograd Province Revolutionary Tribunal
f. 2421   Committee for the Revolutionary Defense of Petrograd
f. 2551   Commissariat for Enlightenment, SK SO
f. 2815   Commissariat for Public Health, SK SO
f. 3390   Extraordinary Assembly of Delegates from Petrograd Factories and Plants
f. 5937   Leningrad Section of the Woodworkers' Union
f. 6261   Leningrad Section of the Food Processors' Union
f. 6276   Petrograd Trade Union Council
f. 7034   Railway Workers Committee of the Nikolaevskii Rail Line
f. 7384   Petrograd Soviet
f. 8098   Petrograd Province Cheka
f. 8816   Petrograd district dumas and duma administrative boards
f. 8957   Commissariat for Agriculture, SK SO
f. 9618   Editorial Board, [project on] the History of the Leningrad Soviet
f. 9672   Editorial Board, [project on] the History of Leningrad Factories and
          Plants

TsGAIPD SPb, Tsentral'nyi gosudarstvennyi arkhiv istoriko-politicheskikh dokumentov Sankt-Peterburga
f. 1   Bolshevik Petersburg Committee
f. 2   Bolshevik Vyborg District Committee

f. 4   Bolshevik Vasilii Island District Committee
f. 6   Bolshevik Petrograd [Petersburg] District Committee
f. 8   Bolshevik Porokhovskii District Committee
f. 10   Bolshevik Okhtinskii District Committee
f. 11   Bolshevik Spasskii District Committee
f. 12   Bolshevik Lesnoi District Committee
f. 13   Bolshevik Novoderevenskii District Committee
f. 15   Bolshevik Kronstadt Committee
f. 16   Bolshevik Committee, Leningrad Province
f. 165   Bolshevik Rozhdestvenskii District Committee
f. 457   Bolshevik Fraction, Petrograd Trade Union Council
f. 999   Bolshevik Narva–Peterhof District Committee
f. 1430   Bolshevik Liteinyi District Committee
f. 1728   Files on individual Bolsheviks
f. 1817   Bolshevik Second City District Committee
f. 1842   Bolshevik First City District Committee
f. 1949   Government Printing Office and Paper Factory (Goznak)
f. 2315   Bolshevik Kolpinskii District Committee
f. 4000   Institute on the History of the Party, Leningrad Oblast Committee
            of the Communist Party of the Soviet Union–Institute of Marxism-
            Leninism Branch

LOGAV, Leningradskii oblastnoi arkhiv v g. Vyborge
f. r-2201   Justice Section, Petrograd Soviet
f. r-2202   Justice Section, Petrograd Province Soviet
f. r-2204   Council of People's Judges for Petrograd Province

RGA VMF, Rossiiskii gosudarstvennyi arkhiv Voenno-Morskogo Flota
f. r-2   Deputy Commander, Naval Forces of the Republic
f. r-5   Administrative Office, People's Commissariat for Naval Affairs
f. r-50   Commander of the Kronstadt Naval Base
f. r-52   Kronstadt Fortress
f. r-92   Headquarters, Baltic Fleet Command
f. r-95   Central Committee of the Baltic Fleet
f. r-96   Council of Baltic Fleet Commissars
f. r-306   Council of Baltic Fleet Flag Officers
f. r-342   Naval General Staff
f. r-661   Kronstadt Soviet
f. r-852   Battleship Group, Baltic Fleet Command
f. r-2244   Shchastny, A. M.

TsGALI SPb, Tsentral'nyi gosudarstennyi arkhiv literatury i isskusstva Sankt-
Peterburga
f. 63   Petrograd Bureau, Russian Telegraph Agency (PETRO, ROSTA), for-
            merly the Petrograd Telegraph Agency (PTA)

TsA FSB RF, Tsental'nyi arkhiv federal'noi sluzhby bezopasnosti Rossiiskoi federatsii
f. 1   All-Russian Extraordinary Commission (VCheka)
No. N-2   Case of the Counterrevolutionary Rebellion in the Second Baltic Fleet
            Detachment, 1918
No. N-8   Case of the Left SR Revolt

No. N-196 Case of Uritskii's Assassination
No. N-199 Case of Volodarskii's Assassination
No. N-685 Case of Maria Spiridonova (1918–1930)
No. N-972 Case of the Attempted Assassination of Lenin, 1 January 1918
No. N-13266 Case of Maria Spiridonova (1937)

AU FSB SPb i LO, Arkhiv upravleniia federal'noi sluzhby bezopasnosti po Sankt-Peterburgu i Leningradskoi oblasti
f. 1   Petrograd Cheka
f. 19/32   Military-Naval Control, Baltic Fleet
No. 3614   Case of A. M. Shchastny
No. 10940   Case of White Guardist Recruitment for "Murman"
No. 22121   Strikes at the Putilov Plant
No. 30377   Case of the Secret Society [Comorra] for the People's Revenge
No. 47037   Case of the Counterrevolutionary Conspiracy in the Mikhailovskii Artillery Academy

RNB SPb RO, Rossiiskaia natsional'naia biblioteka Sankt-Peterburga, rukopisnoe otdelenie

Stenograficheskie otchety zasedanii Petrogradskoi gorodskoi dumy sozyva 20 avgusta 1917 g., vols. 1–3

GOPB, Gosudarstevennaia obshchestvenno-politicheskaia biblioteka
        Leaflet collection

Great Britain

National Archives of the United Kingdom (TNA): Public Records Office (PRO)
ADM   137/1731
ADM   137/1737
ADM   137/3337
ADM   137/4183
ADM   223/637
FO   337/88
FO   371/337
FO   371/395
FO   371/3286
FO   371/3307
FO   371/3315
FO   371/3325
FO   371/3327
FO   371/3329
FO   371/3330
FO   371/3332
FO   371/3334
FO   371/3335
FO   371/3336
FO   371/3337
FO   371/3339
FO   371/3348
FO   371/3350

FO   371/3975
WO   32/5669

United States

Bakhmetiev Archive, Columbia University
        Zenzinov Collection

Hoover Institution on War, Revolution, and Peace, Stanford University
        Lockhart Collection
        Isaac Steinberg Collection

Lilly Library, Indiana University
        Lockhart, R. Mss.

Newspapers

Delo naroda (SR)
Den' (Menshevik)
Derevenskaia bednota (Bolshevik)
Derevenskaia kommuna (Soviet)
Edinstvo (Plekhanov's right socialist Edinstvo group)
Gazeta-kopeika (unaffiliated)
Gazeta rabochego i krest'ianskogo pravitel'stva (Sovnarkom)
Golos trudogo krestianstva (CEC Peasant Section)
Iskra (Menshevik)
Izvestiia Kronshtadtskogo soveta (Kronstadt Soviet)
Izvestiia Petrogradskogo soveta (Soviet)
Izvestiia vserossiiskogo komiteta spaseniia rodiny i revoliutsii (All-Russian Committee for
        Salvation of the Homeland and the Revolution)
Izvestiia vserossiiskogo tsentral'nogo ispolnitel'nogo komiteta i Moskovskogo soveta (Soviet,
        Moscow)
Izvestiia vserossiiskogo tsentral'nogo ispolnitel'nogo komiteta i Petrogradskogo soveta (So-
        viet, Petrograd)
Kommunist (Bolshevik/Left Communist)
Krasnaia gazeta (Petrograd Soviet, morning and evening editions)
Narodnoe delo (SR, Moscow)
Nash vek (Kadet)
Nashe slovo (League for Women's Equal Rights)
Nashi vedomosti (unaffiliated, evening edition)
Novaia Petrogradskaia gazeta (Unaffiliated, morning and evening editions)
Novaia zhizn' (Maxim Gorky's independent social democratic group, Petrograd and
        Moscow editions)
Novosti dnia (unaffiliated, Moscow, evening edition)
Novye vedomosti (unaffiliated, morning and evening editions)
Novyi den' (Socialist)
Novyi luch (Menshevik)
Novyi vechernyi chas (unaffiliated, evening)
Petrogradskaia pravda (Bolshevik, morning and evening editions)
Petrogradskaia vechernaia pochta (unaffiliated, evening edition)
Petrogradskii golos (unaffiliated)
Petrogradskoe ekho (unaffiliated, evening edition)

Pravda (Bolshevik, Moscow)
Rabochaia i krest'ianskaia krasnaia armiia i flot (Soviet, Petrograd/Moscow)
Rabochii i soldat (Petrograd Soviet, evening edition)
Rabotnitsa (Bolshevik)
Revoliutsionnaia rabotnitsa (Left SR)
Russkie vedomosti (unaffiliated, Moscow)
Severnaia kommuna (Soviet, daily and evening editions)
Soldatskaia pravda (Bolshevik)
Sotsial demokrat (Bolshevik, Moscow)
Strana (unaffiliated)
Utro Moskvy (unaffiliated, Moscow)
Vechernaia zvezda (Socialist, evening edition)
Vechernye ogni (unaffiliated, evening edition)
Vechernye vedomosti (unaffiliated, evening edition)
Vechernyi chas (unaffiliated, evening edition)
Vestnik soveta 1-go gorodskogo raiona (First City District Soviet)
Vooruzhennyi narod (Soviet)
Znamia bor'by (Left SR, Petrograd)
Znamia truda (Left SR, Petrograd, Moscow)
Zhizn' (unaffiliated, Moscow)

Contemporary Periodicals, Temporary Publications, Historical Journals

Arkhiv russkoi revoliutsii
Biulleten' komissariata vnutrennykh del SK SO
Biulleten' vserossiiskogo soiuza zashchity uchreditel'nogo sobraniia
Chrezvychainoe sobranie upolnomochennykh fabrik i zavodov g. Petrograda
Ezhenedel'nik chrezvychainykh komissii po bor'be s kontr-revoliutsiei i spekulatsiei
Ezhenedel'nik komissariata finansov i soveta narodnogo khoziaistva Severnoi oblasti
God proletarskoi revoliutsii
Golos minuvshego
Istkusstvo kommuny
Istoricheskie zapiski
Istoriia SSSR
Izvestiia komissariata zdravookhraneniia soiuza kommun severnoi oblasti
Izvestiia TsK KPSS
Krasnaia letopis'
Krasnyi Petrograd
Novyi put'
Otechestvennaia istoriia
Partiinye izvestiia
Plamia
Proletarskaia revoliutsiia
Revolutionary Russia
Russian Review
Slavic Review
Sotsialisticheskii vestnik
Vestnik godovshchiny velikoi raboche-krest'ianskoi revoliutsii
Vestnik oblastnogo komissariata vnutrennykh del (Soiuz kommun Severnoi oblasti)
Vestnik oblastnogo komissariata zemledeliia (Soiuz kommun Severnoi oblasti)
Voenno-istoricheskii zhurnal

Voprosy istorii
Voprosy istorii KPSS
Zhizn' iskusstva

Published Documents

Abrosimova, T. A., T. P. Bondarevskaia, E. T. Leikina, and V. Iu. Cherniaev, eds. *Peter-burgskii komitet RSDRP (b): Protokoly i materialy zasedanii.* St. Petersburg, 2003.
Akademiia nauk SSSR, Institut istorii, Leningradskoe otdelenie. *Raionnye sovety Petro-grada v 1917 godu: Protokoly, rezoliutsii, postanovleniia obshchikh sobranii i zaseda-nii ispolnitel'nykh komitetov.* 3 vols. Moscow–Leningrad, 1964–1966.
Anskii, A., ed. *Protokoly Petrogradskogo soveta professional'nykh soiuzov za 1917 g.* Lenin-grad, 1927.
Anskii, S. "Posle perevorota 25-ogo Oktiabria 1917 g." In *Arkhiv russkoi revoliutsii.* 8:43–55. Berlin, 1923.
Artsybushev, Iu. K. *"Diktatura proletariata" v Rossii: Nabroski s natury Iu. K. Artsy-busheva.* Moscow, 1922.
Belov, G. A., et al., eds. *Iz istorii Vserossiiskoi chrezvychainoi komissii, 1917–1921 gg. Sbornik dokumentov.* Moscow, 1958.
Bernshtam, M. S. *Nezavisimoe rabochee dvizhenie v 1918 godu (dokumenty i materi-aly).* Paris, 1981.
Bol'shevistskoe rukovodstvo. Perepiska. 1912–1927. Moscow, 1996.
Bone, A. *The Bolsheviks and the October Revolution: Minutes of the Central Com-mittee of the Russian Social-Democratic Labour Party (bolsheviks), August 1917–February 1918.* London, 1974.
Bubnov, A. "Oktiabr'skie biulleteny TsK bol'shevikov." *Proletarskaia revoliutsia,* 1921, no. 1:10–19.
Bunyan, James, and H. H. Fisher, eds. *The Bolshevik Revolution, 1917–1918: Docu-ments and Materials.* Stanford, 1965.
Bystranskii, V. "Oktiabr'skaia revoliutsiia—velichaishee sobytie v mirovoi istorii." *God proletarskoi revoliutsii,* November 7, 1918, p. 1.
Cherniaev, V. Iu., ed. *Piterskie rabochie i "diktatura proletariata" oktiabr' 1917–1929: Sbornik dokumentov.* St. Petersburg, 2000.
Chugaev, D. A., ed. *Petrogradskii voenno-revoliutsionnyi komitet: Dokumenty i materi-aly,* Vols. 1–3. Moscow, 1966–1967.
Cromie, F. N. A. *Letters [on Russian Affairs] from Captain Cromie RN.* n. p., 1919.
"Delo rabochego s"ezda," *Izvestiia,* October 25, 1918, p. 5.
Doklad o deiatel'nosti krest'ianskogo otdela vserossiiskogo tsentral'nogo ispolnitel'nogo komi-teta sovetov. Moscow, 1918.
Drezen, A. K., ed. *Baltiiskii flot v Oktiabr'skoi revoliutsii i grazhdanskoi voine.* Lenin-grad, 1932.
Fedorov, I. G. "Epidemiia kholery v Petrograde v 1918 g." *Izvestiia komissariata zdra-vookhraneniia soiuza kommun severnoi oblasti,* 1918, no. 1:82–88.
Fraiman, A. L. *Baltiiskie moriaki v bor'be za vlast' sovetov (noiabr' 1917–dekabr' 1918).* Leningrad, 1968.
———, comp. *Krakh germanskoi okkupatsii na Pskovshchine: Sbornik dokumentov.* Lenin-grad, 1939.
Galili, Z., and A. Nenarokov, eds. *Mensheviki v 1917 godu.* Vol. 3, pt. 2. Moscow, 1994.
———. *Mensheviki v 1918 godu.* Moscow, 1999.

Gorodetskii, E. N., ed. *Vtoroi vserossiiskii s"ezd sovetov rabochikh i soldatskih deputatov (25–26 Oktiabria 1917 g.): Sbornik dokumentov i materialov.* Moscow, 1997.

Institut marksizma-leninizma pri TsK KPSS. *Dekrety Sovetskoi vlasti.* Vols. 1–4. Moscow, 1957–1968.

——. *Leninskii sbornik.* Vol. 11. Moscow–Leningrad, 1929.

——. *Perepiska sekretariata TsK RSDRP (b)-RKP (b) s mestnymi partiinymi organizatsiami.* Vols. 1–4. Moscow, 1957–1969.

——. *Protokoly tsentral'nogo komiteta RSDRP (b), avgust 1917–fevral' 1918.* Moscow, 1958.

——. *Sed'moi ekstrennyi s"ezd RKP (b), mart 1918 goda: Stenograficheskii otchet.* Moscow, 1962.

——. *Shestoi s"ezd RSDRP (bol'shevikov), avgust 1917 goda: Protokoly.* Moscow, 1958.

Iroshnikov M. P., ed. *Dekrety Sovetskoi vlasti o Petrograde, 1917–1918.* Leningrad, 1986.

Istpart, *Protokoly s"ezdov i konferentsii vsesoiuznoi kommunisticheskoi partii (b): Sed'moi s"ezd, mart 1918 goda.* Moscow–Leningrad, 1928.

Iz istorii vserossiiskoi chrezvychainoi komissii, 1917–1921 gg.: Sbornik dokumentov. Moscow, 1958.

"Iz perepiski E. D. Stasovoi i K. T. Novgorodtsevoi (Sverdlovoi), mart–dekabr' 1918." *Voprosy istorii,* 1956, no. 10:85–101.

Keep, John L. H., trans. and ed. *The Debate on Soviet Power: Minutes of the All-Russian Central Executive Committee, Second Convocation, October 1917–January 1918.* Oxford, 1979.

Kowalski, Roman I., ed. *Kommunist: Ezhenedel'nyi zhurnal ekonomiki, politiki i obshchestvennosti,* nos. 1–4 (1918). New York, 1990.

Kreml' za reshetkoi (Podpol'naia Rossiia). Berlin, 1922.

Kudelli, P. F., ed. *Pervyi legal'nyi Peterburgskii komitet bol'shevikov v 1917 g.* Moscow–Leningrad, 1927.

——. *Vtoraia i tret'ia Petrogradskie obshchegorodskie konferentsii bol'shevikov v iiule i oktiabre 1917 goda: Protokoly.* Moscow–Leningrad, 1927.

Latsis, M. *Chrezvychainye komissii po bor'be s kontr-revoliutsii.* Moscow, 1921.

——. *Dva goda bor'by na vnutrennyi front.* Moscow, 1920.

——. *Otchet vserossiiskoi chrezvychainoi komissii za chetyre goda ee deiatel'nosti (20 dekabria 1917–20 dekabria 1921 g.): 1. Organizatsionnaia chast'.* Moscow, 1922.

Lenin, V. I. *Polnoe sobranie sochinenii.* 5th ed. Vols. 34–37, 50. Moscow, 1962, 1965, 1981.

——. *Sochineniia.* 3rd ed. Vol. 22. Moscow–Leningrad, 1931.

Listovki Petrogradskikh bol'shevikov, 1917–1920. Vol. 3. Leningrad, 1957.

Litvin, A. L., ed. *Levye esery i VCheka: Sbornik dokumentov.* Kazan', 1996.

——. *Mensheviki v Sovetskoi Rossii: Sbornik dokumentov.* Kazan', 1998.

Lur'e, M. "Iz istorii bor'by s 'levymi' kommunistami v Petrogradskoi organizatsii bol'shevikov." *Krasnaia letopis',* 1934, no. 2 (59): 100–111.

Makintsian, P., and M. Ia. Latsis., eds. *Krasnaia kniga VChK.* 2nd ed. 2 vols. Moscow, 1989.

Ministerstvo inostranykh del SSSR, *Dokumenty vneshnoi politiki SSSR.* Vol. 1. Moscow, 1957.

——. *Sovetsko-germanskie otnosheniia: Ot peregovorov v Brest-Litovske do podpisaniia Rapal'skogo dogovora.* Vol. 1. Moscow, 1968.

Nikolaevskii, B. I. *Mensheviki v dni oktiabr'skogo perevorota.* New York, 1962.

Ol'minskii, M. "O chrezvychainykh komissiiakh." *Pravda,* October 8, 1918, p. 1.

Osnovnye organizatsii Soveta rabochikh i soldatskikh deputatov. Kronstadt, 1918.

Otchet severnoi oblastnoi konferentsii s 3-ogo po 6-e aprelia. Petrograd, 1918.

Pervaia konferentsiia rabochikh i krasnoarmeiskikh deputatov 1-ogo gorodskogo raiona (stenograficheskie otchety 25 maia–5 iiunia). Petrograd, 1918.

"Pervye shagi bol'shevistskogo Petrogradskogo soveta v 1917 godu: Protokoly zasedanii." *Krasnaia letopis',* 1927, no. 3 (24): 65–82.

Pervyi narodnyi kalendar' na 1919 g. Petrograd, 1919.

Pervyi s"ezd sovetov narodnogo khoziaistva Severnoi oblasti: Stenograficheskii otchet. Petrograd, 1918.

Peters, Ia. Kh. "Krasnyi terror (beseda s Petersom)." *Utro Moskvy,* November 4, 1918, p. 1.

Piatyi sozyv vserossiiskogo tsentral'nogo ispolnitel'nogo komiteta: Stenograficheskii otchet Moscow, 1919.

Piatyi vserossiiskii s"ezd sovetov rabochikh, krest'ianskikh, soldatskikh i kazach'ikh deputatov: Stenograficheskii otchet. Moscow, 1918.

Pipes, Richard, ed. *The Unknown Lenin: From the Secret Archive.* New Haven, 1996.

Pokrovskii, M. N., and Ia. A. Iakovleva, eds. *Vtoroi vserossiiskii s"ezd sovetov R. i S. D.* Moscow–Leningrad, 1928.

———. *Vserossiiskoe uchreditel'noe sobranie.* Moscow–Leningrad, 1930.

"Prezidium Petrogradskogo soveta rabochikh i soldatskikh deputatov, dekabr' 1917g.–ianvar' 1918 g. *Krasnaia letopis',* 1932, no. 1–2 (46–47): 102–109.

Protokoly pervogo s"ezda partii levykh sotsialistov-revoliutsionerov internatsionalistov. Petrograd, 1918.

Protokoly 1-go s"ezda predstavitelei gub. sovdepov i zavedyvaiushchikh gubernskikh otdel upravleniia. Moscow, 1918.

Protokoly zasedanii Ispolnitel'nogo Komiteta Sovetov R., S., Kr., i Kaz. Deputatov II sozyva. Moscow, 1918.

"Protokoly zasedanii TsIK i Biuro TsIK S. R. i S. D. 1-go sozyva posle Oktiabria." *Krasnyi arkhiv,* 1925, vol.10, pp. 95–137.

Protokoly zasedanii vserossiiskogo tsentral'nogo ispolnitel'nogo komiteta 4-go sozyva. Moscow, 1920.

Puti revoliutsii (stat'i, materialy, vospominaniia). Berlin, 1923.

Rashin, A. "Demobilizatsiia promyshlennogo truda v Petrogradskoi gubernii za 1917–18 gg." In *Materialy po statistike truda,* ed. S. G. Strumilin, pp. 32–52. Issue 5. Petrograd, 1919.

Samoilova, K. *Chto dala rabochim i krest'ianam velikaia Oktiabr'skaia revoliutsiia (k godovshchine revoliutsii 26 oktiabria 1917 g.–7 noiabria 1918 g.).* Petrograd, 1918.

Sbornik dekretov i postanovlenii po soiuzu kommun severnoi oblasti. Issue 1. Part 1. Petrograd, 1919.

Sbornik prikazov, postanovlenii, rasporiazhenii, tsirkuliarnykh telegram Narodnogo komissariata vnutrennikh del. Issue 1. *S 25 oktiabria 1917 g. po 1 avgusta 1918 g.* Moscow, 1918.

Shelokhaev, V. V., project director. Ia. V. Leontiev, ed. *Partiia levykh sotsialistov-revoliutsionerov: Dokumenty i materialy.* Vol. 1. Moscow, 2000.

———. N. D. Erofeev, ed. *Partiia sotsialistov-revoliutsionerov: Dokumenty i materialy.* Vols. 1, 3. Part. 2. Moscow, 2000.

———. D. B. Pavlov, ed. *Protokoly tsentral'nogo komiteta konstitutsionno-demokraticheskoi partii, 1915–1920.* Moscow, 1998.

Shestoi vserossiiskii chrezvychainyi s"ezd sovetov rab., kr., kaz. i krasnoarm. deput., stenograficheskii otchet. Moscow, 1919.

"Soveshchanie polkovykh predstavitelei Petrogradskogo garnizona, 29 oktiabria 1917g." *Krasnaia letopis',* 1927, no. 2 (23): 220–225.

Spisok fabrichno-zavodskikh predpriiatii Petrograda. Po dannym na aprel' 1918. Petrograd, 1918.

Statisticheskii sbornik po Petrogradu i Petrogradskoi gubernii. Petrograd, 1922.

Stenograficheskii otchet o rabotakh piatogo s"ezda sovetov rabochikh i krest'ianskikh deputatov Peterburgskoi gubernii 21–23-go Avgusta 1918 goda. Petrograd, 1918.

Stenograficheskii otchet 4-go chrezvychainogo s"ezda sovetov rabochikh, soldatskikh, krest'ianskikh i kazach'ikh deputatov. Moscow, 1920.

Strumilin, S. "Sostav partii Kommunistov v Petrograde v sentiabre 1918 goda." *Petrogradskaia pravda,* December 12, 1918, p. 2.

Tonin, G. L., ed. "Chetvertaia obshchegorodskaia konferentsiia Petrogradskikh bol'shevikov v 1917 g." *Krasnaia letopis',* 1927, no. 3 (24): 58–64.

Tret'ii vserossiiskii s"ezd sovetov rabochikh, soldatskikh, i krest'ianskikh deputatov. St. Petersburg, 1918.

Trilisser, David. "Nel'zia molchat'." *Severnaia kommuna,* December 4, 1918, p. 1.

Trotskii, L. *Sochineniia.* Vol. 17, pt. 1. Moscow–Leningrad, 1926.

Tsentral'noe statisticheskoe upravlenie, Petrogradskoe stolichnoe statisticheskoe biuro. *Materialy po statistike Petrograda.* Issue 2. Petrograd, 1920.

Tsvigun, S. K., et al., eds. *V. I. Lenin i VChK: Sbornik dokumentov (1917–1922 gg.).* Moscow, 1975.

Tvorchestvo revoliutsionnykh rabochikh 2-go gorodskogo raiona: Otchet o rabote sovdepa 2-gor. raiona s pervykh dnei revoliutsii do godovshchiny velikoi oktiabr'skoi revoliutsii. Petrograd, 1918.

Ustav organizatsii sochuvstvuiushchikh Rossiiskoi kommunisticheskoi partii (bol'shevikov). Petrograd, 1918.

V. I. Lenin. Neizvestnye dokumenty. 1891–1922 gg. Moscow, 1999.

Vokrug uchreditel'nogo sobraniia: Sbornik statei i dokumentov. Petrograd, 1918.

Vos'moi s"ezd Rossiiskoi kommunisticheskoi partii (bol'shevikov): Stenograficheskii otchet. Moscow, 1919.

Wade, Rex A., ed. *Documents of Soviet History.* Vol. 1. *The Triumph of Bolshevism, 1917–1919.* Gulf Breeze, Fla., 1991.

Zeman, Z. A. B., ed. *Germany and the Revolution in Russia, 1915–1918: Documents from the Archives of the German Foreign Ministry.* London, 1958.

Zhurnaly Petrogradskoi gorodskoi dumy. Petrograd, 1917.

Zinoviev, G. *Sochineniia: God revoliutsii, fevral' 1917 g.–fevral' 1918 g.* Vol. 7, pt. 1, Leningrad, 1925.

Diaries and Memoirs

Abramovich, R. "Stranitsy istorii: Vikzhel (noiabr' 1917)." *Sotsialisticheskii vestnik,* May 1960, pp. 96–99; June 1960, pp. 118–124.

Aldanov, M. *Kartiny Oktiabr'skoi revoliutsii, istoricheskie portrety, portrety sovremennikov, zagadka Tolstogo.* St. Petersburg, 1999.

Antipov, N. "Ocherki o deiatel'nosti Petrogradskoi chrezvychainoi komissii." *Petrogradskaia pravda,* January 1, 1919, pp. 3–4; January 4, 1919, p. 2; January 4, 1919, pp. 2–3; January 5, 1919, pp. 2–3; January 7, 1919, pp. 2–3; January 12, 1919, p. 2; January 15, 1919, p. 2; January 16, 1919, p. 2; January 22, 1919, pp. 3–4.

Aronson, G. Ia. "Dvizheniia upolnomochennykh ot fabrik i zavodov v 1918 godu." New York [Inter-University Project on the History of the Menshevik Movement], 1960.

Begletsov, Nikolai. "V dni 'krasnogo' terrora." In *Che-Ka: Materialy po deiatel'nosti chrezvychainykh komissii,* pp. 69–84. Berlin, 1922.

Bonch-Bruevich, V. *Na boevykh postakh fevral'skoi i oktiabr'skoi revoliutsii.* Moscow, 1931.

———. *Pereezd Sovetskogo pravitel'stva iz Petrograda v Moskvu (po lichnym vospominaniiam).* Moscow, 1926.

———. *Ubiistvo germanskogo posla Mirbakha i vosstanie levykh eserov (po lichnym vospominaniiam).* Moscow, 1927.

Borman, A. A. "Moskva-1918 (iz zapisok sekretnogo agenta v kremle)." *Russkoe proshloe,* book 1, 1991 pp. 115–149.

Botmer, Karl von. *S Grafom Mirbakhom v Moskve.* Moscow, 1996.

Buchanan, M. *Petrograd.* London, 1918.

Bykhovskii, N. Ia. *Vserossiiskii sovet krest'ianskikh deputatov v 1917 g.* Moscow, 1929.

Chernov, V. M. *Pered burei.* New York, 1953.

Denike Iu. P. "B. O. Bogdanov v nachale 1918." *Sotsialisticheskii vestnik,* January 1960, p. 48.

———. "From the Dissolution of the Constituent Assembly to the Outbreak of the Civil War." In *The Mensheviks from the Revolution of 1917 to the Second World War,* ed. Leopold Haimson, pp. 107–155. Chicago and London, 1974.

———. "I. G. Tsereteli." *Novyi zhurnal,* 1959, no. 57:284 –285.

Dingel'shtedt, F. "Iz vospominanii agitatora Petrogradskogo komiteta RSDRP (b) (s sentiabria 1917 g. po mart 1918 g.)." *Krasnaia letopis',* 1927, no. 1 (22): 55–68.

Dybenko, P. E. *Iz nedr tsarskogo flota k velikomu oktiabriu.* Moscow, 1928.

Eremeev, K. "Nachalo Krasnoi armii (organizatsiia 1 korpusa Krasnoi armii)." *Proletarskaia revoliutsiia,* 1929, no. 2 (29): 154–168.

Flerovskii, I. "Miatezh mobilizovannykh matrosov v Peterburge." *Proletarskaia revoliutsiia,* 1926, no. 8 (55): 218–237.

Garvi, P. A. *Professional'nye soiuzy v Rossii.* New York, 1981.

Gippius, Zinaida. *Dnevniki.* Moscow, 1999.

Gorbunov, N. P. "Kak sozdalsia v Oktiabr'skie dni rabochii apparat soveta narodnykh komissarov." In *Utro strany sovetov,* ed. M. P. Iroshnikov, pp. 146–154. Leningrad, 1988.

Hill, George A. *Go Spy the Land.* London, 1932.

Hoffman, Max. *War Diaries and Other Papers.* Translated by Eric Sutton. Vol. 2. London, 1929.

Iakovlev, V. "Malo-visherskii epizod (Pereezd Sovnarkoma v Moskvu v 1918 g.)." *Krasnaia letopis',* 1934, no. 1 (58): 94–103.

Il'in-Zhenevskii, A. F. *Bol'sheviki u vlasti: Vospominaniia o 1918 gody.* Leningrad, 1929.

———. "Brestskii mir i partii." *Krasnaia letopis',* 1928, no. 1 (25): 48–49.

———. "Tragikomediia uchreditel'nogo sobraniia." *Krasnaia letopis',* 1927, no. 3 (24): 115–139.

Ilyin-Zhenevsky. *The Bolsheviks in Power: Reminiscences of the Year 1918.* Translated and annotated by Brian Pearce. London, 1984.

Ivanov, A. V. "Putilovskii rabochii na prieme u Il'icha." In *Vospominaniia o V. I. Lenine,* 2:336–338. Moscow, 1957.

Izgoev, A. S. "Piat' let v Sovetskoi Rossii (obryvki vospominanii i zametki)." In *Arkhiv russkoi revoliutsii,* 10:5–55. Berlin, 1923.

Izmailovich, A. *Posleoktiabr'skie oshibki.* Moscow, 1918.

Kakhovskaia, I. K. "Delo Eikhorda i Denikina (Iz vospominanii)." In *Puti revoliutsii,* pp. 191–260. Berlin, 1923.

Kedrov, M. "Iz krasnoi tetradi ob Il'iche." In *Vospominaniia o Vladimire Il'iche Lenine,* 2:94–110. Moscow, 1957.

Kokovtsev, V. N. *Iz moego proshlogo: Vospominaniia 1903–1919 gg.* Paris, 1933.

Krylenko, N. V. *Sudoustroistvo RSFSR: Lektsii po teorii i istorii sudoustroistva.* Moscow, 1923.

Lockhart, Bruce, R. H. *British Agent.* New York and London, 1933.

Malakhovskii, V. L. "Perekhod ot Krasnoi gvardii k Krasnoi armii." *Krasnaia letopis',* 1928, no. 3 (27): 5–51.

Malinovskii, Iu. P. "K pereezdu TsK RKP (b) i Sovetskogo pravitel'stva iz Petrograda v Moskvu (mart 1918)." *Voprosy istorii KPSS,* 1968, no. 11:99–103.

Malitskii, A. *Cheka i GPU.* Kharkov, 1923.

Minichev, A. "V dni levo-eserskogo miatezha v Petrograde v 1918 g. (iz vospominanii)." *Krasnaia letopis',* 1928, no. 1 (25): 66–69.

Mstislavskii, S. D. *Five Days Which Transformed Russia.* Bloomington, 1988.

———. *Piat' dnei: Nachalo i konets fevral'skoi revoliutsii.* Moscow, Petersburg, Berlin, 1922.

———. "Vospominaniia S. D. Mstislavskogo." In A. L. Litvin, *Levye esery i VCheka: Sbornik dokumentov,* pp. 187–211. Kazan, 1996.

Nabokov, Vladimir. "Vremennoe pravitel'stvo." In *Arkhiv russkoi revoliutsii,* 1:9–96. Berlin, 1921.

Nelidov, N. D. "Zagovory v Petrograde." *Beloe delo: Letopis' bor'by,* 1928, no. 4:195–218.

Oganovskii, N. "Dnevnik chlena uchreditel'nogo sobraniia." *Golos minuvshego,* 1918, nos. 4–6:143–172.

Orzhekhovskii, V. "Stranichka krasnogo terrora. Petrograd 1918–1919." *Na chuzhoi storone,* 1924, vol. 8, pp. 99–168.

Peters, Ia. Kh. "Itogi Oktiabr'skoi revoliutsii za god: Bor'ba s kontr-revoliutsiei (beseda s tov. Petersom)." *Izvestiia,* November 6, 1918, p. 5.

———. "Vospominaniia o rabote v VChK v pervyi god revoliutsii." *Proletarskaia revoliutsiia,* 1924, no. 10 (33): 5–32.

Podvoiskii, N. I. "Ot krasnoi gvardii k krasnoi armii." *Istorik marksist,* 1938, no. 1: 16–43.

Puchkov, A. S. "Perekhod ot dobrovol'cheskoi k reguliarnoi Krasnoi armii v Petrograde i okruge." *Krasnaia letopis',* 1929, no. 4 (31): 5–38.

———. "Pervye shagi k reguliarnoi Krasnoi armii." *Krasnaia letopis',* 1929, no. 2 (29): 75–100.

Raskolnikov, F. F. "Rasskaz o poteriannom dne." *Novyi mir,* 1933, no. 12:96–104.

———. *Rasskazy Michmana Il'ina.* Moscow, 1934.

———. *Tales of Sub-Lieutenant Ilyin.* Translated and annotated by Brian Pearce. London, 1982.

Reilly, S. *Britain's Master Spy: The Adventures of Sidney Reilly.* New York and London, 1933.

Revoliutsionnaia deiatel'nost' Konkordii Nikolaevnoi Samoilovoi: Sbornik vospominanii. Moscow, 1922.

Robien, Louis de. *The Diary of a Diplomat in Russia, 1917–1918.* New York and Washington, 1969.

Samoilo, A. *Dve zhizni.* Moscow, 1958.

Semenev, G. *Voennaia i boevaia rabota partii sotsialistov-revoliutsionerov.* Moscow, 1922.

Shingarev, A. I. *The Shingarev Diary.* Royal Oak, 1978.

Shklovskii, V. *Sentimental'noe puteshestvie.* Moscow, 1990.

Shliapnikov, D. [Observations of the Events of July 1918 in Moscow], *Za zemliu i voliu* (Kazan), July 16–19, 1918; reprinted in A. L. Litvin, *Levye esery i VCheka: Sbornik dokumentov,* pp. 211–233. Kazan, 1996.

Smolianskii, G. *Obrechennye.* Moscow, 1927.

Sokolov, Boris, "Zashchita vserossiiskogo uchreditel'nogo sobraniia." In *Arkhiv russkoi revoliutsii,* 13:5–70. Berlin, 1924.

Spiridonova, M. "Prosh Proshian." *Katorga i ssylka,* 1924, bk. 8:217–223.

Stashevich, P. "Ledovyi pokhod Baltiiskogo flota." In *Oktiabr'skii shkval: Moriaki Baltiiskogo flota v 1917 goda.* Leningrad, 1927.

Stasova, Elena. *Vospominaniia.* Moscow, 1969.

———. *Stranitsy zhizni i bor'by.* Moscow, 1988.

Steinberg, I. N. *Als ich Volkskommissar war: Episoden aus der rusischen Oktoberrevolution.* Munich, 1929.

———. *In the Workshop of the Revolution.* New York, 1953.

Stupochenko, L. "V Brestskie dni (Vospominaniia ochevidtsa)." *Proletarskaia revoliutsiia,* 1923, no. 4 (16): 94–111.

———. *V Brestskie dni.* Moscow, 1926.

Sukhanov, N. N. *Zapiski o revoliutsii.* Vol. 3. Moscow, 1992.

Sverdlova, K. T. *Iakov Mikhailovich Sverdlov.* Moscow, 1960.

Sviatitskii, N. "Fraktsiia partii S. R., uchreditel'noe sobranie i ee deiatel'nost'." *Partiinye izvestiia,* 1918, no. 5:32–42.

———. "5–6 ianvaria 1918 goda: Iz vospominaniia byvshego esera." *Novyi mir,* 1928, no. 2:220–228.

Trotsky, L. *The Stalin School of Falsification.* New York, 1972.

———. *Lenin.* New York, 1959.

———. *My Life.* New York, 1970.

Vishniak, M. V. *Vserossiiskoe uchreditel'noe sobranie.* Paris, 1932.

Vompe, P. *Dni Oktiabr'skoi revoliutsii i zheleznodorozhniki.* Moscow, 1924.

Williams, Albert Rhys. *Journey into Revolution: Petrograd, 1917–1918.* Chicago, 1969.

Young, Kenneth, ed. *The Diaries of Sir Bruce Lockhart.* Vol. 1, *1915–1938.* London, 1973.

Zenzinov, V. L. *Iz zhizny revoliutsionera.* Paris, 1919.

Secondary Studies

Agar, Augustus. *Baltic Episode: A Classic of Secret Service in Russian Waters.* London, 1963.

Akademiia nauk SSSR, Institut istorii, Leningradskoe otdelenie. *Oktiabr'skoe vooruzhennoe vosstanie: Semnadtsatyi god v Petrograde.* Vol. 2. Leningrad, 1967.

Alekseeva, T., and N. Matveev. *Dovereno zashchishchat' revoliutsii: O G. I. Bokii.* Moscow, 1987.

Bainton, Roy. *Honored by Strangers: The Life of Captain Francis Cromie CB DSO RN— 1882–1918.* Shrewsbury, 2002.

"Bankir iz VChK." In *Ocherki istorii vneshnoi razvedki,* ed. E. M. Primakov, 2:19–24. Moscow, 1997.

Baumgart, Winfried. *Deutsche Ostpolitik 1918: Von Brest-Litowsk bis zum Ende des Ersten Welkrieges.* Vienna and Munich, 1966.

Berar, Eva. "Pochemu bol'sheviki pokinuli Petrograd?" *Minuvshee: Istoricheskii al'manakh,* 1993, no. 14:226–250.

Berberova, Nina. *Zheleznaia zhenshchina, 1892–1974.* New York, 1991.

———. *Moura: The Dangerous Life of Moura Budberg.* Translated by Marian Schwartz and Richard D. Sylvester. New York, 2005.

Berezhkov, V. I. *Piterskie prokuratory: Rukovoditeli VChK–MGB.* St. Petersburg, 1998.

Bordiugov, G. A., and V. A. Kozlov. "Istoricheskaia razvilka vesnoi 1918 g." *Voprosy istorii KPSS,* 1990, no. 8:32–66; no. 9:50–66.

Borrero, Mauricio. *Hungry Moscow: Scarcity and Urban Society in the Russian Civil War, 1917–1921.* New York, 2003.

Brook-Shepherd, Gordon. *The Iron Maze: The Western Secret Services and the Bolsheviks.* London, 1999.

Brovkin, Vladimir N. *Behind the Front Lines of the Civil War: Political Parties and Social Movements in Russia, 1918–1922.* Princeton, N.J., 1994.

———. "Politics, Not Economics, Was the Key." *Slavic Review* 44, no. 2 (1985): 244–250.

Bykov, A., and L. Panov. *Diplomaticheskaia stolitsa Rossii.* Vologda, 1998.

Bykovskii, N. *Vserossiiskii sovet krest'ianskikh deputatov 1917 g.* Moscow, 1929.

Bystrova, A. "Bor'ba za ukreplenie diktatury proletariata: Pervye shagi diktatury proletariata." In *Oktiabr' v Petrograde,* ed. O. N. Lidak. Leningrad, 1933.

Carr, E. H. *The Bolshevik Revolution, 1917–1923.* Vol. 2. Baltimore, Md., 1966.

Chamberlin, William Henry. *The Russian Revolution, 1917–1921.* 2 vols. New York, 1935.

Chistikov, A. N. "U kormila vlasti." In *Petrograd na perelome epokh,* ed. V. A. Shishkin, pp. 9–60. St. Petersburg, 2000.

Chubarian, A. *Brestskii mir.* Moscow, 1964.

Churakov, Dimitri, *Revoliutsiia, gosudarstvo, rabochii protest: Formy, dinamika i priroda massovykh vystuplenii rabochikh v Sovetskoi Rossii. 1917–1918 gody.* Moscow, 2004.

Clements, Barbara Evans. *Bolshevik Feminist: The Life of Aleksandra Kollontai.* Bloomington, 1979.

———. *Bolshevik Women.* Cambridge, 1997.

Cohen, Stephen F. *Bukharin and the Bolshevik Revolution: A Political Biography.* New York, 1973.

Corney, Frederick. *Telling October: Memory and the Making of the October Revolution.* Ithaca, N.Y., 2004.

Craig, Gordon. *Germany, 1866–1945.* New York, 1999.

Daniels, Robert V. *The Conscience of the Revolution: Communist Opposition in Soviet Russia.* Cambridge, Mass., 1960.

Davidov, M. I. *Bor'ba za khleb.* Moscow, 1971.

Davydov, A. Iu. *Nelegal'noe snabzhenie Rossiiskogo naseleniia i vlast' 1917–1921.* St. Petersburg, 2002.

Debo, Richard K. "Lockhart Plot or Dzerzhinskii Plot?" *Journal of Modern History* 43, no. 3 (1970): 413–439.

———. *Revolution and Survival: The Foreign Policy of Soviet Russia 1917–18.* Toronto, 1979.

Drobishev, V. Z. *Glavnyi shtab sotsialisticheskogo promyshlennosti. Ocherki istorii VSNKh, 1917–1932,* Moscow, 1966.

Dumova, N. G. *Kadetskaia kontrrevoliutsiia i ee razgrom.* Moscow, 1982.

Elov, B. "O partiinykh konferentsiiakh RKP Petrogradskoi organizatsii." *Spravochnik Petrogradskogo agitatora,* 1921, no. 10:89–105.

Ezergailis, Andrew. *The Latvian Impact on the Bolshevik Revolution: The First Phase, September 1917 to April, 1918.* New York, 1983.

Fel'shtinskii, Iu. *Krushenie mirovoi revoliutsii: Brestskii mir.* Moscow, 1992.

———. "Ne 'miatezh' a provokatsiia." *Otechestvennaia istoriia,* 1992, no. 3:30–48.

Figes, Orlando. *A People's Tragedy: The Russian Revolution.* New York, 1999.

Fitzpatrick, Sheila. *The Russian Revolution.* Oxford, 1994.

Foglesong, David S. *America's Secret War against Bolshevism: U.S. Intervention in the Russian Civil War, 1917–1919.* Chapel Hill, N.C., 1995.

———. "Xenophon Kalamatiano: An American in Revolutionary Russia." *Intelligence and National Security* 6, no. 1 (1991): 154–195.

Fraiman, A. L. *Forpost sotsialisticheskoi revoliutsii: Petrograd v pervye mesiatsy sovetskoi vlasti.* Leningrad, 1969.

———. *Revoliutsionnaia zashchita Petrograda v fevrale–marte 1918 g.* Moscow–Leningrad, 1964.

Frenkel, Z. G. *Petrograd perioda voiny i revoliutsii. Sanitarnye usloviia i kommunal'noe blagoustroistvo.* Petrograd, 1923.

Galperina, B. D., and V. I. Startsev. "Sovety rabochikh i soldatskikh deputatov v bor'be za ovladenie apparatom gorodskogo obshchestvennogo upravleniia (noiabr' 1917–noiabr' 1918 g.)." In *Rabochie Leningrada v bor'be za pobedu sotsializma,* pp. 62–103. Moscow–Leningrad, 1963.

Getzler, Israel. *Kronstadt, 1917–1921: The Fate of a Soviet Democracy.* Cambridge, 1983.

Gimpel'son, E. G. *Formirovanie Sovetskoi politicheskoi sistemy, 1917–1923.* Moscow, 1995.

Gogolevskii, A. V. *Petrogradskii sovet v gody grazhdanskoi voiny.* Leningrad, 1982.

Gorodetskii, E. N. "Demobilizatsiia armii v 1917–1918 gg." *Istoriia SSSR,* 1958, no. 1:3–31.

———. *Rozhdenie sovetskogo gosudarstva, 1917–1918 gg.* Moscow, 1965.

Gorodetskii, E. N., and Iu. Sharapov. *Sverdlov.* Moscow, 1971.

Gusev, K. V. *Krakh partii levykh eserov.* Moscow, 1963.

———. *V. M. Chernov, Shtrikhi k politicheskomu portretu.* Moscow, 1999.

Hafner, Lutz. "The Assassination of Count Mirbach and the 'July Uprising' of the Left SRs in Moscow, 1918." *Russian Review,* 1991, no. 3:324–344.

Haimson, Leopold H. "The Mensheviks after the October Revolution." Part 1, *Russian Review* (October 1979): 456–473; Part 2 (April 1980): 181–207; Part 3 (July 1980): 462–483.

———. *Russia's Revolutionary Experience, 1905–1917: Two Essays.* New York, 2005.

Holquist, Peter. *Making War, Forging Revolution: Russia's Continuum of Crisis, 1914–1921.* Cambridge, Mass., 2002.

Hughes, Michael. *Inside the Enigma: British Officials in Russia, 1900–1930.* London, 1997.

Iakubovich, M. P. "G. Zinoviev." In *Samizdat Register 2,* ed. Roy A. Medvedev, pp. 65–97. New York, 1981.

Iarov, S. V. *Gorozhanin kak politik, revoliutsiia, voennyi kommunizm i NEP glazami Petrogradtsev.* St. Petersburg, 1999.

———. *Krest'ianin kak politik, krest'ianstvo severo-zapada Rossii v 1918–1919 gg.: Politicheskoe myshlenie i massovyi protest.* St. Petersburg, 1999.

Ignatov, E. *Gorodskie raionnye sovety kak forma uchastiia rabochikh v upravlenii gosudarstvom.* Moscow, 1929.

Iroshnikov, M. P. *Sozdanie sovetskogo tsentral'nogo gosudarstvennogo apparata.* Leningrad, 1967.

Kapchinskii, O. "Kto sluzhil v VCheka-OGPU." *Voenno-istoricheskii arkhiv,* no. 22 (2001): 155–177.

Karpenko, B. "O perepisi naseleniia g. Petrograda 2 iiunia 1918 goda." In Tsentral'noe statisticheskoe upravlenie, Petrogradskoe stolichnoe statisticheskoe biuro, *Materialy po statistike Petrograda,* issue 2, pp. 48–50. Petrograd, 1920.

Keep, John L. H. *The Russian Revolution: A Study in Mass Mobilization.* London, 1976.

Kennan, George F. *Soviet-American Relations, 1917–1920.* Vol. 2, *The Decision to Intervene.* New York, 1967.

———. "The Sisson Documents." *Journal of Modern History* 28, no. 2 (1956): 130–154.

Khmelevskii, V. P. *Severnyi oblastnoi komitet RKP (b).* Leningrad, 1972.

Klopov, E. V. "Daty zasedanii TsK RKP (b) neobkhodimo utochnit' (9 marta 1918)." *Voprosy istorii KPSS,* 1966, no. 11:118–119.

Krasnikova, A. V. *Na zare Sovetskoi vlasti.* Leningrad, 1963.

Kowalskii, Ronald I. *The Bolshevik Party in Conflict: The Left Communist Opposition of 1918.* Pittsburgh, Pa., 1991.

Krukhkovskaia, V. M. *Tsentral'naia gorodskaia duma Petrograda v 1917 g.* Leningrad, 1976.

Kulyshev, Iu. S., and V. I. Nosach. *Partiinaia organizatsiia i rabochie Petrograda v gody grazhdanskoi voiny.* Leningrad, 1971.

Kutuzov, V. A., V. F. Lepetiukhin, V. F. Sedov, and O. N. Stepanov. *Chekisti Petrograda na strazhe revoliutsii.* Leningrad, 1987.

Lavrov, V. M. *"Krest'ianskii parlament" Rossii (Vserossiiskie s"ezdy sovetov krest'ianskikh deputatov v 1917–1918 godakh).* Moscow, 1996.

Leggett, George. *The Cheka: Lenin's Political Police: The All-Russian Extraordinary Commission for Combating Counterrevolution and Sabotage.* Oxford and New York, 1986.

Leonov, S. V. *Rozhdenie Sovetskoi imperii.* Moscow, 1997.

Leont'ev, Ia. V. "Novye istochniki po istorii levoeserskogo terrora." In *Individualnyi politicheskii terror v Rossii XIX–XX v.,* pp. 139–148. Moscow, 1996.

Lewin, Moshe. "More Than One Piece of the Puzzle Is Missing." *Slavic Review* 44, no. 2 (1985): 239–243.

Lih, Lars. *Bread and Authority in Russia, 1914–1921.* Berkeley, 1990.

Lincoln, W. Bruce. *Red Victory: A History of the Russian Civil War.* New York, 1989.

Lindenmeyr, Adele. "The First Soviet Political Trial: Countess Sofia Panina before the Petrograd Revolutionary Tribunal." *Russian Review* (October 2001): 505–525.

Litvin, A. L. *Krasnyi i belyi terror v Rossii, 1918–1922.* Kazan', 1995.

Litvin, A. L., and L. M. Ovrutskii. *Levye esery: Programma i taktika.* Kazan', 1992.

Lur'e, M. "Pervyi s"ezd komitetov derevenskoi bednoty soiuza kommun severnoi oblasti, 3–6 noiabria 1918 goda." *Krasnaia letopis',* 1931, no. 4 (43): 5–46.

Maiorov, S. M. *Bor'ba Sovetskoi Rossii za vykhod iz imperialisticheskoi voiny.* Moscow, 1959.

Malinovskii, Iu. P. "K pereezdu TsK RKP (b) i Sovetskogo pravitel'stva iz Petrograda v Moskvu (mart 1918)." *Voprosy istorii KPSS,* 1968, no. 11:99–103.

Mally, Lynn. *The Culture of the Future: The Proletcult Cult Movement in Revolutionary Russia 1917–1922.* Berkeley, 1990.

Mandel, David. *The Petrograd Workers and the Soviet Seizure of Power: From the July Days 1917 to July 1918.* New York, 1984.

Mawdsley, Evan. *The Russian Civil War.* Boston, 1987.

———. *The Russian Revolution and the Baltic Fleet: War and Politics, February 1917–April 1918.* London, 1978.

Mayer, Arno J. *The Furies: Violence and Terror in the French and Russian Revolutions.* Princeton, N.J., 2000.

McAuley, Mary. *Bread and Justice: State and Society in Petrograd, 1917–1922.* Oxford, 1991.

Medvedev, Roy A. *The October Revolution.* New York, 1979.

Melancon, Michael. "The Left Socialist Revolutionaries and the Bolshevik Uprising." In *The Bolsheviks in Russian Society,* ed. Vladimir Brovkin, pp. 59–80. New Haven, 1997.

Melgunov, S. P. *Krasnyi terror v Rossii.* Moscow, 1990.

Milshtein, A. L. "Rabochie Petrograda v bor'be za ukreplenie sovetov (Perevybory Petrogradskogo soveta v iiune 1918 g.)." In *Rabochie Leningrada v bor'b'e za pobedu sotsializma,* pp. 126 –168. Moscow–Leningrad, 1963.

Mints, I. I. *God 1918.* Moscow, 1982.

Muranov, A. I., and V. E. Zviagintsev. *Dos'e na marshala: Iz istorii zakrytykh sudebnykh protsessov.* Moscow, 1996.

Musaev, V. I. *Prestupnost' v Petrograde v 1917–1921.* St. Petersburg, 2001.

Nenarokov, A. P., ed. *Pervoe Sovetskoe pravitel'stvo, oktiabr' 1917–iul' 1918.* Moscow, 1991.

Nevskii, V., and V. Belov. "Na drugoi den' posle vosstaniia," *Krasnaia letopis',* 1922, no. 2–3:309–315.

Nikolaevskii, B. I. "Stranitsy proshlogo: K 80-letiiu L. O. Tsederbaum-Dan." *Sotsialisticheskii vestnik,* 1958, no. 7/8:149–154.

Nosach, V. I. "Profsoiuzy Petrograda v pervyi god Sovetskoi vlasti." In *Iz istorii velikoi Oktiabr'skoi sotsialistichskoi revoliutsii i sotsialisticheskogo stroitel'stva v SSSR,* ed. V. A. Ovsiakin, ed., pp. 133–154. Leningrad, 1967.

Ocherki istorii Leningradskoi organizatsii KPSS, part.2, Noiabr 1917–1945. Leningrad, 1968.

Osipova, T. V. *Rossiiskoe krest'ianstvo v revoliutsii i grazhdanskoi voine.* Moscow, 2001.

Ovrutskii, L. M., and A. I. Razgon. "Poniat' dukh 6 iiulia." *Otechestvennaia istoriia,* 1992, no. 3:49–61.

———. "Razbitye nadezhdy: levye sotsialisty-revoliutsionery (internatsionalisty)." In *Istorii politicheskikh partii Rossii,* ed. A. I. Zeveleva, pp. 347–371. Moscow, 1994.

Oznobishin, D. V. "Leninskii svod otvetov mestnykh sovetov na zapros SNK o zakliuchenii Brestskogo mira." In *Istochnikovedenie istorii sovetskogo obshchestva,* issue 2, pp. 189–243. Moscow, 1968.

———. *Ot Bresta do Iur'eva.* Moscow, 1966.

Petrov, M. N. *VChK-OGPU: Pervoe desiatiletie (na materialakh severo-zapada Rossii).* Novgorod, 1995.

Pipes, Richard. *Russia under the Bolshevik Regime.* New York, 1993.

———. *Three "Whys" of the Russian Revolution.* New York, 1995.

Porsheva, O. S. *Mentalitet i sotsial'noe povedenie rabochikh, krest'ian i soldat Rossii v period pervoi mirovoi voiny (1914–mart 1918).* Ekaterinburg, 2000.

Potekhin, M. N. *Pervyi sovet proletarskoi diktatury.* Leningrad, 1966.

———. *Petrogradskaia trudovaia kommuna.* Leningrad, 1974.

Protasov, L. G. *Vserossiiskoe uchreditel'noe sobranie: Istoriia rozhdeniia i gibeli.* Moscow, 1997.

Rabinovich, A. "Bol'sheviki i samoubiistvo levykh eserov." In *Oktiabr'skaia revoliutsia: Ot novykh istochnikov k novomu osmysleniiu,* ed. S. V. Tiutiukin, pp. 188–206. Moscow, 1998.

———. "Bol'sheviki, nizy, i sovetskaia vlast': Petrograd, fevral 1917–iiul' 1918." In *Anatomiia revoliutsii,* ed. V. Iu. Cherniaev, Z. Galili, L. Haimson, S. I. Potolov, and Ju. Scherer, pp. 116–133. St. Petersburg, 1994.

———. *Bol'sheviki prikhodiat k vlasti: Revoliutsiia 1917 goda v Petrograde.* Moscow, 1989.

———. "Dos'e Shchastnogo: Trotskii i delo geroia Baltiiskogo flota." *Otechestvennaia istoriia,* 2001, no. 1:61–82.

———. "Moisei Uritskii: Robes'per revoliutsionogo Petrograda?" *Otechestvennaia istoriia,* 2003, no. 1:3–21.

———. "Popytki formirovaniia mnogopartiinogo demokraticheskogo sotsialisticheskogo pravitel'stva v 1917 godu v Rossii." *Istoriia SSSR,* no. 6:191–207.

Rabinovich, S. E. "Bol'sheviki v Krasnoarmeiskikh organizatsii v 1918 godu (Mart–iiun' 1918 g.)." *Krasnaia letopis',* 1930, no. 6 (39): 213–230.

Rabinowitch, Alexander. *The Bolsheviks Come to Power: The Revolution of 1917 in Petrograd.* New York, 1976.

———. "Early Disenchantment with Bolshevik Rule: New Data from the Archives of the Extraordinary Assembly of Delegates from Petrograd Factories." In *Politics and Society under the Bolsheviks,* ed. Kevin McDermott and John Morrison, pp. 188–206. London, 1999.

———. "The Evolution of Local Soviets in Petrograd, November 1917–June 1918: The Case of the First City District Soviet," *Slavic Review* 46, no. 1 (1987): 20–37.

———. "The Evolution of Local Soviets in Urban Russia, 1917–1920: The Case of the Petrograd First City District Soviet." In *Party, State, and Society in the Russian Civil War: Explorations in Social History,* ed. Diane P. Koenker, William G. Rosenberg, and Ronald G. Suny, pp. 133–157. Bloomington, 1989.

———. "The Shchastny File: Trotsky and the Case of the Hero of the Baltic Fleet." *Russian Review,* no. 58 (October 1999): 37–47.

Radkey, O. N. *Russia Goes to the Polls: The Election to the All-Russian Constituent Assembly.* Ithaca, N.Y., 1989.

———. *The Sickle under the Hammer: The Russian Socialist Revolutionaries in the Earliest Months of Soviet Rule.* New York, 1963.

Raleigh, Donald J. *Experiencing Russia's Civil War: Politics, Society, and Revolutionary Culture in Saratov, 1917–1922.* Princeton, N.J., 2002.

Razgon, A. I. "B. D. Kamkov." In *Politicheskaia istoriia Rossii v partiiakh i litsakh,* pp. 228–246. Moscow, 1993.

———. "Pravitel'stvennyi blok." *Istoricheskie zapiski,* vol. 117, 1989, pp. 107–156.

———. *VTsIK Sovetov v pervye mesiatsy diktatury proletariata.* Moscow, 1977.

———. "Zabytye imena." In *Pervoe Sovetskoe pravitel'stvo,* pp. 448–459. Moscow, 1991.

Rigby, T. H. *Lenin's Government: Sovnarkom 1917–1922.* London, 1979.

Rokitianskii, Iakov, and Reinhard Muller. *Krasnyi dissident: Akademik Riazanov–opponent Lenina, zhertva Stalina.* Moscow, 1996.

Roliakov, M. "Soiuz kommun Severnoi oblasti." In *Khoziaistvo Severo-zapadnogo kraia,* 1927, no. 9:11–20.

Rosenberg, William G. *Liberals in the Russian Revolution: The Constitutional Democratic Party, 1917–1921.* Princeton, N.J., 1974.

———. "Russian Labor and Bolshevik Power after October." *Slavic Review* 44, no. 2 (1985): 205–238.

Rupasov, A. I., and A. N. Chistikov. *Sovetsko-finliandskaia granitsa. 1918–1938.* St. Petersburg, 2000.

Sakwa, Richard. *Soviet Communists in Power: A Study of Moscow during the Civil War, 1918–1921.* New York, 1988.

Savitskaia, R. M. "Istochniki o V. I. Lenine po podgotovke i provedenii II vserossiiskogo s"ezda sovetov." In *Velikii Oktiabr': Istoriia, istoriografiia, istochnikovedenie,* pp. 251–267. Moscow, 1978.

Schapiro Leonard. *The Origin of the Communist Autocracy.* Cambridge, 1955.

Serge, Victor. *Year One of the Russian Revolution.* London, 1992.

Service, Robert. *The Bolshevik Party in Revolution: A Study in Organizational Change, 1917–1923.* London, 1979.

———. *Lenin: A Biography.* Cambridge, Mass., 2000.

Shapiro, Leonard. *The Origin of the Communist Autocracy.* New York and Washington, 1965.

Shelavin, K. I. "Iz istorii Peterburgskogo komiteta bol'shevikov v 1918 g." *Krasnaia letopis',* 1928, no. 2 (26): 106–124; 1928, no. 3 (27): 146–172; 1929, no. 1 (28): 68–88; 1929, no. 2 (29): 24–45; 1929, no. 3 (30): 120–153.

Shoshkov, E. N. *Namorsi A. M. Shchastnyi.* St. Petersburg, 2001.

Shteinberg, Valentin. *Ekab Peters.* Moscow, 1989.

Simonian M. N. *Ego professiia revoliutsiia: Dokumental'nyi ocherk o zhizni i deiatel'nosti N. V. Krylenko.* Moscow, 1985.

Sivokhina, T. A. "Obrazovanie i deiatel'nost' krest'ianskoi sektsii VTsIK." *Vestnik Moskovskogo universiteta,* 1969, no. 2:13–25.

Smirnov, N. N. *Tret'ii vserossisskii s"ezd sovetov.* Leningrad, 1988.

Smith, S. A. *Red Petrograd: Revolution in the Factories, 1917–1918.* Cambridge, 1983.

Sobolev, V. A., ed. *Lubianka 2: Iz istorii otechestvennoi kontrrazvedki.* Moscow, 1990.

Sofinov, P. G. *Ocherki istorii VChK.* Moscow, 1960.

Spence, Richard. *Trust No One: The Secret Life of Sidney Reilly.* Los Angeles, 2003.

Spirin, L. M. *Klassy i partii v grazhdanskoi voine v Rossii, 1917–1921.* Moscow, 1969.

———. *Krakh odnoi avantury (miatezh levykh eserov v Moskve 6–7 iiulia 1918).* Moscow, 1971.

Startsev, V. I. *Ocherki po istorii Petrogradskoi krasnoi gvardii i rabochei militsii.* Moscow–Leningrad, 1965.

Stites, Richard. *Revolutionary Dreams: Utopian Vision and Experimental Life in the Russian Revolution.* New York and Oxford, 1989.

Suny, Ronald Grigor. *The Baku Commune: Class and Nationality in the Russian Revolution.* Princeton, N.J., 1972.

Swain, Geoffrey. "Before the Fighting Started: A Discussion on the Theme of 'The Third Way.'" *Revolutionary Russia* (June 1991): 210–234.

———. "The Disillusioning of the Revolution's Praetorian Guard: The Latvian Riflemen, Summer–Autumn 1918." *Europe-Asia Studies* 51, no. 4 (1999): 667–689.

———. *The Origins of the Russian Civil War.* London and New York, 1996.

———. "Vacietis: The Enigma of the Red Army's First Commander." *Revolutionary Russia,* June 2003, pp. 68–86.

Tiutiukin, S. V. *Menshevizm: Stranitsy istorii.* Moscow, 2002.

Tucker, Robert C. *Stalin as Revolutionary.* Norton, 1973.

Ullman, Richard H. *Anglo-American Relations, 1917–1921.* Vol. 1, *Intervention and the War.* Princeton, N.J., 1961.

Uralov, S. G. *Moisei Uritskii: Biograficheskii ocherk.* Leningrad, 1962.

Vladimirova, V. *God sluzhby 'sotsialistov' kapitalistam.* Moscow–Leningrad, 1927.

Volkogonov, Dmitri. *Lenin: A New Biography.* New York, 1944.

Von Geldern, James. *Bolshevik Festivals, 1917–1920.* Berkeley, 1993.

Von Hagen, Mark. *Soldiers in the Proletarian Dictatorship: The Red Army and the Soviet Socialist State, 1917–1930.* Ithaca, N.Y., and London, 1990.

Wade, Rex A. *Red Guards and Workers' Militias in the Russian Revolution.* Stanford, 1984.

———. *The Russian Revolution, 1917.* Cambridge, 2000.

Wheeler-Bennett, John W. *Brest-Litovsk: The Forgotten Peace, March, 1918.* London, 1938.

Wildman, Allan K. *The End of the Russian Imperial Army: The Road to Soviet Power and Peace.* Princeton, N.J., 1987.

Wood, Elizabeth A. *The Baba and the Comrade: Gender and Politics in Revolutionary Russia.* Bloomington, 1997.

Zdanovich, A. A. "Latyshskoe delo: Niuansy raskrytiia 'zagovora poslov'." *Voenno-istoricheskii zhurnal,* 2004, no. 3:25–32.

———. *Otechestvennaia kontrrazvedka, 1914–1920.* Moscow, 2004.

Znamenskii, O. N. *Vserossiiskoe uchreditel'noe sobranie: Istoriia sozyva i politicheskogo krusheniia.* Leningrad, 1976.

Reference Works

Acton, Edward, Vladimir Cherniaev, and William G. Rosenberg, eds. *Critical Companion to the Russian Revolution, 1914–1921.* Bloomington, 1997.

Deiateli SSSR i revoliutsionnogo dvizheniia Rossii, entsiklopedicheskii slovar' granat. Moscow, 1989.

Institut marksizma-leninizma pri TsK KPSS. *Vladimir Il'ich Lenin, Biograficheskaia khronika.* Vols. 5, 6. Moscow, 1974–1975.

Liubimov, I. N. *Revoliutsiia 1917 goda: Khronika sobytii.* Vol. 6, *Oktiabr'–dekabr'.* Moscow, 1930.

Politicheskie partii Rossii konets XIX–pervaia tret' XX veka: Entsiklopediia. Moscow, 1996.

Sankt-Peterburg: Entsiklopediia. St. Petersburg–Moscow, 2004.

Sankt-Peterburg/Petrograd/Leningrad: Entsiklopedicheskii spravochnik. Moscow, 1992.

Volobuev, P. V., chief editor. *Politicheskie deiateli Rossii 1917.* Moscow, 1993.

Other Materials

Boniece, Sally A. "Mariia Spiridonova, 1894–1918: Feminine Martyrdom and Revolutionary Mythmaking." Ph.D. dissertation, Indiana University, Bloomington, 1995.

Shkarovskii, Mikhail. "Beskrovnyi miatezh." Unpublished manuscript.

INDEX

Alexander Rabinowitch, Professor Emeritus of History at Indiana University, Bloomington, is widely acknowledged to be a pioneer in the study and teaching of the revolutionary and Soviet eras in Russian history. He was one of the first Western scholars to conduct research on Communist party history in Soviet archives. His classic book, *The Bolsheviks Come to Power* (1976), was the first major Western work on the Russian revolutions published in the Soviet Union under Gorbachev, and it is still required reading for advanced history students in Russian and Western universities. He is author of *Prelude to Revolution: The Petrograd Bolsheviks and the July 1917 Uprising* (Indiana University Press, 1968) and co-editor of *Russia in the Era of NEP: Explorations in Soviet Society and Culture* (Indiana University Press, 1991). He has lectured at American, European, Russian, and Asian universities and his many essays have appeared in journals, magazines, and newspapers in this country and abroad.